1684

AMERICA

AMERICA

A NARRATIVE HISTORY

VOLUME I

___

GEORGE BROWN TINDALL

═══

W · W · NORTON & COMPANY · NEW YORK · LONDON

*The text of this book is composed in Caledonia, with display
type set in Torino Roman. Composition by New England Ty-
pographic Service, Inc. Manufacturing by R. R. Donnelley.
Book design by Antonina Krass.*

Library of Congress Cataloging in Publication Data

Tindall, George Brown.
America: a narrative history.

Includes bibliographies and index.
1. United States—History.   I. Title.
E178.1.T55   1984   973   83-22165

ISBN 0-393-95356-4

W. W. Norton & Company, Inc., 500 Fifth Avenue, New York, N. Y. 10110

W. W. Norton & Company Ltd., 37 Great Russell Street, London WC1B 3NU

3   4   5   6   7   8   9   0

Time present and time past
Are both perhaps present in time future,
And time future contained in time past.

T. S. Eliot, *Four Quartets*

CONTENTS

10 | NATIONALISM AND SECTIONALISM 359

11 | THE JACKSONIAN IMPULSE 392

12 | THE DYNAMICS OF GROWTH 426

13 | AN AMERICAN RENAISSANCE: ROMANTICISM AND REFORM 465

14 | MANIFEST DESTINY 509

15 | THE OLD SOUTH: AN AMERICAN TRAGEDY 537

MAPS

PREFACE

This book is characterized in its subtitle as "A Narrative History." Since professional historians are currently debating the meaning of this term, I'd like to clarify, at least for students and other nonprofessionals, what the term "narrative" suggests about the approach I've taken here.

In *America: A Narrative History* I have tried to fashion the sprawling American past into a story, one brimming with vivid characters and great events. It is a story of promise and achievement, as well as the irony and tragedy of only partially fulfilled ideals. It is a story the events of which are connected in patterns of influence and consequence, not recounted in isolation from one another. By showing connections among past events, I've tried to bring out for readers their significance, their meaning.

With the narrative approach I've taken I've attempted also to put the reader in contact with the personalities and occurrences of the past. Wherever possible, the characters in this story speak with their own voice, the better to convey the flavor of American history.

Does the story I tell have a simple moral? Sir Isaiah Berlin, a distinguished Oxford don, once took as the theme for an essay on Leo Tolstoy's theory of history a fragment from the Greek poet Archilochus which said: "The fox knows many things, but the hedgehog knows one big thing." I prefer to see myself as one who runs with foxes rather than rolls up with hedgehogs. Yet if there were one single idea I should hope to implant with this text, it would be that the lessons of history are not simple lessons, that history is a complex and elusive subject, and that one should be on guard immediately against theories of single causation or pronouncements that begin "History proves. . . ."

The book in hand is designed to serve as an introduction to

American history. However much one might hope to provide a comprehensive account of all the major themes, one cannot pretend in such a limited scope to exhaust the subject. I do hope, however, that this survey will become a gateway through which readers will be drawn to explore more deeply the vast and compelling story of American history.

George B. Tindall
Chapel Hill, North Carolina

ACKNOWLEDGMENTS

A *New Yorker* cartoon of recent vintage has a publisher telling an aspiring author: "Well, it's good, but people just don't write books all by themselves any more." In truth, people don't. The single name on the title page of this book neglects the credit owed to many others. Joseph J. Ellis of Mount Holyoke College, the book's advisory editor, read successive drafts almost from the first, and supplied a judicious mixture of the criticism an author needs and the reassurance he craves. What is more, as deadlines loomed, he sped the author to completion with timely and well-formulated suggestions on the final chapters. Gary R. Freeze, graduate assistant and factotum at the University of North Carolina at Chapel Hill, helped compile the end-of-chapter bibliographies.

The influences which have contributed to this book—teachers, students, books, journals, documents I have encountered over the years, colleagues more than generous in their responses to inquiries—are more than I could acknowledge in a reasonable space, even if I had the gift of total recall. Historians who have read and commented on parts of the typescript in their areas of expertise include Herman J. Belz (University of Maryland), Stephen Botein (Michigan State University), Don E. Fehrenbacher (Stanford University), Michael F. Holt (University of Virginia), Richard B. Latner (Tulane University), Richard L. McCormick (Rutgers University), Drew R. McCoy (University of Texas), Michael R. McVaugh (University of North Carolina), Robert M. Miller (University of North Carolina), Charles W. Royster (Louisiana State University), Ronald E. Shaw (Miami University of Ohio), Michael B. Stoff (University of Texas), Carl Vipperman (University of Georgia), and Peter F. Walker (University of North Carolina).

David B. Parker and Linda W. Sellars, graduate assistants and copyreaders par excellence, saved me from many grotesque constructions, and Parker further checked points of factual accuracy. Jane Lindley, administrative manager of the Department of History in Chapel Hill, routinely passes miracles at expediting administrative details. Over a period of years a number of people who served in the department's secretarial pool have typed parts of various drafts: Jamie Lewis, Pat Maynor, Rosalie I. Radcliffe, Linda Stephenson, and Mary Woodall. Most of the final draft was typed by Mandy Hollowell and Ceci Long, and by Peter Hardy with the help of the Kenan Research Fund when the department was temporarily understaffed.

In the Louis Round Wilson Library at Chapel Hill, Louise McG. Hall, Mary R. Ishaq, Donna P. Cornick, Ridley Kessler, Jr., and their associates have shown the characteristic tenacity of reference librarians in tracking down elusive references.

The Department of History at Chapel Hill and the National Endowment for the Humanities aided a year's stay at the Center for Advanced Study, Stanford, California, by courtesy of Gardner Lindzey and his associates, which helped me immensely in gathering my thoughts for this book as well as other projects. Especially generous to me there were Deanna Dejan at the word processor; Margaret Amara, librarian; and Bruce Harley, on many missions in the book run to the Stanford University library.

At W. W. Norton & Company, James L. Mairs, vice-president, senior editor, and director of production, acted as impresario straordinario from the inception of the project—organizing, supervising, and coordinating, all the while patiently keeping the author's nose to the grindstone and his morale in repair. A year's leave sponsored by the company helped achieve both ends. Steve Forman performed a variety of editorial tasks with unfailing serenity. Fred Bidgood, the copy editor, proved patient and thorough in preparing the manuscript for publication. George P. Brockway, chairman, and Edwin Barber, director of the College Department, both read and marked up the typescript to the author's advantage. Nora Seton and Amy Boesky looked after essential details at crucial times. Antonina Krass designed an elegant book, and Sydney W. Cohen compiled a useful index.

My son Bruce M. Tindall helped with copyreading at this end. To him and his wife, Susan A. McGrath, to my daughter Blair A. M. Tindall, and to my wife Blossom M. Tindall, my love and gratitude, as always.

AMERICA

1

THE COLLISION OF CULTURES

The earliest Americans are lost in the mists of time, where legends abound. Like people everywhere the Indians told myths of creation, which varied from tribe to tribe: some spoke of a habitation in the sky from which humans and animals had come; still others spoke of miraculous events, such as the union of the Sky Father and Earth Mother. In the Southwest the Pueblo people had a place of worship called the kiva, a stone pit in which a deeper opening symbolized Sipapu, a place of mystery in the north where people entered the world from underground.

Some romancers have had it that the American Indians came from the mythical lost continents of Atlantis (an ancient legend) or Mu (a modern fantasy), others that they drifted across from Asia, Africa, or Europe. Their pedigree has been linked variously, but without firm proof, to the Japanese, Chinese, Hindus, Egyptians, Phoenicians, Moluccans, Polynesians, Scandinavians, black Africans, the ten "lost" tribes of Israel, or to the Welsh who followed a fabled prince Madoc in the twelfth century.

Chance contacts across the waters may have occurred. Ecuadorian pottery, dating from about 3000–2000 B.C., bears a striking resemblance to Japanese pottery of the time. The sweet potato, otherwise a peculiarly American plant, grew in Polynesia before modern times. Still, granting the odds that some cultural traits crossed the oceans, the likelihood—now almost a certainty —is that there was a real place in the north where Indian peoples entered the New World, not from underground but from Siberia to Alaska, either by island-hopping across the Bering Strait or over a broad land bridge (Beringia) from which the waters receded during the Ice Ages.

Beringia must have been the route by which the horse and camel, which apparently evolved first in America, crossed to the

1

Old World before they became extinct in the New, and by which the deer and the elephant (the extinct American mammoth) went the other way. There is no evidence to place the origin of *Homo sapiens* in the New World, nor in the Old World much earlier than 50,000 years ago, although the latter is more controversial. Given the advance and retreat of the ice sheets over North America, a crossing might have been possible 50,000–40,000 years ago, but the most likely time for the latest crossings would have been just after the last heavy ice coverage, 18,000–16,000 years ago, when people could still walk across and then filter southward toward warmth through passes in the melting ice.

Once the ice sheets melted and the sea rose again, these pre-Mongoloid migrants were cut off from the rest of humanity (except for the short-lived Viking settlements on Greenland and Newfoundland) until Columbus came in 1492. For those long eons about the only written records are the relatively late pictographs of Middle America, remnants of a much larger body of writing which the Spanish conquerors destroyed in order to wipe out the memory of heathen beliefs and practices. Most of these writings, mainly Aztec and Mayan, remain undeciphered. The story therefore remains in the realm of prehistory, the domain of archeologists and anthropologists who must salvage a record from the rubble of the past: stone tools and weapons, bones, pottery, figurines, ancient dwellings, burial places, scraps of textiles and basketry, and finally bits of oral tradition and the reports of

Out of the mists of time, a carved jade head of the Olmec culture, found in Chiapas, Mexico. [Museum of the American Indian, Heye Foundation].

THE FIRST MIGRATION

◄──── Principal migration routes

early explorers, all pieced together with the adhesive of informed guesswork.

Pre-Columbian Indian Civilizations

Archeological digs add yearly to the fragments of knowledge about pre-Columbian America. The richest finds have been made on either side of the Isthmus of Panama, where Indian civilization peaked in the high altitudes of Mexico and Peru. Indeed it has been possible to reconstruct a remarkable sequence of events in pre-Columbian Middle America, a story of successive peoples who built great empires and a monumental architecture, supported by large-scale agriculture and a far-flung commerce: the Olmecs, Mayas, Toltecs, Aztecs, Incas, and others.

EARLY CULTURAL STAGES   On either side of these peaks of civilization, Indian life at the time of the Discovery dwindled into more primitive forms. By the best recent estimates about 100–112 million people lived in the Western Hemisphere, about 10–12 million (or 10 percent) in what is now the United States. Their cultures ranged from those of stone-age nomads to the life of set-tled communities which practiced agriculture. Many had passed the earlier cultural stages defined by archeologists as Lithic (Stone Age) and Archaic (hunting and gathering), and had reached the Formative stage of settled agriculture, although none of them ever achieved the heights of the cultures to the south.

The Lithic stage lasted to about 5000 B.C. Remnants of stone choppers and scrapers, similar to artifacts found in Siberia, sug-gest the presence of people long before the development, by about 9500 B.C., of projectile points for use on spears, and later, on arrows. With the invention of projectiles early man entered the age of the big-game hunters, who ranged across most of the Americas, chasing down mammoths, bison, deer, and antelopes.

As hunting and gathering became a way of life diet became more varied. It included a number of small creatures such as ra-coons and opossums, along with fish and shellfish (Archaic hooks, nets, and weirs have been found) and wild plants: nuts, greens, berries, and fruits in season. The Archaic Indians began to settle down in permanent or semipermanent villages; they invented fiber snares, basketry, and mills for grinding nuts; they domesti-cated the dog and the turkey or as some would have it, the dog, who knew a soft touch when he saw one, domesticated its master. In southern California, then as now relatively well-populated, tribes were able to specialize in sea animals, shellfish, and acorns. In some places in fact the Archaic stage persisted into very re-cent times—specifically until August 27, 1911, when a primitive man named Ishi, "the last wild Indian," left the woods and stum-bled into a white settlement seventy miles north of Sacramento, California.

The Formative stage replaced the Archaic, by definition, with the introduction of farming and pottery. In these developments Middle Americans got the jump on the tribes farther north and became the center of innovation and cultural diffusion. By about 5000 B.C. Indians of the Mexican highlands were cultivating or gathering plant foods that became the staples of the New World: chiefly maize (Indian corn), beans, and squash, but also such plants as chili peppers, avocadoes, pumpkins, and many more. These were developed into the forms now familiar by cross-breeding, accidental in part, but believed to have been also the product of experiments by Indian horticulturists. Maize, for in-stance, began as an ancient Mexican grass which cross-bred with another grass to produce teosinte. Countless crosses of maize with teosinte over the centuries produced the types of Indian corn which the Europeans found later.

THE MAYAS, AZTECS, AND INCAS   By about 2000–1500 B.C. permanent towns dependent on farming had appeared in Mexico, and so had pottery, which possibly diffused northward from Ecuador. The more settled life in turn provided leisure for more complex cultures, for the cultivation of religion, crafts, art, science, administration—and warfare. A stratified social structure began to emerge. From about A.D. 300–900 Middle America reached the flowering of its Classic cultures, with great centers of religion, gigantic pyramids, temple complexes, and courts for ceremonial games, all supported by the surrounding peasant villages. Life centered in the cities of Teotihuacán and Monte Alban and the Mayan culture of present-day Yucatán and Guatemala. The Mayas had developed enough mathematics (including a symbol for zero) and astronomy to devise a calendar more accurate than that the Europeans were still using at the time of Columbus. Then, about A.D. 900, for reasons unknown the Classic cultures

PRE-COLUMBIAN
INDIAN CIVILIZATIONS IN
MIDDLE AND SOUTH AMERICA

collapsed and the religious centers were abandoned. The Toltecs, a warlike people, conquered most of the region, but around A.D. 1200 they too withdrew, for reasons unknown.

During the time of troubles that followed, the Aztecs arrived from somewhere to the northwest, founded the city of Tenochtitlán (now Mexico City), traditionally in 1325, and gradually expanded their control over central Mexico. When the Spaniards arrived in 1519, the Aztec Empire under Montezuma II ruled over perhaps 5 million people—estimates range as high as 20 million. They were held in fairly loose subjugation for the sake of trade and tribute, and for the sake of captives to sacrifice on the altars of their bloodthirsty sun god, Huitzilopochtli (symbolized by the hummingbird), to feed and strengthen him for his daily journey across the sky. Because their culture was heir to the technology, arts, and religions of previous peoples in Middle America, the Aztecs are sometimes compared to the ancient Romans, in contrast to the more creative Mayas, who were the Greeks of the New World.

Farther south, in what is now Colombia, the Chibchas built a similar empire on a smaller scale; still farther south the Quechua peoples (better known by the name of their ruler, the Inca) by the fifteenth century controlled an empire that stretched a thousand miles along the Andes Mountains from Ecuador to Chile, connected by an elaborate system of roads and organized under an autocratic government which dominated life about as fully as any totalitarian state of the twentieth century.

INDIAN CULTURES OF NORTH AMERICA   The peoples of the present-day United States reached the Formative stage only in the last thousand years before Christ. There were three identifiable cultural peaks: the Adena-Hopewell culture of the Northeast (800 B.C.–A.D. 600), the Mississippian of the Southeast (A.D. 600–1500); and the Pueblo-Hohokam culture of the Southwest (400 B.C.–present). None of these ever reached the heights of the Classic stage in Middle America, although they showed strong influences from there, and they retreated for the most part back into an Archaic-Formative stage in which the English settlers found the first tribes with which they came in contact.

The halting transition from Archaic to Formative in the eastern woodland cultures is marked in the remains by such innovations as pottery, agriculture, earthen burial mounds, and tobacco and the smoking pipe. The Adena culture, centered in the Ohio Valley, was older but overlapped the similar Hopewell in the same area. The Adena-Hopewell peoples left behind enormous, and to the early settlers mysterious, earthworks and burial mounds—sometimes elaborately shaped like great snakes, birds, or animals. Evidence found in the mounds suggests a developed social structure and a specialized division of labor. There were signs too of an elaborate trade network which spanned the continent. The Hopewellians made ceremonial blades from Rocky Mountain obsidian, bowls from sea shells of the Gulf and Atlantic, ornamental silhouettes of hands, claws, and animals from Appalachian mica, breast plates, gorgets, and ornaments from copper found near Lake Superior. The Northeastern Indians at the time of colonization were distant heirs to the Hopewellian culture after its decline: the Algonquian tribes of the coastal areas and more directly, perhaps even by direct descent, the tribes making up the Iroquois League of Five Nations, a federation formed after 1600 as a result of their first contact with the French.

The Mississippian culture of the Southeast, which centered in the central Mississippi Valley, probably derived its impulse from the Hopewellians, but reached its height later and under greater influence from Middle America—in its intensive agriculture, its pottery, its temple mounds (vaguely resembling pyramids), and its death cults, which involved human torture and sacrifice. The Mississippian culture peaked in the fourteenth and fifteenth centuries, after the European discovery, and possibly collapsed fi-

A wooden carving of a mother carrying a child, found in a Hopewell burial mound in southern Ohio. [Milwaukee Public Museum]

nally as the result of diseases transmitted from European contacts.

All the peoples of the Southeast, and far into the Midwest, were touched by the Mississippian culture, and as late as the eighteenth century tribes of the Southeast still practiced their annual busk, or green corn ceremony, a ritual of renewal in which pottery was smashed, dwellings cleaned out, all fires were quenched, and a new fire kindled in the temple. The Mississippian traditions lingered among the Muskogean peoples of the Gulf area—the Choctaws, Creeks, and Chickasaws—but they also touched the Cherokees (originally Iroquoian) and the Algonquian and eastern Sioux tribes nearer the South Atlantic seaboard.

The greatest capacity for survival in their homeland was displayed by the irrigation-based cultures of the arid Southwest, elements of which persist today and heirs of which (the Hopis, Zuñis, and others) still live in the adobe pueblos of their ancestors. The Formative cultures of the Southwest, the closely related Mogollon, Hohokam, and Anasazi ("the ancient ones," in Navaho language), derived from a desert Archaic culture called Cochise and from contacts with Middle America, perhaps even from pre-Conquest Mexican outposts. The most widespread and best known of the cultures, the Anasazi, centered around the

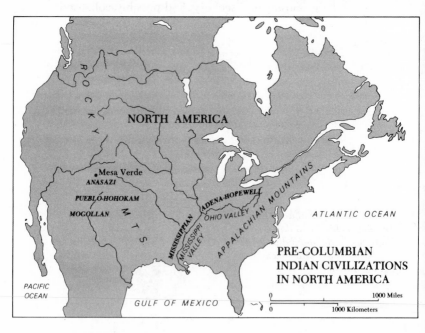

PRE-COLUMBIAN
INDIAN CIVILIZATIONS
IN NORTH AMERICA

Ruins of Anasazi cliff dwellings at MesaVerde, in Colorado. The circular chamber to the left is a ceremonial kiva. [Denver Convention & Visitors Bureau]

"four corners" where the states of Arizona, New Mexico, Colorado, and Utah now meet.

Like other peoples of the Formative stage, they never gave up the Archaic patterns of hunting and gathering, eating small animals, rodents, reptiles, birds, and insects, along with seeds, mesquite beans, pinon nuts, yucca fruits, and berries. With the coming of agriculture they perfected techniques of "dry farming," using the traces of ground water and catching the runoff in garden terraces, or in the case of the Hohokam, extensive irrigation works. Housing evolved from the Mogollon pit houses, which suggested the later kivas where religious observances were held, and developed into the baked-mud adobe structures which grew four and five stories high and were sometimes located, as at Mesa Verde, Colorado, in canyons underneath protective cliffs.

In contrast to the Middle American and Mississippian cultures, Anasazi society lacked a rigid class structure. The religious leaders and warriors labored much as the rest of the people. In fact warfare was little pursued except in self-defense (Hopi means "the peaceful people") and there was little evidence of human sacrifice or human trophies. There is evidence, however, that a lengthy drought (1276–1299) and the pressure of new arrivals from the north about 1300 began to restrict Anasazi territory. Into their peaceful world came the aggressive Navahos and Apaches, followed two centuries later by Spaniards marching up from the South.

When the whites came, even the most developed Indian societies were ill-equipped to resist these dynamic European cultures invading their world. There were large and fatal gaps in their knowledge and technology. Mogollon Indians had invented etching, but the wheel was found in the New World only on a few toys. The Indians of Mexico had copper and bronze but no iron except a few specimens of meteorites. Messages were conveyed by patterns in beads in the Northeast and by knotted cords among the Incas, but there was no alphabet or any true writing save the hieroglyphs of Middle America. The aborigines had domesticated dogs, turkeys, and llamas, but horses were unknown until the Spaniards came astride their enormous "dogs."

Disunity everywhere—civil disorders and rebellions plagued even the Aztecs and Incas—left the peoples of the New World open to division and conquest. North of Mexico, the nearest approach to organized government on a wide scale was the Iroquois League of the Five Nations, with weaker parallels like the Creek Confederacy of the Gulf Plains and the late–sixteenth-century Powhatan Confederacy of Virginia. But as it turned out the centralized societies to the south were as vulnerable as the scattered tribes farther north. The capture or death of their rulers (one usually followed the other) left them in disarray and subjection. The scattered tribes of North America made the whites pay more dearly for their conquest, but when open conflict erupted the bow and arrow were seldom a match for guns anywhere.

EUROPEAN VISIONS OF AMERICA

Long before Columbus, America lived in the fantasies of Europeans. Seneca, the Roman philosopher, wrote in his *Medea:* "An age will come after many years when the Ocean will loose the chain of things, and a huge land lie revealed; when Tiphys will disclose new worlds and Thule no more be the ultimate." Before Seneca the vast unknown beyond Gibraltar had entered the mythology of ancient Greece. In the west, toward the sunset which marked the end of day and symbolically the end of life, was an earthly paradise, a land of plenty and felicity. There

Homer put his Elysian Fields, the blessed abode of the dead, and Hesiod, a poet of the eighth century B.C. (a contemporary of the Olmecs and the North American mound builders), located the distant Hesperides which Father Zeus provided for a "godlike race of hero-men" who lived untouched by toil or sorrow. Whether called the Isles of the Blest, Avalon, or some other name (perhaps, some thought, it was the Garden of Eden), this happy land survived in myth throughout the Middle Ages, coloring the perceptions of explorers. When Sir Thomas More envisaged an ideal society in his book *Utopia* (1516), he placed it on an island in the New World.

Peter Martyr, the earliest European historian of the New World, said in the late fifteenth century that the Indians "seem to live in that golden world of which old writers speak so much: wherein men lived simply and innocently without enforcement of laws, without quarrelings, judges and libels, content only to satisfy nature, without further vexation for knowledge of things to come." This "Noble Savage" (as John Dryden later called him) would haunt the imagination for centuries—his reputation still clings to the popular image of the Indians. And the vision of America as a place of rebirth, a New Eden freed from the historic sins of the Old World, still colors the self-image of the American people.

Fugitive myths of legendary lands and forgotten voyages gripped the medieval imagination and appeared on fanciful maps: St. Brendan's Isles, visited by Irish monks in the sixth century; Antilia, whence Christians had fled the Moors and built seven cities ruled by seven bishops; Brasil; Satanazes; and others —some of them perhaps confused reports of the Azores or Canaries, some even perhaps garbled accounts of real discoveries. Occasionally curious bits of carved wood, even corpses that looked vaguely Chinese, washed up in the Azores—vagrant reminders, like meteorites from space, of worlds unknown.

THE NORSE DISCOVERIES

Norse discoveries of the tenth and eleventh centuries are the earliest that can be verified, and even they dissolved into legend, in stories that no doubt grew in the telling before they were written down centuries later in *The Saga of Eric the Red* and the *Tale of the Greenlanders*. Like Eskimos crossing the Bering Strait to the east, the Norsemen went island-hopping across the North Atlantic to the west. Before A.D. 800 they had reached the

HELLULAND
(Baffin I.)   GREENLAND

NORWAY

ICELAND

FAROE
ISLANDS
SHETLAND ISLANDS

SCOTLAND

MARKLAND
(Labrador)

ENGLAND

NORTH
AMERICA   L'Anse-aux-Meadows

IRELAND

VINLAND
(Newfoundland)

EUROPE

ATLANTIC OCEAN

CAPE COD

NORSE DISCOVERIES

× Norse settlements

0   1000 Miles

0   1000 Kilometers

AFRICA

Faroes, and about A.D. 870 they conquered Iceland from Irish settlers while other Vikings terrorized the coasts of Europe. Around 985 an Icelander named Eric the Red colonized the west coast of an icebound island he deceptively called Greenland— Eric was the New World's first real-estate booster—and about a year later a trader named Bjarni Herjulfson missed Greenland and sighted land beyond. Knowing of this, Leif Ericsson, son of Eric the Red, sailed out from Greenland about A.D. 1001 and sighted the coasts of Helluland (Baffin Island), Markland (Labrador), and Vinland (Newfoundland), where he settled for the winter.

Three attempts to colonize the site followed: one led by Leif's brother Thorvald about 1004–1005, another by Thorfinn Karlsefni about 1009–1010—both abandoned after fierce attacks by natives they called Skraelings—and a third attempt about 1014. According to the *Tale of the Greenlanders*, this venture ended in gruesome tragedy when Leif's demonic sister Freydis baited her jealous husband Thorvald into killing two of his associates (Freydis dispatched their women) so that she could have their ships. After that the colony was abandoned and the sagas told no more of Vinland. Until the 1960s speculation had placed it as far south as Rhode Island or Chesapeake Bay. The riddle was not solved until 1963, when a Norwegian investigator uncovered the ruins of a number of Norse houses at L'Anse aux Meadows, on the northern coast of Newfoundland. This almost surely was the Vinland of the Sagas.

The Norse discoveries have an antiquarian interest, but they had no meaningful relation to later American history unless Columbus heard of them, which is doubtful. The Norsemen withdrew from North America in the face of hostile natives and the Greenland colonies vanished mysteriously in the fifteenth century. Nowhere in Europe had the forces yet developed which would impel men to colonize and subdue the New World.

THE EMERGENCE OF EUROPE

During the five centuries from Ericson to Columbus, Europe emerged slowly from the invasions, disorders, and weakness that had plagued it since the fall of Rome. In the twelfth century, a time often called the High Middle Ages, western Europe achieved comparative stability. The age of discovery, in turn, coincided with the opening of the modern period in European history. Indeed the burst of energy with which Europe spread its power and culture around the world was the epoch-making force of modern times. The expansion of Europe derived from, and in turn affected, the peculiar patterns and institutions which distinguished modern times from the medieval: the revival of learning and the rise of the inquiring spirit; the rise of trade, towns, and modern corporations; the decline of feudalism and the rise of national states; the Protestant Reformation and the Catholic Counter-Reformation; and on the darker side, some old sins— greed, conquest, exploitation, oppression, racism, and slavery— which quickly defiled the fancied innocence of the New Eden.

RENAISSANCE GEOGRAPHY For more than two centuries before Columbus the mind of Europe quickened with the fledgling Renaissance: the rediscovery of ancient classics, the rebirth of secular learning, the spirit of inquiry, all of which spread the more rapidly after Johan Gutenberg's invention of movable type around 1440. Learned men of the fifteenth century held in almost reverential awe the authority of ancient learning. The most direct though by no means the only contribution of antiquity to the age of discovery was in geography. As early as the sixth century B.C. the Pythagoreans had taught the sphericity of the earth, and in the third century B.C. Eratosthenes computed its size very nearly correctly. All this had been accepted in medieval universities on the authority of Aristotle. The story that Columbus was trying to prove this theory is one of those durable falsehoods that will not disappear in the face of the evidence. No informed man of his time thought the earth was flat.

The foremost geographer of ancient times—and of the fifteenth century—was Claudius Ptolemy of Alexandria, whose *Guide to Geography* was compiled in the second century A.D., later preserved by Byzantine scholars, and printed in many Latin editions after 1475. Columbus knew the book and also the work of a leading geographer of his own time, Cardinal Pierre d'Ailly's *Imago Mundi* (*A Picture of the World*), written about 1410 and published in 1485—a copy survives with Columbus's marginal notes. Ptolemy made the earth smaller than Eratosthenes had done and grossly overestimated the extent of Asia. Other writers favored by Columbus, especially the Florentine scholar Toscanelli, with whom he corresponded, brought the Asian coast even nearer to Portugal—to about where America actually was—and thus spurred the idea of sailing west to reach the East.

Progress in the art of navigation came with the revival of learning. The precise origin of the magnetic compass is unknown, but the principle was known by the twelfth century, and in the fifteenth century mariners took to using the astrolabe and crossstaff long used by landlocked astronomers to sight stars and find the latitude. Steering across the open sea, however, remained a matter of dead-reckoning. A ship's master set his course along a given latitude and calculated it as best he could from the angle of the North Star, or with less certainty the sun, estimating speed by the eye. Longitude remained a matter of guesswork, since accurate timepieces were needed to obtain it. Ship's clocks were too inaccurate until the chronometer was developed in the eighteenth century.

THE GROWTH OF TRADE, TOWNS, AND NATION-STATES The forces which would invade and reshape the New World found their focus in the rising towns, the centers of a growing trade which slowly broadened the narrow horizons of feudal Europe. In its farthest reaches this trade, quickened by contacts made during the Crusades, moved either overland or through the eastern Mediterranean all the way to East Asia, whence Europeans imported spices, medicine, silks, precious stones, dye-woods, perfumes, and rugs in return for the wines, glassware, wool, and silver of Europe. The trade gave rise to a merchant class and they in turn gave a boost to the idea of corporations through which the risks and profits might be shared by many stockholders.

The trade was both chancy and costly. Goods commonly

passed from hand to hand, from ships to pack trains and back to ships along the way, subject to levies by all sorts of princes and potentates, with each middleman pocketing whatever he could. The Muslim world, from Spain across North Africa into Central Asia, lay athwart all the more important routes and this added to the hazards. Little wonder, then, that Europeans should dream of an all-water route to the riches of East Asia and the Indies. Interest in the Orient had been further stirred by travelers' stories, of which the best known was the account by the Venetian Marco Polo, written in 1298–1299 and printed more than once in the fifteenth century. Christopher Columbus had a Latin version, with margins heavily annotated in his own hand.

Another spur to exploration was the rise of national states, with kings and queens who had the power and the means to sponsor the search. The growth of the merchant class went hand in hand with the growth of centralized power. Traders wanted uniform currencies, trade laws, and the elimination of trade barriers, and so became natural allies of the sovereigns who could meet their needs. In turn merchants and university-trained professionals supplied the monarchs with money, lawyers, and officials. The Crusades to capture the Holy Land (1095–1270) had also advanced the process. They had brought the West into contact with Eastern autocracy and had decimated the ranks of the feudal lords. And new means of warfare—the use of gunpowder and standing armies—further weakened the independence of the nobility. By 1492 the map of western Europe showed several united kingdoms: France, where in 1453 Louis XI had emerged from the Hundred Years' War as head of a unified state; England, where in 1485 Henry VII emerged victorious after thirty years of civil strife, the Wars of the Roses; Spain, where in 1469 Ferdinand of Aragon and Isabella of Castile united two great kingdoms in marriage; and Portugal, where even earlier, in 1384, John I had fought off the Castilians and assured national independence.

THE VOYAGES OF COLUMBUS

It was in Portugal, with the guidance of John's son, Prince Henry the Navigator, that exploration and discovery began in earnest. About 1418 Prince Henry set up an information service to collect charts and data on winds and currents. In 1422 he sent out his first expedition to map the coast of Africa. Driven partly by the hope of outflanking the Islamic world, partly by the hope of trade, the Portuguese by 1446 reached Cape Verde, by 1471 the equator, and by 1482 the Congo River. In 1488 Bartholomew Diaz rounded the Cape of Good Hope, and in 1498 Vasco da Gama went on to Calicut in India.

Christopher Columbus meanwhile was learning his trade in the school of Portuguese seamanship. Born in 1451 the son of a weaver in Genoa, Italy, Columbus took to the sea at an early age, and made up for his lack of formal education by learning geography, navigation, and Latin (still the universal language of the learned). In 1476 he reached Portugal and went on voyages to Guinea, England, and Iceland, married a girl from Madeira where he made his home for a while, and during the 1480s hatched a scheme to reach the East by sailing west. But Portugal was by then too involved with African explorations. Christopher's brother Bartholomew, a professional mapmaker, hawked the idea in the courts of England and France, but they were busy with other matters. In 1486 Columbus turned to Queen Isabella, and after years of disappointment finally enlisted the support of King Ferdinand's advisor, Luis de Santangel, keeper of the privy purse. Santangel won the support of the Spanish monarchs and himself raised much of the money needed to finance the voyage. The legend that the queen had to hock the crown jewels is as spurious as the fable that Columbus had to prove the earth was round.

Columbus chartered one ship, the *Santa Maria,* and the city of

Columbus encounters the Indians of America. This engraving illustrated the 1493 letter in which Columbus announced his discovery. [New York Public Library]

Palos supplied two smaller caravels, the *Pinta* and *Niña*, exacted in punishment for some offense against the crown. From Palos Columbus sailed to the Canary Islands and by dead-reckoning westward. Early on October 12, 1492, after thirty-three days at sea, a lookout sighted land. It was an island in the Bahamas, called Guanahani (Iguana) by the inhabitants and renamed San Salvador (Holy Savior) by Columbus—later renamed Watlings Island. According to his own reckoning he was near Japan. He therefore continued to search through the Bahamian Cays down to Cuba, a place name which suggested Cipangu (Japan), and then eastward to the island he named Española (or Hispaniola) where he traded for some gold nose-plugs and bracelets with the people he insisted upon calling Indians. The friendly islanders of what Columbus thought an outpost of Asia belonged to the Arawak-language group who, pushed out of South America, had in turn pushed the Siboney Indians into western Cuba and western Hispaniola. Columbus learned of, but did not encounter until his second voyage, the fierce Caribs of the Lesser Antilles. Because of their location the name of the Caribbean Sea was derived from their name; because of their bad habits our word "Cannibal" was derived from a Spanish version of their name (Canibal).

On the night before Christmas the *Santa Maria* ran aground off Hispaniola and Columbus decided to return home with the two caravels, leaving about forty men behind. On the way home he discovered the need to move north and out of the easterly trade winds, which had brought him westward. This course led him to the Azores and thence to Portugal. The Portuguese thus learned of the new lands first, and John II laid claim to the discoveries on the grounds that they probably lay near the Portuguese Azores.

When Columbus finally reached Palos, the news spread rapidly throughout Europe. Ferdinand and Isabella instructed him to prepare for the second voyage and immediately set about shoring up their legal claim. Pope Alexander VI, who was Spanish, issued a papal bull (after *bulla*, or seal), *Inter Caetera*, which drew an imaginary boundary line 100 leagues west of the Azores, and provided that the area beyond should be a Spanish sphere of exploration and possession. Alarmed, the Portuguese monarch dropped his claim but demanded a dividing line farther west. In the Treaty of Tordesillas (1494) Spain accepted a line 370 leagues west of the Cape Verde Islands. In 1500 Pedro Alvares Cabral, a Portuguese captain on his way around Africa, swung southwestward across the Atlantic and sighted the hump of Brazil, which lay within the Portuguese sphere.

Meanwhile Columbus returned in 1493 with seventeen ships
and some 1,200 men, and planted the first Spanish colony on Hispaniola, where he learned that the men left behind on the first
voyage had been killed. He found the Lesser Antilles, explored
the coast of Cuba, discovered Jamaica, and finally returned to
Spain in 1496, leaving his brother Bartholomew in the new colony to found the city of Santo Domingo. On a third voyage in
1498 Columbus found Trinidad and explored the northern coast
of South America. Back in Hispaniola he displayed a disastrous
vacillation about dealing with a rebellion, and was arrested and
sent back to Spain in chains. But he regained enough favor to
lead a fourth voyage in 1502, during which he sailed along the
coast of Central America, still looking in vain for Asia. Marooned
on Jamaica more than a year, he finally returned to Spain in 1504
and in 1506 he died at Valladolid.

To the end Columbus refused to believe that he had discovered anything other than outlying parts of the Orient. Soon after
the first voyage Peter Martyr, a learned Italian at the Spanish
court, wrote letters in which he spoke of a New World, and noted
that the size of the globe suggested something other than India,
but even he did not find this New World inconsistent with the
Indies. Full awareness that a great land mass lay between Europe
and Asia only slowly seeped into the European consciousness,
and by one of history's greatest ironies led the New World to be
named not for its discoverer but for one of the first to argue with
conviction that it was indeed a New World, unknown to Ptole-

my. In 1507 the geographer Martin Waldseemüller published a treatise, *Cosmographiae Introductio (Introduction to Cosmography)*, in which he suggested that the New World should be called America, after Amerigo Vespucci.

Vespucci was a Florentine merchant and navigator sent to Spain as an agent of the ruling de Medici family. He knew Columbus, may have been among those who welcomed him back from the first voyage, and certainly helped outfit his ships for the second and third. Later, by his own accounts, Vespucci himself made four voyages to the New World, although there is firm evidence for only two. Vespucci did not command any of these expeditions, but his distinction as a geographer and an interpreter of what he found exceeded that of Columbus. The great popularity of his writings was important in bringing home to Europe the true nature and extent of the discoveries. This was indeed a New World.

THE GREAT BIOLOGICAL EXCHANGE

The first European contacts with this New World began a diffusion of cultures, an exchange of such magnitude and pace as humanity had never known before and will never know again short of contact with extra-terrestrial life. It was in fact more than a diffusion of cultures: it was a diffusion of distinctive biological systems. If anything, the plants and animals of the two worlds were more different than the people and their ways of life. Europeans, for instance, had never seen such creatures as the fearsome (if harmless) iguana, flying squirrels, fish with whiskers like

An iguana, drawn by John White, one of the earliest English settlers in America. [British Museum]

cats, snakes that rattled "castanets," or anything quite like several other species: bison, cougars, armadillos, opossums, sloths, tapirs, anacondas, electric eels, vampire bats, toucans, Andean condors, or hummingbirds. Among the few domesticated animals, they could recognize the dog and the duck, but turkeys, guinea pigs, llamas, vicuñas, alpacas, and guanacos were all new. Nor did the Indians know of cattle, pigs, sheep, goats, and (maybe) chickens, which soon arrived in abundance. Within a half century, for instance, whole islands of the Caribbean were overrun by pigs, whose ancestors were bred in Spain.

The exchange of plant life worked an even greater change, a revolution in the diets of both hemispheres. Before the Discovery three main staples of the modern diet were unknown in the Old World: maize, potatoes (sweet and white), and many kinds of beans (snap, kidney, lima beans, and others). The white potato, although commonly called "Irish," actually migrated from South America to Europe and only reached North America with Scotch-Irish immigrants of the 1700s. Other New World food plants were manioc (soon a staple in tropical Africa, consumed in the United States chiefly as tapioca), peanuts, squash, peppers, tomatoes, pumpkins, pineapples, sassafras, papayas, guavas, avocadoes, cacao (the source of chocolate), and chicle (for chewing gum). Europeans soon introduced rice, wheat, barley, oats, wine

John White's drawing of plantain, a plant new to the European discoverers of America. [British Museum]

grapes, melons, coffee, olives, bananas, "Kentucky" bluegrass, daisies, and that bane of the homeowner, dandelions.

The beauty of the exchange was that the food plants were more complementary than competitive. They grew in different soils and climates, or on different schedules. Indian corn, it turned out, could flourish almost anywhere—high or low, hot or cold, wet or dry. It spread quickly throughout the world. Before the end of the 1500s American maize and sweet potatoes were staple crops in China. The green revolution exported from the Americas thus helped nourish a worldwide population explosion probably greater than any since the invention of agriculture, something like a fivefold increase from 1630 to 1950, from some 500 million to almost 2.5 billion. Plants originally domesticated by American Indians now make up about a third of the world's food plants.

Europeans, moreover, adopted many Indian devices: canoes, snowshoes, moccasins, hammocks, kayaks, ponchos, dogsleds, toboggans, and parkas. The rubber ball and the game of lacrosse had Indian origins. New words entered the languages of Europeans in profusion: wigwam, teepee, papoose, succotash, hominy, tobacco, moose, skunk, opossum, woodchuck, chipmunk, tomahawk, mackinaw, hickory, pecan, raccoon, and hundreds of others—and new terms in translation: warpath, warpaint, paleface, medicine man, firewater. And the aborigines left the map dotted with place names of Indian origin long after they were gone, from Miami to Yakima, from Penobscot to Yuma.

There were still other New World contributions: tobacco and a number of drugs, including coca (for cocaine and novocaine), curare (a muscle relaxant), and cinchona bark (for quinine), and one common medical device, the enema tube. Indian healers, unlike the snake-oil merchants who traded on their reputation, were seldom quacks. But the white man presented them with exotic maladies they could not handle, for the Indians had lived in blissful ignorance of many infections that plagued Europeans. Even minor European diseases like measles turned killer in the bodies of Indians who had never encountered them and thus had built no immunity. Major diseases like smallpox and typhus killed all the more speedily. According to Thomas Harriot's account from the first colony sent by Sir Walter Raleigh to Roanoke Island, within a few days after Englishmen visited the Indian villages of the neighborhood, "people began to die very fast, and many in short space. . . . The disease also was so strange that they neither knew what it was, nor how to cure it; the like by report of the oldest man in the country never happened before, time out of mind." Now it happened time and time again. The first contacts with some of Columbus's sailors devastated whole communities, and the epidemics spread rapidly into the interior. But the Indians made some restitution. They got the worst of the bargain, but they infected Europeans with syphilis. This, rather than diarrhea, was the true "Montezuma's revenge."

PROFESSIONAL EXPLORERS

Undeterred by new diseases, professional explorers, mostly Italians, hired themselves out to the highest bidder to look for that open sesame to riches, a western passage to the Orient. One after another these men probed the shorelines of America during the early sixteenth century in the vain search for an opening, and thus increased by leaps and bounds European knowledge of the vast expanse of the new discoveries. The first to sight the North American continent was John Cabot, or Giovanni Caboto, a Venetian and possibly a native of Genoa, whom Henry VII of England sponsored after having missed a chance to sponsor Columbus. Acting on the theory that Cathay was opposite England, Cabot sailed from Bristol across the North Atlantic in 1497 and fetched up at Cape Breton or southern Newfoundland. Cabot never returned from a second voyage in 1498, but his landfall at what the king called "the newe founde lande" gave England the basis for a later claim to all of North America. For many years little was done to follow up the discovery except by fishermen who more and more exploited the teeming waters of the Grand Banks after 1500—men from England, Portugal, France, and Spain. In 1513 the Spaniard Vasco Nuñez de Balboa became the first European to sight the Pacific Ocean, but only after he had crossed the Isthmus of Panama on foot.

The Portuguese, who from their base in the Azores explored the coasts of Newfoundland and Labrador, and named the latter, meanwhile stole the march by going the other way. In 1498, while Columbus prowled the Caribbean, Vasco da Gama reached the East by sailing around Africa and soon afterward set up the trading posts of a commercial empire stretching from India to the Moluccas (or Spice Islands) of Indonesia. The Spaniards, however, reasoned that the line of demarcation established by the Treaty of Tordesillas ran around the other side of the earth as well. Hoping to show that the Moluccas lay near South America within the Spanish sphere, Ferdinand Magellan, a Portuguese seaman in the employ of Spain, set out to find a pas-

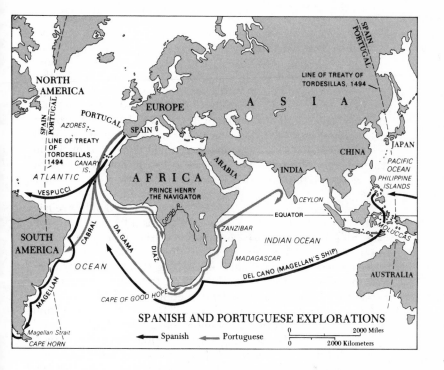

NORTH
AMERICA

EUROPE

A   S   I   A

LINE OF TREATY OF
TORDESILLAS, 1494

SPAIN
PORTUGAL

PORTUGAL

AZORES

SPAIN

CHINA

JAPAN

PACIFIC
OCEAN

SPAIN
PORTUGAL

LINE OF TREATY
OF
TORDESILLAS,
1494

CANARY
IS.

AFRICA

ARABIA

INDIA

PHILIPPINE
ISLANDS

ATLANTIC

VESPUCCI

PRINCE HENRY
THE NAVIGATOR

CEYLON

EQUATOR

SOUTH
AMERICA

OCEAN

CABRAL

DA GAMA

DIAZ

Congo R.

ZANZIBAR

MADAGASCAR

INDIAN OCEAN

MOLUCCAS

DEL CANO (MAGELLAN'S SHIP)

AUSTRALIA

MAGELLAN

CAPE OF GOOD HOPE

SPANISH AND PORTUGUESE EXPLORATIONS

Magellan Strait

CAPE HORN

◄— Spanish   ◄— Portuguese

0   2000 Miles

0   2000 Kilometers

sage through or around southern South America. Departing
Spain in 1519, he found his way through the dangerous strait
which now bears his name, then moved far to the north before he
found winds to bear him westward. On a journey far longer than
he had bargained for, he touched upon Guam and eventually
made a landfall in the Philippines, where he lost his life in a fight
with the natives.

Led by Magellan's navigator, Sebastian del Cano, however,
the remaining two ships made their way to the Moluccas, picked
up a cargo of spices, and one of them, the *Victoria*, returned to
Spain in 1522. This first voyage around the globe quickened
Spanish ambitions for empire in the East, but after some abortive
attempts at establishing themselves there, the Spaniards, beset
by war with France, sold Portugal their claims to the Moluccas.
From 1565, however, Spaniards would begin to penetrate the
Philippines, discovered by Magellan and named for the Spanish
prince who became Philip II. In the seventeenth century the English and the Dutch would oust Portugal from most of its empire,
but for a century the East Indies was Portuguese.

THE SPANISH EMPIRE

And the New World was Spanish, except for Brazil. The Caribbean Sea was the funnel through which Spanish power entered the New World. Columbus himself founded the first colony on Hispaniola in 1493; a few years later his brother Bartholomew started to build a castle (ruins of which still exist) at Santo Domingo, which became the capital of the Indies. From there colonization proceeded eastward to Puerto Rico (1508) and westward to Cuba (1511–1514).

CORTÉS'S CONQUEST   In the islands, Spaniards found only Archaic cultures. On the mainland, however, it was different, for there they found civilizations in some ways equal to their own, but almost as vulnerable as the Archaic cultures to their power. The great adventure of mainland conquest began in 1519, when Hernando Cortés and 600 men landed on the site of Vera Cruz, which he founded, and then, far exceeding his orders, set about a daring conquest of the Aztec Empire. The 200-mile march from Vera Cruz through difficult mountain passes to the Aztec capital of Tenochtitlán (Mexico City), and the subjugation of the Aztecs, was one of the most remarkable feats in human history.

But Cortés had some advantages and made the most of them. An acute judge of character and a gifted diplomat as well as military leader, he landed in a region where the people were still fighting off the spread of Aztec power and were ready to embrace new allies. To the Aztecs and their enemies alike, Cortés seemed to fulfill legends of the Toltec god Quetzalcoatl, who was due to return in the form of a white man and conquer the Aztecs. By a combination of threats and wiles, after several battles Cortés was able to enter Tenochtitlán peacefully and to make the emperor, Montezuma, his puppet. This state of affairs lasted until the spring of 1520, when the Aztecs rebelled and stoned Montezuma to death. The Spaniards lost about a third of their men in the streets as they fought their way out. Their allies remained loyal, however, and Cortés gradually regrouped. In 1521 he took the city again and with it the new emperor, Cuauhtemoc. After that the resistance collapsed, and Cortés and his officers simply replaced the former Aztec overlords as rulers over the Indian empire.

In doing so they set the style for other conquistadores to follow. Within twenty years his emulators had established a Spanish empire far larger than Rome's had ever been. Between 1522 and

A Navajo representation of Spanish conquistadors on the march, located in Canyon de Chelly, Arizona. [Shelly Grossman/Woodfin Camp & Associates]

1528 various lieutenants of Cortes, the most notable being Pedro de Alvarado, conquered the remnants of Mayan-Toltec culture in Yucatán and Guatemala. In 1531 Francisco Pizarro took a band of soldiers down the Pacific coast from Panama toward Cuzco, the seat of the Inca. Along the way he was able to play off against each other the supporters of rival claimants to the throne of the Inca, and to capture the leading claimant Atahualpa, seize his treasure, and execute him in 1533 after a trial on trumped-up charges of usurpation, idolatry, polygamy, and other crimes. From Peru, conquistadores extended Spanish authority through Chile by about 1553, and to the north, in present-day Colombia, conquered the Chibcha Empire in 1536–1538.

The Spanish were great believers in form. Before entering upon each new conquest, Spanish generals read a *Requerimiento* (Requirement) to the native people. This curious document recited Christian history from the creation to the time of Pope Alexander VI, and called upon the Indians to accept the authority of the Castilian crown, as granted by the pope. Failure to do so would result in subjugation and loss of property, and even more dire consequences. "The resultant deaths and damages shall be your fault," the paper added, not that of the Spaniards. The *Requerimiento* was repeatedly pronounced before battle, and while it may have helped to salve consciences, it required a strange naïvete. "It is not Christianity that leads them on," the great Spanish dramatist Lope de Vega had the devil say in his play *The New World*, "but rather gold and greed."

The course of empire was nevertheless marked by Spain's centuries-long crusade to expel the Islamic Moors from their foothold in the Iberian peninsula. By coincidence it was in 1492, the very year of discovery, that the Catholic monarchs captured the last Moorish stronghold, Granada, and there ordered the expulsion of all Jews (previously tolerated by the Moors) unless they converted to Christianity.

SPANISH AMERICA   The conquest of America thus seemed almost like an extension of this crusade into a new world—first conquest, then evangelization, by force if need be. The conquistadores transferred to America and there elaborated a system known as the *encomienda,* whereby Christian knights had acquired rights over land and people captured from the Moors. In America favored officers took over Indian villages or groups of villages. As *encomenderos* they were called upon to protect and care for the villages and support a missionary clergy. In turn they could levy tribute in goods and labor. Spanish America therefore developed from the start a society of extremes: conquistadores and encomenderos who sometimes found wealth beyond the dreams of avarice, if more often just a crude affluence, and subject peoples who were held in poverty.

What were left of them, that is. By the mid-1500s Indians were nearly extinct in the West Indies, reduced more by European diseases than by Spanish exploitation. To take their place the colonizers as early as 1503 began to bring in black slaves from Africa, the first in a melancholy traffic that eventually would bring over 9 million people across the Atlantic in bondage. In all of Spain's New World empire, by one informed estimate, the Indian population dropped from about 50 million at the outset to 4 million in the seventeenth century, and slowly rose again to 7.5 million. Whites, who totaled no more than 100,000 in the mid–sixteenth century, numbered over 3 million by the end of the colonial period.

The Indians did not always want for advocates, however. Catholic missionaries in many cases offered a sharp contrast to the conquistadores. Setting examples of self-denial, they went out into remote areas, often without weapons or protection, to spread the gospel—and often suffered martyrdom for their efforts. Among them rose defenders of the Indians, the most noted of whom was Bartolomeo de las Casas, a priest in Hispaniola (1502–1514) and later bishop of Chiapas, Guatemala, author of *A Brief Relation of the Destruction of the Indies* (1552). Las Casas won some limited reforms from the Spanish government, but ironically had a more lasting influence in giving rise to the so-called Black Legend of Spanish cruelty which the enemies of Spain gleefully spread abroad, often as a cover for their own abuses.

From such violently contrasting forces Spanish America gradually developed into a settled society, the independent conquistadores replaced quickly by a second generation of bureaucrats, the *encomienda* replaced by the *hacienda* (a great farm or ranch), as the claim to land became a more important source of wealth than the claim to labor. The empire was organized first into two great regions, the Viceroyalties of New Spain and Perú; eventually the Viceroyalties of New Granada and La Plata were split off from the latter. From the outset these were understood to be separate realms of the Castilian crown, united with Spain and with each other only in the person of the monarch. And from the outset, in sharp contrast to the later English experience, the crown took an interest in regulating every detail of colonial administration. After 1524 the Council of the Indies, directly under the crown, issued laws for America, served as the appellate court for civil cases arising in the colonies, and had general oversight of the bureaucracy. Trade, finances, and taxation were closely watched by the *Casa de Contratación*, or House of Trade, set up at Seville in 1503.

The culture that grew up in Spanish America would be fundamentally unlike the English-speaking world that would arise to the north. In fact a difference already existed in pre-Columbian America, with largely nomadic tribes to the north and the more settled and complex civilizations in Mesoamerica. On the latter world the Spaniards imposed an overlay of their own peculiar ways, but without uprooting the deeply planted cultures they found. Just as Spain itself harbored reminders of the one-time Arab rule, so in the New World reminders of the Aztec and Incan cultures lingered. Catholicism, which for long centuries had absorbed pagan gods and transformed pagan feasts into such holy days as Christmas and Easter, in turn adapted Indian beliefs and rituals to its own purposes. The Mexican Virgin of Guadalupe, for instance, evoked memories of feminine divinities in native cults. Thus Spanish America, in the words of Mexican writer Octavio Paz, became a land of superimposed pasts. "Mexico City was built on the ruins of Tenochtitlán, the Aztec city that was built in the likeness of Tula, the Toltec city that was built in the likeness of Teotihuacán, the first great city on the American continent. Every Mexican bears within him this continuity, which goes back two thousand years."

SPANISH EXPLORATIONS   For more than a century after Columbus no European power other than Spain had more than a brief foothold in the New World. Spain had not only the advantage of having sponsored the discovery, but of having stumbled onto those parts of America that would bring the quickest returns. While France and England remained preoccupied with domestic quarrels and religious conflict, Spain had forged an intense national unity. Under Charles V, heir to the throne of Austria and the Netherlands, and Holy Roman Emperor to boot, Spain dominated Europe as well as America. The treasures of the Aztecs and the Incas added to her power, but eventually they would prove to be a mixed blessing. The easy reliance on American gold and silver undermined the basic economy of Spain and tempted the government to live beyond its means, while American bullion contributed to price inflation throughout Europe.

To the north of Mexico the Spaniards never got a secure footing, but the "Spanish borderlands" of the southern United States from Florida to California preserve many reminders of the Spanish presence. Spanish mariners probably saw the coast of North America before 1500 (a crude outline which might have been Florida shows on a map of 1502), but the earliest known exploration of the Florida coast was made in 1513 by Juan Ponce de Leon, then governor of Puerto Rico, who later tried but failed to plant a colony on the Gulf coast in 1521. Meanwhile Spanish explorers skirted the Gulf coast from Florida to Vera Cruz, scouted the Atlantic coast from Cuba to Newfoundland, and established a short-lived colony on the Carolina coast.

Sixteenth-century knowledge of the interior came mostly from would-be conquistadores who sought but found little to plunder in the hinterlands. The first, Pánfilo de Narváez, landed in 1528 at Tampa Bay, marched northward to Appalachee, an Indian village in present-day Alabama, then back to the coast near St. Marks, where his party contrived crude vessels in hope of reaching Mexico. Wrecked on the coast of Texas, a few survivors under Nuñez Cabeza de Vaca worked their way painfully overland and after eight years stumbled into a Spanish outpost in western Mexico. Hernando de Soto followed their example in 1540–1543. With 600 men he landed on the Florida west coast, hiked up as far as western North Carolina, then westward beyond the Mississippi, and on up the Arkansas River. In the spring of 1542 de Soto died near the site of Memphis; the next year the survivors floated down the Mississippi and 311 of the original band found their way to Mexico. In 1540 Francisco Vasquez de Coronado, inspired by rumors of gold, traveled northward into New Mexico and eastward across Texas and Oklahoma

SPANISH EXPLORATIONS
OF THE MAINLAND

- •••• Balboa 1513
- ▬▬ Ponce de León 1513
- ▬·▬ Cortéz 1519
- ▬▬ Narvaez 1528
- ▬▬ Pizarro 1531-1533
- ▬ ▬ Cabeza de Vaca 1535-1536
- •••••• De Soto 1539-1542
- ▬ ▬ Coronado 1540-1542

0   1000 Miles
0   1000 Kilometers

as far as Kansas. He came back in 1542 without gold but with a
more realistic view of what lay in those arid lands.

The first Spanish base in the present United States came in response to French encroachments on Spanish claims. In 1562
French Huguenots established a short-lived colony at Port
Royal, South Carolina, and two years later another at Fort Caroline, Florida. The following year, 1565, a Spanish outpost,
named St. Augustine, became the first European town in the
present-day United States, and is now its oldest urban center except for the pueblos of New Mexico. While other outposts failed,
St. Augustine survived as a defensive outpost perched on the
edge of a continent.

In New Mexico missionary efforts began in 1581, and the first major colonization drive in 1598. Santa Fe, the capital and second-oldest European city in the United States, was founded in 1609 or 1610. An Indian uprising in 1680, the great Pueblo Revolt, temporarily chased the Spaniards out, but they returned in the 1690s. Spanish outposts on the Florida and Texas Gulf coasts and in California did not come until the eighteenth century.

THE PROTESTANT REFORMATION

While Spain built her empire, a new movement was growing elsewhere in Europe, the Protestant Reformation, which would embitter national rivalries, and by encouraging serious challenges to Catholic Spain's power, profoundly affect the course of early American history. When Columbus sailed in 1492 all of western Europe acknowledged the authority of the Catholic church and its pope in Rome. The unity of Christendom began to crack in 1517, however, when Martin Luther, a German monk and theologian, posted on the church door in Wittenberg his "Ninety-five Theses" in protest against abuses in the church and especially against the sale of indulgences for the remission of sins. Sinful men, Luther argued, could win salvation neither by good works nor through the mediation of the church, but only by faith in the redemptive power of Christ and through a direct relationship to God—the "priesthood of all believers." And the only true guide to the will of God was the Bible.

Fired with these beliefs, Luther set out to reform the church and ended by splitting it. Lutheranism spread rapidly among the people and their rulers—some of them with an eye to seizing church properties—and when the pope expelled Luther from the church in 1520, reconciliation became impossible. The German states fell into conflict over religious differences until 1555, when they finally patched up a peace whereby each prince determined the religion of his subjects. Generally, northern Germany became Lutheran, along with Scandinavia. The principle of close association between church and state thus carried over into Protestant lands, but Luther had unleashed ideas that ran beyond his personal control.

Other Protestants pursued Luther's doctrine to its logical end and preached religious liberty for all. Further divisions on doctrinal matters led to the appearance of various sects of Anabaptists, who rejected infant baptism, and other offshoots including the Mennonites, Amish, Dunkers, Familists, and Schwenkfelders. There already existed, moreover, another group, the

Martin Luther preaching. On the right, church officials—popes, cardinals, and monks—are caught in the mouth of hell. On the left are those saved through simple faith. [Bettmann Archive]

Moravians, who followed the teachings of Jan Hus, a Czech reformer martyred for his beliefs nearly a century before Luther.

CALVINISM   Soon after Luther began his revolt a number of Swiss cantons, influenced by the teachings of Huldreich Zwingli in Zurich, began to throw off the authority of Rome. In Geneva the reform movement looked to John Calvin, a Frenchman who had fled to Switzerland and who brought his adopted city under the sway of his beliefs. In his great theological work, *The Institutes of the Christian Religion* (1536), Calvin set forth a stern doctrine. All men, he taught, were damned by the original sin of Adam, but the sacrifice of Christ made possible their redemption by faith. The experience of faith, however, was open only to those who had been elected by God and thus predestined to salvation from the beginning of time. It was a hard doctrine, but the infinite wisdom of God was beyond human understanding.

Calvinism required a stern moral code, for the outward sign of true faith was correct behavior. If this did not of itself prove that one was of the elect, an immoral life clearly proved the opposite. Calvin therefore insisted upon strict morality and hard work, a teaching which especially suited the rising middle class. Moreover, he taught that men serve God through any legitimate calling, and permitted laymen a share in the governance of the church through a body of elders and ministers called the consistory or presbytery. The doctrines of Calvin became the basis for the beliefs of the German Reformed and Dutch Reformed churches, the Presbyterians in Scotland, some of the Puritans in England, and the Huguenots (or Confederates) in France. Through these and other groups Calvin later exerted more effect upon religious belief and practice in the English colonies than any other single leader of the Reformation.

THE REFORMATION IN ENGLAND   In England the Reformation, like so many other things, followed a unique course. The Church of England, or Anglican church, took form through a gradual process of Calvinizing English Catholicism. Rejection of papal authority came about at first, however, for purely political reasons. Henry VIII (1509–1547), the second of the Tudor dynasty, had in fact won from the pope the title of Defender of the Faith, for his *Defense of the Seven Sacraments* (1521), a refutation of Luther's ideas. But Henry's marriage to Catherine of Aragon had produced no male heir, and for that reason he required an annulment. In the past popes had found ways to accommodate such requests, but Catherine was the aunt of Charles V, king of Spain and emperor of the Holy Roman Empire, whose support was vital to the church's cause on the continent, so the pope refused. Unwilling to accept the rebuff, Henry severed the connection with Rome, named a new archbishop of Canterbury who granted the annulment, and married the lively Anne Boleyn. And she, in one of history's great ironies, presented him not with the male heir he sought, but a daughter, who as Elizabeth I would reign from 1558 to 1603 over one of England's greatest eras.

Elizabeth could not be a Catholic, for in the Catholic view she was illegitimate. During her reign, therefore, the Church of England became Protestant, but in its own way. The structure of organization, the bishops and archbishops, remained much the same, but the doctrine and practice changed: the Latin liturgy became, with some changes, the English *Book of Common Prayer*, the cult of saints was dropped, and the clergy were permitted to marry. The thirty-nine Articles of Faith, prepared by a committee of bishops and announced in 1571, defined the Anglican creed in Protestant terms, though sometimes evasively. For the sake of unity the "Elizabethan Settlement" allowed some latitude in theology and other matters, but this did not satisfy all. The episcopate, on the one hand, tried to enforce the letter of the law, stressing traditional practice. Many others, however, especially those under Calvinist influence from the continent, wished to "purify" the church so that it more nearly fit their

Elizabeth I, who ruled England during the springtime of its power. She is portrayed here standing on a map of England. [National Portrait Gallery, London]

views of biblical authority. Some of these Puritans would later despair of the effort to reform the Anglican church and would leave England to build their own churches in America.

CHALLENGES TO SPANISH EMPIRE

The Spanish monopoly of New World colonies remained intact throughout the sixteenth century, but not without challenge from national rivals spurred now by the emotion unleashed by the Protestant Reformation. The French were the first to pose a serious challenge, and Huguenot (Protestant) seamen from the great ports of France promised to build France into a major seapower. Spanish treasure ships from the New World held out a tempting lure to French corsairs, and at least as early as 1524 one of them was plundered off the Azores by a French privateer. In 1524 Francis I sent an Italian named Giovanni da Verrazzano in search of a passage to Asia. Sighting land (probably at Cape Fear, North Carolina), Verrazzano ranged along the coast as far north as Maine. On the way he viewed Pamlico Sound across the North Carolina Outer Banks, and beguiled by hope, mistook it for the Pacific Ocean. On a second voyage in 1538, his career came to an abrupt end in the West Indies at the hands of the fierce Caribs.

Unlike the Verrazzano voyages, those of Jacques Cartier about a decade later led to the first French effort at colonization. On three voyages (1534, 1535–1536, and 1541–1542) Cartier explored the Gulf of St. Lawrence and up the St. Lawrence River looking for the Kingdom of Saguenay, another fantasy compounded of European greed and Indian tall tales. Twice he got as far as present Montréal, and twice wintered at or near the site of Québec, near which a short-lived French colony appeared in 1542–1543. From that time forward, however, French kings lost interest in Canada, France after mid-century plunged into religious civil wars, and the colonization of Canada had to await the coming of Samuel de Champlain, the "Father of New France," after 1600.

From the mid-1500s forward, greater threats to Spanish power arose from the growing strength of the Dutch and English. The provinces of the Netherlands, which had passed by inheritance to the Spanish king, and which had become largely Protestant, rebelled against Spanish rule in 1567. A protracted and bloody struggle for independence was interrupted by a twelve-year truce which ended the war in 1609 for a time, but Spain did not accept the independence of the Dutch Republic until 1648.

Almost from the beginning of the revolt the Dutch "Sea Beggars," privateers working out of both English and Dutch ports, plundered Spanish ships in the Atlantic and carried on illegal trade with the Spanish colonies. The Dutch "Sea Beggars" soon had their counterpart in the Elizabethan "Sea Dogges": John Hawkins, Francis Drake, and others. While Elizabeth steered a tortuous course to avoid open war with Catholic Spain, she encouraged both Dutch and English captains in smuggling and piracy. Sir John Hawkins, first of the great Sea Dogs, got his start as a smuggler in 1562 when he picked up some 300 black slaves in Sierra Leone and traded them at a profit in Hispaniola. Two years later he took a cargo to the Spanish Main (in Venezuela and Panamá). A third voyage, in 1567–1568, however, ended in disaster when a Spanish fleet surprised him at Vera Cruz. Only two of his five ships escaped, commanded respectively by Hawkins and his cousin, Francis Drake, whose exploits soon overshadowed his own.

Drake now abandoned the pretense of legal trade and set out to loot Spanish treasure. In 1577 he embarked in the *Golden*

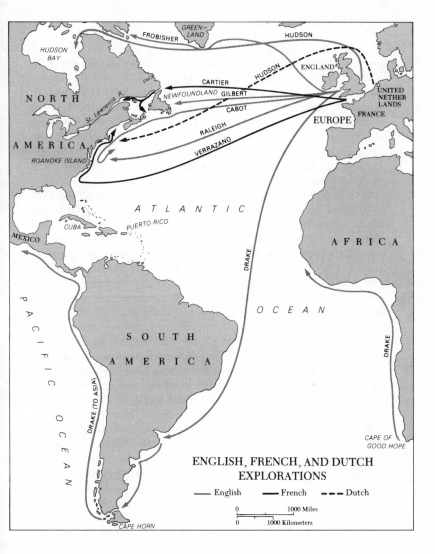

ENGLISH, FRENCH, AND DUTCH
EXPLORATIONS

——— English　　——— French　　- - - Dutch

0　　　　　　　1000 Miles
0　　　　　1000 Kilometers

Hind on his famous adventure around South America to raid
Spanish towns along the Pacific and surprise a treasure ship from
Perú. Continuing in a vain search for a passage back to the Atlantic, he was driven out to sea. He closed with the American coast
at about 43° north and spent seven weeks at Drake's Bay in
"New Albion," as he called California. Eventually he found his
way westward around the world and back home in 1580. Elizabeth, who had secretly backed the voyage, shared a profit of
4,600 percent, and knighted Sir Francis upon his return.

THE ARMADA'S DEFEAT   Such depredations continued for some twenty years before circumstances finally provoked open war. In 1568 Elizabeth's cousin Mary, "Queen of Scots," ousted by Scottish Presbyterians in favor of her infant son, fled to refuge in England. Mary, who was Catholic, had a claim to the English throne by descent from Henry VII, and soon became the focus for Spanish-Catholic intrigues to overthrow Elizabeth. Finally, after an abortive plot to kill Elizabeth and elevate Mary to the throne, the queen yielded to the demands of her ministers and had Mary beheaded in 1587.

In revenge Philip II decided to crush once and for all the Protestant power of the north and began to gather his ill-fated Armada, whereupon Francis Drake swept down upon Cadiz and destroyed part of the fleet before it was ready. His "singeing of the King of Spain's beard" postponed for a year the departure of the "Invincible Armada," which set out in 1588. From the beginning it was a case of incompetence and mismanagement compounded by bad luck. The Spanish idea of naval warfare was to bring rival ships together for what in effect was an infantry battle at sea. The heavy Spanish galleons, however, could not cope with the smaller and faster English vessels commanded by Drake and others. The English harried the Spanish ships through the English Channel on their way to the Netherlands, where the Armada was to pick up an army of invasion. But caught up in a powerful "Protestant Wind" from the south, the storm-tossed fleet never got there. It was swept into the North Sea instead, and what was left of it finally found its way home around the British Isles, leaving wreckage scattered on the shores of Scotland and Ireland.

Defeat of the Armada marked the beginning of English supremacy on the sea and cleared the way for English colonization. It was the climactic event of Elizabeth's reign, and it brought to a crescendo the surging patriotism that had been born of the epic conflict with Spain. The great literature of the Elizabethan age reflected a spirit of confidence and pride. The historical plays of William Shakespeare, especially, celebrated the glories of the House of Tudor and linked them to the spirit of the nation: "This blessed plot, this earth, this realm, this England." England was in the springtime of her power, filled with a youthful zest for new worlds and new wonders that were opening up before the nation.

ENGLISH EXPLORATIONS   A significant figure in channeling this energy was Richard Hakluyt the Younger, an Oxford clergyman, who as a youth was inspired by the example of his cousin, the elder Richard Hakluyt, to collect and publish accounts of the great voyages of exploration. He set out systematically to read whatever accounts he could find in Latin, Greek, Italian, Spanish, Portuguese, French, and English. In the process he rescued some accounts from destruction. In 1582 Hakluyt brought out his first book, *Divers Voyages touching the discoverie of America,* and in the summer of the Armada he finished *The Principall Navigations, voiages and discoveries of the English Nation.*

Hakluyt, moreover, became an active promoter of colonization. In 1584, at the request of Sir Walter Raleigh, he prepared for the queen *A Discourse of Western Planting* (first published three centuries later) in which he pleaded for colonies to accomplish diverse objects: to extend the reformed religion, to expand trade, to employ the idle, to supply England's needs from her own dominions, to provide bases in case of war with Spain, to enlarge the queen's revenues and navy, and to discover a Northwest Passage to the Orient.

While Hawkins and Drake ransacked the Spanish Main, other seamen renewed the search for the Northwest Passage, inspired by Sir Humphrey Gilbert's *A discourse of a Discoverie for a New Passage to Cataia.* Three voyages by Martin Frobisher (1576–1578) and three by John Davis (1585–1587) discovered new lands (and Eskimos) to the west of Greenland, but no passage. The history of English colonization must begin with Gilbert and his half-brother, Sir Walter Raleigh. In 1578 Gilbert, who had long been a confidant of the queen, secured a royal patent to possess and hold "heathen and barbarous landes countries and territories not actually possessed of any Christian prince or people." Significantly the patent guaranteed to Englishmen and their descendents in such a colony the rights and privileges of Englishmen "in suche like ample manner and fourme as if they were borne and personally residaunte within our sed Realme of England." And laws had to be "agreable to the forme of the lawes and pollicies of England." Gilbert, after two false starts, finally set out with a colonial expedition in 1583, intending to settle near Narragansett Bay. He landed in Newfoundland, took possession of the land for Elizabeth by right of John Cabot's discovery, read his commission to some mystified fishermen on the shore, and after losing his largest vessels, because the season was far advanced he resolved to return home with the other two. On the last day of his life he was seen with a book in his hand—probably Sir Thomas More's *Utopia,* which inspired his last recorded words. From the deck of his pinnace *The Squirrel,* Gilbert shouted across to the other ship the haunting words: "We are as near to heaven by sea as by land.'' The following night his ship vanished and was never seen again.

RALEIGH'S LOST COLONY   The next year, 1584, Raleigh persuaded the queen to renew Gilbert's patent in his own name, and sent out Capts. Philip Amadas and Arthur Barlowe with an English-naturalized Portuguese pilot, Simon Ferdinando, to reconnoiter a site. Sailing by way of the West Indies, they came to the Outer Banks of North Carolina, which Verrazzano had visited sixty years before, found an inlet to Pamlico Sound, and discovered Roanoke Island, where the soil seemed fruitful and the natives friendly. The Outer Banks afforded some protection, and rivers to the interior encouraged dreams of a route to the Pacific. In 1585 Raleigh's first colony went out under the command of Sir Richard Grenville with Ralph Lane as governor. Grenville went via the West Indies, plundering Spanish vessels to help defray the cost, and left the colonists on Roanoke Island before returning to England. They survived a mild winter, but the following June friction with the natives led to a fight, and when Francis

The English arrival at the Outer Banks. Roanoke Island is at left. The engraving is by Theodore de Bry, based on a drawing by John White. [Library of Congress]

Drake arrived to warn them of a threatened Spanish attack, the colonists decided to go home. Soon afterward Grenville returned, but not finding the colonists, left fifteen men behind to hold the fort and departed.

Raleigh immediately set about trying again, and in 1587 sponsored a colony of 117, including women and children, under Gov. John White. The plan was to pick up Grenville's men at Roanoke and proceed to Chesapeake Bay, since Roanoke was inaccessible to large vessels. But Simon Ferdinando, claiming the season was too far advanced—and probably eager to get on with plundering Spanish vessels—insisted that the colony remain at Roanoke. After a month in Roanoke, Governor White returned to England to get supplies, leaving behind his daughter Elinor and his grandaughter Virginia Dare, the first English child born in the New World. White, however, could not get back because of the war with Spain. He finally returned in 1590 to find the city of "Ralegh" abandoned and despoiled.

No trace of the colonists was ever found, nor any of the men Grenville left behind, and any theory as to their fate is only a wild surmise. Hostile Indians may have destroyed the colony, or hostile Spaniards—who certainly planned to attack—may have done the job. The only clue was one word carved on a doorpost, "Croatoan," the name of a friendly tribe of Indians and also of their island, the present Ocracoke. A romantic legend later developed that the colonists joined the Croatan Indians, finally were absorbed by them, and were among the ancestors of the present Lumbee Indians of Robeson County, North Carolina. There is no solid evidence for this, and while some may have gone south, the main body of colonists appears to have gone north to the southern shores of the Chesapeake Bay, as they had talked of doing, and lived there for some years until killed by Powhatan. But none of them was ever seen again. Unless some remnant of the Lost Colony did survive in the woods, there was still not a single Englishman in North America when Queen Elizabeth died in 1603.

FURTHER READING

Many scholars have at one time or another looked at pre-Columbian Amerindian life in the Western Hemisphere. Probably the most readable and comprehensive of the anthropological accounts is Harold E. Driver's *Indians of North America* (1970).° Alfred L.

° These books are available in paperback editions.

Kroeber's *Cultural and Natural Areas of Native North America* (1939) remains a fundamental guide for the dynamics of Indian culture. A good recent historical treatment is Alvin M. Joseph, Jr.'s *The Indian Heritage of America* (1968). A more topical use of the same material is Wilcomb E. Washburn's *The Indian In America* (1975).° Also useful is the ancient text by James Adair, *History of the American Indians, Particularly Those Nations Adjoining to the Mississippi, East and West Florida, Georgia, South and North Carolina, and Virginia* (1755, 1968).

Several works explore the theme of cultural conflict. Henry Warner Bowden's *American Indians and Christian Missions: Studies in Cultural Conflict* (1981) is short and interpretative. More theoretical is Richard Drinnon's *Facing West: The Metaphysics of Indian Hating and Empire Building* (1980).° Karen O. Kupperman's *Settling with the Indian: The Meeting of English and Indian Cultures in America, 1580–1640* (1980), stresses the racist nature of the conflict. Charles Gibson's *The Aztecs under Spanish Rule* (1964)° examines similar developments in Latin America, while Nathan Wachtel's *The Vision of the Vanquished* (1977) looks at the Indian point of view.

For evidence that Viking explorers came to North America before Columbus, see Frederick J. Pohl's *The Viking Settlements of North America* (1972) and Paul H. Chapman's *The Norse Discovery of America* (1981).° Michael A. Musmano's *Columbus Was First* (1966) counters such evidence. Interpretations of the conflicting evidence about early cultural contacts is presented in Carroll L. Riley et al. (eds.), *Man across the Sea: Problems of Pre-Columbian Contacts* (1971).

A number of fine overviews of European exploration are available. The most comprehensive are two volumes by Samuel E. Morison, *The European Discovery of America: The Northern Voyages, A.D. 500–1600* (1971), and *The Southern Voyages, A.D. 500–1600* (1974). Briefer, but a good outline of the forces of exploration, is John H. Parry's *The Age of Reconnaisance* (1963).° More specific are David B. Quinn's *North America from Earliest Discovery to First Settlements* (1977), John H. Parry's *The Spanish Seaborne Empire* (1966), and Charles R. Boxer's *The Portuguese Seaborne Empire* (1969). Scholarship on Columbus is best handled by Samuel E. Morison's *Columbus, Admiral of the Sea* (2 vols., 1942),° which was condensed into *Christopher Columbus, Mariner* (1956).°

The structure and form of European conquest and settlement is examined in Clarence H. Haring's *The Spanish Empire in America* (1947), which stresses the institutional framework of imperial government, and James Long's *Conquest and Commerce: Spain and England in the Americas* (1975), which compares the process of colonization of the two nations. See also William J. Eccles's *France in America* (1972)° and Charles Gipson's *Spain in America* (1966).° The most comprehensive view of how European mercantile tendencies led to "modernization" of the rest of the world is presented in Louis Hartz's *The Founding of New Society: Studies in the History of the United States, Latin America, South Africa, Canada, and Australia* (1964).

The English efforts which led to the Roanoke Island colony are documented in two books by David B. Quinn: *Raleigh and the British Empire*

(1947), and the aforementioned *England and the Discovery of America* (1974). For background on the motives for English exploration and settlement, consult Alfred L. Rowse's *The Expansion of Elizabethan England* (1955), John Phillips Kenyon's *Stuart England* (1978), and Carl Bridenbaugh's *Vexed and Troubled Englishmen, 1590–1642* (1968).° The link between English settlements like Roanoke and the Irish experience is explored in David B. Quinn's *The Elizabethans and the Irish* (1966). Robert R. Reynolds looks at the economic motivations which led to explorations in *Europe Emerges: Transition toward an Industrial World-Wide Society, 600–1750* (1961).

2

ENGLAND AND HER COLONIES

The England which Elizabeth bequeathed to her successor, like the colonies it would plant, was a unique blend of elements. The language and the people themselves mixed Germanic and Latin ingredients. The Anglican church mixed Protestant theology and Catholic forms in a way unknown on the continent. And the growth of royal power paradoxically had been linked with the rise of English liberties, in which even Tudor monarchs took pride. In the course of their history the English people have displayed a genius for "muddling through," a gift for the pragmatic compromise that defied logic but in the light of experience somehow worked.

THE ENGLISH BACKGROUND

Set off from the continent by the English Channel, that "moat defensive to the house" in Shakespeare's words, England had safe frontiers after the union of the English and Scottish crowns in 1603. In her comparative isolation, England developed institutions to which the continent had few parallels, except perhaps among the Dutch. By 1600 the decline of feudal practices was far advanced. The great nobles, decimated by the Wars of the Roses, had been brought to heel by Tudor monarchs and their ranks filled with men loyal to the crown. In fact the only nobles left, strictly speaking, were those few peers of the realm who sat in the House of Lords. All others were commoners, and among their ranks the aristocratic pecking order ran through a great class of landholding squires, distinguished mainly by their wealth and bearing the simple titles of "esquires" and "gentlemen," as did many well-to-do townsmen. They in turn mingled

James I, the successor to Queen Elizabeth and the first of England's Stuart kings. [National Portrait Gallery, London]

IACOBVS D.G. MAGNÆ BRITANNIÆ FRANCIÆ
SCOTIÆ ET HYBERNIÆ REX. ANNO MDCXXI.

freely and often intermarried with the classes of yeomen (small freehold farmers) and merchants.

ENGLISH LIBERTIES   It was to these middle classes that the Tudors looked for support and, for want of bureaucrats or a standing army, for local government. Chief reliance in the English counties was on the country gentlemen, who usually served without pay. Government therefore allowed a large measure of local initiative. Self-rule in the counties and towns became a habit—one that, along with the offices of justice of the peace and sheriff, English colonists took along as part of their cultural baggage.

Even the Tudors, who acted as autocrats, preserved the forms of constitutional procedure. In the making of laws the king's subjects consented through representatives in the House of Commons. By custom and practice the principle was established that the king taxed his subjects only with the consent of Parliament. And by its control of the purse strings Parliament would draw other strands of power into its hands. This structure of habit broadened down from precedent to precedent to form a constitution that was not written in one place, or for that matter, not fully written down at all. The *Magna Carta* of 1215, for instance, had been a statement of privileges wrested by certain nobles from the king, but it became part of a broader tradition that the people as a whole had rights which even the king could not violate.

A further buttress to English liberty was the great body of common law, which had developed since the twelfth century in royal courts established to check the arbitrary caprice of local nobles. Without laws to cover every detail, judges had to exercise their own ideas of fairness in settling disputes. Decisions once made became precedents for later decisions, and over the years a body of judge-made law developed, the outgrowth more of experience than of abstract logic. Through the courts the principle evolved that a subject could be arrested or his goods seized only upon a warrant issued by a court, and that he was entitled to a trial by a jury of his peers (his equals) in accordance with established rules of evidence.

ENGLISH ENTERPRISE   The liberties of Englishmen inspired a certain initiative and vigor of which prosperity and empire were born. The ranks of entrepreneurs and adventurers were constantly replenished by the young sons of the squirearchy, cut off from the estate which the oldest son inherited by the law of primogeniture (or first born). The growth of commerce featured at first the growth of the trade in woolen cloth built up after 1400 by the Company of Merchant Adventurers, which greatly expanded markets on the continent, working chiefly through Antwerp. The company was the prototype of the regulated company, actually a trade association of merchants who sold on their own accounts under the regulation of the company, which secured markets and privileges.

With time, however, investors formed joint-stock companies, ancestors of the modern corporation, in which stockholders shared the risks and profits, sometimes in a single venture but more and more on a permanent basis. When the cloth market became saturated in the mid-1500s, English merchants began to scan broader horizons for new outlets, new goods, new patterns of trade, and found themselves incurring greater risks. Some of the larger companies managed to get royal charters which entitled them to monopolies in certain areas and even governmental powers in their outposts: the Muscovy Company (1555), the Levant Company (1581), the Barbary Company (1585), the Guinea Company (1588), and the East India Company (1600). Companies like these would become the first instruments of colonization.

For all the vaunted glories of English liberty and enterprise, it was not the best of times for the common people of the realm. For more than two centuries serfdom had been on the way to extinction, as the feudal duties of serfs were commuted into rents. But while tenancy gave a degree of independence, it also gave landlords the ability to increase demands and, as the trade in woolen products grew, to enclose farmlands and evict the tenants in favor of sheep. The enclosure movement of the sixteenth century thus gave rise to the great numbers of sturdy beggars and rogues who people the literature of Elizabethan times and gained immortality in Mother Goose: "Hark, hark, the dogs do bark. The beggars have come to town." The problem was met only in part by Elizabethan poor laws which obligated each parish to care for its own (a practice passed on to the colonies), and the needs of this displaced population became another argument for colonial expansion—the more because the cloth market weakened and the nation's economy sought other outlets.

THE ENGLISH CIVIL WAR   With the death of Elizabeth the Tudor line ran out and the throne fell to the first of the Stuarts, whose dynasty spanned most of the seventeenth century, a turbulent time during which, despite many distractions at home, the English planted an overseas empire. In 1603 James VI of Scotland, son of the ill-fated Mary, Queen of Scots, and great-great-grandson of Henry VII, became James I of England—as Elizabeth had planned. A man of ponderous erudition, James fully earned his reputation as the "wisest fool in all Christendom." He lectured Englishmen on every topic but remained blind to English traditions and sensibilities. Where the Tudors had wielded absolute power through constitutional forms, the learned James demanded a more consistent logic and advanced at every chance the theory of divine right, beginning with a lecture to his first Parliament. Where the Puritans hoped to find a Presbyterian ally, they found instead a testy autocrat. "No bishop, no king," he told them, and promised to "harry them out of the land." He even offended Anglicans by sensibly deciding to end Elizabeth's war with Catholic Spain—and old privateers by suppressing what had now become piracy.

Charles I, who succeeded his father in 1625, proved even more stubborn about royal prerogative, ruled without Parliament from 1628 to 1640, and levied taxes by royal decree. The archbishop of Canterbury, William Laud, directed a systematic persecution of Puritans but finally overreached himself when he tried to impose Anglican worship on Presbyterian Scots. In 1638 Scotland rose in revolt and in 1640 Charles called Parliament to

Charles I. [The Louvre, Paris]

rally support and raise money. The "Long Parliament" (new elections had been delayed now for twenty years) impeached Laud instead, condemned to death the king's chief minister, the earl of Strafford, and abolished the "prerogative courts" established by the crown. In 1642, when the king tried to arrest five members of Parliament, civil war broke out between the "Roundheads" who supported Parliament and the "Cavaliers" who supported the king.

In 1646 royalist resistance collapsed and parliamentary forces captured the king. Parliament, however, could not agree on a permanent settlement. A dispute arose between Presbyterians and Independents (who preferred a congregational church government), and in 1648 the New Model Army purged the Presbyterians, leaving a "Rump Parliament" which then instigated the trial and execution of Charles I on charges of treason.

Oliver Cromwell, commander of the army, became in effect a

military dictator, ruling first through a council chosen by Parliament (the Commonwealth) and after forcible dissolution of Parliament as Lord Protector (the Protectorate). Cromwell extended religious toleration to all except Catholics and Anglicans, but his arbitrary governance and his moralistic codes made the regime more and more unpopular. When, after his death in 1658, his son proved too weak to carry on, the army once again took control, permitted new elections for Parliament, and supported the restoration of the monarchy under Charles II, son of the martyred king, in 1660.

Charles accepted as terms of the Restoration settlement the principle that he must rule jointly with Parliament, and managed by tact or shrewd maneuvering to hold his throne. His younger brother, the duke of York, was less flexible. Succeeding as James II in 1685, he openly avowed Catholicism and assumed the same unyielding stance as the first two Stuarts. Englishmen could bear it so long as they expected one of his Protestant daughters, Mary or Anne, to succeed him, but in 1688 the birth of a son who would be reared a Catholic finally brought matters to a crisis. Leaders of Parliament invited Mary and her husband William of Orange, a Dutch prince, to assume the throne jointly, and James fled the country.

By this "Glorious Revolution" Parliament finally established its independence of royal control. Under the Bill of Rights, in 1689, William and Mary gave up the prerogatives of suspending laws, erecting special courts, keeping a standing army, or levying taxes except by Parliament's consent. They further agreed to frequent sessions and freedom of speech in Parliament, freedom of petition to the crown, and restrictions against excessive bail and cruel and unusual punishments. Under the Toleration Act of 1689 a degree of freedom of worship was extended to all Christians except Catholics and Unitarians, although dissenters from the established church still had few political rights. In 1701 the Act of Settlement ensured a Protestant succession through Queen Anne (1702–1727). And by the Act of Union in 1707 England and Scotland became the United Kingdom of Great Britain.

SETTLING THE CHESAPEAKE

During these eventful years all but one of the thirteen North American colonies and several more in the islands of the Caribbean had their start. After the ill-fated efforts of Gilbert and Raleigh, the joint-stock company of merchants and gentlemen became the chief vehicle of colonization. In 1606 James I

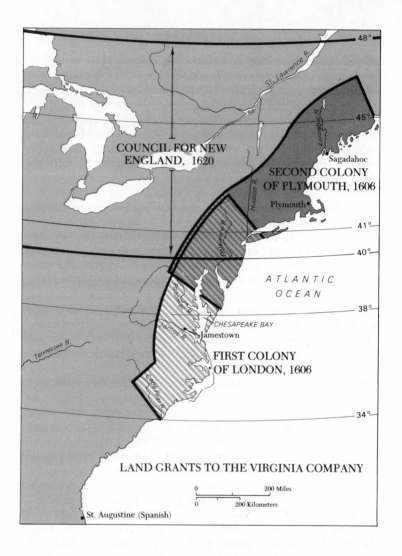

COUNCIL FOR NEW
ENGLAND, 1620

SECOND COLONY
OF PLYMOUTH, 1606

Sagadahoc

Plymouth

ATLANTIC
OCEAN

CHESAPEAKE BAY

Jamestown

FIRST COLONY
OF LONDON, 1606

LAND GRANTS TO THE VIRGINIA COMPANY

St. Lawrence R.

Kennebec R.

Hudson R.

Delaware R.

Potomac R.

James R.

Tennessee R.

Cape Fear R.

48°

45°

41°

40°

38°

34°

0   200 Miles

0   200 Kilometers

St. Augustine (Spanish)

chartered a Virginia Company with two divisions, the First Colony of London and the Second Colony of Plymouth. The London group could plant a settlement between the Thirty-fourth and Thirty-eighth Parallels, the Plymouth group between the Forty-first and Forty-fifth Parallels, and either between the Thirty-eighth and Forty-first Parallels, provided they kept a hundred miles apart. The stockholders expected a potential return from gold and other minerals; products, such as wine, citrus fruits, and olive oil, to free England from dependence on Spain; trade with the Indians; pitch, tar, potash, and other forest products needed for naval stores; and perhaps a passage to Cathay. Some investors dreamed of finding another Aztec or Inca Empire, but there were in fact relatively few Indians in eastern North America; some thought of a pirate base for plundering Spanish treasure ships. Few if any foresaw what the first English colony would actually become: a place to grow tobacco.

From the outset the pattern of English colonization would diverge from the Spanish. For one thing the English had a different model in their experience. The Spanish had retaken their homeland from the Moors and in the process worked out patterns of colonization later used in America. The English, after four centuries of sporadic intervention in Ireland, proceeded under Elizabeth to conquer the Irish by military force. While the interest in America was growing, the English were already involved in planting settlements, or "plantations" in Ireland. Within their own pale (or limit) of settlement the English set about reconstructing their familiar way of life insofar as possible. The term "wild Irish," which today seems more comic than serious, was then taken in dead earnest. The English went to Ireland, one historian said, with "a preconceived idea of a barbaric society and they merely tailored the Irishman to fit this ideological straitjacket." In English eyes, Irish Catholicism was mere paganism. What the English saw as a "savage nation" that lived "like beastes" could therefore be subjected without compunction. The same pattern would apply to the Indians of North America. In America, moreover, the English settled along the Atlantic seaboard, where the native populations were relatively sparse. There was no Aztec or Inca Empire to conquer and rule. Even without the example of Ireland, the colonists would have no alternative to setting up their own "pales" of settlement.

VIRGINIA   In August 1607 the Plymouth Company landed about 100 men at Sagadahoc on the Kennebec River in Maine, but abandoned the site after a hard winter of Indian hostility, bungling, and short supplies. Meanwhile the London Company, under the vigorous lead of Sir Thomas Smith, a prominent merchant, had already planted the first permanent colony in Virginia. On December 20, 1606, three ships borrowed from the Muscovy Company—the *Susan Constant*, the *Godspeed*, and the *Discovery*—sailed out from the Thames River with about 144 men. On May 6, 1607, having traveled south via the West Indies to catch the trade winds, they sighted the capes of Chesapeake Bay. Following instructions, they chose a river with a northwest bend—in hope of a passage to Cathay—and settled about 100 miles from the sea to hide from marauding Spaniards. The river

EARLY VIRGINIA AND MARYLAND

- Original grant to Lord Baltimore
- ---- Present-day boundary of Maryland

they called the James, and the settlement, Jamestown. Contrary to instructions to choose an island, they settled on a peninsula where the 105 survivors could see any approach from downstream and defend a narrow neck of land against the Indians. They were defenseless, however, from the mosquitoes of the neighboring swamps.

The colonists set about building a fort, thatched huts, a storehouse, and a church. Capt. Christopher Newport explored the James up to the falls near present Richmond, where he reached the limits of tribes dominated by Powhatan, and then sailed home, leaving the colonists perched on the edge of the wilderness. The colonists set to planting, but they were either townsmen unfamiliar with farming or, fully two-thirds of them, "gentleman" adventurers who scorned manual labor. Ignorant of woodlore, they could not exploit the abundant game and fish. Supplies from England were undependable, although Newport returned twice in 1608, and only John Smith's leadership and their trade with the Indians, who taught them to grow maize, enabled them to survive.

The Indians of the region were loosely organized in what Thomas Jefferson later called the "Powhatan Confederacy." Neither that nor the title "emperor" which the English gave to their *weroance* accurately conveys the structure of their society. Powhatan, chief of the Pamunkey tribe, had merely extended an insecure hegemony over some thirty tribes in the coastal area.

Despite occasional clashes with the colonists, the Indians adopted a stance of watchful waiting. The reason probably was that Powhatan at first hoped for trade and alliance with newcomers who might serve his purposes, and realized too late their growing design to possess the country.

The colonists, as it happened, had more than a match for Powhatan in Capt. John Smith, a man of humble origins but rare powers, a soldier of fortune whose tales of exploits in eastern Europe are so extravagant as to strain belief, except that they stand up wherever they can be checked against other evidence. When the colonists opened their sealed instructions, they found that Smith, who had quarreled with the expedition's leaders and had been clapped into chains on board ship, was to be a member of the governing council. The council was at first beset by disagreement and vacillation, but by force of will and ability Smith was soon in charge. With the colonists on the verge of starvation, he imposed discipline, forced all to work on pain of expulsion, bargained with the Indians, fought off a season of gold fever, explored and mapped the Chesapeake region. Despite his efforts, however, only 53 of the 120 were alive at the end of 1608.

In 1609 the Virginia Company moved to reinforce the Jamestown colony. A new charter redefined the colony's boundaries

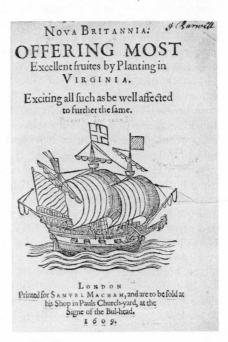

One of the Virginia Company's attempts to attract settlers to Jamestown. [Library of Congress]

and replaced the largely ineffective council with an all-powerful governor whose council was only advisory. In a dramatic promotion the company lured new subscribers from all ranks of society and attracted new settlers with the promise of free land after seven years of labor. The company in effect had given up hope of prospering except through the sale of lands which would rise in value as the colony grew. The governor, the noble Lord De La Warr (Delaware), sent as interim governor Sir Thomas Gates. In May 1609 Gates set out with a fleet of nine vessels and about 500 passengers and crew. On the way Gates was shipwrecked on Bermuda, where he and the other survivors wintered in comparative ease, subsisting on fish, fowl, and wild pigs. (Their story was transformed by William Shakespeare into his play *The Tempest.*)

Part of the fleet did reach Jamestown, however, and deposited some 400 settlers, who overwhelmed the remnant of about 80. These leaderless settlers, said one observer, included "many unruly gallants packed thether by their friends to escape il destinies." But their destinies were "il" indeed. All chance that John Smith might control things was lost when he suffered a gunpowder burn and sailed back to England in October 1609. The consequence was anarchy and the "starving time" of the winter of 1609–1610, during which most of the colonists, weakened by hunger, fell prey to pestilence. By May, when Gates and his companions made their way to Jamestown on two small ships painfully built in Bermuda, only about 60 remained alive. All poultry and livestock (including horses) had been eaten, and one man was even said to have dined on his wife. Jamestown was falling into ruins, the Indians had turned hostile, and the decision was made to give it up.

In June 1610, as the colonists made their way down the river, Lord Delaware providentially arrived with three ships and 150 men, whereupon instead of leaving Virginia, the colonists returned to Jamestown and hived off the first new settlements upstream at Henrico (Richmond) and two more downstream near the mouth of the river. It was a critical turning point for the colony, whose survival required a combination of stern measures and not a little luck. Effective leadership came with Delaware, and after his departure, under his deputies. In 1611 Thomas Gates took charge and established a strict system of *Lawes Divine, Moral, and Martiall,* inaccurately called "Dale's Code," after Thomas Dale who enforced them as marshal. Severe even by the standards of a ruthless age, the code enforced a militaristic discipline needed for survival.

Under Governors Dale (1614–1616) and Samuel Argall

(1617–1618) the colony limped along until it gradually found a reason for being: tobacco. In 1612 John Rolfe had begun to experiment with the harsh and biting Virginia tobacco. Eventually he got hold of some seed for the more savory Spanish varieties, and by 1616 the weed had become an export staple. Meanwhile Rolfe had made another contribution to stability by marrying Pocahontas, the daughter of Powhatan. Pocahontas had been a familiar figure in the streets of Jamestown almost from the beginning. In 1607, then only twelve, she figured in perhaps the best-known story of the settlement, the rescue of John Smith, who attributed to his own charm and English superiority what was perhaps the climax to a ritual threat of execution, a bit of play-acting to impress Smith with Powhatan's authority. In 1613, however, on a foray to extort corn from the Indians, Dale's men had captured Pocahontas and held her for ransom. To fend off the crisis, Rolfe proposed marriage to Pocahontas, Powhatan agreed, and a wary peace ensued. Distinguished Virginians still boast of their descent from the Indian "princess."

Sir Edwin Sandys, a prominent member of Parliament, replaced Thomas Smith as head of the company in 1618 and set about a series of reforms. First of all he inaugurated a new headright policy. Anybody who bought a share in the company at $12\frac{1}{2}$ shillings, or anybody who could transport himself to Virginia, could have fifty acres, and fifty more for any servants he might send or bring. The following year, 1619, was memorable in several ways. The company now relaxed the tight regimen of the *Lawes* and promised that the settlers should have the "rights of Englishmen," including a representative assembly. A new governor, Sir George Yeardley, arrived with instructions to put the new order into effect, and on July 30, 1619, the first General Assembly of Virginia, including the governor, six councilors, and twenty-two burgesses, met in the church at Jamestown and deliberated for five days, "sweating & stewing, and battling flies and mosquitoes." It was an eventful year in two other respects. The promoters also saw a need to send out wives for the men who, Sir Edwin Sandys noted, "By defect thereof (as is credibly reported) stay there but to get something and then return for England." During 1619 a ship arrived with ninety young women, to be sold to likely husbands of their own choice for the cost of transportation (about 125 pounds of tobacco). And a Dutch man-of-war, according to an ominous note in John Rolfe's diary, stopped by and dropped off "20 Negars," the first blacks known to have reached English America. It would be another year before the fabled *Mayflower* came.

THE INCONVENIENCIES
THAT HAVE HAPPENED TO SOME PER-
SONS WHICH HAVE TRANSPORTED THEMSELVES
from *England* to *Virginia*, vvithout prouisions neceſſary to ſuſtaine themſelues, hath
greatly hindred the *Progreſſe of that noble Plantation: For preuention of the like diſorders*
heereafter, that no man ſuffer, either through ignorance or miſinformation; it is thought re-
quiſite to publiſh this ſhort declaration : wherein is contained a particular of ſuch neceſ-
ſaries, as either priuate families or ſingle perſons ſhall haue cauſe to furniſh themſelues with, for their better
ſupport at their firſt landing in *Virginia*; whereby alſo greater numbers may receiue in part,
directions how, to prouide themſelues.

	Apparrell.	li.	s.	d.
	One Monmouth Cap —————	00	01	10
	Three falling bands —————	—	01	03
	Three ſhirts —————	—	07	c6
	One waſte-coate —————	—	02	02
	One ſuite of Canuaſe —————	—	07	06
	One ſuite of Frize —————	—	10	00
	One ſuite of Cloth —————	—	15	00
	Three paire of Iriſh ſtockins —————	—	04	—
Apparrell for	Foure paire of ſhooes —————	c8	c8	
one man, and	One paire of garters —————	00	10	
ſo after the	One doozen of points —————	00	03	
rate for more.	One paire of Canuaſe ſheets —————	08	00	
	Seuen ells of Canuaſe, to make a bed and			
	boulſter, to be filled in *Virginia* 8s.			
	One Rug for a bed 8 s. which will the bed	c8	00	
	ſeruing for two men, halfe is —————			
	Fiue ells coorſe Canuaſe, to make a bed at			
	Sea for two men, to be filled with ſtraw,			
	iiij. s. —————		05	00
	One coorſe Rug at Sea for two men, will			
	coſt vj. s. is for one —————			
		04	00	00

	Victuall.			
	Eight buſhels of Meale —————	02	00	00
For a whole	Two buſhels of peaſe at 3.s. —————	06	00	
yeere for one	Two buſhels of Oatemeale 4.s. 6.d. —————	09	00	
man, and ſo	One gallon of *Aquauitæ* —————	02	06	
for more after	One gallon of Oyle —————	03	06	
the rate.	Two gallons of Vineger 1. s. —————	02	00	
		03	03	00

	Armes.			
	One Armour compleat, light —————	17	00	
For one man,	One long Peece, fiue foot or fiue and a halfe,			
but if halfe of	neere Musket bore —————	01	02	—
your men	One ſword —————	05	—	
haue armour	One belt —————	01	—	
it is ſufficient	One bandaleere —————	01	06	
ſo that all	Twenty pound of powder —————	18	00	
haue Peeces	Sixty pound of ſhot or lead, Piſtoll and			
and ſwords.	Gooſe ſhot —————	05	00	
		03	09	06

	Tooles.	li.	s.	d.
	Fiue broad howes at 2.s. a piece —————	—	10	—
	Fiue narrow howes at 16.d. a piece —————	—	06	c8
	Two broad Axes at 3.s. 8.d. a piece —————	—	07	c4
	Fiue felling Axes at 18.d. a piece —————	—	07	06
	Two ſteele hand ſawes at 16.d. a piece —————	—	02	08
	Two two-hand ſawes at 5. s. a piece —————	—	10	—
	One whip-ſaw, ſet and filed with box, file,			
	and wreſt —————	—	10	—
For a family	Two hammers 12.d. a piece —————	—	02	00
of 6. perſons	Three ſhouels 18.d. a piece —————	—	04	06
and ſo after	Two ſpades at 18.d. a piece —————	—	03	—
the rate for	Two augers 6.d. a piece —————	—	01	00
more.	Sixe chiſſels 6.d. a piece —————	—	03	00
	Two percers ſtocked 4.d. a piece —————	—	00	c8
	Three gimlets 2.d. a piece —————	—	00	06
	Two hatchets 21.d. a piece —————	—	03	06
	Two froues to cleaue pale 18.d. —————	—	03	00
	Two hand-bills 20. a piece —————	—	03	04
	One grindleſtone 4.s. —————	—	04	00
	Nailes of all ſorts to the value of —————	02	00	—
	Two Pickaxes —————	—	03	—
		06	02	c8

	Houſhold Implements.			
	One Iron Pot —————	00	c7	—
	One kettle —————	—	06	—
For a family	One large frying-pan —————	—	02	c6
of 6. perſons,	One gridiron —————	—	01	06
and ſo for	Two skillets —————	—	05	—
more or leſſe	One ſpit —————	—	02	—
After the rate.	Platters, diſhes, ſpoones of wood —————	—	04	—
		01	c8	00
	For Suger, Spice, and fruit, and at Sea for 6.men —	00	12	06

For Suger, Spice, and fruit, and at Sea for 6.men —

So the full charge of Apparrell, Victuall, Armes, Tooles, and houſhold ſtuffe, and after this rate for each perſon, will amount vnto about the ſumme of — | 13 | 10 | —
The paſſage of each man is — | 06 | 00 | —
The fraight of theſe proviſions for a man, will bee about halfe a Tun, which is — | 01 | 10 | —
So the whole charge will amount to about — | 20 | 00 | 00

Nets, hookes, lines, and a tent muſt be added, if the number of people be grea-
ter, as alſo ſome kine.
And this is the vſuall proportion that the Virginia Company doe
beſtow vpon their Tenants which they ſend.

Whoſoeuer tranſports himſelfe or any other at his owne charge vnto *Virginia*, ſhall for each perſon ſo tranſported before Midſummer 1625.
haue to him and his heires for euer fifty Acres of Land vpon a firſt, and fifty Acres vpon a ſecond diuiſion.

Imprinted at London by FELIX KYNGSTON. 1622.

*The Virginia Company recommended that prospective settlers bring
to America these "provisions necessary to sustain themselves." At
bottom is the company's new headright policy. [New York Public
Library]*

Despite its successes the company again fell upon evil days.
Sandys quarreled with other leaders in the company, and in 1622
Powhatan's brother and successor, Opechancanough, led a concerted uprising which killed 347, including John Rolfe. Some
14,000 people had migrated to the colony since 1607, but the
population in 1624 stood at a precarious 1,132. Despite the
broad initial achievements of the company, after about 1617 a
handful of insiders had engrossed large estates and began to monopolize the indentured workers. In a tobacco boom of those

years some made fortunes, but most of the thousands sent out died before they could prove themselves. At the behest of Sandys's opponents, the king appointed a commission to investigate, and on its recommendation a court dissolved the company. Virginia became a royal colony.

The king did not renew instructions for an assembly, but his governors found it impossible to rule the troublesome Virginians without one, and annual assemblies met after 1629, although not recognized by the crown for another ten years. After 1622, relations with the Powhatan Confederates continued in a state of what the governor's council called "perpetual enmity" until the aging Opechancanough staged another concerted attack in 1644. The English suffered as many casualties as they had twenty-two years before, but put down the uprising with such ferocity that nothing quite like it happened again.

Sir William Berkeley, who arrived as governor in 1642, presided over the colony's growth for most of the next thirty-four years. The brawling populace of men on the make over which he held sway was a far cry from the cultivated gentry of the next century. But among them were the Byrds, Carters, Masons, and Randolphs who made the fortunes that nurtured the celebrated aristocrats of later generations.

MARYLAND In 1634, ten years after Virginia became a royal colony, a neighboring settlement appeared on the northern shores of Chesapeake Bay, the first proprietary colony, granted to Lord Baltimore by Charles I and named Maryland in honor of Queen Henrietta Maria. Sir George Calvert, the first Lord Baltimore, had announced in 1625 his conversion to Catholicism and sought the colony as a refuge for English Catholics who were subjected to discriminations at home. He had in fact undertaken to colonize Newfoundland in 1623 under a previous grant, but that colony was abandoned after a successful clash with the French followed by the severe winter of 1628–1629. Calvert had tried Virginia too. In October 1629 he had landed with his family and some followers at Jamestown, but was ordered to leave because he refused to take the Oaths of Allegiance and Supremacy to the monarch.

Nevertheless he kept the favor of King Charles and sought a charter in the region, which was issued in 1632 after his death. His son, Cecilius Calvert, the second Lord Baltimore, actually founded the colony. The charter, which set a precedent for later proprietary grants, gave the recipient the same powers bestowed upon the bishop of Durham in the past. In a region near the Scottish border, the warlike bishop had ruled almost as an independent monarch, but the charter specified that the laws must be in accordance with those of England. References to religion were vague except for a mention that chapels should be established according to the ecclesiastical law of England.

In 1634 Calvert planted the first settlement at St. Mary's on a small stream near the mouth of the Potomac. St. Mary's in fact was already there, a native settlement purchased from friendly Indians along with the cleared fields around it. Calvert brought Catholic gentlemen as landholders, but a majority of the servants from the beginning were Protestants. The charter gave Calvert power to make laws with the consent of the freemen (all property holders). The first legislative assembly met in 1635, and divided into two houses in 1650, with governor and council sitting separately. This was instigated by the predominantly Protestant freemen—largely servants who had become landholders, or immigrants from Virginia. The charter also empowered the proprietor to grant manorial estates, and Maryland had some sixty before 1676, but the Lords Baltimore soon found that to draw settlers they had to offer farms. Because of their flexibility, the Calverts bent rather than broke in the prevailing winds. Ousted from the proprietorship only for brief periods under Cromwell and William III, they continued even then to hold their property rights and coined a fortune in America before the end of the colonial period. The colony was meant to rely on mixed farming, but its fortunes, like those of Virginia, soon came to depend on tobacco.

SETTLING NEW ENGLAND

The Virginia Company of Plymouth never got back to colonization after the Sagadahoc failure in 1607, although it did bestir itself to hire John Smith as an explorer. After his return from a visit in 1614 Smith published *A Description of New England* (1616) and thus named the region. Having watched the London Company's transition from commerce to real estate, the leader of the Plymouth Company, Sir Ferdinando Gorges, reorganized his moribund enterprise into the Council for New England (1620), which had the right to issue land grants between the Fortieth and Forty-eighth Parallels.

PLYMOUTH The first permanent settlers landed in New England by no design of the council, which had some notion of creating vast feudal domains for its members. In fact they landed there by no design of their own—at least none that they acknowledged.

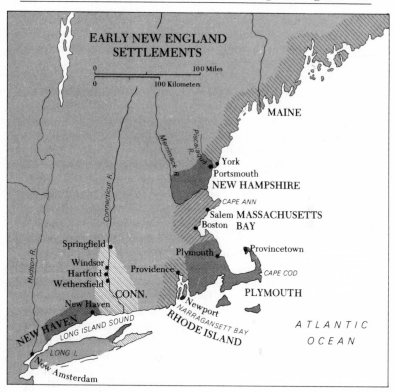

EARLY NEW ENGLAND
SETTLEMENTS

0 _____ 100 Miles
0 _____ 100 Kilometers

MAINE

Merrimack R.
Piscataqua R.

York
Portsmouth
NEW HAMPSHIRE

CAPE ANN

Salem MASSACHUSETTS
Boston BAY

Connecticut R.

Springfield
Windsor
Hartford
Wethersfield

Hudson R.

CONN.

New Haven

Providence

Plymouth

Provincetown

CAPE COD

PLYMOUTH

NEW HAVEN

LONG ISLAND SOUND

Newport
NARRAGANSETT BAY
RHODE ISLAND

ATLANTIC
OCEAN

LONG I.

New Amsterdam

They meant to go to Virginia, they said. The Pilgrims who established Plymouth colony belonged to the most extreme and uncompromising sect of Puritans, the Separatists, who had severed all ties with the Church of England. They stemmed from a congregation established in 1602 at Scrooby in eastern England, members of which had slipped away to Holland in 1607 to escape persecution. The Calvinistic Dutch granted them asylum and toleration, but restricted them mainly to unskilled labor. After ten years in Leyden they had wearied of the struggle. Watching their children gradually turn into Dutchmen, drifting away to become sailors, soldiers, or worse, so that "their posterity would be in danger to degenerate and be corrupted," they longed for English ways and the English flag. If they could not have them at home, perhaps they might transplant them to the New World. King James would not promise outright toleration if they set up a colony, but did agree to leave them alone, or as he put it, to "connive at them."

The Leyden group got the support of London merchants, led by Thomas Weston, who secured a land patent from the Virginia Company and set up a joint-stock company. In July 1620 a group of thirty-five Pilgrims led by William Bradford left Leyden on the *Speedwell*. At Southampton, England, a larger ship, the *Mayflower*, and a larger group of colonists joined them. At Plymouth, however, they had to abandon the leaky *Speedwell* and in September they crammed the *Mayflower* with their party of 101, both "saints" and "strangers," the latter including John Alden, a cooper, and Miles Standish, a soldier hired to organize their defenses. A stormy voyage led them in November to Cape Cod, far north of Virginia. Heading south, they encountered rough waters and turned back to seek safety at Provincetown. "Being thus arrived at safe harbor, and brought safe to land," William Bradford wrote in his history, *Of Plymouth Plantation*, "they fell upon their knees and blessed the God of Heaven who had brought them over the vast and furious ocean, and delivered them from all the perils thereof, again to set their feet on the firm and stable earth, their proper element." Exploring parties then scouted Cape Cod Bay and hit upon a place John Smith had called Plymouth for their settlement. Since they were outside the jurisdiction of any organized government, forty-one of the Pilgrim Fathers entered into a formal agreement to abide by laws made by leaders of their own choosing—the Mayflower Compact of November 21, 1620.

On December 26 the *Mayflower* reached Plymouth harbor and stayed there until April to give shelter and support while the Pilgrims raised and occupied their dwellings amid the winter snows. Nearly half the colonists died of exposure and disease, but friendly relations with the neighboring Wampanoag Indians proved their salvation. In March 1621 an Indian named Samoset walked into the settlement and later introduced Squanto, who spoke English and showed the colonists how to grow maize. A few years earlier Squanto had been kidnapped aboard a passing English ship and sold into slavery in Spain, whence he had somehow found his way back to England and, aboard a trading ship, back home, where he found himself to be the sole survivor of the Pawtuxet tribe, which had been wiped out by a pestilence in 1617. By autumn the Pilgrims had a bumper crop of corn, a flourishing fur trade, and a supply of lumber for shipment. To celebrate they held a harvest feast in company with Chief Massasoit and the Wampanoags. But after the ship *Fortune* arrived with thirty-five new colonists, the enlarged group again faced hunger before a food supply arrived in the spring. To make matters worse, on the way home the *Fortune* lost its cargo of furs and lumber to a French privateer.

But the colony soon stabilized. In 1621 it got a land patent from the Council for New England. Two years later it gave up its original communal economy to the extent that each settler was to provide for his family from his own land. A group of settlers bought out the sponsoring merchants in 1626 and promised to pay the purchase price in nine annual installments, although final settlement was delayed until 1648. In 1630 Governor Bradford secured a new title, the "Bradford Patent," from the Council for New England, which confirmed possession and defined the boundaries more clearly.

Throughout its separate existence, until absorbed into Massachusetts in 1691, the Plymouth colony remained in the anomalous position of holding a land grant but no charter of government from any English authority. The government grew instead out of the Mayflower Compact, which was neither exactly a constitution nor a precedent for later constitutions, but rather the obvious recourse of a group who had made a covenant (or agreement) to form a church and who believed that God had made a covenant with men to provide a way to salvation. Thus the civil government grew naturally out of the church government, and the members of each were identical at the start. The signers of the compact at first met as the General Court, which chose the governor and his assistants (or council). Later others were admitted as members, or "freemen," but only church members were eligible. Eventually, as the colony grew, the General Court became in 1639 a body of representatives from the various towns.

Plymouth Colony's population never rose above 7,000, and after ten years it was still overshadowed by its larger neighbor, Massachusetts Bay Colony. Plymouth's area, Cape Cod and the neighboring mainland, had relatively poor land, lacked ready access to furs from the interior, and was not in the best location for fisheries. But its imprint on the national mind would be greater than its size would warrant—William Bradford's unpretentious history, *Of Plymouth Plantation* (completed in 1651) brought the colony vividly to life. And Plymouth invented Thanksgiving—at least later generations persuaded themselves that its 1621 harvest festival was the first Thanksgiving.

During the decade of the 1620s a scattering of settlements appeared along the neighboring coasts, mainly fishing posts occupied only in season, plus a few rugged hermits like Samuel Maverick, who engaged in fishing, fur trading, and sometimes a little farming on his island in Massachusetts Bay. The Pilgrims got their first neighbors when Thomas Weston, who had helped them get a start, sent about fifty "rude and lusty fellows" via Plymouth to Wessagussett (now Weymouth), but that lasted only one winter. Another try by one Captain Wollaston at Mount Wollaston (now part of Quincy) likewise failed, and Wollaston moved to Virginia. He left behind Thomas Morton, who persuaded some thirty men to stay in what he renamed Merry Mount. There, only twenty-five miles from Plymouth, Morton's company of Indian traders brought Renaissance England to the New World, "drinking and dancing about" a maypole, in Governor Bradford's words, "inviting the Indean women for their consorts, dancing and frisking together . . . and worse practices." But his chief sin was selling the Indians firewater and firearms. It was all too much for the Pilgrims, who sent Miles Standish ("Captaine Shrimpe," in Morton's satiric account) to seize the reprobate and send him back to England in 1628.

MASSACHUSETTS BAY   Massachusetts Bay Colony, the Puritan Utopia, had its genesis in one of the fishing posts near Plymouth. In 1623 a group of Dorchester merchants with a patent from the Council for New England set up a permanent fishing village on Cape Ann. For three years they occupied the site of the present Gloucester, but the venture proved unprofitable and the promoters withdrew. In 1626 a remnant of about thirty moved down to Naumkeag (later Salem) under the leadership of Roger Conant, a devout Puritan. Back in Dorchester the Rev. John White, a moderate Puritan and a leading force in the Gloucester settlement, held to his hope for a Christian mission to the English fishermen and Indians along the coast. In answer to White's appeal, a group of Puritans and merchants formed the New England Company in 1628, and got a land patent from the Council for New England. Then to confirm its legality the company turned to Charles I, who issued a charter in 1629 under the new name of Massachusetts Bay Company.

The New England Company already had sent new settlers to Salem, including John Endecott as governor. Leaders of the company at first looked upon it mainly as a business venture, but a majority faction led by John Winthrop, a well-to-do lawyer from East Anglia recently discharged from a government job, resolved to use the colony as a refuge for persecuted Puritans and as an instrument for building a "wilderness Zion" in America. The charter had one fateful omission: the usual proviso that the company maintain its home office in England. Winthrop's group

therefore decided to take the charter with them, thereby trans-
ferring the entire government of the colony to Massachusetts
Bay, where they hoped to ensure Puritan control. By the Cambridge Agreement of 1629 twelve leaders resolved to migrate on
these conditions, and the company's governing body agreed.

In March 1630 the *Arbella,* with Gov. John Winthrop and the
charter aboard, embarked with six other ships for Massachusetts.
In a sermon, "A Model of Christian Charity," delivered on board
the *Arbella,* Winthrop told his fellow Puritans "we must consider
that we shall be a city upon a hill"—an example to all people. By
the end of 1630 seventeen ships bearing 1,000 more arrived. As
new settlers poured in, Salem was joined by a new settlement,
Charlestown, where Winthrop moved, and soon Mystic, Newton, Watertown, and Dorchester. Boston, on the Shawmut Peninsula, became the chief city and capital. The *Arbella* migrants
thus proved but the vanguard of a massive movement, the Great
Migration, that carried some 40,000–50,000 Englishmen to the
New World over the next decade, fleeing persecution and economic depression at home. They went not only to New England
and the Chesapeake, but now also to new English settlements in
the Lesser Antilles: St. Christopher (first settled in 1624), Barbados (1627), Nevis (1632), Montserrat (1632), and Antigua
(1632). The West Indian islands started out to grow tobacco but
ended up in the more profitable business of producing cane
sugar.

The transfer of the Massachusetts charter, whereby an English
trading company evolved into a provincial government, was a
unique venture in colonization. Power in the company rested
with the General Court, which elected the governor and assistants. The General Court consisted of shareholders, called freemen (those who had the "freedom of the company"), but of
those who came, few besides Winthrop and his assistants had
such status. This suited Winthrop and his friends, but then 108
more settlers asked to be admitted as freemen. Rather than risk
trouble, the inner group invited applications and finally admitted
118 in 1631. A further provision was made at that time that only
church members, a limited category, could become freemen.

At first the freemen were limited to the choice of assistants
who chose the governor and deputy governor. The procedure
violated provisions of the charter, but Winthrop kept the document hidden and few knew of the exact provisions. In the Watertown Protest of 1632, the people of one town objected to paying
taxes levied by the governor and assistants "for fear of bringing
themselves and posterity into bondage." Winthrop rebuked

THE

OATH
OF A
FREE-MAN

I A.B. being by Gods Providence an Inhabitant and
FREEMAN within the Iurifdiction of this Common
wealth; doe freely acknowledge myfelfe to be fubject to the
Government thereof.
AND therefore doe here fweare by the Great and Dreadful
NAME of the Everliving GOD, that I will be true and
faithfull to the fame, and will accordingly yield affiftance &
fupport thereunto with my perfon and eftate as in equity I am
bound; and will alfo truly endeavour to maintaine & preferve
all the liberties & priviledges thereof, fubmitting myfelfe to
the wholefome Lawes & Orders made and eftablifhed by the
fame. +++ AND further that I will not Plot or practife any
evill againft it, or confent to any that fhall fo doe: but will
timely difcover and reveal the fame to lawfull authority now
here eftablifhed, for the fpeedy preventing thereof.

M OREOVER I doe folemnly bind myfelfe in the
fight of GOD, that when I fhall be called to give
my voyce touching any fuch matter of this State in which
FREEMEN are to deale +++ I will give my vote and
fuffrage as I fhall judge in mine own confcience may beft
conduce and tend to the publicke weale of the body without
refpect of perfon or favour of any man.
So help me GOD in the LORD IESVS CHRIST.

Printed at Cambridge in New England:
by Order of the Generall Courte:
Moneth the Firft - 1639

*The Oath of a Free-Man: "I will give my vote and suffrage as I shall judge
in mine own conscience . . ." (1639). [American Antiquarian Society]*

them, but that year restored to the body of freemen election of
the governor and his deputy. Controversy simmered for two
more years until 1634, when each town sent two delegates to
Boston to confer on matters coming before the General Court.
There they demanded to see the charter, which Winthrop reluctantly produced, and they read that the power to pass laws and
levy taxes rested in the General Court. Winthrop argued that the
body of freemen had grown too large, but when it met, the General Court responded by turning itself into a representative body
with two or three deputies to represent each town. They also

chose a new governor, and Winthrop did not resume the office until three years later.

A final stage in the evolution of the government, a two-house legislature, came in 1644 when, according to Winthrop, "there fell out a great business upon a very small occasion." The "small occasion" involved a classic melodrama which pitted a poor widow against a well-to-do merchant over ownership of a stray sow. The General Court, being the supreme judicial as well as legislative body, was the final authority in the case. Popular sympathy and the deputies favored the widow, a Mrs. Sherman, but the assistants disagreed. The case was finally settled out of court, but the assistants feared being outvoted on some greater occasion. They therefore secured a separation into two houses and Massachusetts thenceforth had a bicameral assembly, the deputies and assistants sitting apart, with all decisions requiring a majority in each house.

Thus over a period of fourteen years the Massachusetts Bay Company, a trading corporation, was transformed into the governing body of a commonwealth. Membership in a Puritan church replaced the purchase of stock as the means of becoming a freeman, which was to say, a voter. The General Court, like Parliament, became a representative body of two houses, the House of Assistants corresponding roughly to the House of Lords, the House of Deputies to the House of Commons. The charter remained unchanged, but practice under the charter was quite different from the original expectation.

RHODE ISLAND   More by accident than design Massachusetts became the staging area for the rest of New England as new colonies grew out of religious quarrels within the fold. Puritanism created a volatile mixture: on the one hand the search for God's will could lead to a stubborn orthodoxy; on the other hand it could lead troubled consciences to diverse, radical, even bizarre convictions. Young Roger Williams, who arrived in 1631, was among the first to cause problems, ironically because he was the purest of Puritans, troubled by the failure of Massachusetts Nonconformists to repudiate the Church of England. He held a brief pastorate in Salem, then tried Separatist Plymouth, where according to Governor Bradford he "began to fall into strange opinions," specifically questioning the king's right to grant Indian lands "under a sin of usurpation of others' possession," and returned to Salem. Williams's belief that a true church must have no truck with the unregenerate led him eventually to the absurdity that no true church was possible, unless perhaps consisting of his wife and himself—and he may have had doubts about her.

But bizarre as Williams's beliefs may have been, they led him to principles that later generations would honor for other reasons. The purity of the church required complete separation of church and state and freedom from coercion in matters of faith. Williams therefore questioned the authority of government to impose an oath of allegiance and rejected laws imposing religious conformity. Such views were too advanced even for the radical church of Salem, which finally removed him, whereupon Williams retorted so hotly against churches that were "ulcered and gangrened" that the General Court in 1635 banished him to England. Governor Winthrop, however, out of personal sympathy, permitted him to slip away with a few followers among the Narragansett Indians, whom he had befriended. In the spring of 1636 Williams established the town of Providence at the head of Narragansett Bay, the first permanent settlement in Rhode Island.

Anne Hutchinson fell into dispute with the Puritan leaders for different reasons. The articulate wife of a well-to-do settler, she called groups together in her home to discuss the sermons of the Rev. John Cotton. In the course of the talks it began to appear that she held to a belief in an inner light from the Holy Spirit. Only Cotton, it seemed, along with her brother-in-law, the Rev. John Wheelwright, preached the appropriate "covenant of grace"; the others had a "covenant of works." Her adversaries likened her beliefs to the Antinomian heresy, technically a belief that one is freed from the moral law by the dispensation of grace in the gospel. The important point here was that Mrs. Hutchinson offended authority. Upon being hauled before the General Court, she was lured into convicting herself by claiming direct divine inspiration—blasphemy to the orthodox. Banished in 1638, she too took refuge in Narragansett country with a group of followers under William Coddington, who founded Pocasset (Portsmouth) on Aquidneck Island. Eventually she went to Long Island, under Dutch jurisdiction, and died there in an Indian attack in 1643. Her fate, Winthrop wrote, was "a special manifestation of divine justice."

When dissentions split Portsmouth, Coddington founded Shawomet (Warwick) on the mainland below Providence, and another Massachusetts outcast, Samuel Gorton, established Newport at the southern end of Aquidneck. Thus the colony of Rhode Island and Providence Plantations grew up in Narragansett Bay. It was a disputatious lot of dissenters who agreed mainly on one thing: that the state had no right to coerce belief. In 1640 they formed a confederation and in 1644 secured their first charter—from the Puritan Parliament. Williams lived until 1683, an active and beloved citizen of the commonwealth he founded in a society which, during his lifetime at least, lived up to his principles of religious freedom and a government which rested on the consent of the people.

CONNECTICUT   Connecticut had a more orthodox start in groups of Puritans seeking better lands and access to the fur trade farther west. In 1633, ignoring Fort Good Hope which the Dutch had established near the present-day site of Hartford, a group from Plymouth settled Windsor, ten miles farther up the Connecticut River. In 1636, activated by the leadership of Thomas Hooker, three entire church congregations from Watertown, Dorchester, and Newton (now Cambridge) trekked westward by the "Great Road," driving their hogs and cattle like the westering pioneers of a later day, and moved respectively to the Connecticut River towns of Wethersfield, Windsor, and Hartford, which earlier arrivals had laid out the previous year. A fourth group, from Roxbury, founded Springfield. Meanwhile in 1635 John Winthrop, Jr., had planted another town at the mouth of the river—Saybrook, named after its two proprietors, Lord Saye and Sele and Lord Brooke, who had acquired a grant from the Council for New England.

For a year the settlers in the river towns were governed under a commission from the Massachusetts General Court, but finding that only Springfield lay within Massachusetts, the inhabitants of Wethersfield, Windsor, and Hartford organized the self-governing colony of Connecticut in 1637. The impulse to organize came when representatives of the towns met to consider ways of meeting the danger of attack from the Pequot Indians, who lived east of the river. Before the end of the year the Pequots had attacked Wethersfield, and the settlers, with help from Massachusetts, responded with ferocity, surprising and burning the chief Pequot town on the Mystic River and slaughtering some 400 men, women, and children; stragglers were sold into slavery. All but a remnant of the Pequots perished in the holocaust.

In 1639 the Connecticut General Court adopted the "Fundamental Orders of Connecticut," a series of laws which provided for a government like that of Massachusetts, except that voting was not limited to church members. New Haven had by then appeared within the later limits of Connecticut. A group of English Puritans, led by their minister John Davenport and the wealthy merchant Theophilus Eaton, had migrated first to Massachusetts and then, seeking a place to establish themselves in commerce, to New Haven on Long Island Sound in 1638. Mostly city dwellers, they found themselves reduced to hardscrabble farming, despite their intentions. The New Haven colony became the most rigorously Puritan of all. Like all the other offshoots of Massachusetts, it too lacked a charter and maintained a self-governing independence until 1662, when it was absorbed into Connecticut under the terms of that colony's first royal charter.

NEW HAMPSHIRE AND MAINE   To the north of Massachusetts, most of what are now New Hampshire and Maine was granted in 1622 by the Council for New England to Sir Ferdinando Gorges and Capt. John Mason and their associates. In 1629 Mason and Gorges divided their territory at the Piscataqua River, Mason taking the southern part which he named New Hampshire. The first settlement had already appeared at Rye in 1623, the same year as the Gloucester fishing settlement. It remains uncertain whether Rye was deserted or merged with a colony later founded nearby at Strawberry Bank, and still later known as Portsmouth. In the 1630s Puritan immigrants began filtering in, and in 1638 the Rev. John Wheelwright, one of Anne Hutchinson's group, founded Exeter. Maine consisted of a few scattered and small settlements, mostly fishing stations, the chief of them being York.

An ambiguity in the Massachusetts charter brought the proprietorships into doubt, however. The charter set the boundary three miles north of the Merrimack River and the Bay colony took that to mean north of the river's northermost reach, which gave it a claim on nearly the entire Gorges-Mason grant. During the English time of troubles in the early 1640s Massachusetts took over New Hampshire, and in the 1650s extended its authority to the scattered settlements in Maine. This led to lawsuits with the heirs of the proprietors and in 1677 English judges and the Privy Council decided against Massachusetts in both cases. Two years later New Hampshire became a royal colony, but Massachusetts bought out the Gorges heirs and continued to control Maine as its proprietor. A new Massachusetts charter in 1691 finally incorporated Maine into Massachusetts.

The English Civil War in America

Before 1640 English settlers in New England and around Chesapeake Bay had established two great beachheads on the

Oliver Cromwell, England's Lord Protector from 1653 until his death in 1658. [British Information Service]

Atlantic coast, separated by the Dutch colony of New Netherland in between. After 1640, however, the struggle between king and Parliament distracted attention from colonization and migration dwindled to a trickle of emigrants for more than twenty years. During the time of civil war and Cromwell's Puritan dictatorship the struggling colonies were left pretty much to their own devices, especially in New England where English Puritans saw little need to intervene. In 1643 four of the New England colonies—Massachusetts, Plymouth, Connecticut, and New Haven—looked to their own safety by forming the New England Confederation. The purpose was mainly joint defense against the Dutch, French, and Indians, but the colonies agreed also to support the Christian faith, to render up fugitives, and to settle disputes through the machinery of the Confederation. Two commissioners from each colony met annually to transact business. In some ways the Confederation behaved like a sovereign power. It made treaties with New Netherland and French Acadia, and in 1653 voted a war against the Dutch who were supposedly stirring the Indians against Connecticut. Massachusetts, far from the scene of trouble, failed to cooperate, however, and the Confederation was greatly weakened by the inaction of its largest member. The commissioners nevertheless continued to meet annually until 1684, when Massachusetts lost its charter.

Virginia and Maryland remained almost as independent as New England. At the behest of Gov. William Berkeley, the Virginia Burgesses in 1649 denounced the execution of Charles and recognized his son, Charles II, as the lawful king. In 1652, however, the Assembly yielded to parliamentary commissioners backed by a parliamentary fleet and overruled the belligerent governor. In return for the surrender the commissioners let the Assembly choose its own council and governor, and the colony grew rapidly in population during its years of independent government—some of the growth came from the arrival of royalists who found a friendly haven in the Old Dominion, despite its capitulation to the Puritans.

The parliamentary commissioners who won the submission of Virginia proceeded to Maryland, where the proprietary governor faced particular difficulties with his Protestant majority, largely Puritan but including some earlier refugees from Anglican Virginia. At Governor Stone's suggestion the Assembly had passed, and the proprietor had accepted, the Maryland Toleration Act of 1649, an assurance that Puritans would not be molested in their religion. In 1652 Stone yielded to the commissioners, who nevertheless removed him temporarily, revoked the Toleration Act, and deprived Lord Baltimore of his governmental rights, though not of his lands and revenues. Still, the more extreme Puritan elements were dissatisfied and a brief clash in 1654 brought civil war to Maryland, deposing the governor. But the Calverts had a remarkable skill at retaining favor. Oliver Cromwell took the side of Lord Baltimore and restored him to full rights in 1657, whereupon the Toleration Act was reinstated. The act deservedly stands as a landmark to human liberty, albeit enacted more out of expediency than conviction, and although it limited toleration to those who professed belief in the Holy Trinity.

Although Cromwell let the colonies go their own way, he was not indifferent to the nascent empire. He fought trade wars with the Dutch and harassed England's traditional enemy, Catholic Spain, in the Caribbean. In 1655 he sent out an expedition which conquered Jamaica from the Spaniards, thereby improving the odds for English privateers and pirates who pillaged Spanish ships—and often any others that chanced by.

The Restoration of King Charles II in England was followed by an equally painless restoration of previous governments in the colonies. The process involved scarcely any change, since little had occurred under Cromwell. The Virginia Assembly gladly restored Governor Berkeley to his office, an act soon confirmed by the crown. The king promptly confirmed Lord Baltimore in his rights, which Cromwell had already restored. Emigration rapidly expanded population in both colonies. Fears of reprisals against Puritan New England proved unfounded, at least for the time being. Agents hastily dispatched by the colonies won reconfirmation of the Massachusetts charter in 1662 and the very first royal charters for Connecticut and Rhode Island in 1662 and 1663. All three retained their status as self-governing corporations. Plymouth still had no charter, but went unmolested. New Haven, however, disappeared as a separate entity, absorbed into the colony of Connecticut.

SETTLING THE CAROLINAS

The Restoration of the Merry Monarch opened a new season of enthusiasm for colonial expansion, directed mainly by royal favorites. Within twelve years the English had conquered New Netherland, had settled Carolina, and very nearly filled out the shape of the colonies. In the middle region formerly claimed by the Dutch, four new colonies sprang into being: New York, New Jersey, Pennsylvania, and Delaware. Without exception the new colonies were proprietary, awarded by the king to men who had remained loyal, or had contributed to his restoration, or in

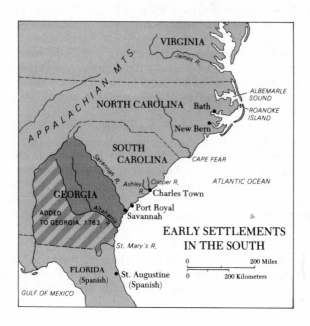

one case to whom he was indebted. In 1663 he granted Carolina to eight True and Absolute Lords Proprietors: Sir John Colleton, a Barbadian planter and prime mover of the enterprise; George Monk, the duke of Albemarle, Cromwell's army commander who engineered the Restoration; Edward Hyde, earl of Clarendon; Sir Anthony Ashley-Cooper, later earl of Shaftesbury; Lord John Berkeley and his brother, Gov. William Berkeley of Virginia; William Craven, earl of Craven; and Sir George Carteret. The list is nearly a complete rollcall of the movers and shakers in Restoration expansion. Six of the eight were connected with the Royal African and Hudson's Bay Companies. Two—Carteret and Lord Berkeley—became the proprietors of New Jersey, and six, including Berkeley and Carteret, became proprietors of the Bahamas. Five served on the Council of Trade, six on the Council for Foreign Plantations, both important committees of the Privy Council.

NORTH CAROLINA   Carolina was from the beginning made up of two widely separated areas of settlement, which finally became separate colonies. The northernmost part, long called Albemarle, had been entered as early as the 1650s by stragglers who drifted southward from Virginia. For half a century Albemarle remained a remote scattering of settlers along the shores of Albemarle Sound, isolated from Virginia by the Dismal Swamp and lacking easy access for ocean-going vessels. For many years its reputation suffered from the belief that it served as a rogue's harbor for the offscourings of Virginia. Later the aristocratic William Byrd, who helped survey the dividing line between Virginia and North Carolina, dubbed the neighboring colony Lubberland: "Surely there is no place in the world where the inhabitants lived with less labor than in North Carolina. . . . When the weather is mild, they stand leaning with both their arms upon the cornfield fence and gravely consider whether they had best go and take a small beat at the hoe but generally find reasons to put it off. . . ." Albemarle had no governor until 1664 when Sir William Berkeley exercised proprietary authority to appoint William Drummond, no assembly until 1665, and not even a town until a group of French Huguenots founded the village of Bath in 1704.

SOUTH CAROLINA   The proprietors neglected Albemarle from the outset, and focused on more promising sites to the south. They proposed to find settlers who had already been seasoned in the colonies, and from the outset Barbadians showed a lively inter-

*Advertisement for
settlers showing the
proprietors' interest in
South Carolina. [Univer-
sity of North Carolina]*

est. Colleton had connections in Barbados, where the rise of large-scale sugar production had persuaded small planters to try their luck elsewhere. Sir Anthony Ashley-Cooper finally spurred the enterprise by persuading his colleagues to take on more of the financial burden of settlement. In 1669 three ships left London with about 100 settlers recruited in England. The expedition sailed first to Barbados, to pick up more settlers, then north to Bermuda. The goal was Port Royal, at what is now the southern tip of South Carolina, but the settlers decided to go farther north to put more distance between themselves and Spanish St. Augustine. The choice fell on a place several miles up the Ashley River, where Charles Town remained from 1670 to 1680, when it was moved across and downstream to Oyster Point, overlooking Charleston Harbor where, as proud Charlestonians later claimed, the Ashley and Cooper Rivers "join to form the Atlantic Ocean."

The government of this colony rested on one of the most curious documents of colonial history, the "Fundamental Constitutions of Carolina," drawn up by Lord Ashley with the help of his secretary, John Locke. Its cumbersome frame of government and

A view of Charles Town, South Carolina. [New York Public Library]

its provisions for a nobility of proprietors, landgraves, and cassiques had little effect in the colony except to encourage a practice of large land grants, but from the beginning smaller "headrights" were given to every immigrant who paid his own way. The provision which had greatest effect was a grant of religious toleration, designed to encourage immigration, which gave South Carolina a greater degree of indulgence (extending even to Jews and heathens) than either England or any other colony except Rhode Island, and when it was established, Pennsylvania.

For two decades the South Carolina proprietors struggled to find a staple crop. Indeed the colonists at first had trouble providing their own subsistence. The first profitable enterprise was the Indian trade developed by Dr. Henry Woodward, who had left an expedition to live among the Indians and learn their languages four years before the founding of Charles Town. Through his contacts with the coastal tribes of Cusabos and Coosas, later with the Westoes along the Savannah River, enterprising colonists built up a flourishing trade in deerskins and redskins. Ambitious Barbadians, case-hardened by African slavery in the tropics, dominated the colony and did not scruple at organizing a major trade in Indian slaves, whom the Westoes obligingly drove to the coast for shipment to the West Indians. The first major export other than furs and slaves was cattle, and a staple crop was not developed until the introduction of rice in the 1690s. Meanwhile the continuing Indian trade led to repeated troubles with the proprietors, who tried in vain to regulate Indian affairs and stabilize the colony. Ultimately the struggle would lead to a rebellion against proprietary rule and an appeal to the crown to take charge. South Carolina became a separate royal colony in

1719. North Carolina remained under proprietary rule for ten more years, until the proprietors surrendered their governing rights to the crown in 1729.

SETTLING THE MIDDLE COLONIES AND GEORGIA

NEW NETHERLAND BECOMES NEW YORK   Charles II resolved early to pluck out that old thorn in the side of the English colonies— New Netherland. The Dutch colony was older than New England, and had been planted when the two Protestant powers enjoyed friendly relations in opposition to Catholic Spain. The Dutch East India Company (organized in 1620) had hired an English captain, Henry Hudson, to seek the elusive passage to Cathay. Coasting North America in 1609, Hudson had discovered Delaware Bay and explored the river named for him, to a point probably beyond Albany where he and a group of Mohawks made merry with brandy. From the contact stemmed a lasting trade relation between the Dutch and the Iroquois nations, a group of whom had met a hostile reception from the French explorer Champlain the year before. In 1614 the Dutch established fur-trading posts on Manhattan Island and upriver at Fort Orange (later Albany). Ten years later a newly organized West India Company began permanent settlement, the first on Governor's Island. In 1626 Gov. Peter Minuit purchased Man-

The earliest view of Fort New Amsterdam, at the southern tip of Manhattan, around 1636–1639. [New York Public Library]

hattan from the resident Indians and Fort Amsterdam appeared at the lower end of the island. The village of New Amsterdam, which grew up around the fort, became the capital of New Netherland.

Dutch settlements gradually dispersed in every direction where furs might be found. They moved not only into surrounding locales like Staten Island and Long Island, but north around Fort Orange, south around Fort Nassau on the Delaware, and eastward to Fort Good Hope on the Connecticut River, which was soon surrounded by New England settlers and eventually surrendered to them in 1653. In 1638 a Swedish trading company established Fort Christina at the site of the present Wilmington and scattered a few hundred settlers up and down the Delaware River. The Dutch, at the time allied to the Swedes in the Thirty Years' War, made no move to challenge the claim until 1655, when a force outnumbering the entire Swedish colony subjected them without bloodshed to the rule of New Netherland. The chief contribution of the short-lived New Sweden to American culture was the idea of the log cabin, which the Swedes and a few Finnish settlers with them had brought over from the woods of Scandinavia.

The West India Company was interested mainly in the fur trade and less in agricultural settlements. In 1629, however, the company provided that any stockholder might obtain a large estate (a patroonship) if he peopled it with fifty adults within four years. The patroon was obligated to supply cattle, tools, and buildings. His tenants, in turn, paid him rent, used his grist mill, gave him first option on surplus crops, and submitted to a court he established. It amounted to transplanting the feudal manor into the New World, and met with as little luck as similar efforts in Maryland and South Carolina. Volunteers for serfdom were hard to find when there was land available elsewhere, and the only successful patroonship was that of Kiliaen van Rensselaer, a pearl merchant of Amsterdam, who secured lands covering what are now two counties around Albany. Most settlers took advantage of the company's provision that one could have as farms (*bouweries*) all the lands one could improve.

The government of the colony was under the almost absolute control of a governor sent out by the company, subject to little check from his council or from the directors back in Holland. The three successors to Minuit—Wouter Van Twiller, William Kieft, and Peter Stuyvesant—proved stubborn autocrats, either corrupt or inept, especially at Indian relations. They depended on a small professional garrison for defense, and the inhabitants (including a number of English on Long Island) betrayed almost total indifference in 1664 when Governor Stuyvesant called them to arms against a threatening British fleet. Almost defenseless, old soldier Peter Stuyvesant blustered and stomped about on his wooden leg, but finally surrendered without a shot and stayed on quietly at his farm in what had become the colony of New York.

The plan of conquest had been hatched by the king's brother, the duke of York and Albany, later King James II. As lord high admiral and an investor in the African trade, York had already engaged in harassing Dutch shipping and forts in Africa. When he and his advisors counseled that New Netherland could easily be reduced, Charles II simply granted the region to his brother as proprietor, permitted the hasty gathering of a force, and the English transformed New Amsterdam into New York and Fort Orange into Albany, replaced Stuyvesant with Col. Richard Nicolls, and held the country thereafter, except for a brief Dutch reoccupation in 1673–1674. The Dutch, however, left a permanent imprint on the land and the language: the Dutch vernacular faded away but place names like Block Island, Wall Street (the original wall was for protection against Indians), Broadway (Breede Wegh) remained, along with family names like Rensselaer, Roosevelt, and Van Buren. The Dutch presence lingered in the Dutch Reformed church; in words like boss, cooky, crib, snoop, stoop, spook, and kill (for creek); in the legendary Santa Claus, Rip Van Winkle, and the picturesque Dutch governors, preserved in the satirical caricatures of Washington Irving's *Knickerbocker History*.

NEW JERSEY Shortly after the conquest, still in 1664, the duke of York granted his lands between the Hudson and the Delaware Rivers to Sir George Carteret and Lord John Berkeley (brother of Virginia's governor), and named the territory for Carteret's native island of Jersey. The New Jersey proprietorship then passed through a sequence of incredible complications. In 1674 Berkeley sold his share to a Quaker leader Edward Byllynge, whose affairs were so encumbered that their management fell to three trustees, one of whom was William Penn, another prominent Quaker. In 1676 by mutual agreement the colony was divided by a diagonal line into East and West New Jersey, with Carteret taking the east—a division that corresponded to New Jersey's status later as hinterland and commuter bedroom for New York and Philadelphia. Finally in 1682 Carteret sold out to a group of twelve, including Penn, who in turn brought into

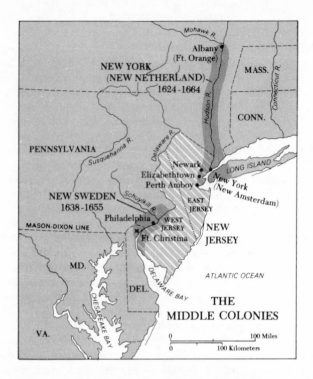

THE
MIDDLE COLONIES

partnership twelve more proprietors, for a total of twenty-four!
In East New Jersey, peopled at first by perhaps 200 Dutch who
had crossed the Hudson, new settlements gradually arose: some
disaffected Puritans from New Haven founded Newark, Carteret's brother brought a group to found Elizabethtown (Elizabeth), and a group of Scots founded Perth Amboy. In the west,
which faces the Delaware, a scattering of Swedes, Finns, and
Dutch remained, soon to be overwhelmed by swarms of English
Quakers. In 1702 East and West Jersey were united as a royal
colony.

PENNSYLVANIA AND DELAWARE   The Quaker sect, as the Society of
Friends was called in ridicule, was the most influential of many
radical groups that sprang from the turbulence of the English
Civil War. Founded by George Fox about 1647, the Quakers
carried further than any other group the doctrine of individual
inspiration and interpretation—the "inner light," they called it.
Discarding all formal sacraments and formal ministry—each
spoke only as the spirit moved him—they refused deference to
persons of rank, used the familiar "thee" and "thou" in address-
ing everyone, refused to take oaths because that was contrary to

Scripture, and embraced pacifism. Quakers were subjected to persecution—often in their zeal they seemed to invite it—but never inflicted it on others. Their toleration extended to complete religious freedom for all, of whatever belief or disbelief, and to the equality of sexes and the full participation of women in religious affairs.

In 1673 George Fox had returned from an American visit with the vision of a Quaker commonwealth in the New World and had infected others with his idea. The entrance of Quakers into the New Jersey proprietorships had encouraged Quakers to migrate, especially to the Delaware River side. And soon, across the river, arose Fox's "Holy Experiment," William Penn's Quaker Commonwealth, the colony of Pennsylvania. William Penn was the son of Admiral Sir William Penn who had supported Parliament in the Civil War and led Cromwell's conquest of Jamaica but later helped in the Restoration. Young William was reared as a proper gentleman, but as a student at Oxford had turned to Quakerism. His father disowned him, but after a reconciliation, sent him off to France to get his mind on other things. It worked for a while, but Penn later came back to the faith.

A Quaker meeting. Note the presence of women, evidence of Quaker views on the equality of the sexes. [Museum of Fine Arts, Boston]

Upon his father's death he inherited the friendship of the Stuarts and a substantial estate, including a claim of £16,000 his father had lent the crown. Whether in settlement of the claim or out of simple friendship he got from Charles II in 1681 proprietary rights to a tract extending westward from the Delaware for five degrees of longitude and from the "beginning" of the forty-third degree on the north to the "beginning" of the fortieth degree on the south. The land was named, at the king's insistence, for Penn's father: Pennsylvania (literally Penn Woods). The boundary overlapped lands granted to both New York and Maryland. The New York boundary was settled on the basis of the duke of York's charter at 42° North, but the Maryland boundary remained in question until 1767 when a compromise line (nineteen miles south of the Fortieth Parallel) was surveyed by Charles Mason and Jeremiah Dixon—the celebrated Mason-Dixon Line.

When Penn assumed control there was already a scattering of Dutch, Swedish, and English settlers on the west bank of the Delaware, but Penn was soon making vigorous efforts to bring in more settlers. He published glowing descriptions of the colony, which were translated into German, Dutch, and French. They were favorably received, especially by members of Pietist sects whose beliefs paralleled those of the Quakers. By the end of 1681 Penn had about 1,000 settlers in his province, and in October of the next year arrived himself with 100 more. By that time a town was growing up at the junction of the Schuylkill and Delaware Rivers, which Penn called Philadelphia (the City of Brotherly Love). Because of the generous terms on which Penn offered land, because indeed he offered aid to emigrants, the colony grew rapidly.

Indian relations were unusually good from the beginning, because of the Quakers' friendliness and because of Penn's careful policy of purchasing land titles from the Indians. Penn even took the trouble to learn the language of the Delawares, something few white men even tried. For some fifty years the settlers and the natives lived side by side in peace, in relationships of such trust that Quaker farmers sometimes left their children in the care of Indians when they were away from home.

The government, which rested on three Frames of Government promulgated by Penn in 1682, 1683, and 1701, resembled that of other proprietary colonies, except that the councilors as well as the assembly were elected by the freemen (taxpayers and property owners) and the governor had no veto—although Penn did. "Any government is free . . . where the laws rule and the people are a party to the laws," Penn wrote in the 1682 Frame of Government. He hoped to show that a government could run in accordance with Quaker principles, that it could maintain peace and order without oaths or wars, that religion could flourish without an established church and with absolute freedom of conscience. Because of its tolerance, Pennsylvania became a refuge not only for Quakers but for a variety of dissenters—as well as Anglicans—and early reflected the ethnic mixture of Scotch-Irish and Germans that became common to the middle colonies and the southern backcountry. Penn himself stayed only two years in the colony, and although he returned in 1699 for two more years, he continued at home the life of an English gentleman—and Quaker.

In 1682 the duke of York also granted Penn the area of Delaware, another part of the Dutch territory. At first Delaware became part of Pennsylvania, but after 1701 was granted the right to choose its own assembly. From then until the American Revolution it had a separate assembly, but had the same governor as Pennsylvania.

GEORGIA Georgia was the last of the British continental colonies to be established, half a century after Pennsylvania. In 1663, despite Spanish claims in the area, Charles II had granted the area from the Thirty-first to Thirty-sixth Parallels to the Carolina proprietors, but in 1732 George II gave the land between the Savannah and Altamaha Rivers to the twenty-one trustees of Georgia. In two respects Georgia was unique among the colonies; it was set up as both a philanthropic experiment and as a military buffer against Spanish Florida. Gen. James E. Oglethorpe, who accompanied the first colonists as resident trustee, represented both concerns: as a soldier who organized the defenses, and as a philanthropist who championed prison reform and sought a colonial refuge for the poor and persecuted.

In 1733 a band of 120 colonists founded Savannah near the mouth of the Savannah River. Carefully laid out by Oglethorpe, the old town with its geometrical pattern and its numerous little parks remains a monument to the city planning of a bygone day. A group of Protestant refugees from Salzburg began to arrive in 1734, followed by a number of Germans and German-speaking Moravians and Swiss, who made the colony for a time more German than English. The addition of Scottish Highlanders, Portuguese Jews, Welsh, Piedmontese, and others gave the early colony a cosmopolitan character much like that of its neighbor across the river.

A view of Savannah in 1734. The town's layout was carefully planned.
[The Mariners' Museum, Newport News, Va.]

As a buffer against Florida the colony succeeded, but as a philanthropic experiment it failed. Efforts to develop silk and wine production had little success. Land holdings were limited to 500 acres, rum was prohibited, and the importation of slaves forbidden, partly to leave room for servants brought on charity, partly to ensure security. But the utopian rules soon collapsed. The regulations against rum and slavery were widely disregarded, and finally abandoned in 1742 and 1749 respectively. By 1759 all restrictions on landholding were removed.

In 1753 the trustees' charter expired and the province reverted to the crown. As a royal colony Georgia acquired for the first time an effective government. The province developed slowly over the next decade, but grew rapidly in population and wealth after 1763. Instead of wine and silk, Georgians exported rice, indigo, lumber, naval stores, beef, and pork, and carried on a lively trade with the West Indies. Georgia's products fitted well into the British economic system and Georgians prospered. The colony, which got off to such a late start, had become a roaring success.

THRIVING COLONIES

Sir John Seeley, a British historian of a later date, once wrote that England acquired an empire "in a fit of absence of mind." The determined propaganda of Richard Hakluyt and his disciples, the elaborate plans of Gilbert, Raleigh, and their successors, tend to belie such a claim, but the record of the colonies almost validates it.

In the abstract it seems an unlikely way to build an empire, but after a late start the English outstripped both the French and the Spanish in the New World. The lack of plan was the genius of English colonization, for it gave free rein to a variety of human impulses. The centralized control imposed by the monarchs of Spain and France got them off the mark more quickly but eventually led to their downfall because it hobbled innovation and responsiveness to new circumstances. The British acted by private investment and with a minimum of royal control. Not a single colony was begun at the direct initiative of the crown. In the English colonies poor immigrants had a much greater chance of getting at least a small parcel of land. The English, unlike their rivals, welcomed people from a variety of nationalities and dissenting sects who came in search of a new life or a safe harbor. And a degree of self-government made the English colonies more responsive to new circumstances—if sometimes stalled by controversy.

The compact pattern of English settlement contrasted sharply with the pattern of Spain's far-flung conquests or France's far-reaching trade routes to the interior by way of the St. Lawrence and Mississippi Rivers (discussed in Chapter 4). Geography reinforced England's bent for concentrated occupation and settlement of its colonies. The rivers and bays which indented the coasts served as veins of communication along which colonies first sprang up, but no great river offered a highway to the far interior. About a hundred miles back in Georgia and the Carolinas, and nearer the coast to the north, the "fall line" of the rivers presented rocky rapids which marked the head of navigation and the end of the coastal plain. About a hundred miles beyond that, and farther back in Pennsylvania, stretched the rolling expanse of the Piedmont, literally the foothills. And the final backdrop of English America was the Appalachian Mountain range, some 200 miles from the coast in the south, reaching down to the coast at points in New England, with only one significant break—up the Hudson-Mohawk Valley of New York. For 150 years the farthest outreach of settlement stopped at the slopes of the mountains.

Quebec

N E W   F R A N C E

MAINE

Montreal

St. Lawrence R.

L.
CHAMPLAIN

MAHICAN

ABNAKI

NEW YORK

NEW HAMPSHIRE

LAKE ONTARIO

MOHAWK
ONEIDA
ONONDAGA   Mohawk R.
CAYUGA
SENECA   *IROQUOIS*   Albany

Connecticut R.

Hudson R.

Boston

MASSACHUSETTS BAY

WAMPANOAG

PLYMOUTH

Hartford

Providence

MOHEGAN

RHODE ISLAND

New Haven

CONNECTICUT

New York

PENNSYL-
VANIA

Delaware R.

Susquehanna R.

NEW JERSEY

Philadelphia
Wilmington

DELAWARE

M O U N T A I N S

MARYLAND

Potomac R.

MARYLAND

DELAWARE

NANTICOKE

VIRGINIA

St. Mary's

POWHATAN

James R.

Jamestown

TUSCARORA

NORTH
CAROLINA

WACCAMAW

SOUTH
CAROLINA

A T L A N T I C   O C E A N

EUROPEAN SETTLEMENTS AND
INDIAN TRIBES IN EARLY AMERICA

0   200 Miles

0   200 Kilometers

To the east lay the wide expanse of ocean, which served as a highway for the transit of civilization from Europe to America, but also as a barrier beyond which civilization took to new paths in a new environment.

FURTHER READING

Several general interpretations handle the sweep of English settlement during the early colonial period. The first volume of Charles M. Andrews's *The Colonial Period of American History* (1934–1937) is detailed and comprehensive. Shorter and more interpretative are Daniel J. Boorstin's *The Americans: The Colonial Experience* (1958),° David Hawke's *The Colonial Experience* (1966), and John E. Pomfret and Floyd M. Shumway's *The Founding of the American Colonies, 1583–1600* (1970). Pomfret and Shumway put the most emphasis on the early settlement patterns. Worth consultation are relevant passages from the fifteen-volume *The British Empire before the Revolution* (1936–1970), by Lawrence H. Gipson.

As noted in Chapter 1 Carl Bridenbaugh's *Vexed and Troubled Englishmen, 1500–1642* (1968)° helps explain why so many sought a new home in a strange land. Vital to perceiving how social conditions produced turmoil is Peter Laslett's *The World We Have Lost* (1965).° A study of the political institutions of the time is Wallace Notestein's *The English People on the Eve of Colonization, 1603–1630* (1951). English constitutional traditions and their effect on the colonists are examined in Julian H. Franklin's *John Locke and the Theory of Sovereignty* (1978) and Davis S. Lovejoy's *The Glorious Revolution in America* (1972).° John Phillips Kenyon documents the internal dynamics of English politics in *Stuart England* (1978).°

Carl Bridenbaugh's *Jamestown, 1544–1699* (1980), traces the English experience on the Chesapeake. P. L. Barbour's *The Three Worlds of Captain John Smith* (1964) is full of interesting detail. Alden Vaughan's *American Genesis: Captain John Smith and the Founding of Virginia* (1975) is shorter. The early chapters of Edmund S. Morgan's *American Slavery / American Freedom* (1975)° also shed light on the English experience in Virginia.

George Langdon's *Pilgrim Colony: A History of New Plymouth, 1620–1691* (1966), focuses on the development of the second American settlement. Still useful and enlightening is William Bradford's narrative of the Pilgrim experience, *Of Plymouth Plantation,*° edited in 1952 by Samuel E. Morison.

Scholarship abounds on the development of Puritanism. To learn about the English roots of the movement, see Charles H. and Katherine George's *The Protestant Mind of the English Reformation* (1961). More

° These books are available in paperback editions.

analytical and psychological is Michael Walzer's *The Revolution of the Saints: A Study in the Origins of Radical Politics* (1965).° The works of Perry Miller demonstrate how Puritan ideology evolved once transplanted to the New World. See especially Miller's *The New England Mind* (2 vols.; 1939, 1954).° More concise, yet complex and rewarding, is his *Errand into the Wilderness* (1964).° The problem of translating idea into governance is treated in Edmund S. Morgan's *The Puritan Dilemma: The Story of John Winthrop* (1958)° and George L. Haskin's *Law and Authority in Early Massachusetts* (1960).

The problem of dissent in a theocracy is handled in works on the establishment of other New England colonies. Start with Edmund S. Morgan's *Roger Williams, The Church, and the State* (1967).° Further explanation can be found in Emery Battis's *Saints and Sectarians: Anne Hutchinson and the Antinomian Controversey in Massachusetts Bay Colony* (1962). The religious theme in the settlement of Connecticut is also handled in Mary J. A. Jones's *Congregational Commonwealth* (1968).

No comprehensive work explores the overall pattern of settlement of the Middle Colonies, yet good scholarship exists for each colony. Thomas J. Condon's *New York Beginnings: The Commercial Origins of New Netherlands* (1968) examines the Dutch connection. The influence of Quakers can be studied through Gary B. Nash's *Quakers and Politics: Pennsylvania, 1681–1726* (1968), and Edwin B. Bronner's *William Penn's "Holy Experiment"* (1962). Also helpful are volumes on the early history of each colony. Consult Michael Kammen's *Colonial New York* (1975), Joseph E. Illick's *Colonial Pennsylvania* (1976), John E. Pomfret's *Colonial New Jersey* (1973), and John A. Munroe's *A History of Delaware* (1979).

Settlement of the areas along the south Atlantic is traced in Wesley F. Craven's *The Southern Colonies in the Seventeenth Century, 1607–1689* (1949),° and Clarence L. Ver Steeg's *Origins of the Southern Mosaic* (1975). Aubrey C. Land et al., *Law, Society, and Politics in Early Maryland* (1977), explore early Maryland. The early chapters of Hugh Lefler and William S. Powell's *Colonial North Carolina* (1973) and M. Eugene Sirman's *Colonial South Carolina* (1966) cover the activities of the Lords Proprietors. To study Olgethorpe's aspirations, consult Paul S. Taylor's *Georgia Plan: 1732–1752* (1972).

3 ⤠

COLONIAL WAYS OF LIFE

THE SHAPE OF EARLY AMERICA

POPULATION GROWTH England's first footholds in America were bought at a fearful price. The beachhead in Virginia, one historian pointed out, "cost far more casualties, in proportion to numbers engaged, than did the conquest of any of the Japanese-held islands in World War II." But once the seasoning time was past and the colony was on its feet, Virginia and all its successors grew at a prodigious rate. After Virginia put down the last major Indian uprising in 1644, its population quadrupled from about 8,000 to 32,000 over the next thirty years, then more than doubled, to 75,000, by 1704. Throughout the mainland colonies the yearly growth rate during the eighteenth century ran about 3 percent. In 1625 the English colonists numbered little more than 2,000 in Virginia and Plymouth together; by 1700 the population in the colonies was perhaps 250,000, and during the eighteenth century it doubled at least every twenty-five years. By 1750 the number had passed 1 million; by 1775 it stood at about 2.5 million. In 1700 the English at home outnumbered the colonists by about 20 to 1; by 1775, on the eve of the American Revolution, the ratio was about 3 to 1.

The prodigious increase of colonial population did not go unnoticed of course. In 1770 Ezra Stiles, the future president of Yale College, predicted in his diary that English would "become the vernacular Tongue of more people than any one Tongue on Earth, except the Chinese." Benjamin Franklin of Pennsylvania, a keen observer of many things, published in 1751 his *Observations Concerning the Increase of Mankind* in which he pointed out two facts of life which distinguished the colonies from Europe: land was plentiful and cheap; labor was scarce and dear. Just the opposite conditions prevailed in the Old World. From this reversal of conditions flowed many if not most of the changes which European culture underwent in the New World—not the least being that good fortune beckoned the immigrant and induced the settlers to replenish the earth with large families. Where labor was scarce, children could lend a hand, and once they were grown could find new land for themselves if need be. Colonists tended, as a result, to marry and start new families at an earlier age.

THE BIRTH RATE   At the time many English women never married at all, and those who did often waited until their mid or later twenties, and men until even later. But in England women outnumbered men, while in the first waves of colonial settlement the sex ratio was reversed. The result was that the average age at marriage for colonial women dropped to twenty or twenty-one, for men to twenty-five or twenty-six, and the birth rate rose accordingly, since those who married earlier had time for about two additional pregnancies during the childbearing years. Later a gradual reversion to a more even sex ratio brought the average age at marriage back toward the European norm. Even so, given the better economic prospects in the colonies, a greater number of American women married and the birth rate remained higher

Mr. John Freake, *and* Mrs. Elizabeth Freake and Baby Mary. *Elizabeth married John at age nineteen; Mary, born when Elizabeth was thirty-two, was the Freakes' eighth and last child. [The Worcester Art Museum]*

than in Europe, probably around 45–50 births per 1,000 women per year in the colonies in contrast to about 28 per 1,000 in Europe.

THE DEATH RATE What was equally important, however, was a startlingly lower death rate in the New World. Infants generally had a better chance to reach maturity, and adults had a better chance to reach old age. In seventeenth-century New England, apart from childhood mortality, men would expect to reach seventy and women nearly that age. The difference was less because of what Massachusetts Gov. William Shirley called the "Healthfulness of the Climates on this Continent" than because of the character of the settlements. Since the land was more bountiful, famine seldom occurred after the first year, and while the winters were more severe than in England, firewood was plentiful. Being younger on the whole—the average age in the colonies in 1790 was sixteen!—Americans were less susceptible to disease than were Europeans. More widely scattered, they were also less exposed to disease. This began to change, of course, as population centers grew and trade and travel increased. By the mid–eighteenth century the colonies were beginning to have levels of contagion much like those in Europe. In 1735–1737, for instance, a diphtheria epidemic swept the northern colonies, taking the lives of thousands. In this case the lack of previous ex-

94. Gravestone of Mary Briant and children by an unidentified artist. The epitaph reads HERE LYES Ẏ [the] BODY / OF Mʳˢ MAˑRY BRIˑANᵀ / WIFE OF Mʳ THOˑMAS / BRIˑANT WHO DYED / NOˑUEMBER THE 30ᵗʰ / 1724 AGED 39 YEAREˢ / & IN HAR ARMS DOTH / LYE Ẏ CORPS OF TWO / LOVELY BABES BORN / OF HAR 8 DAYS BEˑFORˢ / HAR DEATH ONE A SOˣ / NATHAⁿⁱᵉˡ DYED Ẏ DAY / BEFORE HAR A DᴀUGHⁱʳ / NAMᴱᴰ HANˣᴬᴴ DYED A FEW OURˢ AFⁱᵉʳ HAR. 1724. Norwell, Massachusetts. Slate, 29″ x 23¼″.

The death rate in colonial America was relatively low, but Mary Briant's gravestone bears testimony to the ever-present spectre of childhood mortality. [The Warder Collection] posure now left the young especially vulnerable for want of a chance to develop immunity.

The greatest variations on these patterns occurred in the earliest testing times of the southern colonies. During the first century after the Jamestown settlement, down to about 1700, a high rate of mortality and a chronic shortage of women meant that the population increase there could be sustained only by immigration. In the southern climate English settlers proved vulnerable to malaria, dysentery, and a host of other diseases. The mosquito-infested rice paddies of the Carolina tidewater were notoriously unhealthy. And ships which docked at the Chesapeake tobacco plantations brought in with their payloads unseen cargoes of smallpox, diphtheria, and other infections. Given the higher mortality, families were often broken by the early death of parents. One consequence was to throw children on their own at an earlier age. Another was probably to make the extended family support network, if not the extended household, more important in the South.

SEX RATIOS AND THE FAMILY   Whole communities of religious or ethnic groups migrated more often to the northern colonies than to the southern, bringing more women in their company. There was no mention of any women at all among the first arrivals at Jamestown. Virginia's seventeenth-century sex ratio of two or three white males to each female meant that many men never married, although nearly every adult woman did. Counting only the unmarried, the ratio went to about eight men for every woman. In South Carolina around 1680 the ratio stood at about three to one, but since about three-quarters of the women were married, it was something like seven to one for singles.

A population made up largely of bachelors without strong ties to family and to the larger community made for instability of a high order in the first years. And the high mortality rates of the early years further loosened family ties. While the first generations in New England proved to be long-lived, and many more children there knew their grandparents than in the motherland, young people in the seventeenth-century South were apt never to see their grandparents and in fact to lose one or both of their parents before reaching maturity. But after a time of seasoning, immunities built up. Eventually the southern colonies reverted to a more even sex ratio and family sizes approached those of New England. In eighteenth-century Virginia, Col. William Byrd of Westover asserted, matrimony thrived "so excellently" that an "Old Maid or an Old Bachelor are as scarce among us and reckoned as ominous as a Blazing Star." And early marriage remained common. The most "antique Virgin" Byrd knew was his own daughter, of about twenty.

Survival was the first necessity and for the 90–95 percent of colonists who farmed, a subsistence or semi-subsistence economy remained the foundation of being. Life moved more by the rhythms of the seasons, the rising and setting of the sun, than by the dictates of the clock. Not only food, but shelter, implements, utensils, furnishings, and clothing had to be made at home from the materials at hand. As the primary social and economic unit, the family became a "little commonwealth" which took on functions performed by the community in other times and places. Production, religion, learning, health care, and other activities centered around the home. Fathers taught their sons by example how to farm, hunt, and fish. Mothers taught their daughters how to tend to the chickens, the gardens, and the countless household chores that fell to the women of that time. Extended kinship ties added meaning to life and stability to communities. Such lineal family values tended to inhibit the constant mobility (social and geographic) and risk-taking so often assumed to be a peculiarly American characteristic.

Though colonists began in the early years to manifest such traditional American traits as practicality, acquisitiveness, restlessness, and a propensity for violence, it would be far too easy to read back into colonial times exaggerated notions of American individualism. Whatever the changes to be wrought by environment, the earliest settlers were transplanted Europeans whose ideas and practices adjusted to new circumstances only by degrees. Clusters of ethnic and religious groups which sprang up, such as the "tribal cult" of Puritans in New England, or the settlements of Germans in Pennsylvania, suggest that European values persisted in the New World for some time. Conditions in America did cause changes in family life, the implications of which social historians have only begun to work out, but this much seems clear. The conjugal unit, or nuclear family of parents and children, was not a new development in the colonies but the familiar arrangement in both England and America. The household that included an extended family of three or more generations was rare, although given the greater life span, large networks of kinship ties did develop. These networks included servants attached to households, who were often young kinspeople apprenticed to learn a trade.

THE SOCIAL HIERARCHY   The earliest settlers also brought in their cultural baggage certain fixed ideas of hierarchy and rank that had been part of their culture. People of the lower orders deferred to their "betters" almost without question. Devereux Jarratt, son of a carpenter and later an Episcopal evangelist, recalled that in the Virginia of his youth: "We were accustomed to look upon, what were called *gentle folks*, as beings of a superior order. . . . Such ideas of the differences between *gentle* and *simple*, were, I believe, universal among all of my rank and age. . . ." John Winthrop, looking out from a higher station in life, asserted it to be God's will that "in all times some must be rich, some poore, some high and eminent in power and dignitie, others meane and in subjection." But from Jamestown onward persons of "meane" birth like John Smith revealed rare qualities when confronted with the wilderness. The breadth of opportunity to be plucked from danger impelled settlers to shake off the sense of limitations that haunted the more crowded lands of Europe. J. Hector St. John de Crevecoeur, a French immigrant, wrote from his New York farm in the 1780s: "A European, when he first arrives, seems limited in his intentions, as well as in his views; but he very suddenly alters his scale; . . . he no sooner breathes our air than he forms schemes, and embarks in designs he never would have thought of in his own country."

Still, the new experience of social mobility took some getting used to. The fear lingered that it threatened the equilibrium of society, and efforts persisted to keep the "meaner sort" in their place. But attempts to regulate dress as the outward sign of social class ran up against a human weakness for finery. Even in Puritan New England, which got an undeserved credit for austerity, the scorn of fancy dress was reserved mainly for those who affected to rise above their station. In 1651 the Massachusetts General Court declared its "utter detestation and dislike" that persons of mean condition "should take upon them the garb of gentlemen." and prescribed fines for those with estates of less than £200 who wore gold or silver lace or silver buttons and other such finery.

WOMEN IN THE COLONIES The status of women too altered in the new conditions of life. The acute shortage of women in the early years made them the more highly valued, and by many accounts brought subtle improvements in their status—a condition which tended to move with successive frontiers westward. The general labor shortage meant that both women and children were treated more indulgently than in the Europe of their times, not that their standing in the law or in their assigned roles in society was drastically altered. "Here, as in England," the historian Julia Cherry Spruill wrote, "women were without political rights, and generally wives were legal nonentities" whose property the husband controlled—although single women and widows had practically the same legal rights as men.

Despite the conventional mission of women to serve in the domestic sphere, the scarcity of labor opened new lines of action. Quite a few women by necessity or choice went into gainful occupations. In the towns they commonly served as tavern hostesses and shopkeepers, but occasional notices in colonial papers listed women also in such employments as doctors, printers, upholsterers, glaziers, painters, silversmiths, tanners, and shipwrights—often but not always widows carrying on their husbands' trade. Some managed plantations, again usually carrying on in the absence of husbands. One exceptional early case was "Mistress Margarett Brent, Spinster," of Maryland, who arrived in 1638 with two brothers and a sister. All four came on their own ventures, the Mistresses Brent bringing in servants and patenting large tracts of land. Margaret Brent ran her plantation so well that her brothers entrusted their affairs to her in their absence. As executrix of Gov. Leonard Calvert's estate she settled his complex affairs and arranged to pay the local militia and avert a mutiny. As "his Lordship's Attorney" she boldly demanded a vote in the Assembly the better to see after his affairs. The governor, in response, acknowledged her gifts, but denied her re-

Prudence Punderson's needlework The First, Second, and Last Scene of Mortality *(c. 1776), illustrating the domestic path, from cradle to coffin, followed by most colonial women. [Connecticut Historical Society]*

quest. When she became perhaps the first American suffragette, she had overstepped the bounds of acceptance.

The colonists everywhere had much in common. But as the land filled with population behind the frontier, the differences of geography and climate, and the diverse human elements entering the New World, produced ways of life that differed from north to south, from east to west. New England evolved into a center of fishing and commerce, the Puritan and the Yankee; the southern colonies into the land of tobacco and rice, the country gentleman and the black slave; the Middle Colonies into the colonial "breadbasket" of wheat and barley, the home of the Quaker, the Dutchman, and the Scotch-Irish.

SOCIETY AND ECONOMY IN THE SOUTHERN COLONIES

STAPLES The southern colonies had one unique advantage—the climate. They could grow exotic staples (market crops) that withered in northern latitudes and were prized by the mother country. Virginia, as Charles I put it, was "founded upon smoke." Within four years of John Rolfe's first experiments the passion for the "joviall weed" reached such heights that Gov. Thomas Dale required two acres of corn as a prerequisite for growing it. By 1619 production had reached 20,000 pounds, and in the year of the Glorious Revolution, 1688, it was up to 18 million pounds.

After 1690 rice was as much the staple in South Carolina as tobacco in Virginia or sugar in Barbados. The process of its naturalization is obscure. One cherished story is that the colony conjured the industry from a single bag of seed from Madagascar, but there are other stories of seed from India and Africa (black slaves, already familiar with rice growing in Africa, may have taught whites their method) and there is solid evidence that the Lords Proprietors planned experiments with rice from the beginning. From whatever source the rice came, the rise and fall of tidewater rivers made the region ideally suited to a crop which required alternate flooding and draining of the fields. In 1699 the young colony exported at least 366 tons of rice, according to the customs collector Edward Randolph.

Much later, in the 1740s, another exotic staple appeared—indigo, the blue dyestuff which found an eager market in the British woolens industry. An enterprising young lady named Eliza Lucas, daughter of the governor of Antigua, produced the first crop on her father's Carolina plantation, left in her care when she was only seventeen. She thereby founded a major industry, and as the wife of Charles Pinckney, later brought forth a major dynasty which flourished in the golden age of Charleston.

From the southern woods came harvests of lumber and naval stores (tar, pitch, and turpentine) as well. From their early leadership in the latter trade North Carolinians would later derive the nickname of Tar Heels. In the interior a fur trade flourished, and in the Carolinas, a cattle industry that pretokened the later industry on the Great Plains—with cowboys, roundups, brandings, and long drives to market.

English customs records showed that for the years 1698–1717 South Carolina and the Chesapeake colonies bought English goods averaging £154,000 in value annually, and sent back American goods averaging £246,000 leaving a balance of £92,000 in favor of the colonies. But the balance was more than offset by "invisible" charges: freight payments to shipper, profits, commissions, storage charges, and interest payments to English merchants, insurance premiums, inspection and customs duties, and outlays to purchase indentured servants and slaves. Thus began a pattern that would plague the southern staple-crop system into the twentieth century. Planter investments went into land and slaves while the profitable enterprises of shipping, trade, investment, and manufacture fell under the sway of outsiders.

LAND   Land could be had almost for the asking throughout the colonial period, although many a frontier squatter who succumbed to the lure ignored the formalities of getting a deed. In colonial law land titles rested ultimately upon grants from the crown, and in colonial practice the evolution of land policy in the first colony set patterns that were followed everywhere save in New England. In 1614 when Governor Dale gave each of the Virginia Company's colonists three acres for his own use, it was the beginning of a policy that every colonist could claim a plot of his own. In 1618 the company, lacking any assets other than land, promised each investor a fifty-acre "share-right" for £12.10s, and each settler a "headright" for paying his own way or for bringing in others. When Virginia became a royal colony in 1624, the headright system continued to apply, administered by the governor and his council. Lord Baltimore adopted the same practice in Maryland, and successive proprietors in the other southern and middle colonies adopted variations on the plan.

As time passed certain tracts were put up for sale and throughout the colonies special grants (often sizable) went to persons of rank or persons who had performed some meritorious service, such as fighting the Indians. Since land was plentiful and population desired, the rules tended to be generously interpreted and carelessly applied. With the right connections, persons or companies might engross handsome estates and vast speculative tracts in the interior, looking toward future growth and rising land values. From the beginning of colonization—in fact before the beginning—the real-estate boomer was a stock figure in American history, and access to power was often access to wealth. But by the early 1700s acquisition of land was commonly by purchase under more or less regular conditions of survey and sale by the provincial government. The later national land surveys followed the southern practice.

The first grants were made without any conditions attached, but at an early date the crown and proprietors decided to recover something from the giveaways by the levy of annual quit-rents on the land. In the Middle Ages such payments would quit (release) the tenant from military and other duties to his lord. In the New World, however, such levies had no roots in a feudal tradition and came to be a point of chronic protest, resistance, and evasion. But they remained on the books.

Some promoters of colonization, including Ferdinando Gorges, Lord Baltimore, and the Lords Proprietors of Carolina, had dreams of reviving the feudal manor in the New World. Their plans went awry, it is commonly said, because of the New World environment. With land aplenty, there was little call to volunteer for serfdom. Yet in unexpected ways the southern colonies gave rise to something analogous, a new institution with a new name: the plantation. The word originally carried the meaning of colony. The plantations in the New World were the colonies and planters were the settlers who had "planted" them. Gradually the name attached itself to individual holdings of large size.

If one distinctive feature of the South's staple economy was a good market in England, another was a trend toward large-scale production. Those who planted tobacco soon discovered that it quickly exhausted the soil, thereby giving an advantage to the planter who had extra fields to rotate in beans and corn or to leave fallow. With the increase of the tobacco crop, moreover, a fall in prices meant that economies of scale might come into play —the large planter with lower cost per unit might still make a profit. Gradually he would extend his holdings along the river-fronts, and thereby secure the advantage of direct access to the ocean-going vessels that moved freely up and down the water-

An idyllic view of a tidewater plantation. Note the easy access to ocean-going vessels. [Metropolitan Museum of Art]

ways of the Chesapeake, discharging goods from London and taking on hogsheads of tobacco. So easy was the access in fact that the Chesapeake colonies never required a city of any size as a center of commerce, and the larger planters functioned as merchants and harbormasters for their neighbors.

LABOR If the planter found no volunteers for serfdom, and if wage labor was scarce and expensive, one could still purchase an indentured servant for £6 to £30 (a substantial sum, which in much of the seventeenth and eighteenth centuries would equal perhaps 900 to 5,000 pounds of tobacco) and get his labor for a term of years. Voluntary indentured servitude accounted for probably half the arrivals of white settlers in all the colonies outside New England. The name derived from the indenture, or contract, by which a person could bind himself to labor in return for transportation to the New World. Usually one made the contract with a shipmaster who would then sell it to a new master upon arrival. Not all went voluntarily. The London underworld developed a flourishing trade in "kids" and "spirits," who were enticed or spirited into servitude. On occasion orphans were bound off to the New World; from time to time the mother country sent convicts into colonial servitude, the first as early as 1617. After 1717, by act of Parliament, convicts guilty of certain crimes could escape the hangman by "transportation." Most of these, like Moll Flanders, the lusty heroine of Daniel Defoe's novel, seem to have gone to the Chesapeake. And after 1648 political and military offenders met a like fate, beginning with some captives of the Parliamentary armies.

In due course, however, the servant reached the end of his term, usually after four to seven years, claimed the freedom dues set by custom and law—some money, tools, clothing, food—and took up land of his own. And with the increase of the colonies, servants had a wider choice of destination. Pennsylvania became more often the chosen land, "one of the best poor man's countries in the world," in the verdict of Judge William Allen.

SLAVERY But captive Africans, although they might cost a bit more, had no choice and served for life. Slavery, long a dying institution in Europe, had undergone a revival in Spanish America a full century before the Jamestown colony. It gradually evolved in the Chesapeake after 1619, when a Dutch vessel dropped off twenty Negroes in Jamestown. Some of the first were treated as indentured servants, with a limited term, and achieved freedom and landownership. They themselves sometimes acquired slaves and white indentured servants. But gradually, with rationalizations based on color difference or heathenism, the practice of perpetual slavery became the custom of the land. Evidence that

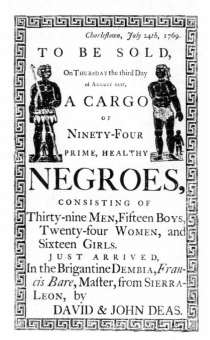

Advertisement for the sale of slaves—men, boys, women, and girls. [American Antiquarian Society]

in 1640 blacks were being held in hereditary life service appears in Virginia court records. In 1660 and 1661, and 1663 in Maryland, the colonial Assembly recognized slavery by laws that later expanded into elaborate and restrictive slave codes. In South Carolina, by contrast, Barbadians after 1670 simply transplanted the institution of slavery full-blown from the Caribbean before they discovered its value in the rice paddies, where indentured servants could hardly be enticed to work in the mud and heat.

The sugar islands of the French and British Antilles and the cane fields of Portuguese Brazil had the most voracious appetite for human cargoes, using them up in the tropical heat and miasmas on the average within seven years. By 1675 the English West Indies had over 100,000 slaves while the colonies in North America had only about 5,000. But as the staple crops became established on the American continent, the demand for slaves grew. And as readily available lands diminished, Virginians were less eager to bring in indentured servants who would lay claim to them at the end of their service. Though British North America took less than 5 percent of the total slave imports to the Western Hemisphere during the more than three centuries of that squalid traffic—399,000 out of some 9,566,000—it offered better chances for survival if few for human fulfillment. The natural increase of black immigrants in America approximated that of whites by the end of the colonial period.

Negro slavery was recognized in the laws of all the colonies, but flourished in the Tidewater South—one colony, South Carolina, had a black majority through most of the eighteenth century. By one estimate, about 40 percent of the slaves imported into North America came in through Sullivan's Island in Charleston Harbor, which was to black Americans what New York's Castle Garden and Ellis Island were later to millions of European immigrants or San Francisco's Angel Island to Asians. To say that black Africans made up the largest single group of non-English immigrants to the colonies, however, would be to ignore the great ethnic diversity of unwilling arrivals from lands as remote from each other as Angola and Senegambia, the west coast of Africa, and the area around the hump in between. About half the total came from Congo-Angola and the Bight of Biafra, and nearly all the rest from the Atlantic coast up to Senegambia. Thrown indiscriminately together, people who spoke Mandingo, Wolof, Ibo, Hausa, Kongo, and countless other tongues added to those who spoke various European and Indian languages to make the most relentless melting pot. As a result, diverse peoples developed a new identity as Afro-Americans, though not without leaving obscurely entwined in the fabric of American culture

The survival of African culture among American slaves is evident in this late–eighteenth-century painting of a South Carolina plantation. The musical instruments, pottery, and clothing are of African origin, probably Yoruba. [The Abby Aldridge Rockefeller Folk Art Center, Williamsburg, Va.]

more strands of African heritage than historians and anthropologists can ever disentangle. Among the more obvious were new words that entered the language, such as tabby, tote, cooter, goober, yam, banana, and the names of the Coosaw, Peedee, and Wando Rivers.

Most of the slaves were fated to become fieldhands, but not all did. Blacks from the lowlands of Africa used their skills as boatmen in the coastal waterways. Some had linguistic skills that made them useful interpreters. Others tended cattle and swine in the wilderness, or hacked away at the forests and operated sawmills. In a land which had to construct itself they became skilled artisans: blacksmiths, carpenters, coopers, bricklayers, and the like. Some of the more fortunate entered domestic service.

Slavery and the growth of a biracial South had economic, political, and cultural effects far into the future, and set America on the way to significant conflicts. Questions about the beginnings still have a bearing on the present. Did a deep-rooted color prejudice lead to slavery, for instance, or did the existence of slavery produce the prejudice? Clearly slavery evolved because of the desire for a supply of controlled labor, and Englishmen fell in with a trade established by the Portuguese and Spanish more than a century before—the very word "Negro" is Spanish for "black." But while Englishmen often enslaved Indian captives, they did not bring their white captives into slavery. Color was the crucial difference, or at least the crucial rationalization.

One historian has marshalled evidence that the seeds of slavery were already planted in Elizabethan attitudes. Englishmen associated the color black with darkness and evil; they stamped the different appearance, behavior, and customs of Africans as "savagery." At the very least such perceptions could soothe the consciences of people who trade in human flesh. On the other hand most of the qualities which colonial Virginians imputed to blacks to justify slavery were the same qualities that Englishmen assigned to their own poor to explain *their* status: their alleged bent for laziness, improvidence, treachery, and stupidity, among other shortcomings. Similar traits, moreover, were imputed by ancient Jews to the Canaanites and by the Mediterranean peoples of a later date to the Slavic captives sold among them. The names Canaanite and Slav both became synonymous with slavery—the latter lingers in our very word for it. Such expressions would seem to be the product of power relationships and not the other way around. Dominant peoples repeatedly assign ugly traits to those they bring into subjection.

THE GENTRY   By the early eighteenth century Virginia and South Carolina were moving into the golden age of the Tidewater gentry, leaving the more isolated and rustic colony of North Carolina as "a valley of humiliation between two mountains of conceit." The first rude huts of Jamestown had given way to frame and brick houses. Some of the seventeenth-century homes, like Governor Berkeley's Green Springs or Nathaniel Bacon's "Castle," were spacious, but even the most prosperous generally lived in houses of four to seven small rooms. It was only as the seventeenth century yielded to the eighteenth that the stately country seats in the Georgian, or "colonial," style began to emerge along the banks of the great rivers: Tuckahoe, Stratford, Westover, Berkeley, Carter's Grove, Nomini Hall, and others which still stand as monuments to a graceful age. The great mansions, flanked by storehouses and servants' quarters, characteristically faced both ways, looking down to the waterfront dock and the expanse of river, and to a landward front where a drive from the road led up to the imposing steps and doorways. In South Carolina the mansions along the Ashley, Cooper, and Wando, or along the tidal creeks that set the Sea Islands imperceptibly off from the mainland, came to be noted for

The Westover mansion (1730), built in Virginia by William Byrd II.
[Museum of Modern Art]

their spacious gardens and avenues of moss-hung live oaks. The Charleston town houses of the gentry varied the Georgian style by turning their sides to the street and adding to their fronts long piazzas in the West Indian style to catch the sea breezes.

The new aristocracy patterned its provincial lifestyle after that of the English country gentlemen. The great houses became centers of sumptuous living and legendary hospitality to neighbors and passing strangers. In their zest for the good life the planters kept in touch with the latest refinements of London style and fashion, living on credit extended for the next year's crop and the years' beyond that, to such a degree that in the late colonial period Thomas Jefferson called the Chesapeake gentry "a species of property annexed to certain English mercantile houses." Dependence on outside capital became a chronic southern problem lasting far beyond the colonial period.

In season the carriages of the Chesapeake elite rolled to the villages of Annapolis and Williamsburg, and the city of Charleston became the center of political life and high fashion where the new-issue aristocrats could reel and roister for days on end and patronize the taverns, silversmiths, cabinetmakers, milliners, and tailors. Through much of the year the outdoors beckoned planters to the pleasures of hunting and fishing and horsemanship. Gambling on horse races, cards, and dice became consuming passions for men and women alike. But a cultivated few courted high culture with a diligence that violated genteel indulgence. William Byrd II of Westover pursued learning with the same passion that he pursued the ladies, if not with the same flourish. He built a library of some 3,600 volumes and often rose early to keep up his Latin, Greek, and Hebrew. Robert "King" Carter of Nomini Hall practiced music several hours a day. The

Pinckneys of the Carolina low country, when they were at home, practiced their musical instruments and read from such authors as Vergil, Milton, Locke, Addison, Pope, and Richardson. Such families commonly sent their sons—and often their daughters— abroad for an education, usually to England, sometimes to France.

RELIGION   The first colonists in Virginia brought with them the Rev. Robert Hunt, an Anglican minister, but only in Virginia (1619) and Maryland (1692) was the Church of England established (tax supported) before the end of the seventeenth century. In the early eighteenth century it became the established church in all the South—and some counties of New York and New Jersey, despite the presence of many dissenters. In the new environment, however, the Anglican church evolved into something quite unlike the state church of England. The scattered population and the absence of bishops made centralized control difficult. After 1632 the bishop of London held theoretical jurisdiction over the colonial churches, but regulation was generally entrusted to governors more concerned with political matters.

In practice therefore, if not in theory, the Anglican churches became as independent of any hierarchy as the Congregationalists of New England. Governance fell to lay boards of vestrymen, who chose the ministers, and usually held them on a tight rein by granting short-term contracts. In Virginia ministerial salaries depended on the taxes paid in the parish, and in 1662 were set uniformly at the value of 13,333 pounds of leaf; the salary therefore fluctuated with the price of tobacco. Often the parishes were too large for an effective ministry. Isolated chapels might have lay readers and get only infrequent visits by clergymen. Standards were often lax, and the Anglican clergy around the Chesapeake became notorious for its "sporting parsons," addicted to foxhunting, gambling, drunkenness, and worse. Some parishes went for long periods without ministers: ordination by a bishop could be had only in England, and the pay was too uncertain.

No bishop ever resided in the colonies, and only a bishop could ordain ministers or confirm members, a fact which of itself caused a falling off. Certain functions of supervision and discipline, however, could be delegated to "commissaries," the first and most noted of whom was James Blair, who brought some order into Virginia's church affairs after 1689. At his death in 1743 only two parishes lacked ministers. Commissary Thomas Bray, appointed to Maryland in 1696, spent less than a year in the colony during which he established a library in nearly every parish, but was more significant for work back in England which led King William to charter the Society for the Propagation of the Gospel in Foreign Parts (the SPG, sometimes called the "Venerable Society"). The first missionary of the SPG arrived in South Carolina on Christmas Day 1702; from then until 1783 the SPG sponsored a total of 309 missionaries, who worked especially in New England and the Middle Colonies where the Anglican church was weakest. The missionaries kept up a sporadic agitation to have a bishop assigned to the colonies, but none ever was. Opposition came from various quarters: most of the colonists were dissenters; some in England feared that the appointment of bishops might make the colonies more independent, some in the colonies that it would make them less so; commercial and landed interests feared that it might make the colonies less attractive to dissenters, and so inhibit growth.

SOCIETY AND ECONOMY IN NEW ENGLAND

TOWNSHIPS   By contrast to the seaboard planters who transformed the English manor into the southern plantation, the Puritans transformed the English village into the New England town. Land policy in New England had a stronger social and religious purpose than elsewhere. Towns shaped by English precedent and Puritan policy also fitted the environment of a rockbound land, confined by sea and mountains and unfit for large-scale cultivation.

Neither headrights nor quitrents ever took root in New England. There were cases of large individual grants, but the standard system was one of township grants to organized groups. A group of settlers, often gathered already into a church, would petition the General Court for a town (what elsewhere was commonly called a "township") then divide it according to a rough principle of equity—those who invested more or had larger families might receive more land—retaining some pasture and woodland in common and holding some for later arrivals. In some early cases the towns arranged each settler's land in separate strips after the medieval practice, but with time land was commonly divided into separate farms to which landholders would move out, away from the close-knit village. And still later, by the early eighteenth century, the colonies used their remaining land as a source of revenue by selling townships to proprietors whose purpose, more often than not, was speculation and resale.

This colonial woodcut suggests the tremendous effort required by basic farming in New England. [New York Public Library]

ENTERPRISE The life of the New England farmer was typically a hardscrabble subsistence. Simply clearing the glacier-scoured soil of rocks might require sixty days of hard labor per acre. The growing season was short, and no exotic staples grew in that hard climate. If the town resembled the English village, the crops too were those familiar to the English countryside: wheat, barley, oats, some cattle and swine, and where the woodland predators could be killed off—especially on islands like Nantucket or Martha's Vineyard—sheep grazed on the land. By the end of the seventeenth century New England farmers were developing some surpluses for export but never any staples that met the demands of the English market.

With virgin forests ready for conversion into masts, lumber, and ships, and rich fishing grounds that stretched northward to Newfoundland, it is little wonder that New Englanders turned to the sea for livelihood—the fisheries in fact antedated settlement by more than a century. The Chesapeake region afforded a rich harvest of oysters, but New England by its proximity to waters frequented by cod, mackerel, halibut, and other varieties became the more important maritime center. Marblehead, Salem, Ipswich, and Charlestown early became important commercial fishing towns. Whales too abounded in New England waters and supplied whale oil for lighting and lubrication, as well as ambergris, a secretion used in perfumes. New England ships eventually were chasing whales from Baffin Bay to Antarctica and out across the Pacific.

The fisheries, unlike the farms, supplied a staple of export to Europe, while lesser grades of fish went to the West Indies as food for slaves. Fisheries encouraged the development of shipbuilding, and experience at seafaring spurred commerce which led to wider contacts in the Atlantic world and a certain cosmopolitanism which clashed with more provincial aspects of the Puritan utopia.

Abundant forests near the shore yielded lumber, masts, pitch, and tar, and as early as July 4, 1631, John Winthrop launched a ship of sixty tons, the *Blessing of the Bay,* which marked the beginning of an American merchant marine. By the mid–seventeenth century shipyards had developed at Boston, Salem, Dorchester, Gloucester, Portsmouth, and other towns. New England remained the center of shipbuilding throughout the colonial period. Lumber provided not only raw material for ships but a prime cargo. As early as 1635 what may have been the first sawmill appeared at Portsmouth, New Hampshire. Sawmills soon abounded throughout the colonies, often together with gristmills using the same source of waterpower.

TRADE   Commercially the colonies by the end of the seventeenth century had become part of a great North Atlantic connection, trading not only with the British Isles and the British West Indies, but also—and often illegally—with Spain, France, Portugal, Holland, and their colonies from America to the shores of Africa. Out of necessity the colonists had to import manufac-

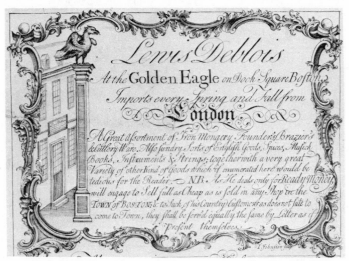

A Boston merchant's trade card (1757). Note the manufactured goods imported from London, to be sold "full as cheap as is sold in any shop in the town of Boston." [Winterthur Museum]

tured goods from Britain and Europe: hardware, machinery, paint, instruments of navigation, various household items. The function of the colonies as a market for English goods was important to the mother country. The central problem for the colonies was to find the means of paying for the imports—the eternal problem of the balance of trade.

The mechanism of trade in New England and the Middle Colonies differed from that of the South in two respects: their lack of staples to exchange for English goods was a relative disadvantage, but the abundance of their own shipping and mercantile enterprise worked in their favor. After 1660, in order to protect English agriculture and fisheries, the English government raised prohibitive duties against certain major exports of these colonies: fish, flour, wheat, and meat, while leaving the door open to timber, furs, and whale oil. Consequently New York and New England in the years 1698–1717 bought more from England than they sold there, incurring an unfavorable trade balance of about £66,000 sterling.

The northern colonies met the problem partly by using their own ships and merchants, thus avoiding the "invisible" charges for trade and transport, and by finding other markets for the sta-

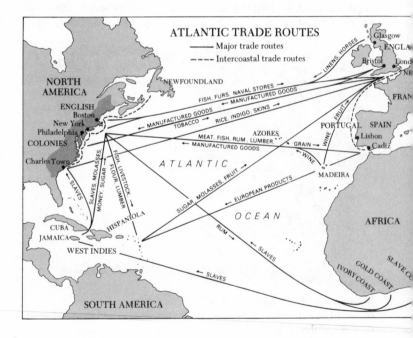

ATLANTIC TRADE ROUTES
—— Major trade routes
---- Intercoastal trade routes

ples excluded from England, thus acquiring goods or bullion to pay for imports from the mother country. American lumber and fish therefore went to southern Europe, Madeira, and the Azores for money or in exchange for wine; lumber, rum, and provisions went to Newfoundland; and all of these and more went to the West Indies, which became the most important outlet of all. American merchants could sell fish, bread, flour, corn, pork, bacon, beef, and horses to West Indian planters who specialized in sugarcane. In return they got money, sugar, molasses, rum, indigo, dyewoods, and other products, much of which went eventually to England. This gave rise to the famous "triangular trade" (more a descriptive convenience than a rigid pattern) in which New Englanders shipped rum to the west coast of Africa and bartered for slaves, took the slaves on the "Middle Passage" to the West Indies, and returned home with various commodities including molasses, from which they manufactured rum. In another version they shipped provisions to the West Indies, carried sugar and molasses to England, and returned with manufactured goods from Europe.

The generally unfavorable balance of trade left a chronic shortage of hard money, which drifted away to pay for imports and invisible charges. Since England restricted the export of bullion, such coins as found their way to the colonies were mostly foreign: the Portuguese johannes (or "joe") and moidore, the French pistole, and most important of all, the Spanish piece of eight (eight reals) or the Spanish milled dollar which later took its place—the ancestor of the American dollar. Colonists reckoned in terms of English pounds, shillings, and pence, but it has been said that they were more a medium of expression than a medium of exchange.

Various expedients met the shortage of currency: the use of wampum or commodities, the monetary value of which colonial governments tried vainly to set by law. From 1652 to 1684 Massachusetts coined silver "pine tree" shillings, but lost the right after the loss of its charter in 1684. Promissory notes of individuals or colonial treasurers often passed as a crude sort of paper money. Most of the colonies at one time or another issued bills of credit, on promise of payment later (hence the dollar "bill"), and after South Carolina took the lead in 1712, most set up land banks which issued paper money for loans to farmers on the security of their lands, which were mortgaged to the banks. Colonial farmers began to recognize that an inflation of paper money led to an inflation of crop prices, and therefore asked for more and more paper. Thus began in colonial politics what was to become a recurrent issue in later times, the question of currency inflation. Wherever the issue arose, debtors commonly favored growth in the money supply, which would make it easier for them to settle accounts, whereas creditors favored a limited money supply, which would increase the value of their capital. In 1741, therefore, in response to influential creditors of Massachusetts, Parliament extended the Bubble Act of 1720 to the colonies. That act, passed in response to speculative frauds in England like the South Sea Bubble, outlawed joint-stock companies not authorized by Parliament. Ten years later, in 1751, Parliament outlawed legal tender paper money in New England, and in 1764 throughout the colonies.

RELIGION   It has been said that in New England one was never far from the smell of fish and brimstone. The Puritans for many years had a bad press. By the standards of later ages they were judged bigots, but they had come to America to escape error, not to tolerate it in their New Zion. And the picture of the dour Puritan, hostile to anything that gave pleasure, is false. Puritans, especially those of the upper class, wore colorful clothing, enjoyed secular music, and imbibed prodigious quantities of rum. "Drink is in itself a good creature of God," said the Rev. Increase Mather, " . . . but the abuse of drink is from Satan." The architecture and household articles of Puritan New England have a continuing aesthetic appeal. The things of the world, in the Puritan view, were made by God and to be enjoyed by man. Sin lay not so much in their use as in their misuse. At the same time man had an obligation to work in this world, and worldly success was important.

The Puritans who settled Massachusetts, unlike the Separatists of Plymouth, proposed only to form a purified version of the Anglican church. They believed that they could remain loyal to the Church of England, the unity of church and state, and the principle of compulsory uniformity. But their remoteness from England led them directly, in fact very quickly, to a congregational form of church government identical with that of the Pilgrim Separatists, and for that matter little different from the practice of southern Anglicans.

Certain things in the Puritan faith were pregnant with meaning for the future. In the Puritan's version of Calvin's theology God had voluntarily entered into a covenant, or contract, with men through which his creatures could secure salvation. By analogy, therefore, an assembly of true Christians could enter into a church covenant, a voluntary union for the common worship of

God. From this it was a fairly short step to the idea of a voluntary union for purposes of government. The history of New England affords examples of several such limited steps towards constitutional government: the Mayflower Compact, the Cambridge Agreement of John Winthrop and his followers, the Fundamental Orders of Connecticut, and the informal arrangements whereby the Rhode Island settlers governed themselves until they secured a charter in 1663.

The covenant theory contained certain germs of democracy in both church and state, but democracy was no part of Puritan political science which, like so much else in Puritan belief, began with original sin. Because of man's depravity government became necessary for his restraint. "If people be governors," asked the Rev. John Cotton, "who shall be governed?" The Puritan was dedicated to seeking not the will of the people but the will of God. The ultimate source of authority was the Bible, God's revelation to man. But the Bible had to be known by right reason, which was best applied by those trained to the purpose. Hence most Puritans deferred to an intellectual elite for a true knowledge of God's will. Church and state were but two aspects of the same unity, the purpose of which was to carry out God's will on earth. The New England way might thus be summarized in the historian Perry Miller's phrase as a kind of "dictatorship of the regenerate."

The church exercised a pervasive influence over the life of the town, but unlike the Church of England it had no temporal power. Thus while Puritan New England has often been called a theocracy, the church technically was entirely separated from the state—except that the residents were taxed for its support. And if not all inhabitants were church members, they were impelled, indeed required, to be present for church services. So complete was the consensus of church member and nonmember alike that the closely knit communities of New England have been called peaceable kingdoms. It was a peace, however, under which there bubbled a volcano of soul-searching.

The Puritan lived anything but what Plato had called "the unexamined life." He was assailed by doubts, by a fear of falling away, by the haunting fear that despite his best outward efforts he might not be one of God's elect. Add that to the long winters which kept the family cooped up during the dark, cold months, and one has a formula for seething resentments and recriminations which, for the sake of peace in the family, had to be projected outward toward neighbors. The New Englanders of those peaceable kingdoms therefore built a reputation as the most litigious people on the face of God's earth, continually quarreling over fancied slights, business dealings, and other issues, and building in the process a flourishing legal profession.

SOCIAL STRAINS   All the while, social strains were growing in the community, a consequence of population pressure on the land. In the close-knit towns of New England the fragmentation of family ties seems to have been slowed by the peculiar circumstances of the community. Studies of Andover, Dedham, and Plymouth, Massachusetts, among other towns, suggest that at least in the seventeenth century family ties grew stronger and village life more cohesive than in the homeland. The conjugal unit prevailed, but intermarriage of families blurred the line between family and community. And among the first settlers, fathers exercised strong patriarchal control over their sons through their control of the land. They kept the sons in the town, not letting them set up their own households or get title to their farmland until they reached middle age.

In New England as elsewhere the tendency was to subdivide the land among all the children. But by the eighteenth century, with land scarcer, the younger sons were either getting control of property early or else moving on. Often the younger male children were forced out, with family help and blessings, to seek land elsewhere or new kinds of work in the commercial cities. With the growing pressure on land in the settled regions, poverty was becoming visible in what had once seemed a country of unlimited opportunity.

The emphasis on a direct accountability to God, which lay at the base of all Protestant theology, itself caused a persistent tension and led believers to challenge authority in the name of private conscience. Massachusetts repressed such heresy in the 1630s, but it resurfaced during the 1650s among Quakers and Baptists, and in 1659–1660 the colony hanged four Quakers who persisted in returning after they were expelled. These acts caused such revulsion—and an investigation by the crown—that they were not repeated, although heretics continued to face harassment and persecution.

More damaging to the Puritan Utopia was the increasing worldliness of New England, which placed growing strains on church discipline. More and more children of the "visible saints" found themselves unable to give the required testimony of regeneration. In 1662 an assembly of ministers at Boston accepted the "Half-Way Covenant," whereby baptized children of church members could be admitted to a "halfway" membership and secure baptism for their own children in turn. Such members, however, could neither vote nor take communion. A further blow to Puritan hegemony came with the Massachusetts royal charter of 1691, which required toleration of dissenters and based the right to vote on property rather than on church membership.

The strains which built up in Massachusetts's transition from Puritan utopia to royal colony reached an unhappy climax in the witchcraft hysteria at Salem Village (later Danvers) in 1692. The general upheaval in the colony's political, economic, social, and religious life was compounded in that locale by a conflict of values between a community rooted in the subsistence farm economy and the thriving port of Salem proper.

Seething insecurities in the community made it receptive to accusations by adolescent girls that they had been bewitched. Before the hysteria ran its course ten months later, nineteen people (including some men) had been hanged, one man pressed to death by heavy stones, and more than 100 others jailed. The fascination of horror has drawn a disproportionate amount of attention to the witchcraft delusions. It should be noted, however, that most people in the Western world at that time believed in witches who served the devil and his demons. But nearly everybody responsible for the Salem executions later recanted and nothing quite like it happened in the colonies again. In Europe witches were still being executed in the eighteenth century.

Society and Economy in the Middle Colonies

AN ECONOMIC MIX Both geographically and culturally the Middle Colonies stood between New England and the South, blending their own influences with elements derived from the older regions on either side. In so doing they more completely reflected the diversity of colonial life and more fully foreshadowed the pluralism of the later American nation than the regions on either side. Their crops were those of New England but more bountiful, owing to better land and a longer growing season, and they developed surpluses of foodstuffs for exports to the plantations of the South and the West Indies: wheat, barley, oats, and other cereals, flour, and livestock. Three great rivers—the Hudson, Delaware, and Susquehanna—and their tributaries gave the Middle Colonies a unique access to their backcountry and to the fur trade of the interior, where New York and Pennsylvania long enjoyed friendly relations with the Iroquois, Delaware, and other tribes of the area. As a consequence the region's commerce rivaled that of New England, and indeed Philadelphia eventually supplanted Boston as the largest city of the colonies.

Land policies followed the headright system of the South, with all the later embellishments of favoritism to influential speculators. One of the most successful of these was James Logan, a man of staggering erudition, secretary to William Penn, then Pennsylvania commissioner of property and holder of numerous other offices from which positions of influence he set himself up as one of the leading merchants and landholders—and owner of the largest private library—in the colonies. In New York the early royal governors, especially Lord Cornbury, went him one better. They carried forward, in practice if not in name, the Dutch device of the patroonship, granting to influential favorites vast estates on Long Island and up the Hudson and Mohawk Valleys. These realms most nearly approached the Old World manor, self-contained domains farmed by tenants who paid feudal dues to use the landlords' mills, warehouses, smokehouses, and wharfs. But with free land elsewhere, New York's population languished and the new waves of immigrants sought the promised land of Pennsylvania.

AN ETHNIC MIX   In the makeup of their population the Middle Colonies stood apart from both the mostly English Puritan settlements and the biracial plantation colonies to the South. In New York and New Jersey, for instance, Dutch culture and language lingered for some time to come, along with the Dutch Reformed church. Up and down the Delaware River the few Swedes and Finns, the first settlers, were overwhelmed by the influx of English and Welsh Quakers, followed in turn by the Germans and Scotch-Irish.

The Germans came mainly from the Rhineland Palatinate, which had been devastated and impoverished first in the Thirty Years' War (1618–1648), then in the repeated wars of Louis XIV (1667–1713). Penn's brochures on the bounties of Pennsylvania circulated in German translation, and his promise of religious freedom brought a response from persecuted sects, especially the Mennonites, German Baptists whose beliefs resembled those of the Quakers. In 1683 Francis Daniel Pastorius brought a group of Mennonites to found Germantown near Philadelphia. They were but the vanguard of a swelling migration in the eighteenth century which included Lutherans, Reformed Calvinists, Moravians, Dunkers, and others, a large proportion of whom paid their way as indentured servants, or "redemptioners," as

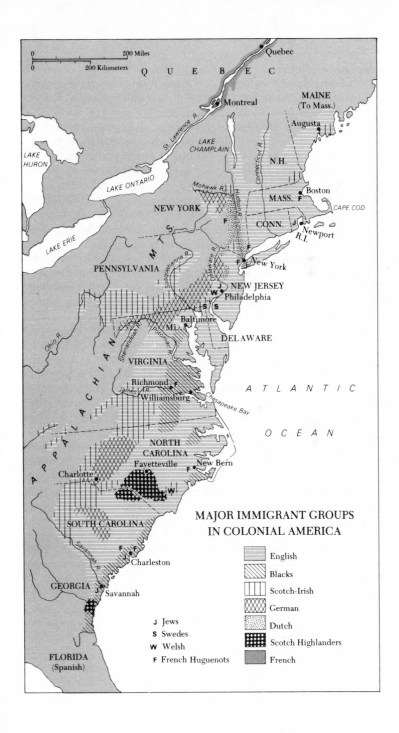

MAJOR IMMIGRANT GROUPS
IN COLONIAL AMERICA

	English
	Blacks
	Scotch-Irish
	German
	Dutch
	Scotch Highlanders
	French

J Jews
S Swedes
W Welsh
F French Huguenots

they were commonly called. Back of Philadelphia they created a belt of settlement in which the "Pennsylvania Dutch" (a corruption of *Deutsch*, meaning German) predominated, and a channel for the dispersion of German population through the colonies.

The Scotch-Irish began to arrive later and moved still farther out in the backcountry. "Scotch-Irish" is an enduring misnomer for Ulster Scots, Presbyterians transplanted to confiscated lands in Northern Ireland to give that country a more Protestant tone. The Ulster plantation dated from 1607–1609, the years when Jamestown was fighting for survival. A century later the Ulster Scots were on the move again, in flight from economic disaster caused by English tariffs, especially the Woolens Act of 1699. This time they looked mainly to Pennsylvania.

The Germans and Scotch-Irish became the largest non-English elements in the colonies, but other groups enriched the diversity of population in New York and the Quaker colonies: French Huguenots (Calvinists whose privilege of toleration was revoked in 1685), Irish, Welshmen, Swiss, Jews, and others. New York had inherited from the Dutch a tradition of toleration which had given the colony a motley population before the English conquest: French-speaking Walloons and Frenchmen, Germans, Danes, Portuguese, Spaniards, Italians, Bohemians, Poles, and others, including some New England Puritans. The Protestant Netherlands had given haven to the Sephardic Jews expelled from Spain and Portugal, and enough of them found their way into New Netherland to found a synagogue there.

What could be said of Pennsylvania as a refuge for the persecuted might be said as well of Rhode Island and South Carolina, which practiced a similar religious toleration. Newport and Charleston, like New York and Philadelphia, became centers of minuscule Jewish populations. French Huguenots made their greatest mark on South Carolina, more by their enterprise than by their numbers, and left implanted in the life of the colony such family names as Huger, Porcher, DeSaussure, Legare, Lanneau, and Lesesne. A number of Highland Scots came directly from their homeland rather than by way of Ulster, especially after suppression of a rebellion in 1745 on behalf of the Stuart pretender to the throne, "Bonnie Prince Charlie." A large group of them went to Fayetteville, North Carolina, where Gaelic-speaking Scots settled beside Lumbee Indians who had spoken English for nearly a century.

The eighteenth century was the great period of expansion and population growth in British North America, and during those years a large increase of the non-English stock took place. A rough estimate of the national origins of the white population, based on linguistic analysis of family names in the census of 1790, found it to be 60.9 percent English, 14.3 percent Scots and Scotch-Irish, 8.7 percent German, 5.4 percent Dutch, French, and Swedish, 3.7 percent Irish, and 7 percent miscellaneous or unassigned. If one adds to the 3,172,444 whites in the first census the 756,770 nonwhites, not even considering uncounted Indians, it seems likely that little more than half the populace, and perhaps fewer, could trace their origins to England. Of the blacks about 75 percent had been transported from the bend of African coastline between the Senegal and Niger Rivers; most of the rest came from Congo-Angola.

THE BACKCOUNTRY   Pennsylvania in the eighteenth century became the great distribution point for the diverse ethnic groups of European origin, just as the Chesapeake and Charleston became the distribution points for African peoples. Before the mid–eighteenth century, population in the Pennsylvania backcountry was coming up against the Appalachian barrier and, following the line of least resistance, the Scotch-Irish and Germans filtered southward across western Maryland, down the Shenandoah valley of Virginia, and on into the Carolina and Georgia backcountry. Germans were first in the upper Shenandoah Valley, and to the south of them Scotch-Irish filled the lower valley. Migrants of both stocks continued to move into the Carolina and Georgia backcountry, while others found their way up from Charleston.

Along the fringes of the frontier were commonly found the Scotch-Irish, who had acquired in their homeland and in Ulster a stubborn fighting spirit that brooked no nonsense from the "savages" of the woods. And out on the cutting edge life might be in that "state of nature" described by Thomas Hobbes: "poor, nasty, brutish, and short." It was a lonely life of scattered settlements, isolated log cabins set on plots of land which the pioneer owned or at least occupied, furnished with crude furniture hacked out with axe and adze and pieced together with pegs. The frontier regions bred a rough democracy, because most people were on a nearly equal status, and instilled a stubborn individualism in people who got accustomed to deciding things for themselves. With time, of course, neighborhoods grew up within visiting distance, animal and Indian trails broadened into wagon roads, crossroads stores grew up into community gathering places where social intercourse could be lubricated with the whiskey that was omnipresent on the Scotch-Irish frontier.

The backcountry of the Piedmont, and something much like it on up to northern New England (Maine, New Hampshire, and what would become Vermont), became a fourth major region that stretched the length of the colonies across the abstract imaginary boundaries which separated the political units. Government was slow to reach these remote settlements, and the system of "every man for himself" sometimes led frontier communities into conditions of extreme disorder.

COLONIAL CITIES

During the seventeenth century the colonies remained in comparative isolation, evolving subtly distinctive ways and unfolding separate histories. Boston and New York, Philadelphia and Charleston were more likely to keep in closer touch with London than with each other. The Carolina upcountry had more in common with the Pennsylvania backcountry than either had with Charleston or Philadelphia. Colonial cities faced outward to the Atlantic. Since commerce was their chief reason for being, they hugged the coastline or, like Philadelphia, sprang up on streams where ocean-going vessels could reach them. Never holding more than 10 percent of the colonial population, they exerted an influence in commerce, politics, and civilization generally out of proportion to their size.

Five major port cities outdistanced the rest. By the end of the colonial period Philadelphia, with some 30,000 people (counting adjacent suburbs), was the largest city in the colonies and second only to London in the British Empire. New York, with about 25,000, ranked second, Boston numbered 16,000, Charles Town 12,000, and Newport 11,000. Falling in a range of about 8,000 down to 4,000 were secondary ports and inland towns like New Haven and Norwich, Connecticut; Norfolk; Baltimore; Lancaster, Pennsylvania; Salem; New London; Providence; and Albany.

THE SOCIAL AND POLITICAL ORDER   The upper crust of urban society were the merchants who bartered the products of American farms and forests for the molasses and rum of the West Indies, the wines of Madeira, the manufactured goods of Europe, and the slaves of Africa. Their trade in turn stimulated the activities of rum distilling, ropewalks, sail lofts, instrumentmakers, and ship chandlers who supplied vessels leaving port. After the merchants, who constituted the chief urban aristocracy, came a middle class of craftsmen, retailers, innkeepers, and small jobbers

who met a variety of needs. And at the bottom of the pecking
order were sailors, unskilled workers, and some artisans.

Class stratification in the cities became more pronounced as
time went by. One study of Boston found that in 1687 the richest
15 percent of the population owned 52 percent of the taxable
wealth; by 1771 the top 15 percent owned about two-thirds and
the top 5 percent owned some 44 percent of the wealth. In Philadelphia the concentration of wealth was even more pronounced.

Problems created by urban growth are nothing new. Colonial
cities had problems of traffic which required not only paved
streets and lighting but regulations to protect children and animals in the streets from reckless riders. Regulations restrained
citizens from creating public nuisances by tossing their garbage
into the streets. Fires that on occasion swept through closely
packed buildings led to preventive standards in building codes,
restrictions on burning rubbish, and the organization of volunteer and finally professional fire companies. Crime and violence
made necessary more police protection than the constable and
watch duty which at first was required of ordinary citizens. And
in cities the poor became more visible than in the countryside.
Colonists brought with them the English principle of public responsibility. The number of Boston's poor receiving public assistance rose from 500 in 1700 to 4,000 in 1736, New York's from

*Fighting a fire in colonial New York, from the certificate of the Hand in
Hand Fire Company, New York (1762). [New York Public Library]*

250 in 1698 to 5,000 in the 1770s. Most of it went to "outdoor" relief in the form of money, food, clothing, and fuel, but alms-houses also appeared in colonial cities.

Town governments were not always equal to their multiple tasks. Of the major cities, Boston and Newport had the common New England system of town meetings and selectmen, while New York after 1791 had an elected council responsive to the citizens, although its mayor and other officials were still appointed by the governor. Philadelphia, however, fell under a self-perpetuating closed corporation in which the common run of citizens had no voice, and colonial Charles Town never achieved status as a municipal corporation at all, but remained under the thumb of the South Carolina Assembly.

CITY LIFE IN THE COLONIES   Little of the colonial population lived far from the navigable streams, except in the interior. The first roads were likely to be Indian trails, which themselves often followed the tracks of bison and perhaps the ancient mastodon through the forests. The trails widened with travel, then became roads by order of provincial and local authorities. Land travel at first had to go by horse or by foot. The first stagecoach line for the public, opened in 1732, linked Burlington and Perth Amboy, New Jersey, connecting by water to Philadelphia and New York, respectively. That same year a guidebook published in Boston, Thomas Prince's *The Vade Mecum for America*, gave roads connecting from Boston through Providence, New York, Philadelphia, and eventually on to Williamsburg and Charleston, with connecting branches. From the main ports good roads might reach thirty or forty miles inland, but all were dirt roads subject to washouts and mudholes. There was not a single hard-surfaced road during the entire colonial period, aside from city streets.

Taverns were an important adjunct of colonial travel, since movement by night was too risky, and they became social and political centers to which the local people repaired to learn news from travelers, to discuss the current issues, to socialize, drink, and gamble. Postal service through the seventeenth century was almost nonexistent—people entrusted letters to travelers or sea captains. Massachusetts set up a provincial postal system in 1677, and Pennsylvania in 1683. In 1691 King William favored Thomas Neale with a monopoly of postal service in Massachusetts, New York, and Pennsylvania, and Neale's deputy, Andrew Hamilton of Philadelphia, established a weekly service from Portsmouth, New Hampshire, to Philadelphia. The system proved unprofitable though, and Neale abandoned his monopoly in 1707. Under a Parliamentary Law of 1710, however, the postmaster of London was authorized to name a deputy in charge of the colonies and a system eventually extended the length of the Atlantic seaboard. Benjamin Franklin, who served as deputy-postmaster from 1753 to 1774, speeded up the service with shorter routes and night-traveling post riders, and increased the volume by inaugurating lower rates.

More reliable deliveries gave rise to newspapers in the eighteenth century. The first printing press was set up at Cambridge, Massachusetts, in 1638, in connection with Harvard College; it produced mainly religious tracts and sermons. The first newspaper to endure was the Boston *News-Letter* (1704), which started when William Campbell, postmaster of Boston, began writing letters to friends around Massachusetts to keep them informed of current events. Before 1745 twenty-two newspapers had been started, seven in New England, ten in the Middle Colonies, five in the South, including the *American Weekly Mercury* (1719) of Philadelphia; the *New England Courant* (1721) of Boston published by James Franklin, older brother of Benjamin; Ben's own *Pennsylvania Gazette* (acquired 1729), the *South Carolina Gazette* (1732) published by former Franklin printers Thomas Whitmarsh and Louis Timothy, John Peter Zenger's New York *Weekly Journal* (1733), and the *Virginia Gazette* (1736).

An important landmark in the progress of freedom of the press was Zenger's trial for seditious libel for publishing criticisms of New York's governor, William Cosby. Imprisoned for ten months and brought to trial in 1735, he was defended by the aged Andrew Hamilton of Philadelphia, whose cleverness made him perhaps the original "Philadelphia lawyer." The established rule in English common law held that one might be punished for criticism which fostered "an ill opinion of the government." The jury's function was only to determine whether or not the defendant had published the opinion. Hamilton startled the court with his claim that Zenger had published the truth—which the judge ruled an unacceptable defense. Cosby was so unpopular, however, that the jury considered the attacks on him true and held the editor not guilty. The libel law remained standing as before, but editors thereafter were emboldened to criticize officials more freely. No more such cases of any consequence arose.

THE ENLIGHTENMENT

DISCOVERING THE LAWS OF NATURE   It was the cities that, through their commercial contacts, through their newspapers, and through many-fold activities, became the centers for the dissemination of fashion and ideas. In the world of ideas a new fashion was abroad: the Enlightenment. During the first century of English colonization the settlers' contemporaries in Europe went through a scientific revolution in which the old Ptolemaic view of an earth-centered universe was overthrown by the new heliocentric (sun-centered) system of Polish astronomer Nicolaus Copernicus. A climax to the revolution came with Sir Isaac Newton's *Principia* (*Mathematical Principles of Natural Philosophy,* 1687), which set forth his theory of gravitation. Newton had, in short, hit upon the design of a mechanistic universe moving in accordance with natural laws which could be grasped by human reason and explained by mathematics.

By analogy from Newton's world machine one could reason that natural laws governed all things—the orbits of the planets and also the orbits of human relations: politics, economics, and society. Reason could make men aware, for instance, that the natural law of supply and demand governed economics or that natural rights to life, liberty, and property determined the limits and functions of government.

Much of enlightened thought could be reconciled with established beliefs—the idea of natural law existed in Christian theology, and religious people could reason that the worldview of Copernicus and Newton simply showed forth the glory of God. Puritan leaders accepted Newtonian science from the start. Yet if one carried the idea to its ultimate logic, one might find God eliminated or at best reduced to the position of a remote Creator —as the French *philosophe* Voltaire put it, as master clockmaker who planned the universe and set it in motion. Evil in the world, one might reason further, resulted not from original sin and innate depravity so much as from an imperfect understanding of the laws of nature. Man, John Locke argued in his *Essay on Human Understanding* (1690), is largely the product of his environment, the human mind a blank tablet on which experience is written. The evils of a corrupt society therefore might corrupt the mind. The way to improve both society and human nature was by the application and improvement of Reason—which was the highest Virtue (enlightened thinkers often capitalized both words).

THE ENLIGHTENMENT IN AMERICA Whether or not one pursued all this to the outermost reaches of its logic, such ideas affected the climate of thought in the eighteenth century. The premises of Newtonian science and the Enlightenment, moreover, fitted the

American experience. In the New World people no longer moved in the worn grooves of tradition that defined the roles of priest or peasant or noble. Much of their experience had already been with observation, experiment, and the need to think anew. America was therefore receptive to the new science. Anybody who pretended to a degree of learning revealed a curiosity about natural philosophy, and some carried it to considerable depth.

John Winthrop, Jr. (1606–1676), three times governor of Connecticut, wanted to establish industries and mining in America. These interests led to his work in chemistry and membership in the Royal Society of London. He owned probably the first telescope brought to the colonies. His cousin, John Winthrop IV (1714–1779), was a professional scientist, Hollis Professor of Mathematics and Natural Philosophy at Harvard, who introduced to the colonies the study of calculus and ranged over the fields of astronomy, geology, chemistry, and electricity. Cadwallader Colden, last royal governor of New York, studied and wrote in the fields of botany and physics. David Rittenhouse of Philadelphia, a clockmaker, became a self-taught scientist who built two orreries and probably the first telescope made in America. John Bartram of Philadelphia spent a lifetime traveling and studying American plant life, and gathered in Philadelphia a botanical garden now part of the city's park system.

FRANKLIN'S INFLUENCE   Benjamin Franklin stood apart from all these men as the person who epitomized the Enlightenment, in the eyes of both Americans and Europeans, more than any other single person. It was fitting that Franklin came from Pennsylvania, which in the eyes of Voltaire had fulfilled the Quaker virtues of toleration and simplicity. William Penn, Voltaire wrote, had "brought to the world that golden age of which men talk so much and which probably has never existed anywhere except in Pennsylvania." Franklin came from the ranks of the common man and never lost the common touch, a gift that accounted for his success as a publisher. Born in Boston in 1706, son of a candle and soap maker, apprenticed to his older brother, a printer, Franklin ran away at the age of seventeen. In Philadelphia, before he was twenty-four he owned a print shop where he edited and published the *Pennsylvania Gazette*, and when he was twenty-seven he brought out *Poor Richard's Almanac*, still mined for its homely maxims on success and happiness. Before he retired from business at the age of forty-two, Franklin, among other achievements, had founded a library, invented a stove, set up a fire com-

Benjamin Franklin as a leading figure in the Enlightenment. The electrical storm alludes to his famous experiments with electricity. [Philadelphia Museum of Art]

pany, helped start the academy which became the University of Pennsylvania, and started a debating club which grew into the American Philosophical Society. After his early retirement he intended to devote himself to public affairs and the sciences.

The course of events allowed him less and less time for science, but that was his passion. Franklin's *Experiments and Observations on Electricity* (1751) went through many editions in several languages and established his reputation as a leading thinker and experimenter. His speculations extended widely to the fields of medicine, meteorology, geology, astronomy, physics, and other aspects of science. He invented the Franklin stove, the lighting rod, and a glass harmonica for which Mozart and Beethoven composed. In his travels as colonial agent to London and later American ambassador to France, his insatiable curiosity led to suggestions (some of them later adopted) for improvements in ship design. Franklin's university had been the printshop, and the triumph of this untutored genius further confirmed the Enlightenment trust in the powers of Nature.

EDUCATION IN THE COLONIES   The heights of abstract reasoning, of course, were remote from the everyday concerns of most colonists. For the colonists at large, education in the traditional ideas and manners of society—even literacy itself—remained primarily the responsibility of family and church, and one not always accepted. The modern conception of universal free education as a responsibility of the state was a slow growth and failed to win universal acceptance until the twentieth century. Yet there is evidence of a widespread concern almost from the beginning that steps needed to be taken lest the children of settlers grow up untutored in the wilderness.

Conditions in New England proved most favorable for the establishment of schools. The Puritan emphasis on Scripture reading, which all Protestants shared in some degree, implied an obligation to ensure literacy. The great proportion of highly educated people in Puritan New England (Massachusetts probably had a greater proportion of college graduates in the early seventeenth century than in the twentieth) ensured a common respect for education. And the compact towns of that region made schools more feasible than among the scattered people of the southern colonies. In 1635 the inhabitants of Boston established the Boston Latin Grammar School, which had a distinguished career to the twentieth century, and the same year the General Court voted to establish a college which, begun in 1638, grew into Harvard University. In 1647 the colony enacted the famous "ye olde deluder Satan" Act (designed to thwart the Evil One) which required every town of fifty or more families to set up a grammar school (a Latin school that could prepare a student

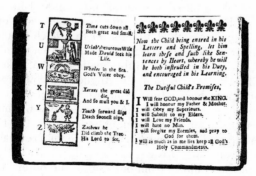

*A New England primer (1727). From books such
as this, the New England child was "both instructed
in his Duty, and encouraged in his learning."
[New York Public Library]*

for college). Although the act was widely evaded, it did signify a serious purpose to promote education. Massachusetts Bay set an example which the rest of New England emulated.

The Dutch in New Netherland were nearly if not equally as active as the New England Puritans, and more active than the English who succeeded them after 1664. In Pennsylvania the Quakers never heeded William Penn's instructions to establish public schools, but did respect the usefulness of education and financed a number of private schools teaching practical as well as academic subjects. In the southern colonies efforts to establish schools were hampered by the more scattered populations, and in parts of the backcountry by indifference and neglect. Some of the wealthiest planters and merchants of the Tidewater sent their children to England or hired tutors, who in some cases would also serve the children of neighbors. In some places wealthy patrons or the people collectively managed to raise some kind of support for "old field" schools and academies at the secondary level.

THE GREAT AWAKENING

STIRRINGS In the new currents of learning and the Enlightenment, however, many people seemed to be drifting away from the old moorings of piety. And if the Lord had allowed great Puritan and Quaker merchants of Boston and Philadelphia to prosper, the haunting fear arose that the devil had lured them into the vain pursuit of worldly gain. Intellectually the educated classes were falling into deism and skepticism. And out along the fringes of settlement there grew up a great backwater of the unchurched, people who had no minister to preach or administer sacraments or perform marriages, who fell into a primitive and sinful life, little different from the heathens who lurked in the woods. Charles Woodmason, an Anglican divine, called the backcountry preachers in the Carolinas "ignorant wretches, who cannot write." A Baptist communion service was to him like "A Gang of frantic Lunatics broke out of Bedlam." By the 1730s the sense of falling-away had prepared the time for a revival of faith, the Great Awakening, a wave of evangelism that within a few years swept the colonies from one end to the other, America's first mass movement.

In 1734–1735 a rehearsal for the event came in a remarkable spiritual refreshing that occurred in the congregation of Jon-

*The Rev. Jonathan Edwards awoke
many congregants to their plight in
sermons such as "Sinners in the
Hands of an Angry God."*
[Yale University Art Gallery]

athan Edwards, a Congregationalist minister of Northampton in
western Massachusetts. Edwards's vivid descriptions of the tor-
ments of hell and the delights of heaven inspired his congregants.
About the same time William Tennant arrived from Ulster and in
Neshaminy, Pennsylvania, set up a "Log College" for the education of ministers to serve the Scotch-Irish Presbyterians around
Philadelphia. The Log College specialized in turning out zealots
who scorned complacency and proclaimed the need for revival.

The catalyst of the Great Awakening, however, was a twenty-
seven-year-old Anglican minister, George Whitefield, whose
reputation as an evangelist preceded him to the colonies. In the
autumn of 1739 he arrived in Philadelphia, and late in that year
preached to crowds of as many as 6,000 around Philadelphia.
After visiting in Georgia, he made a triumphal procession northward to New England, drawing great crowds and releasing
"Gales of Heavenly Wind" that dispersed sparks throughout the
colonies. Young and magnetic, possessed of a golden voice, a dramatic actor in the pulpit who impersonated the agonies of the
damned and the joys of the regenerate, he swept audiences with
his unparalleled eloquence. Even the skeptical Ben Franklin,
who went to see the show in Philadelphia, found himself so carried away that he emptied his pockets into the collection plate
—perhaps the highest possible tribute to Whitefield's per-
suasiveness. The core of his message was the need to experience
a "new birth"—the need for a sudden and emotional moment of
conversion and salvation—and the dangers of an unconverted
ministry which had not experienced such rebirth.

Imitators sprang up everywhere, some of whom carried the language and histrionics to extremes. Graduates of the Log College denounced the "pharisaical preachers" who were themselves unconverted. The Rev. James Davenport, an itinerant Congregationalist of New England, set about stomping on the devil. The churched and unchurched flocked to the meetings, and seized of the terror and ecstacy, groveled on the floor or lay unconscious on the benches, to the chagrin of more decorous churchgoers. One never knew, the more traditional clergymen warned, whence came these enthusiasms—perhaps they were delusions sent by the Evil One to discredit the true faith.

PIETY AND REASON Everywhere the Awakening brought splits, especially in the more Calvinistic churches. Presbyterians divided into the "Old Side" and "New Side"; Congregationalists into "Old Lights" and "New Lights." New England would never be the same. The more traditional clergy found its position being undermined as church members chose sides and either dismissed their ministers or deserted them. Many of the "New Lights" went over to the Baptists, and others flocked to Presbyterian or, later, Methodist groups, which in turn divided and subdivided into new sects.

New England Puritanism was now finally divided. The precarious tension in which the Founders had held the elements of piety and reason was now sundered. Jonathan Edwards, the great theologian of the Awakening and perhaps of all American history, led the movement toward piety and justified the emotional extravagance of the conversion experience as something beyond the ability of the human frame to stand without physical manifestation. But he was an intellectual, himself never given to those excesses nor to the histrionics of Whitefield. Edwards's magnum opus was an elaborate theological reconciliation of Calvinism and the Enlightenment: *Of Freedom of the Will* (1754). Indeed, one curious and paradoxical sequel of the revival was the growth in New England churches of the "New Divinity," which spun out the ramifications of the revival theology in such recondite fashion that whole congregations got lost in the fog. In consequence New England was infiltrated more and more by Baptists, Presbyterians, Anglicans, and other denominations, but the revival tradition which had its chief theologian in New England paradoxically scored its most lasting victories along the chaotic frontiers of the middle and southern colonies.

In the more sedate churches of Boston, moreover, the principle of reason got the upper hand in a reaction against the excesses of revival emotion. Bostonian ministers like Charles Chauncey and Jonathan Mayhew assumed the lead in preaching a doctrine of rationality. They reexamined Calvinist theology and found it too forbidding and irrational that men could be forever damned by predestination. The rationality of Newton and Locke, the idea of natural law, crept more and more into their sermons. They were already on the road to Unitarianism and Universalism.

In reaction to taunts that the "born-again" ministers lacked learning, the Awakening gave rise to the denominational colleges that became so characteristic of American higher education. The three colleges already in existence had grown earlier from religious motives: Harvard, founded in 1636, because the Puritans dreaded "to leave an illiterate ministry to the church when our present ministers shall lie in the dust"; the College of William and Mary, in 1693, to serve James Blair's purpose of strengthening the Anglican ministry; and Yale College, in 1701, set up to serve the Puritans of Connecticut, who felt that Harvard was drifting from the strictest orthodoxy. The Presbyterian College of New Jersey, later Princeton University, was founded in 1746 as successor to William Tennent's Log College. In close succession came King's College (1754) in New York, later Columbia University, an Anglican institution; the College of Rhode Island (1764), later Brown University, Baptist; Queen's College (1766), later Rutgers, Dutch Reformed; and Congregationalist Dartmouth (1769), the outgrowth of an earlier school for Indians. Among the colonial colleges only the University of Pennsylvania, founded as the Philadelphia Academy in 1754, arose from a secular impulse.

The Great Awakening, like the Enlightenment, set in motion currents that still flow in American life. It implanted permanently in American culture the evangelical principle and the endemic style of revivalism. The movement weakened the status of the old-fashioned clergy and encouraged the believer to exercise his own judgment, and thereby weakened habits of deference generally. By adding to the proliferation of denominations it added to the need for toleration of dissent. But in some respects the counterpoint between the Awakening and the Enlightenment, between the principles of piety and reason, paradoxically led by different roads to similar ends. Both emphasized the power and right of the individual to judge things for himself, and both aroused millennial hopes that America would become the promised land in which men might attain to the perfection of piety or reason, if not of both.

FURTHER READING

Scholarship in colonial social history traditionally offers a varied fare. Since most works concentrate on specific themes and particular locales, a comprehensive social analysis of the 1600s awaits its historian. Timothy H. Breen's *Puritans and Adventurers: Change and Persistence in Early America* (1980)° traces the steadfastness of early settlement patterns in both the northern and southern colonies, but concentrates on Virginia and Massachusetts. James A. Henretta's *The Evolution of American Society, 1700–1815* (1973),° brings together much recent research on the eighteenth century. Sketches of everyday life and social conditions appear in the overviews listed in Chapter 2, particularly Daniel Boorstin's *The Americans: The Colonial Experience* (1958).° Richard F. Hofstadter's *America At 1750: A Social Portrait* (1971)° is valuable for the later colonial period.

Until recently Puritan communities received the bulk of scholarly attention. Studies of the New England town include Darrett B. Rutman's *Winthrop's Boston: Portrait of a Puritan Town, 1630–1649* (1965);° Summer Powell's *Puritan Village* (1963),° on the origins and social structure of Sudbury, Mass.; Kenneth A. Lockridge's *A New England Town: The First One Hundred Years* (1970),° which looks at the relationship of family and authority in Dedham, Mass.; Philip Greven's *Four Generations: Population, Land, and Family in Colonial Amherst, Massachusetts* (1970);° and Paul Boyer and Stephen Nissenbaum's *Salem Possessed* (1974),° which conects the famous witch trials to changes in community structure and economic base.

All five books just listed stress patterns of structural development in Massachusetts during the seventeenth century. Broader in cultural interpretation are Richard S. Dunn's *Puritans and Yankees: The Winthrop Dynasty of New England, 1630–1717* (1982),° Timothy H. Breen's *The Character of the Good Ruler: Puritan Political Ideals in New England, 1630–1730* (1982),° and E. Digby Balzell's *Puritan Boston and Quaker Philadelphia* (1982).° For an interdisciplinary approach, see John Demos's *Entertaining Satan: Witchcraft and the Culture of Early New England* (1982).° For a comparison of the Puritans and the Pilgrims, see John Demos's *A Little Commonwealth: Family Life in Plymouth Colony* (1970).°

The descendants of these early settlers are described in Michael Zuckerman's *Peaceable Kingdoms: Massachusetts Towns in the Eighteenth Century* (1970),° Edward Cook's *Fathers of the Towns: Leadership and Community Structure in Eighteenth Century New England* (1976), and Robert A. Gross's *The Minutemen and Their World* (1976).°

For the social history of the southern colonies, see Wesley F. Craven's *The Southern Colonies in the Seventeenth Century* (1949).° Valuable for the eighteenth century is Carl Bridenbaugh's *Myths and*

Realities: Societies of the Colonial South (1963),° which advances the idea that more than one "South" was developing.

The best southern social history is intertwined with analysis of the origins of slavery. Begin with Edmund S. Morgan's *American Slavery / American Freedom: The Ordeal of Colonial Virginia* (1975),° which examines the impact of social structure, environment, and labor patterns in a biracial context. Peter H. Wood weaves a similar social mosaic for South Carolina in *Black Majority: Negroes in Colonial South Carolina from 1670 through the Stono Rebellion* (1974).° More specific on the racial nature of the origins of slavery are Winthrop Jordan's *White over Black: American Attitudes toward the Negro, 1550–1812* (1968),° and David B. Davis's *The Problem of Slavery in Western Culture* (1966).° The mechanics of the slave market are handled in Philip D. Curtin's *The Atlantic Slave Trade* (1969).° Black viewpoints are also presented in Gerald Mullin's *Flight and Rebellion: Slave Resistance in Eighteenth Century Virginia* (1972),° and Timothy H. Breen and Stephen Innes's *"Myne Own Ground": Race and Freedom on Virginia's Eastern Shore, 1640–1676* (1980),° a short and insightful work on free blacks. Lewis C. Gray's *History of Agriculture in the Southern United States to 1860* (vol. 1, 1933) handles the specifics of plantation agriculture. David W. Galenson's *White Servitude in Colonial America* (1981) looks at the indentured labor force.

Patterns of trade during the colonial period have principally been approached from the mercantile viewpoint. James F. Shepherd and Gary M. Walter, in *The Economic Rise of Early America* (1979), emphasize the connection between maritime commerce and interior development. Problems with the monetary system are treated in Curtis P. Nettels's *The Money Supply of the American Colonies before 1720* (1934). Trade connections with Europe are stressed in Ralph Davis's *Rise of the Atlantic Economy* (1973).° How the staple tobacco affected both commerce and cultivation can be studied in Jacob M. Price's *France and the Chesapeake* (2 vols.; 1973). The interaction of trade and politics in America's first cities is the subject of Carl Bridenbaugh's *Cities in the Wilderness* (1955) and Gary B. Nash's *The Urban Crucible* (1979).°

Land policies and the Turner thesis have also received recent attention. Charles S. Grant's *Democracy in the Connecticut Frontier Town of Kent* (1961)° challenges the interpretation that frontier settlements enjoyed a greater degree of equality. James T. Lemon explores land holding patterns in one county of Pennsylvania in *The Best Poor Man's Country* (1972).° The impact of land pressures and tenancy is explored in P. O. Walker's *Land and People* (1978) and Sung Bok Kim's *Landlord and Tenant in Colonial New York* (1978). The political implications of land pressures are documented for the Middle Colonies in Patricia Bonomi's *A Factious People* (1971).° The ethnic composition of landholders is studied in Robert V. Wells's *The population of the British Colonies before 1776* (1975).

An overview of cultural patterns is provided in Louis B. Wright's *Cultural Life of the American Colonies, 1607–1763* (1957).° Henry F. May's *The Enlightenment in America* (1976)° examines intellectual trends. For the role of Benjamin Franklin in American culture, consult first the full-length biographies by Carl Van Doren, *Benjamin Franklin* (1938), and Charles C. Sellers, *Benjamin Franklin in Portraiture* (1962). Shorter but instructive is Verner W. Crane's *Benjamin Franklin and a Rising People* (1954). Franklin's reputation as a scientist is treated in Alfred O. Aldridge's *Franklin and His French Contemporaries* (1957). Lawrence Cremin's *American Education: The Colonial Experience, 1607–1783* (1970),° surveys educational development at several levels. Joseph J. Ellis's *The New England Mind in Transition: Samuel Johnson of Connecticut, 1696–1772* (1973), examines the role religion played in the development of higher education.

A concise introduction to the events and repercussions of the Great Awakening is J. M. Bumsted and John E. Van de Wetering's *What Must I Do To Be Saved?* (1976). Studies of the revival which concentrate on New England include Richard Bushman's *From Puritan to Yankee: Character and Social Order in Connecticut* (1967)° and C. C. Goen's *Revivalism and Separtism in New England, 1740–1800* (1962). Alan Heimert's *Religion and the American Mind from the Great Awakening to the Revolution* (1966) emphasizes the relationships of faith and belief to later political behavior. The political impact of the new religious enthusiasm in Virginia is handled in Rhys Isaac's *The Transformation of Virginia, 1740–1790* (1982).° Perry Miller analyzes Jonathan Edward's theological influence in *Jonathan Edwards* (1958). More recent is Patricia J. Tracy's *Jonathan Edwards, Pastor* (1980),° which stresses the Northampton minister's relations to his community. To understand the conflicts of authority between dissenters and the established churches in the colonies, consult Carl Bridenbaugh's *Mitre and Sceptre: Transatlantic Faiths, Ideas, Personalities, and Politics, 1689–1775* (1962), William G. McLoughlin's *Isaac Backus and the American Pietistic Tradition* (1967), and Charles S. Bolton's *Southern Anglicanism: The Church of England in Colonial South Carolina* (1982).

4

THE IMPERIAL PERSPECTIVE

In 1757, 150 years after the Jamestown beginnings, Edmund Burke wrote: "The settlement of our colonies was never pursued upon any regular plan; but they were formed, grew, and flourished, as accidents, the nature of the climate, or the dispositions of private men happened to operate." Burke's statement was true. For the better part of the seventeenth century England remained too disrupted by the running struggle between Parliament and the Stuarts ever to perfect either a colonial policy or effective agencies of imperial control. Intervention in colonial affairs was a matter of ad hoc commissions, experimentation, and "muddling through," a practice at which the British had a certain skill and not little luck. Slowly a plan of colonial administration emerged after the Restoration and began to fall into a semblance of order under William III, but even so it fell short of coherence and efficiency.

English Administration of the Colonies

Throughout the colonial period the king stood as the source of legal authority in America, and titles derived ultimately from royal grants. All colonies except Georgia got charters from the king before the Glorious Revolution, and thus before the crown lost supremacy to Parliament. The colonies therefore continued to stand as "dependencies of the crown" and the important colonial officials held office at the pleasure of the crown. And Georgia's status conformed to the established practice.

The king exercised his authority through the Privy Council, a body of some thirty to forty advisors appointed by and responsible solely to him, and this group became the first agency of colonial supervision. But the Privy Council was too large and too burdened to keep track of the details. So in 1634 Charles I entrusted colonial affairs to eleven members, the Lords Commissioners for Plantations in General, with William Laud, archbishop of Canterbury, as its head. The Laud Commission grew in part out of the troubles following the dissolution of the Virginia Company and in part out of Laud's design to impose political and religious conformity on New England. In 1638 his commission ordered Massachusetts to return its charter and answer charges that colonial officials had violated the provisions. Sir Ferdinando Gorges, appointed governor-general of New England, planned to subdue the region by force if necessary, and might have nipped the Puritan experiment in the bud except for the troubles at home which prevented further action.

The Civil War in England, which lasted from 1641 to 1649, was followed by Cromwell's Puritan Commonwealth and Protectorate, and both gave the colonies a respite from efforts at royal control. A Parliamentary Council for the Colonies, set up in 1643, and various Parliamentary committees and commissions, never exercised more than a shadowy authority. Puritan New England was naturally well disposed toward the Parliamentary cause, and in 1652 Cromwell dispatched an expedition to the colonies which forced the West Indies, Virginia, and Maryland to recognize Parliamentary authority but left them otherwise unmolested.

THE MERCANTILE SYSTEM If Cromwell showed little concern for colonial administration, he had a lively concern for colonial trade, which had fallen largely to Dutch shipping during the upheavals in England. Therefore in 1651 Parliament adopted a Navigation Act which excluded nearly all foreign shipping from the English and colonial trade. It required that all goods imported into England or the colonies must arrive on English ships and that the majority of the crew must be English. In all cases colonial ships and crews qualified as English. The act excepted European goods, which might come in ships of the country which produced the goods, but only from the place of origin or the port from which they were usually shipped.

On economic policy, if nothing else, Restoration England under Charles II took its cue from Cromwell. The New Parliament quickly adopted and then elaborated the mercantile system he had effected. The mercantile system, or mercantilism, became in the seventeenth and eighteenth centuries the operative theory of all major European powers—although the term itself was a later invention—and more than a trace of it remains in national policies today. In a world of national rivalries, the reasoning went, power and wealth went hand in hand. To be strong a state should be wealthy. To be wealthy it should enlarge its stores of gold and silver. To get and keep gold and silver the state should limit foreign imports and preserve a favorable balance of trade. And to accomplish these things the state should encourage manufacturers, through subsidies and monopolies if need be; it should develop and protect its own shipping; and it should make use of colonies as sources of raw materials and markets for its own finished goods. Mercantilists held that the total of the world's wealth, as reflected in the total stock of gold and silver, remained essentially fixed. All that changed was the nation's share of that stock. The theory lacked a conception of what today is a commonplace—that economic growth might enlarge wealth regardless of gold and silver.

Next came the Navigation Act of 1660, which amounted to a reenactment of Cromwell's act of 1651, but with a new twist. Ships' crews now had to be not half but three-quarters English, and certain enumerated articles were to be shipped only to England or other English colonies. These were things needed but not produced by the mother country. The list included at first tobacco, cotton, indigo, ginger, rustick and other dyewoods, and sugar. Later the enumeration expanded to include, among other things, rice, naval stores, hemp, masts and yards, copper ores, and furs. Not only did England (and the colonies) become the only outlet for these colonial exports, but three years later the Navigation Act of 1663 sought to make England the funnel through which all colonial imports had to be routed as well. The act was sometimes called the Staple Act because it made England the staple (market or trade center) for goods sent to the colonies. Everything shipped from Europe to America had to stop off in England, be landed, and pay duty before reshipment. There were few exceptions: only servants, horses, and provisions from Scotland; wine from Madeira and the Azores; and salt for fisheries. A third major act rounded out the trade system. The Navigation Act of 1673 (sometimes called the Plantation Duty Act) required that every captain loading enumerated articles give bond to land them in England, or if they were destined for another colony, that he pay on the spot a duty roughly equal to that paid in England.

ENFORCING THE NAVIGATION ACTS   The Navigation Acts set forth policy in provisions that were simple and straightforward enough. And they supplied a convenient rationale for a colonial system: to serve the economic needs of the mother country. Their enforcement in scattered colonies was something else again, however. So in the age of Charles II a bureaucracy of colonial administrators began to emerge, but it took shape slowly, and in fact never achieved full delineation. After the Restoration of 1660, supervision of colonial affairs fell once again to the Privy Council, or rather to a succession of its committees. In 1675, however, Charles II introduced some order into the chaos when he designated certain privy councilors the Lords of Trade and Plantations, whose name reflects the overall importance of economic factors. The Lords of Trade were to make the colonies abide by the mercantile system and to seek out ways to make them more profitable to England and the crown. To these ends they served as the clearinghouse for all colonial affairs, building up an archive and a bureaucracy of colonial experts supervised by their secretary, William Blathwayte. By advice rather than by direct authority, at least in theory, they named governors, wrote or reviewed the governors' instructions, and handled all reports and correspondence dealing with colonial affairs.

Within five years of the Plantation Duty Act, between 1673 and 1678, collectors of customs appeared in all the colonies and in 1683 a surveyor-general of the customs in the American colonies was named. The most notorious of these, insofar as the colonists were concerned, was Edward Randolph, the first man to make an entire career in the colonial service and the nemesis of

William Burgis's view of Boston shows the importance of shipping and its regulation in the colonies, especially Massachusetts Bay. [Winterthur Museum]

insubordinate colonials for a quarter century. Randolph's first assignment was as courier from the Lords of Trade. He arrived at Boston in June 1676 to demand that Massachusetts send agents to answer complaints that it had usurped the proprietary rights in New Hampshire and Maine. More was at stake, however. Since the Restoration the colony had ignored gentle hints that it bring its practices more in line with fundamental elements of the Restoration compromise. Massachusetts had accepted the formality of conducting judicial proceedings in the king's name. It dragged its heels, however, on adopting an Oath of Allegiance, repealing laws counter to English law, allowing use of the Anglican *Book of Common Prayer*, or making property instead of church membership the voting test. The expanding commercial interests of New England counseled prudence and accommodation, but the Puritan leaders harbored a persistent distrust of Stuart designs on their Wilderness Zion.

After a brief stay, Randolph submitted a report bristling with hostility. The Bay Colony had not only ignored royal wishes, it had tolerated violations of the Navigation Acts, refused appeals from its courts to the Privy Council, and had operated a mint in defiance of the king's prerogative. Massachusetts officials had told him, Randolph reported, "that the legislative power is and abides in them solely to act and make laws by virtue" of their charter. Continuing intransigence from Massachusetts led the Lords of Trade to begin legal proceedings against the colonial charter in 1678, although the issue remained in legal snarls for another six years. Meanwhile Randolph returned in 1680 to establish the royal colony of New Hampshire, then set up shop as the king's collector of customs in Boston, whence he dispatched repeated accounts of colonial recalcitrance. Eventually, in 1684, the Lords of Trade won a court decision which annulled the charter of Massachusetts.

THE DOMINION OF NEW ENGLAND   Temporarily, its government was placed in the hands of a special royal commission. Then in 1685 Charles II died, to be succeeded by his brother, the duke of York, as James II, the first Catholic sovereign since the death of Queen Mary in 1558. Plans long maturing in the Lords of Trade for a general reorganization of colonial government fitted very well the autocratic notions of James II, who asserted his prerogatives more forcefully than his brother and seemed to have less fear that he might have "to embark on his travels" again. The new king therefore readily approved a proposal to create a Dominion of New England and to place under its sway all colonies down through New Jersey. Something of the sort might have been in store for Pennsylvania and the southern colonies as well if the reign of James II had lasted longer. In that case the English colonies might have found themselves on the same tight leash as the colonies of Spain or France.

The Dominion was to have a government named altogether by royal authority, a governor and council who would rule without any assembly at all. The royal governor, Sir Edmond Andros, who had already served briefly as governor of New York, appeared in Boston in 1686 to establish his rule, which he soon extended over Connecticut and Rhode Island, and in 1688 over New York and the Jerseys. Andros was a soldier, accustomed to taking—and giving—orders. He seems to have been honest, efficient, and loyal to the crown, but totally without tact in circumstances which called for the utmost diplomacy—the uprooting of long-established institutions in the face of popular hostility.

His measures inspired increasing resentment, especially in Massachusetts. Taxation was now levied without the consent of the General Court, and when residents of Ipswich, led by the Rev. John Wise, protested against taxation without representation, a number of them were imprisoned or fined. Andros suppressed town governments. He proceeded to establish enforcement of the trade laws and subdue smuggling with the help of Edward Randolph, that omnipresent servant of the crown. And most ominous of all, Andros and his lieutenants took over one of the Puritan churches for Anglican worship in Boston. Puritan leaders believed, with good reason, that he proposed to break their power and authority. Andros might have found a moderate party in the prosperous and comfortable merchants, concerned for their businesses perhaps more than for their religion, but his enforcement of the Navigation Acts enraged them as well.

In any case the Dominion was scarcely established before word came of the Glorious Revolution of 1688–1689. James II in the homeland, like Andros in New England, had aroused resentment by arbitrary measures and, what was more, by openly parading his Catholic faith. The birth of a son, sure to be reared a Catholic, put the opposition on notice that James's system would survive him. The Catholic son, rather than the Protestant daughters, Mary and Anne, would be next in line for the throne. Parliamentary leaders, their patience exhausted, invited Mary and her husband, the Dutch stadtholder, William of Orange, to assume the throne as joint monarchs. James, his support dwindling, fled the country.

THE GLORIOUS REVOLUTION IN AMERICA   When news reached Boston that William had landed in England, Boston staged its own Glorious Revolution, as bloodless as that in England. Andros and his councilors were arrested and Massachusetts reverted to its former government. In rapid sequence the other colonies that had been absorbed into the Dominion followed suit. All were permitted to retain their former status except Massachusetts and Plymouth which, after some delay, were united under a new charter in 1691 as the royal colony of Massachusetts Bay. In New York, however, events took a different course. There, Francis Nicholson, serving as Andros's lieutenant-governor, was deposed by a group led by a German immigrant, Jacob Leisler, who assumed the office of governor pending word from England. When ambiguous letters came from William authorizing a continuation of the government, Leisler believed that they gave him power, and for two years he kept the province under his control with the support of the militia which had mobilized to overthrow Nicholson. Finally, in 1691, the king appointed a new governor, but an unfortunate tragedy ensued, which turned upon misunderstandings and poor timing. Leisler hesitated to turn over authority, and on this pretext the new governor charged him with treason. Leisler and his son-in-law, Jacob Milborne, were hanged on May 16, 1691. Four years too late, in 1695, Parliament exonerated them of all charges. For years to come Leisler and anti-Leisler factions would poison the political atmosphere of New York.

No effort was made to resume the disastrous policy of the Dominion of New England, but a remnant of that design, so to speak, was salvaged in the policy of bringing more colonies under royal control to the extent that the crown appointed the governor. Massachusetts was first, in 1691. New York kept the status of royal colony it had achieved upon the accession of James II. In Maryland after the Glorious Revolution, a local rebellion against the Catholic proprietor gave the occasion to appoint a royal governor in 1691. Maryland, however, reverted to proprietary status in 1715 after the fourth Lord Baltimore became Anglican. Pennsylvania had an even briefer career as a royal colony, 1692–1694, before reverting to Penn's proprietorship. New Jersey became royal in 1702, South Carolina in 1719, North Carolina in 1729, and Georgia in 1752.

The Glorious Revolution had significant long-term effects on American history in that the Bill of Rights and Toleration Act, passed in 1689, influenced attitudes and the course of events in the colonies even though they were not legally binding there.

And what was more significant for the future, the overthrow of James II set an example and a precedent for revolution against the monarch. In defense of that action the philosopher John Locke published his *Two Treatises on Government* (1690), which had an enormous impact on political thought in the colonies. The *First Treatise* refuted theories of the divine right of kings. The more important *Second Treatise* set forth Locke's contract theory of government. People were endowed with certain natural rights, the reasoning went—basically the rights to life, liberty, and property. Without government, in a state of nature, such rights went without safeguard. Hence men came together and by mutual agreement established governments among themselves. Kings were parties to such agreements, and bound by them. When they violated the rights of the people, therefore, the people had the right—in extreme cases—to overthrow the monarch and change their government.

The idea that governments emerged by contract out of a primitive state of nature is of course hypothetical, not a documented account of events. What Locke was seeking, as the historian Carl Becker put it, was "not the historical origin, but the rational justification, of government." But in the American experience governments had actually grown out of contractual arrangements such as he described: for instance, the Mayflower Compact, the Cambridge Agreement, the Fundamental Orders of Connecticut. The royal charters themselves constituted a sort of contract between the crown and the settlers. Locke's writings in any case appealed to colonial readers, and his philosophy probably had

John Locke. [National Portrait Gallery, London]

more influence in America than in England. It might be an over-statement, but a plausible case can be made that Locke's theories established a tradition, a consensus within which American institutions operated by almost universal consent, at least from the time of independence and to some extent before. Other works of political philosophy which had a wide influence in the colonies were James Harrington's *Oceana* (1656), a republican utopia, and Algernon Sidney's *Discourse on Government* (1698).

AN EMERGING COLONIAL SYSTEM   The accession of William and Mary brought on a recapitulation and refinement of the existing Navigation Acts and administrative system. In 1696 two developments created at last the semblance, and to some degree the reality, of a coherent colonial system. First, the Navigation Act of 1696, "An Act for preventing Frauds and regulating Abuses in the Plantation Trade," restated the existing restrictions on colonial commerce but added certain provisions designed to tighten the enforcement: a special oath by governors to enforce the Navigation Acts, the use by customs officials of "writs of assistance" (general search warrants which did not have to specify the place to be searched), and the trial of accused violators in Admiralty Courts, which Edward Randolph had recommended because juries habitually refused to convict. Admiralty cases were decided by judges whom the governors appointed.

Second, also in 1696, by executive order William III created the Board of Trade (Lords Commissioners of Trade and Plantations) to take the place of the Lords of Trade and Plantations. The new board included eight privy councilors and additional members from outside. Colonial officials were required to report to the board, and its archives constitute the largest single collection of materials on colonial relations with the mother country from that time on.

The functions of the Board of Trade, which continued through the remainder of the colonial period, were again primarily advice and policy-making. Since its main purpose was to make the colonies serve the mother country's economy, the board investigated the enforcement of the Navigation Acts, and recommended ways to limit colonial manufactures and to encourage the production of raw materials. In 1705, for instance, at the board's behest Parliament enacted a bounty for the production of naval stores, ship timber, masts, and hemp. Similar payments were later extended to encourage the production of rice, indigo, and other commodities. The board examined all colonial laws and made recommendations for their disallowance by the crown.

In all, 8,563 colonial laws eventually were examined and 469 of them were actually disallowed. The board also made recommendations for official appointments in the colonies.

SALUTARY NEGLECT From 1696 to 1725 the board met regularly and worked vigorously toward subjecting the colonies to a more efficient royal control. After 1725, however, the board entered a period of relative inactivity. After the death of Queen Anne the throne went in turn to the Hanoverian monarchs, George I (1714–1727) and George II (1727–1760), German princes who were next in the Protestant line of succession by virtue of descent from James I. Under these monarchs, the cabinet (a kind of executive committee in the Privy Council) emerged as the central agency of administration. Robert Walpole, as first minister (1721–1742), deliberately followed a policy of not rocking the boat lest he endanger the Hanoverian settlement, a policy which Edmund Burke later called "a wise and salutary neglect." The board became chiefly an agency of political patronage, studded with officials who took an interest mainly in their salaries. Under the earl of Halifax the board experienced a revival after 1748, and from 1752 to 1761 actually had power to appoint colonial governors, but generally decreased in significance thereafter.

In the course of the eighteenth century other administrative agencies and offices became involved in certain aspects of colonial government. The most important of these was the secretary of state for the Southern Department. After about 1700 he was the chief administrative official with supervision over colonial matters. Royal governors were responsible to him for colonial defense and military matters. At the same time the secretary had responsibility for Mediterranean affairs and relations with France and Spain, which of course often involved colonial matters—and colonial wars. But the secretary was too busy with diplomacy to give sustained attention to the colonies, and indeed none showed much energy, except the elder William Pitt, who held the office while also first minister. The duke of Newcastle, who served (1727–1748) during the decades of salutary neglect, was, according to a contemporary, a man who lost an hour in the morning every day and spent the rest of the day running around trying to find it.

Colonial Governments

Government within the colonies, like colonial policy, evolved without plan, but colonial governments at least had in the English government a body of precedent to fall back on. In broad outline the governor, council, and assembly in each colony corresponded to the king, lords, and commons of the mother country. At the outset all the colonies except Georgia had begun as projects of trading companies or feudal proprietors holding charters from the crown, but eight colonies eventually relinquished or forfeited their charters and became royal provinces. In these the governor was named by the crown. In Maryland, Pennsylvania, and Delaware he remained the choice of a proprietor, although each had an interim period of royal government. Connecticut and Rhode Island remained the exceptions, the last of the corporate colonies, which elected their own governors to the end of the colonial period. In the corporate and proprietary colonies, and in Massachusetts, the charter served as a rough equivalent to a written constitution. Rhode Island and Connecticut in fact kept their charters as state constitutions after independence. Over the years certain anomalies appeared, as colonial governments diverged from that of England. On the one hand the governors retained powers and prerogatives which the king had lost in the course of the seventeenth century. On the other hand the assemblies acquired powers, particularly with respect to appointments, which Parliament had yet to gain.

POWERS OF THE GOVERNORS   The crown never vetoed acts of Parliament after 1707, but the colonial governors still held an absolute veto and the crown could disallow (in effect, veto) colonial legislation by action of the Board of Trade. With respect to the assembly, the governor still had the power to determine when and where it would meet, to prorogue (adjourn or recess) sessions, and to dissolve the assembly for new elections or to postpone elections indefinitely at his pleasure. The crown, however, was pledged to summon Parliament every three years and call elections at least every seven, and could not prorogue sessions. The royal or proprietary governor, moreover, nominated for life appointment the members of his council (except in Massachusetts, where they were chosen by the lower house) and the council functioned as both the upper house of the legislature and the highest court of appeal within the colony. With respect to the judiciary, in all but the charter colonies the governor still held the prerogative of creating courts and of naming and dismissing judges, powers explicitly denied the king in England. The assemblies, however, generally made good their claim that courts should be created only by legislative authority, although the crown repeatedly disallowed acts to grant judges life tenure in order to make them more independent.

As chief executive the governor could appoint and remove officials, command the militia and naval forces, grant pardons, and as his commission often put it, "execute everything which doth and of right ought to belong to the governor"—which might cover a multitude of powers. In these things his authority resembled the crown's, for the kings still exercised executive authority and had the power generally to name all administrative officials. This often served as a powerful means of royal influence in Parliament, since the king could appoint members or their friends to lucrative offices. And while the arrangement might seem to another age a breeding ground for corruption or tyranny, it was often viewed in the eighteenth century as a stabilizing influence, especially by the king's friends. But it was an influence less and less available to the governors. On the one hand colonial assemblies nibbled away at their power of appointment; on the other hand the authorities in England more and more drew the control of colonial patronage into their own hands.

POWERS OF THE ASSEMBLIES   Unlike the governor and council, chosen by an outside authority, the colonial assembly represented an internal choice. Whether called the House of Burgesses (Virginia), of Delegates (Maryland), of Representatives (Massachusetts), or simply Assembly, the lower houses were chosen by popular vote in counties or towns or, in South Carolina, parishes. Although the English Toleration Act of 1689 did not apply to the colonies, religious tests for voting tended to be abandoned thereafter (the Massachusetts charter of 1691 so specified) and the chief restriction left was a property qualification, based on the notion that only men who held a "stake in society" could vote responsibly. Yet the property qualifications generally set low hurdles in the way of potential voters. Property holding was widespread, and a greater proportion of the population could

Currency issued by Massachusetts Bay. Colonial assemblies grew powerful through their control of the purse. [American Antiquarian Society]

vote in the colonies than anywhere else in the world of the eighteenth century.

Women, children, and blacks were excluded—as a matter of course—and continued to be excluded for the most part into the twentieth century, but the qualifications excluded few adult free white males. Virginia, which at one time permitted all freemen to vote, in the eighteenth century required only the ownership of 25 acres of improved land or 100 acres of wild land (available from speculators for a total of about £3), or the ownership of a "house" and part of a lot in town, the ownership of a £50 estate, or a service in a five-year apprenticeship in Williamsburg or Norfolk. Qualifications for membership in the assembly ran somewhat higher, and in an age which still held to habits of deference, officeholders tended to come from the more well-to-do —a phenomenon not unknown today—but there were exceptions. One unsympathetic colonist observed in 1744 that the New Jersey Assembly "was chiefly composed of mechanicks and ignorant wretches; obstinate to the last degree." In any case, gentlefolk who ran for office found then as now that a certain respect for the sensibilities of humbler men paid off in votes.

Colonial politics of the eighteenth century recapitulated English politics of the seventeenth. In one case there had been a tug of war between king and Parliament, ending with the supremacy of Parliament, confirmed by the Glorious Revolution. In the other case colonial governors were still trying to wield prerogatives which the king had lost in England, a fact of which the assemblies were fully informed. They also knew all the arguments for the "rights" and "liberties" of the people and their legislative bodies, and against the dangers of despotic power. A further anomaly in the situation was the undefined relationship of the colonies to Parliament. The colonies had been created by authority of the crown and their governmental connections ran to the crown, yet Parliament on occasion passed laws which applied to the colonies, and were tacitly accepted by the colonies.

By the early eighteenth century the assemblies, like Parliament, held two important strands of power—and they were perfectly aware of the parallel. First, they held the power of the purse string in their right to vote on taxes and expenditures. Second, they held the power to initiate legislation and not merely, as in the early history of some colonies, the right to act on proposals from the governor and council. These powers they used to pull other strands of power into their hands when the chance presented itself. Governors were held on a tight leash by the assembly's control of salaries, his and others, which were voted annually and sometimes not at all. Only in four southern colonies did governors have some freedom from this coercion. In South Carolina and Georgia they were paid from crown funds, and in North Carolina and Virginia out of permanent funds drawn from colonial revenues: an export tax of two pence per hogshead of tobacco in Virginia and the more uncertain returns from quit-rents in North Carolina.

But even in those colonies the assemblies controlled other appropriations, and by refusing to vote money forced governors to yield up parts of the traditional executive powers. Assemblies, because they controlled finance, demanded and often got the right to name tax collectors and treasurers. Then they stretched the claim to cover public printers, Indian agents, supervisors of public works and services, and other officers of the government. By specifying how appropriations should be spent they played an important role even in military affairs and Indian relations, as well as other matters. Indeed in the choice of certain administrative officers they pushed their power beyond that of Parliament in England, where appointment remained a crown prerogative.

All through the eighteenth century the assemblies expanded their power and influence, sometimes in conflict with the governors, sometimes in harmony with them, and often in the course of routine business, passing laws and setting precedents the collective significance of which neither they nor the imperial authorities fully recognized. Once established, however, these laws and practices became fixed principles, parts of the "constitution" of the colonies. Self-government became first a habit, then a "right."

TROUBLED NEIGHBORS

The English conquest of North America would have been a different story, maybe a shorter and simpler story, had the English first encountered a stronger Indian presence. Instead, in the coastal regions they found scattered and mutually hostile groups which were subject to a policy of divide and conquer. Some, perhaps most, of the Indians guessed at the settlers' purpose quickly, like those, Powhatan told John Smith, "who do inform me your coming is not for trade, but to invade my people and possess my country." But tempted by trade goods or the promise of alliances, or intimidated by a show of force, they let things drift until the English were too entrenched to push back into the sea.

The Puritans and their Indian allies, the Narragansetts, mount a ferocious attack on the Pequots at Mystic, Connecticut (1637). [The Library Company of Philadelphia]

During the first half of the seventeenth century the most severe tests of the colonists' will to prevail came with the Virginia troubles of 1622 and 1644 and Connecticut's Pequot War of 1637. In both colonies Indian leaders had a desperate sense of last-chance efforts to save their lands; in both they failed. For the Pequots the results were virtual extermination—Puritan savagery in killing and enslaving Pequots was so great as to offend even the Englishmen's allies, the Narrangansetts, who had never seen such total war. In Virginia, according to a census taken in 1669, only eleven of twenty-eight tribes described by John Smith in 1608 and only about 2,000 of some 30,000 Indians remained in the colony. Indian resistance had been broken for the time.

Then in the mid-1670s both New England and Virginia went through another time of troubles: an Indian war in New England, and in Virginia a civil war masquerading as an Indian war. For a long time in New England the Indian fur trade had contributed to peaceful relations, but the growth of settlement and the decline of the animal population was reducing the eastern tribes to relative poverty. Colonial government encroached repeatedly, forcing Indians to acknowledge English laws and customs, including Puritan codes of behavior, and to permit English arbitration of disputes. On occasion colonial justice imposed fines, whippings, and worse. At the same time Puritan missionaries reached out to the tribes and one, John Eliot, translated the Bible into the Algonquian language. By 1675, several thousand converts had settled in special "praying Indian" towns.

CONFLICTS WITH THE INDIANS   The spark that set New England ablaze was struck by the murder of one Sassamon, a "praying Indian" who had attended Harvard, later strayed from the faith while serving King Philip of the Wampanoag tribe, and then returned to the Christian fold. King Philip (Metacomet to the Wampanoags) was a son of Chief Massasoit, who had early befriended the Pilgrims. Now King Philip became their enemy when Plymouth Colony tried and executed three Wampanoags for the murder of Sassamon. In retaliation the tribesmen attacked the settlement of Swansea on the fringes of Plymouth.

Thus began "King Philip's War," which the land-hungry leaders of Connecticut and Massachusetts quickly enlarged by attacking the peaceful Narragansetts at their chief refuge in Rhode Island—a massacre the Rhode Island authorities were helpless to prevent. From June to December 1675, Indian attacks ravaged the interior of Massachusetts and Plymouth, and guerrilla war continued through 1676. At one point Indians put to the torch a town within twenty miles of Boston. Finally, depleted supplies and the casualty toll wore down Indian resistance. In August Philip himself was tracked down and killed. The rest was a matter of mopping up pockets of resistance, but fighting went on until 1678 in New Hampshire and Maine. New England might have perished if King Philip had formed an effective coalition, but his failure to do so was typical of Indian wars. Indians who survived the slaughter had to submit to colonial authority and accept confinement to ever-dwindling plots of land.

BACON'S REBELLION   The news from New England added to tensions among settlers strung out into the interior of Virginia, and contributed to the tangled events thereafter known as Bacon's Rebellion. Virginia had the makings of trouble at the time in depressed tobacco prices and in the crowds of freed servants who found the best lands already taken. Just before the outbreak, Gov. William Berkeley had remarked in a letter: "How miserable that man is that Governes a People where six parts of seaven at least are Poore, Endebted, Discontented and Armed." And, he might have added, greedily eyeing lands north of the York River guaranteed to the Chesapeake tribes in 1646.

The discontent turned to violence in July 1675 when a petty squabble between a frontier planter and the Doeg Indians on the Potomac led to the murder of the planter's herdsman, and in turn retaliation by frontiersmen who killed ten or more Doegs and, by mistake, fourteen Susquehannocks. Soon a force of Virginia and Maryland militiamen laid siege to the Susquehannocks, murdered in cold blood five chieftains who came out for a parley, and then let the enraged survivors get away to take their revenge on frontier settlements. Scattered attacks continued on down to the James, where Nathaniel Bacon's overseer was killed.

By then, their revenge accomplished, the Susquehannocks pulled back. What followed had less to do with a state of war than with a state of hysteria. Berkeley proposed that the assembly support a series of forts along the frontier. But that would not slake the thirst for revenge—nor would it open new lands to settlement. Besides, it would be expensive. Some thought Berkeley was out to preserve a profitable fur trade, although there is no evidence that he was deeply involved personally. At this point in May 1676 Nathaniel Bacon assumed command of a group of frontier vigilantes. The twenty-nine-year-old Bacon had been in Virginia only two years, but he had been well set up by an English father relieved to get him out of the country. He was also a member of the governor's council. Later historians would praise him as "The Torchbearer of the Revolution" and leader of the

King Charles II proclaims Nathaniel Bacon and his accomplices, "being persons of mean and desperate fortunes," guilty of high treason. [The Warder Collection]

first struggle of common man versus aristocrat, of frontier versus tidewater. Instead he was the spoiled son of a rich squire who had a talent for trouble, who led punitive expeditions against peaceful Indians, and whose main achievement was to persuade the friendly Occaneechees to destroy a small band of Susquehannocks just before he treacherously slaughtered the Occaneechees themselves.

After that the events had little to do with Indians, except some friendly Pamunkeys, who also felt Bacon's wrath. Bacon was early in the line of one hoary American tradition. Indians, he said, were "all alike," and therefore apparently fair game. Hoping to rally support against Bacon, Governor Berkeley called elections for a new assembly, which met in June 1676. Bacon was elected, had a brief reconciliation with Berkeley, and rejoined the governor's council, but failed to get the commission he demanded as commander of the militia. He fled Jamestown, aroused his own men to intimidate Berkeley, and eventually attacked and burned Jamestown in September only to fall ill and die of swamp fever a month later.

Berkeley quickly regained control and subdued the leaderless rebels. In the process he hanged twenty-three of them and confiscated several estates. In London, report had it, King Charles II said: "That old fool has hang'd more men in that naked Country than he had done for the Murther of his Father." For such severity the king recalled Berkeley to England and a royal commission made treaties of pacification with the remaining Indians, some of whose descendants still live on tiny reservations guaranteed them in 1677. One consequence of the fighting, however, was to open new lands to the colonists and to confirm the power of an inner group of established landholders who sat in the council.

The more powerful tribes all along had been back in the interior: mainly the Iroquois Confederation of the Hudson and Mohawk Valleys, the Cherokees of the southern Appalachians and foothills, and the Creeks farther south. By the time settlement pressed against these lands the English beachheads had grown into a formidable power. But the Indians had grown in strength too. Thrust suddenly by European traders from the Stone Age into the Iron Age, they had adopted into their cultures firearms, steel knives, iron utensils, and alchohol, and into their populations survivors of the eastern tribes. During the first century of settlement they had also learned the subtleties of international diplomacy, weighing the relative advantages of English, French, and Spanish trade goods and alliances, and learning to play the balance-of-power games that the great powers played in Europe.

NEW FRANCE   Permanent French settlement in the New World began the year after the Jamestown landing, far away in Québec where the explorer Samuel de Champlain unfurled the *fleur-de-lis* on the shores of the St. Lawrence River in 1608, and three years later at Port Royal, Acadia (later Nova Scotia). While Acadia remained a remote outpost, New France expanded well beyond Québec, from which Champlain pushed his explorations up the great river and into the Great Lakes as far as Lake Huron, and southward to the lake which still bears his name. There, in 1609, he joined a band of Huron and Ottawa allies in a fateful encounter, fired his arquebus into the ranks of their Iroquois foes, and kindled an enmity which pursued New France to the end. Shortly afterward the Iroquois had a more friendly meeting with Henry Hudson near Albany, and soon acquired their own firearms from Dutch, and later English, traders. Thenceforth the Iroquois stood as a buffer against any French designs to move toward the English of the Middle Colonies, and as a constant menace on the flank of the French waterways to the interior.

Until his death in 1653 Champlain governed New France under a sequence of trading companies, the last being the Company of a Hundred Associates which the king's minister, Cardinal Richelieu, formed in 1627 of men chosen for their close loyalty to the crown. The charter imposed a fatal weakness that hobbled New France to its end. The company won a profitable monopoly of the fur trade, but it had to limit the population to French Catholics. Neither the enterprising, seafaring Huguenots of coastal France nor foreigners of any faith could populate the country. Great seigneurial land grants went to persons who promised to bring settlers to work the land under feudal tenure. The colony therefore remained a scattered patchwork of dependent peasants, Jesuit missionaries, priests, soldiers, officials, and *coureurs de bois* (literally, runners of the woods) who ranged the interior in quest of furs.

In 1663 King Louis XIV and his chief minister, Jean Baptiste Colbert, changed New France into a royal colony and pursued a plan of consolidation and stabilization. Colbert dispatched new settlers, including shiploads of young women to lure disbanded soldiers and *coureurs de bois* into settled matrimony. He sent out tools and animals for farmers, nets for fishermen, and tried to make New France self-sufficient in foodstuffs. The population grew from about 4,000 in 1665 to about 15,000 in 1690. Still, Louis de Buade, Count Frontenac, who was governor from 1672 to 1682 and 1689 to 1698, held to a grand vision of French empire in the interior, spurring on the fur traders and missionaries and converting their outposts into military stations in the wilderness: Fort Detroit appeared at the far end of Lake Erie, Fort Michilimackinac at the far end of Lake Huron.

FRENCH LOUISIANA From the Great Lakes explorers moved southward. In 1673 Louis Joliet and Père Marquette, a Jesuit priest, ventured into Lake Michigan, up the Fox River from Green Bay, then down the Wisconsin to the Mississippi, and on as far as the Arkansas River. Satisfied that the great river flowed to the Gulf of Mexico, they turned back for fear of meeting with Spaniards. Nine years later, in 1682, Robert Cavalier, sieur de la Salle, went all the way to the Gulf and named the country Louisiana after the king.

Settlement of the Louisiana country finally began in 1699 when Pierre le Moyne, sieur d'Iberville, landed a colony at Biloxi, Mississippi. In 1702 the main settlement was moved to Mobile Bay and in 1710 to the present site of Mobile, Alabama. In 1717 Louisiana annexed the Illinois villages near Fort Louis (1690–1691), settled originally from Canada. For nearly half a century the chief mover and shaker in Louisiana was Jean Baptiste le Moyne, sieur de Bienville, a younger brother of d'Iberville. Bienville arrived with the first settlers in 1699, when he was only eighteen, and left the colony for the last time in 1743, when he was sixty-two. Sometimes called the "Father of Louisiana," he served periodically as governor or acting governor and always as advisor during those years. In 1718 he founded New Orleans, which became the capital in 1722. Louisiana, first a proprietary and then a corporate colony, became a royal province in 1732.

"France in America had two heads," the historian Francis Parkman wrote, "one amid the snows of Canada, the other amid the canebrakes of Louisiana." The French thus had one enormous advantage: access to the great water routes which led to the heartland of the continent. Because of geography as well as deliberate policy, however, French America remained largely a howling wilderness inhabited by a mobile population of traders, trappers, missionaries—and, mainly, Indians. In 1750 when the English colonies numbered about 1.5 million, the French population was no more than 80,000. Yet in some ways the French had the edge on the British. They offered European goods in return for furs, encroached far less upon Indian lands, and so won allies against the English who came to possess the land. French governors could mobilize for action without any worry about quarreling assemblies or ethnic and religious diversity. The British may have had the edge in population, but their separate colo-

THE FRENCH
IN NORTH AMERICA

English possessions
French possessions
Spanish possessions

•••••• Route of Marquette and Joliet, 1673

—— Route of La Salle, 1682

0   300 Miles
0   300 Kilometers

nies often worked at cross purposes. The Middle Colonies, for instance, protected by the Iroquois buffer, could afford to ignore the French threat—for a long time at least. Whenever conflict threatened, colonial assemblies seized the time to extract new concessions from their governors. Colonial merchants, who built up a trade supplying foodstuffs to the French, persisted in smuggling supplies even in wartime.

THE COLONIAL WARS

Colonists of the two nations came into conflict from the beginning of settlement. The Acadians clashed with Englishmen in Maine, across the Bay of Fundy, and suspiciously eyed the *Bostonnais*. Only a thin stretch of woods separated New England from Québec and Montréal, and an English force briefly occupied Québec from 1629 to 1632. Between New York and Québec, Lake Champlain supplied an easy water route for invasion in either direction, but the Iroquois stood athwart the path. Farther south the mountainous wilderness widened into an almost impenetrable buffer. On the northernmost flank, the isolated Hudson's Bay Company offered British competition for the fur trade of the interior, and both countries laid claim to Newfoundland. On the southernmost flank, the British and French jockeyed for position in the Caribbean sugar islands.

But for most of the seventeenth century the two continental empires developed in relative isolation from each other, and for most of that century the homelands remained at peace with each other. After the Restoration, Charles II and James II pursued a policy of friendship with Louis XIV—and secretly took pensions from His Catholic Majesty. The Glorious Revolution of 1688, however, worked an abrupt reversal in English diplomacy. William III, the new king, as stadtholder of the Dutch Republic, had fought a running conflict against the ambitions of Louis XIV in the Netherlands and the German Palatinate. His ascent to the throne brought England almost immediately into a Grand Coalition against Louis in the War of the League of Augsburg, sometimes called the War of the Palatinate, known in the colonies simply as King Williams's War (1689–1697), the first of four great European and intercolonial wars over the next sixty-four years: the War of the Spanish Succession (Queen Anne's War, 1701–1713); the War of the Austrian Succession (King George's War, 1744–1748); and the Seven Years' War (the French and Indian War, which lasted nine years in America, 1754–1763). In all except the last, which the historian Lawrence Gipson called the "Great War for Empire," the battles in America were but a sideshow to greater battles in Europe, where British policy riveted on keeping a balance of power against the French. The alliances shifted from one fight to the next, but Britain and France were pitted against each other every time.

KING WILLIAM'S WAR   In King William's War scattered fighting occurred in the Hudson Bay posts, most of which fell to the

French, and in Newfoundland, which fell to a French force under d'Iberville, soon to be the founder of Louisiana. The French aroused their Indian allies to join in scattered raids along the northern frontier, beginning with a surprise attack which destroyed Schenectady, New York, in the winter of 1690. In Massachusetts, Capt. William Phips, about to become the first royal governor, got up an expedition which took Acadia. New York's acting governor, Jacob Leisler, laid plans with agents from Massachusetts, Plymouth, and Connecticut for concerted attacks on Québec. But a New England expedition via the St. Lawrence bogged down in futility when the New York contingent failed to show up. The New York expedition via Lake Champlain never got under way for want of support from other colonies or the Iroquois allies, who refused to move in the face of a smallpox outbreak. The war finally degenerated into a series of frontier raids and ended ingloriously with the Treaty of Ryswick (1697), which returned the colonies to their prewar status.

QUEEN ANNE'S WAR But fighting resumed only five years later. In 1700 the Spanish crown passed to Philip of Anjou, grandson of Louis XIV and potential heir to the throne of France. Against this new threat to the balance of power—a possible union of France and Spain—William III organized a new alliance, but the War of the Spanish Succession began after his death and was known to the colonists as Queen Anne's War. This time the Iroquois, tired of fighting the French, remained neutral and the French respected New York's immunity from attack. The brunt of this war therefore fell on New England and South Carolina. In Charleston the colonists raised a force which destroyed the Spanish town of St. Augustine in 1702, but withdrew after failing to reduce its fort of San Marcos. In 1706 Charleston fought off a counterattack, and for the next seven years a sporadic border war raged between South Carolina and Florida, the English with Yemassee and Creek allies taking the war nearly to St. Augustine.

South Carolina's Indian allies in fact constituted most of a force which responded to North Carolina's call for help in the Tuscarora War (1711–1713). The Tuscaroras, a numerous people who had long led a settled life in the Tidewater, suddenly found their lands invaded in 1709 by Germans and Swiss under Baron de Graffenried, who founded New Bern. The war began when the Tuscaroras fell upon the new settlements with devastating effect. It ended with even more devastating effect when slave merchants of South Carolina mobilized their Indian allies to kill about 1,000 Tuscaroras and enslave another 700. The survivors found refuge in the north, where they became the sixth nation of the Iroquois Confederacy.

In New England the exposed frontier from Maine to Massachusetts suffered repeated raids during Queen Anne's War. In the winter of 1704 the villages of Wells, Maine, and Deerfield, Massachusetts, were sacked by French and Indian forces, and the settlers were either slaughtered or taken on desperate marches through the snow to captivity among the Indians or the Canadians. Once again Port Royal fell in 1710, and once again a British force moved upriver toward Québec, but gave up the effort after eight transports ran aground. Things went better for the English in the Caribbean, where they took control of St. Christopher, and in Europe, where John Churchill, duke of Marlborough, led allied forces to brilliant victories in Germany and the Netherlands.

In the complex Peace of Utrecht (1713) England accepted Philip of Anjou as king of Spain, but only with the proviso that he renounce the throne of France. England also took from Spain the stronghold of Gibraltar and the island of Minorca. Louis XIV gave up most of his claims in Germany and recognized British title to the Hudson Bay, Newfoundland, Acadia (now Nova Scotia), and St. Christopher, as well as the British claim to sovereignty over the Iroquois (nobody consulted the Iroquois). The French renounced any claim to special privileges in the commerce of Spanish or Portuguese America. Spain agreed not to transfer any of its American territory to a third party, and granted to the British the *asiento*, a contract for supplying Spanish America 4,800 slaves annually over a period of thirty years and the right to send one ship a year to the great fair at Porto Bello in Panama—concessions which opened the door for British smuggling, a practice which grew into a major cause of friction and, eventually, of renewed warfare.

In the South the frontier flared up once more shortly after the war. The former Yemassee and Creek allies, outraged by the continuing advance of settlement, attacked the Charleston colony. The Yemassee War of 1715 was the southern equivalent of King Philip's War in New England, a desperate struggle which threatened the colony's very existence. Once again, however, the Indians were unable to present a united front. The Cherokees remained neutral for the sake of their fur trade and the defeated Yemassees retired into Florida or mingled with the Creeks who retreated beyond the Chattahoochee River, leaving open the country in which the new colony of Georgia appeared eighteen years later.

KING GEORGE'S WAR BEGINS   In the generation of nominal peace after Queen Anne's War the European colonists jockeyed for position, intrigued with the Indians, and set up fortified posts at strategic points in the wilderness. The third great international war began in 1739 with a preliminary bout between England and Spain, called the War of Jenkins' Ear in honor of an English seaman who lost an ear to a Spanish guardacosta and exhibited the shriveled member as part of a campaign to arouse London against Spain's rudeness to smugglers. The war began with a great British disaster, a grand expedition against Porto Bello in Panama, for which thousands of colonists volunteered and in which many died of yellow fever. One of the survivors, Lawrence Washington of Virginia, memorialized the event by naming his estate Mount Vernon, after the ill-starred but popular admiral in command. Along the southern frontier the new colony of Georgia, less than a decade old, now served its purpose as a military buffer. Gen. James Oglethorpe staged a raid on St. Augustine and later fought off Spanish counterattacks against Frederika, but Charleston remained secure.

In 1744 France entered the war, which merged with another general European conflict, the War of the Austrian Succession, or King George's War in the colonies. Once again border raids flared along the northern frontier. Gov. William Shirley of Massachusetts mounted an expedition under William Pepperell of Maine, a prominent merchant with a genius for management, and reduced the French Fort Louisbourg on Cape Breton after a lengthy siege. It was a costly conquest, but the war ended in stalemate. In the Treaty of Aix-la-Chappelle (1748) the British exchanged Louisbourg for Madras, which the French had taken in India.

In the brief respite that followed before the climactic struggle, the focus of attention turned to the Ohio Valley. French penetration had moved westward by the Great Lakes and down the Mississippi, but the Ohio, with short portages from Lake Erie to its headwaters, would make a shorter connecting link for French America. But during the 1740s fur traders from Virginia and Pennsylvania had begun to penetrate into that disputed region. Some 300 of them operated in the country by 1749, according to the French commander of Fort Miami, south of Detroit. Not far behind were the Pennsylvania and Virginia land speculators. "The English," one French agent warned the Indians, "are much less anxious to take away your peltries than to become masters of your lands." Pennsylvania, because of the Quaker impulse, gave less support to its speculators than Virginia, which laid claim to the country through a quirk in the 1609 charter which described boundaries leading "westward and Northwestward" to the South Sea; it was their northern boundary, they said, which led "Northwestward." Virginians had organized several land companies, most conspicuously the Ohio Company, to which the king granted 200,000 acres along the upper Ohio in 1749, with a promise of 300,000 more. The company forthwith dispatched a Pennsylvania frontiersman to seek out the best lands.

The French resolved to act before the British advance became a dagger pointed at the continental heartland. In 1749 Celoron de Blainville proceeded down the Alleghany and Ohio Rivers to spy out the land, woo the Indians, and bury leaden plates with inscriptions stating the French claim. Magic engravings hardly made the soil French, but in 1753 a new governor, the Marquis Duquesne, arrived in Canada and set about making good on the claim with a chain of forts in the region.

THE FRENCH AND INDIAN WAR When news of these trespasses reached Williamsburg, Governor Dinwiddie sent out an emissary to warn off the French. An ambitious young adjutant-general of the Virginia militia, Maj. George Washington, whose older brothers owned a part of the Ohio Company, volunteered for the mission. With a few companions, Washington made his way to Fort LeBoeuf and returned with a polite but firm refusal. Dinwiddie then sent one Capt. William Trent with a small force to erect a fort at the strategic fork where the Alleghany and Monongahela Rivers meet to form the great Ohio. No sooner was Trent started than a larger French force appeared, ousted him, and proceeded to build Fort Duquesne on the same strategic site. Meanwhile Washington had been organizing a force of volunteers, and in the spring of 1754 he went out with an advance guard and a few Indian allies. Near Great Meadows they fell into a skirmish with a French detachment. Who fired first is unknown, and perhaps irrelevant, but it marked the first bloodshed of a long—and finally decisive—war which reached far beyond America. Washington fell back with his prisoners and hastily constructed a stockade, Fort Necessity, which soon fell under siege by a larger force from Fort Duquesne. On July 4, 1754, Washington surrendered and was permitted to withdraw with his survivors. With that disaster in the backwoods a great world war had begun, but Washington came out of it with his reputation intact—and he was world-famous at the age of twenty-two.

Back in London the Board of Trade already had taken notice of the growing conflict in the backwoods, and had called a meeting in Albany, New York, of commissioners from all the colonies as

Benjamin Franklin saw the importance of uniting the colonies against the French in 1754. His symbol of the need to unite would become popular again twenty years later, when the colonies faced a different threat. [Historical Society of Pennsylvania]

far south as Maryland to confer on precautions. The Albany Congress (June 19 to July 10, 1754), which was sitting when the first shots sounded at Great Meadows, ended with little accomplished. The delegates conferred with Iroquois chieftains and sent them away loaded with gifts in return for some half-hearted promises of support. The congress is remembered mainly for the Plan of Union worked out by a committee under Benjamin Franklin and adopted by unanimous vote of the commissioners. The plan called for a chief executive, a kind of supreme governor to be called the President-General of the United Colonies, appointed and supported by the crown, and a supreme assembly called the Grand Council, with forty-eight members chosen by the colonial assemblies. This federal body would oversee matters of defense, Indian relations, and trade and settlement in the west, and would levy taxes to support its programs.

It must have been a good plan, Franklin reasoned, since the assemblies thought it gave too much power to the crown and the crown thought it gave too much to the colonies. At any rate the assemblies either rejected or ignored the plan, and the Board of Trade never had to face a decision. Only two substantive results came out of the congress. Its idea of a supreme commander for British forces in America was adopted, as was its advice that New Yorker William Johnson, a friend of the Iroquois, be made British superintendent of the northern Indians.

In London the government decided to force a showdown in

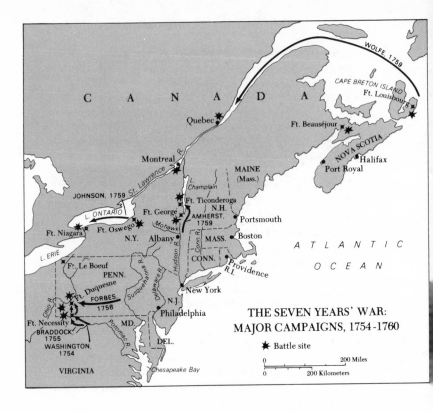

THE SEVEN YEARS' WAR:
MAJOR CAMPAIGNS, 1754-1760

★ Battle site

0   200 Miles
0   200 Kilometers

America, but things went badly at first. In 1755 the British fleet
failed to halt the landing of reinforcements in Canada, but scored
one success in Nova Scotia with the capture of Fort Beauséjour
and then buttressed their hold on the country by expelling most
of its French population. Some 5,000–7,000 Acadians who refused to take an oath of allegiance were scattered through the
colonies from Maine to Georgia. Impoverished and homeless,
many of them by desperate expedients found their way to
French Louisiana, where they became the "Cajuns" (a corruption of "Acadians") whose descendants still preserve the language of Molière along the remote bayous.

The backwoods, however, became the scene of one British disaster after another over the next three years. In 1755 a new British commander-in-chief, Gen. Edward Braddock, arrived in
Virginia with two regiments of regulars. With the addition of
some colonial troops, including Washington as a volunteer staff
officer, Braddock hacked a road through the wildernesses from
the upper Potomac to the vicinity of Fort Duquesne. Hauling

heavy artillery to invest the French fort, along with a wagon train of supplies, Braddock's men achieved a great feat of military logistics, and were on the verge of success when, seven miles from Fort Duquesne, the surrounding woods suddenly came alive with Indians and Frenchmen in Indian costume. Beset on three sides by concealed enemies, the wagon train broke down in blind panic and the British forces retreated in disarray, abandoning most of their artillery and supplies. Braddock lost his life in the encounter, and his second in command retreated with the remaining British regulars to the safety of Philadelphia.

After that, Indian attacks flared up along the frontier. Among the first to seize the chance to even old scores were the Delawares, once befriended by Penn, later cheated out of their lands by his successors. Scotch-Irish and German refugees fled eastward as the Delawares burned, killed, and pillaged in their settlements. Pennsylvania Quakers, stubbornly pacifist, insisted that compromise was still possible, but finally, under British pressure, bent their principles only to the extent of withdrawing from the Pennsylvania Assembly and letting the war party vote the money and measures needed to fight back.

A WORLD WAR   For two years war raged along the frontier without becoming the cause of war in Europe. In 1756, however, the colonial war merged with what became the Seven Year's War in

A 1755 cartoon boasts of British superiority to the French. The British lion at left stands over "his dominions"—Ohio, Virginia, Nova Scotia— protecting them from invasion. [Library of Congress]

Europe. There, Empress Maria Theresa of Austria, still brooding over the loss of territory in the last conflict, worked a diplomatic revolution by bringing Austria's old enemy France, as well as Russia, into an alliance against Frederick the Great of Prussia. Britain, ever mindful of the European balance of power, now deserted Austria to ally with Frederick. The onset of war brought into office a new British government with the popular and eloquent William Pitt as war minister. Pitt's ability and assurance ("I know that I can save England and no one else can") instilled confidence at home and abroad. The grandson of "Diamond" Pitt, once governor of Madras in India, Pitt committed his main forces to the war for overseas empire while providing subsidies to Frederick, who was desperately fighting off attacks from three sides.

Soon the force of British sea power began to cut off French reinforcements and supplies to the New World—and the trading goods with which they bought Indian allies. Pitt improved the British forces, gave command to young men of ability, and carried the battle to the enemy. In 1758 the tides began to turn. Fort Louisbourg fell. The Iroquois, sensing the turn of fortunes, pressed their dependents, the Delawares, to call off the frontier attacks. Gen. John Forbes organized a new expedition against Fort Duquesne and pushed a new wilderness road directly westward from Philadelphia. Having learned caution from Braddock's defeat, he kept his scouts alert on his flanks and proceeded slowly to set up supply posts along the way and send out emissaries to court the Indians. When he finally reached his goal, the outnumbered French chose discretion as the better part of valor, burned Fort Duquesne, and deserted the scene. On the site arose the British Fort Pitt, and later the city of Pittsburgh.

In 1759 the war reached its climax in a three-pronged offensive against Canada, along what had become the classic invasion routes: via Niagara, Lake Champlain, and up the St. Lawrence. British forces were earmarked for each. On the Niagara expedition British forces were joined by a group of Iroquois under William Johnson, who commanded the capture of Fort Niagara after the British commander fell in the field. The loss of Niagara virtually cut the French lifeline to the interior. On Lake Champlain Gen. Jeffrey Amherst took Fort George and Fort Ticonderoga, then paused to refortify and await reinforcements for an advance northward.

Meanwhile the most decisive battle was shaping up at Québec. Commanding the expedition up the St. Lawrence was Gen. James Wolfe, a dedicated professional soldier who at the age of thirty-three had already spent more than half his life in military

The decisive British assault on Québec (1759). [National Army Museum, London]

service. For two months Wolfe probed the defenses of Québec, seemingly impregnable on its fortified heights and defended by alert forces under Gen. Louis Joseph de Montcalm. Finally Wolfe found a path by which he led his force up the cliffs behind Québec under cover of darkness on the night of September 12–13 and emerged on the Plains of Abraham, athwart the main roads to the city. There, in a set battle more like the warfare of Europe than the skirmishes of the backwoods, his forces waited out the French advance until it was within close range, then loosed a simultaneous volley followed by one more which devastated the French ranks—and ended French power in North America for all time. News of the victory was clouded by the word of Wolfe's—and Montcalm's—death in the battle, but it reached London along with similar reports from India, where Gen. Robert Clive of the East Indian Company had reduced French outposts one by one, secured Bengal, and established the base for an expanding British control of India. It was the *annus mirabilis*, the miraculous year 1759, during which Great Britain secured an empire on which the sun never set.

The war dragged on until 1763, but the rest was a process of mopping up. Montréal, the last important vestige of French control in North America, fell in 1760, and while the frontiers remained active with the scattered Indian raids, the game was up for the French. In the South, where little significant action had occurred, the Cherokee nation flared into belated hostility, but Jeffrey Amherst, dispatched now to Charleston, moved toward the mountains with a force of British regulars and provincials and broke Cherokee resistance in 1761. In the North, just as peace

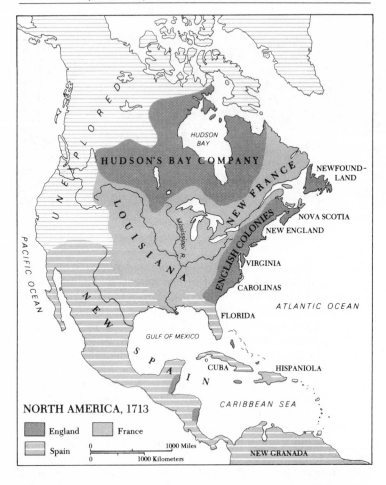

NORTH AMERICA, 1713

England   France

Spain

0   1000 Miles

0   1000 Kilometers

was signed, a chieftain of the Ottawas, Pontiac, conspired to confederate all the Indians of the frontier and launched a series of attacks that were not finally suppressed until 1764, after the backwoods had been ablaze for ten years.

Just six weeks after the capture of Montréal in 1760 King George II died and his grandson ascended to the throne as George III. George III resolved to take a more active role than his Hanoverian predecessors. Under the guidance of his former tutor and chief advisor, the Scottish earl of Bute, he resolved to seek peace and forced Pitt out of office. Pitt had wanted to carry the fight to the enemy by declaring war on Spain before the

NORTH AMERICA, 1763

England

Spain

— Proclamation Line of 1763

0   1000 Miles
0   1000 Kilometers

French could bring that other Bourbon monarchy into the conflict. He was forestalled, but Spain belatedly entered in 1761 and during the next year met the same fate as the French: in 1762 British forces took Manila in the Philippines and Havana in Cuba.

THE PEACE OF PARIS   An end to war came in the Peace of Paris of 1763. Bute as first minister accepted a more generous settlement than Pitt was willing to do, but nevertheless it was a peace that ended French power in North America and all but eliminated it in India, where France retained only a few trading posts. In America Britain took all French North American possessions east of the Mississippi River, and all of Spanish Florida, east and west. France ceded Louisiana to Spain in compensation for Spain's loss of the Floridas. This left France no territory on the continent of North America. In the West Indies France gave up Tobago, Dominica, Grenada, and St. Vincent. British power reigned supreme over North America east of the Mississippi, but a fatal irony would pursue the British victory.

In gaining Canada the British government put in motion a train of events that would end twenty years later with the loss of all the rest of British America. France, humiliated in 1763, thirsted for revenge. In London, Benjamin Franklin, agent for the colony of Pennsylvania, 1764–1775, found the French minister inordinately curious about America and suspected him of wanting to ignite the coals of controversy. Less than three years after Franklin left London, and only fifteen years after the conquest of New France, he would be in Paris arranging an alliance on behalf of Britain's rebellious colonists.

FURTHER READING

The student with a serious interest in the structure of colonial government and the global context of colonial development should begin with Charles M. Andrew's *The Colonial Period of American History* (vol. 4, 1938), which details the evolution of the British imperial system. Also see the relevant volumes of Lawrence H. Gipson's *The British Empire before the American Revolution* (1936–1970) to place the British colonies in the context of European imperial politics. Other works which cover much the same ground are George L. Beer's *The British Colonial System* (1908) and Leonard W. Labaree's *Royal Government in America* (1930).

The economics motivating colonial policies are covered in Eli Heckscher's *Mercantilism* (2 vols.; 1935). The problems of colonial customs administration are explored by George L. Beer's *The English Navigation Acts* (1939) and Thomas C. Barrow's *Trade and Empire* (1967). Michael G. Hall's *Edward Randolph and the American Colonies* (1969)° examines the same problems through the career of one imperial official.

The effect of imperial policies on colonial politics is covered in A. G. Olson's *Anglo-American Politics, 1660–1775* (1973), which traces the rise of party-like factions on the provincial level. For details on conflicts between those factions and the Crown, see Ian K. Steele's *Politics of Colonial Policy: The Board of Trade in Colonial Administration, 1696–1720* (1968). Jerome R. Reich's *Leisler's Rebellion* (1953) looks at the factional nature of that dispute. A good account of Bacon's Rebellion is found in Edmund S. Morgan's *American Slavery / American Freedom:*

° These books are available in paperback editions.

The Ordeal of Colonial Virginia (1975).° The Andros crisis is treated in Viola F. Barnes's *The Dominion of New England* (1923). Other views of Crown-colonial relations include Wilcomb E. Washburn's *The Governor and the Rebel* (1957), which emphasizes Crown concerns over management of Indian affairs, and Stephen Webb's *The Governors-General* (1977), which argues that the Crown was more concerned with military administration than commercial regulation.

Historians of early Indian wars have taken several different approaches to the topic. Richard Slotkin's *Regeneration through Violence* (1973)° links the colonists' treatment of Indians with later national character traits. Alden Vaughan defends the treatment of Indians by the Puritans in *New England Frontier: Puritans and Indians, 1620–1675* (1965).° Francis Jennings counters this thesis in *The Invasion of America* (1975).° Allen Trelease documents the viewpoints of provincial officials in *Indian Affairs in Colonial New York: The Seventeenth Century* (1960). Other interesting works include George Hunt's *The Wars of the Iroquois* (1940)° and Douglas E. Leach's *Flintlock and Tomahawk: New England in King Phillip's War* (1958).°

A good introduction to the imperial phase of the colonial conflicts is Howard H. Peckman's *The Colonial Wars, 1689–1762* (1964). More analytical is Douglas E. Leach's *Arms for Empire: A Military History of the British Colonies in North America* (1973). Paul E. Kopperman's *Braddock at the Monongahela* (1976) is a good biography of that unfortunate general. The viewpoint of the French can be learned through William J. Eccles's *The Canadian Frontier, 1534–1760* (1969), and Charles E. O'Neill's *Church and State in French Colonial Louisiana* (1966). No understanding of these wars is complete without reading the majestic works of Francis Parkman, *France and England in North America*. The most rewarding single volume is *Montcalm and Wolfe* (1885).°

5

FROM EMPIRE TO INDEPENDENCE

The Heritage of War

Seldom if ever since the days of Elizabeth had England thrilled with such pride as in the closing years of the Great War for Empire. The victories of 1759 had delivered Canada and India to British control. In 1760 the young and vigorous George III ascended to the throne and confirmed once again the Hanoverian succession. Even the downfall of Pitt, who lost favor in 1761, failed to check the momentum of his war machine, which ousted the Spanish from Manila and Havana in 1762. And in 1763 the Peace of Paris, even though it brought England less than Pitt would have liked, confirmed the possession of a great new empire.

The colonists shared in the ebullience of patriotism. But the moment of euphoria was all too brief. It served to mask festering resentments and new problems which were the heritage of the war. Underneath the pride in the British Empire an American nationalism was maturing. Ben Franklin foresaw a time, he said, when the capital of the British Empire would be on the Hudson instead of the Thames. But Americans were beginning to think and speak of themselves more as Americans than as English or British. With a great new land to exploit, they could look to the future with confidence. They had a new sense of importance after starting and fighting a vast world war with such success. Some harbored resentment, justified or not, at the haughty air of British soldiers and slights received at their hands, and many in the early stages of the war lost their awe of British soldiers who were at such a loss in frontier fighting. Those feelings became all the stronger as they lost the need of further protection against the foreign enemy.

166

Imperial forces, nevertheless, had borne the brunt of the war and had won it for the colonists, who had supplied men and materials reluctantly, and who persisted in trading with the enemy. Molasses in the French West Indies, for instance, continued to draw New England ships like flies. The trade was too important for the colonists to give up, but more than Pitt could tolerate, although he put up with the colonies' reluctance to support even their own forces. Along with patrols, one important means of disrupting this trade was the use of "writs of assistance,"general search warrants that allowed officers to enter any place during daylight hours to seek evidence of illegal trade. When the death of George II invalidated the writs in 1760, Boston merchants hired James Otis to fight in the courts against renewal. He lost, but in the process advanced the radical precept that any act of Parliament which authorized such "instruments of slavery" was against the British Constitution, against natural equity, and therefore void.

Neither at Albany in 1754 nor later in the war had the colonies been able, or even seriously sought, to form a concerted plan of action. They had relied on the imperial authorities to name a commander-in-chief, to formulate strategy, to bear most of the cost, and to set up superintendents of Indian affairs north and south. The assemblies had used the exigencies of war, though, to extract still more power from the governors and turn themselves more than ever into little parliaments. When the war ended Virginia was still embroiled in what came to be called the "parson's cause." Since the seventeenth century the Virginia clergy had been paid in tobacco, but after a crop failure in 1755 the legislature converted payment to cash at two pence per pound of tobacco—well below the market price of about six pence. After the Privy Council disallowed the Two Penny Act in 1759, several clergymen brought suit for full payment at market value. In the most celebrated suit, that of James Maury in Hanover County, a young lawyer named Patrick Henry swayed the jury against Maury with his logic that the king's disallowing a beneficial law had broken the compact with his people and had forfeited all right to obedience. The jury awarded the Reverend Maury one pence.

The peace which secured an empire laid upon the British ministry a burden of new problems. How should they manage the defense and governance of the new possessions? What disposition should they make of the western lands? How were they to service an unprecedented debt of nearly £140 million built up during the war, and bear the new burdens of administration and defense? And—the thorniest problem of all, as it turned out—

what role should the colonies play in all this? The problems were of a magnitude and complexity to challenge men of the greatest statemanship and vision, but those qualities were rare among the ministers of George III.

British Politics

In the British politics of the day nearly everybody who was anybody called himself a Whig, even King George. Whig had been the name given to those who opposed James II, led the Glorious Revolution of 1688, and secured the Protestant Hanoverian succession in 1714. By the time of the Glorious Revolution even their Tory adversaries had had enough of James II, but the Tories continued to bear the stigma of support for the Stuart cause and their influence waned. The Whigs were the champions of liberty and parliamentary supremacy, but with the passage of time Whiggism had drifted into complacency and leadership settled upon an aristocratic elite of the Whig gentry. This dominant group of landholding families was concerned mostly with the pursuit of personal place and advantage, and with local questions rather than great issues of statecraft. In the absence of party organization, parliamentary politics hinged on factions bound together by personal loyalties, family connections, and local interests, and on the pursuit of royal patronage.

In the administration of government an inner "Cabinet" of the

King George III, at age thirty-three. [Courtauld Institute of Art]

king's ministers had been supplanting the unwieldy Privy Council as the center of power ever since the Hanoverian succession. The kings still had the prerogative of naming their ministers, and they used this prerogative to form coalitions of men who controlled enough factions in the House of Commons to command majorities for the government's measures, though the king's ministers were still technically responsible to the king rather than to parliamentary majorities. George III resolved to take a more active role in the process than the first two Georges, who had abandoned initiative to the great Whig families—George I in part because he barely spoke English.

In 1761 the new king made the earl of Bute, a Scottish lord, his first minister. Bute held the trust of the king as a longtime confidant and political mentor, but as a lord he was disqualified from the House of Commons and had little influence there. In 1763, moreover, just as the great war came to an end, Bute wearied of parliamentary intrigues and stepped aside. For the remainder of that decade the king turned first to one and then to another leader, ministries came and went, and the government fell into instability just as the new problems of empire required solutions. Ministries rose and fell because somebody offended the king, or because somebody's friend failed to get a job. Colonial policy remained marginal to the chief concerned of British politics. The result was first inconsistency and vacillation, followed by stubborn inflexibility.

WESTERN LANDS

No sooner was peace arranged in 1763 than events thrust the problem of the western lands upon the government in an acute form. The Indians of the Ohio region, half unable to believe that their French friends were helpless and fully expecting the reentry of English settlers, grew restless and receptive to the warnings of the visionary Delaware Prophet and his disciple, Pontiac, chief of the Ottawa. In May 1763 Pontiac's effort to seize Fort Detroit was betrayed and failed, but the western tribes joined Pontiac's conspiracy to reopen frontier warfare and within a few months wiped out every British post in the Ohio region except Detroit and Fort Pitt. A relief force under Col. Henry Bouquet lifted the siege of Fort Pitt in August and Pontiac abandoned the attack on Detroit in November, but the outlying settlements suffered heavy losses before British forces could stop the attacks. Pontiac himself did not agree to peace until 1766.

THE PROCLAMATION OF 1763   To keep the peace, the ministers in London reasoned, further settlement could wait another day. The immediate need was to stop Pontiac's warriors and reassure the Indians. There were influential fur traders, moreover, who preferred to keep the wilderness as a game preserve. The pressure for expansion might ultimately prove irresistible—British and American speculators were already dazzled by the prospects—but there would be no harm in a pause while things settled down and a new policy evolved. The king's ministers therefore brought forward, and in October the king signed, the Royal Proclamation of 1763, drafted by the earl of Shelburne, head of the Board of Trade. The order drew a Proclamation Line along the crest of the Appalachians beyond which settlers were forbidden to go and colonial governors were forbidden to authorize surveys or issue land grants. It also established the new British colonies of Quebec and East and West Florida, the last two consisting mainly of small settlements at St. Marks and St. Augustine respectively, now peopled mainly by British garrisons.

The line did not long remain intact. In 1768 the chief royal agents for Indian affairs north and south negotiated two treaties, at Fort Stanwix, New York, and at Hard Labor, South Carolina, by which the Iroquois and Cherokees gave up their claims to lands in the Ohio region—a strip in western New York, a large area of southwestern Pennsylvania, and between the Ohio and the Tennessee farther south. In 1770, by the Treaty of Lochaber, the Cherokees agreed to move the line below the Ohio still farther westward. Land speculators, including Benjamin Franklin, Sir William Johnson, and a number of British investors, soon formed a syndicate and sought a vast domain covering most of present West Virginia and eastern Kentucky, where they proposed to establish the colony of Vandalia. The Board of Trade lent its support, but the formalities were not completed before Vandalia vanished in the revolutionary crisis.

SETTLERS PUSH WEST   Regardless of the formalities, hardy backwoodsmen pushed on over the ridges; by 1770 the town of Pittsburgh had twenty log houses and a small village had appeared on the site of Wheeling. In 1769 another colony was settled on the Watauga River by immigrants from southwestern Virginia, soon joined by settlers from North Carolina. The Watauga colony turned out to be within the limits of North Carolina, but so far removed from other settlements that it became virtually a separate republic under the Watauga Compact of 1772; North Carolina took it into the new district of Washington in 1776.

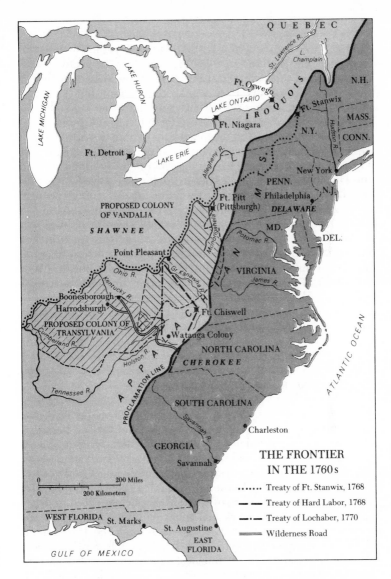

THE FRONTIER
IN THE 1760s

······· Treaty of Ft. Stanwix, 1768

— — — Treaty of Hard Labor, 1768

—·—·— Treaty of Lochaber, 1770

════ Wilderness Road

Another opening came south of the Ohio into the dark and bloody ground of Kentucky, which had been something of a neutral hunting ground shared by the northern and southern tribes. The Shawnees, who lived north of the Ohio, still claimed rights there despite the Iroquois and Cherokee concessions. In 1774 conflicts on the northwestern frontier of Virginia led the last royal governor, Lord Dunmore, to organize two expeditions against the Shawnees. In a battle at Point Pleasant, where the Kanawha empties into the Ohio, Gen. Andrew Lewis fought off an attack and the defeated war chiefs of the Shawnees forced their leader, Cornstalk, to surrender their claims. James Harrod of Pennsylvania soon rebuilt his settlement at Harrodsburg which had been destroyed during the fighting, and Judge Richard Henderson of North Carolina formed a plan to settle the area on a larger scale. He organized the Transylvania Company in 1774, and in 1775 bought from the Cherokees a dubious title to the land between Kentucky and Cumberland Rivers. Next he sent out a band of men under the most famous frontiersman of them all, Daniel Boone, to cut the Wilderness Road from the upper Holston River via the Cumberland Gap in southwestern Virginia on up to the Kentucky River. Along this road settlers moved up to Boonesborough and Henderson set about organizing a government for his colony of Transylvania. But his claim was weak. Transylvania sent a delegation to the Continental Congress, which refused to receive it, and in 1776 Virginia responded to a petition from the Harrodsburg settlers and organized much of present Kentucky into a county of Virginia.

GRENVILLE AND THE STAMP ACT

GRENVILLE'S COLONIAL POLICY   Meanwhile, as Shelbourne was drafting the Proclamation of 1763, a new ministry had begun to grapple with the problems of imperial finances. The new chief minister, George Grenville, first lord of the Treasury, was a man much like the king: industrious, honest, meticulous, and obtuse. His opinions, the king himself observed, were "seldom formed from any other motives than such as may be expected to originate in the mind of a clerk in a counting house." Grenville apparently took without question the need for redcoats to defend the frontier, although the colonies had been left mostly to their own devices before 1754. But he faced estimates of £300,000 annually for American defense, on top of an already staggering debt. He had already tried to find new revenues at home, one result being a cider tax so unpopular that it helped to drive him briefly out of office. It would not be the last time that British or American officials would learn that taxes on drink, fortified or otherwise, stirred deadly passions.

With the large tax burden at home and a much lighter one in the colonies, Grenville reasoned that the Americans were obli-

George Grenville, first lord of
the treasury, whose tax policy
aroused colonial opposition.
[Christ Church, Oxford]

gated to share the cost of their own defense. As he began to tote
up the accounts he learned that the American customs service
spent £8,000 to collect only a fourth that amount in revenue.
Clearly evasion and inefficiency, not to mention corruption,
were rampant, and the service needed tightening. Grenville directed absentee customs agents to pack themselves off to America
and cease hiring deputies. He issued stern orders to colonial officials and set the navy to patrolling the coasts. In Parliament he
secured an Act for the Encouragement of Officers Making Seizures (1763) which set up a new vice-admiralty court in Halifax
with jurisdiction over all the colonies, a court which had no
juries of colonists sympathetic to smugglers. The old habits of
salutary neglect in the enforcement of the Navigation Acts were
coming to an end, causing no little annoyance to American shippers.

Strict enforcement of the old Molasses Act of 1733 posed a
serious threat to New England's mercantile prosperity, which in
turn created markets for British goods. The sixpence duty had
been set prohibitively high, not for purposes of revenue but to
prevent trade with the French sugar islands. Yet the rum distilleries consumed more molasses than the British West Indies provided, and as Gov. Francis Bernard of Massachusetts wrote to the
king: "Even illegal trade, where the balance is in favor of British
subjects, makes its final return to Great Britain." Grenville recognized that the sixpence duty, if enforced, would be ruinous to
a major colonial enterprise, and put through a new Revenue Act
of 1764, commonly known as the Sugar Act, which cut the duty

in half, from sixpence to threepence. This, he reasoned, would reduce the temptation to smuggle or to bribe the customs officers. In addition the Sugar Act levied new duties on imports of foreign textiles, wines, coffee, indigo, and sugar. The act, Grenville estimated, would bring in about £45,000 a year which would go "toward defraying the necessary expenses of defending, protecting, and securing, the said colonies and plantations." For the first time Parliament had adopted duties frankly designed to raise revenues in the colonies and not merely incidental to regulation of trade.

One other measure in Grenville's new design of colonial policy had an important impact on the colonies: the Currency Act of 1764. The colonies faced a chronic shortage of hard money, which kept going out to pay debts in England. To meet the shortage they resorted to issuing their own paper money. British creditors, however, feared payment in a depreciated currency. To alleviate their fears, Parliament in 1751 had forbidden the New England colonies to make their currency legal tender. Now Grenville extended the prohibition to all the colonies. The result was a decline in the value of existing paper money, since nobody was obligated to accept it in payment of debts, even in the colonies. The deflationary impact of the Currency Act, combined with new duties and stricter enforcement, delivered a severe shock to a colonial economy already suffering a postwar business decline.

THE STAMP ACT   But Grenville's new design was still incomplete. The Sugar Act would defray only a fraction of the cost of maintaining the 10,000 troops to be stationed in the colonies. Grenville announced when he introduced the act that he had in mind still another measure to raise money in America, a stamp tax. Early in 1765 he presented his plan to agents of the colonies in London. They protested unanimously, but had no response to his request for an alternative. And neither he nor they seemed to have any inkling of the storm it would arouse. Benjamin Franklin, representing four colonies, even proposed one of his friends as a stamp agent.

On February 13, 1765, Grenville laid his proposal before Parliament. It aroused little interest or debate. Only three speeches were delivered in opposition, but one of them included a fateful phrase. Col. Isaac Barré, who had served with Wolfe at Québec, said that British agents sent out to the colonies had "caused the blood of these sons of liberty to recoil within them." Nevertheless the act passed the Commons by a vote of 205 to 49. The act

A British revenue stamp (1765).
[Library of Congress]

created revenue stamps ranging in cost from threepence to £6, and required that they be fixed to printed matter and legal documents of all kinds: newspapers, pamphlets, broadsides, almanacs, bonds, leases, deeds, licenses, insurance policies, ship clearances, college diplomas, even dice and playing cards. The requirement would go into effect on November 1, 1765.

In March 1765 Grenville put through the measure that completed his design, the Quartering Act, in effect still another tax. This act required the colonies to supply British troops with provisions and to provide them barracks or submit to their use of inns and vacant buildings. It applied to all colonies, but affected mainly New York, headquarters of the British forces.

WHIG IDEOLOGY IN THE COLONIES   The cumulative effect of Grenville's measures raised colonial suspicions to a fever. Unwittingly this plodding minister of a plodding king had stirred up a storm of protest and set in train a profound and searching exploration of English traditions and imperial relations. If anything, the colonists were more impregnated with Whiggery than the English. They had absorbed it from the polemics of John Trenchard and Thomas Gordon, authors of *Cato's Letters* (1720–1723), Joseph Addison's play *Cato* (1713), Viscount Bolingbroke, Algernon Sidney, the histories of Paul Rapin and Catherine Macaulay, and above all from John Locke's justification of the Glorious Revolution, his *Two Treatises on Government* (1690). They knew that English history had been a struggle by Parliament to preserve life, liberty, and property against royal tyranny.

They also knew from their religious heritage and by what Patrick Henry called "the lamp of experience" that human nature is corruptible and lusts after power. The safeguard against abuses, in the view of those who called themselves "True Whigs," was not to rely on human goodness but to check power with power. And the British Constitution had embodied these principles in a mixed government of kings, lords, and commons, each serving as a check on the others. Even on the continent of Europe enlightened philosophers looked with admiration upon English liberties. A character in Mozart's opera, *The Abduction from the Seraglio*, announced: "I am an Englishwoman, born to freedom." The French writer Montesquieu, in his *Spirit of the Laws*, mingled the idea of a mixed government (king, lords, commons) with his own notion of the separation of powers (executive, legislative, judicial). The colonists, like Montesquieu, embraced the Enlightenment philosophy of natural law and natural rights. But if the Enlightenment found lodgment in their minds, the Whig interpretation of history and human nature was built into their bones. In the end it saved them from the facile optimism and the pursuit of utopia which would lure the French revolutionaries into the horrors of the Terror.

But in 1764 and 1765 it seemed to the colonists that Grenville had loosed upon them the very engines of tyranny from which Parliament had rescued England in the seventeenth century, and by imposition of that very Parliament! A standing army was the historic ally of despots, and now with the French gone and Pontiac subdued, several thousand soldiers remained in the colonies: to protect the colonists or to subdue them? It was beginning to seem clear that it was the latter. Among the fundamental rights of Englishmen were trial by jury and the presumption of innocence, but vice-admiralty courts excluded juries and put the burden of proof on the defendant. Most important, Englishmen had the right to be taxed only by their elected representatives. Parliament claimed that privilege in England, and the colonial assemblies had long exercised it in America. Now Parliament was out to usurp the assemblies' power of the purse strings.

THE QUESTION OF REPRESENTATION In a flood of colonial pamphlets, speeches, and resolutions, debate on the Stamp Tax turned mainly on the point expressed in a slogan familiar to all Americans: "no taxation without representation," a cry that had been raised years before in response to the Molasses Act of 1733. In 1764 James Otis, now a popular leader in the Massachusetts assembly, set fourth the argument in a pamphlet, *The Rights of the British Colonists Asserted and Proved.* Grenville had one of his subordinates, Thomas Whately, prepare an answer which developed the ingenious theory of "virtual representation." If the colonies had no vote in Parliament, neither did most Englishmen who lived in boroughs that had developed since the last appointment. Large cities had grown up which had no right to elect a member, while old boroughs with little or no population still returned members. Nevertheless each member of Parliament represented the interests of the whole country and indeed the whole empire. Charleston, for instance, had fully as much representation as Manchester, England.

To the colonists virtual representation was nonsense, justified neither by logic nor by their own experience. In America, to be sure, the apportionment of assemblies failed to keep pace with the westward movement of population, but it was based more nearly on population and—in contrast to British practice—each member was expected to live in the district he represented. In a pamphlet widely circulated during 1765 Daniel Dulany, a young lawyer of Maryland, suggested that even if the theory had any validity for England, where the interests of electors might be closely tied to those of nonelectors, it had none for colonists 3,000 miles away, whose interests differed and whose distance from Westminster made it impossible for them to influence members. James Otis went more to the heart of the matter. If such considerable places as Manchester, Birmingham, and Sheffield were not represented, he said, "they ought to be."

PROTEST IN THE COLONIES Soon after passage of the Stamp Act, Benjamin Franklin wrote back to his radical friend Charles Thomson in Philadelphia: "We might as well have hindered the sun's setting. But since 'tis down . . . let us make as good a night of it as we can." In reply Thomson predicted "the works of darkness" in the night. The Stamp Act became the chief target of colonial protest. The Sugar Act affected mainly New England, but the Stamp Act imposed a burden on all the colonists who did any kind of business. And it affected most of all the articulate elements in the community: merchants, planters, lawyers, printer-editors—all strategically placed to influence opinion.

Through the spring and summer of 1765 popular resentment found outlet in mass meetings, parades, bonfires, and other demonstrations. The protest enlisted farmers, artisans, laborers, businessmen, dock workers, and seamen alarmed at the disruption of business. Lawyers, editors, and merchants like Christopher Gadsden of Charleston and John Hancock of Boston took the lead or lent support. In North Carolina Governor Tryon reported the mobs to be composed of "gentlemen and planters." They began to assume a name adopted from Colonel Barré's speech: Sons of Liberty. They met underneath "Liberty Trees"—in Boston a great elm on Hanover Square, in Charleston a live oak in Mr. Mazyck's pasture. They erected "Liberty poles" topped by the Phrygian liberty cap, the ancient Roman *pileus* which was presented to freed slaves. One day in mid-August, nearly three months before the effective date of the Stamp Act, an effigy of Boston's stamp agent Andrew Oliver swung from the Liberty Tree and in the evening a mob carried it through the streets, destroyed the stamp office, and used the wood to burn the effigy. Somewhat later another mob sacked the home of Lt.-Gov. Thomas Hutchinson and the local customs officer. Oliver, thoroughly shaken, resigned his commission and stamp agents throughout the colonies felt impelled to follow his example.

By November 1, its effective date, the Stamp Act was a dead letter. Business went on without the stamps. Newspapers appeared with the skull and crossbones in the corner where the stamp belonged. After passage of the Sugar Act a movement had begun to boycott British goods. Now the adoption of non-importation agreements became a universal device of propaganda and pressure on British merchants. Sage and sassafras took the place of tea. Homespun garments became the fashion as symbols of colonial defiance.

The general revolt gave impulse to the idea of colonial unity, as colonists discovered that they had more in common with each other than with London. In May, long before the mobs went into action, the Virginia House of Burgesses had struck the first blow against the Stamp Act in the Virginia Resolves, a series of resolutions inspired by young Patrick Henry's "torrents of sublime eloquence." Virginians, the burgesses declared, were entitled to the rights of Englishmen, and Englishmen could be taxed only by their own representatives. Virginians, moreover, had always been governed by laws passed with their own consent. Newspapers spread the resolutions throughout the colonies, along with even more radical statements that were kept out of the final version, and other assemblies hastened to copy Virginia's example. On June 8, 1765, the Massachusetts House of Representatives issued a circular letter inviting the various assemblies to send delegates to confer in New York on appeals for relief from the king and Parliament.

Nine responded, and from October 7 to 25 the Stamp Act Congress of twenty-seven delegates conferred and issued expressions of colonial sentiment: a Declaration of the Rights and Grievances of the Colonies, a petition to the king for relief, and a petition to Parliament for repeal of the Stamp Act. The delegates acknowledged that the colonies owed a "due subordination" to Parliament, but they questioned "whether there be not a material distinction . . . between the necessary exercise of Parliamentary jurisdiction in general Acts, for the amendment of the Common Law and the regulation of trade and commerce throughout the whole empire, and the exercise of that jurisdiction by imposing taxes on the colonies." Parliament, in short, might have powers to legislate for the regulation of the empire, but it had no right to levy taxes, which were a free gift granted by the people through their representatives.

REPEAL OF THE ACT   The storm had scarcely broken before Grenville's ministry was out of office, dismissed not because of the colonial turmoil but because they had fallen out with the king over the distribution of offices. In July 1765 the king installed a new minister, the marquis of Rockingham, leader of the "Rockingham Whigs," the "old Whig" faction which included men like Barré and Edmund Burke who sympathized with the colonists' views. Rockingham resolved to end the quarrel by repealing the Stamp Act, but he needed to move carefully in order to win a ma-

The Repeal, or the Funeral Procession of Miss Americ-Stamp *(1766).*
Grenville carries the dead Stamp Act in its coffin. In the background,
trade with America starts up again. [John Carter Brown Library, Brown
University]

jority. Simple repeal was politically impossible without some affirmation of parliamentary authority. When Parliament assembled early in the year, William Pitt demanded that the Stamp Act be repealed "absolutely, totally, and immediately," but urged that Britain's authority over the colonies "be asserted in as strong terms as possible," except on the point of taxation. Rockingham steered a cautious course, and seized upon the widespread but false impression that Pitt accepted the principle of "external" taxes on trade but rejected "internal" taxes within the colonies. Benjamin Franklin, summoned before Parliament for interrogation in what was probably a rehearsed performance, helped to further the false impression that this was the colonists' view as well, an impression easily refuted by reference to the colonial resolutions of the previous year.

In March 1766 Parliament passed the repeal, but in order to pacify Grenville's following without offending the Pitt supporters, Rockingham accepted the Declaratory Act, which asserted the full power of Parliament to make laws binding the colonies "in all cases whatsoever." It was a cunning evasion which made no concession with regard to taxes, but made no mention of them either. It left intact in the minds of many members the impression that a distinction had been drawn between "external" and "internal" taxes, and that impression would have fateful consequences for the future. For the moment, however, the Declaratory Act seemed little if anything more than a gesture to save face. Amid the rejoicing and relief on both sides of the Atlantic there were no omens that the quarrel would be reopened within a year. To be sure, the Sugar Act remained on the books, but Rockingham reduced the molasses tax from three pence to one pence, less than the cost of a bribe.

Fanning the Flames

But the king continued to have his ministers play musical chairs. Rockingham fell for the same reasons as Grenville, a quarrel over appointments, and the king invited Pitt to form a ministry including the major factions of Parliament and rewarded him with the title of earl of Chatham. Burke compared the coalition to pigs gathered at a trough. The ill-matched combination would have been hard to manage even if Pitt had remained in charge, but the old warlord began to slip over the fine line between genius and madness, leaving direction to the indolent duke of Grafton, who headed the cabinet after Pitt resigned in 1768. For a time in 1767 the guiding force in the ministry was

Charles Townshend, chancellor of the Exchequer, whose "abilities were superior to those of all men," according to Horace Walpole, "and his judgement below that of any man." The erratic Townshend took advantage of Pitt's absence to reopen the question of colonial taxation and seized upon the notion that "external" taxes were tolerable to the colonies—not that he believed it for a moment.

THE TOWNSHEND ACTS   In May and June 1767 Townshend put his plan through the House of Commons and in September he died, leaving behind a bitter legacy: the Townshend Acts. First, he set out to bring the New York assembly to its senses. That body had defied the Quartering Act and refused to provide billets or supplies for the king's troops. Parliament, at Townshend's behest, suspended all acts of the assembly until it yielded. New York protested but finally caved in, inadvertently confirming the suspicion that too much indulgence had encouraged colonial bad manners. Townshend followed up with the Revenue Act of 1767, which levied duties ("external taxes") on colonial imports of glass, lead, paints, paper, and tea. Third, he set up a Board of Customs Commissioners at Boston, the colonial headquarters of smuggling. Finally, he reorganized the Vice-Admiralty Courts, providing four in the continental colonies—at Halifax, Boston, Philadelphia, and Charleston.

Christian Remick's watercolor of the Boston Commons shows British troops encamped. [New York Public Library]

The Townshend duties were something of a success on the ledger books, bringing in revenues of £31,000 at a cost of about £13,000. But the intangible costs were greater. For one thing the duties taxed goods exported from England, indirectly hurting British manufacturers, and had to be collected in colonial ports, increasing collection costs. But the greater cost was a new drift into ever-greater conflict. The Revenue Act of 1767 posed a more severe threat to colonial assemblies than Grenville's taxes, for Townshend proposed to apply these moneys to pay governors and other officers and release them from dependence on the assemblies.

DICKINSON'S *LETTERS*   The Townshend Acts took the colonists by surprise, and the storm gathered more slowly than it had two years before. But once again citizens resolved to resist, to boycott British goods, to wear homespun, to develop their own manufactures. Once again the colonial press spewed out expressions of protest, most notably the essays of John Dickinson, a Philadelphia lawyer who hoped to resolve the dispute by persuasion. Late in 1767 his twelve *Letters of a Pennsylvania Farmer* (as he chose to style himself) began to appear in the *Pennsylvania Chronicle*, from which they were copied in other papers and in pamphlet form. His argument simply repeated with greater detail and more elegance what Daniel Dulany and the Stamp Act Congress had already said. The colonists held that Parliament might regulate commerce and collect duties incidental to that purpose, but it had no right to levy taxes for revenue whether they were internal or external. Dickinson used the language of moderation throughout. "The cause of Liberty is a cause of too much dignity to be sullied by turbulence and tumult," he argued. The colonial complaints should "speak at the same time the language of affliction and veneration."

SAMUEL ADAMS AND THE SONS OF LIBERTY   But the affliction grew and the veneration waned. British ministers could neither conciliate moderates like Dickinson nor cope with firebrands like Samuel Adams of Boston, who was now emerging as the supreme genius of revolutionary agitation. Adams, a Harvard graduate, son of a moderately well-off family, had run down the family brewery and failed at everything else except politics. At Harvard he had chosen as the subject for his master's degree "whether it be lawful to resist the Supreme Magistrate, if the Commonwealth be otherwise preserved." Now he was obsessed with the conviction that Parliament had no right to legislate at all for the colonies, that Massachusetts must return to the spirit of its Puritan founders and defend itself from a new design against its liberties.

While other men tended their private affairs, Adams was whipping up the Sons of Liberty and organizing protests in the Boston town meeting and the provincial assembly. Early in 1768 he and James Otis formulated another Massachusetts Circular Letter, which the assembly dispatched to the other colonies. The letter restated the illegality of parliamentary taxation, warned that the new duties would be used to pay colonial officials, and invited the support of other colonies. In London the earl of Hillsborough, just appointed to the new office of secretary of state for the colonies, only made bad matters worse. He ordered the assembly to withdraw the letter. The assembly refused, by a vote of 92 to 17, and was dissolved. The consequence was simply more discussion of the need for colonial cooperation. In Charleston the John Wilkes Club drank toasts to the antirescinders, the "glorious ninety-two."

Among Townshend's legacies the new Board of Customs Commissioners at Boston offered still more confirmation of Adams's suspicions. Customs officers had been unwelcome in Boston since the arrival of Edward Randolph a century before. But the irascible Randolph at least had the virtue of honesty. His successors cultivated the fine art of what one historian has called "customs racketeering." Under the Sugar Act, collectors profited from illegal cargoes and exploited technicalities. One diabolical ploy was to neglect certain requirements, then suddenly insist on a strict adherence. In May 1768 they set a trap for Sam Adams's friend and patron John Hancock, a well-to-do merchant. On the narrow ground that Hancock had failed to post a bond before loading his sloop *Liberty* (always before he had posted bond after loading) they seized the ship. A mob gathered to prevent its unloading. The commissioners towed the ship to Castle William in the harbor and called for the protection of British troops. In September 1768 two regiments of redcoats arrived in Boston. Clearly they were not there to protect the frontiers. On the day the soldiers arrived, a convention of delegates from Massachusetts towns declared their "aversion to an unnecessary Standing Army, which they look upon as dangerous to their Civil Liberty."

To members of Parliament the illegal convention smacked of treason, but it gave them little reason to believe that any colonial jury would ever convict the likes of Sam Adams. Consequently by formal resolution Parliament recommended that the king get information on "all treasons, or misprison of treason" committed in Massachusetts and appoint a special commission to judge the evidence under a forgotten act passed during the reign of Henry VIII by which the accused could be taken to England for trial. The king never acted on the suggestion, but the threat was unmistakable. In mid-May 1769 the Virginia assembly passed a new set of resolves reasserting its exclusive right to tax Virginians, challenging the constitutionality of an act which would take a man across the ocean for trial, and calling upon the colonies to unite in the cause. Virginia's governor promptly dissolved the assembly, but the members met independently, dubbed themselves a "convention" after Boston's example, and adopted a new set of nonimportation agreements. Once again, as with the Virginia Resolves against the Stamp Act, most of the other assemblies followed the example.

In London events across the Atlantic still evoked only marginal interest. The king's long effort to reorder British politics to his liking was coming to fulfillment, and that was the big news. In 1769 new elections for Parliament finally produced a majority of the "King's Friends," held to his cause by pelf and patronage. And George III found a minister to his taste in Frederick, Lord North, the plodding chancellor of the Exchequer who had replaced Townshend. In 1770 the king dismissed the Grafton coalition and installed a cabinet of the King's Friends, with North as first minister. North, who venerated the traditions of Parliament, was no stooge for the king, but the two worked in harmony.

THE BOSTON MASSACRE The impact of colonial boycotts on English commerce had persuaded Lord North to modify the Townshend Acts, just in time to halt a perilous escalation of conflict. The presence of soldiers in Boston had been a constant provocation. Bostonians copied the example of the customs officers and indicted soldiers on technical violations of local law. Crowds heckled and ridiculed the "lobster backs." On March 5, 1770, in the square before the customs house, a group began taunting and snowballing the sentry on duty. His call for help brought Capt. Robert Preston with reinforcements. Then somebody rang the town firebell, drawing a larger crowd to the scene. At their head was Crispus Attucks, a runaway mulatto slave who had worked for some years on ships out of Boston. Finally one soldier was knocked down, rose to his feet, and fired into the crowd. When the smoke cleared away five people lay on the ground dead or dying and eight more were wounded. The cause of resistance now had its first martyrs, and the first to die was the runaway

A broadside published by the Boston Gazette *describes "The* BLOODY
MASSACRE . . . *in King Street, Boston" (March 1770). Paul Revere's
engraving illustrates the Massacre. The coffins bear the initials of those
killed. [New-York Historical Society]*

slave, Crispus Attucks. Gov. Thomas Hutchinson, at the insistence of a mass meeting in Faneuil Hall, moved the soldiers out of town to avoid another incident. Those involved in the shooting were indicted for murder, but they were defended by John Adams, Sam's cousin, who thought they were the victims of circumstance, provoked, he said, by a "motley rabble of saucy boys, negroes and mulattoes, Irish teagues and outlandish Jack tars." All were acquitted except two, who got light punishment for manslaughter.

News of the Boston Massacre sent shock waves up and down the colonies. "No previous outrage had given a general alarm," wrote Mercy Otis Warren in her *History of the American Revolution* (1805). The incident "created a resentment which emboldened the timid" and "determined the wavering." But late in April news arrived that Parliament had repealed all the Townshend duties save one. The cabinet, by a fateful vote of five to four, had advised keeping the tea tax as a token of parliamentary authority. Colonial diehards insisted that pressure should be kept on British merchants until Parliament gave in altogether, but the nonimportation movement soon faded. Parliament, after all, had given up the substance of the taxes, with one exception, and much of the colonists' tea was smuggled in from Holland anyway.

For two years little more was done to disturb relations. Discontent simmered down and suspicions began to fade on both sides of the ocean. The Stamp Act was gone, as were all the Townshend duties except that on tea, and Lord Hillsborough disclaimed any intent to seek further revenues. But most of the Grenville-Townshend innovations remained in effect: the Sugar Act, the Currency Act, the Quartering Act, the Vice-Admiralty Courts, the Boards of Customs Commissioners. The redcoats had left Boston but they remained nearby and the British navy still patrolled the coast. Each remained a source of irritation and the cause of occasional incidents. There was still tinder awaiting a spark, and colonial patriots remained alert to resist new impositions.

DISCONTENT ON THE FRONTIER

Through the years of agitation, parts of the backcountry had stirred with quarrels that had nothing to do with the Stamp and Townshend Acts. Rival land claims to the east of Lake Champlain pitted New York against New Hampshire, and the Green

Mountain Boys led by Ethan Allen against both. Eventually the denizens of the area would simply set up shop on their own, as the state of Vermont, created in 1777 although not recognized as a member of the Union until 1791. In Pennsylvania sporadic quarrels broke out with land claimants who held grants from Virginia and Connecticut, whose boundaries under their charters overlapped those granted to William Penn, or so they claimed. A more dangerous division in Pennsylvania arose when a group of frontier ruffians took the law into their own hands. Outraged at the lack of frontier protection during Pontiac's rebellion because of Quaker influence in the assembly, a group called the "Paxton Boys" took revenge by the massacre of peaceful Conestoga Indians in Lancaster County, then threatened the so-called Moravian Indians, a group of Moravian converts near Bethlehem. When the Moravian Indians took refuge in Philadelphia, some 1,500 Paxton Boys marched on the capital, where Benjamin Franklin talked them into returning home by promising that more protection would be forthcoming.

Farther south, frontiersmen of South Carolina had similar complaints about the lack of settled government and the need for protection against horse thieves, cattle rustlers, and Indians. The backcountrymen organized societies called "Regulators" to administer vigilante justice in the region and refused to pay taxes until they got effective government. In 1769 the assembly finally set up six new circuit courts in the region and revised the fees, but still did not respond to the backcountry's demand for representation.

In North Carolina the protest was less over the lack of government than over the abuses and extortion inflicted by appointees from the eastern part of the colony. Farmers felt especially oppressed at the refusal either to issue paper money or to accept produce in payment of taxes, and in 1768 organized as Regulators to resist. Efforts to stop seizures of property and other court proceedings led to more disorders and an enactment, the Johnston Bill, which made the rioters guilty of treason. In the spring of 1771 Gov. William Tryon led 1,200 militiamen into the Piedmont center of Regulator activity. There he met and defeated some 2,000 ill-organized Regulators in the Battle of Alamance, which cost eight killed on each side. One insurgent, James Few, was executed on the battlefield. Twelve others were convicted of treason and six hanged. While this went on, Tryon's men ranged through the backcountry forcing some 6,500 Piedmont settlers to sign an oath of allegiance.

In South Carolina, while Regulators protested in the interior, tensions between the colony and the imperial authorities never quite broke. There, in 1769, the very year the assembly was responding to the backcountry demands, it also voted £1,500 for the radical Bill of Rights Society in England to pay the debts of the government's outspoken critic, John Wilkes. When the king's ministers instructed the governor and council to assert themselves in the matter, royal government in South Carolina reached an impasse. The assembly passed its last annual tax law in 1769, and after 1771 passed no legislation at all.

A Worsening Crisis

Two events in June 1772 broke the period of quiescence in the quarrels with the mother country. Near Providence, Rhode Island, a British schooner, the *Gaspee*, patrolling for smugglers, accidentally ran aground. Under cover of darkness a crowd from the town boarded the ship, removed the crew, and set fire to the vessel. A commission of inquiry was formed with authority to hold suspects (for trial in England, it was rumored, under that old statute of Henry VIII), but nobody in Rhode Island seemed to know anything about the affair. Four days after the burning, on June 13, 1772, Gov. Thomas Hutchinson told the Massachusetts assembly that his salary thenceforth would come out of the customs revenues. Soon afterward word came that judges of the Superior Court would be paid from the same source, and no longer be dependent on the assembly for their income. The assembly expressed a fear that this portended "a despotic administration of government."

The existence of the *Gaspee* commission, which bypassed the courts of Rhode Island, and the independent salaries for royal officials in Massachusetts both suggested to the residents of other colonies that the same might be in store for them. The discussion of colonial rights and parliamentary encroachments gained momentum once again. To keep the pot boiling, in November 1772 Sam Adams got the Boston Town Meeting to form a committee of correspondence which issued a statement of rights and grievances and invited other towns to do the same. Committees of correspondence sprang up across Massachusetts and spread into other colonies. In March 1773 the Virginia assembly proposed the formation of such committees on an intercolonial basis, and a network of the committees spread across the colonies, keeping in touch, mobilizing public opinion, and keeping colonial resentments at a simmer. In unwitting tribute to their effectiveness,

Daniel Leonard, a Massachusetts loyalist, called the committees "the foulest, subtlest, and most venomous serpent ever issued from the egg of sedition."

THE BOSTON TEA PARTY   Lord North soon provided them with the occasion to bring resentment from a simmer to a boil. In May 1773 he undertook to help some friends through a little difficulty. North's scheme was a clever contrivance, perhaps too clever, designed to bail out the East India Company which was foundering in a spell of bad business. The company had in its British warehouses some 17 million pounds of tea. Under the Tea Act of 1773 the government would refund the British duty of twelve pence per pound on all that was shipped to the colonies and collect only the existing three pence duty payable at the colonial port. By this arrangement colonists could get tea more cheaply than Englishmen could, for less even than the black-market Dutch tea. North, however, miscalculated in assuming that price alone would govern colonial reaction. And he erred even worse by permitting the East India Company to serve retailers directly though its own agents or consignees, bypassing the wholesalers who had handled it before. Once that kind of monopoly was established, colonial merchants began to wonder, how soon would the precedent apply to other commodities?

The committees of correspondence, with strong support from colonial merchants, alerted people to the new danger. The government was trying to purchase acquiescence with cheap tea. Before the end of the year large consignments went out to major colonial ports. In New York and Philadelphia popular hostility forced company agents to resign. With no one to receive the tea, it went back to England. In Charleston it was unloaded into warehouses—and later sold to finance the Revolution. In Boston, however, Governor Hutchinson and Sam Adams resolved upon a test of will. The ships' captains, alarmed by the radical opposition, proposed to turn back. Hutchinson, two of whose sons were among the consignees, refused permission until the tea was landed and the duty paid. On November 30, gathered in Old South Church, the Boston Town Meeting warned officials not to assist the landing, although they were legally bound to seize the cargo after twenty days in port, which expired on December 16. On that night a group of men hastened from the hall to Griffin's Wharf where, thinly disguised as Mohawk Indians, they boarded the three ships and threw the tea overboard—cheered on by a crowd along the shore. Like those who had burned the *Gaspee*, they remained parties unknown—except to hundreds of Boston-

*Destruction of tea in Boston Harbor, December 16, 1773. [American
Antiquarian Society]*

ians. One participant later testified that Sam Adams and John
Hancock were there—he had exchanged the countersign with
Hancock: an Indian grunt followed by "me know you." About
£15,000 worth of tea went to the fishes.

Given a more deft response from London the Boston Tea Party
might easily have undermined the radicals' credibility. Many
people, especially merchants, were aghast at the wanton destruction of property. A town meeting in Bristol, Massachusetts,
condemned the action. Ben Franklin called on his native city to
pay for the tea and hasten into sackcloth and ashes. But the British authorities had reached the end of patience. "The colonists
must either submit or triumph," George III wrote to Lord North,
and North hastened to make the king's judgment a self-fulfilling
prophecy.

THE COERCIVE ACTS   In March 1774 North laid before Parliament
four measures to discipline Boston, and Parliament enacted them
in April. The Boston Port Act closed the port from June 1, 1774,
until the tea was paid for. An Act for the Impartial Administration of Justice let the governor transfer to England the trial of any
official accused of committing an offense in the line of duty—no

more redcoats would be tried on technicalities. A new Quartering Act directed local authorities to provide lodging for soldiers, in private homes if necessary. Finally, the Massachusetts Government Act made the colony's council and law-enforcement officers all appointive; sheriffs would select jurors and no town meeting could be held without the governor's consent, except for the annual election of town officers. In May, Gen. Thomas Gage arrived to replace Hutchinson as governor and assume command of British forces.

The actions were designed to isolate Boston and make an example of the colony. Instead they hastened development of a movement for colonial unity. "Your scheme yields no revenue," Edmund Burke had warned Parliament; "it yields nothing but discontent, disorder, disobedience. . . ." At last, it seemed to colonists, their worst fears were being confirmed. If these "Intolerable Acts," as the colonists labeled the Coercive Acts, were not resisted, the same thing would be in store for the other colonists. Still further confirmation of British designs came with news of the Quebec Act, passed in June. The Quebec Act set up a totally unrepresentative government to the north under an appointed governor and council, and gave a privileged position to the

A 1774 engraving representing the tumultuous events in America. Lord North, with the Boston Port Bill in his pocket, pours tea down America's throat. America spits it back. Looking on (at left) are Spain and France, with interest, and (at right) the English military, with concern. [New York Public Library]

Catholic church. The measure was actually designed to deal with the peculiar milieu of a colony peopled mainly by Frenchmen, unused to representative assemblies, but it seemed merely another indicator of designs for the rest of the colonies. What was more, the act placed within the boundaries of Quebec the western lands north of the Ohio River, lands in which Pennsylvania, Virginia, and Connecticut had charter claims. Soon afterward came an announcement of new regulations which restricted sale of ungranted lands in the colonies and provided for relatively high quitrents on such lands.

Meanwhile colonists rallied to the cause of Boston, taking up collections and sending provisions. In Williamsburg, when the Virginia assembly met in May, a young member of the Committee of Correspondence, Thomas Jefferson, proposed to set aside June 1, the effective date of the Boston Port Act, as a day of fasting and prayer in Virginia. The governor immediately dissolved the assembly, whose members retired down Duke of Gloucester Street to the Raleigh Tavern and drew up a resolution for a "Continental Congress" to make representations on behalf of all the colonies. Similar calls were coming from Providence, New York, Philadelphia, and elsewhere, and in June the Massachusetts assembly suggested a meeting at Philadelphia, in September. Shortly before George Washington left to represent Virginia at the meeting, he wrote to a friend: " . . . the crisis is arrived when we must assert our rights, or submit to every imposition, that can be heaped upon us, till custom and use shall make us as tame and abject slaves, as the blacks we rule over with such arbitrary sway."

THE CONTINENTAL CONGRESS   On September 5, 1774, the First Continental Congress assembled in Philadelphia's Carpenter's Hall. They numbered fifty-five in all, elected by provincial congresses or irregular conventions, and representing twelve continental colonies, all but Georgia, Quebec, Nova Scotia, and the Floridas. Peyton Randolph of Virginia was elected president and Charles Thomson, "the Sam Adams of Philadelphia," became secretary, but not a member. The Congress agreed to vote by colonies, although Patrick Henry urged the members to vote as individuals on the grounds that they were not Virginians or New Yorkers or whatever, but Americans. In effect the delegates functioned as a congress of ambassadors, gathered to concert forces on common policies and neither to govern nor rebel but to adopt and issue a series of resolutions and protests.

The Congress gave serious consideration to a plan of union introduced by Joseph Galloway of Pennsylvania. His proposal followed closely the plan of the Albany Congress twenty years before; to set up a central administration of a governor-general appointed by the crown and a grand council chosen by the assemblies to regulate "general affairs." All measures dealing with America would require approval of both this body and Parliament. The plan was defeated only by a vote of six to five. Meanwhile a silversmith from Boston, Paul Revere, had come riding in from Massachusetts with the radical Suffolk Resolves, which Congress proceeded to endorse. Drawn up by Joseph Warren and adopted by a convention in Suffolk County, the resolutions declared the Intolerable Acts null and void, called upon Massachusetts to arm for defense, and called for economic sanctions against British commerce.

In place of Galloway's plan the Congress adopted a Declaration of American Rights which conceded only Parliament's right to regulate commerce and those matters which were strictly imperial affairs. It proclaimed once again the rights of Englishmen, denied Parliament's authority with respect to internal colonial affairs, and proclaimed the right of each assembly to determine the need for troops within its own province. In addition Congress sent the king a petition for relief and issued addresses to the people of Great Britain and the colonies. Finally it adopted the Continental Association of 1774 which recommended that every county, town, and city form committees to enforce a boycott on all British goods. In taking its stand Congress had adopted what later would be called the dominion theory of the British Empire, a theory long implicit in the assemblies' claim to independent authority but more recently formulated in two widely circulated pamphlets by James Wilson of Pennsylvania (*Considerations on the Nature and Extent of the Legislative Authority of the British Parliament*) and Thomas Jefferson of Virginia (*Summary View of the Rights of British America*). Each had argued that the colonies were not subject to Parliament but merely to the crown; each like England itself was a separate realm, a point further argued after Congress adjourned in the *Novanglus Letters* of John Adams, published in Massachusetts. Another congress was called for May 1775.

In London few members of Parliament were ready to comprehend, much less accept, such "liberal and expanded thought," as Jefferson called it. In the House of Lords, William Pitt, earl of Chatham, did urge acceptance of the American view on taxation, however, and suggested a compromise under which the Continental Congress might vote a revenue for the crown. In the

Commons, Edmund Burke, in a brilliant speech on conciliation, urged merely an acceptance of the American view on taxation as consonant with English principles. The real question, he argued, was "not whether you have the right to render your people miserable; but whether it is not your interest to make them happy."

But neither house was in a mood for such points. Instead they declared Massachusetts in rebellion, forbade the New England colonies to trade with any nation outside the empire, and excluded New Englanders from the North Atlantic fisheries. Lord North's Conciliatory Resolution, adopted February 27, 1775, was as far as they would go. Under its terms, Parliament would refrain from any but taxes to regulate trade and would grant to each colony the duties collected within its boundaries provided the colonies would contribute voluntarily to a quota for defense of the empire. It was a formula, Burke said, not for peace but for new quarrels.

SHIFTING AUTHORITY

But events were already moving beyond conciliation. All through the later months of 1774 and early 1775 the patriot defenders of American rights were seizing the initiative. The uncertain and unorganized Loyalists, if they did not submit to nonimportation agreements, found themselves confronted with persuasive committees of "Whigs," with tar and feathers at the ready. In October 1774 the Massachusetts House of Representatives, meeting in defiance of Governor Gage, restyled itself the Provincial Congress and named John Hancock head of a Committee of Safety with power to call up the militia. The militia, as much a social as a military organization in the past, now took to serious drill in formations, tactics, and marksmanship, and organized special units of Minute Men ready for quick mobilization. Everywhere royal officials were losing control as provincial congresses assumed authority and colonial militias organized, raided military stores, gathered arms and gunpowder. In Massachusetts the authority of General Gage scarcely extended beyond Boston.

LEXINGTON AND CONCORD   On April 14 Gage received secret orders from the earl of Dartmouth, who had replaced Hillsborough as colonial secretary, to proceed against the "open rebellion" that existed in the colony, even at the risk of conflict. Leaders of the provincial congress, whom Gage was directed to arrest, were mostly beyond his reach, but Gage decided to move

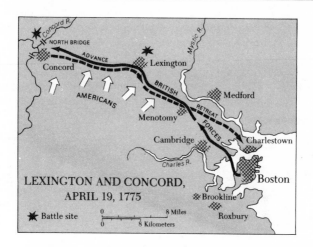

quickly against the militia's supply depot at Concord, about twenty miles away. On the night of April 18 Lt.-Col. Francis Smith and Maj. John Pitcairn of the marines gathered 700 men on Boston Common and set out by way of Lexington. But local patriots got wind of the plan, and Boston's Committee of Safety sent Paul Revere and William Dawes by separate routes on their famous ride to spread the alarm. Revere reached Lexington about midnight and alerted John Hancock and Sam Adams, who were hiding there. Joined by Dawes and Dr. Samuel Prescott, who had been visiting in Lexington, he rode on toward Concord. A British patrol intercepted the trio, but Prescott got through with the warning.

At dawn on the morning of April 19 the British advance guard found Capt. John Parker and about seventy Minute Men lined up on the village green at Lexington. Parker, lacking specific orders, had left the road to Concord unobstructed, and apparently intended only a silent protest, but Pitcairn rode onto the green ordering the militia to disperse. The Americans had already begun quietly backing away when somebody fired a shot and the British soldiers loosed a volley into the Minute Men, leaving eight dead and ten wounded. The British officers hastily got their men under control and back on the road to Concord. There the Americans already had carried off most of their stores, but the British destroyed what they could—including a Liberty Pole. At Concord's North Bridge the growing American forces inflicted fourteen casualties on a British platoon, and about noon Smith began marching his forces back to Boston. The road back

(Above): *Amos Doolittle's 1775 engraving shows Major Pitcairn directing the fire of British troops on the Minute Men at Lexington. [New York Public Library]* (Below): *Doolittle here shows American farmers firing on the British as they retreat to Boston. [New York Public Library]*

had turned into a gauntlet as the embattled farmers from "every Middlesex village and farm" sniped from behind stone walls, trees, barns, houses, all the way back to Charlestown peninsula. By nightfall the survivors were safe under the protection of the fleet and army at Boston, having lost 273 men along the way, the Americans 95.

THE SPREADING CONFLICT When the Second Continental Congress convened at Philadelphia on May 10, 1775, Boston was under siege by the Massachusetts militia, commanded by Gen. Artemus Ward. On the very day that Congress met, Fort Ticonderoga in New York was surprised and taken by a force of "Green Mountain Boys" under Ethan Allen of Vermont and Massachusetts volunteers under Benedict Arnold of Connecticut, who held a commission from the Massachusetts Committee of Safety. The British yielded, Allen said, to his demand "in the name of the great Jehovah and the Continental Congress." Two days later the force took Crown Point, north of Ticonderoga.

The Continental Congress, with no legal authority and no resources, met amid reports of spreading warfare and had little choice but to assume the de facto role of a revolutionary government. The Congress accepted a request that it "adopt" the motley army gathered around Boston and on June 15 named George Washington to be general and commander-in-chief of a Continental Army. In the original organizational plan, four major-generals and eight brigadiers were commissioned. To support the enterprise Congress resorted to a familiar colonial expedient, paper money, and voted to issue $2 million with the colonies pledged to redemption in proportion to their population.

On June 17, the very day that Washington got his commission, the colonials and British force engaged in their first major fight, the Battle of Bunker Hill. While Congress deliberated, both American and British forces in and around Boston had grown. Militiamen from Rhode Island, Connecticut, and New Hampshire joined in the siege. British reinforcements included three major-generals—Sir William Howe, Sir Henry Clinton, and John Burgoyne—who brought Gage belated orders to proceed against Concord. On the day before the battle American forces began to fortify the high ground of Charlestown peninsula, overlooking Boston. Breed's Hill was the battle location, nearer to Boston than Bunker Hill, the site first chosen (and the source of the battle's erroneous name). Gage, at the urging of Henry Clinton, ordered a frontal assault, with British forces moving in formation against murderously accurate fire from the militiamen. On the third attempt, when the colonials began to run out of gunpowder, a bayonet charge ousted them. The British took the high ground, but at the cost of 1,054 casualties among about 2,000 men. The colonials lost about 400 in casualties and prisoners.

When Washington arrived to take charge things had again reached a stalemate, and so remained through the winter, until early March. At that time American forces occupied Dorchester

Heights to the south and brought the city under threat of bombardment with cannon and mortars. Gen. William Howe, who had long since replaced Gage as British commander, reasoned that discretion was the better part of valor and retreated by water to Halifax, Nova Scotia. The last British forces, along with fearful American Loyalists, embarked on March 17, 1776, which Boston afterward celebrated as Evacuation Day—a double holiday for the Boston Irish. By that time British power had collapsed nearly everywhere, and the British forces faced not the suppression of a rebellion but the reconquest of a continent.

While Boston remained under siege the Continental Congress held to the dimming hope that compromise was still possible. On July 5 and 6, 1775, the delegates issued two major documents: an appeal to the king thereafter known as the Olive Branch Petition, and a Declaration of the Causes and Necessity of Taking Up Arms. The Olive Branch Petition, written by John Dickinson, professed continued loyalty to George III and begged him to restrain further hostilities pending a reconciliation. The Declaration, also largely Dickinson's work, traced the controversy, denounced the British for the unprovoked assault at Lexington, and rejected independence but affirmed the colonists' purpose to fight for their rights rather than submit to slavery. When the Olive Branch Petition reached London the outraged king refused even to look at it. On August 22 he ordered the army at Boston to regard the colonists "as open and avowed enemies." The next day he issued a proclamation of rebellion.

Before the end of July 1775 the Congress authorized an attack on Québec in the vain hope of rallying support from the French inhabitants. One force, under Richard Montgomery, advanced by way of Lake Champlain; another, under Benedict Arnold, struggled through the Maine woods. Together they held Québec under siege from mid-September until their final attack was repulsed on December 30, 1775. Montgomery was killed in the battle and Arnold wounded.

In the South, Virginia's Governor Dunmore raised a Loyalist force, including slaves recruited on promise of freedom, but met defeat in December 1775. After leaving Norfolk he returned on January 1, 1776, and burned most of the town. In North Carolina, Loyalist Scottish Highlanders, joined by some former Regulators, were dispersed by a Patriot force at Moore's Creek Bridge. The Loyalists had set out for Wilmington to join an expeditionary force under Lord Cornwallis and Sir Henry Clinton. That plan frustrated, the British commanders decided to attack Charleston instead, but the Patriot militia there had partially finished a palmetto log fort on Sullivan's Island (later named in honor of its commander, Col. William Moultrie). When the British fleet attacked on June 28, 1776, the spongy palmetto logs absorbed the naval fire and Fort Moultrie's cannon returned it with devastating effect. The fleet, with over 200 casualties and every ship damaged, was forced to retire. South Carolina honored the palmetto by putting it on the state flag.

As the fighting spread north into Canada and south into Virginia and the Carolinas, the Continental Congress assumed, one after another, the functions of government. As early as July 1775 it appointed commissioners to negotiate treaties of peace with Indian tribes and organized a Post Office Department with Benjamin Franklin as postmaster-general. In October it authorized formation of a navy, in November a marine corps. A committee appointed in November began to explore the possibility of foreign aid. In March 1776 the Continental Navy raided Nassau in the Bahamas, and Congress further authorized privateering operations against British vessels. But the delegates continued to hold back from the seeming abyss of independence. Yet through late 1775 and early 1776 word came of one British action after another that proclaimed rebellion and war. In December 1775 a Prohibitory Act declared the colonies closed to all commerce, and word came that the king and cabinet were seeking mercenaries in Europe, and getting them in Germany. Eventually almost 30,000 Germans served, about 17,000 of them from the principality of Hesse-Kassel, and "Hessian" became the name applied to them all. Parliament remained deaf to the warnings of Burke, Pitt, John Wilkes, Charles James Fox, and other members that reconquest would not only be costly in itself but that the effort might lead to another great war with France and Spain.

COMMON SENSE   In January 1776 Thomas Paine's pamphlet *Common Sense* was published anonymously in Philadelphia. Paine had arrived there thirteen months before. Coming from a humble Quaker background, Paine had distinguished himself chiefly as a drifter, a failure in marriage and business. At age thirty-seven he set sail for America with a letter of introduction from Benjamin Franklin and the purpose of setting up a school for young ladies. When that did not work out, he moved into the political controversy as a freelance writer, and with *Common Sense* proved himself the consummate revolutionary rhetorician. Until his pamphlet appeared the squabble had been mainly with Parliament. Paine directly attacked allegiance to the monarchy which had remained the last frayed connection to Britain, and refocused the hostility previously vented on Parliament. The common sense of the matter, it seemed, was that King George III and the King's Friends bore the responsibility for the malevolence toward the colonies. Monarchy, Paine boldly proclaimed, rested upon usurpation; its origins would not bear looking into. One honest man, he said, was worth more "than all the crowned ruffians that ever lived." Americans should consult their own interests, abandon George III, and declare their independence: "The blood of the slain, the weeping voice of nature cries,'TIS TIME TO PART."

INDEPENDENCE

Within three months more than 100,000 copies were in circulation. "*Common Sense* is working a powerful change in the minds of men," George Washington said. "A few more flaming arguments as Falmouth and Norfolk and the principles of *Common Sense* will not leave many in doubt." A visitor to North Carolina's Provincal Congress could "hear nothing praised but *Common Sense* and independence." One by one the provincial governments authorized their delegates in Congress to take the final step: Massachusetts in January, South Carolina in March, Georgia and North Carolina in April, Virginia in May. On June 7 Richard Henry Lee of Virginia moved a resolution "that these

The Continental Congress votes Independence, July 2, 1776. [American Antiquarian Society]

United Colonies are, and of right ought to be, free and independent states. . . ." Lee's resolution passed on July 2, a date that "will be the most memorable epoch in the history of America," John Adams wrote to his wife Abigail. The memorable date, however, became July 4, 1776, when Congress adopted Thomas Jefferson's Declaration of Independence, a statement of political philosophy which remains a dynamic force to the present day.

JEFFERSON'S *DECLARATION* Jefferson's summary of the prevailing political sentiment, prepared on behalf of a committee of John Adams, Benjamin Franklin, Roger Sherman, and Robert R. Livingston, was an eloquent restatement of John Locke's contract theory of government, the theory in Jefferson's words that governments derived "their just Powers from the consent of the people," who were entitled to "alter or abolish" those which denied their "unalienable rights" to "life, Liberty, and the pursuit of Happiness." The appeal was no longer simply to "the rights of Englishmen" but to the broader "laws of Nature and Nature's God." But at the same time the Declaration implicitly supported the theory that the British Empire was a federation united only through the crown. Parliament, which had no proper authority over the colonies, was never mentioned by name. The enemy was a king who had "combined with others to subject us to a jurisdiction foreign to our constitution, and unacknowledged by our laws. . . ." The document set forth "a history of repeated injuries and usurpations, all having in direct object the establishment of an absolute Tyranny over these States." The "Representatives of the United States of America," therefore, declared the thirteen "United Colonies" to be "Free and Independent States."

"WE ALWAYS HAD GOVERNED OURSELVES" So it had come to this, thirteen years after Britain acquired domination of North America. Historians have been fruitful in advancing theories and explanations: trade regulation, the restrictions on western lands, the tax burden, the burden of debts to British merchants, the fear of an Anglican bishop, the growth of a national consciousness, the lack of representation in Parliament, ideologies of Whiggery and the Enlightenment, the evangelistic impulse, Scottish moral philosophy, the abrupt shift from a mercantile to an "imperial" policy after 1763, class conflict, revolutionary conspiracy. Each of them separately and all of them together are subject to challenge, but each contributed something to collective grievances that rose to a climax in a gigantic failure of British statesmanship. A conflict between British sovereignty and American rights had

Jefferson's draft of the Declaration of Independence. [Library of Congress] come to a point of confrontation that adroit statesmanship might have avoided, sidestepped, or outflanked. Irresolution and vacillation in the British ministry finally gave way to the stubborn determination to force an issue long permitted to drift. The colonists, conditioned by the Whig interpretation of history, saw these developments as the conspiracy of a corrupted oligarchy —and finally, they decided, of a despotic king—to impose an "absolute Tyranny."

Perhaps the last word on how it came about should belong to an obscure participant, Levi Preston, a Minute Man of Danvers, Massachusetts. Asked sixty-seven years after Lexington and Concord about British oppressions, he responded, as his young interviewer reported later: " 'What were they? Oppressions? I didn't feel them.' 'What, were you not oppressed by the Stamp Act?' 'I never saw one of those stamps, and always understood that Governor Bernard put them all in Castle William. I am certain I never paid a penny for one of them.' 'Well, what then about the tea-tax?' 'Tea-tax! I never drank a drop of the stuff; the boys threw it all overboard.' 'Then I suppose you had been reading Harrington or Sidney and Locke about the eternal principles of liberty.' 'Never heard of 'em. We read only the Bible, the Catechism, Watts's Psalms and Hymns, and the Almanack.' 'Well, then, what was the matter? and what did you mean in going to the fight?' 'Young man, what we meant in going for those redcoats was this: we always had governed ourselves, and we always meant to. They didn't mean we should.' "

FURTHER READING

Interpretations of America's path to independence have displayed some of the most influential scholarship of recent times. Jack P. Greene, ed., *The Reinterpretation of the American Revolution* (1968),° brings together many of the recent theories. Also valuable are Stephen G. Kurtz and James H. Hutson, eds., *Essays on the American Revolution* (1973),° and Alfred T. Young, ed., *The American Revolution: Explorations in the History of American Radicalism* (1976).° Young is particularly good for further reading on political conflicts such as the Regulator controversy.

Narrative surveys of the events covered in this chapter include John C. Miller's *Origins of the American Revolution* (1943) and Lawrence H. Gipson's *The Coming of the Revolution* (1954),° the latter a condensation of material from a multivolume study of British imperial policy. The

° These books are available in paperback editions.

early chapters of Robert Middlekauff's *The Glorious Cause: The American Revolution, 1763–1789* (1982), are also helpful.

The perspective of Great Britain remains important for understanding why revolution erupted. Sir Lewis Namier's *England in the Age of the American Revolution* (1961)° provides a sound introduction for both politics and society. More emphasis is put on politics in George H. Guttridge's *English Whiggism and the American Revolution* (1963) and John Brewer's *Party Ideology and Popular Politics at the Accession of George III* (1976). Studies of relations between the Mother Country and its colonies include R. R. Palmer's *The Age of the Democratic Revolution: A Political History of Europe and America, 1760–1800* (2 vols.; 1959, 1964), Ian R. Christie and Benjamin W. Labaree's *Empire or Independence, 1760–1776* (1976),° and Bernard Donoughue's *British Politics and the American Revolution: The Path to War* (1964). J. A. Ernest's *Money and Politics in America, 1755–1775* (1973), deals with fiscal policy.

How Americans came to an intellectual justification for revolt is traced in Bernard Bailyn's *The Ideological Origins of the American Revolution* (1967),° and in the opening chapters of Gordon S. Wood's *The Creation of the American Republic, 1776–1787* (1969).° To understand how these views deterred the outbreak of violence for so long, see Pauline Maier's *From Resistance to Revolution: Colonial Radicals and the Development of American Opposition to Great Britain, 1765–1776* (1972).° Biographical studies of the men who held such views include John C. Miller's *Sam Adams* (1936), Richard R. Beeman's *Patrick Henry* (1974), Merrill Petersen's *Thomas Jefferson and the New Nation* (1970),° Dumas Malone's *Jefferson, The Virginian* (1948),° Peter Shaw's *The Character of John Adams* (1976),° Eric Foner's *Tom Paine and Revolutionary America* (1976),° and Pauline Maier's *The Old Revolutionaries: Political Lives in the Age of Samuel Adams* (1980).°

A number of books deal with specific events in the chain of crises. Edmund S. and Helen Morgan's *Prologue to Revolution: The Stamp Act Crisis* (1953)° gives the colonial perspective on that crucial event, while P. D. G. Thomas's *British Politics and the Stamp Act Crisis* (1975) emphasizes imperial motives. Also valuable are Benjamin W. Larabee's *The Boston Tea Party* (1964)° and Hiller Zobel's *The Boston Massacre* (1970).° Carl Becker's *The Declaration of Independence* (1922)° remains the best introduction to the events in Philadelphia. Also valuable is the relevant chapter in Merrill Jensen's *The Founding of a Nation* (1968). More interpretative about the contents of the Declaration is Garry Wills's *Inventing America: Jefferson's Declaration of Independence* (1978).°

Colony-level studies also give a clearer perspective to the events of the Revolution. A traditional standard is Carl Becker's *The History of Political Parties in the Province of New York, 1760–1776* (1909). More recent are Patricia U. Bonomi's *A Factious People: Politics and Society in Colonial New York* (1971),° James H. Hutson's *Pennsylvania Politics, 1746–1770: The Movement for Royal Government and its Consequences* (1972), Rhys Isaac's *The Transformation of Virginia, 1740–1790*

(1982),° A. Roger Ekirch's *"Poor Carolina": Politics and Society in Colonial North Carolina, 1729–1776* (1981), William Pencok's *War, Politics, and Revolution in Provincial Massachusetts* (1981), and Edward Countryman's *A People in Revolution: The American Revolution and Political Society in New York, 1760–1790* (1981).

The events across the Appalachians are chronicled concisely by Jack M. Sosin in *The Revolutionary Frontier* (1967). Michael A. Lafaro's *The Life and Adventures of Daniel Boone* (1978) presents a brief but thorough account of that pioneer.

Military affairs in the early phases of the war are handled in John Shy's *Toward Lexington: The Role of the British Army in the Coming of the Revolution* (1965)° and Don Higginbotham's *The War for American Independence* (1971),° as well as other works listed in Chapter 6. In particular, see the early chapters of Charles Royster's *A Revolutionary People at War* (1979)° for the link between rebellion and ideology.

6 ✐

THE AMERICAN REVOLUTION

1776: Washington's Narrow Escape

On July 2, 1776, the day that Congress voted for independence, British redcoats landed on the undefended Staten Island. They were the vanguard of a gigantic effort to reconquer America and the first elements of an enormous force that gathered around New York Harbor over the next month. By mid-August Gen. William Howe, with the support of a fleet under his older brother, Admiral Richard, Lord Howe, had some 32,000 men at his disposal, including 9,000 "Hessians"—the biggest single force ever mustered by the British in the eighteenth century. Washington had expected the move and transferred most of his men from Boston, but could muster only about 19,000 Continentals and militiamen. With such a force New York was indefensible, but Congress wanted it held, and in making gestures of resistance Washington exposed his men to entrapments from which they escaped more by luck and Howe's caution than by any strategic genius of the American commander. Washington was still learning his trade, and the New York campaign afforded some expensive lessons.

FIGHTING IN NEW YORK AND NEW JERSEY The first conflicts took place on Long Island, where the Americans wanted to hold Brooklyn Heights, from which the city might be bombarded. In late August, however, Howe inflicted heavy losses in preliminary battles and forced Washington to evacuate Long Island to reunite his dangerously divided forces. A timely rainstorm, with winds and tides, kept the British fleet out of the East River and made possible a withdrawal to Manhattan under cover of darkness.

George Washington, commander-in-chief of the Continental Army. [Washington/Custis/Lee Collection, Washington and Lee University]

After their success on Long Island the brothers Howe sought a parley with commissioners from the Continental Congress. At the Staten Island Peace Conference on September 11 they met with Benjamin Franklin, John Adams, and Edmund Rutledge, but it soon became clear that the Howes were empowered, in effect, only to negotiate a surrender. Pardons were offered to those who returned to British allegiance and vague promises of fair treatment were advanced—but only after all "extralegal" congresses and conventions were dissolved. The Americans chose to fight on against the odds.

The odds were overwhelming, and they might have been decisive if Howe had moved quickly to pen Washington in lower Manhattan. The main American force, however, withdrew northward to the mainland and retreated slowly across New Jersey and over the Delaware River into Pennsylvania. In the retreat marched a volunteer, Thomas Paine. Having opened an eventful year with his pamphlet *Common Sense*, he composed in Newark *The American Crisis* (the first of several *Crisis* papers) which now appeared in Philadelphia:

> These are the times that try men's souls: The summer soldier and the sunshine patriot will, in this crisis, shrink from the service of his country; but he that stands it NOW deserves the love and thanks of man and woman. Tyranny, like Hell, is not easily conquered. Yet we have this consolation with us, that the harder the conflict, the more glorious the triumph.

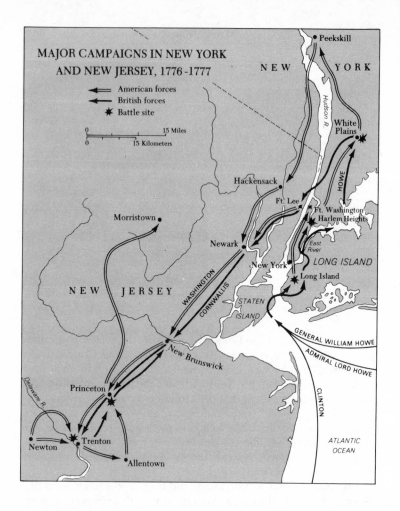

MAJOR CAMPAIGNS IN NEW YORK
AND NEW JERSEY, 1776-1777

American forces
British forces
★ Battle site

15 Miles
15 Kilometers

The pamphlet, ordered read in the Revolutionary camps, resolved by its eloquence the hesitation of many and helped restore the shaken morale of the Patriots—as events would soon do more decisively.

General Howe, firmly ensconced in New York (which the British held throughout the war), established outposts in New Jersey and to the east at Newport, and settled down to wait out the winter. But Washington was not yet ready to go into winter quarters. Instead he daringly seized the initiative. On Christmas night 1776 he slipped across the icy Delaware with some 2,400 men (an episode immortalized in the heroic and fanciful painting of Emmanuel Leutze) and near dawn at Trenton surprised a garrison of 1,500 Hessians still befuddled from too much holiday cheer. It was a total rout from which only 500 royal soldiers escaped death or capture. At nearby Princeton on January 3 the Americans met and drove off three regiments of British redcoats, and finally took refuge in winter quarters at Morristown, in the hills of northern Jersey. The campaigns of 1776 had ended, after repeated defeats, with two minor victories which inspirited the Patriot cause. Howe had missed his great chance, indeed several chances, to bring the rebellion to a speedy end.

AMERICAN SOCIETY AT WAR

THE LOYALISTS Before Trenton, General Howe may have thought that Washington's army was on the verge of collapse and that he need not embitter the colonials and endanger the future restoration by inflicting needless casualties. During the summer and fall of 1776, in fact, New Jersey civilians assumed that the rebellion was collapsing and thousands hastened to sign an oath of allegiance. But the British setbacks at Trenton and Princeton reversed the outlook, and with the British withdrawal New Jersey quickly went back under insurgent control. Through most of the war, in New Jersey and in other colonies, the British would be chasing that elusive will-o'-the-wisp, the Tory majority that Loyalists kept telling them was out there waiting only for British regulars to show the flag.

That the Loyalists were numerous is evident from the departure during or after the war of roughly 100,000 of them, or more than 3 percent of the total population. One plausible estimate had it that opinion was about evenly divided three ways among Patriots or Whigs (as the revolutionaries called themselves), Tories (as Patriots called the Empire Loyalists), and an indifferent middle swayed mostly by the better organized and more energetic radicals. A more likely guess, taking note of the trouble both sides had with recruitment, would be that the middle ground was held by a majority of the populace. Neither side showed great enthusiasm for the struggle. And there was a like division in British opinion. The aversion of so many Englishmen to the war was one reason for the government's hiring German mercenaries, the "Hessians."

The historian Wallace Brown has estimated the total number of Loyalists to have been no more than 7.6–18 percent of the total white adult population. Toryism was "a distinctly urban and seaboard phenomenon" with a clear "commercial, officeholding, and professional bias." But Tories came from all walks of life. Governors, judges, and other royal officials were almost totally loyal; colonial merchants might be tugged one way or the other, depending on how much they had benefited or suffered from mercantilist regulation; the great planters were swayed one way by dependence on British bounties, another by their debts to British merchants. In the backcountry of New York and the Carolinas many humble folk rallied to the crown. Where planter aristocrats tended to be Whig, as in North Carolina, backcountry farmers (many of them recently Regulators) leaned to the Tories. Calculations of self-interest, of course, did not always govern. Sentiment and conviction could be, and often were, the roots of loyalty.

THE MOMENTUM OF WAR   The American Revolution has ever since seemed to most Americans a fight between the Americans and the British, but the War for Independence was also very much a civil war which set brother against brother and divided such families as the Randolphs of Virginia, the Morrises of Pennsylvania, and the Otises of Massachusetts. Benjamin Franklin's illegitimate son, William Temple, royal governor of New Jersey, was a Tory. The fratricidal hate that often goes with civil war gave rise to some of the most bloodcurdling atrocities in the backcountry of New York and Pennsylvania and in Georgia where Tory Rangers and their Indian allies went marauding against frontier Whigs. Whigs responded in kind against units of Loyalist militia or regulars. Once begun, the retaliation and counterretaliation of guerrilla warfare developed a momentum of its own.

In few places, however, were there enough Tories to establish control without the presence of British regulars, and nowhere for very long. Time and again the British forces were frustrated by both the failure of Loyalists to materialize in strength and the collapse of Loyalist militia units once regular detachments pulled out. Even more disheartening was what one British officer called "the licentiousness of the troops, who committed every species of rapine and plunder," and thereby converted potential friends into enemies. British and Hessian regulars, brought up in a hard school of warfare, tended to treat all civilians as hostile. Loyalist militiamen, at the same time, where loath to let any rebel sympathizers slip back into passivity, and so prodded them into active hostility. On the other side the Patriot militia kept springing to life whenever redcoats appeared nearby, and all adult white males, with few exceptions, were obligated under state law to serve when called. With time even the most apathetic would be pressed into a commitment, if only to turn out for drill. And sooner or later nearly every colonial county was touched by military action that would call for armed resistance. The war itself, then, whether through British and Loyalist behavior or the call of the militia, mobilized the apathetic majority into at least an appearance of support for the American cause. This commitment, even if sham, could seldom be reversed once made.

MILITIA AND ARMY   Americans were engaged in the kind of fighting that had become habitual when they were colonists. To repel an attack, the militia somehow materialized; the danger past, it evaporated. There were things to take care of at home and no time for concern about other battles over the horizon. They "come in, you cannot tell how," George Washington said in exasperation, "go, you cannot tell when, and act you cannot tell where, consume your provisions, exhaust your stores, and leave you at last at a critical moment." The militia was usually best at bushwhacking. All too often the green troops would panic in a formal line of battle, and so were commonly placed in the front ranks in the hope that they would get off a shot or two before they turned tail.

The Continental Army, by contrast, was on the whole well trained and dependable, whipped into shape by such foreign volunteers as the marquis de Lafayette and the baron von Steuben. Although some 230,000 enlistees passed through the army, many of those were repeaters who came in for tenures as brief as three months. Washington's army fluctuated in size from around 10,000 troops to as high as 20,000 and as low as 5,000. At times he could put only 2,000–3.000 in the field. Line regiments were

Soldiers in the Continental Army. [The Anne S. K. Brown Military Collection]

organized, state by state, and the states were supposed to keep them filled with volunteers, or conscripts if need be, but Washington could never be sure that his requisitions would be met.

PROBLEMS OF FINANCE AND SUPPLY The same uncertainty beset the army and Congress in their quest for supplies. None of the states came through with more than a part of its share, and Congress reluctantly let army agents take supplies directly from farmers in return for Quartermaster Certificates, which promised future payment. Congress managed to raise some $9 million from the domestic sale of bonds, some $11 million from foreign loans, and about $6 million in requisitions on the states. Since these totals were far short of the war's cost the only expedient left was paper money. In June 1775 Congress began the issuance of Continental currency and kept the printing presses running until nearly $250 million was outstanding before the end of 1779. The states issued about another $200 million. By 1780 the Continental dollar had depreciated so badly that Congress called in the notes, taking them for payments in place of silver at ratio of $40 in paper to $1 in silver. Over $100 million came in under that proviso, but new notes were issued in their place to the amount of about $4.5 million.

With goods scarce and money so plentiful, prices in terms of "Continentals" rose sharply. During the winter of 1777–1778 Washington's men would suffer terribly, less because of actual shortages than because farmers preferred to sell for British gold and silver. Congress did better at providing munitions than at providing other supplies. In 1777 Congress established a government arsenal at Springfield, Massachusetts, and during the war states offered bounties for the manufacture of guns and powder. Still, most munitions were supplied either by capture during the war or by importation from France, where the government was all too glad to help rebels against its British archenemy.

During the harsh winter at Morristown (1776–1777) Washington's army very nearly disintegrated as enlistments expired and deserters fled the hardships. Only about 1,000 Continentals and a few militiamen stuck it out. With the spring thaw, however, recruits began arriving to claim the bounty of $20 and 100 acres of land offered by Congress to those who would enlist for three years or for the duration of the conflict, if less. With some 9,000 regulars Washington began sparring and feinting with Howe in northern New Jersey. Howe had been maturing other plans, however, and so had other British officers.

1777: SETBACKS FOR THE BRITISH

Divided counsels, overconfidence, poor communications, and vacillation plagued British planning for the campaigns of 1777. After the removal of General Gage during the siege of Boston, there was no commander-in-chief. Guy Carleton held an independent command in Canada, but it transpired that he was not even in charge of plans for his own theater. Instead his subordinate, the vainglorious "Gentleman Johnny" Burgoyne, had rushed back to London at the end of 1776 with news of Carleton's cautious withdrawal from Ticonderoga. In London, Burgoyne won the ear of Lord George Germain, the secretary of state for the colonies, who endorsed Burgoyne's plan and put him in command of the northern armies. Burgoyne proposed to advance southward to the Hudson while another force moved eastward from Oswego down the Mohawk Valley. Howe, meanwhile, could lead a third force up the Hudson from New York City. This three-pronged offensive would bisect the colonies along the Hudson River line.

Howe in fact had proposed a similar plan, combined with an attack on New England, and had he stuck to it, might have cut the colonies in two and delivered them a disheartening blow. But he changed his mind and decided to move against the Patriot capital, Philadelphia, expecting that the Pennyslvania Tories would then rally to the crown and secure the colony. Germain had approved that plan too, confident that some 3,000 troops left in New York would be enough to divert Patriot strength from Burgoyne. Howe and Germain, it turned out, were both wrong in their expectations. Howe, moreover, finally decided to move on Philadelphia from the south, by way of Chesapeake Bay, and that put his forces even father away from Burgoyne.

Howe's plan succeeded, up to a point. He took Philadelphia—or as Benjamin Franklin put it, Philadelphia took him. The Tories there proved less numerous than he expected. Washington, sensing Howe's purpose, withdrew most of his men from New Jersey to meet the new threat. At Brandywine Creek, south of Philadelphia, Howe pushed Washington's forces back on September 11 and eight days later occupied Philadelphia. Washington counterattacked against a British encampment at Germantown on October 4, but reinforcements from Philadelphia under General Lord Cornwallis arrived in time to repulse the attack. Washington retired into winter quarters at Valley Forge

Quebec

C A N A D A

Montreal

MAINE
(Mass.)

ST. LEGER

St. Lawrence R.

BURGOYNE

Richelieu R.

LAKE
CHAMPLAIN

VT.

N.H.

Connecticut R.

Crown Point
Ft. Ticonderoga

LAKE
ONTARIO
Ft. Oswego

N. Y.

GATES

LAKE
GEORGE

Ft. Stanwix

ST. LEGER

ARNOLD

Saratoga

Oriskany

Mohawk R.

Freeman's Farm
Albany

Bennington

MASS.

Boston

Kingston

CONN.

R.I.

Susquehanna R.

Delaware R.

WASHINGTON

Hudson R.

PENN.

LONG ISLAND

Princeton

New York

Valley Forge
(WINTER QUARTERS)
Brandywine

Trenton
Germantown
Philadelphia

Wilmington

N.J.

ATLANTIC OCEAN

HOWE

MD.

DEL.

HOWE

VA.

CHESAPEAKE BAY

MAJOR CAMPAIGNS OF 1777:
Saratoga and Philadelphia

⟵ American forces

⟵ British forces

★ Battle site

0   100 Miles

0   100 Kilometers

while Howe and his men remained for the winter in the relative comfort of Philadelphia, twenty miles away. But Howe had gained a pyrrhic victory, while Burgoyne to the north was stumbling into disaster.

SARATOGA   Burgoyne moved southward along the Richelieu River toward Lake Champlain with about 9,500 men, and sent Lt.-Col. Barry St. Leger westward with a band of 900 regular, Tories, and Canadian scouts. At Oswego they picked up nearly a thousand Iroquois allies and headed eastward for Albany. The American army in the north, like Washington's army at Morristown, had dwindled during the winter, and when Burgoyne brought cannon to Mount Defiance, overlooking Fort Ticonderoga, the Continentals prudently abandoned the fort but with substantial loss of powder and supplies. An angry Congress thereupon removed Gen. Philip Schuyler from command of the northern forces and replaced him with Horatio Gates, a favorite of the New Englanders. Fortunately for the American forces Burgoyne delayed at Ticonderoga while reinforcements of Continentals and militia arrived from the south and from New England.

Before Gates arrived, Burgoyne had already experienced two serious reversals. At Oriskany, New York, on August 6, a band of militia repulsed an ambush by St.Leger's Tories and Indians, and gained time for Benedict Arnold to bring a thousand Continentals to the relief of Fort Stanwix. St. Leger's Indians, convinced they faced an even greater force than they actually did, deserted him, and the Mohawk Valley was secured for the Patriot forces. To the east, at Bennington, Vermont (August 16) a body of New England militia repulsed a British foraging party with heavy losses. American reinforcements continued to gather, and after two sharp battles at Freeman's Farm (September 19 and October 7) Burgoyne pulled back to Saratoga, where Gates's forces surrounded him. On October 17,1777, Burgoyne capitulated. By the terms of the surrender his 5,000 soldiers laid down their arms on their word that they would embark for England, under parole (or promise) not to participate further in the war—a genial eighteenth-century practice that saved a lot of upkeep on prisoners-of-war. American leaders, however, feared that the returned prisoners would only be replaced by others stationed in England, and reneged on this agreement. Some of the Hessians were released to assume American residence but the main forces were taken away as prisoners to Virginia. Burgoyne himself was permitted to go home.

ALLIANCE WITH FRANCE   On December 2 news of the American triumph reached London; two days later it reached Paris, where it was celebrated almost as if it were a French victory. It was a signal awaited by both French officials and American agents there. The French foreign minister, the comte de Vergennes, had watched the developing Anglo-American crisis with great anticipation. In September 1775 he had sent a special agent to Philadelphia to encourage the colonists and hint at French aid. In November of that year the Continental Congress set up a Committee of Secret Correspondence, later called the Committee for Foreign Affairs, a forerunner of the State Department. The committee employed Massachusetts colonial agent Arthur Lee as its envoy in London. Then in March 1776 it sent Silas Deane, a Connecticut merchant, to buy munitions and other supplies and inquire about French aid. In September 1776 the committee named Deane, Lee, and Benjamin Franklin its commissioners to France.

In May 1776 the French took their first step toward aiding the colonists. King Louis XVI turned over a million livres to Pierre Augustin Caron de Beaumarchais (author of *The Barber of Seville* and *The Marriage of Figaro*) for clandestine help to the Americans. Assuming the guise of Roderigue Hortalez and Company, ostensibly a trading enterprise, Beaumarchais was soon guiding fourteen ships with war matériel to America; most of the Continental Army's powder in the first years of the war came from this source. The Spanish government added a donation, but soon established its own supply company in Bilbao: Don Diego de Gardoqui and Sons. When the word from Saratoga arrived, Beaumarchais got so carried away in his haste to tell Louis XVI that he wrecked his carriage.

Vergennes now saw his chance to strike a sharper blow at France's enemy and entered into serious negotiations with the American commissioners. On February 6, 1778, they signed two treaties; a Treaty of Amity and Commerce, in which France recognized the United States and offered trade concessions, including important privileges to American shipping, and a Treaty of Alliance. Under the latter both agreed, first, that if France entered the war, both countries would fight until American independence was won; second, that neither would conclude a "truce or peace" without "the formal consent of the other first obtained"; and third, that each guaranteed the other's possessions in America "from the present time and forever against all other powers." France further bound herself to seek neither Canada nor other British possessions on the mainland of North America.

Vergennes at first tried to get Spain to act with him. When she hesitated he took the plunge alone. By June 1778 British vessels had fired on French ships and the two nations were at war. In 1779, after extracting French promises to help her get back territories taken by the British in the previous war, including Gibraltar, Spain entered the war as an ally of France, but not of the United States. In 1780 Britain declared war on the Dutch, who persisted in a profitable trade with the French and Americans. The embattled farmers at Concord had indeed fired the "shot heard round the world." Like Washington's encounter with the French in 1754, it was the start of another world war, and the fighting now spread to the Mediterranean, Africa, India, the West Indies, and the high seas.

1778: Both Sides Regroup

After Saratoga, Lord North knew that the war was unwinable, but the king refused to let him either resign or make peace. North did propose a gesture of conciliation, but his ministry and Parliament moved in such a dilatory fashion that the Franco-American Alliance was signed before the gesture could be made. On March 16, 1778, the House of Commons finally adopted a program which in effect granted all the American demands prior to independence. Parliament repealed the Townshend tea duty, the Massachusetts Government Act, and the Prohibitory Act, and authorized a peace commission which the earl of Carlisle was appointed to head. Further delays followed before the Carlisle Commission reached Philadelphia in June, a month after Congress had ratified the French treaties. The Congress refused to begin any negotiations until independence was recognized or British forces withdrawn, neither of which the commissioners could promise.

Unbeknownst to the Carlisle commissioners, the crown had already authorized the evacuation of Philadelphia, a withdrawal which further weakened what little bargaining power they had. After Saratoga, General Howe had resigned his command and Sir Henry Clinton had replaced him, with orders to pull out of Philadelphia, and if necessary, New York, but to keep Newport. He was to supply troops for an attack on the French island of St. Lucia and send an expedition to Georgia. In short, he was to take a defensive stand except in the South, where the government believed a latent Tory sentiment in the backcountry needed only the British presence for its release. The ministry was right, up to a point, but the sentiment turned out once again, as in other theaters of war, to be weaker that it seemed.

For Washington's army at Valley Forge the winter had been a season of suffering greater than the previous winter at Morristown. While the great diplomatic achievement was maturing in Paris, the American force, encamped near Philadelphia, endured cold, hunger, and disease. Many deserted or resigned their commissions. Washington had to commandeer foodstuffs. The winter was marked by dissension in Congress and the army, and by some sentiment to make Washington the scapegoat for the Patriots' plight. Despite rumors of a movement to replace him, there seems never to have developed any concerted effort to do so. One incident, which went down in history as the "Conway Cabal," apparently never amounted to anything more than a letter in which Gen. Thomas Conway criticized Washington and hinted at his hope that Horatio Gates would replace the commanding general. Gates disavowed any connection with the affair, except as recipient of the letter. Conway himself resigned from the service and later apologized to Washington after being wounded by another officer in a duel resulting from the affair.

As winter drew to an end the army's morale was strengthened by promises from Congress of extra pay and bonuses after the war, its spirit revived by the good news from France, and its fighting trim sharpened by the Prussian baron von Steuben who began to drill it in March. As General Clinton withdrew his forces eastward toward New York, Washington began to move out in pursuit across New Jersey. On June 28 he caught up with the British at Monmouth Court House and engaged them in an indecisive battle, with about 300 casualties on either side. Clinton then slipped away into New York while Washington took up a position at White Plains, north of the city. From that time on the northern theater, scene of the major campaigns and battles in the first years of the war, settled into a long stalemate, interrupted by minor and mostly inconclusive engagements.

ACTIONS ON THE FRONTIER The one major American success of 1778 occurred far from the New Jersey battlefields, out to the west where British garrisons at Forts Niagara and Detroit had set frontier Tories and Indians to raiding western settlements. At Detroit Col. William Hamilton won the sobriquet "hair buyer" for his offers to pay for American scalps. Early in 1778 young George Rogers Clark took 175 frontiersmen and a flotilla of flatboats down the Ohio River, marched through the woods, and on the evening of July 4 took Kaskaskia by surprise. The French inhabitants, terrified at first, "fell into transports of joy" at news of the French alliance. Within a month, and without bloodshed,

Recruiting soldiers for the Continental Army. An appeal to those interested in "viewing the different parts of this beautiful continent, in the honourable and truly respectable character of a soldier," and then returning home "with his pockets FULL of money and his head COVERED with laurels."
[Historical Society of Pennsylvania]

Clark took Cahokia (opposite St. Louis), Vincennes, and some minor outposts in what he now called the County of Illinois in the state of Virginia. After the British retook Vincennes in December, Clark marched his men (almost half French volunteers) through icy rivers and flooded prairies, sometimes in water neck deep, and laid siege to an astonished British garrison there. Then Clark, the hardened woodsman, tomahawked Indian captives in sight of the fort to show that the British afforded no protection. He spared the British captives when they surrendered, however, including the notorious Colonel Hamilton. Clark is often credited with having conquered the West for the new nation, but there is no evidence that the peace negotiators in 1782 knew about his exploit.

While Clark's captives traveled eastward to Williamsburg, a much larger punitive expedition moved against the Iroquois country. On July 3, 1778, as Clark neared Kaskaskia, hundreds of Tory Rangers and Senecas (reputedly the most ferocious of the Iroquois) swept down from Fort Niagara into the Wyoming Valley of Pennsylvania, annihilated some "regular"and militia defenders, and took more than 200 scalps. The Tories and Indians continued to terrorize frontier settlements all through the summer until a climatic attack in November ravaged Cherry Valley, only fifty miles from Albany, New York. In response to the frontier outcries the Continental Congress instructed Washington to chastise the Iroquois. The task was entrusted to an expedition of 4,000 men under Gen. John Sullivan and James Clinton. At Newtown (now Elmira) Sullivan met and defeated the only serious opposition on August 29, 1779, and proceeded to carry out Washington's instruction that the Iroquois country be not "merely overrun but destroyed."

WESTERN CAMPAIGNS, 1778 -1779

⇐ American forces   △ Cherokee settlements

◀━ British forces

✴ Battle site   Tory-Seneca raids (1778)

0   200 Miles

0   200 Kilometers

The American force devastated about forty Seneca and Cayuga villages together with their orchards and food stores. So ruthless and complete was the destruction that large numbers of the Indians were thrown completely upon their British allies for scant supplies from Fort Niagara. The action broke the power of the Iroquois federation for all time, but it did not completely pacify the frontier. Sporadic encounters with various tribes of the region continued to the end of the war.

A similar fate befell the Cherokees farther south. In early 1776 a delegation of northern Indians—Shawnees, Delawares, and Mohawks—talked the Cherokees into striking at frontier settlements in Virginia and the Carolinas. Swift retaliation followed. In August, South Carolina forces burned the lower Cherokee towns and destroyed all the corn they could get their hands on. Virginia and North Carolina forces brought a similar destruction upon the middle and upper towns. Once again, in 1780, a Virginia–North Carolina force wrought destruction on Cherokee towns lest the Indians go to the aid of General Cornwallis, killing twenty-nine and burning over 1,000 towns and 50,000 bushels of corn, along with other supplies. By weakening the major Indian tribes along the frontier, the American Revolution, among its other results, cleared the way for rapid settlement of the trans-Appalachian West.

The War in the South

At the end of 1778 the focus of British action shifted suddenly to the south. The whole region from Virginia to the Carolinas had been free from any major action for over two years. Now the British would test King George's belief that a sleeping Tory power in the South needed only the presence of a few regulars to awaken it. So Lord George Germain conveyed to General Clinton His Majesty's plan to take Savannah and roll northward gathering momentum from the Loyalist countryside. For a while the idea seemed to work, but it ran afoul of two things: first, the Loyalist strength was less than estimated; and second, the British forces behaved so harshly as to drive even loyal men into rebellion.

SAVANNAH AND CHARLESTON   In November 1778, in accord with the king's desire, Clinton dispatched 3,500 men from New York and New Jersey under Lt.-Col. Archibald Campbell to join Gen. Augustin Prevost's Florida Rangers in attacking Savannah. So small was the defending force of Continentals and militia that Campbell quickly overwhelmed the Patriots and took the town. Almost as quickly, with the help of Prevost, Campbell brushed aside opposition in the interior; Gov. James Wright returned and reestablished the royal government in Georgia. There followed a byplay of thrust and parry between Prevost and South Carolina forces. Prevost finally drove toward Charleston, his redcoats plundering plantation houses along the way. The pillage so delayed his army that in May 1779 Prevost fetched up against impregnable defenses on Charleston Neck and narrowly escaped entrapment by Gen. Benjamin Lincoln's Continentals.

The seesaw campaign took a major turn when General Clinton brought new naval and land forces southward to join a massive amphibious attack which bottled up General Lincoln on the Charleston peninsula. On May 12, 1780, Lincoln was compelled to surrender the city and its 5,500 defenders, the largest army surrendered since Saratoga and the greatest single American loss of the war. At this point Congress, against Washington's advice, turned to the victor of Saratoga, Horatio Gates, to take command and sent him south. Charles Lord Cornwallis, dispatched with one of three columns to subdue the Carolina interior, surprised Gates's force at Camden, South Carolina, and threw his new army into a rout, led by Gates himself all the way back to Hillsborough, North Carolina, 160 miles away. It had come to pass as Gates's friend and neighbor Charles Lee had warned after Saratoga: "Beware that your Northern laurels do not turn to Southern willows."

THE CAROLINAS   Cornwallis had South Carolina just about under control, but his cavalry leaders Banastre Tarleton and Patrick Ferguson, who mobilized Tory militiamen, overreached themselves in their effort to subdue the Whigs. "Tarleton's Quarters" became bywords for savagery, because "Bloody Tarleton" gave little quarter to vanquished foes. Ferguson sealed his own doom when he threatened to march over the mountains and hang the leaders of the Watauga country. Instead the "overmountain men" went after Ferguson and, allied with other backcountry Whigs, caught him and his Tories on Kings Mountain, just inside South Carolina. There, on October 7, 1780, they devastated his force of about 1,100. By then feelings were so strong that American irregulars continued firing on Tories trying to surrender and later inflicted indiscriminate slaughter on Tory prisoners. Kings Mountain, an unaccustomed victory, is sometimes called the turning point of the war in the South. Its effect, by proving that

MAJOR CAMPAIGNS IN THE SOUTH, 1778-1781

YORKTOWN, 1781

American forces
British forces
Battle site

0   100 Miles
0   100 Kilometers

the British were not invincible, was to embolden small farmers to join guerrilla bands under partisan leaders like Francis Marion, "the Swamp Fox."

While the overmountain men were closing on Ferguson, Congress had chosen a new commander for the southern theater, Gen. Nathanael Greene, the "fighting Quaker" of Rhode Island. A man of infinite patience, skilled at managing men and saving supplies, careful to avoid needless risks, he was suited to a war of attrition against the British forces. From Charlotte, where he arrived in December, Greene moved his army eastward toward the Pee Dee River, to a site picked by his engineer, the Polish volunteer Thaddeus Kosciuszko. As a diversion he sent Gen. Daniel Morgan with about 700 men on a sweep to the west of Cornwallis's headquarters at Winnsboro. Taking a position near Cowpens, Morgan found himself swamped by militia units joining him faster than he could provide for them. Tarleton caught Morgan and his men on January 17, 1781, with the rain-swollen Broad River at their backs—a position Morgan took deliberately to force the green militiamen to stand and fight. Once the battle was joined, Tarleton mistook a readjustment in the American line for a militia panic, and rushed his men into a destructive fire. Tarleton and a handful of cavalry escaped, but more than 100 of his men were killed and more than 700 taken prisoner.

Morgan then fell back into North Carolina linked up with Greene's main force at Guilford Court House (now Greensboro), and then led Cornwallis on a wild goose chase up to the Dan River where, once the Americans had crossed, the British could not follow. His supplies running low, Cornwallis drew back to Hillsborough. When reinforcements of militiamen from Virginia and the Carolinas arrived, Greene returned to Guilford Court house and offered battle on March 15, 1781. There he placed his militiamen at the front of the line, asking them only to fire three shots before they drew back. As he feared, they fled the field, but in the process drew the pursuing redcoats into an enfilading fire from either side. Having inflicted heavy losses, Greene prudently withdrew to fight another day. Cornwallis was left in possession of the field, but at a cost of nearly 100 men killed and more than 400 wounded. In London, when the word arrived, parliamentary leader Charles James Fox echoed King Pyrrhus: "Another such victory and we are undone."

Cornwallis marched off toward the coast at Wilmington to lick his wounds and take on new supplies. Greene then resolved to go back into South Carolina in the hope of drawing Cornwallis after him or forcing the British to give up the state. There he joined forces with the guerrillas already active on the scene, and in a series of brilliant actions kept losing battles while winning the war: "We fight, get beat, rise, and fight again," he said. By September he had narrowed British control in the Deep South to Charleston and Savannah, although for more than a year longer Whigs and Tories slashed at each other in murderous backcountry actions.

Meanwhile Cornwallis had headed north away from Greene, reasoning that Virginia must be eliminated as a source of reinforcement before the Carolinas could be subdued. In May 1781 he marched north into Virginia. There, since December, Benedict Arnold, now a British general, was engaged in a war of maneuver with American forces under Lafayette and von Steuben. Arnold, until the previous September, had been American commander at West Point; there he nursed grievances over an official reprimand for extravagances as commander of reoccupied Philadelphia, and plotted to sell out the American stronghold to the British. The American capture of the British go-between, Maj. John André, revealed Arnold's plot. Forewarned, Arnold joined the British in New York while the hapless André was hanged as a spy.

YORKTOWN   When Cornwallis linked up with Arnold at Petersburg, their combined forces rose to 7,200, far more than the small American force there. British raiders went out deep into Virginia, and one sortie by Tarleton nearly captured Governor Jefferson and his legislature at Charlottesville. When American reinforcements arrived under Anthony Wayne, captor of Stony Point in 1779, Cornwallis moved back toward the coast to establish contact with New York. In a fatal miscalculation, he picked Yorktown as a defensible site. There seemed to be little reason to worry about a siege, with Washington's main land force attacking New York and the British navy in control of American waters.

To be sure, there was a small American navy, but it was no match for the British fleet. Washington had started it with some fishing vessels during the siege of Boston, but American privateers, acting under state or Continental authority, proved far more troublesome. Most celebrated then and after were the exploits of Capt. John Paul Jones, who crossed the Atlantic in 1778 with his sloop of war *Ranger* and gave the British navy some bad moments in its home waters. In France, Benjamin Franklin got Jones an old Indiaman which the captain named the *Bonhomme Richard* in honor of Franklin's Poor Richard. Off England's Flamborough Head on September 23, 1779, Jones won a desperate battle with the British frigate *Serapis*, which he captured and occupied before his own ship sank. This was the occasion for his stirring and oft-repeated response to a British demand for surrender: "I have not yet begun to fight."

Still, such heroics were little more than nuisances to the British. But at a critical point, thanks to the French navy, the British lost control of the Chesapeake waters. For three years Washington had waited to get some military benefit from the French alliance. In 1780 the French finally landed a force of about 6,000 at Newport, which the British had given up to concentrate on the South, but the French army under the comte de Rochambeau sat there for a year, blockaded by the British fleet. But in 1781 the elements for combined action suddenly fell into place. In May, as

Cornwallis moved into Virginia, Washington persuaded Rochambeau to join forces for an attack on New York. The two armies linked up in July, but before they could strike at New York, word came from the West Indies that Admiral De Grasse was bound for the Chesapeake with his entire French fleet and some 3,000 soldiers. Washington and Rochambeau immediately set out toward Yorktown, all the while preserving the semblance of a flank movement against New York.

On August 30 De Grasse's fleet reached Yorktown and landed his troops to join Lafayette's force already watching Cornwallis. On September 6, the day after a British fleet under Admiral Thomas Graves appeared, De Grasse gave battle and forced Graves to give up his effort to relieve Cornwallis, whose fate was quickly sealed. Graves departed four days later for repairs in New York. De Grasse then sent ships up the Chesapeake to ferry down Washington's and Rochambeau's armies, which brought the total allied forces to more than 16,000, or better than double the size of Cornwallis's army. The siege began on September 28. On October 14 two major redoubts guarding the left of the British line fell to French and American attackers, the latter led by Washington's aide Alexander Hamilton. A British counterattack on October 16 failed to retake them, and later that day a squall forced Cornwallis to abandon a desperate plan to escape across the York River. On October 17, 1781, four years to the day after Saratoga, he sued for peace, and on October 19 the British force of almost 8,000 marched out, their colors cased. Gen. Benjamin Lincoln, captured at Charleston, later returned in a prisoner exchange and now Washington's second in command, directed them to the field of surrender as the band played somber tunes along with the English nursery rhyme, "The World Turned Upside Down":

> If buttercups buzzed
> after the bee;
> If boats were on land,
> Churches on sea;
> If ponies rode men,
> and grass ate the cow;
> If cats should be chased,
> into holes by the mouse;
> If mammas sold their babies,
> To gypsies for half a crown;
> If summer were spring
> And the other way round;
> Then all the world would be upside down.

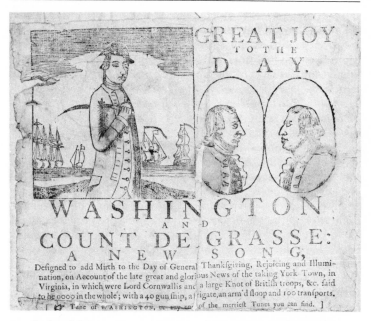

Broadside celebrating America's victory at Yorktown. [Winterthur Museum]

NEGOTIATIONS

Whatever lingering hopes of victory the British may have harbored vanished at Yorktown. "O God, it's all over," Lord North groaned at news of the surrender. On February 27, 1782, the House of Commons voted against further prosecution of the war and on March 5 passed a bill authorizing the crown to make peace. On March 20 Lord North resigned and a new ministry was made up of the old friends of the Americans headed by the duke of Rockingham, who had brought about repeal of the Stamp Act. The new colonial minister, Lord Shelburne, became chief minister after Rockingham's death in September, and directed negotiations with American commissioners.

As early as 1779 the Continental Congress had authorized John Adams to conduct peace negotiations, but he and Vergennes were at odds almost from the beginning, and the French foreign minister used his influence in Philadelphia to get a new five-man commission with instructions to rely on Vergennes for advice. Only three members of the commission were active, however: Adams, who was on state business in the Netherlands;

John Jay, minister to Spain; and Franklin, already in Paris. Thomas Jefferson stayed home because of his wife's fatal illness, and Henry Laurens, held prisoner in the Tower of London after capture on the high seas, arrived late in the negotiations. Franklin and Jay did most of the work. In April 1782 Lord Shelburne sent a special representative, Richard Oswald, to Paris for conversations with Franklin. When Jay arrived, however, he was still smarting from snubs he had received in Madrid and intensely suspicious of Vergennes.

The French commitment to Spain complicated matters. Spain and the United States were both allied with France, but not with each other. America was bound by its alliance to fight on until the French made peace, and the French were bound to help the Spanish recover Gibraltar from England. Unable to deliver Gibraltar, or so the tough-minded Jay reasoned, Vergennes might try to bargain off American land west of the Appalachians in its place. Jay's distrust quickened when Vergennes's secretary informally suggested just such a bargain and left secretly for London. Fearful that the French were angling for a separate peace with the British, Jay persuaded Franklin to play the same game. Ignoring their instructions to consult fully with the French, they agreed to further talks provided Oswald were authorized "to treat with the Commissioners appointed by the Colonys, under the title of Thirteen United States." On November 30, 1782, the talks produced a preliminary treaty with Great Britain. If it violated the spirit of the alliance, it did not violate the strict letter of the treaty with France, for Vergennes was notified the day before it was signed and final agreement still depended on a Franco-British settlement.

THE PEACE OF PARIS   Early in 1783 France and Spain gave up on Gibraltar and reached an armistice. The final signing of the Peace of Paris came on September 3, 1783. In accord with the bargain already struck, Great Britain recognized the independence of the United States and agreed to a Mississippi River boundary to the west. Both the northern and southern borders left ambiguities that would require further definition in the future. Florida, as it turned out, passed back to Spain—along with the island of Minorca in the Mediterranean. France regained Senegal in Africa and the island of Tobago in the West Indies, both of which she had lost in 1763. The British further granted Americans the "liberty" of fishing off Newfoundland and in the St. Lawrence Gulf, and the right to dry their catches on the unsettled coasts of Labrador, Nova Scotia, and the Magdalen Islands. On the matter

North America, 1783

RUSSIANS

UNEXPLORED

HUDSON
BAY

Claimed
by
Spain,
Russia,
and
England

Claimed by
England and U.S.
Lake-of-the-Woods

NEWFOUND-
LAND

Claimed by
England
and U.S.

St. Lawrence R.

ST. PIERRE
& MIQUELON (France)

MAGDALEN
IS.

NOVA SCOTIA

Boston

UNITED

New York

STATES

Mississippi R.

L O U I S I A N A

PACIFIC OCEAN

Claimed by U.S.
and Spain

Charleston

Savannah

ATLANTIC
OCEAN

M E X I C O

FLORIDA

GULF OF MEXICO

CUBA

HISPANIOLA

BRITISH
HONDURAS

HAITI
(France)

NORTH AMERICA,
1783

CARIBBEAN SEA

CENTRAL AMERICA

England   United States

Spain

0   1000 Miles

0   1000 Kilometers

SOUTH AMERICA

of debts, the best the British could get was a promise that British merchants should "meet with no legal impediment" in seeking to collect them. And on the tender point of Loyalists whose property had been confiscated, the negotiators agreed that Congress would "earnestly recommend" to the states the restoration of confiscated property. Each of the last two points was little more than a face-saving gesture for the British.

On November 24 the last British troops left New York City, and on December 4 they evacuated Staten Island and Long Island. That same day Washington took leave of his officers at Fraunces Tavern in New York. On December 23 he appeared before the Continental Congress, meeting in Annapolis, to resign his commission. Before the end of the next day he was back at Mount Vernon, home in time for Christmas.

THE POLITICAL REVOLUTION

REPUBLICAN IDEOLOGY   The Americans had won their War for Independence. Had they undergone a political revolution as well? One answer was given years later by John Adams: "The Revolution was affected before the war commenced. The Revolution was in the minds and hearts of the people. . . . This radical change in the principles, opinions, sentiments, and affections of the people, was the real American Revolution." A movement which began as a struggle for the rights of Englishmen had become a fight for independence in which those rights found expression in governments which were new yet deeply rooted in the colonial experience and the prevailing viewpoints of Whiggery and the Enlightenment. Such ideas as the contract theory of government, the sovereignty of the people, the separation of powers, and natural rights found their way quickly, almost automatically, into the new frames of government that were devised while the fight went on—amid other urgent business.

The American Revolution was unique, Louis Hartz wrote in *The Liberal Tradition in America*, not for "the freedom to which it led, but the established feudal structure it did not have to destroy." Unlike France, Alexis de Tocqueville later said, the Americans did not have to "endure a democratic revolution." In a sense they had been born free, and they saw their revolution as in the main a defense of their liberty and property against what seemed a tyrannical and corrupt government. Still, the revolutionary controversies forced Americans to think out things once taken as a matter of course. Political thinking had to catch up with colonial institutions and practices, but once that process began it carried a momentum of its own.

The very idea of republican government was a far more radical departure in that day of kings and emperors than it would seem to later generations. The idea was rooted in that radical element of British Whiggery which a later historian labeled the eighteenth-century Commonwealthmen, a group which invoked the spirit of republican thinkers in Cromwell's England, the late Roman Republic, and classical antiquity. In the focus of republican thinking Americans began to see themselves in a new light, no longer the rustic provincials in a backwater of European culture but rather the embodiment of the virtue so long praised by intellectuals. "Those who labor in the earth," Jefferson wrote in his *Notes on the State of Virginia* (1781), "are the chosen people of God, if ever He had a chosen people, whose breasts He has

made His peculiar deposit for substantial and genuine virtue."
As free citizens of a republic, unshackled by dependence on the
favor of the court, the American would cast off corruptions of the
Old World and usher in a new reign of liberty and bliss, not only
for themselves but for all mankind. Reality, of course, was bound
to fall short of such millennial hopes, but the republican ideal
served to focus and reinforce the new American vision.

NEW STATE CONSTITUTIONS   At the onset of the fighting every colony saw the departure of governors and other officials, and
usually the expulsion of Loyalists from the assemblies, which
then assumed power as provincial "congresses" or "conventions." But they were acting as revolutionary bodies without any
legal basis for the exercise of authority. In two of the states this
presented little difficulty. Connecticut and Rhode Island, which
had been virtually little republics as corporate colonies, simply
purged their charters of any reference to colonial ties. Massachusetts followed their example until 1780. In the other states
the prevailing notions of social contract and popular sovereignty
led to written constitutions which specified the framework and
powers of government. One of the lessons of the Revolution, it
seemed, had been that one should not rely on the vague body of
law and precedent which made up the unwritten constitution of
Britain. The colonies in fact had had written constitutions in the
form of their charters. Constitution making got under way even
before independence. In May 1776 Congress advised the colonies to set up new governments "under the authority of the people." At first the authority of the people was exercised by
legislatures which simply adopted constitutions and promulgated
them. But they had little more status than ordinary statutory law,
it could be argued, since the people had no chance to express
their wishes directly.

When the Massachusetts assembly hastily submitted a constitution to the towns for approval, however, it was rejected. Massachusetts thereupon invented what became a standard device
for American constitution making: a body separate from and superior to the legislature to exercise the people's sovereignty. In
1779–1780 Massachusetts elected a special convention, chosen
for the specific purpose of making a constitution. The invention
of the constitutional convention was an altogether original contribution to the art of government, and one that other states copied. The resultant document went out to the town meetings with
the provision that two-thirds or more would have to ratify it,
which they did. The Massachusetts Constitution of 1780 de-

clared: "The body politic is formed by a voluntary association of individuals; it is a social compact, by which the whole people covenants with each citizen, and each with the whole people that all shall be governed by certain laws for the common good."

The first state constitutions varied mainly in detail. They formed governments much like the colonial governments, with elected governors and senates instead of appointed governors and councils. Generally they embodied, sometimes explicitly, a separation of powers as a safeguard against abuses, and generally they included a Bill of Rights which protected the time-honored rights of petition, freedom of speech, trial by jury, freedom from self-incrimination, and the like. Most tended to limit the powers of governors and increase the powers of·the legislatures, which had led the people in their quarrels with the colonial governors. Pennsylvania went so far as to eliminate the governor and upper house of the legislature altogether, and operated until 1790 with a unicameral legislature limited only by a house of "censors" who reviewed its work every five years.

THE ARTICLES OF CONFEDERATION   The central government, like the state governments, grew out of an extralegal revolutionary body. The Continental Congress exercised governmental powers by common consent and without any constitutional sanction before March 1781. In a sense it had much the character of a diplomatic congress, composed of delegates named annually by the state legislatures. Plans for a permanent frame of government were started very early, however. Richard Henry Lee's motion for independence included a call for a plan of confederation. As early as July 12, 1776, a committee headed by John Dickinson produced a draft constitution, the "Articles of Confederation and Perpetual Union." For more than a year Congress debated the articles in between more urgent matters and finally adopted them on November 15, 1777, subject to ratification by all the states. All states ratified promptly except Maryland, which stubbornly insisted that the seven states claiming western lands should cede them to the authority of Congress. Maryland did not relent until early 1781, when Virginia gave up its claims under the old colonial charter to the vast region north of the Ohio River. New York had already given up a dubious claim based on its "jurisdiction" over the Iroquois, and the other states eventually gave up their charter claims, although Georgia did not until 1802.

When the Articles of Confederation became effective in March 1781 they did little more than legalize the status quo.

"The United States in Congress Assembled" had a multitude of responsibilities but little authority to carry them out. It had full power over foreign affairs and questions of war and peace; it could decide disputes between the states; it had authority over coinage, postal service, and Indian affairs, and responsibility for the government of the western territories. But it had no power to enforce its resolutions and ordinances upon either states or individuals. And it had no power to levy taxes, but had to rely on requisitions which state legislatures could ignore at their will.

The states, after their battles with Parliament, were in no mood for a strong central government. The Congress in fact had less power than the colonists had once accepted in Parliament, since it could not regulate interstate and foreign commerce. For certain important acts, moreover, a special majority was required. Nine states had to approve measures dealing with war, privateering, treaties, coinage, finances, or the army and navy. Amendments to the articles required unanimous ratification by all the states. The Confederation had neither an executive nor a judicial branch; there was no administrative head of government (only the president of the Congress, chosen annually) and no federal courts.

THE SOCIAL REVOLUTION

On the general frame of government there was in America a consensus—the forms grew so naturally out of experience and the prevalent theories. On other points, however, there was disagreement. As the historian J. Franklin Jamieson put it, in what might be taken almost as a general law of revolutions: "The stream of revolution, once started, could not be confined within narrow banks, but spread abroad upon the land." The more conservative Patriots would have been content to replace royal officials with the rich, the well-born, and the able, and let it go at that. But more radical elements, which had been quickened by the long agitations, raised the question not only of home rule but who shall rule at home, to cite the oft-quoted phrase of the historian Carl Becker.

EQUALITY AND ITS LIMITS   The spirit of equality borne by the Revolution found outlet in several directions, one of which was simply a weakening of old habits of deference. One Colonel Randolph of Virginia told of being in a tavern when a rough group of farmers came in, spitting and pulling off their muddy boots without regard to the sensibilities of the gentlemen present: "The spirit of independence was converted into equality," Randolph wrote, "and every one who bore arms, esteems himself upon a footing with his neighbors. . . . No doubt each of these men considers himself, in every respect, my equal." No doubt each did.

What was more, participation in the army or militia activated and politicized people who had taken little interest in politics before. The large number of new political opportunities that opened up led more ordinary citizens into participation than ever before. The social base of the new legislatures was much broader than that of the old assemblies.

Men fighting for their liberty found it difficult to justify the denial to others of the rights of suffrage and representation. The property qualifications for voting, which already admitted an overwhelming majority of white males, were lowered still further. In Pennsylvania, Delaware, North Carolina, Georgia, and Vermont any taxpayer could vote, although commonly officeholders had to meet higher property requirements. Men who had argued against taxation without representation found it hard to justify denial of proportionate representation for the back-country, which generally enlarged its presence in the legislatures. New men thrown up by the revolutionary turmoil often replaced older men, some of whom had been Loyalists. More often than not the newcomers were men of lesser property. Some states concentrated much power in a legislature chosen by a wide suffrage, but not even Pennsylvania went quite so far as universal manhood suffrage. Others, like New York and Maryland, took a more conservative stance.

New developments in land tenure which grew out of the Revolution extended the democratic trends of suffrage requirements. Confiscations resulted in the seizure of Tory estates by all the state legislatures. Some were quite large, such as the estates of the Penn family, of Lord Fairfax in Virginia, and James DeLancey in New York. William Pepperrell of Maine lost a spread on which he could ride for thirty miles. These lands, however, were of small consequence in contrast to the unsettled lands formerly at the disposal of crown and proprietors, now in the hands of popular assemblies, much of which was used for bonuses to veterans of the war. Western lands, formerly closed by the Proclamation of 1763 and the Quebec Act of 1774, were soon thrown open for settlers.

THE PARADOX OF SLAVERY   The revolutionary principles of liberty and equality, moreover, had clear implications for the enslaved blacks. Jefferson's draft of the Declaration had indicted the king for having violated the "most sacred rights of life and liberty of a distant people, who never offended him, captivating them into slavery in another hemisphere," but the clause was struck out "in complaisance to South Carolina and Georgia." The clause was in fact inaccurate in completely ignoring the implication of American slaveholders and slavetraders in the traffic. Before the Revolution, only Rhode Island, Connecticut, and Pennsylvania had halted the importation of slaves. After independence all the states except Georgia stopped the traffic, although South Carolina later reopened it.

Black soldiers or sailors were present at most of the major battles, from Lexington to Yorktown; some were on the Loyalist side. Lord Dunmore, governor of Virginia, anticipated a general British policy in 1775 when he promised freedom to slaves, as well as indentured servants, who would bear arms for the Loyalist cause. Taking alarm at this, General Washington at the end of 1775 reversed an original policy of excluding blacks from American forces—except the few already in militia companies—and Congress quickly approved. Only two states, South Carolina and Georgia, held out completely against the policy, but by a rough estimate few if any more than about 5,000 were admitted to the American forces in a total of about 300,000, and most of those were free blacks from northern states. They served mainly in white units, although Massachusetts did organize two all-black companies and Rhode Island one. Slaves who served in the cause of independence got their freedom and in some cases land bounties. But the British army, which freed probably tens of thousands, was a greater instrument of emancipation than the American forces. Most of the newly freed blacks found their way to Canada or to British colonies in the Caribbean.

In the northern states, which had fewer slaves than the southern, the doctrines of liberty led swiftly to emancipation for all either during the fighting or shortly afterward. Vermont's Constitution of 1777 specifically forbade slavery. The Massachusetts Constitution of 1780 proclaimed the "inherent liberty" of all, and a court decision in 1783 freed one Quock Walker on the grounds that slavery could not legally exist under that provision. Elsewhere north of the Mason-Dixon line gradual emancipation became the device for freeing the slaves. Pennsylvania in 1780 provided that all children born thereafter to slave mothers would become free at age twenty-eight. In 1784 Rhode Island provided freedom for all born thereafter, at age twenty-one for males, eighteen for females. New York lagged until 1799 in granting freedom to mature slaves born after enactment, but an

Elizabeth Freeman (Mumbet). A former slave, Elizabeth Freeman won her freedom in a Massachusetts court by claiming that the "inherent liberty" of all applied to slaves as well. [Massachusetts Historical Society]

act of 1817 set July 4, 1827, as the date for emancipation of all remaining slaves.

South of Pennsylvania the potential consequences of emancipation were so staggering—South Carolina had a black majority—that whites refused to be stampeded by abstract philosophy. Yet even there slaveholders like Washington, Jefferson, Patrick Henry, and others were troubled. "I am not one of those . . . " Henry Laurens of South Carolina wrote his son, "who dare trust in Providence for defense and security of their own liberty while they enslave and wish to continue in slavery thousands who are as well entitled to freedom as themselves." Jefferson wrote in his *Notes on Virginia* (1785): "Indeed I tremble for my country when I reflect that God is just; that his justice cannot sleep forever." But he, like many other white southerners, was riding the tiger and did not know how to dismount. The furthest antislavery sentiment carried the southern states was to relax the manumission laws under which owners might free their slaves.

THE STATUS OF WOMEN   The logic of liberty applied to the status of women as much as to that of blacks, but wrought even less change in their sphere. Women joined in prewar campaigns to boycott British goods—in fact their support was essential to success in that cause. The war drew women at least temporarily into new pursuits. They plowed fields, kept shop, and melted down pots and pans to make shot. Esther Reed of Philadelphia organized a ladies' association which raised money to provide comforts for the troops. The fighting was man's work, but women served the armies in various support roles, such as handling supplies and serving as couriers. Wives often followed their husbands to camp, and on occasion took their places in the line, as Margaret Corbin did at Fort Washington when her husband fell at his artillery post, or Mary Ludwig Hays (better known as Molly Pitcher) did when hers collapsed of heat fatigue. An exceptional case was that of Deborah Sampson, who joined a Massachusetts regiment as Robert Shurtleff and served from 1781 to 1783 by the "artful concealment" of her sex.

Early in the struggle, on March 31, 1776, Abigail Adams wrote to her husband John: "In the new Code of Laws which I suppose it will be necessary for you to make I desire you would remember the Ladies. . . . Do not put such unlimited power into the hands of the Husbands." Since men were "Naturally Tyrannical," she wrote, "why then, not put it out of the power of the vicious and the Lawless to use us with cruelty and indignity with impunity." Otherwise, "If particular care and attention is not paid to the Ladies we are determined to foment a Rebellion, and will not hold ourselves bound by any Laws in which we have no voice, or Representation." Husband John replied playfully: "We have been told that our Struggle has loosened the bands of Government every where." But Abigail's letter offered the "first Intimation that another Tribe more numerous and powerful than all the rest were grown discontented." But he continued: "Depend upon it, we know better than to repeal our Masculine systems."

And one is hard put to find evidence that the legal status of women benefited from equalitarian doctrine. There is local evidence that in parts of New England divorces were easier to get, but married women still forfeited control of their own property to their husbands, and women gained no political rights except in one state, apparently by accident. New Jersey's state constitu-

Abigail Adams, in a portrait by Gilbert Stuart. [National Gallery of Art]

tion of 1776 defined voters as all "free inhabitants" who could meet property requirements, and some women began voting in the 1780s and continued to do so until 1807, when the state disfranchised both women and blacks. Although some limited advances were made in education, it was a slow process. The chief contribution of the Revolution seems to have been less in substantive gains for women than in a growing willingness to challenge old shibboleths, in the spirit of Abigail Adams. In an essay "On the Equality of the Sexes" (written in 1779, published in 1790), Judith Sargent Murray wrote: "We can only reason from what we know, and if an opportunity of acquiring knowledge hath been denied us, the inferiority of our sex cannot fairly be deduced from thence." Some groundwork was being laid for future battles, but meaningful victories in the cause of equality between the sexes remained in the future.

FREEDOM OF RELIGION   The Revolution also set in motion a transition from the toleration of religious dissent to a complete freedom of religion in the separation of church and state. The Anglican church, established in five colonies and parts of two others, was especially vulnerable because of its association with the crown and because dissenters outnumbered Anglicans in all the states except Virginia. And all but Virginia removed tax support for the church before the fighting was over. In 1776 the Virginia Declaration of Rights guaranteed the free exercise of religion, and in 1786 the Virginia Statute of Religious Freedom (written by Thomas Jefferson) declared that: "no man shall be compelled to frequent or support any religious worship, place or ministry whatsoever," that none should in any way suffer for his religious opinions and beliefs, "But that all men shall be free to profess, and by argument to maintain, their opinions in matters of religion."

New England, with its Puritan heritage, was in less haste to disestablish the Congregational church, although the rules were already being relaxed enough by the 1720s to let Quakers and Baptists assign their tax support to their own churches. New Hampshire finally discontinued tax support for its churches in 1817, Connecticut in 1818, Maine in 1820, and Massachusetts in 1833. Certain religious requirements for officeholding lingered here and there on the law books: Massachusetts and Maryland required a declaration of Christian faith; Delaware had a Trinitarian test; New Jersey and the Carolinas held that officeholders must be Protestants. But in most cases these requirements disappeared before many more years.

In churches as well as in government the Revolution set off a period of constitution making, as some of the first national church bodies emerged. In 1784 the Methodists, who at first were an offshoot of the Anglicans, came together in a general conference at Baltimore under Bishop Francis Asbury. The Anglican church, rechristened Episcopal, gathered in a series of meetings which by 1789 had united the various dioceses in a federal union under Bishop Samuel Seabury of Connecticut; in 1789 also the Presbyterians held their first general assembly in Philadelphia. The following year, 1790, the Catholic church had its first bishop in the United States when John Carroll was named bishop of Baltimore. Other churches would follow in the process of coming together on a national basis.

EMERGENCE OF AN AMERICAN CULTURE

For all the weakness of the central government, the Revolution generated a nascent sense of common nationality. At the time of the French and Indian War Andrew Burnaby, an English traveler, observed: "Fire and water are not more heterogeneous than the different colonies in North America. Nothing can exceed the jealousy . . . which they possess in regard to each other." But the Revolution taught Americans to think "continentally," as Alexander Hamilton put it. As early as the Stamp Act Congress of 1765, Christopher Gadsden, leader of the Charleston radicals, had said: "There ought to be no New England man, no New Yorker, known on the Continent; but all of us Americans." In the first Continental Congress Patrick Henry asserted that such a sense of identity had come to pass: "The distinctions between Virginians, Pennsylvanians, New Yorkers, and New Englanders are no more. I am not a Virginian but an American."

The concrete experience of the war reinforced the feeling. Soldiers who went to fight in other states inevitably broadened their horizons. John Marshall, future chief justice, served first in the Virginia militia and then in the Continental Army in the middle states and endured the winter of 1777–1778 at Valley Forge. He later wrote: "I found myself associated with brave men from different states who were risking life and everything valuable in a common cause. I was confirmed in the habit of considering America as my country and Congress as my government." American nationalism, like American independence, was the creation of the Revolution.

At the same time the Revolution itself marked the start of a national tradition, one that would ultimately reach back and incorporate colonial heroes in its legends. The Revolution produced symbols of unity in, for instance, the Declaration of Independence and the flag, designed by Francis Hopkinson, a Philadelphia lawyer and poet, and a pantheon of heroes whose deeds and whose stirring cries echoed down the years: Sgt. William Jasper's vaulting the palmetto fort on Sullivan's Island to retrieve the fallen flag; Patrick Henry's exhorting his countrymen to choose liberty or death; Nathan Hale's speaking his perhaps apocryphal last words before the British hanged him for a spy: "I only regret that I have but one life to lose for my country." It detracted not a bit from the effect of those cries that both paraphrased lines from Addison's *Cato* nor that William Prescott's admonition at Bunker Hill not to fire "until you see the whites of their eyes" echoed Frederick the Great. And at least some were American originals: John Parker's telling the Minute Men at Lexington, "Don't fire unless fired upon, but if they mean to have a war let it begin here!"; John Paul Jones's defiantly responding to the call for surrender, "I have not yet begun to fight!"; or Richard Henry Lee's postwar tribute to the dead Washington, "first in war, first in peace, and first in the hearts of his countrymen."

ARTS IN THE NEW NATION   The marquis de Chastellux, a French aristocrat who fought in the cause, thought the Revolution in America had generated "more heroes than she [America] has marble and artists to commemorate them." The Revolution provided the first generation of native artists with inspirational subjects. It also filled them with high expectations that individual freedom would release creative energies and vitalize both commerce and the arts. The hope that America would become the future seat of empire and the arts had excited the colonials at least since the appearance of the Anglican divine George Berkeley's celebrated "Verses on the Prospect of Planting Arts and Learning in America" (published in 1752), which included the oft-quoted line: "Westward the course of empire takes its way." Nathaniel Ames's *Almanac* for 1758 took up the theme in unmeasured terms: "The Curious have observed, that the Progress of Humane Literature (like the Sun) is from the East to the West." Soon the course of the arts and sciences would alter the face of the land. "O! Ye unborn Inhabitants of America," the *Almanac* continued, "when your Eyes behold the sun after he has rolled the seasons round for two or three centuries more, you will know that in Anno Domini 1758, we dream'd of your Times."

At the Princeton commencement in 1771 two graduating seniors and budding young authors, Philip Freneau and Hugh Henry Brackenridge, classmates of James Madison and Aaron Burr, presented "A Poem on the Rising Glory of America" in which they reviewed once again the westward transit of culture and foretold in America "the final stage . . . of high invention and wond'rous art, which not the ravages of time shall waste." The Revolution itself raised expectations yet higher. As David Ramsay put it in his *History of the American Revolution* (1789), the conflict with England "gave a spring to the active powers of the inhabitants, and set them on thinking, speaking and acting, in a line far beyond that to which they had been accustomed." The result, one historian has noted, was a sudden efflorescence of the arts: "By the time the country inaugurated its first president in 1789" it had also produced "its first novel, first epic poem, first composer, first professionally acted play, first actor and dancer, first museum, its first important painters, musical-instrument makers, magazine engravers—indeed most of the defining features of traditional high culture."

If, as it happened, no American artist of the time quite measured up to the highest expectations, many of them in the inspiration of the moment chose patriotic themes and celebrated the new nation. Ironically, the best American painters of the time spent all or most of the Revolution in England, studying with Benjamin West of Pennsylvania and John Singleton Copley of

Charles Willson Peale founded the world's first popular museum of natural science and art. Peale began the museum in his Philadelphia home in 1784. His idea of opening a museum to all was revolutionary. [Elise Peale Patterson de Gelpi-Toro]

Massachusetts, both of whom had set up shop in London before the outbreak. Even John Trumbull, who had served in the siege of Boston and the Saratoga campaign, somehow managed a visit to London during the war before returning to help his brother supply the Continentals. Later he adopted patriotic themes in *The Battle of Bunker Hill*, and his four panels in the Capitol Rotunda at Washington: *The Declaration of Independence*, *The Surrender of General Burgoyne*, *The Surrender of General Cornwallis*, and *The Resignation of General Washington*. Charles Willson Peale, who fought at Trenton and Princeton and survived the winter at Valley Forge, produced a virtual portrait gallery of Revolutionary War figures. Over twenty-three years he painted George Washington seven times from life and produced in all sixty portraits of him. Peale's portrait of Washington after the battle of Princeton (painted in 1779) is believed to be the most faithful representation of the general at the time of the War of Independence.

The poet John Trumbull (cousin of the painter) produced perhaps the most successful creative work on the Revolution in *M'Fingal* (1776), a mock heroic satire on American Tories. At the time its ironic tone suited the public temper less than *Common Sense*, but it went through many editions after the war. Joel Barlow, associated with Trumbull in a literary group called the Hartford Wits, later composed an ambitious patriotic epic, *The Vision of Columbus* (1787), enlarged and revised as *The Columbiad* (1807), designed to show America as "the noblest and most elevated part of the earth." Widely hailed at the time as an instant classic, it was pretentious and almost unreadable. Barlow is better remembered for *The Hasty Pudding* (1796), a mock epic which celebrated American simplicity in contrast to Old World sophistication. The Revolution-era poems of Philip Freneau, such as his elegy "To the Memory of Brave Americans," "Eutaw Springs," and "The Memorable Victory of Paul Jones," capture better than any others the patriotic emotions of the war.

EDUCATION   The most lasting effect of postwar nationalism may well have been its mark on education. In the colonies there had been a total of nine colleges, but once the Revolution was over, eight more sprang up in the 1780s and six in the 1790s. Several of the revolutionary state constitutions had provisions for state universities. Georgia's was the first chartered, in 1785, but the University of North Carolina (chartered in 1789) was the first to open, in 1795. An interest in general systems of public schools stirred in some of the states, especially in Pennsylvania and Virginia. Jefferson worked out an elaborate plan for a state system that would provide a rudimentary education for all, and higher levels of education for the talented, up through a state university. The movement for public education, however, would reach fruition much later. At the time, and well into the next century, no state would have a system of schools in the present-day sense.

Education played an important role in broadening and deepening the sense of nationalism, and no single element was as important, perhaps as the spelling book, an item of almost universal use. Noah Webster of Hartford, while teaching at Goshen, New York, prepared an elementary speller published in 1783. By 1890 more than 60 million copies of his "Blue Back Speller" had been printed, and the book continued to sell well into the twentieth century. In his preface Webster issued a cultural Declaration of Independence: "The country," he wrote, "must in some future time, be as distinguished by the superiority of her literary improvements, as she already is by the liberality of her civil and ecclesiastical constitutions." Volume II of Webster's *Grammatical Institute*, a grammar, appeared in 1784, and Volume III, a reader, in 1785, crammed with selections from the speeches of Revolutionary leaders who, he said, were the equals of Cicero and Demosthenes. Other titles, *The American Spelling Book* (the "Blue Back") and *An American Selection of Lessons in Reading and Speaking,* pursued a growing fashion in textbooks of using the word American in the title: American arithmetics as well as spellers appeared. Jedediah Morse, author of *American Geography* (1789), said that the country needed its own textbooks so that the people would not be affected with monarchical and aristocratic ideas.

In a special sense American nationalism was the embodiment of an idea. This first new nation, unlike the rising nations of Europe, was not rooted in antiquity. Its people save the Indians, had not inhabited it over the centuries, nor was there any nation of a common descent. "The American national consciousness," Hans Kohn wrote in *The Idea of Nationalism*, " . . . is not a voice crying out of the depth of the dark past, but is proudly a product of the enlightened present, setting its face resolutely toward the future." And American nationalism embodied a universal idea, with implications for all the world.

Many people, at least since the time of the Pilgrims, had thought America to be singled out for a special identity, a special mission. Jonathan Edwards said God had singled out America as "the glorious renovator of the world," and still later John Adams proclaimed the opening of America "a grand scheme and design in Providence for the illumination and the emancipation of the slavish part of mankind all over the earth." The mission had subtly changed, but it was still there. It was now a call to lead the way for all mankind toward liberty and equality. Meanwhile, however, Americans had to come to grips with more immediate problems created by their new nationhood.

FURTHER READING

The war of the Revolution is the subject of many good surveys. Two which scholars use often are Don Higginbotham's *The War of American Independence* (1971)° and John R. Alden's *The American Revolution, 1775–1783* (1954). Military history buffs should also turn to Christopher Ward's *The War of the Revolution* (2 vols.; 1952) for its details of maneuvers and its clear maps. Another perspective is provided by memoirs and reports of the actual participants in George F. Scheer and Hugh Rankin's *Rebels and Redcoats* (1957).° Briefer accounts are found in Howard Peckham's *The War for Independence* (1958)° and Willard M. Wallace's *Appeal to Arms* (1951).° The British side of the conflict is handled by Piers MacKesy in *The War for America* (1964). Action at sea is the subject of Gardner W. Allen's *A Naval History of the American Revolution* (2 vols.; 1913). Perceptive analysis of the values and goals which led Americans to fight appears in Don Higginbotham, ed., *Reconsiderations on the American Revolution* (1978), as well as John Shy's *A People Numerous and Armed* (1976),° Charles Royster's *A Revolutionary People at War* (1979),° and Lawrence D. Cress's *Citizens in Arms* (1982).

Biographical studies of the major military figures include James T. Flexner's *George Washington in the American Revolution* (1968), Ira D. Gruber's *The Howe Brothers and the American Revolution* (1972),° William Willcox's *Portrait of a General: Sir Henry Clinton in the War of Independence* (1964), Franklin Wickwire's *Cornwallis and the War of Independence* (1970), Samuel E. Morison's *John Paul Jones: A Sailor's Biography* (1959),° Theodore Thayer's *Nathanael Greene: Strategist of the American Revolution* (1960), and Don Higginbotham's *Daniel Morgan: Revolutionary Rifleman* (1961). Material on George Rogers Clark can be found in Jack Sosin's *The Revolutionary Frontier, 1763–1783* (1967).

Why some Americans remained loyal to the Crown is the subject of Bernard Bailyn's *The Ordeal of Thomas Hutchinson* (1974),° Robert M. Calhoon's *The Loyalists in Revolutionary America* (1973), and William H. Nelson's *The American Tory* (1962).° Paul H. Smith's *Loyalists and Redcoats* (1964) traces the military role of the Tories, and Wallace Brown's *The King's Friends* (1965) argues that the loyalists came from all classes of colonial society.

Edmund S. Morgan's *The Birth of the Republic, 1763–1789* (1956),°

° These books are available in paperback editions.

provides a concise introduction to the political events which led rebellious colonists to form a new nation. Herbert Aptheker's *The American Revolution, 1763–1783* (1960), gives a Marxist interpretation to the same events. A more detailed focus on the ideology of Republicanism is in Gordon S. Wood's *The Creation of the American Republic, 1776–1787* (1969).° Merrill Jensen's *The Articles of Confederation* (1940)° is a good introduction to the first attempt at nation forming. Also see a more recent work by Jensen, *The American Revolution within America* (1974). State-level studies of revolutionary politics include some of the works cited for Chapter 5, as well as the following: Fletcher Greene's *Constitutional Developments in the South Atlantic States* (1930), Jackson Turner Main's *The Upper House in Revolutionary America, 1763–1788* (1967) and *The Sovereign States, 1775–1783* (1973), and Robert Brown's *Middle Class Democracy and the Revolution in Massachusetts, 1691–1780* (1955).°

The effort to trace the social effects of the Revolution goes back at least to J. Franklin Jameson's, *The American Revolution Considered as a Social Movement* (1925).° Richard B. Morris's *The American Revolution Reconsidered* (1967)° works at updating and modifying Jameson. A radical view of the social conflicts of the period is found in some of the essays in Alfred Young (ed.), *The American Revolution* (1976).° Jackson Turner Main's *The Social Structure of Revolutionary America* (1965)° looks at the quantitative evidence for the emergence of social equality, while Rhys Isaac's *The Transformation of Virginia, 1740–1790* (1982),° examines the social conflicts in that pivotal state. The question of disestablishment and religious liberty is treated in essays by Sidney Mead, *The Lively Experiment* (1963). Relevant chapters in Winthrop Jordan's *White over Black* (1968)° address the issue of emancipation during the Revolutionary period. One of the few recent community-level studies of change is Robert A. Gross's *The Minute Men and Their World* (1976).° Mary Beth Norton's *Liberty's Daughters* (1980)° documents the role women played in securing independence, and Lynne Withey's *Dearest Friend: A Life of Abigail Adams* (1981) portrays the role played by one very important Revolutionary woman. Joy and Richard Buel's *The Way of Duty: A Woman and Her Family in Revolutionary America* (1984) shows the impact of the Revolution on the lives of a remarkable New England family.

The standard introduction to diplomacy remains Samuel F. Bemis's *The Diplomacy of the American Revolution* (1935).° Richard B. Morris's *The Peacemakers* (1965)° examines more closely the negotiations for the Treaty of Paris, and William C. Stinchcombe details the events of American diplomats in *The American Revolution and the French Alliance* (1969).

SHAPING A FEDERAL UNION

THE CONFEDERATION

Speaking to his fellow graduates at the Harvard commencement in 1787, young John Quincy Adams lamented "this critical period" when the country was "groaning under the intolerable burden of . . . accumulated evils." More than a century later the popular writer and lecturer John Fiske used the same phrase, the "critical period," as the title for a history of the United States under the Articles of Confederation. For many years it was the fashion among historians to dwell upon the weaknesses of the Confederation and the "accumulated evils" of the time to the neglect of the major achievements.

The Congress of the Confederation, to be sure, had little if any more governmental authority than the United Nations would have 200 years later. "It could ask for money but not compel payment," as one historian wrote, "it could enter into treaties but not enforce their stipulations; it could provide for raising of armies but not fill the ranks; it could borrow money but take no proper measures for repayment; it could advise and recommend but not command." In foreign affairs and the domestic economy the Congress was virtually helpless to cope with problems of diplomacy and postwar depression which would have challenged the resources of a much stronger government. It was not easy to find men of stature to serve in such a body, and often hard to gather a quorum of those who did. Yet in spite of its handicaps the Confederation Congress somehow managed to keep afloat and to lay important foundations for the future. It concluded the Peace of Paris in 1783. It created the first executive departments. And it formulated principles of land distribution and territorial government which guided expansion ultimately all the way to the Pacific coast.

Throughout most of the War for Independence the Congress remained distrustful of executive power. It assigned administrative duties to its committees and thereby imposed an almost intolerable burden on conscientious members. At one time or another John Adams, for instance, served on some eighty committees. In 1781, however, anticipating ratification of the Articles of Confederation, Congress began to set up three departments: Foreign Affairs, Finance, and War, in addition to a Post Office Department which had existed since 1775. Each was to have a single head responsible to Congress. For superintendent of finance Congress chose Robert Morris, a prominent Philadelphia merchant who by virtue of his business connections and a talent for financial sleight-of-hand brought a semblance of order into the federal accounts. The other departments had less success to their credit, and indeed lacked executive heads for long periods. The first secretary for foreign affairs, Robert R. Livingston, left that post in May 1783 and was not replaced by John Jay until the following summer. Given enough time and stability, however, Congress and the department heads might have evolved something like the parliamentary cabinet system. As it turned out, these agencies were the beginnings of the government departments that came into being later under the Constitution.

FINANCE   But as yet there was neither president nor prime minister, only the presiding officer of Congress and its secretary, Charles Thomson, the "Sam Adams of Philadelphia," who served continuously from 1774 to 1789. The closest thing to an executive head of the Confederation was Robert Morris, who as superintendent of finance in the final years of the war became the most influential figure in the government, and who had ideas of making both himself and the Confederation more powerful. He envisioned a coherent program of taxation and debt management to make the government financially stable; "a public debt supported by public revenue will prove the strongest cement to keep our confederacy together," he confided to a friend. It would wed to the support of the federal government the powerful influence of the public creditors. Morris therefore welcomed the chance to enlarge the debt by issuing new securities in settlement of wartime claims. Because of the government's precarious finances, these securities brought only ten to fifteen cents on the dollar, but with a sounder treasury—certainly with a tax power

Robert Morris, the most influential figure in the Confederation government, in a portrait by Charles Willson Peale. [Independence National Historical Park Collection]

—they could be expected to rise in value, creating new capital with which to finance banks and economic development.

In 1781, as part of his overall plan, Morris secured a congressional charter for the Bank of North America, which would hold federal deposits, lend money to the government, and issue banknotes that would be a stable currency. A national bank, it was in part privately owned and was expected to turn a profit for Morris and other shareholders, in addition to performing a public service. But his program depended ultimately on a secure income for the government, and foundered on the requirement of unanimous approval for amendments to the Articles of Confederation. During the war he nearly got for Congress the power to levy a 5 percent import duty, but Rhode Island's refusal to ratify an amendment stood in the way. Once the war was over the spur of military need was gone. Local interests and the fear of a central authority—a fear strengthened by the recent quarrels with king and Parliament—hobbled action.

To carry their point, Morris and his nationalist friends in 1783 risked a dangerous gamble. Washington's army, encamped at Newburgh on the Hudson River, had grown restless in the final winter of the war. Their pay was in arrears as usual, and past experience gave them reason to fear that claims to bounties and life pensions for officers might never be honored once their services were no longer needed. In January 1783 a delegation of officers appeared in Philadelphia with a petition for redress. Soon they found themselves drawn into a scheme to line up the army and public creditors with nationalists in Congress and confront the states with the threat of a coup d'état unless they yielded more power to Congress. Horatio Gates and other high officers were drawn into the network and circulated an inflammatory address against any further "milk and water" petitions. Alexander Hamilton, congressman from New York and former aide to General Washington, sought to bring his old commander into the plan.

Washington sympathized with the purpose. If congressional powers were not enlarged, he had told a friend, "the band which at present holds us together, by a very feeble thread, will soon be broken, when anarchy and confusion must ensue." But Washington was just as deeply convinced that a military coup would be both dishonorable and dangerous. When he learned that some of the plotters had planned an unauthorized meeting of officers, he summoned a meeting first and confronted the issue. Drawing his spectacles from his pocket, he began: "I have grown not only gray but blind in the service of my country." When he had finished his dramatic and emotional address, his officers, with Gates in the chair, unanimously adopted resolutions denouncing the recent "infamous propositions" and the Newburgh Conspiracy came to a sudden end. By the middle of June all those who had enlisted for the duration were furloughed with three months' pay in the personal notes of Superintendent Morris, and Washington awaited the British evacuation of New York with a skeleton force serving time enlistments.

A body of Pennsylvania recruits provided a sorry aftermath to the quiet dispersal. Their pay in arrears, about eighty militiamen mutinied, marched from Lancaster to Philadelphia, and with reinforcements from regiments there, conducted a threatening demonstration in front of Independence Hall. When state authorities failed to provide a guard, for fear the militia would join the mutiny, the Congress after three days fled to Princeton, later adjourned to Annapolis, then Trenton, and in 1785 finally settled in New York. Moving from place to place, often unable to muster a quorum, the Congress struggled on with growing futility. An amendment to give Congress power to levy duties for twenty-five years, proposed in 1783, met the same fate as the previous amendment. In 1784 Morris resigned as superintendent of finance and a committee took charge once again.

The Confederation never did put its finances in order. The Continental currency had long since become a byword for worthlessness. It was never redeemed. The debt, domestic and foreign, grew from $11 million to $28 million as Congress paid off citizens' and soldiers' claims. Each year Congress ran a deficit on its operating expenses. Since the Confederation remained unable to pay off its securities, some of the states agreed to assume the burden of their citizens. They accepted in payment of taxes and imposts the indents (certificates) which Congress issued in lieu of interest payments—and Congress then took back the indents in payment of requisitions on the states, up to a fourth of the total amount due. Some of the states accepted federal securities in payment for state securities or for land. The foreign debt alone ran up to $11 million, but in spite of everything, Congress somehow managed to find the money to pay interest on loans from Dutch bankers and kept open a line of credit at least from that source.

LAND POLICY The one source from which Congress might hope ultimately to draw an independent income was the sale of western lands. But throughout the Confederation period that income remained more a fleeting promise of the future than an accomplished fact. The Confederation nevertheless dealt more effectively with the western lands than with anything else. There Congress had direct authority, at least on paper. Thinly popu-

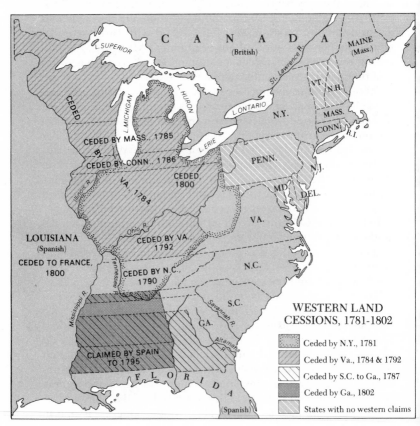

WESTERN LAND
CESSIONS, 1781-1802

Ceded by N.Y., 1781
Ceded by Va., 1784 & 1792
Ceded by S.C. to Ga., 1787
Ceded by Ga., 1802
States with no western claims

lated by Indians, Frenchmen, and a growing number of American squatters, the region north of the Ohio River had long been the site of overlapping claims by colonies and speculators. The Revolution itself had been brought on in no small part by disagreement over western lands and British feelings that the colonies should be taxed for their administration and defense. In 1784 Virginia's cession of lands north of the Ohio was complete, and by 1786 all states had abandoned their claims in the area except for a 120-mile strip along Lake Erie, which Connecticut held until 1800 as its "Western Reserve," in return for giving up its claims in the Wyoming Valley of Pennsylvania.

As early as 1779 Congress had made a basic commitment in principle not to pursue a colonial policy in the future national domain. The delegates resolved instead that western lands ceded by the states "shall be . . . formed into distinct Republican states," equal in all respects to other states. Between 1784 and 1787 policies for the development of the West emerged in three major ordinances of the Confederation Congress. These documents, which rank among its most positive achievements—and among the most important in American history—set precedents that the United States followed in its expansion all the way to the Pacific. Thomas Jefferson in fact was prepared to grant self-government from an early stage, when settlers would meet and choose their own officials. Under the ordinance of 1784, when the population equaled that of the smallest existing state the territory would achieve full statehood. Congress, however, rejected Jefferson's specific provision for ten future states with bizarre if melodious names like Assenisipia and Cherronesus, although three of the suggestions later turned up on the map with only slight alteration: Michigania, Illinoia, and Washington.

In the Land Ordinance of 1785 the delegates outlined a plan of land surveys and sales which would eventually stamp a rectangular pattern on much of the nation's surface, a pattern still visible from the air in many parts of the country because of the layout of roads and fields. Wherever Indian titles had been extinguished, the Northwest was to be surveyed into townships six miles square along east-west and north-south lines. Each township in turn was divided into 36 lots (or sections) one mile square (or 640 acres). The 640-acre sections were to go at auction for no less than $1 per acre or $640 total, and without provision for credit. Such terms favored land speculators, of course, since few dirt farmers had that much money or were able to cultivate that much land. In later years new land laws would make smaller plots available at lower prices, but in 1785 Congress was faced with an

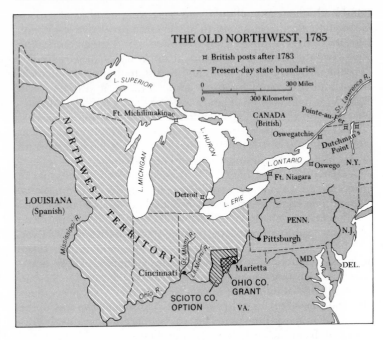

THE OLD NORTHWEST, 1785

¤ British posts after 1783
--- Present-day state boundaries

0   300 Miles
0   300 Kilometers

L. SUPERIOR

Ft. Michilimakinac ¤

NORTHWEST

L. MICHIGAN

L. HURON

CANADA
(British)

Pointe-au-Fer ¤

St. Lawrence R.

Oswegatchie ¤

Dutchman's
Point ¤

L. ONTARIO   ¤ Oswego   N.Y.

¤ Ft. Niagara

LOUISIANA
(Spanish)

TERRITORY

Detroit ¤

L. ERIE

PENN.

Mississippi R.

Gt. Miami R.

Lt. Miami R.

Pittsburgh

N.J.

Cincinnati

MD

DEL.

Marietta

OHIO CO.
GRANT

SCIOTO CO.
OPTION

Ohio R.

VA.

empty treasury. In each township, however, Congress did reserve the income from the sixteenth section for the support of schools—a significant departure at a time when public schools were rare.

In seven ranges to the west of the Ohio River, an area in which recent treaties had voided Indian titles, surveying began. But before any land sales occurred a group of speculators from New England presented Congress a seductive offer. Organized in Boston under the leadership of Gen. Samuel Parsons the group took the name of the Ohio Company and sent the Rev. Manasseh Cutler to present their plan. He proved a persuasive lobbyist, and in 1787 Congress voted a grant of 1.5 million acres for about $1 million in certificates of indebtedness to Revolutionary War veterans. The arrangement had the dual merit, Cutler argued, of reducing the debt and encouraging new settlement and sales. Further, to ensure passage the lobbyist cut in several congressmen on another deal, the Scioto Company, which got an option on 5 million acres more. In April 1788 the Ohio Company's first settlers floated downstream from Pittsburgh on a flatboat aptly named the *May-flower* and established Marietta. The Scioto Company never took up its option, but that did not prevent its

European agent, the poet Joel Barlow, from selling lands it did not own—with the help of an Englishman named, of all things, Playfair! In 1790 several hundred French settlers arrived only to find that they had no title to the lands they had supposedly bought. A sympathetic Congress relieved their distress by voting them a grant of land. In 1788 a New Jersey speculator named John Cleves Symmes got an option on lands between the Great and the Little Miami Rivers and soon had Cincinnati and several other villages under way.

A TOWNSHIP IN THE OLD NORTHWEST

6	5	4	3	2	1
7	8	9	Income reserved for school support		
18	17	16	15	14	13
19	20	21	22	23	24
30	29	28	27	26	25
31	32	33	34	35	36

Numbering system adopted in 1796

A township is 36 square miles

A section is 1 square mile (640 acres)

THE NORTHWEST ORDINANCE   Spurred by the plans for land sales and settlement, Congress drafted a new and more specific frame of territorial government to replace Jefferson's ordinance of 1784. The new plan backed off from Jefferson's recommendation of early self-government. Because of the trouble that might be expected from squatters who were clamoring for free land, the Northwest Ordinance of 1787 required a period of colonial tutelage. At first the territory fell subject to a governor, a secretary, and three judges, all chosen by Congress. Eventually there would be three to five territories in the region, and when any one had 5,000 free male adults it could choose an assembly and Congress would name a council of five from ten names proposed by the assembly. The governor, named by the central authority, would have a veto and so would Congress. The resemblance to the old royal colonies is clear, but there were two significant differences. For one, the Ordinance anticipated statehood when any territory's population reached 60,000. For another, it included a bill of rights which guaranteed religious freedom, representation in proportion to population, trial by jury, habeas corpus, and the application of common law. And finally, the Ordinance excluded slavery permanently from the Northwest—a proviso Jefferson had failed to get accepted in his Ordinance of 1784. This proved a fateful decision. As the progress of emancipation in the existing states gradually freed all slaves above the Mason-Dixon line, the Ohio River boundary of the Old Northwest extended the line between freedom and slavery all the way to the Mississippi.

In the lands south of the Ohio River a different line of development occurred. Title to the western lands remained with Georgia, North Carolina, and Virginia for the time being, but settlement proceeded at a far more rapid pace during and after the Revolution, despite the Indians' fierce resentment of encroachments on their hunting grounds. Substantial centers of population grew up around Harrodsburg and Boonesboro in the Kentucky Blue Grass and along the Watauga, Holston, and Cumberland Rivers, as far west as Nashborough (Nashville). In the Southwest active movements for statehood arose early. North Carolina tentatively ceded its western claims in 1784, whereupon the Holston settlers formed the short-lived state of Franklin, which became little more than a bone of contention between rival speculators until North Carolina reasserted control in 1789, shortly before the cession of its western lands became final.

Indian claims too were being extinguished. The Iroquois and Cherokees, badly battered during the Revolution, were in no position to resist encroachments. By the Treaty of Fort Stanwix (1784) the Iroquois were forced to cede land in western New York and Pennsylvania. In the Treaty of Hopewell (1785) the Cherokees gave up all claims in South Carolina, much of western North Carolina, and large portions of present-day Kentucky and Tennessee. Also in 1785 the major Ohio tribes gave up their claim to most of Ohio, except for a chunk bordering the western part of Lake Erie. The Creeks, pressed by the state of Georgia to cede portions of their lands in 1784–1785, went to war in the summer of 1786 with covert aid from Spanish Florida. But when Spanish aid diminished, the Creek chief Alexander McGillivray traveled to New York and in 1791 finally struck a bargain which gave the Creeks favorable trade arrangements with the United States, but did not restore the lost lands.

TRADE AND THE ECONOMY   In its economic life, as in planning westward expansion, the young nation dealt with difficult problems vigorously. Congress had little to do with achievements in the economy but neither could it bear the blame for a depression that wracked the country for several years during the transition to independence, the result of the war and separation from the British Empire. In New England and much of the backcountry fighting seldom interrupted the tempo of farming, and the producers of foodstuffs especially benefited from rising prices and wartime demands. The southern Tidewater suffered a loss of slave labor, much of it carried off by the British. Returns from indigo and naval stores declined with the loss of British bounties, but in the long run rice and tobacco benefited from an enlarged foreign market for their products.

Merchants suffered far more wrenching adjustments than the farmers. Cut out of the British mercantile system, they had to find new outlets for their trade. Circumstances that impoverished some enriched those who financed privateers, supplied the armies on both sides, and hoarded precious goods while demand and prices soared. By the end of the war a strong sentiment for free trade had developed in both Britain and America. In the memorable year 1776 the Scottish economist Adam Smith brought out *The Wealth of Nations*, a classic manifesto against mercantilism. Some British statesmen embraced the new gospel, but the public and Parliament still clung to the conventional wisdom of mercantilism for many years to come.

British trade with America did resume, and American ships were allowed to deliver American products and return to the United States with British goods. American ships could not carry British goods anywhere else, however. The pent-up demand for familiar goods created a bull market in exports to America, fueled by British credits and the hard money that had come into America from foreign aid, the expenditures of foreign armies, or wartime trade and privateering. The result was a quick cycle of boom and bust, a buying spree followed by a currency shortage and economic troubles that lasted several years.

In colonial days the chronic deficit in trade with Britain could be offset by the influx of coins from trade with the West Indies. Now American ships found themselves excluded altogether from the British West Indies, and therefore from the old triangular trades. But the islands still demanded wheat, fish, lumber, and other products from the mainland, and American shippers had not lost their talent for smuggling, at which the islanders connived. Already American shippers had begun exploring new outlets, and by 1787 their seaports were flourishing more than ever. Freed from the old colonial restraints, they now had the run of the seven seas. Trade treaties opened new markets with the Dutch (1782), Swedes (1783), Prussians (1785), and Moroccans (1787), and American shippers found new outlets on their own in Europe, Africa, and Asia. The most spectacular new development, if not the largest, was trade with China. It began in 1784–1785, when the *Empress of China* sailed from New York to Canton and back, around the tip of South America. Profits from its cargo of silks and tea encouraged the outfitting of other ships which carried ginseng root and other American goods to exchange for the luxury goods of the Orient.

The dislocations in trade and the need for readjustment, one historian noted, "produced bitter complaints in the newspapers and led to extravagant charges against both state and central governments, but in no case do the records of imports and exports and ship tonnages bear out the cries of havoc." By 1790 American commerce and exports had far out run the trade of the colonies. American merchants had more ships than before the war. Agricultural exports were twice what they had been. Although most of the exports were the products of American forests, fields, and fisheries, during and after the war more Americans had turned to small-scale manufacturing, mainly for domestic markets. By 1787, when Tench Coxe of Philadelphia, a promoter of manufactures, set out to summarize major American enterprises, he ended with dozens of products from ships and ironwork to shoes, textiles, and soap.

DIPLOMACY   The achievements of the flourishing young nation are more visible in hindsight than they were at the time. Until 1787 the shortcomings and failures remained far more apparent —and the advocates of a stronger central government were extremely vocal on the subject. In diplomacy, despite the achievement of trade treaties by 1787 with France, Holland, Sweden, Prussia, and Morocco, there remained the nagging problems of relations with Great Britain and Spain, both of which still kept posts on United States soil and intrigued with Indians and white settlers in the West. The British, despite the peace treaty of 1783, held on to a string of forts from Lake Champlain to Michilimackinac. From these they kept a hand in the fur trade and a degree of influence with the Indian tribes whom they were suspected of stirring up to make sporadic attacks on the frontier. They gave as a reason for their continued occupation the failure of Americans to pay their debts, conveniently ignoring the point that the peace treaty had included only a face-saving gesture which committed Congress to recommend that the states place no legal impediment in the way of their collection. Impediments continued, nonetheless. A common question in Virginia, George Mason said, was: "If we are now to pay the debts due to British merchants, what have we been fighting for all this while?"

Another major irritant was the confiscation of Loyalist property. Under the peace treaty Congress was obligated to stop persecutions, to guarantee immunity for twelve months during which Loyalists could return and wind up their affairs, and to recommend that the states return confiscated property. Persecutions, even lynchings, of Loyalists still occurred until after the end of the war. Some Loyalists returned unmolested, however, and once again took up their lives in their former homes. By the end of 1787, moreover, all the states at the request of Congress had rescinded the laws that were in conflict with the peace treaty.

The British refused even to dispatch an ambassador to the new nation before 1791. As early as 1785, however, the United States took the initiative by sending over that confirmed rebel, John Adams, as ambassador to the Court of St. James's. He was politely received by George III himself, but spent three years in futile efforts to settle the points at issue: mainly the forts, debts, and the property rights of Loyalists. Unknown to Adams the British even toyed with the idea of annexing Vermont through intrigues with the Allen brothers, Ethan and Levi. The area, claimed by New Hampshire, had been awarded by the Privy Council to New York, but the influential Allen brothers, with large land claims at stake, ignored the ruling, then took the lead in organizing the state of Vermont in 1777. When Congress refused to recognize Vermont for fear of offending New York, the Allens began dickering with the British. Eventually, however, nothing came of it all. New York gave up its claim in 1790 and Vermont became the fourteenth state in 1791.

With Spain the chief points at issue were the southern boundary and the right to navigate the Mississippi. According to the preliminary treaty with Britain the United States claimed a line as far south as the Thirty-first Parallel; Spain held out for the line running eastward from the mouth of the Yazoo River (at 32° 22′ N), which she claimed as the traditional boundary—and which would have been the boundary if Britain had retained Florida. Spanish forces, which had taken Natchez from the British during the war, continued to occupy that town in territory claimed by the United States. The American treaty with Britain had also specified the right to navigate the Mississippi River to its mouth, but the international boundary ran down the middle of the river most of its length and the river was entirely within Spanish Louisiana in its lower reaches. The right to navigation was a matter of importance because of the growing settlements in Kentucky and Tennessee, but in 1784 Louisiana's Governor Miro closed the river to American commerce and began to intrigue with the Creeks, Choctaws, Chickasaws, and other Indians of the Southwest against the frontiersmen, and with the frontiersmen against the United States. Gen. James Wilkinson, a Kentucky land speculator, further enriched himself with Spanish gold in return for promises to conspire for secession of the West and perhaps its annexation by Spain. But Wilkinson was a professional slyboots, with an instinct for trouble, whose loyalties ran mainly to his own pocketbook. And he was not the only man on the make who was double-dealing with the Spaniards.

In 1785 the Spanish government sent as its ambassador to the United States Don Diego de Gardoqui, whose father's trading company had been the front for Spanish aid during the Revolution. Gardoqui entered into lengthy but fruitless negotiations with John Jay, the secretary for foreign affairs, whom he had first met in Madrid during the war. Jay had instructions to get free navigation of the Mississippi and the Spanish acceptance of the 31° boundary; Gardoqui had instructions not to give them. But he did ply Jay and his wife with gifts and flattery. Finally, in hope of getting trade concessions from Spain, Jay sought permission from Congress to give up navigation of the Mississippi—an idea planted by Gardoqui in the knowledge that it would be divisive. It was granted, but only by a vote of seven to five, with the southern states holding out against such a sacrifice in the interest of northern merchants. Since the ratification of a treaty required the vote of nine states, the negotiations collapsed and the issues remained unsettled for nearly another decade.

THE CONFEDERATION'S PROBLEMS   The problems of trans-Appalachian settlers, however, seemed remote from the everyday concerns of most Americans. What touched them more closely were the economic dislocations and the currency shortage. Merchants who found themselves excluded from old channels of imperial trade began to agitate for reprisals. State governments, in response, laid special tonnage duties on British vessels and special tariffs on the goods they brought. But state action alone failed to work for want of uniformity. British ships could be diverted to states whose duties were less restrictive. Efforts to meet this problem by taxing British goods that flowed across state lines created an impression that states were involved in commercial

*A North Carolina hundred-dollar bill (1778).
Rampant inflation during the Revolution reduced
the value of paper money, creating economic
problems the Confederation could not solve.
[American Antiquarian Society]*

war with each other, although the duties seldom affected American goods. The need, it seemed to commercial interests, was for a central power to regulate trade. In 1784 Congress proposed to amend the Articles of Confederation so as to permit uniform navigation acts, but Rhode Island and North Carolina objected. The amendment, like all others, failed of ratification—not for want of support but for want of unanimity.

Mechanics and artisans who were developing an infant industry with products ranging from crude iron nails to the fine silver bowls of Paul Revere wanted to go further, to take reprisals against British goods as well as British ships. They sought, and in various degrees obtained from the states, tariffs against foreign goods that competed with theirs. The country would be on its way to economic independence, they argued, if only the specie that flowed into the country had been invested in domestic manufactures instead of being paid out for foreign goods. Nearly all the states gave some preference to American goods, but again the lack of uniformity in their laws put them at cross purposes, and so urban mechanics along with merchants were drawn into the movement for a stronger central government in the interest of uniform regulation.

The shortage of cash gave rise also to some more immediate demands for paper currency as legal tender, for postponement of tax and debt payments, for laws to "stay" the foreclosure of mortgages. Farmers, who had profited during the war, found themselves squeezed by depression and mounting debts while merchants sorted out and opened up their new trade routes. Creditors demanded hard money, but specie was in short supply —and paper money was almost nonexistent after the depreciation of the Continental currency. The result was an outcry for relief, and around 1785 the demand for paper money became the most divisive issue in state politics. Debtors demanded it, and in some cases, most notably South Carolina, merchants supported it because in that state they could use the paper but did not have to take it in payment of old debts. In Pennsylvania public creditors demanded paper as a device to collect their claims against the state. Paper, they reasoned, was better than nothing. Creditors elsewhere generally opposed such action, however, because it was likely to mean payment in a depreciated currency.

In 1785–1786, seven states provided for issues of paper money. In spite of the cries of calamity at the time the money never seriously depreciated in Pennsylvania, New York, and South Carolina. It served in five states—Pennsylvania, New York, New Jersey, South Carolina, and Rhode Island—as a means of credit to hard-pressed farmers through state loans on farm mortgages. It was variously used to fund state debts and to pay off the claims of veterans. North Carolina used some of it to buy tobacco for sale abroad to raise specie, but in that case swindlers bilked the state with overpriced leaf and collected veterans' claims with forged certificates.

Sharp depreciation finally discredited the issue in the Tar Heel state, which was second in notoriety only to Rhode Island, where the debtor party ran wild. In 1786 the Rhode Island legislature issued £100,000 in paper, the largest issue of any state in proportion to population, and declared it legal tender in payment of all debts. Creditors fled the state to avoid being paid in worthless paper, merchants closed their doors while mobs rioted against them, and a "forcing act" denied trial by jury and levied fines against anyone who refused to take the money at face value. Eventually a test case reached the state's supreme court, and in *Trevett v. Weeden* (1787) the court ruled the law unconstitutional. The case stands as a landmark, the first in which a court exercised the doctrine of judicial review in holding a state law unconstitutional. The forcing act was then repealed and the legal tender clause finally repealed in 1789.

SHAYS'S REBELLION Newspapers throughout the country ran accounts of developments in Rhode Island, and that little common-

Daniel Shays and Job Shattuck, leaders of the revolt of western Massachusetts farmers against tax and debt policy (1787). [National Portrait Gallery, Smithsonian Institution]

wealth, stubbornly cross-grained since the days of Roger Williams, became the prime example of democracy run riot—until its hotspur neighbor, Massachusetts, provided the final proof (some said) that the country was poised on the brink of anarchy: Shays's Rebellion. There the trouble was not too much paper money but too little, and too much taxation. After 1780 Massachusetts had remained in the grip of a rigidly conservative regime. Ever-larger poll and land taxes were levied to pay off a heavy debt, held mainly by wealthy creditors in Boston, and the taxes fell most heavily upon beleaguered farmers and the poor in general. When the legislature adjourned in 1786 without providing either paper money or any other relief from taxes and debts, three western counties erupted into spontaneous revolt. Armed bands closed the courts and prevented foreclosures, and a tatterdemalion "army" under Daniel Shays, a destitute farmer and war veteran, advanced upon the federal arsenal at Springfield in January 1787.

A small militia force, however, scattered the approaching army with a single volley of artillery which left four dead. Gen. Benjamin Lincoln, arriving soon after with reinforcements from Boston, routed the remaining Shaysites at Petersham. The Shaysites nevertheless had a victory of sorts. The state legislature omitted direct taxes the following year, lowered court fees, and exempted clothing, household goods, and tools from the debt process. But a more important consequence was the impetus the rebellion gave to conservatism and nationalism.

Rumors, at times deliberately inflated, blew up out of all proportion a pathetic rebellion of desperate men. The rebels were linked to the conniving British and accused of seeking to pillage the wealthy. What was more, the rebellion set an ominous example. "There are combustibles in every State," Washington wrote, "which a spark might set fire to." Of the disorders he asked: "Good God! Who, besides a Tory, could have foreseen, or a Briton predicted them?" The answer, of course, was nearly every political philosopher of the Whig or Enlightened persuasion who was dear to the men of the Revolution. Anarchy, they taught, was the nemesis of republics, mob rule the sequel to unchecked democracy. Shays therefore was the harbinger of greater evils to come unless the course of events were altered. Not that all the leaders of the time agreed. Jefferson was, if anything, too complacent. From his post in Paris, where one of history's great bloodbaths would soon take place, he wrote to a friend back home: "The tree of liberty must be refreshed from time to time with the blood of patriots and tyrants."

CALLS FOR A STRONGER GOVERNMENT   The advocates of a stronger central authority already had gained momentum from the adversities of the times. Public creditors, merchants, and mechanics had a self-interest in a stronger central government, and many public-spirited men saw it as the only alternative to anarchy. Gradually they were breaking down the ingrained fear of a tyrannical central authority with the evidence that tyranny might come from other quarters. And one thing readers of another century must remember, conditioned as we are to see potential conflict between human rights and property rights, is that the American of the eighteenth century considered the security of property to be the foundation stone of liberty. What the eighteenth-century American might forget, however, was that the Shaysites were fighting in defense of their property too.

Already, well before the outbreaks in New England, the nationalist movement had come to demand a convention to revise the Articles of Confederation. Such a convention had been the subject of fruitless discussions in Congress, initiated by Charles Pinckney of South Carolina, but the initiative finally came from an unexpected quarter. In March 1785 commissioners from the states of Virginia and Maryland had met at Mount Vernon upon Washington's invitation to settle outstanding questions about the navigation of the Potomac and Chesapeake Bay. Washington had a personal interest in the river flowing by his door: it was a potential route to the West, with its upper reaches close to the upper reaches of the Ohio, where his military career had begun thirty years before. The delegates agreed on interstate cooperation, and Maryland suggested a further pact with Pennsylvania and Delaware to encourage water communication between the Chesapeake and the Ohio River; the Virginia legislature agreed, and at Madison's suggestion invited all thirteen states to send delegates for a general discussion of commercial problems. Nine states named representatives, but those from only five appeared at the Annapolis Convention in September 1786—Maryland itself failed to name delegates and neither the New England states nor the Carolinas and Georgia were represented. Apparent failure was turned into success, however, by the alert Alexander Hamilton, representing New York, who presented a resolution for still another convention in Philadelphia to consider all measures necessary "to render the constitution of the Federal Government adequate to the exigencies of the Union."

ADOPTING THE CONSTITUTION

THE CONSTITUTIONAL CONVENTION After stalling for several months Congress fell in line on February 21, 1787, with a resolution endorsing as "expedient" a convention "for the sole and express purpose of revising the Articles of Confederation." By then five states had already named delegates; before the meeting six more states had acted. New Hampshire delayed until June and its delegates arrived in July. Independent-minded Rhode Island kept aloof throughout. On the appointed date (May 14, 1787) only the delegates from Pennsylvania and Virginia were present, but twenty-nine delegates from nine states began work on May 25. Altogether seventy-three men were elected by the state legislatures, fifty-five attended at one time or another, and after four months thirty-nine signed the Constitution they had drafted.

The durability and flexibility of that document testify to the remarkable quality of the men who made it, an assembly of "demi-gods" according to Jefferson, who was himself absent as a diplomat in France. They were surprisingly young: forty-two was the average age, although they ranged from the twenty-seven-year-old Jonathan Dayton of New Jersey to the eighty-one-year-old Benjamin Franklin, president of the state of Pennsylvania. They were even more surprisingly mature and foresighted: many of them were widely read in history, law, and political philosophy, familiar with the writings of Vattel, Locke, and Montesquieu, aware of the confederacies of the ancient world, and at the same time practical men of experience, tested in the fires of the Revolution. "Experience must be our only guide," John Dickinson said. "Reason may mislead us." Washington and

James Madison was only thirty-six when he assumed a major role in the drafting of the Constitution. This miniature is by Charles Willson Peale (c. 1783). [Library of Congress]

Franklin were the most famous of them at the time, and both, especially Washington, lent prestige and inspired confidence. More active in the debates were James Madison, the ablest political philosopher in the group; George Mason, author of the Virginia Bill of Rights; the witty and eloquent Gouverneur Morris and James Wilson of Pennsylvania, the latter one of the ablest lawyers in the colonies and next in importance in the convention only to Washington and Madison; Roger Sherman of Connecticut; and Elbridge Gerry of Massachusetts. Conspicuous by their absence were John Adams and Thomas Jefferson, then serving in London and Paris, and during most of the convention, Alexander Hamilton, since he could not vote once his two states'-rights colleagues from New York had gone home for good.

The delegates' differences on political philosophy for the most part fell within a narrow range. On certain fundamentals they generally agreed: that government derived its just powers from the consent of the people, but that society must be protected from the tyranny of the majority; that the people at large must have a voice in their government, but that checks and balances must be provided to keep any one group from arrogating power; that a stronger central authority was essential, but that all political power was easily subject to abuse. They believed that even the best of men were selfish by nature, and they harbored few illusions that government could be founded altogether upon a trust in goodwill and virtue. Since governments existed to restrain men, James Madison said, their very existence was "a reflection upon human nature." Yet by a careful arrangement of checks and balances, by checking power with power, the Founding Fathers hoped to devise institutions that could somehow constrain the sinfulness of individuals.

THE VIRGINIA AND NEW JERSEY PLANS   At the outset the delegates made Washington their president by unanimous vote, and William Jackson their secretary. One of the first decisions was to meet behind closed doors, in order to discourage outside pressures and speeches to the galleries. The secrecy of the proceedings was remarkably well kept, and since Jackson's journal was a skeleton record of motions and votes, knowledge of the debates comes mainly from extensive notes kept by James Madison. It was Madison, too, who drafted the proposals which set the framework of the discussions. These proposals, which came to be called the "Virginia Plan," were presented on May 29 by Edmund Randolph, governor of the state and delegate to the convention. The Virginia plan embodied a revolutionary proposal for the delegates to scrap their instructions to revise the Articles of Confederation and to submit an entirely new document to the states. The plan proposed separate legislative, executive, and judicial branches, and a truly national government to make laws binding upon individual citizens and to coerce states as well. Congress would be divided into two houses, a lower house chosen by popular vote and an upper house chosen by the lower house from nominees of the state legislatures. Congress could disallow state laws under the plan and would itself define the extent of its and the states' authority.

On June 15 William Paterson submitted the alternative New Jersey or small-state plan, which proposed to keep the existing structure of Congress, but to give it power to levy taxes and regulate commerce and authority to name a plural executive (with no veto) and a Supreme Court. The different plans presented the convention with two major issues: whether to amend the Articles or draft a new document, and whether to have congressional representation by states or by population. On the first point the Convention voted, June 19, to work toward a national government as envisioned by the Virginians. On the powers of this government there was little disagreement save in detail. Experience with the Articles had persuaded the delegates that an effective government, as distinguished from a confederation, needed the power to levy taxes, to regulate commerce, to raise an army and navy, and to make laws binding upon individual citizens. The lessons of the 1780s suggested to them, moreover, that in the interest of order and uniformity the states must be denied certain powers: to issue money, to abrogate contracts, to make treaties or wage war, to levy tariffs or export duties.

Disagreement then turned less on philosophy than on geography. The first clash in the convention involved the issue of representation. Delegates from the larger states generally favored the Virginia plan, which would give them greater representation; those from the smaller states rallied behind the New Jersey plan, which would preserve an equal vote to each state. In hindsight the issue was a false one, since differing interests have seldom ranged the states into blocs according to size, but at the time it was the most divisive single question to rise in the convention and one that might have wrecked the whole enterprise had it not been resolved. The solution was the "Great Compromise," sometimes called the "Connecticut Compromise," proposed by Roger Sherman, which gave both groups their way. The larger states won apportionment by population in the House of Representatives; the smaller states got equality in the Senate, but with the vote there by individuals and not by states.

Geographic division cut another way in a struggle between northern and southern delegates which turned upon slavery and the regulation of trade, an omen of sectional controversies to come in future years. Southerners, with slaves so numerous in their states, wanted them counted as part of the population in determining the number of their representatives. Northerners were happy enough to have slaves counted in deciding each state's share of direct taxes but not for purposes of representation. On this issue the Confederation Congress had supplied a handy precedent when it sought an amendment to make population rather than land values the standard for requisitions. The proposed amendment to the Articles would have counted three-fifths of the slaves. The delegates, with little dissent, agreed to incorporate the same three-fifths ratio in the new Constitution as a basis for apportioning both representatives and direct taxes. A more sensitive issue was presented by an effort to prevent the central government from stopping the foreign slave trade. Again, since slavery had not yet become the overriding issue it later became, the question was fairly readily settled by establishing a time limit. "The morality or wisdom of slavery," said Oliver Ellsworth of Connecticut, "are considerations belonging to the states themselves." Congress could not forbid the foreign slave trade before 1808, but could levy a tax of $10 a head on all slaves imported. In both provisions, a sense of delicacy dictated the use of euphemisms. The Constitution spoke of "free Persons" and "all other persons," of "such persons as any of the States Now existing shall think proper to admit," and of persons "held to Service of Labor." The odious word "slavery" did not appear in the Constitution until the Thirteenth Amendment (1865) abolished the "peculiar institution" by name.

The final decision on the slave trade was linked to a compromise on the question of the broader congressional power to regulate commerce. Northern states, where the merchant and shipping interests were most influential, were prepared to give Congress unlimited powers, but the southerners feared that navigation acts favoring American shipping might work at the expense of getting southern commodities to the market by reducing foreign competition with northern shippers. Southerners therefore demanded that navigation acts be passed only by a two-thirds vote, but finally traded this demand for a prohibition on congressional power to levy export taxes and for a twenty-year, instead of a ten-year, delay on power to prohibit the slave trade.

THE SEPARATION OF POWERS   Their essential agreement on the need for a new frame of government kept the delegates from lapsing into quarelling factions: they were determined to seek accommodation. The details of governmental structure, while causing disagreement, occasioned far less trouble than the basic issues pitting the large and small states, the northern and southern states. Existing state constitutions, and the convention's resolve to disperse power with checks and balances, encouraged a consensus on the separation of powers among legislative, executive, and judicial branches. The American version of checks and

Signing the Constitution, September 17, 1787. *Thomas Pritchard Rossiter's painting shows George Washington presiding over what Thomas Jefferson called "an assembly of demi-gods." [Independence National Historical Park Collection]*

balances did not correspond to the old Whig model which separated powers among British commons, lords, and king, since Americans had neither lords nor a king—and the new document would specifically forbid titles of nobility—but there were parallels. The Founding Fathers expected the lower house to be closest to the people from whom they rose by election every two years. The upper house, chosen by state legislatures, was at one remove from the voters. Staggered terms of six years further isolated senators from the passing fancies of public passion by preventing the choice of a majority in any given year. Senators were expected to be, if not an American House of Lords, at least something like the colonial councils, a body of dignitaries advising the president as the councils had advised the governors.

And the president was to be an almost kingly figure. He was subject to election every four years, but his executive powers corresponded to those which British theory still extended to the king; in practice his powers actually exceeded the monarch's powers. This was the sharpest departure from the recent experience in state government, where the office of governor had commonly been downgraded because of the recent memory of struggles with the colonial executives. The president had a veto over acts of Congress, subject to being overridden by a two-thirds vote in each house, although the royal veto had long since fallen into complete disuse. He was commander-in-chief of the armed forces, and responsible for the execution of the laws. He could make treaties with the advice and consent of two-thirds of the Senate. He had power to appoint diplomats, judges, and other officers with the consent of a Senate majority. He was instructed to report annually on the state of the nation and was authorized to recommend legislation, a provision which presidents eventually would take as a mandate to form and promote extensive programs. Unlike the king, however, he could be removed for cause, by action short of revolution. The House could impeach (indict) him—and other civil officers—on charges of treason, bribery, or "other high crimes and misdemeanors," and the Senate could remove him by a two-thirds vote upon conviction. The presiding officer at the trial of a president would be the chief justice, since the usual presiding officer of the Senate (the vice-president) would have a personal stake in the outcome.

The convention's nationalists—men like Madison, James Wilson, and Hamilton—wanted to strengthen the independence of the executive by entrusting the choice to popular election. At least in this instance the nationalists, often accused of being the aristocratic party, favored a bold new departure in democracy.

But an elected executive was still too far beyond the American experience. Besides, a national election would have created enormous problems of organization and voter qualification. Wilson suggested instead that the people of each state choose presidential electors equal to the number of their senators and representatives. Others proposed that the legislators make the choice. Finally, late in the convention, it was voted to let the legislature decide the method in each state. Before long nearly all the states were choosing the electors by popular vote, and the electors were acting as agents of party will, casting their votes as they had pledged before the election. This method was contrary to the original expectation that the electors would deliberate and make their own choices.

On the third branch of government, the judiciary, there was surprisingly little debate. Both the Virginia and New Jersey plans had called for a Supreme Court, which the Constitution established, providing specifically for a chief justice of the United States and leaving up to Congress the number of other justices. The only dispute was on courts "inferior" to the Supreme Court, and that too was left up to Congress. Although the Constitution nowhere authorized the courts to declare laws void when they conflicted with the Constitution, the power of judicial review was almost surely intended by the framers, and was soon exercised in cases involving both state and federal laws. Article VI declared the federal constitution, federal laws, and treaties to be the "supreme law of the land," state laws or constitutions to the contrary notwithstanding. At the time the advocates of states' rights thought this a victory, since it eliminated the proviso in the Virginia plan for Congress to settle all conflicts with state authority. As it turned out the clause became the basis for an important expansion of judicial review.

While the Constitution extended vast new powers to the national government, the delegates' mistrust of unchecked power is apparent in repeated examples of countervailing forces: the separation of the three branches of government, the president's veto, the congressional power of impeachment and removal, the Senate's power over treaties and appointments, the courts' implied right of judicial review. In addition the new frame of government reserved to the states large areas of undivided sovereignty—a reservation soon made explicit by amendment —and specifically forbade Congress to pass bills of attainder (legislative acts depriving persons of property) or ex post facto laws (laws adopted after the event to make past deeds criminal).

The most glaring defect of the Articles of Confederation, the rule of unanimity which defeated every effort to amend them, led the delegates to provide a less forbidding though still difficult method of amending the new Constitution. Amendments could be proposed either by two-thirds vote of each house or by a convention especially called upon application of two-thirds of the legislatures. Amendments could be ratified by approval of three-fourths of the states acting through their legislatures or special conventions. The national convention has never been used, however, and state conventions have been called only once—to ratify the repeal of the Eighteenth Amendment (the Prohibition amendment).

THE FIGHT FOR RATIFICATION The old rule of unanimity, if applied to ratification of the Constitution itself, would almost surely have doomed its chances at the outset. The final article of the original Constitution therefore provided that it would become effective upon ratification by nine states (not quite the three-fourths majority required for amendment). Conventions were specified as the proper agency for ratification, since legislatures might be expected to boggle at giving up any of their powers. The procedure, insofar as it bypassed the existing Articles of Confederation, constituted a legal revolution, but it was one in which the Confederation Congress joined. After fighting off efforts to censure the convention for exceeding its authority, the Congress submitted its work to the states on September 28, 1787.

The first nationwide political struggle of United States history, or rather thirteen separate struggles over the same issue, began in the fall of 1787. Advocates of the new Constitution, who might properly have been called Nationalists, assumed the more reassuring name of Federalists. Opponents, who really favored more of a federal system, became Antifederalists. The initiative which the Federalists took in assuming their name was characteristic of the whole campaign. They got the jump on their critics. Their leaders, who had been members of the convention, were already familiar with the document and the arguments on each point. They were not only better prepared but better organized, and on the whole, made up of the more articulate elements in the community.

Much ink has been spilled by historians in debating the motivation of the advocates of the new Constitution. For more than a century the tendency prevailed to idolize the Founding Fathers who created what the nineteenth-century British statesman William Gladstone called "the most wonderful work ever struck off

at a given time by the brain and purpose of man." In 1913, however, Charles A. Beard's book *An Economic Interpretation of the
Constitution* advanced the amazing thesis that the Philadelphia
"assembly of demi-gods" was made up of humans who had a selfish interest in the outcome. They held large amounts of depreciated government securities and otherwise stood to gain from
the power and stability of the new order.

Beard argued that the delegates represented an economic
elite of those who held mainly "personalty" against those who
held mainly "realty." The first group was an upper crust of lawyers, merchants, speculators in western lands, holders of depreciated government securities, and creditors generally whose
wealth was mostly in "paper": mortgages, stocks, bonds, and the
like. The second group consisted of small farmers and planters
whose wealth was mostly in land and slaves. The holders of western lands and government bonds stood to gain from a stronger
government. Creditors generally stood to gain from the prohibitions against state currency issues and against the impairment of
contract, provisions clearly aimed at the paper money issues and
stay laws (granting stays, or postponements, on debt payments)
then effective in many states.

Beard's thesis was a useful antidote to hero worship, and still
contains a germ of truth, but he rested his argument too heavily
on the claim that holders of personalty predominated in the convention. Most of the delegates, according to evidence unavail-
able to Beard, had no compelling stake in paper wealth, and most
were far more involved in landholding. After doing exhaustive
research into the actual holdings of the Founding Fathers, the
historian Forrest McDonald announced in his book *We the People: The Economic Origins of the Constitution* that Beard's "economic interpretation of the Constitution does not work." Many
prominent nationalists, including the "Father of the Constitution," James Madison himself, had no bonds, western lands, or
much other personalty. Some opponents of the Constitution, on
the other hand, held large blocks of personalty. McDonald did
not deny that economic interests figured in the process, but they
functioned in a complex interplay of state, sectional, group, and
individual interests which turned largely on how well people had
fared under the Confederation.

There is evidence, however, in the voting and in the makeup
of the ratifying conventions of divisions between "localist" and
"cosmopolitan" elements, as the historian Jackson T. Main labeled them, who held to opposing worldviews because of their
contrasting experiences. The localist tended to be a person "of

narrow horizons—most often rural and sparsely educated—
whose experience is limited to his own neighborhood," whereas
the cosmopolitan was a person "of broad outlook, usually urban,
urbane, and well-educated, who has traveled widely and has had
extensive contacts with the world because of his occupation, the
offices he has held, or his interests."

A large proportion of the localists were, to be sure, small
farmers, but their leaders were often men of substance who were
temperamentally or ideologically opposed to centralization.
Two decades before Beard's interpretation appeared, the historian O. G. Libby had mapped out the vote on ratification state by
state and had observed that a line drawn fifty miles inland from
Maine to Georgia would separate "pretty accurately" the Federalist tidewater from the Antifederalist interior. In general the
idea works. Small farmers and frontiersmen saw little to gain
from the promotion of interstate commerce and much to lose
from prohibitions on paper money and stay laws, and many of

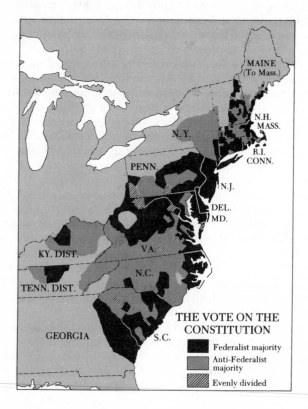

THE VOTE ON THE
CONSTITUTION

- ■ Federalist majority
- ▨ Anti-Federalist majority
- ▨ Evenly divided

them feared that an expansive land policy was likely to favor speculators.

There were, however, some notable exceptions. Some farmers in New Hampshire and western Massachusetts, for instance, felt they had an interest in promoting interstate commerce up and down the Connecticut River. In Virginia the Shenandoah Valley, running northeastward, encouraged strong ties with Maryland and Pennsylvania. Some parts of the frontier looked to a stronger government for defense against Indians: in the state of Georgia, for instance, fear of the Creek Indians motivated unanimous ratification by a state convention eager to promote a stronger central government—which, as it turned out, soon reached an understanding with the Creeks.

Charles A. Beard hardly made a new discovery in finding that people are selfish, but it would be simplistic to attribute all human action to hidden economic interest. One must give some credence to the possibility that people mean what they say and are often candid about their motives, especially in large matters of public affairs. The most notable circumstance of the times in fact was that, unlike so many revolutions, the American Revolution led not to general chaos and terror but, in the words of the social critic Hannah Arendt, to "a spontaneous outbreak of constitution-making." From the 1760s through the 1780s there occurred a prolonged debate over the fundamental issues of government which in its scope and depth—and in the durability of its outcome—is without parallel.

THE FEDERALIST   Among the supreme legacies of that debate was *The Federalist*, a collection of essays originally published in the New York press between October 1787 and July 1788. Instigated by Alexander Hamilton, the eighty-five articles published under the name "Publius" included about thirty by James Madison and five by John Jay. The authorship of some remain in doubt. Written in support of ratification, the essays defended the principle of a supreme national authority, but at the same time sought to reassure doubters that the people and the states had little reason to fear usurpations and tyranny by the new government. In perhaps the most famous single essay, No. Ten, Madison argued that the very size and diversity of the country would make it impossible for any single faction to form a majority which could dominate the government. Republics, the conventional wisdom of the times insisted, could work only in small, homogeneous countries like Switzerland and the Netherlands. In larger countries they would descend into anarchy and tyranny through the influence of factions. Quite the contrary, Madison insisted. Given a balanced federal polity they could work in large and diverse countries probably better. "Extend the sphere," he wrote, "and you take in a greater variety of parties and interests; you make it less probable that a majority of the whole will have a common motive to invade the rights of other citizens. . . ."

The Federalists did try to cultivate a belief that the new union would contribute to prosperity, in part to link their movement with the economic recovery already under way. The Antifederalists, however, talked more of the dangers of power in terms that had become familiar during the long struggles with Parliament and the crown. They noted the absence of a Bill of Rights protecting the rights of individuals and states. They found the process of ratification highly irregular, as it was—indeed illegal under the Articles of Confederation. Patrick Henry "smelt a rat" from the beginning. Not only did he refuse to attend the Constitutional Convention, he demanded later that it be investigated as a conspiracy. The Antifederalist leaders—men like Henry and Richard Henry Lee of Virginia, George Clinton of New York, Sam Adams and Elbridge Gerry of Massachusetts, Luther Martin of Maryland—were often men whose careers and reputations had been established well before the Revolution. The Federalist leaders, on the other hand, were more likely to be younger men whose careers had begun in the Revolution and who had been "nationalized" in the fires of battle—men like Hamilton, Madison, and Jay.

The disagreement between the two groups, however, was more over means than ends. Both sides for the most part agreed that a stronger national authority was needed, and that it required an independent income to function properly. Both were convinced that the people must erect safeguards against tyranny, even the tyranny of the majority. Few of its supporters liked the Constitution in its entirety, but felt that it was the best obtainable; few of its opponents found it unacceptable in its entirety. Once the new government had become an accomplished fact, few diehards were left who wanted to undo the work of the Philadelphia convention.

THE DECISION OF THE STATES Ratification gained momentum before the year 1787 was ended, and several of the smaller states were among the first to act, apparently satisfied that they had gained all the safeguards they could hope for in equality of representation in the Senate. Delaware's convention was first, and ratified the Constitution unanimously on December 7; Penn-

sylvania approved by 46 to 23 on December 12; New Jersey
on December 18 and Georgia on January 2 were unanimous;
Connecticut voted in favor, 128 to 40, on January 9. Massachusetts, still sharply divided in the aftermath of Shays's Rebellion,
was the first state in which the outcome was close. There the
Federalists carried the day by winning over two hesitant leaders
of the popular party. They dangled before John Hancock the possibility of becoming vice-president, and won the acquiescence of
Samuel Adams when they agreed to recommend amendments
designed to protect human rights, including one that would specifically reserve to the states all powers not granted to the new
government. Massachusetts approved, by 187 to 168 on February 6. Maryland ratified on April 26, by 63 to 11; South Carolina
on May 23, by 149 to 73. In New Hampshire one session had
failed to agree, and the Federalists had won a delay during which
they mobilized greater strength. On June 21, 1788, the reassembled delegates voted ratification by 57 to 47.

New Hampshire was the ninth to ratify, and the Constitution
could now be put into effect, but the union could hardly succeed
without the approval of Virginia, the largest state, or New York,
the third largest, which occupied a key position geographically.
Both states had a strong opposition. In Virginia Patrick Henry

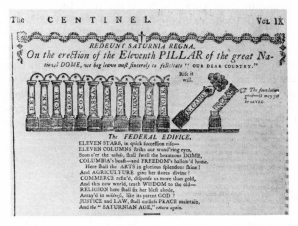

This cartoon from the August 2, 1788, Massachusetts
Centinel announces New York's vote to ratify the
Constitution. It took almost two years for Rhode Island
to complete "the beauteous DOME." [New-York Historical
Society]

became the chief spokesman of backcountry farmers who feared the powers of the new government, but wavering delegates were won over by the same strategem as in Massachusetts. When it was proposed that the convention should recommend a Bill of Rights, Edmund Randolph, who had refused to sign the finished document, announced his conversion to the cause. Virginia's convention ratified on June 25, by a vote of 89 to 79. In New York, as in New Hampshire, Hamilton and the other Federalists worked for a delay, in the hope that action by New Hampshire and Virginia would persuade the delegates that the new framework would go into effect with or without New York. On July 26, 1788, they carried the day by the closest margin thus far, 30 to 27. North Carolina and Rhode Island remained the only holdouts, and North Carolina stubbornly withheld action until amendments composing a Bill of Rights were actually submitted by Congress. On November 21, 1789, North Carolina joined the new government, which was already under way, 194 to 77. Rhode Island, true to form, continued to hold out, and did not relent until May 29, 1790. Even then the vote was the closest of all, 34 to 32.

Upon notification that New Hampshire had become the ninth state to ratify, the Confederation Congress began to draft plans for an orderly transfer of power. On September 13, 1788, Congress adopted an ordinance which placed the seat of the new government in New York and fixed the date for elections: January 7, 1789, for choice of electors; February 4 for their balloting. March 4, 1789, was the date set for the meeting of the new Congress. Each state would set the date for electing its first members. On October 10, 1788, the Confederation Congress transacted its last business and passed into history.

"Our constitution is in actual operation," the elderly Ben Franklin wrote to a friend; "everything appears to promise that it will last; but in this world nothing is certain but death and taxes."

Further Reading

The traditional view that multiple crises led America from Confederation to Constitution began with John Fiske's *The Critical Period of American History* (1888). Merrill Jensen's *The New Nation* (1950) presents a more recent, "consensus" view that downplays the extent of crisis. Overviews of the political events of the 1780s can be found in

Jensen's *The Articles of Confederation* (1940),° and Andrew C. McLaughlin's *The Confederation and the Constitution* (1962).° Relevant chapters of Gordon S. Wood's *The Creation of the American Republic, 1776–1787* (1969),° trace the changing contours of political philosophy during these years. The behavior of Congress is the subject of both H. James Henderson's *Party Politics in the Continental Congress* (1974) and Jack N. Rakove's *The Beginnings of National Politics* (1979).°

More specific treatments of the events of the 1780s are Frederick W. Marks III's *Independence on Trial* (1973), which deals with the problems of foreign commerce among the various states, and E. James Ferguson's *The Power of the Purse: A History of American Public Finance, 1776–1790* (1961), which analyzes the difficulties of putting together a credit system. Clarence L. Van Steeg's biography, *Robert Morris: Revolutionary Financier* (1954),° examines the role of that central figure.

To understand what individual states faced during the period, see Richard P. McCormick's *Experiment in Independence: New Jersey in the Critical Period, 1781–1789* (1950), and Florence Parker Simister's *The Fire's Center: Rhode Island in the Revolutionary Era, 1763–1790* (1978). Robert S. Taylor's *Western Massachusetts in the Revolution* (1954) and Marion L. Starkey's *A Little Rebellion* (1955) provide background on Shays's Rebellion. A brief account of the state of Franklin is in Noel B. Gerson's *Franklin: America's Lost State* (1968). For a view of public sentiment during the period, see Joseph J. Ellis's *After the Revolution: Profiles of American Culture* (1979),° as well as Oscar and Lillian Handlin's *A Restless People: America in Rebellion, 1770–1787* (1982).

As noted in the text, Charles A. Beard's *An Economic Interpretation of the Constitution* (1913)° remained powerfully influential for more than a generation. More recent challenges to Beard include Robert E. Brown's *Charles Beard and the Constitution* (1956)° and Forrest McDonald's *We the People: The Economic Origins of the Constitution* (1958).° Also helpful is McDonald's *E Pluribus Unum: The Formation of the American Republic, 1776–1790* (1965).° Other interpretations are found in Leonard W. Levy (ed.), *Essays on the Making of the American Constitution* (1969), Merrill Jensen's *Making of the American Constitution* (1964), and Robert E. Brown's *Reinterpretation of the Formation of the American Constitution* (1963). Catherine Drinker Bowen's *Miracle at Philadelphia* (1966)° is a readable narrative of the convention proceedings.

Recent scholarship treats both sides of the ratification argument. The best introduction to the Federalist viewpoint remains in their own words, edited by Benjamin F. Wright, *The Federalist* (1961). Garry Wills's *Explaining America: The Federalist* (1981)° provides an interpretation of what they wrote. Biographies of Federalist writers are also helpful, among them Jacob Ernest Cook's *Alexander Hamilton* (1982), Forrest McDonald's *Alexander Hamilton: A Biography* (1979),° and Irving Brant's *James Madison: The Nationalist, 1780–87* (1948).

Most recently Herbert J. Storing and Murray Day have completed a

° These books are available in paperback editions.

multivolume compendium of the anti-Federalist documents. Their slim, but incisive, introduction is *What the Anti-Federalists Were For* (1981). Also see Robert A. Rutland's *The Ordeal of the Constitution: The Anti-Federalists and the Ratification Struggle of 1787–1788* (1966) and Jackson Turner Main's *The Anti-Federalists: Critics of the Constitution, 1781–1788* (1961).° For the Bill of Rights which emerged from the ratification struggles, see Robert A. Rutland's *The Birth of the Bill of Rights, 1776–1791* (1955).

For discussions of the problem of slavery in forming the Constitution, see the relevant sections of Donald Robinson's *Slavery in the Structure of American Politics, 1765–1820* (1982),° and James McGregor Burns's *The Vineyard of Liberty: The American Experiment* (1982).°

8

THE FEDERALISTS:
WASHINGTON AND ADAMS

A New Government

On the appointed date, March 4, 1789, the new Congress of the United States, meeting in New York, could muster only eight senators and thirteen representatives. A month passed before both chambers gathered a quorum. Only then could the temporary presiding officer of the Senate count the ballots and certify the foregone conclusion that George Washington, with sixty-nine votes, was the unanimous choice of the electoral college for president. John Adams, with thirty-four votes, the second-highest number, became vice-president.

Washington's journey from Mount Vernon to New York, where he was inaugurated on April 30, turned into a triumphal procession which confirmed the universal confidence he commanded, and the hopeful expectancy with which the new experiment was awaited. But Washington himself confessed to feeling like "a culprit who is going to his place of execution," burdened with dread that so much was expected of him. When he delivered the inaugural address he trembled visibly and at times seemed barely able to make out the manuscript in front of him.

SYMBOLS OF AUTHORITY The task before the president and the Congress was to create a government anew. From the Confederation Washington inherited but the shadow of a bureaucracy: a foreign office with John Jay and two clerks; a Treasury Board with little or no treasury; a secretary of war with an army of 672 officers and men, and no navy at all; a dozen or so clerks who had

Mary Varick's sampler celebrates George Washington's inauguration as president of the United States in 1789. [Museum of the City of New York]

served the old Congress; a heavy debt and almost no revenue, and no machinery for collecting one. There was an acute realization that anything done at the time would set important precedents for the future. Even the question of an etiquette appropriate to the dignity and authority of the new government occupied Congress to a degree that later Americans (and not a few at the time) would regard as absurd. A committee of Congress went so far as to suggest for a presidential title "His Highness, the President of the United States and Protector of Rights of the Same." A solemn discussion of the issue in Congress ended happily when the House of Representatives addressed the chief executive simply by his constitutional title: "President of the United States." One irreverent wag in the Congress suggested privately that a form of address appropriate to the vice-president's appearance would be "Your Rotundity."

The Congress nevertheless agreed with John Vining of Delaware, who said on the floor of the House: "there are cases in which generosity is the best economy, and no loss is ever sustained by a decent support of the Magistrate. A certain appearance of parade and external dignity is necessary to be supported." To that end Congress set the president's salary at $25,000, an income far above that of any other official and probably all but a few Americans. The president obliged them with a show of pomp and circumstance. On public occasions he ap-

A 1790 reception at President Washington's house in New York. The formality of the occasion fit the man, and, many thought, the newly created office. [The Brooklyn Museum]

peared in a coach drawn by four horses, sometimes six, escorted by liveried retainers. He held formal dinners for "official characters and strangers of distinction," but took no invitations himself. Every Tuesday from 3 to 4 p.m. he held a formal levee, clothed in black velvet, his hair in full dress, powdered and gathered, wearing yellow gloves and a finely polished sword, holding a cocked hat with cockade and feather. Visiting in Boston, Washington stubbornly declined to visit Gov. John Hancock until Hancock paid a call on him, thus making the point that a president takes precedence over a mere governor. Mixed emotions greeted the show of ceremony. Some members of Congress continued to fear that another president might make "that bold push for the throne" predicted by Patrick Henry. The antimonarchists did stop a move to stamp coins with the head of the incumbent president—preferring an emblem of Liberty instead.

GOVERNMENTAL STRUCTURE   More than matters of punctilio occupied the First Congress, of course. In framing the structure of government it was second in importance only to the Constitutional Convention itself. During the summer of 1789 Congress authorized executive departments, corresponding in each case to those already formed under the Confederation. To head the Department of State Washington named Thomas Jefferson, recently back from his mission to France. As head of the Department of War, Gen. Henry Knox continued in substantially the same position he had occupied since 1785. To head the Department of the Treasury, Washington picked his old wartime aide Alexander Hamilton, now a prominent lawyer in New York. The new position of attorney-general was occupied by Edmund Randolph, former governor of Virginia. Unlike the other three Randolph headed no department but served as legal advisor to the government, and on such a meager salary that he was expected to continue a private practice on the side. Almost from the beginning Washington routinely called these men to sit as a group for discussion and advice on matters of policy. This was the origin of the president's cabinet, an advisory body for which the constitution made no formal provision—except insofar as it provided for the heads of departments.

The structure of the court system, like that of the executive departments, was left to Congress, except for a chief justice and Supreme Court. Congress determined to set the membership of the highest court at six: the chief justice and five associate justices. There was some sentiment for stopping there and permitting state courts to determine matters of federal law, but the Congress decided in favor of thirteen Federal District Courts. From these, appeals might go to one of three Circuit Courts, composed of two Supreme Court justices and the district judge, meeting twice a year in each district. Members of the Supreme Court, therefore, became intinerant judges riding the circuit during a good part of the year. All federal cases originated in the District Court, and if appealed on issues of procedure or legal interpretation, went to the Circuit Courts and from there to the Supreme Court. There were only two exceptions, both specified in the Constitution: the Supreme Court had original jurisdiction in cases involving states or foreign ambassadors, ministers, and consuls. As the first chief justice Washington named John Jay, who served until 1795.

THE BILL OF RIGHTS In the House of Representatives James Madison made a Bill of Rights one of the first items of business. The lack of such provisions had been one of the Antifederalists' major objections to the Constitution as originally proposed. While at first Madison believed that the absence of a Bill of Rights made little difference (events proved him wrong), he recognized the need to allay the fears of Antifederalists and to meet the moral obligation imposed by those ratifying conventions which had approved the Constitution with the understanding that amendments would be offered. In all 210 amendments had been suggested. From the Virginia proposals Madison drew the first eight amendments, modeled after the Virginia Bill of Rights which George Mason had written in 1776. These all provided safeguards for certain fundamental rights of individuals. The Ninth and Tenth Amendments addressed themselves to the demand for specific statements that the enumeration of rights in the Constitution "shall not be construed to deny or disparage others retained by the people" and that "powers not delegated to the United States by the Constitution, nor prohibited by it to the states, are reserved to the States respectively, or to the people." The Tenth Amendment was taken almost verbatim from the Articles of Confederation. The House adopted, in all, seventeen amendments; the Senate, after conference with the House, adopted twelve; the states in the end ratified ten, which constitute the Bill of Rights, effective December 15, 1791.

RAISING A REVENUE Revenue was the government's most critical need and the Congress, at Madison's lead, undertook a revenue measure as another of the first items of business. Madison proposed a modest duty for revenue only, but the demands of manufacturers in the northern states for higher duties to protect them from foreign competition forced a compromise. Madison's proposed ad valorem duty of 5 percent (of the goods' value) applied to most items, but reached 7 1/2 percent on certain listed items, and specific duties as high as 50 percent were placed on thirty items: steel, nails, hemp, molasses, ships, tobacco, salt, indigo, and cloth among them. Madison linked the tariff to a proposal for a mercantile system which would levy extra tonnage duties on foreign ships, an especially heavy duty on countries which had no commercial treaty with the United States.

Madison's specific purpose was to levy economic war against Great Britain, which had no such treaty but had more foreign trade with the new nation than any other country. Northern businessmen, however, were in no mood for a renewal of economic pressures, for fear of disrupting the economy. Secretary of the Treasury Hamilton agreed with them. In the end the only discrimination built into the Tonnage Act of 1789 was between American and all foreign ships: American ships paid a duty of 6¢ per ton; American-built but foreign-owned ships paid 30¢; and foreign-built and owned ships paid 50¢ per ton. The disagreements created by the trade measures were portents of quarrels yet to come: whether foreign policy should favor Britain or France, and the more persistent question of whether tariff and tonnage duties should penalize farmers with higher prices and freight rates in the interest of northern manufacturers and ship-owners. The latter in turn became a sectional question of South versus North.

HAMILTON'S VISION OF AMERICA

But the first provision for a revenue, linked as it was to other issues, was but the beginning of the effort to get the country on a sound financial basis. In finance, with all its broad implications for policy in general, it was Alexander Hamilton who, in the words of the historian Joseph Charles, more than any other man "bent the twig and inclined the tree." The first secretary of the treasury was in a sense the protégé of the president, a younger man who had been his aide during four years of the Revolution. Born out of wedlock on the island of Nevis, deserted by a ne'er-do-well father, Hamilton was left an orphan on St. Croix at thirteen by the death of his mother. With the help of friends and relatives, Hamilton found his way at seventeen to New York, attended King's College (later Columbia University), entered the revolutionary agitations as speaker and pamphleteer, and joined the service, where he came to the attention of the commander. "George Washington was an aegis essential to me," Hamilton wrote later, after the president's death. Married to the daughter of Gen. Philip Schuyler, he studied law, passed the bar examination, established a legal practice in New York, and became a self-made aristocrat, serving as collector of revenues and member of

Alexander Hamilton in 1796. [National Portrait Gallery, Smithsonian Institution]

the Confederation Congress. An early convert to nationalism, he had a big part in promoting the Constitutional Convention. A hero of the siege of Yorktown, he remained forever after a frustrated military genius, hungry for greater glory on the field of battle.

In a series of classic reports submitted to Congress in the two years from January 1790 to December 1791, Hamilton outlined his program for government finances and the economic development of the United States. The reports were soon adopted, with some alterations in detail but little in substance. The only exception was the last of the series, the Report on Manufactures, and that one outlined a neomercantilist program which eventually would become government policy, whatever brave talk of laissez-faire might accompany it.

ESTABLISHING THE PUBLIC CREDIT   Hamilton submitted the first and most important of his reports to the House of Representatives on January 14, 1790, at the invitation of that body. This First Report on the Public Credit, as it has since been called, was the cornerstone of the Hamiltonian program. It recommended two things mainly: first, funding of the federal debt at face value, which meant that the government's creditors could turn in securities for new interest-bearing bonds; and second, the federal government's assumption of state debts from the Revolution to the amount of $21 million. The report raised a multiplicity of issues about the national and state debts, and provided the material for lengthy discussions and debates before its substance was adopted on August 4, 1791. Then in short order came three more reports: on December 13, 1790, a Second Report on Public Credit, which included a proposal for an excise tax on distilled spirits to aid in raising revenue to cover the nation's debts (Hamilton meant this tax also to establish the precedent of an excise tax, and to rebuke elements that had been least friendly to his program). On the following day another report from Hamilton recommended a national bank, a revival of the Robert Morris idea that had led to the Bank of North America. On January 28, 1791, the secretary suggested a national mint—which was established the following year. And finally, on December 5, 1791, as the culmination of his basic reports, the Report on Manufactures proposed an extensive program of government aid and encouragement to the development of manufacturing enterprises.

Each of Hamilton's reports excited vigorous discussion and disagreement. His program was substantially the one Robert Morris had urged upon the Confederation a decade before, and one which Hamilton had strongly endorsed at the time. "A national debt," Hamilton had written Morris in 1781, "if it is not excessive, will be to us a national blessing; it will be a powerful cement of our union. It will also create a necessity for keeping up taxation to a degree which without being oppressive, will be a spur to industry; remote as we are from Europe and shall be from danger, it were otherwise to be feared our popular maxims would incline us to great parsimony and indulgence." Payment of the national debt, in short, would be not only a point of national honor and sound finance, ensuring the country's credit for the future; it would also be an ocasion to assert a national taxing power and thus instill respect for the authority of the national government.

Few in Congress would dispute this logic, although a number of members had come expecting at least some degree of debt repudiation to lessen the burden. What troubled them more were questions of simple equity, questions which Hamilton took pains to anticipate and answer in the First Report itself. Since many of the bonds had fallen into the hands of speculators, especially after the appearance of the First Report sent agents of speculators (including members of Congress) scurrying to buy them up, was it fair that the original purchasers, who had been forced into selling their bonds at a reduced price, should lose the benefit of the restoration of governmental credit? Hamilton answered the argument on both practical and moral grounds. Not only would it be impossible to judge who might have benefited from selling bonds and investing the proceeds in more productive ways, but speculators were entitled to consideration for the risk they had taken and the faith they had shown in the government.

SECTIONAL DIFFERENCES EMERGE   It was on this point, however, that Madison, who had been Hamilton's close ally in the movement for a stronger government, broke with him for the second time (their first break had been over the issue of tonnage duties), and as in the first case the difference here had ominous overtones of sectionalism. Madison did not question that the debt should be paid; he was troubled, however, that speculators and "stock-jobbers" would become the chief beneficiaries, and troubled further by the fact that the far greater portion of the debt was held north of the Mason-Dixon line. Madison, whom Hamilton had expected to take the lead for his program in the House, therefore advanced an alternative plan to give a larger share to the first owners than to the later speculators. "Let it be a liberal one in favor of the present holders," he suggested. "Let them have the highest price which has prevailed in the market; and let the residue belong to the original sufferers." Madison's opposition touched off a vigorous debate, but Hamilton carried his point by a margin of three to one when the House brought it to a vote.

Madison's opposition to the assumption of state debts got more support, however, and set up a division more clearly along sectional lines. The southern states, with the exception of South Carolina, had whittled down their debts. New England, with the largest unpaid debts, stood to be the greatest beneficiary of the assumption scheme. Rather than see Virginia victimized, Madison held out an alternative. Why not, he suggested, have the government assume state debts as they stood in 1783 at the conclusion of the peace? Debates over this issue deadlocked the whole question of debt funding and assumption through much of 1790.

A resolution finally came when Hamilton accosted Thomas Jefferson on the steps of the president's home and suggested a compromise with the Virginians. The next evening, at a dinner arranged by Jefferson, Hamilton and Madison reached an understanding. In return for northern votes in favor of locating the permanent capital on the Potomac, Madison pledged to seek enough southern votes to pass the assumption, with the further arrangement that those states with smaller debts would get in effect outright grants from the federal government to equalize the difference. With these arrangements enough votes were secured to carry Hamilton's funding and assumption schemes. The capital would be moved to Philadelphia for ten years, after which time it would be settled at a Federal City on the Potomac, the site to be chosen by the president. In August 1790 Congress finally passed the legislation for Hamilton's plan.

A NATIONAL BANK   By this vast program of funding and assumption Hamilton had called up from nowhere, as if by magic, a great sum of capital. As he put it in his original report, a national debt "answers most of the purposes of money." Transfers of government bonds, once the debt was properly funded, would be "equivalent to payments in specie." This feature of the program was especially important in a country which had, from the first settlements, suffered a shortage of hard money and in which foreign coins circulated widely for another half century. But having established the public credit, Hamilton moved on to a related measure essential to his vision of national greatness. He called for the creation of a national bank, which by issuance of banknotes (paper money) might provide a uniform circulating medium. Government bonds held by the bank would back up the value of its new banknotes, needed as a medium of exchange because of the chronic shortage of specie. The national bank, chartered by Congress, would remain under governmental surveillance, but private investors would purchase four-fifths of the $10 million capital and name twenty of the twenty-five directors; the government would take the other fifth of the capital and name five directors. Government bonds would be received in payment for three-fourths of the stock in the bank, and the other fourth would be payable in gold and silver.

The bank, Hamilton explained, would serve many purposes. Its notes would become a stable circulating currency, uniform in value because redeemable in gold and silver upon demand. Moreover, the bank would provide a source of capital for loans to fund the development of business and commerce. Bonds, which might otherwise be stowed away in safes, would instead become the basis for a productive capital in the form of banknotes available for loan at low rates of interest, the "natural effect" of which would be "to incease trade and industry." What is more, the existence of the bank would serve certain housekeeping needs of the government: a safe place to keep its funds, a source of "pecuniary aids" in sudden emergencies, and the ready transfer of

The first Bank of the United States in Philadelphia. Proposed by Hamilton, the bank opened in 1791. [Library of Congress]

funds to and from branch offices by means of bookkeeping entries which would obviate the tedious "transportation and retransportation" of metals for payment of bills and taxes.

Once again Madison rose to lead the opposition. Madison could find no authority in the Constitution for such a bank. He himself had proposed in the Constitutional Convention a grant of power to charter corporations, but no specific provisions had been adopted. That was enough to raise in President Washington's mind serious doubts as to the constitutionality of the measure, which Congress passed fairly quickly over Madison's objections. Before signing the bill into law, therefore, the president sought the advice of his cabinet and found there an equal division of opinion. The result was the first great and fundamental debate on constitutional interpretation. Should there be a strict or a broad construction of the document? Were the powers of Congress only those explicitly stated or were there others implied by the language of the Constitution? The argument turned chiefly on Article 1, Section 8, which authorized Congress to "make all laws which shall be necessary and proper for carrying into execution the foregoing Powers."

Such language left room for serious disagreement and led to a direct confrontation between Jefferson, with whom Attorney-General Edmund Randolph agreed, and Hamilton, who had the support of Secretary of War Henry Knox. Jefferson pointed to the Tenth Amendment, which reserved to the states and the people powers not delegated to Congress. "To take a single step beyond the boundaries thus specially drawn around the powers of Congress, is to take possession of a boundless field of power, no longer susceptible of any definition." A bank might be a convenient aid to Congress in collecting taxes and regulating the currency, but it was not, as Article 1, Section 8, specified, *necessary*.

Hamilton had not expected the constitutionality of the bank to become a decisive issue, and in his original report had neglected the point, but he was prepared to meet his opponents on their own ground. In a lengthy report to the president, Hamilton insisted that the power to charter corporations was included in the sovereignty of any government, whether or not expressly stated. The word "necessary," he explained, often meant no more than "needful, requisite, incidental, useful, or conducive to." And in a classic summary, he expressed his criterion on constitutionality: "This criterion is the *end*, to which the measure relates as a *mean*. If the *end* be clearly comprehended within any of the specified powers, collecting taxes and regulating the currency, and if the measure have an obvious relation to that *end*, and is not forbidden by any particular provision of the Constitution, it may safely be deemed to come within the compass of the national authority. . . ."

The president, influenced by the fact that the matter under consideration came within the jurisdiction of the secretary of the treasury, accepted Hamilton's argument and signed the bill. And he had indeed, in Jefferson's words, opened up "a boundless field of power" which in coming years would lead to a further broadening of implied powers with the approval of the Supreme Court. Under John Marshall the Court would eventually adopt Hamilton's words almost verbatim. On July 4, 1791, the bank's stock was put up for sale and in what seemed to Jefferson a "delirium of speculation" was sold within a few hours, with hundreds of buyers turned away. It cost the government itself nothing until later, for its subscription of $2 million was immediately returned by the bank in a loan of the same amount, with ten years for repayment.

ENCOURAGING MANUFACTURES   But Hamilton's imagination and his ambitions for the new country remained unexhausted. In the last of his great reports, the Report on Manufactures, he set in place the capstone of his design, an argument for the active encouragement of manufacturing to provide productive uses for the new capital he had created by his funding, assumption, and banking schemes. A reading of this report will lay to rest any idea that the Founding Fathers abandoned mercantilism to embrace the newfangled laissez-faire attitudes of Adam Smith. "The extreme embarrassments of the United States during the late War, from an incapacity of supplying themselves, are still matter of keen recollection," Hamilton wrote. Multiple advantages would flow from the development of manufactures: the diversification of labor in a country given over too exclusively to farming; greater use of machinery; work for those not ordinarily employed, such as women and children; the promotion of immigration; a greater scope for the diversity of talents in business; a more ample and various field for enterprise; and a better domestic market for the products of agriculture.

To secure his ends Hamilton was ready to use the means to which other countries had resorted, and which he summarized: protective tariffs, or in Hamilton's words, "protecting duties," which in some cases might be put so high as to be prohibitive; restraints on the export of raw materials; bounties and premiums to

encourage certain industries; tariff exemptions for the raw materials of manufacturing, or "drawbacks" (rebates) to manufacturers where duties had been levied for revenue or other
purposes; encouragements to inventions and discoveries; regulations for the inspection of commodities; and finally, the encouragement of internal improvements in transportation, the
development of roads, canals, and navigable streams.

Some of his tariff proposals were enacted in 1792. Otherwise
the program was filed away—but not forgotten. It became an arsenal of arguments for the advocates of manufactures in years to
come, in Europe as well as in America. An outline can hardly do
justice to what was a complex state paper which anticipated and
attempted to demolish all counterarguments, among them the
ominous question which kept arising with Hamilton's schemes:
"Ideas of a contrariety of interests between the northern and
southern regions of the Union," which he found "in the Main as
unfounded as they are mischievous." If, as seemed likely from
experience and circumstances, the northern and middle states
should become the chief scenes of manufacturing, they would
create robust markets for agricultural products, some of which
the southern states were peculiarly qualified to produce. North
and South would both benefit, he argued, as commerce moved
between these regions more than along the established channels
across the Atlantic, thus strengthening the Union: "every thing
tending to establish *substantial* and *permanent order* in the affairs
of a Country, to increase the total mass of industry and opulence,
is ultimately beneficial to every part of it."

HAMILTON'S ACHIEVEMENT Largely owing to the skillful Hamilton, whom a close student of the Federalist period called "the
greatest administrative genius in America, and one of the greatest administrators of all time," the Treasury Department, which
employed half or more of the civil servants at the time, was established on a basis of integrity and efficiency. The Revolutionary War debt was put on the way to retirement, a "Continental"
became worth something after all (if only at a ratio of 100 to 1 in
payments to the government), the credit of the government was
secure, government securities sold at par, and foreign capital
began to flow in once again. And prosperity, so elusive in the
1780s, began to flourish once again, although President Washington cautioned against attributing "to the Government what is
due only to the goodness of Providence."

Still, the suspicion would not die down that Hamilton's was a
program designed to promote a class and sectional interest, and

some even thought a personal interest. There is, however, no evidence that Hamilton benefited personally in any way from his program, although Assistant Treasury Secretary William Duer, unbeknownst to Hamilton, did leak word of the funding and assumption message to favored friends in time for them to reap a speculative harvest from the rise in values. Duer himself later became involved in deals which landed him in prison. There is no reason to believe that Hamilton's conscious aim was to benefit either a section or a class at the expense of the government. He was inclined toward a truly nationalist outlook. As a result of his early years in the islands he lacked the background of narrow localism that most of his contemporaries shared to some degree, although his failure to take that factor into full account was one of his weaknesses. Indeed he would have favored a much stronger central government, including a federal veto on state action, even a constitutional monarchy if that had been practicable. But, ironically, given his background of illegitimacy and poverty, Hamilton believed that throughout history a minority of the strong dominated the weak. There was always a ruling group, perhaps military or aristocratic, and Hamilton had the wit to see now the rising power of commercial capitalism. He was in many ways a classic Whig who, like Britain's ruling oligarchy of the eighteenth century, favored government by the rich and well-born. The mass of the people, he once said "are turbulent and changing; they seldom judge or determine right." And once, in his cups, he went further: "Your people, sir, is a great beast!" To tie the government closely to the rich and the well-born, then, was but to secure the interest of good government and to guard the public order against the potential turbulence which always haunted him.

Hamilton's achievement, however, was to tie more closely to the government those who were already on its side—and to overlook, or even antagonize, those who had their doubts. Hamilton never came to know the people of the small villages and farms, the people of the frontier. They were absent from his world, despite his own humble beginnings in the islands. And they, along with the planters of the South, would be at best only indirect beneficiaries of his programs. Below the Potomac the Hamiltonian vision excited little enthusiasm except in South Carolina, which had a large state debt to be assumed and a sizable concentration of mercantile interests at Charleston. There was, in short, a vast number of people who were drawn into opposition to Hamilton's new engines of power. In part they were southern, in part backcountry, and in part a politically motivated faction opposing Hamilton in New York.

THE REPUBLICAN ALTERNATIVE

In this split over the Hamiltonian program lay the seeds of the first political parties of national scope. Hamilton became the embodiment of the party known as the Federalists; Madison and Jefferson became the leaders of those who took the name Republican and thereby implied that the Federalists really aimed at a monarchy. Parties were slow in developing, or at least in being acknowledged as legitimate. All the political philosophers of the age deplored the spirit of party or faction. The concept of a loyal opposition, of a two-party system as a positive good, was yet to be formulated. Parties, or factions, as eighteenth-century Englishmen and colonists knew them, were bodies of men bent upon self-aggrandizement through the favor of the government. They smelled of jobbery and corruption. So it cannot be said that either side in the disagreement over national policy deliberately set out to create a party system, which indeed would not be firmly established nor widely accepted as a public good until the next century was more than a quarter spent.

But there were important differences of both philosophy and self-interest which simply would not dissolve. At the outset Madison, who had collaborated with Hamilton in the movement for a national government and the writing of *The Federalist,* assumed leadership of Hamilton's opponents in the Congress. The states meant more to Madison than to Hamilton, who would as soon have seen a consolidated central government. And Madison, like Thomas Jefferson, was rooted in Virginia, where opposition to the funding schemes flourished. In December 1790 the Virginia Assembly bluntly protested Hamilton's funding schemes in a resolution drafted by Patrick Henry: "In an agricultural country like this . . . to erect, and concentrate, and perpetuate a large monied interest . . . must in the course of human events produce one or other of two evils, the prostration of agriculture at the feet of commerce, or a change in the present from of federal government, fatal to the existence of American liberty. . . . Your memorialists can find no clause in the Constitution authorizing Congress to assume the debts of the States!" To Hamilton this was "the first symptom of a spirit which must either be killed, or will kill the Constitution of the United States."

After the compromise which had assured passage of the funding and assumption, Madison and Jefferson moved into ever more irreconcilable opposition to Hamilton's policies: his move to place an excise tax on whiskey, which laid a burden especially on the trans-Appalachian farmers whose grain went into that potable and portable liquid; his proposal for the bank; and his report on manufactures. Against the last two both men raised constitutional objections. As the differences developed, hostility between Jefferson and Hamilton grew and festered, to the distress of President Washington. Jefferson, the temperamentally shy and retiring secretary of state, then emerged as the leader of the opposition to Hamilton's policies; Madison continued to direct the opposition in Congress.

JEFFERSON'S AGRARIAN VIEW   Thomas Jefferson, twelve years Hamilton's senior, was in almost every respect his opposite. In contrast to Hamilton, the careerist, the self-made aristocrat, Jefferson was to the manor born, son of a successful surveyor and land speculator, his mother a Randolph, from one of the First Families in Virginia. In contrast to Hamilton's ordered intensity, Jefferson conveyed a certain sense of aristocratic carelessness and a breadth of cultivated interests that ranged perhaps more widely in science, the arts, and the humanities than those of any contemporary, even Franklin. Jefferson read or spoke seven languages. He was an architect of some distinction (Monticello, the Virginia Capitol, the University of Virginia are monuments to his talent), a man who understood mathematics and engineering, an inventor, an agronomist. In his *Notes on Virginia* (1785) he displayed a knowledge of geography, paleontology, zoology, botany, and archeology. He collected paintings and sculpture. He knew music and practiced the violin, although some wit said only Patrick Henry played it worse.

Thomas Jefferson, in a portrait by Rembrandt Peale (1800). [White House Collection]

Philosophically, Hamilton and Jefferson personified the two poles of a great dialectic that formed the character of the Union in the first generation under the Constitution, and defined certain fundamental issues of American life which still echo two centuries later. Hamilton foresaw a diversified capitalistic economy, agriculture balanced by commerce and industry, and was thus the better prophet. Jefferson feared the growth of cities which would be filled with crowds and divided into a capitalistic aristocracy on the one hand and a depraved proletariat on the other. Hamilton feared anarchy and loved order; Jefferson feared tyranny and loved liberty.

What Hamilton wanted for his country was a strong central government, run by the rich and well-born actively encouraging capitalistic enterprise. What Jefferson wanted was a republic of yeoman farmers: "Those who labor in the earth," he wrote, "are the chosen people of God, if ever he had a chosen people, whose breasts He has made His peculiar deposit for genuine and substantial virtue." Where Hamilton was the old-fashioned English Whig, Jefferson, who spent several years in France, was the enlightened *philosophe*, the natural radical and reformer who attacked the aristocratic relics of entail and primogeniture in Virginia; opposed an established church; proposed an elaborate plan for public schools; prepared a more humane criminal code; and was instrumental in eliminating slavery from the Old Northwest, although he kept the slaves he had inherited. On his tomb were finally recorded the achievements of which he was proudest: author of the Declaration of Independence and the Virginia Statute of Religious Freedom, and founder of the University of Virginia.

Jefferson set forth his vision of what America should be in his *Notes on Virginia* in 1785: "While we have land to labor then, let us never wish to see our citizens occupied at a work-bench, or twirling a distaff. . . . For the general operations of manufacture, let our work-shops remain in Europe. It is better to carry provisions and materials to work-men there, than bring them to the provisions and materials, and with them their manners and principles. . . . The mobs of great cities add just so much to the support of pure government, as sores do to the strength of the human body."

PARTY DISPUTES   The one thing that Jefferson and Hamilton had in common, it seemed, was their mutual enmity, which began with disagreement in the cabinet and soon became widely visible in a journalistic war of words between two editors with the curiously similar names of Fenno and Freneau. John Fenno's *Gazette of the*

United States, founded in 1789, "to endear the General Government to the people," became virtually the official administration organ, extolling Hamilton and his policies at every opportunity, and holding contracts for government printing. Philip Freneau, poet and journalist, was enticed to Philadelphia from New York in 1791 to found the *National Gazette* and given a sinecure as translator for Jefferson's Department of State. Each man was compromised by his connection, but each loyally supported his benefactor out of real conviction.

In their quarrel Hamilton unwittingly identified Jefferson more and more in the public mind as the leader of the opposition to his policies; Madison was still a relatively obscure congressman whose central role in the Constitutional Convention was yet unknown. In the summer of 1791 Jefferson and Madison set out on a "botanizing" excursion up the Hudson, a vacation which many Federalists feared was a cover for consultations with Gov. George Clinton, the Livingstons, and Aaron Burr, leaders of the faction in New York which opposed the aristocratic party of the De Lanceys, Van Rensselaers, and Philip Schuyler, Hamilton's father-in-law. While the significance of that single trip was blown out of proportion, there did ultimately arise an informal alliance of Jeffersonian Republicans in the south and New York which would become a constant if sometimes awkward feature of the party and its successor, the Democratic party.

Still, there was no opposition to Washington, who longed to end his exile from Mount Vernon and even began preparing a farewell address, but was urged by both Hamilton and Jefferson to continue in public life. He was the only man who could transcend party differences and hold things together with his unmatched prestige and the infinite confidence the American people placed in him. In 1792 Washington was unanimously reelected, but in the scattering of second votes the Republican Clinton got fifty electoral votes to Adams's seventy-seven.

CRISES FOREIGN AND DOMESTIC

In Washington's second term the problems of foreign relations came to center stage, brought there by the consequences of the French Revolution, which had begun during the first months of Washington's presidency. Americans followed events in France with almost universal sympathy, up to a point. By the spring of 1792, though, the hopeful experiment in liberty, equality, and fraternity had transmogrified itself into a monster that plunged France into war with Austria and Prussia and began devouring its own children along with its enemies in the Terror of 1793–1794.

After the execution of King Louis XVI in January 1793, Great Britain entered into the coalition of monarchies at war with the French Republic. For the next twenty-two years Britain and France were at war, with only a brief respite, until the final defeat of French forces under Napoleon in 1815. The war presented Washington, just beginning his second term, with an awkward decision. By the treaty of 1778 the United States was a perpetual ally of France, obligated to defend her possessions in the West Indies. But Americans wanted no part of the war; on this much Hamilton and Jefferson could agree. Hamilton had a simple and direct answer to this problem: simply declare the alliance invalid because it was made with a government that no longer existed. Jefferson preferred to delay and use the alliance as a bargaining point with the British. But in the end Washington followed the advice of neither. Taking a middle course, on April 22, 1793, the president issued a neutrality proclamation that evaded even the word "neutrality." It simply declared the United States "friendly and impartial toward the belligerent powers" and warned American citizens that "aiding or abetting hostilities" or other unneutral acts might be prosecuted.

CITIZEN GENÊT At the same time, Washington accepted Jefferson's argument that the United States should recognize the new French government (becoming the first country to do so) and receive its new ambassador, Citizen Edmond Charles Genêt. Early in 1793 Citizen Genêt landed at Charleston, where he immediately organized a Jacobin Club, officially recognized in Paris by his fellow radicals. Along the route to Philadelphia the enthusiastic reception accorded by his sympathizers gave Genêt an inflated notion of his potential, not that he needed encouragement. In Charleston he began to authorize privateers to bring in British prizes, and in Philadelphia he continued the process. He intrigued with frontiersmen and land speculators, including George Rogers Clark, with an eye to an attack on Spanish Florida and Louisiana, and issued military commissions in an Armée du Mississippi and an Armée des Florides.

Genêt quickly became an embarrassment even to his Republican friends. Jefferson decided that the French minister had overreached himself when he violated a promise not to outfit a captured British ship as a privateer and sent out the *Little Sarah*, rechristened the *Petite Democrate*. When, finally, Genêt threatened in a moment of anger to appeal his cause directly to the American people over the head of their president, the cabinet unanimously agreed that he had to go and in August 1793 Washington demanded his recall. Meanwhile a new party of radicals had gained power in France and sent over its own minister, Citizen Fauchet, with a warrant for Genêt's arrest. Instead of returning to risk the guillotine, Genêt sought asylum, married the daughter of Governor Clinton, settled down as a country gentleman on the Hudson, and died years later an American citizen.

Genêt's foolishness and the growing excesses of the French radicals were fast cooling American support for their revolution. To Hamilton's followers it began to resemble their worst nightmares of democratic anarchy and infidelity. The French made it hard even for Republicans to retain sympathy, but they swallowed hard and made excuses. "The liberty of the whole earth was depending on the issue of the contest," the genteel Jefferson wrote, "and . . . rather than it should have failed, I would have seen half the earth devastated." Nor did the British make it easy for Federalists to rally to their side. Near the end of 1793 they informed the American government that they intended to occupy their northwest posts indefinitely and announced Orders in Council under which they seized the cargoes of American ships with provisions for or produce from the French islands. Given the offenses by both sides, it is hard to comprehend the degree to which the French and British causes polarized American opinion and the two parties. In the contest, it seemed, one either had to be a Republican and support liberty, reason, and France, or become a Federalist and support order, faith, and Britain. And the division gave rise to some curious anomalies: slaveholding planters joined the yelps for Jacobin radicals who dispossessed their aristocratic counterparts in France, and rang the tocsin in protest against British seizures of New England ships; Massachusetts shippers still profited from the British trade and kept quiet. Boston, once a hotbed of revolution, became a bastion of Federalism.

JAY'S TREATY   Early in 1794 the Republican leaders in Congress were gaining support for a plan of commercial retaliation to bring the British to their senses, when the British gave Washington a timely opening for a settlement. They announced abandonment of the Orders under which American brigs and schooners were being seized in wholesale lots, and on April 16, 1794, Washington named Chief Justice John Jay as a special envoy to Great Britain. Jay left with instructions to settle all major issues:

to secure British abandonment of the western posts, reparations for the losses of American shippers, compensation for slaves carried away in 1783, and a commercial treaty which would legalize American commerce with the British West Indies.

Jay entered the negotiations with his bargaining power compromised by both Federalists and Republicans. In Philadelphia Hamilton indiscreetly told the British minister that the United States had no intention of joining the Armed Neutrality recently formed by Scandinavian countries to uphold neutral rights. In Paris the new American minister, James Monroe, spoke before the National Assembly and embraced both its president and its revolution. The British in turn demanded from Jay greater assurances that America would keep neutral.

To win his objectives, Jay was obliged in fact to be more than neutral and to concede the British definition of neutral rights. He accepted the principles that naval stores were contraband, that provisions could not go in neutral ships to enemy ports, and the "Rule of 1756" by which trade with enemy colonies prohibited in peacetime could not be opened in wartime. Britain also gained most-favored-nation treatment in American commerce and a promise that French privateers would not be outfitted in American ports. Finally, Jay conceded that the old American debts to British merchants would be adjudicated and paid by the American government. In return for these concessions he won three important points: British evacuation of the northwest posts by 1796, reparations for the seizures of American ships and cargoes in 1793–1794, and legalization of trade with the British West Indies. But the last of these (Article XII) was so hedged with restrictions that the Senate eventually struck it from the treaty. Only ships of seventy tons or less could enter the trade, and the United States had to promise not to re-export any molasses, sugar, coffee, cocoa, or cotton. Jay, of course, knew nothing of the future importance of the cotton gin Eli Whitney had just invented.

A public outcry of rage greeted the terms of the treaty when they were leaked and published in the Philadelphia *Aurora*. Even Federalist shippers, ready for settlement on almost any terms, were disappointed at the limitations on their privileges in the West Indies. But much of the outcry was simply expression of disappointment by Republican partisans who sought an escalation of conflict with "perfidious Albion." Some of it was the outrage of Virginia planters at the concession on debts to British merchants and the failure to get reparations for lost slaves. Given the limited enthusiasm of Federalists—Washington himself

John Jay hanged in effigy by opponents to his treaty (1795). [The Warder Collection]

wrestled with doubts over the treaty—Jay remarked he could travel across the country by the light of his burning effigies. Yet the Senate debated the treaty in secret, and in the end quiet counsels of moderation prevailed. Without a single vote to spare, Jay's Treaty got the necessary two-thirds majority on June 24, 1795, with Article XII (the provision regarding the West Indies) expunged. Washington still hesitated but finally signed the treaty as the best he was likely to get and out of fear that subsequent escalation of conflict caused by a refusal would throw the United States into the role of a French satellite. In the House opposition to the treaty went so far as to demand that the president produce all papers relevant to the treaty, but the president refused on the grounds that treaty approval was solely the business of the Senate. He thereby set an important precedent of executive privilege (a term not used at the time), and the House finally relented, supplying the money to fund the treaty on a close vote.

THE FRONTIER STIRS   Other events also had an important bearing on Jay's Treaty, adding force to its settlement of the Canadian frontier and strengthening Spain's conviction that she too needed to reach a settlement of long-festering problems along the southwestern frontier. While Jay was haggling in London, frontier conflict with Indians was moving toward a resolution. Early in 1790 the northwestern tribes routed an American army under Gen. Josiah Harmar along the Maumee River. The next year Gen. Arthur St. Clair, governor of the Northwest Territory, gathered an army of militiamen and "men collected from the streets . . . from the stews and brothels of the cities," and went out to meet an even worse disaster. On November 4, 1791, the Indians surprised the American camp along the Wabash, singled out the officers, few of whom survived, and threw the militia into panic. Only about half of his men escaped unhurt. St. Clair himself, disabled by gout and propped up with pillows in a wagon to watch battle, barely escaped. The defeat resulted in the first congressional investigating committee, which finally put the blame on contractors who failed to supply the army properly.

Conditions along the northwestern frontier, on down into Kentucky, remained unsettled for three more years. Finally Washington named General Wayne, known as "Mad Anthony" since the storming of Stony Point in 1779, to head another expedition. In the fall of 1793 Wayne marched into Indian country with some 2,600 men, built Fort Greenville, and with reinforcements from Kentucky went on the offensive in 1794. On August, 4, 1794, the Indians, reinforced by some Canadian militia, at-

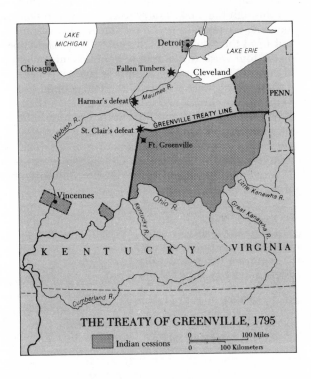

THE TREATY OF GREENVILLE, 1795

Indian cessions

0   100 Miles

0   100 Kilometers

tacked Wayne's force at the Battle of Fallen Timbers, but this time the Americans were ready and repulsed them with heavy losses, after which American detachments laid waste their fields and villages. Dispersed and decimated, they finally agreed to the Treaty of Greenville, signed in August 1795. In the treaty, at the cost of a $10,000 annuity, the United States bought from twelve tribes the rights to the southeastern quarter of the Northwest Territory (now Ohio and Indiana) and enclaves at the sites of Vincennes, Detroit, and Chicago.

THE WHISKEY REBELLION   Wayne's forces were still mopping up after the Battle of Fallen Timbers when the administration resolved on another show of strength in the backcountry against the so-called Whiskey Rebellion. Hamilton's excise tax on strong drink, levied in 1791, had excited strong feeling along the frontier since it taxed a staple crop of the very people who had the least to gain from Hamilton's program. Their grain was more easily transported to market in concentrated liquid form than in bulk. The tax was another part of Hamilton's scheme to pick the pockets of the poor to enrich fat speculators, as the frontiersmen saw it. All through the backcountry from Georgia to Pennsylvania and beyond, the tax gave rise to resistance and evasion. In the summer of 1794 the rumblings of discontent broke into open rebellion in the four western counties of Pennsylvania, where vigilantes organized to terrorize revenuers and taxpayers. They blew up the stills of those who paid the tax, robbed the mails, stopped court proceedings, and in a meeting held at Braddock's Field, threatened an assault on Pittsburgh. On August 7, 1794, President Washington issued a proclamation ordering them home and calling out 12,900 militiamen from Virginia, Maryland, Pennsylvania, and New Jersey. Getting no response from the "Whiskey Boys," he issued a proclamation on September 24 for suppression of the rebellion.

Pittsburgh, July 20, 1794.

FINDING the opposition to the revenue law more violent than I expected, regretting the mischief that has been done, and may from the continuation of measures, seeing the opposition changed from disguised rabble to a respectable party, think it my duty and do resign my commission.

ROBERT JOHNSON.

Robert Johnson resigns his commission as collector of the whiskey tax in Pittsburgh, 1794. [Carnegie Library, Pittsburgh]

Under the command of Gen. Henry Lee, a force larger than any Washington had ever commanded in the Revolution marched out from Harrisburg across the Alleghenies with Hamilton in their midst, itching to smite the insurgents. To his disappointment the rebels vaporized like rye mash when the heat was applied, and the troops met with little more opposition than a few liberty poles. By dint of great effort and much marching they finally rounded up twenty prisoners whom they paraded down Market Street in Philadelphia and clapped into prison. Eventually two of these were found guilty of treason, but were pardoned by Washington on the grounds that one was a "simpleton" and the other "insane." The government had made its point and gained "reputation and strength," according to Hamilton, by suppressing a rebellion which, according to Jefferson, "could never be found," but it was at the cost of creating or confirming new numbers of Republicans who scored heavily in the next Pennsylvania elections. Nor was it the end of whiskey rebellions, which continued in an unending war of wits between moonshiners and revenuers down to the day of twentieth-century rum-runners in hopped-up stock cars.

PINCKNEY'S TREATY   While these stirring events were transpiring in the Keystone State, Spain was suffering some setbacks to her schemes farther south. Spanish intrigues among the Creeks, Choctaws, Chickasaws, and Cherokees were keeping up the same turmoil the British fomented along the Ohio. Washington had sought to buy peace by payment of $100,000 and a commission as brigadier-general to the Creek chief, Alexander McGillivray, the half-blooded son of a Scottish trader, but it was to no avail. In 1793, therefore, John Sevier and some settlers from East Tennessee took it upon themselves to teach the proud Cherokees a lesson by leveling a few of their villages, and in 1794 James Robertson with some Tennesseans from around Nashville smote them again, burning and killing without pity.

The collapse of Spain's own designs in the west combined with Britain's concessions to the north to give some second thoughts to the Spanish, who were preparing to make peace with the French and switch sides in the European war. Among the more agreeable fruits of Jay's talks, therefore, were new parleys with the Spanish government, culminating in the Treaty of San Lorenzo (1795) in which the Spanish Government conceded every substantial point at issue. United States Minister Thomas Pinckney won acceptance of a boundary at the Thirty-first Parallel, free navigation of the Mississippi, the right to deposit goods at

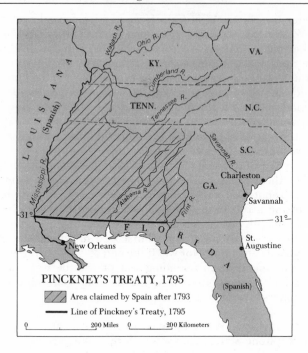

PINCKNEY'S TREATY, 1795

///// Area claimed by Spain after 1793
——— Line of Pinckney's Treaty, 1795

0 _____ 200 Miles   0 _____ 200 Kilometers

New Orleans for three years with promise of renewal, a commission to settle American claims against Spain, and a promise on each side to refrain from inciting Indian attacks on the other. Ratification of the Pinckney Treaty ran into no opposition at all.

Now that Jay and Pinckney had settled things with Britain and Spain, and General Wayne in the Northwest and the Tennessee settlers to the south had smashed the Indians, the West was open for a renewed surge of settlers. New lands, ceded by the Indians in the Treaty of Greenville, revealed Congress once again divided on land policy. There were two basic viewpoints on the matter, one that the public domain should serve mainly as a source of revenue, the other that it was more important to accommodate settlers with low prices, maybe free land, and get the country settled. In the long run the evolution of policy would be from the first toward the second viewpoint, but for the time being the government's need for revenue took priority.

Opinions on land policy, like other issues, separated Federalists from Republicans. Federalists involved in speculation might prefer lower land prices, but the more influential Federalists like Hamilton and Jay preferred to build the population of the eastern states first, lest the East lose political influence and lose a labor force important to the future growth of manufactures. Men of their persuasion wanted high land prices to enrich the treasury, sale of relatively large parcels of land to speculators rather than small amounts to actual settlers, and the development of compact settlements. In addition to his other reports, Hamilton had put out one on the public lands in which he emphasized the need for governmental revenues. Jefferson and Madison at this point were prepared reluctantly to go along for the sake of reducing the national debt, but Jefferson expressed the hope for a plan by which the lands could be more readily settled. In any case, he suggested, frontiersmen would do as they had done before: "They will settle the lands in spite of everybody." The Daniel Boones of the West, always moving out beyond the settlers and surveyors, were already proving him right.

But for the time Federalist policy prevailed. In the Land Act of 1796 Congress resolved to extend the rectangular surveys ordained in 1785, but it doubled the price to $2 per acre, with only a year in which to complete payment. Half the townships would

A farm newly cleared and settled in the West (1793). [New York Public Library]

go in 640-acre sections, making the minimum cost $1,280, and alternate townships would be sold in blocks of eight sections, or 5,120 acres, making the minimum cost $10,240. Either was beyond the means of most ordinary settlers, and a bit much even for speculators who could still pick up state lands at lower prices. By 1800 government land offices had sold fewer than 50,000 acres under the act. Continuing pressures from the West led to the Land Act of 1800 (introduced by a nonvoting territorial delegate from Indiana named William Henry Harrison) which reduced the minimum sale to 320 acres and spread the payments over four years. Thus with a down payment of $160 one could get a farm. All lands went for the minimum price if they did not sell at auction within three weeks. Under the Land Act of 1804 the minimum unit was reduced to 160 acres, which became the traditional homestead, and the price per acre went down to $1.64.

WASHINGTON'S FAREWELL By 1796 President Washington had decided that two terms in office were enough. Tired of the political quarrels and the venom of the partisan press, he was ready to retire once and for all to Mount Vernon. He would leave behind a formidable record of achievement: the organization of a national government with demonstrated power, establishment of the national credit, the recovery of territory previously withheld by Britain and Spain, stabilization of the northwestern frontier, the admission of three new states: Vermont (1791), Kentucky (1792), and Tennessee (1796). With the help of Jay and especially Hamilton, Washington set about preparing a valedictory address, using a draft prepared by Madison four years before.

Washington's Farewell Address, dated September 17, 1796, was not delivered as a speech. It was first published in the Philadelphia *Daily American Advertiser* two days later. It stated first his resolve to decline being considered for a third term. After that, most of the message dwelled on domestic policy, and particularly on the need for unity among the American people in backing their new government. Washington decried the spirit of sectionalism. "In contemplating the causes which may disturb our union," he wrote in one prescient passage, "it occurs as a matter of serious concern that any ground should have been furnished for characterizing parties by geographical discriminations—*Northern* and *Southern*, *Atlantic* and *Western*—whence designing men may endeavor to excite a belief that there is a real difference of local interests and views." He decried as strongly the spirit of party, while acknowledging a body of opinion that parties were "useful checks upon the administration of the government, and serve to keep alive the spirit of liberty." From the natural tendency of men there would always be enough spirit of party, however, to serve that purpose. The danger was partisan excess: "A fire not to be quenched, it demands a uniform vigilance to prevent its bursting into a flame, lest, instead of warming, it should consume."

In foreign relations, he said, America should show "good faith and justice toward all nations" and avoid either "an habitual hatred or an habitual fondness" for other countries. Europe, he noted, "has a set of primary interests which to us have none or a very remote relation. Hence she must be engaged in frequent controversies, the causes of which are essentially foreign to our concerns." The United States should keep clear of those quarrels. It was, moreover, "our true policy to steer clear of permanent alliances with any portion of the foreign world." A key word here is "permanent." Washington enjoined against any further permanent arrangements like that with France, still technically in effect. He did not speak of "entangling alliances"—that phrase would be used by Thomas Jefferson in his first inaugural address—and in fact specifically advised that "we may safely trust to temporary alliances for extraordinary emergencies."

Washington himself had not escaped the "baneful effects" of the party spirit, for during his second term the Republican press came to link him with the Federalist partisans. For the first time in his long career Washington was subjected to sustained, and often scurrilous, criticism. According to Benjamin F. Bache, grandson of Franklin and editor of the Philadelphia *Aurora,* the president was "a man in his political dotage" and "a supercilious tyrant." Washington never responded to such abuse in public but in private he went into towering rages. The effect of such abuse was to hasten his resolve to retire. On the eve of that event the *Aurora* proclaimed that "this day ought to be a Jubilee in the United States. . . . If ever a nation was debauched by a man, the American Nation has been debauched by Washington."

THE ADAMS YEARS

With Washington out of the race, the United States had its first partisan election for president. The logical choice of the Federalists would have been Washington's protégé Hamilton, the chief architect of their programs. But like many a later presidential candidate, Hamilton was not "available," however will-

ing. His policies had left scars and made enemies. Nor did he
suffer fools gladly, a common affliction of Federalist leaders, including the man on whom the choice fell. In Philadelphia, a
caucus of Federalist congressmen chose John Adams as heir apparent with Thomas Pinckney of South Carolina, fresh from his
triumph in Spain, as nominee for vice-president. The Republicans drafted Jefferson (any other choice would have been a surprise) and added geographical balance with Aaron Burr of New
York, an ally of Clinton.

The rising strength of the Republicans, largely due to the
smouldering resentment of Jay's Treaty, very nearly swept Jefferson into office, and perhaps would have but for the public appeals of the French ambassador Adet for his election—an action
which, like the indiscretions of Citizen Genêt, backfired. Then,
despite a Federalist majority among the electors, Alexander
Hamilton thought up an impulsive scheme which very nearly
threw the election away after all. Between Hamilton and Adams
there had been no love lost since the Revolution, when Adams

THE PROVIDENTIAL DETECTION

*An anti-Republican cartoon shows the American
eagle arriving just in time to stop Thomas
Jefferson from burning the Constitution on the
"Altar to Gallic Despotism." [American
Antiquarian Society]*

had joined the movement to remove Hamilton's father-in-law, General Schuyler, from command of the Saratoga campaign. Thomas Pinckney, Hamilton thought, would be more subject to influence than the strong-minded Adams. He therefore sought to have South Carolina Federalists withhold a few votes from Adams and bring Pinckney in first. The Carolinians more than co-operated—they divided their vote between Pinckney and Jefferson—but New Englanders got wind of the scheme and dropped Pinckney. The upshot of Hamilton's intrigue was to cut Pinckney out of both offices and put Jefferson back in the capital as vice-president with sixty-eight votes, second to Adams's seventy-one.

Adams had behind him a distinguished career as a Massachusetts lawyer, a leader in the revolutionary movement and the Continental Congress, a diplomat in France, Holland, and Britain, and as vice-president. In two treatises on politics, the three-volume *Defense of the Constitution of Government of the United States* (1787–1788) and the less formidable *Discourse on Davila°* (1790), he had formally committed to paper a political philosophy that put him somewhere between Jefferson and Hamilton. He shared neither the one's faith in the common people nor the other's fondness for an aristocracy of "paper wealth . . . the madness of the many for the profit of the few." He favored the classic mixture of aristocratic, democratic, and monarchical elements though his use of "monarchical" interchangeably with "executive" exposed him to the attacks of Republicans who saw a monarchist in every Federalist. At times, in his manner and appearance, Adams was made out by his enemies to be a pompous ass, but his fondness for titles and protocol arose from a reasoned purpose to exploit men's "thirst for distinction." He was always haunted by a feeling that he was never properly appreciated—and he may have been right. He tried to play the role of disinterested executive which he outlined in his philosophy. And on the overriding issue of his administration, war and peace, he kept his head when others about him were losing theirs—probably at the cost of his reelection.

WAR WITH FRANCE   Adams inherited from Washington his cabinet —the precedent of changing personnel with each new administration had not yet been set—and with them a party division, for three of the department heads looked to Hamilton for counsel: Timothy Pickering at State, Oliver Wolcott at the Treasury, and

°An Italian historian.

John Adams. [Adams National Historic Site, Quincy, Mass.]

James McHenry at the War Department. Adams also inherited a menacing quarrel with France, a by-product of the Jay Treaty. When Jay accepted the British position that food supplies and naval stores—as well as war matériel—were contraband subject to seizure, the French reasoned that American cargoes in the British trade were subject to the same interpretation and loosed their corsairs in the West Indies with even more devastating effect than the British had in 1793–1794. By the time of Adams's inauguration in 1797 the French had plundered some 300 American ships, and had broken diplomatic relations. As ambassador to Paris, James Monroe had become so pro-French and so hostile to the Jay Treaty that Washington had felt impelled to remove him for his indiscretions. France then had refused to accept Monroe's replacement, Charles Cotesworth Pinckney, and ordered him out of the country.

Adams immediately acted to restore relations in the face of an outcry for war from the "High Federalists," including Secretary of State Pickering. Hamilton, to whom the group generally looked as their leader, agreed with Adams on this point and approved his last-ditch effort for a settlement. In October 1797 C. C. Pinckney returned to Paris with John Marshall and Elbridge Gerry (a Massachusetts Republican) for further negotiations. After long, nagging delays, the three commissioners were accosted by three French counterparts (whom Adams labeled X, Y, and Z in his report to Congress), agents of Foreign Minister Talleyrand, a past master of the diplomatic shakedown. The three delicately let it be known that negotiations could begin only if there were a loan of $12 million, a bribe of $250,000 to the five directors then heading the government, and suitable apologies for remarks recently made in Adams's message to Congress.

Such bribes were common eighteenth-century diplomatic practice—Washington himself had bribed a Creek chieftain and ransomed American sailors from Algerian pirates, each at a cost of $100,000—but Talleyrand's price was high merely for a promise to negotiate. The answer, according to the commissioners' report, was "no, no, not a sixpence." When the XYZ Affair broke in Congress and the public press, this was translated into the more stirring slogan first offered as a banquet toast by Robert Goodloe Harper: "Millions for defense but not one cent for tribute." And the expressions of hostility toward France rose to a crescendo—even the most partisan Republicans were hard put to make any more excuses, and many of them joined a cry for war. An undeclared naval war in fact raged in the West Indies (with some engagements in the Mediterranean and Indian Ocean) from 1798 to 1800, but Adams resisted a formal declaration of war. The French would have to bear the onus for that. Congress, however, authorized the capture of armed French ships, suspended commerce with France, and renounced the alliance of 1778, which was already a dead letter. Adams used the occasion to strengthen American defenses.

An American navy had ceased to exist at the end of the Revolution. Except for revenue cutters of the Treasury Department, no armed ships were available when Algerian brigands began to war on American commerce in 1794. As a result Congress had authorized the arming of six ships. These were incomplete in 1796 when Washington bought peace with the Algerians, but Congress allowed work on three to continue: the *Constitution*, the *United States*, and the *Constellation*, all completed in 1797. In 1798 Congress authorized a new Department of the Navy, headed first by Benjamin Stoddert, a Baltimore merchant. By the end of 1798 the number of naval ships had increased to twenty and by the end of 1799 to thirty-three. But before the end of 1798 an undeclared naval war had begun in the West Indies with the French capture of the American schooner *Retaliation* off Guadeloupe in November 1798.

While the naval war went on, a new army was authorized in 1798 as a 10,000-man force to serve three years. Adams called Washington from retirement to be its commander, agreeing to Washington's condition that he name his three chief subordinates. Washington sent in the names of Hamilton, Charles C. Pinckney, and Henry Knox. In the old army the three ranked in precisely the opposite order, but Washington insisted that Hamilton be his second in command. Adams relented, but resented the slight to his authority as commander-in-chief. The rift among Federalists thus widened further. Because of Washington's age, the choice meant that Hamilton would command the army in the field, if it ever took the field. But recruitment went slowly until well into 1799, by which time all fear of French invasion was dispelled. Hamilton continued to dream of imperial glory, though, planning the seizure of Louisiana and the Floridas to keep them out of French hands, even the invasion of South America, but these remained Hamilton's dreams.

Peace overtures began to come from Talleyrand even before the naval war was fully under way. In the autumn of 1798 Elbridge Gerry returned from Paris with the word. Adams decided to act on the information and took it upon himself, without consulting the cabinet, to name the American minister to the Netherlands, William Vans Murray, special envoy to Paris. The Hamiltonians, infected with a virulent attack of war fever, fought the nomination but finally compromised, in face of Adams's threat to resign, on a commission of three. Adams named Chief Justice Oliver Ellsworth and Gov. William R. Davie of North Carolina to accompany Murray. After a long delay they left late in 1799 and arrived to find themselves confronting a new government under First Consul Napoleon Bonaparte. By the Convention of 1800 they got the best terms they could from the triumphant Napoleon. In return for giving up all claims of indemnity for American losses they got the suspension of the French alliance and the end of the quasi-war. The Senate ratified, contingent upon outright abrogation of the alliance, and the agreement became effective on December 21, 1801.

THE WAR AT HOME   The real purpose of the French crisis all along, the more ardent Republicans suspected, was to create an excuse to put down the domestic opposition. The Alien and Sedition Acts of 1798 lent credence to their suspicions. These four measures, passed in the wave of patriotic war fever, limited freedom of speech and the press, and the liberty of aliens. Proposed by the High Federalists in Congress, they did not originate with Adams but had his blessing. Three of the four acts reflected hostility to foreigners, especially the French and Irish, a large number of whom had become active Republicans and were suspected of revolutionary intent. The Naturalization Act changed from five to fourteen years the residence requirement for citizenship. The Alien Act empowered the president to expel "dangerous" aliens on pain of imprisonment. The Alien Enemy Act authorized the president in time of declared war to expel or imprison enemy aliens at will. Finally, the Sedition Act defined as high misdemeanor any combination or conspiracy against legal measures of the government, including interference with federal officers and insurrection or riot. What is more, the law forbade writing, publishing, or speaking anything of "a false, scandalous and malicious" nature against the government or any of its officers.

Considering what Federalists and Republicans said about each other, the act, applied rigorously, could have caused the imprisonment of nearly the whole government itself. But the purpose was transparently partisan, designed to punish Republicans whom Federalists could scarcely distinguish from Jacobins and traitors. To be sure, perfervid Republican journalists were resorting to scandalous lies and misrepresentations, but so were Federalists; it was a time when both sides seemed afflicted with paranoia. But the fifteen indictments brought, with ten convictions, were all directed at Republicans and some for trivial matters. In the very first case Luther Baldwin of New Jersey was fined $100 for wishing out loud that the wad of a salute cannon might hit President Adams in his rear. The most conspicuous targets of prosecution were Republican editors, including Thomas Cooper, James Callender, and William Duane. Another target was a congressman, Matthew Lyon of Vermont, a rough-and-tumble Irishman who published censures of Adams's "continual grasp for power" and "unbounded thirst for ridiculous pomp, foolish adulation, and selfish avarice." For such libels Lyon got four months and a fine of $1,000, but from his cell he continued to write articles and letters for the Republican papers. The few convictions under the act only created martyrs to the cause of freedom of speech and the press, and exposed the vindictiveness of Federalist judges.

Lyon and the others based a defense on the unconstitutionality of the Sedition Act, but Federalist judges were scarcely inclined to entertain such notions. It ran against the Republican grain, anyway, to have federal courts assume the authority to declare laws unconstitutional. To offset the Alien and Sedition Acts, therefore, Jefferson and Madison conferred and brought forth drafts of what came to be known as the Kentucky and Virginia Resolutions. These passed the legislatures of the two states in November and December 1798, while further Kentucky Resolutions, adopted in November 1799, responded to counterresolutions from northern states. These resolutions, much alike in their arguments, denounced the Alien and Sedition Acts as unconstitutional and advanced what came to be known as the state compact theory. Since the Constitution arose as a compact among the states, the resolutions argued, it followed logically that the states should assume the right to say when Congress had exceeded its

Republican Rep. Matthew Lyon and the Connecticut Federalist Roger Griswald go at each other on the floor of the House (1798). Lyon soon became a target of the Sedition Act. [New York Public Library]

powers. The Virginia Resolutions, drafted by Madison, declared that states "have the right and are in duty bound to interpose for arresting the progress of the evil." The second set of Kentucky Resolutions, in restating the states' right to judge violations of the Constitution, added: "That a nullification of those sovereignties, of all unauthorized acts done under color of that instrument, is the rightful remedy."

The doctrines of interposition and nullification, revised and edited by later theorists, were destined to be used for causes unforeseen by the authors of the Kentucky and Virginia Resolutions. Years later Madison would disclaim the doctrine of nullification as developed by John C. Calhoun, but his own doctrine of "interposition" would resurface as late as the 1950s as a device to oppose racial integration. At the time, it seems, both men intended the resolutions to serve chiefly as propaganda, the opening guns in the political campaign of 1800. Neither Kentucky nor Virginia took steps to nullify or interpose its authority against enforcement of the Alien and Sedition Acts. Instead both called upon the other states to help them win a repeal. Jefferson counseled against any thought of violence, which was "not the kind of opposition the American people will permit." He assured fellow Virginian John Taylor that "the reign of witches" would soon end, that it would be discredited by the arrival of the tax collector more than anything else.

In 1798 Congress had imposed a direct tax on houses, land, and slaves. The Alien and Sedition Acts touched comparatively few individuals, but the tax reached every property holder in the country. In eastern Pennsylvania the general discontent with the tax reached the stage of armed resistance in Fries's Rebellion, an incident that scarcely deserves so impressive a name. John Fries, a Pennsylvania Dutch auctioneer, had led a group of armed men to force the release of two tax evaders imprisoned at Bethlehem. To suppress this "insurrection" President Adams sent army regulars and militiamen into Northampton County. But like the Whiskey Rebellion five years before, the insurrection evaporated. The soldiers found not a rebellion but John Fries conducting an auction. He was arrested and brought to trial with two others on inflated charges of treason. The three men were found guilty twice, a second trial having been granted on appeal, and twice sentenced to hang. President Adams, however, decided that the men had not committed treason and granted them a pardon along with a general pardon to all participants in the affair.

REPUBLICAN VICTORY Thus as the presidential election of 1800 approached, grievances were mounting against Federalist policies: taxation to support an army that had little to do but chase Pennsylvania farmers, the Alien and Sedition Acts which cast the Republicans in the role of defending liberty, the lingering fears of "monarchism," the hostilities aroused by Hamilton's programs, the suppression of the Whiskey Rebellion, and Jay's Treaty. When Adams decided for peace in 1800, he probably doomed his one chance for reelection: a wave of patriotic war fever with a united party behind him. His decision gained him much goodwill among the people at large, but left the Hamiltonians unreconciled and his party divided. In May 1800 the Federalists summoned enough unity to name as their candidates Adams and C. C. Pinckney, brother of Thomas Pinckney, who ran in 1796; they agreed to cast all their electoral votes for both. But the Hamiltonians continued to snipe at Adams and his policies. Soon after his renomination Adams removed two of them from his cabinet—Secretary of State Timothy Pickering and Secretary of War James McHenry—replacing them with two Virginians: John Marshall and Samuel Dexter. Hamilton struck back with a pamphlet questioning Adams's fitness to be president, citing his "disgusting egotism." Intended for private distribution among Federalist leaders, the pamphlet reached the hands of Aaron Burr, who put it in circulation.

Jefferson and Burr, as the Republican candidates, once again represented the alliance of Virginia and New York. Jefferson, perhaps even more than Adams, became the target of villification as a Jacobin and an atheist. His election, people were told, would bring "dwellings in flames, hoary hairs bathed in blood, female chastity violated . . . children writhing on the pike and halberd." Jefferson kept quiet, refused to answer the attacks, and directed the campaign by mail from his home at Monticello. He was advanced as the farmers' friend, the champion of states' rights, frugal government, liberty, and peace.

Adams proved more popular than his party, whose candidates generally fared worse than the president, but the Republicans edged him out by seventy-three electoral votes to sixty-five. The decisive states were New York and South Carolina, either of which might have given the victory to Adams. But in New York

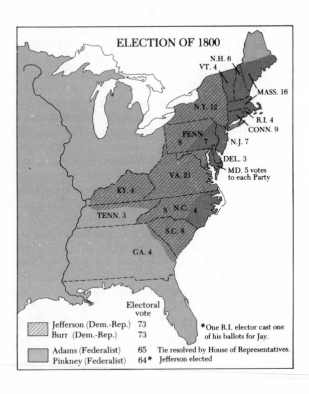

ELECTION OF 1800

N.H. 6
VT. 4
MASS. 16
N.Y. 12
R.I. 4
CONN. 9
PENN. 8 7
N.J. 7
DEL. 3
VA. 21
MD. 5 votes to each Party
KY. 4
TENN. 3
N.C. 4
S.C. 8
GA. 4

	Electoral vote	
Jefferson (Dem.-Rep.)	73	
Burr (Dem.-Rep.)	73	
Adams (Federalist)	65	Tie resolved by House of Representatives.
Pinkney (Federalist)	64*	Jefferson elected

*One R.I. elector cast one of his ballots for Jay.

Burr's organization by vigorous activity won control of the legislature, which cast the electoral votes. In South Carolina, Charles
Pinckney (cousin to the Federalist Pinckneys) won over the legislature by well-placed promises of Republican patronage. Still,
the result was not final, for Jefferson and Burr had tied with seventy-three votes each, and the choice of the president was
thrown into the House of Representatives, where Federalist die-
hards tried vainly to give the election to Burr. This was too much
for Hamilton, who opposed Jefferson but held an even lower
opinion of Burr. Burr refused to assent to the Federalist movement, but neither would he renounce it. Eventually the deadlock
was broken when a confidant of Jefferson assured James A.
Bayard of Delaware that Jefferson would refrain from wholesale
removals of Federalists and uphold the new fiscal system. Bayard
resolved to vote for Jefferson, and several other Federalists
agreed simply to cast blank ballots, permitting Jefferson to win
without any of them actually having to vote for him.

Before the Federalists relinquished power on March 4, 1801,
their "lame duck" Congress passed the Judiciary Act of 1801.
This act provided that the next vacancy on the Supreme Court
should not be filled, created sixteen Circuit Courts with a new
judge for each, and increased the number of attorneys, clerks,
and marshals. Before he left office Adams named John Marshall
to the vacant office of Chief Justice and appointed good Federalists to all the new positions, including forty-two justices of the
peace for the new District of Columbia. The Federalists, defeated and destined never to regain national power, had in the
words of Jefferson "retired into the judiciary as a stronghold."

FURTHER READING

The best introduction to the early Federalists remains John C.
Miller's *The Federalist Era, 1789–1800* (1960).° Where Miller stresses
narrative detail, more recent works analyze the ideological debates
among the nation's first leaders. Richard Buel, Jr.'s *Securing the Revolution: Ideology in American Politics, 1789–1815* (1972),° and John
Zvesper's *Political Philosophy and Rhetoric: A Study of the Origins of
American Party Politics* (1977) trace the persistence of ideas first fostered during the Revolutionary crisis. Older but valuable studies of the
early parties include Joseph Charles's *The Origins of the American Party
System* (1956),° Richard Hofstadter's *The Idea of a Party System* (1969),

°These books are available in paperback editions.

and William D. Chambers's *Political Parties in a New Nation, the American Experience, 1776–1809* (1963).

The 1790s may be best understood through the views and behavior of national leaders. Among the studies of Federalist leaders are a number of biographies of Alexander Hamilton: Jacob Ernest Cook's *Alexander Hamilton* (1982), Forrest McDonald's *Alexander Hamilton: A Biography* (1979),° Gerald Stourzh's *Alexander Hamilton and the Idea of a Republican Government* (1970), Broadus Mitchell's *Alexander Hamilton: The National Adventure, 1788–1804* (1962), and John C. Miller's *Alexander Hamilton: Portrait in Paradox* (1959). For the nation's first president, consult the two volumes by James T. Flexner, *George Washington and the New Nation* (1969) and *George Washington: Anguish and Farewell* (1972). Forrest McDonald's *The Presidency of George Washington* (1974) is also helpful. The second president is handled in Page Smith's *John Adams* (2 vols.; 1962), Martin J. Dauer's *The Adams Federalists* (1969), and Stephen G. Kurtz's *The Presidency of John Adams: The Collapse of Federalism, 1795–1800* (1957).

The opposition viewpoint is the subject of Lance Banning's *The Jeffersonian Persuasion: Evolution of a Party Ideology* (1978). Noble E. Cunningham, Jr.'s *The Jeffersonian Republicans: The Formation of Party Organization, 1789–1801* (1957),° and Lawrence S. Kaplan's *Jefferson and France* (1967) help clarify political views. Biographies include Irving Brant's *James Madison: Father of the Constitution, 1787–1800* (1950), and Merrill Petersen's *Thomas Jefferson and the New Nation* (1970).°

State-level studies illuminate how the conflicts spread beyond the national capital. Consult Harry Tinkcom's *The Republicans and Federalists in Pennsylvania, 1790–1801: A Study in National Stimulus and Local Response* (1950), Paul Goodman's *The Democratic-Republicans of Massachusetts: Politics in a Young Republic* (1964), Alfred F. Young's *The Democratic Republicans of New York: The Origins, 1763–1797* (1967), and Norman Risjord's *Chesapeake Politics, 1781–1800* (1978).

The study of Federalist foreign policy begins with the work of Samuel F. Bemis: *Jay's Treaty* (1923) and *Pinckney's Treaty* (1926).° More recent is Jerald A. Combs's *The Jay Treaty* (1970). Surveys include Lawrence S. Kaplan's *Colonies into Nation: American Diplomacy, 1763–1801* (1972), Paul A. Varg's *Foreign Policies of the Founding Fathers* (1963), and Felix Gilbert's *To the Farewell Address: Ideas of Early American Foreign Policy* (1961). Albert H. Bowman's *Struggle for Neutrality* (1974) is more interpretative. Alexander De Conde breaks down foreign policies in the two Federalist administrations in *Entangling Alliance: Politics and Diplomacy under George Washington* (1958) and *The Quasi-War: The Politics and Diplomacy of the Undeclared War with France, 1797–1801* (1966).

Specific domestic issues are handled in several works. Leland D. Baldwin's *Whiskey Rebels: The Story of a Frontier Uprising* (1939) treats that incident. Patricia Watlingon's *The Partisan Spirit* (1972) examines the Kentucky Resolutions. Harry Ammon looks at the domestic conflicts engendered by *The Genet Mission* (1973).° The treatment of Indians in the old Northwest is handled in Richard H. Kohn's *Eagle and Sword: The Federalists and the Creation of the Military Establishment in America, 1783–1802* (1975). For the Alien and Sedition Acts, consult James Morton Smith's *Freedom's Fetters: The Alien and Sedition Laws and American Civil Liberties* (1956)° and Leonard W. Levy's *Legacy of Suppression: Freedom of Speech and Press in Early American History* (1960). Daniel Sisson's *The American Revolution of 1800* (1974) and Morton Borden's *The Federalism of James A. Bayard* (1955) are good on the election of 1800. The bureaucratic perspective is found in Leonard D. White's *The Federalists: A Study in Administrative History* (1948).°

9

REPUBLICANISM:
JEFFERSON AND MADISON

A New Capital

On March 4, 1801, Thomas Jefferson became the first president to be inaugurated in the new Federal City, Washington, District of Columbia. The location of the city on the Potomac had been the fruit of Jefferson's and Madison's compromise with Hamilton on the assumption of state debts. Choice of the site had been entrusted to President Washington, who picked a location upstream from Mount Vernon and reaching from the village of Georgetown, Maryland, which it included, to the East Branch (now the Anacostia River). The District of Columbia at first took in land on the Virginia side of the Potomac, making it precisely ten miles by ten, but that portion was later ceded back to Virginia. In 1791 Maj. Pierre L'Enfant, a French engineer who had served in the Revolution, drew up the original plan for the district. Followed in its essence, the design called for a gridwork of parallel streets overlaid with diagonal avenues which radiated from various centers, most conspicuously Jenkins's Hill (site of the Capitol) and the site of the Executive Mansion, which faced each other along the length of Pennsylvania Avenue. L'Enfant also planned a third focus for the site of the Supreme Court, symbolizing the three branches of government, but that part of the plan was later abandoned, and the Court long occupied a room in the Capitol basement.

In accordance with the requirement of Congress, work progressed on the public buildings and the city during the 1790s,

This Plan of the City of Washington *shows L'Enfant's detailed gridwork pattern of "Grand Avenues and Streets" (1800). [New York Public Library]*

and President Adams moved into his new home in September 1800. Abigail arrived at the "great castle" in October. It was "in a beautiful situation" with a view of the Potomac and Alexandria, but all the rooms were new and unfinished. By November the Adams family had to keep thirteen fires daily, she said, "or sleep in wet and damp places." Nearby Georgetown, D.C., where Abigail was obliged to market, was "the very dirtyest hole . . . for a place of any trade, or respectability of inhabitants." When Jefferson took office, Washington was still an unprepossessing array of buildings around two centers, Capitol Hill and the Executive Mansion. Between them was a swampy wilderness traversed by the Tiber River and by Pennsylvania Avenue, still full of stumps and mud holes, but with a stone walkway which offered a vantage from which to shoot ducks, snipe, partridge, and, after rains, the perch in the Tiber River! The Congress, having met in eight different towns and cities since 1774, had at least found a permanent home, but as yet enjoyed few amenities. There were only a few sad houses, "most of them small miserable huts," according to Oliver Wolcott, Adams's secretary of the treasury. To a

French acquaintance Sen. Gouverneur Morris wrote: "We lack here only houses, wine cellars, learned men, amiable women, and other trifles to make our city perfect . . . it is the best city in the world to live in—in the future." There were two places of amusement, one a racetrack, the other a theater filled with "tobacco smoke, whiskey breaths, and other strenches, mixed up with the effluvia of stables, and miasmas of the canal. . . . " Practically deserted much of the year, the town came to life only when Congress assembled.

JEFFERSON IN OFFICE

The inauguration of Jefferson befitted the surroundings. The new president left his lodgings and walked two blocks to the unfinished Capitol, entered the Senate chamber and took the oath from Chief Justice John Marshall, read his inaugural address in a barely audible voice, and returned to his boarding house for dinner and the common table. John Adams was absent. He had quietly slipped away, which was just as well according to his descendant, the historian Henry Adams, since "he would have seemed, in his successor's opinion, as little in place as George III would have appeared at the inauguration of President Washington." A tone of simplicity and conciliation ran through Jeffer-

Republican victory banner. The American eagle proclaims Jefferson president, and John Adams "No More." [Smithsonian Institution]

son's inaugural address, its seeming artlessness the product of three laborious drafts: "We are all Republicans—we are all Federalists. If there be any among us who would wish to dissolve this Union or to change its republican form, let them stand undisturbed as monuments of the safety with which error of opinion may be tolerated where reason is left free to combat it."

After this eloquent affirmation of freedom, he proceeded to a ringing affirmation of republican govenment: "I know, indeed, that some honest men fear that a republican government cannot be strong; that this government is not strong enough. But would the honest patriot, in the full tide of successful experiment, abandon a government which has so far kept us free and firm, on the theoretic and visionary fear that this government, the world's best hope, may by possibility want energy to preserve itself? I trust not. I believe this, on the contrary, the strongest government on earth. I believe it is the only one where every man . . . would meet invasions of the public order as his own personal concern. Sometimes it is said that man cannot be trusted with the government of himself. Can he, then, be trusted with the government of others? Or have we found angels in the form of kings to govern him? Let history answer this question."

Jefferson's "happy faculty of condensing whole chapters into aphorisms," as one of his biographers put it, was displayed in his summary of the "essential principles" that would guide his administration: "Equal and exact justice to all men. . . ; peace commerce, and honest friendship with all nations, entangling alliances with none. . . ; freedom of religion; freedom of the press; and freedom of person, under the protection of the habeas corpus; and trial by juries impartially selected. . . . The wisdom of our sages and the blood of our heroes have been devoted to their attainment."

The deliberate display of republican simplicity at Jefferson's inauguration would become the style of his administration. He took pains to avoid the occasions of pomp and circumstance which had characterized Federalist administrations and which to his mind suggested the trappings of kingship. Presidential messages went to Congress in writing lest they resemble the parliamentary speech from the throne. The practice also allowed Jefferson, a notoriously bad public speaker, to exploit his skill as a writer.

Jefferson discarded the coach and six in which Washington and Adams had gone to state occasions and rode about the city on horseback, often by himself. But this was, at least in part, therapy recommended by a doctor, and in part because Washington's

A watercolor of the president's house in 1800. Jefferson called it "big enough for two emperors, one pope, and the grand lama in the bargain." [The Warder Collection]

rutted streets were hardly the place for a carriage. The formal levee was abandoned for an informal weekly reception to which all were invited. Dinners at the White House were held around a circular table, so that none should take precedence, and at social affairs the new president simply ignored the rules of protocol for what he called the rule of *pele mele,* in which the only custom observed was that the ladies went ahead of the men. "When brought together in society, all are perfectly equal," Jefferson said.

It was not that Jefferson had ceased to be the Virginia gentleman, nor that he had abandoned elegant manners or the good life. The cuisine of his French chef and the wines for his frequent dinners strained his budget to the point that he had to borrow money and he left office with a debt which was to pursue him the rest of his life. The dinners also strained the patience of British Minister Anthony Merry, who had already taken umbrage at being received by a president "standing in slippers down at the heels, and both pantaloons, coat and underclothes indicative of an indifference to appearance." Perhaps it was a calculated slight to the minister of George III, who had behaved rudely when the author of the Declaration was presented to him in 1786.

Jefferson liked to think of his election as the "Revolution of 1800," but the margin had been close and the policies which he followed were more conciliatory than revolutionary. That they suited the vast majority of the people is attested to by his overwhelming reelection in 1804. Perhaps the most revolutionary thing about Jefferson's presidency was the orderly transfer of power in 1801, an uncommon event in the world of that day.

"The changes of administration," a Washington lady wrote in her diary, "which in every age have most generally been epochs of confusion, villainy and bloodshed, in this our happy country take place without any species of distraction, or disorder." Jefferson placed in policy-making positions men of his own party, and was the first president to pursue the role of party leader, assiduously cultivating congressional support at his dinner parties and otherwise. It was a role he had not so much sought as fallen into; he still shared the eighteenth-century distrust of the party spirit. In the cabinet the leading fixtures were Secretary of State James Madison, a longtime neighbor and political collaborator, and Secretary of the Treasury Albert Gallatin, a Pennsylvania Republican whose financial skills had won him the respect of Federalists. In an effort to cultivate Federalist New England, Jefferson chose men from that region for the positions of attorney-general, secretary of war, and postmaster-general.

In lesser offices, however, Jefferson refrained from wholesale removal of Federalists, preferring to wait until vacancies appeared, a policy which led to his rueful remark that vacancies obtained "by death are few; by resignation, none." But the pressure from Republicans was such that he often yielded and removed Federalists, trying as best he could to assign some other than partisan causes for the removals. In one area, however, he managed to remove the offices rather than the appointees. In 1802 Congress repealed the Judiciary Act of 1801, and so abolished the circuit judgeships and other offices to which Adams had made his "midnight appointments." A new judiciary act restored to six the number of Supreme Court justices, and set up six circuit courts, each headed by a justice.

MARBURY V. MADISON   It was in the judiciary, however, that Jefferson suffered the chief setbacks of his first term, especially in the case of *Marbury v. Madison*, a case of little intrinsic significance but one which set a precedent of great import. The case involved the appointment of one William Marbury as Justice of the peace in the District of Columbia. Marbury's commission, signed by President Adams two days before he left office, was still undelivered when Madison took office as secretary of state, and Jefferson directed him to withhold it. Marbury then sued for a court order (a writ of mandamus) directing Madison to deliver his commission. The Court's unanimous opinion, written by John Marshall, held that Marbury was entitled to his commission, but then denied that the Court had jurisdiction in the case. Section 13 of the Judiciary Act of 1789, which gave the Court original jurisdiction in mandamus proceedings, was unconstitutional, the court ruled, because the Constitution specified that the Court should have original jurisdiction only in cases involving ambassadors or states. With one bold stroke Marshall avoided an awkward confrontation with an administration which might have defied his order and at the same time established the precedent that the Court could declare a federal law invalid on the grounds that it violated provisions of the Constitution. The precedent of judicial review was not followed again for fifty-four years, but the principle was fixed for want of a challenge.

PARTISAN SQUABBLES   The decision, about which Jefferson could do nothing, confirmed his fear of the judges' tendency to "throw an anchor ahead, and grapple further hold for future advances of power." In 1804 Republicans finally determined to use the impeachment power against two of the most partisan Federalist judges, and succeeded in ousting one of the two. The Republican House brought impeachments against District Judge John Pickering of New Hampshire and Justice Samuel Chase. Pickering was clearly insane, not a high crime or misdemeanor, but he was also given to profane and drunken harangues from the bench, which the Senate quickly decided was. In any event he was incompetent.

The case against Justice Chase, a much bigger matter, was less cut and dried. That he was highhanded and intemperate there was no question. Chase had presided at the sedition trials of two Republican editors, ordering a marshal to strike off the jury panel "any of those creatures or persons called democrats," and once attacked the Maryland consitution from the bench because it granted manhood suffrage, under which "our republican Constitution will sink into a mobocracy." But neither Jefferson nor the best efforts of John Randolph of Roanoke as prosecutor for the House could persuade two-thirds of the senators that Chase's vindictive partisanship constituted "high crimes and misdemeanors." His removal indeed might have set off the partisanship of Republicans in a political carnival of reprisals. His acquittal discouraged further efforts at impeachment, however, which Jefferson pronounced a "farce," after the failure to remove Chase.

DOMESTIC REFORMS   Aside from these setbacks, however, Jefferson for a while had things pretty much his own way. His first term was a succession of triumphs in both domestic and foreign affairs. He did not set out to dismantle Hamilton's program root and branch. Under Gallatin's tutoring he learned to accept the national bank as an essential convenience, and did not push a measure for the bank's repeal which more dogmatic Republicans sponsored. It was too late of course to undo Hamilton's funding and debt assumption operations, but none too soon in the opinion of both Jefferson and Gallatin to set the resultant debt on the way to extinction. At the same time Jefferson insisted on the repeal of the whiskey tax and other Federalist excises. Gallatin, former champion of the "whiskey boys" in Pennsylvania politics, had a change of heart after he took over the treasury, but Jefferson was adamant. The excises were repealed in 1802 and Jefferson won the undying gratitude of bibulous backwoodsmen.

Without the excises, frugality was all the more necessary to a government dependent for revenue chiefly on customs duties and the sale of western lands. Happily for Gallatin's treasury, both flourished. The tragedy of war that had engulfed Europe brought a continually increasing traffic to American shipping and thus revenues to the customs. And settlers flocked into the western lands, which were coming more and more within their reach. The admission of Ohio to statehood in 1803 increased to seventeen the number of states.

By the "wise and frugal government" promised in the inaugural, Jefferson and Gallatin reasoned, the United States could live within its income, like a prudent husbandman. The basic formula was simple: cut back expenses on the military. A standing army was a menace to a free society anyway, and therefore should be kept to a minimum and defense left, in Jefferson's words, to "a well-disciplined militia, our best reliance in peace, and for the first moments of war, till regulars may relieve them. . . ." The navy, which the Federalists had already reduced after the quasi-war with France, ought to be reduced further. Coastal defense, Jefferson argued, should rely on fortifications and a "mosquito fleet" of small gunboats.

In 1807 the record of Jeffersonian reforms was crowned by an act which outlawed the foreign slave trade as of January 1, 1808, the earliest date possible under the Constitution. At the time South Carolina was the only state that still permitted the trade, having reopened it in 1803. But for years to come an illegal traffic would continue. By one informal estimate perhaps 300,000 slaves were smuggled in between 1808 and 1861.

THE BARBARY PIRATES Issues of foreign relations intruded on Jefferson early in his term. Events in the Mediterranean quickly gave him second thoughts about the need for a navy. On the Barbary Coast of North Africa the rulers of Morocco, Algeria, Tunis, and Tripoli had for years filled their coffers by means of piracy and extortion. After the Revolution American shipping in the Mediterranean became fair game, no longer protected by British payments of tribute. The new American government yielded up protection money too, first to Morocco in 1786, then to the others in the 1790s. In May 1801, however, the pasha of Tripoli upped his demands and declared war on the United States by the symbolic gesture of chopping down the flagpole at the United States Consulate. Rather than give in to this, Jefferson sent warships to blockade Tripoli, and a wearisome warfare dragged on until 1805, punctuated in 1804 by the notable exploit of Lt. Stephen Decatur who slipped into Tripoli harbor by night and set fire to the frigate *Philadelphia*, which had been captured (along with its crew) after it ran aground. Before the war ended William Eaton, consul at Tunis, staged an unlikely land invasion of Tripoli from Egypt. With fifteen United States Marines, about forty Greek soldiers, and some restless Arabs, he advanced across the desert and took Derna. But in 1805 the pasha settled for $60,000 ransom and released the crew of the *Philadelphia* (mostly British subjects) whom he had held hostage more than a year. It was still tribute, but less than the $300,000 the pasha had demanded at first, and much less than the cost of the war.

THE LOUISIANA PURCHASE   It was an inglorious end to a shabby affair, but well before it was over events elsewhere had conspired to produce the greatest single achievement of the Jefferson administration, the Louisiana Purchase of 1803, which more than doubled the territory of the United States by bringing into its borders the entire Mississippi Valley west of the river itself. Louisiana, settled by the French, had been ceded to Spain in 1763. Since that time the dream of retaking Louisiana had stirred in the minds of Frenchmen. In 1800 Napoleon Bonaparte secured its return in exchange for a promise (never-fulfilled) to set up a Spanish princess and her husband in Italy as rulers of an enlarged Tuscany. When unofficial word of the deal reached Washington in May 1801, Jefferson hastened Robert R. Livingston, the new minister to France, on his way. Spain in control of the Mississippi outlet was bad enough, but Napoleon in control could only mean serious trouble. "There is on the globe one single spot the possessor of which is our natural and habitual enemy," Jefferson wrote Livingston. "The day that France takes possession of New Orleans . . . we must marry ourselves to the British fleet and nation," not at all the happiest prospect Jefferson ever faced.

Livingston had instructions to talk the French out of it, if it was not too late. If Louisiana had become French he should try to get West Florida (once part of French Louisiana) either from France or with French help. Late Secretary of State Madison told him to seek a price for New Orleans and the Floridas, but Spain still held the Floridas, as it turned out. On into 1803 long and frustrating talks dragged out. Early that year James Monroe was made minister plenipotentiary to assist Livingston in Paris, but no sooner had he arrived in April than Napoleon's minister, Talleyrand, surprised Livingston by asking if the United States would like to buy the whole of Louisiana. Livingston, once he could regain his composure, snapped at the offer.

Napoleon's motives in the whole affair can only be surmised. At first he seems to have thought of a New World empire, but that plan took an ugly turn in French Sainte Domingue (later Haiti). There during the 1790s the revolutionary governments of France had lost control to a black revolt. In 1802, having just patched up the temporary Peace of Amiens with the British, Napoleon thought to improve the occasion by sending a force to subdue the island. By a ruse of war the French captured the black leader, Toussaint l'Ouverture, but then fell victim to guerrilas and yellow fever. Napoleon's plan may have been discouraged too by the fierce American reaction when the Spanish governor of Louisiana closed the Mississippi to American traffic in October 1802, on secret orders from Madrid. In the end Napoleon's purpose seems to have been simply to cut his losses, turn a quick profit, mollify the Americans, and go back to reshaping the map of Europe.

By the treaty of cession, dated April 30, 1803, the United States paid 60 million francs, approximately $11¼ million, for Louisiana. By a separate agreement the United States also agreed to assume French debts owed to American citizens up to 20 million francs, or $3¾ million—making the total price about $15 million. In defining the boundaries of Louisiana the treaty was vague. Its language could be stretched to provide a tenuous claim on Texas and a much stronger claim on West Florida, from Baton Rouge on the Mississippi past Mobile to the Perdido River on the east. When Livingston asked about the boundaries, Talleyrand responded: "I can give you no direction. You have made a noble bargain for yourselves, and I suppose you will make the most of it." Napoleon himself observed: "If an obscurity did not exist, perhaps it would be good policy to put it there."

The turn of events had indeed presented Jefferson with a noble bargain, a great new "empire of liberty," but also with a constitutional dilemma. Nowhere did the Constitution provide for or even mention the purchase of territory. By a strict construction, which Jefferson had professed, no such power existed. Jefferson at first thought to resolve the matter by amendment, but his advisers argued against delay lest Napoleon change his mind. The power to purchase territory, they reasoned, resided in the power to make treaties. Jefferson relented, trusting, he said, "that the good sense of our country will correct the evil of loose construction when it shall produce ill effects." New England Federalists boggled at the prospect of new states that would probably strengthen the Jeffersonian party and centered their fire on a proviso that the inhabitants be "incorporated in the Union" as citizens. In a reversal that foretokened many future reversals on constitutional issues, Federalists found themselves arguing strict construction of the Constitution while Republicans brushed aside such scruples in favor of implied power.

In October 1803 the Senate ratified the treaty by an overwhelming vote of 26 to 6. Both houses of Congress voted the necessary money and made provision for the govenment of the new territory. On December 20, 1803, Gov. William C. C. Clairborne and Gen. James Wilkinson took formal possession of Louisiana from a French agent who had taken over from Spanish authorities only three weeks before. For the time the Spanish kept West Florida, but within a decade it would be ripe for the plucking. In 1808 Napoleon put his brother on the throne of Spain. With the Spanish colonial administration in disarray, American settlers in 1810 staged a rebellion in Baton Rouge and proclaimed the Republic of West Florida, quickly annexed and occupied by the United States as far eastward as the Pearl River. In 1812 the state of Louisiana absorbed the region—still known as the Florida parishes. In 1813, with Spain itself a battlefield for French and British forces, General Wilkinson took over the rest of West Florida, now the Gulf coast of Mississippi and Alabama. Legally, the American government has claimed ever since, all these areas were included in the original Louisiana Purchase.

EXPLORING THE CONTINENT As an amateur scientist long before he was president, Jefferson had nourished an active curiosity about the Louisiana country, its geography, its flora and fauna, its prospects for trade. In January 1803 he asked Congress for money to send an exploring expedition to the far northwest, beyond the Mississippi, in what was still foreign territory. Congress approved and Jefferson assigned as commanders Meriwether Lewis, who as the president's private secretary had been groomed for the job, and another Virginian, William Clark, the much younger brother of George Rogers Clark.

During the winter of 1803–1804 a party of soldiers gathered at St. Louis and in May 1804 the "Corps of Discovery," numbering nearly fifty, set out to ascend the Missouri River. Six months later, near the Mandan Sioux villages in what was later North Dakota, they built Fort Mandan and wintered there in relative comfort, sending back downriver a barge loaded with specimens such as the prairie dog, previously unknown to science, and the magpie, previously unknown in America. Jefferson kept the great horns of a wapiti to display at Monticello. In the spring they added to the main party a French guide, who was little help, and his remarkable Shoshone wife, Sacajawea ("Canoe Launcher"),

EXPLORATIONS OF THE LOUISIANA PURCHASE

▄▄▄ Lewis and Clark, 1804–1806
--- Pike, 1805–1806
——— Pike, 1806–1807

0   300 Miles
0   300 Kilometers

an enormous help as interpreter and go-between with the Indians of the region, and set out once again upstream. At the head of the Missouri they took the north fork, thenceforth the Jefferson River, crossed the continental divide at Lemhi Pass and in dugout canoes descended the Snake and Columbia Rivers to the Pacific. Near the later site of Astoria at the mouth of the Columbia they built Fort Clatsop in which they spent another winter. The following spring they headed back by almost the same route, and after a swing through the Yellowstone country returned to St. Louis in September 1806, having been gone nearly two and a half years.

No longer was the Far West unknown country. Although it was nearly a century before a good edition of the *Journals of Lewis and Clark* appeared in print, many of their findings came out piecemeal, including an influential map in 1814. Convinced that they had found a practical route for the China trade, Lewis and Clark were among the last to hold out hope for a water route through the continent. Their reports of friendly Indians and abundant pelts attracted traders and trappers to the region very quickly, and also gave the United States a claim to the Oregon country by right of discovery and exploration. It would have strained the genius even of a Talleyrand to extend a claim to the Louisiana country beyond the Rocky Mountains.

From the Journals of Lewis and Clark, *this is Clark's sketch of a Chinook alâkân, or candlefish, discovered on February 24, 1806. [The Warder Collection]*

While Lewis and Clark were gone, Jefferson sent other explorers up the Ouachita and Red Rivers, but with little profit to geographical knowledge. More important were the travels of Lt. Zebulon Pike. Sent out by General Wilkinson in 1805–1806 to find the source of the Mississippi River, he mistakenly picked a tributary, later discoveries showed, but contributed to knowledge of the upper Mississippi Valley. Then, during 1806–1807, he went out to the headwaters of the Arkansas River as far as Colorado, discovered Pike's Peak but failed in an attempt to climb it, and made a roundabout return by way of Santa Fe, courtesy of Spanish soldiers who captured his party. Pike's account, while less reliable and less full than that of Lewis and Clark, appeared first and gave Americans their first overall picture of the Great Plains and Rocky Mountains. It also contributed to the widespread belief that the arid regions of the West constituted a Great American Desert, largely unfit for human habitation.

POLITICAL SCHEMES   Jefferson's policies, including the Louisiana Purchase, brought him almost solid support in the South and West. Even New Englanders were moving to his side. By 1809 John Quincy Adams, the son of the second president, would become a Republican! Die-hard Federalists read the handwriting on the wall. The acquisition of a vast new empire in the west would reduce New England to insignificance in political affairs, and along with it the Federalist cause. Under the leadership of Sen. Timothy Pickering, a group of Massachusetts bitter-enders called the Essex Junto began to think about secession from the Union, an idea that would simmer in certain New England circles for another decade. Rather than accede to a Union formed in the image of Jeffersonian Republicanism, they would withdraw.

Soon they hatched a scheme to link New York with New England and contacted Vice-President Aaron Burr, who had been on the outs with the Jeffersonians long since and who was, as ever, ready for subterranean schemes. Their plan depended on Burr's election as governor of New York. In April 1804, however, Burr was overwhelmed by the regular Republican candidate. The extreme Federalists it turned out, could not even hold members of their own party to the plan, which Hamilton bitterly opposed on the grounds that Burr was "a dangerous man, and one who ought not to be trusted with the reins of government." When Hamilton's remarks appeared in the public press, Burr's demand for an explanation led to a duel at Weehawken, New Jersey, in which Hamilton was mortally wounded. Hamilton personally opposed dueling but his romantic streak and sense of honor compelled him to demonstrate his courage, long since established beyond any question at Yorktown. He went to his death, as his son had done in a similar affair the previous year, determined not to fire at his opponent. Burr was unhampered by such scruples. The death of Hamilton ended both Pickering's scheme and Burr's political career— but not his intrigues.

Meanwhile the presidential campaign of 1804 got under way when a congressional caucus of Republicans on February 25 renominated Jefferson and chose George Clinton for vice-president. Opposed by the Federalists Charles Coteworth Pinckney and Rufus King, Jefferson and Clinton won 162 of 176 electoral votes. Only Connecticut and Delaware recorded solid opposition. Jefferson's policy of conciliation had made him a national rather than a sectional candidate. With some pride, Jefferson said in his second inaugural address that he had carried out the general policies announced in the first: "The suppression of unnecessary offices, of useless establishments and expenses, enabled us to discontinue our internal taxes. . . . What farmer, what mechanic, what laborer ever sees a tax-gatherer of the United States?"

DIVISIONS IN THE REPUBLICAN PARTY

RANDOLPH AND THE *TERTIUM QUID*   "Never was there an administration more brilliant than that of Mr. Jefferson up to this period," said John Randolph of Roanoke. "We were indeed in the full tide of successful experiment." But the Republican landslide had a sequel that would often follow such victories in later years. Freed from a strong opposition—Federalists made up only a quarter of the new Congress—the majority began to lose some of its cohesion. Cracks appeared in the Republican facade, portents of major fissures that would finally split the party as the Federalists faded into oblivion. Ironically, John Randolph of Roanoke, a Jeffersonian mainstay in the first term, became the most conspicious of the dissidents. A brilliant but erratic Virginian, left frustrated by a hormonal deficiency, given to fits of insanity in his later years, gifted with a talent for invective delivered in a shrill soprano voice, the Virginia congressman flourished best in opposition. Few of his colleagues had the stomach for one of his tongue-lashings.

Randolph, too much a loner for leadership, was spokesman for a shifting group of "Old Republicans," whose adherence to party principles had rendered them more Jeffersonian than Jefferson

The mercurial John Randolph of Roanoke, in a silhouette drawn from life by William H. Brown. [New York Public Library]

himself. Their philosopher was John Taylor of Carolina, a Virginia planter-pamphleteer whose fine-spun theories of states' rights and strict construction had little effect at the time but delighted the logic-choppers of later years. Neither Randolph nor Taylor could accept his leader's pragmatic gift for adjusting principle to circumstance.

Randolph first began to smell a rat in the case of the Yazoo Fraud, a land scheme which originated in Georgia but entangled speculators from all over. In 1795 the Georgia legislature had sold to four land companies, in which some of the legislators were involved, 35 million acres in the Yazoo country (Mississippi and Alabama) for $500,000 (little more than a penny an acre). A new legislature rescinded the sale the following year, but not before some of the land claims had been sold to third parties. When Georgia finally ceded her western lands to federal authority in 1802, Jefferson sought a compromise settlement of the claims but Randolph managed to block passage of the necessary measures and in the ensuing quarrels was removed as Speaker of the House. The snarled Yazoo affair plagued the courts and Congress for another decade. Finally, in the case of *Fletcher v. Peck* (1810), Chief Justice Marshall ruled that the original sale, however fraudulent, was a legal contract. The repeal impaired the obligation of contract and was therefore unconstitutional. Final settlement came in 1814 when Congress awarded $4.2 million to the speculators.

Randolph's definitive break with Jefferson came in 1806,

when the president sought an appropriation of $2 million for a thinly disguised bribe to the French to win their influence in persuading Spain to yield the Floridas to the United States. "I found I might co-operate or be an honest man—I have therefore opposed and will oppose them," Randolph said. Thereafter he resisted Jefferson's initiatives almost out of reflex. Randolph and his colleagues were sometimes called "Quids," or the *Tertium Quid* (the "third something"), and their dissents gave rise to talk of a third party, neither Republican nor Federalist. But they never got together. Some of the dissenters in 1808 backed James Monroe against Madison for the presidential succession, but the campaign quickly fizzled.

THE BURR CONSPIRACY   John Randolph may have got enmeshed in dogma, but Aaron Burr was never one to let principle stand in the way. Born of a distinguished line of Puritans, including grandfather Jonathan Edwards, he cast off the family Calvinism early to pursue the main chance—and the women. Sheer brilliance and opportunism carried him to the vice-presidency. With a leaven of discretion he might easily have become heir-apparent to Jefferson, but a taste for intrigue was the tragic flaw in his character. Caught up in dubious schemes of Federalist die-hards in 1800 and again in 1804, he ended his political career once and for all when he killed Hamilton.

Searching then for new worlds to conquer, he turned to the West, and before he left office as vice-president he hatched the scheme that came to be known as the Burr Conspiracy. Just what he was up to probably will never be known, because Burr himself very likely was keeping some options open. He may have been getting up an expedition to conquer Mexico—some American freebooters had already pounced on Texas—or West Florida; he perhaps was out to organize a secession of Louisiana and set up an independent republic. On various pretexts he won the ear of the British and Spanish ministers in Washington (with whom he planted hints of a coup d'état in Washington), a variety of public figures in the East, and innumerable westerners, including two future presidents (William Henry Harrison and Andrew Jackson), and that noblest villain of them all, Gen. James Wilkinson, now governor of the Louisiana Territory but still in the pay of the Spanish government.°

In the summer of 1805 Burr sailed on a flatboat downriver all the way to New Orleans, propounding different schemes, lining

---

°The present state of Louisiana was then the Territory of Orleans. Wilkinson governed the rest of the Louisiana Purchase.

Aaron Burr, the brilliant but
erratic vice-president. [New Jersey
Historical Society]

up adventurers and dupes. By the summer of 1806 he was in
Lexington, Kentucky, recruiting for an expedition to take up a
land claim he had purchased in Arkansas, a likely staging area for
a military enterprise or a fallback position if things went wrong.
He arranged, but did not actually attend, the assembling of men,
boats, and supplies on an island belonging to one of his confederates, a rich Irish refugee named Harmon Blennerhassett. Off they
went, some sixty strong, to be joined downstream by Burr. But
by now Burr's adventure had a cast of thousands, which was
bound to cause talk. Rumors began to reach Jefferson, and in November 1806 so did a letter from Wilkinson warning of "a deep,
dark, wicked and wide-spread conspiracy." Wilkinson was double-dealing with Spain and America, but Jefferson never suspected him of being anything but a patriot.

In January 1807, as Burr neared Natchez with his motley
crew, he learned that Wilkinson had betrayed him and that Jefferson had ordered his arrest. He cut out cross-country toward
Pensacola, but was caught and taken off to Richmond for a trial,
which, like the conspiracy, had a stellar cast. Charged with treason by the grand jury, Burr was brought for trial before Chief
Justice Marshall, then riding circuit. The issue revealed both
Marshall and Jefferson at their partisan worst. Marshall was convinced that the "hand of malignity" was grasping at Burr, while
Jefferson, determined to get a conviction at any cost, published
relevant affidavits in advance and promised pardons to conspirators who helped convict Burr. Marshall in turn was so indiscreet
as to attend a dinner given by the chief defense counsel at which
Burr himself was present.

The case established two major constitutional precedents. First, Jefferson ignored a subpoena requiring him to appear in court with certain papers in his possession. He refused, as Washington had refused, to submit papers to the Congress on grounds of executive privilege. Both believed that the independence of the executive branch would be compromised if the president were subject to a court writ, a position since sustained by law. The second major precedent was the rigid definition of treason. On this Marshall adopted the strictest of constructions. Treason under the Constitution consists of "levying war against the United States or adhering to their enemies" and requires "two witnesses to the same overt act" for conviction. Since the prosecution failed to produce two witnesses to an overt act of treason by Burr, the jury brought in a verdict of not guilty.

Whether or not Burr escaped his just deserts, Marshall's strict construction of the Constitution protected the United States, as the authors of the Constitution clearly intended, against the capricious judgments of "treason" that governments through the centuries have used to terrorize dissenters. As to Burr, with further charges pending, he skipped bail and took refuge in France, but returned unmolested in 1812 to practice law in New York. He survived to a virile old age. At age eighty, shortly before his death, he was divorced on grounds of adultery.

WAR IN EUROPE

Oppositionists of whatever stripe were more an annoyance than a threat to Jefferson. The more intractable problems of his second term were created by the renewal of the European war in 1803, which helped resolve the problem of Louisiana but put more strains on Jefferson's desire to avoid "entangling alliances" and the quarrels of Europe. In 1805 Napoleon's smashing defeat of Russian and Austrian forces at Austerlitz made him the master of western Europe. The same year Lord Nelson's defeat of the French and Spanish fleets in the Battle of Trafalgar secured Britain's control of the seas. The war resolved itself into a battle of elephant and whale, Napoleon dominant on land, the British dominant in the water, neither able to strike a decisive blow at the other, and neither restrained by an overly delicate sense of neutral rights or international law.

HARASSMENT BY BRITAIN AND FRANCE For two years after the renewal of hostilities things went well for American shipping, which took over trade with the French and Spanish West Indies.

But in the case of the *Essex* (1805), a British prize court ruled that the practice of shipping French and Spanish goods through American ports while on their way elsewhere did not neutralize enemy goods. Such a practice violated the British rule of 1756 (laid down by the British courts during the Seven Years' War) under which trade closed in time of peace remained closed in time of war. Goods shipped in violation of the rule, the British held, were liable to seizure at any point under the doctrine of continuous voyage. In 1807 the commercial provisions of Jay's Treaty expired and James Monroe, ambassador to Great Britain, failed to get a renewal satisfactory to Jefferson. After that, the British interference with American shipping increased, not just to keep supplies from Napoleon's continent but also to hobble competition with British merchantmen.

In a series of Orders in Council adopted in 1806 and 1807 the British ministry set up a paper blockade of Europe from Copenhagen to Trieste. Vessels headed for continental ports had to get licenses and accept British inspection or be liable to seizure. Napoleon retaliated with his "Continental System," proclaimed in the Berlin Decree of 1806 and the Milan Decree of 1807. In the first he declared a blockade of the British Isles and in the second he ruled that neutral ships which complied with British regulations were subject to seizure when they reached continental ports. The situation presented American shippers with a dilemma. If they complied with the demands of one side they were subject to seizure by the other.

It was humiliating, but the prospects for profits were so great that shippers ran the risk. For seamen the danger was heightened by a renewal of the practice of impressment. The use of press gangs to kidnap men in British (and colonial) ports was a long-standing method of recruitment for the British navy. The seizure of British subjects from American vessels became a new source of recruits, justified on the principle that British subjects remained British subjects for life: "Once an Englishman, always an Englishman." Mistakes might be made, of course, since it was sometimes hard to distinguish British subjects from native Americans; indeed a flourishing trade in fake citizenship papers had arisen in American ports. The humiliation of impressment was mostly confined to merchant vessels, but on at least two occasions before 1807 vessels of the American navy had been stopped on the high seas and seamen removed.

In the summer of 1807 the British *Leopard* accosted the American frigate *Chesapeake* off Norfolk, just outside territorial waters, and after its captain refused to be searched, the *Leopard* fired upon the *Chesapeake* at the cost of three killed and eighteen

Jefferson's Embargo, pictured here as a pesky snapping turtle (Ograbme), stops a tobacco trader. [New York Public Library]

wounded. The *Chesapeake*, unready for battle, was forced to strike its colors. A British search party seized four men, one of whom was later hanged for desertion from the British navy. Soon after the *Chesapeake* limped back into Norfolk, the Washington *Federalist* editorialized: 'We have never, on any occasion, witnessed the spirit of the people excited to so great a degree of indignation, or such a thirst for revenge. . . ." Public wrath was so aroused that Jefferson could have had war on the spot. Had Congress been in session, he might have been forced into war. But Jefferson, like Adams before him, resisted the war fever and suffered politically as a result.

THE EMBARGO   Jefferson resolved to use public indignation as the occasion for an effort at "peaceable coercion." In December 1807, in response to his request, Congress passed the Embargo Act, which stopped all export of American goods and prohibited American ships from clearing for foreign ports. The constitutional basis of the embargo was the power to regulate commerce, which in this case Republicans interpreted broadly as the power to prohibit commerce. "Let the example teach the world that our firmness equals our moderation," said the *National Intelligencer*, "that having resorted to a measure just in itself, and adequate to its object, we will flinch from no sacrifices which the honor and good of the nation demand from virtuous and faithful citizens."

But Jefferson's embargo was a failure from the beginning for want of a will to make the necessary sacrifices. The idealistic spirit which had made economic pressures effective in the prerevolutionary crises was lacking. Trade remained profitable despite the risks, and violation of the embargo was almost laughably easy. Enforcement was lax, and loopholes in the act permitted ships to clear port under the pretense of engaging in coastal trade or whaling, or under an amendment passed a few months after the act, for the purpose of bringing home American property stored in foreign warehouses. Some 800 ships left on such missions, but few of them returned before the embargo expired. Trade across the Canadian border flourished. As it turned out, France was little hurt by the act. Napoleon in fact exploited it to issue the Bayonne Decree (1808), which ordered the seizure of American ships in continental ports on the pretext that they must be British ships with false papers. Or if they truly were American, Napoleon slyly noted, he would be helping Jefferson enforce the embargo. Some British manufacturers and workers were hurt by the lack of American cotton, but they carried little weight with the government, and British shippers benefited. With American ports closed, they found a new trade in Latin American ports thrown open by the colonial authorities when Napoleon occupied the mother countries of Spain and Portugal.

The coercive effect was minimal, and the embargo revived the moribund Federalist party in New England, which renewed the charge that Jefferson was in league with the French. The em-

This 1807 Federalist cartoon compares Washington, on the left, to Jefferson, on the right. Washington is flanked by the British lion and the American eagle, while Jefferson is flanked by a snake and a lizard. Below Jefferson are volumes by French philosophers. [New-York Historical Society]

bargo, one New Englander said, was "like cutting one's throat to cure the nosebleed." At the same time agriculture in the south and west suffered for want of outlets for grain, cotton, and tobacco. After fifteen months of ineffectiveness, Jefferson finally accepted failure and on March 1, 1809, signed a repeal of the embargo shortly before he relinquished the "splendid misery" of the presidency.

In the election of 1808 the succession passed to another Virginian, Secretary of State James Madison. Presidential trial balloons for James Monroe and George Clinton, launched by the Quids, never got off the ground, and Jefferson used his influence in the caucus of Republican congressmen to win the nomination for Madison. Clinton was again the candidate for vice-president. The Federalists, backing Charles Cotesworth Pinckney and Rufus King of New York, revived enough as a result of the embargo to win 47 votes to Madison's 122.

THE DRIFT TO WAR   Madison was entangled in foreign affairs from the beginning. Still insisting on neutral rights and freedom of the seas, he pursued Jefferson's policy of "peaceful coercion" by different but no less ineffective means. In place of the embargo Congress had substituted the Non-Intercourse Act, which reopened trade with all countries except France and Great Britain and authorized the president to reopen trade with whichever of these gave up its restrictions. British Minister David M. Erskine assured Madison's secretary of state that Britain would revoke its restrictions on June 10, 1809. With that assurance, Madison reopened trade with Britain, but Erskine had acted on his own and the foreign secretary, repudiating his action, recalled him. Nonintercourse resumed, but it proved as ineffective as the embargo. In the vain search for an alternative, Congress on May 1, 1810, reversed its ground and adopted a measure introduced by Nathaniel Macon of North Carolina, Macon's Bill No. 2, which reopened trade with the warring powers but provided that if either dropped its restrictions nonintercourse would be restored with the other.

This time Napoleon took a turn at trying to bamboozle Madison. Napoleon's foreign minister, the duc de Cadore, informed the American minister in Paris that he had withdrawn the Berlin and Milan Decrees, but the carefully worded Cadore letter had strings attached: revocation of the decrees depended on withdrawal of the British Orders in Council. The strings were plain to see, but either Madison misunderstood or, more likely, went along in hope of putting pressure on the British. The British refused to give in, but Madison clung to his policy despite Napoleon's continued seizure of American ships. The seemingly hopeless effort did indeed finally work. With more time, with more patience, with a transatlantic cable, Madison's policy would have been vindicated without resort to war. On June 16, 1812, the British foreign minister, facing economic crisis, announced revocation of the Orders in Council. Britain preferred not to risk war with the United States on top of its war with Napoleon. But on June 1 Madison had asked for war, and by mid-June the Congress concurred.

THE WAR OF 1812

CAUSES The main cause of the war—the demand for neutral rights—seems clear enough. Neutral rights were the main burden of Madison's war message and the main reason for a mounting hostility toward the British. Yet the geographical distribution of the vote for war raises a troubling question. The preponderance of the vote for war came from members of Congress representing the agricultural regions from Pennsylvania southward and westward. The maritime states of New York and New England, the region that bore the brunt of British attacks on American trade, gave a majority against the declaration of war. One explanation for this seeming anomaly is simple enough. The farming regions were afflicted by the damage to their markets for grain, cotton, and tobacco, while New England shippers made profits in spite of British restrictions.

Other plausible explanations for the sectional vote, however, include frontier Indian depredations which were blamed on the British, western land hunger, and the desire for new lands in Canada and the Floridas. Indian troubles were endemic to a rapidly expanding West. Land-hungry settlers and speculators kept moving out ahead of government surveys and sales in search of fertile acres. The constant pressure to open new lands repeatedly forced or persuaded Indians to sign treaties they did not always understand, causing stronger resentment among tribes that were losing more and more of their lands. It was an old story, dating from the Jamestown settlement, but one that took a new turn with the rise of two Shawnee leaders, Tecumseh and his twin brother Tenskwatawa, "the Prophet."

Tecumseh, according to Gov. William Henry Harrison of the Indiana Territory, was "one of those uncommon geniuses, which spring up occasionally to produce revolutions and overturn the order of things." He saw with blazing clarity the consequences of Indian disunity, and set out to form a confederation of tribes to

Tecumseh, the Shawnee leader who tried to unite the tribes in defense of their land. He was killed in 1813 at the Battle of the Thames. [Museum of Natural History]

defend Indian hunting grounds, insisting that no land cession was valid without the consent of all tribes since they held the land in common. His brother supplied the inspiration of a religious revival, calling upon the Indians to worship the "Master of Life," to resist the white man's firewater, and lead a simple life within their means. By 1811 Tecumseh had matured his plans and headed south to win the Creeks, Cherokees, Choctaws, and Chickasaws to his cause.

Governor Harrison saw the danger. He gathered a force and set out to attack Tecumseh's capital on the Tippecanoe River, Prophet's Town, while the leader was away. On November 7, 1811, the Indians attacked Harrison's encampment on the Tippecanoe River, although Tecumseh had warned against any fighting in his absence. The Shawnees were finally repulsed in a bloody engagement which left about a quarter of Harrison's men dead or wounded. Only later did Harrison realize that he had inflicted a defeat on the Indians, who had become demoralized and many of whom had fled to Canada. Harrison then burned their town and destroyed all its stores. Tecumseh's dreams went up in smoke, and Tecumseh himself fled to British protection in Canada.

The Battle of Tippecanoe reinforced suspicions that the British were inciting the Indians. Actually the incident was mainly Harrison's doing. With little hope of help from war-torn Europe, Canadian authorities had steered a careful course, discouraging warfare but seeking to keep the Indians' friendship and fur trade. To eliminate the Indian menace, frontiersmen reasoned, they needed to remove its foreign support. The province of Ontario was like a pistol pointed at the United States. Conquest of Canada would accomplish a twofold purpose. It would eliminate British influence among the Indians and open a new empire for land-hungry Americans. It was also the only place, in case of war, where the British were vulnerable to American attack. East Florida, still under the Spanish flag, posed a similar menace. Spain was too weak or unwilling to prevent sporadic Indian attacks across the frontier. The British too were suspected of smuggling through Florida and intriguing with the Indians on the southwest border.

One historian of the quarrels with Britain has suggested that "scholars have overemphasized the tangible, rational reasons for action and . . . have given too little heed to such things as national pride, sensitivity, and frustration, although the evidence for this sort of thing leaps to the eye." Madison's drift toward war was hastened by the rising temperature of war fever. In the Congress which assembled in November 1811 a number of new members from southern and western districts began to ring the changes, holding forth on "national honor" and British perfidy. Among them were Henry Clay of Kentucky, who became Speaker of the House, Richard M. Johnson of Kentucky, Felix Grundy of Tennessee, and John C. Calhoun of South Carolina. John Randolph of Roanoke christened them the "War Hawks." After they entered the House, Randolph said "We have heard but one word —like the whip-poor-will, but one eternal monotonous tone—Canada! Canada! Canada!"

PREPARATIONS As it turned out, the War Hawks would get neither Canada nor Florida. For James Madison had carried into war a country that was ill-prepared both financially and militarily. In 1811, despite earnest pleas from Treasury Secretary Gallatin, Congress had let the twenty-year charter of the Bank of the United States expire. A combination of strict-constructionist Republicans and anglophobes, who feared the large British interest in the bank, did it in. Also, state banks were often mismanaged, resulting in deposits lost through bankruptcy. Trade had approached a standstill and tariff revenues had declined. Loans were needed for about two-thirds of the war costs while northeast opponents to the war were reluctant to lend money. Government bonds were difficult to float.

War had been likely for nearly a decade, but Republican economy had prevented preparations. When, finally, late in 1811 the administration decided to fill up the army to its authorized strength of 10,000 and add an additional force of 10,000, Madison still faced the old arguments against the danger of a standing army. Sen. William B. Giles of Virginia, one of the Old Republicans, suggested an additional force of 25,000 to serve five years. His purpose was to embarrass the administration, because such a volunteer force probably could not be raised and would strain the country's resources. The War Hawks nevertheless supported the measure, and in a law passed on January 9, 1812, increased the authorized force to 35,000. But when the war began the army numbered only 6,700 men, ill-trained, poorly equipped, and led by poorly prepared officers. The senior officers were still in large part veterans of the Revolution. The ranking general, Henry Dearborn, was a veteran of Bunker Hill, sixty-one at the outbreak of war.

The navy, on the other hand, was in comparatively good shape, with able officers and trained men whose seamanship had been tested in the fighting against France and Tripoli. Its ships were well outfitted and seaworthy—all sixteen of them. In the first year of the war it was the navy that produced the only American victories in isolated duels with British vessels, but their effect was mainly an occasional lift to morale. Within a year the British had blockaded the coast, except for New England where they hoped to cultivate antiwar feeling, and most of the little American fleet was bottled up in port.

THE WAR IN THE NORTH   The only place where the United States could effectively strike at the British was Canada. Only once, however, had a war in that arena proved decisive, late in the French and Indian War, when Wolfe took Quebec and strangled the French Empire in America. A similar instinct for the jugular was Madison's best hope: a quick attack on Quebec or Montreal would cut Canada's lifeline, the St. Lawrence River. Instead the old history of the indecisive colonial wars was repeated, for the last time.

Instead of striking directly at the lifeline, the administration opted for a three-pronged drive against Canada: along the Lake Champlain route toward Montreal, with Gen. Henry Dearborn in command; along the Niagara River, with forces under Gen. Stephen Van Rensselaer; and into Upper Canada from Detroit, where Gen. William Hull and some 2,000 men arrived in early July. In Detroit, Hull deliberated and vacillated while his position worsened and the news arrived that Fort Michilimakinac, isolated at the head of Lake Huron, had surrendered on July 17. British Gen. Isaac Brock cleverly played upon Hull's worst fears. Gathering what redcoats he could to parade in view of Detroit's defenders, Brock let it be known that thousands of Indian allies were at the rear and that once fighting began he would be unable to control them. Fearing massacre, Hull surrendered his entire force on August 16, 1812.

Along the Niagara front, General Van Rensselaer was more aggressive than Hull. On October 13 an advance party of 600

THE WAR OF 1812:
Major Northern Campaigns

⟵ American forces   ⟵ British forces

✶ Battle site

LAKE SUPERIOR
Ft. Michilimakinac
LAKE HURON
LAKE MICHIGAN
MICHIGAN TERRITORY
CANADA
York (Toronto)
LAKE ONTARIO
The Thames
BROCK, JULY 1812
Ft. Niagara
Queenstown Heights
RENSSELAER OCT. 1812
N.Y.
Detroit
LAKE ERIE
Ft. Dearborn
Maumee R.
HULL, AUG. 1812
HARRISON, OCT. 1813
PERRY, SEPT. 1813
Put-in-Bay
Presque Isle (Erie)
PENN.
Pittsburgh
Wabash R.
INDIANA TERRITORY
OHIO
Ohio R.
KY.
Susquehanna R.
MD.
Baltimore
Ft. McHenry ✶
Washington D.C. ✶
Potomac R.
VIRGINIA
Chesapeake Bay
ROSS, AUG. 1814
DEL.
N.J.
CONN.
MASS.
Hudson R.
VT.
N.H.
Plattsburgh
Lake Champlain
PREVOST, AUG.-SEPT. 1814
Montreal
St. Lawrence R.
Quebec
BRITISH BLOCKADE

0   200 Miles
0   200 Kilometers

Americans crossed the Niagara River, and worked their way up
the bluffs on the Canadian side to occupy Queenstown Heights.
The stage was set for a major victory, but the New York militia
refused to reinforce Van Rensselaer's men on the claim that their
military service did not obligate them to leave the country. They
complacently remained on the New York side and watched their
outnumbered countrymen be mowed down by a superior force
on the other side.

On the third front, the old invasion route via Lake Champlain,
the trumpet once more gave an uncertain sound. At first, when
word came that British had revoked the Orders in Council, General Dearborn accepted a temporary armistice. On November 19
he finally led his army north from Plattsburgh toward Montreal.
He marched them up to the border, where the militia once again
stood on its alleged constitutional rights and refused to cross, and
then marched them down again.

Madison's navy secretary now pushed vigorously for American
control of inland waters. At Presque Isle (Erie), Pennsylvania,
twenty-eight-year-old Commodore Oliver H. Perry, already a
fourteen-year veteran who had seen action against Tripoli, was
fetching up hardware from Pittsburgh and building a squadron

from the wilderness lumber. By the end of the summer Perry had achieved superiority and set out in search of the British, whom he found at Put-in Bay, near the mouth of the Sandusky, on September 10, 1813. Perry refused to quit when his flagship was shot out from under him. He transferred to another vessel, carried the battle to the enemy, and finally accepted surrender of the entire British squadron. To Gen. William Henry Harrison he sent the long-awaited message: "We have met the enemy and they are ours."

American naval control of waters in the region soon made Upper Canada (north of Lake Erie) untenable to the British. They gave up Detroit in September, and were dissuaded from falling back all the way to the Niagara only by the protests of Tecumseh and his Indian allies. When they took a defensive stand at the Battle of the Thames (October 5), General Harrison inflicted a defeat which eliminated British power in Upper Canada and released the Northwest from any further threat. In the course of the battle, Tecumseh fell and his dream of Indian unity died with him.

THE WAR IN THE SOUTH   In the Southwest too the war flared up in 1813. In April, before moving north, Gen. James Wilkinson had occupied the remainder of Spanish West Florida, where British agents had been active, on the claim that it was part of the Louisiana Purchase. In July 1813 a group of American settlers clashed with the Creeks at Burnt Corn, north of Pensacola, and on August 30 the Creeks attacked Fort Mims, on the Alabama River above Mobile, killing almost half the people in the fort. The news found Andrew Jackson home in bed recovering from a street brawl with Thomas Hart Benton, later senator from Missouri. As major-general of the Tennessee militia, Jackson summoned about 2,000 volunteers and set out on a campaign which utterly crushed the Creek resistance. The decisive battle came on March 27, 1814, at the Horseshoe Bend of the Tallapoosa River, in the heart of the upper Creek country. In the Treaty of Fort Jackson signed that August, the Creeks ceded two-thirds of their lands to the United States, including part of Georgia and most of Alabama.

Four days after the Battle of Horseshoe Bend, Napoleon's empire collapsed. Now free to deal with America, the British developed a threefold plan of operations for 1814. They would launch a two-pronged invasion of America via Niagara and Lake Champlain to increase the clamor for peace in the Northeast, extend the naval blockade to New England, subjecting coastal towns to raids, and seize New Orleans to cut the Mississippi River, lifeline of the West. Uncertainties about the peace settlement in Europe, however, prevented the release of British veterans for a wholesale descent upon the New World. War weariness, after a generation of conflict, countered the British thirst for revenge against the former colonials. British plans were stymied also by the more resolute young commanders Madison had placed in charge of strategic areas by the summer of 1814.

MACDONOUGH'S VICTORY   The main British effort was planned for the invasion via Lake Champlain. From the north Gen. George Prevost, governor-general of Canada, advanced with the finest army yet assembled on American soil: fifteen regiments of regulars, plus militia and artillerymen, a total of about 15,000. The front was saved only by Prevost's vacillation and the superb ability of Commodore Thomas Macdonough, commander of the American naval squadron on Lake Champlain. A land assault might have taken Plattsburgh and forced Macdonough out of his protected position nearby, but England's army bogged down while its flotilla engaged Macdonough in a deadly battle on September 11.

The British concentrated superior firepower from the flagship, the *Confiance*, on Macdonough's ship, the *Saratoga*. With

John Bull making a new Batch of ships to send to the lakes. *The figure at the right tells John Bull, "If you send all you've got to the Lakes, it will only make fun for the Yankeys to take them." [New York Public Library]*

his starboard battery disabled, Macdonough executed a daring maneuver known as "winding ship." He turned the *Saratoga* around while at anchor and brought its undamaged port broadside into action with devastating effect. The *Saratoga* was so damaged that it had to be scuttled, but the battle ended with the entire British flotilla either destroyed or captured. After reading the news, the duke of Wellington informed the British ministry: "That which appears to me to be wanting in America is not a general, or a general officer and troops, but a naval superiority on the Lakes." Lacking this advantage the duke thought the British had no right "to demand any concession of territory from America."

FIGHTING IN THE CHESAPEAKE   Meanwhile, however, American forces suffered the most humiliating experience of the war, the capture and burning of Washington, D.C. With attention focused on the Canadian front, the Chesapeake Bay offered the British a number of inviting targets, including Baltimore, now the fourth-largest city in America. Under the command of Gen. Robert Ross, a British force landed without opposition in June at Benedict, Maryland, and headed for Washington, forty miles away. To defend the capital the Americans had a force of about 7,000, including only a few hundred regulars and 400 sailors. At Bladensburg, Maryland, the American militia melted away in the face of the smaller British force. Only Commodore Joshua Barney's sailors held firm, pounding the British with five twenty-four-pound guns, but the sailors were forced to retire after half an hour.

On the evening of August 24, 1814, the British marched unopposed into Washington, where British officers ate a meal prepared for President and Mrs. Madison, who had joined the other refugees in Virginia. The British then burned the White House, the Capitol, and all other government buildings except the Patent Office. A tornado the next day compounded the damage, but a violent thunderstorm dampened both the fires and the enthusiasm of the British forces, who left to prepare a new assault on Baltimore.

The attack on Baltimore was a different story. With some 13,000 men, chiefly militia, some of them stragglers from Bladensburg, American forces fortified the heights behind the city. About 1,000 men held Fort McHenry, on an island in the harbor. The British landed at North Point, where an advance group of American militia inflicted severe casualties, including a mortal wound to General Ross. When the British finally came into sight of the city on September 13, they halted in the face of American defenses. All through the following night the fleet bombarded Fort McHenry to no avail, and the invaders abandoned the attack on the city as too costly to risk. Francis Scott Key, a Washington lawyer, watched the siege from a vessel in the harbor. The sight of the flag still in place at dawn inspired Key to draft the verses of "The Star Spangled Banner." Later revised and set to the tune of an English drinking song, it was immediately popular and eventually became the national anthem.

THE BATTLE OF NEW ORLEANS   The British failure at Baltimore followed by three days their failure on Lake Champlain, and their offensive against New Orleans had yet to run its course. Along the Gulf coast Andrew Jackson had been busy shoring up the defenses of Mobile and New Orleans. In November, without authorization, he invaded Spanish Florida and took Pensacola to end British intrigues there. Back in Louisiana by the end of November, he began to erect defenses on the approaches to New Orleans, anticipating a British approach by the interior to pick up Indian support and control the Mississippi. Instead the British

THE WAR OF 1812: Major Southern Campaigns

fleet, with some 7,500 European veterans under Gen. Sir Edwin Pakenham, entered Lake Borgne to the east of New Orleans, and eventually reached a level plain on the banks of the Mississippi just south of New Orleans.

Pakenham's painfully careful approach—he waited until all his artillery was available—gave Jackson time to throw up earthworks bolstered by cotton bales for protection. It was an almost invulnerable position, but Pakenham, contemptuous of Jackson's array of frontier militiamen, Creole aristocrats, free Negroes, and pirates, rashly ordered his veterans forward in a frontal assault at dawn on January 8, 1815. His redcoats ran into a murderous hail of artillery shells and deadly rifle fire. Before the British withdrew about 2,000 had died on the field, including Pakenham himself, whose body, pickled in a barrel of rum, was returned to the ship where his wife awaited news of the battle.

The Battle of New Orleans occurred after a peace treaty had already been signed, but this is not to say that it was an anticlimax or that it had no effect on the outcome of the war, for the treaty was yet to be ratified and the British might have exploited to advantage the possession of New Orleans had they won it. But the battle assured ratification of the treaty as it stood, and both governments acted quickly.

This engraving of Pakenham's death at the Battle of New Orleans (January 8, 1815) is based on a painting done at the scene. [New York Public Library]

THE TREATY OF GHENT   Peace efforts had begun in 1812 even before hostilities got under way. The British, after all, had repealed their Orders in Council two days before the declaration of war and confidently expected at least an armistice. Secretary of State Monroe, however, told the British that they would have to give up the outrage of impressment as well. Meanwhile Czar Alexander of Russia offered to mediate the dispute, hoping to relieve the pressure on Great Britain, his ally against France. Madison then sent Albert Gallatin and James Bayard to join John Quincy Adams, American ambassador to Russia, in St. Petersburg. They arrived in July 1813, but the czar was at the warfront, and they waited impatiently until January 1814, but then the British refused mediation. England soon offered to negotiate directly, however. In February, Madison appointed Henry Clay and Jonathan Russell to join the other three commissioners in talks which finally got under way in the Flemish city of Ghent in August.

In contrast to the array of talent gathered in the American contingent, the British diplomats were nonentities, really messengers acting for the Foreign Office, which was more concerned with the effort to remake the map of Europe at the Congress of Vienna. The Americans had more leeway to use their own judgment, and sharp disagreements developed which had to be patched up by Albert Gallatin. The sober-sided Adams and the hard-drinking, poker-playing Clay, especially, rubbed each other the wrong way. The American delegates at first were instructed to demand abandonment of impressment and paper blockades, and to get indemnities for seizures of American ships. The British opened the discussions with demands for territory in New York and Maine, removal of American warships from the Great Lakes, an autonomous Indian buffer state in the Northwest, access to the Mississippi River, and abandonment of American fishing rights off Labrador and Newfoundland. If the British insisted on such a position, the Americans informed them, the negotiations would be at an end.

But the British were stalling, awaiting news of victories to strengthen their hand. They withdrew the demand for an Indian buffer state and substituted *uti possidetis* (retention of occupied territory) as a basis for settlement. This too was rejected. The Americans countered with a proposal for the *status quo ante bellum* (the situation before the war). The news of American victory on Lake Champlain arrived in October and weakened the British resolve. Their will to fight was further weakened by a continuing power struggle at the Congress of Vienna, by the eagerness of

British merchants to renew trade with America, and by the war-weariness of a tax-burdened public. The British finally decided that the game was not worth the candle. One by one demands were dropped on both sides until the envoys agreed to end the war, return the prisoners, restore the previous boundaries, and to settle nothing else. The questions of fisheries and disputed boundaries were referred to commissions for future settlement. The Treaty of Ghent was signed on Christmas Eve 1814.

THE HARTFORD CONVENTION   While the diplomats converged on a peace settlement, an entirely different kind of meeting took place in Hartford, Connecticut. An ill-fated affair, the Hartford Convention represented the climax of New England's dissaffection with "Mr. Madison's war." New England had managed to keep aloof from the war and extract a profit from illegal trading and privateering. New England shippers monopolized the import trade and took advantage of the chance to engage in active trade with the enemy. After the fall of Napoleon, however, the British extended their blockade to New England, occupied Maine as far as the Penobscot River, and conducted several raids along the coast. Even Boston seemed threatened. Instead of rallying to the American flag, however, Federalists in the Massachusetts legislature on October 5, 1814, voted for a convention of New England states to plan independent action. The Constitution, they said, "has failed to secure to this commonwealth, and as they believe, to the Eastern sections of this Union, those equal rights and benefits which are the greatest objects of its formation."

On December 15 the Hartford Convention assembled with delegates chosen by the legislatures of Massachusetts, Rhode Island, and Connecticut, with two delegates from Vermont and one from New Hampshire: twenty-two in all. The convention included an extreme group, Timothy Pickering's "Essex Junto," who were prepared for secession from the Union, but it was controlled by a more moderate group led by Harrison Gray Otis, interested only in a protest in language reminiscent of Madison's Virginia Resolutions of 1798. As the ultimate remedy for their grievances they proposed seven constitutional amendments designed to limit Republican influence: abolishing the three-fifths compromise, requiring a two-thirds vote to declare war or admit new states, prohibiting embargoes lasting more than sixty days, excluding the foreign-born from federal offices, limiting the president to one term, and forbidding successive presidents from the same state.

Their call for a later convention in Boston carried the unmistakable threat of secession if the demands were ignored. Yet the threat quickly evaporated. When messengers from Hartford reached Washington, they found the battered capital celebrating the good news from Ghent and New Orleans. The consequence was a fatal blow to the Federalist party, which never recovered from the stigma of disloyalty and narrow provincialism stamped on it by the Hartford Convention.

THE WAR'S AFTERMATH Conveniently forgotten in the celebrations of peace were the calamities to which the Jeffersonian neglect of national defense had led. For all the fumbling ineptitude with which the War of 1812 was fought, it generated an intense feeling of patriotism. Despite the standoff with which it ended at Ghent, the American public came out of the war with a sense of victory, courtesy of Andrew Jackson and his men at New Orleans. Remembered were the heroic exploits of American frigates in their duels with British ships. Remembered too were the vivid words of the dying Capt. James Lawrence on the *Chesa-*

The War of 1812 created a new feeling of nationalism: "We Owe Allegiance to No Crown." [Collection of Davenport West, Jr.]

peake ("Don't give up the ship") and Oliver H. Perry on Lake Erie ("We have met the enemy and they are ours"), and the stirring stanzas of "The Star Spangled Banner." Under Republican leadership the nation had survived a "Second War of Independence" against the greatest power on earth, and emerged with new symbols of nationhood and a new pantheon of heroes. After forty years of independence, it dawned on the world that the new republic might be here to stay, and that it might be something more than a pawn in European power games.

As if to underline the point, Congress authorized a quick and decisive blow at the pirates of the Barbary Coast. During the War of 1812 the dey of Algiers had once again set about plundering American ships on the claim that he was getting too little tribute. On March 3, 1815, little more than two weeks after the Senate ratified the Peace of Ghent, Congress authorized hostilities against the pirates. On May 10 Capt. Stephen Decatur sailed from New York with ten vessels. In the Mediterranean he first seized two Algerian ships and then sailed boldly into the harbor of Algiers. On June 30, 1815, the dey of Algiers agreed to cease molesting American ships and to give up all United States prisoners. In July and August Decatur's show of force induced similar treaties from Tunis and Tripoli. This time there was no tribute; this time, for a change, the Barbary pirates paid indemnities for the damage they had done. This time victory put an end to the piracy and extortion in that quarter, permanently.

One of the strangest results of a strange war and its aftermath was a reversal of roles by the Republicans and Federalists. Out of the wartime experience the Republicans had learned some lessons in nationalism. Certain needs and inadequacies revealed by the war had "Federalized" Madison, or perhaps "re-Federalized" the Father of the Constitution. Perhaps, Madison reasoned, a peacetime army and navy would not be such an unmitigated evil. Madison now preferred to keep something more than a token force. The lack of a national bank had added to the problems of financing the war. Now Madison wanted it back. The rise of new industries during the war led to a clamor for increased tariffs. Madison went along. The problems of overland transportation in the West had revealed the need for internal improvements. Madison agreed, but on that point kept his constitutional scruples. He wanted a constitutional amendment. So while Madison embraced nationalism and broad construction of the Constitution, the Federalists took up the Jeffersonians' position of states' rights and strict construction. It was the first great reversal of roles in constitutional interpretation. It would not be the last.

FURTHER READING

One of the classics of American history remains the survey of the Republican years found in Henry Adams's *History of the United States during the Administration of Thomas Jefferson* [and] *James Madison* (9 vols.; 1889–1891). Marshall Smelser's *The Democratic Republic, 1801–1815* (1968),° presents a more modern overview. Closer attention to the Jeffersonians themselves is paid by Noble E. Cunningham, Jr.'s *The Republicans in Power: Party Operations, 1801–1809* (1963). James S. Young's *The Washington Community 1800–1828* (1966)° provides an interesting approach to both the mechanics of Jeffersonian politics and the design of the new national capital. Also helpful is Morton Borden's *Parties and Politics in the Early Republic, 1789–1815* (1967).°

Students of Jefferson have been assiduous and productive. The standard modern biography is the multivolume work by Dumas Malone, *Jefferson and His Times* (6 vols.; 1948–1981).° Malone covers this period in *Jefferson, The President* (2 vols.; 1970, 1974).° Forrest McDonald's *The Presidency of Thomas Jefferson* (1976) and Merrill Petersen's *Thomas Jefferson and the New Nation* (1970)° present shorter, yet incisive, views. Fawn Brodie's *Thomas Jefferson: An Intimate Biography* (1974)° takes a psychological approach to a complex man. Good introductions to the life of Jefferson's friend and successor are found in Ralph Ketcham's *James Madison* (1971) and Irving Brant's *The Fourth President: A Life of James Madison* (1970). Raymond Walters, Jr.'s *Albert Gallatin: Jeffersonian Financier and Diplomat* (1957)° assesses both Jeffersonian presidents and studies one of their chief allies. Another look at the Jeffersonian influence is Robert E. Shalhope's *John Taylor of Caroline: Pastoral Republican* (1980).

David Hackett Fischer's *The Revolution of American Conservatism: The Federalist Party in the Era of Jeffersonian Democracy* (1965),° Shaw Livermore, Jr.'s *The Twilight of Federalism: The Disintegration of the Federalist Party* (1962), and Linda K. Kerber's *Federalists in Dissent* (1970)° document how the Federalists behaved while out of power. James M. Banner's *To the Hartford Convention* (1970) analyzes their opposition to the War of 1812. A regional study is James H. Broussard's *The Southern Federalists, 1800–1816* (1979).

Events of the Jeffersonian years are given greater detail in more specialized studies. The concept of judicial review and the courts can be studied in Richard Ellis's *The Jeffersonians and the Judiciary* (1971)° and Charles G. Haines's *The American Doctrine of Judicial Supremacy* (1932). The most comprehensive work on John Marshall remains Albert J. Beveridge's *The Life of John Marshall* (4 vols.; 1919). For the Louisiana Purchase, consult E. Wilson Lewis's *Louisiana in French Diplomacy, 1759–1804* (1934), and Alexander De Conde's *The Affairs of Louisiana* (1976). Bernard De Voto (ed.), *The Journals of Lewis and Clark* (1953), is highly readable but Bernard W. Sheehan's *Seeds of Ex-*

°These books are available in paperback editions.

tinction: Jeffersonian Philanthrophy and the American Indian (1973)° is more analytical about the Jeffersonians and the opening of the West. Thomas P. Abernethy's *The Burr Conspiracy* (1954) and Milton Lomask's *Aaron Burr: The Years from Princeton to Vice President, 1756–1805* (1979) and *The Conspiracy and the Years of Exile, 1805–1836* (1982) trace the career of that remarkable American.

Bradford Perkins's *Prologue to War: England and the United States, 1805–1812* (1961),° concentrates on the diplomacy of the Jeffersonian years. More specific is Burton Spivak's *Jefferson's English Crisis: Commerce, the Embargo, and the Republican Revolution* (1979). Lawrence S. Kaplan's *Jefferson and France: An Essay on Politics and Political Ideas* (1967) is also insightful. Jefferson's first diplomatic decisions are treated in Ray W. Irwin's *Diplomatic Relations of the United States and the Barbary Powers* (1931). A review of the events which brought on war in 1812 is presented in Robert A. Rutland's *Madison's Alternatives: The Jeffersonian Republicans and the Coming of War, 1805–1812* (1975). Also helpful are Roger H. Brown's *The Republic in Peril: 1812* (1964)° and Julius W. Pratt's *Expansionists of 1812* (1925). Accounts of the military conflicts are found in J. K. Mahan's *The War of 1812* (1972), Reginald Horsman's *The War of 1812* (1969), and Harry L. Cole's *The War of 1812* (1965).° Two recent works which concentrate on specific aspects of the war are Alan Lloyd's *The Torching of Washington: The War of 1812* (1975) and Robert V. Remini's *Andrew Jackson and the Course of American Empire, 1767–1821* (1977).° Samuel F. Bemis's *John Quincy Adams and the Foundations of American Foreign Policy* (1949)° and F. L. Engleman's *The Peace of Christmas Eve* (1962) handle the peace negotiations.

10 ✐

NATIONALISM AND SECTIONALISM

ECONOMIC NATIONALISM

When did the United States become a nation? There is no easy answer to the question, for a sense of nationhood was a gradual growth and one always subject to cross-currents of localism, sectionalism, and class interest, as indeed it still is. Americans of the colonies and the early republic by and large identified more closely with the local community and at most the province or state in which they resided than with any larger idea of empire or nation. Among the colonies there was no common tie equal to the connection between each and the mother country. The Revolution gave rise to a sense of nationhood, but that could hardly be regarded as the dominant idea of the Revolution. Men who, like Hamilton, were prepared to think continentally, strengthened the federal Union by the Constitution, but Jefferson's "Revolution of 1800" revealed the countervailing forces of local and state interest. Jefferson himself, for instance, always spoke of Virginia as "my country."

Immediately after the War of 1812, however, there could no longer be any doubt that an American nation existed. Nationalism found expression in economic policy and culture after 1815. An abnormal economic prosperity after the war led to a feeling of well-being and enhanced the prestige of the national government. Jefferson's embargo ironically had given impulse to the factories that he abhorred. The policy of "peaceful coercion" followed by the wartime constraints on trade had caused capital in New England and the middle states to drift from commerce toward manufacturing. The idea became more prevalent that the strength of the country was dependent on a more balanced economy. After a generation of war, shortages of farm commodities in

Samuel Slater's cotton-spinning mill at Pawtucket, Rhode Island, pictured here between 1810 and 1819. Mills like this proliferated after the War of 1812. [Rhode Island Historical Society]

Europe forced up the prices of American products and stimulated agricultural expansion, indeed a wild speculation in farmlands. Southern cotton, tobacco, and rice came to account for about two-thirds of American exports. At the same time planters and farmers could buy in a postwar market which was being flooded with cheap English goods. The new American manufacturers would seek protection from this competition.

President Madison, in his first annual message to Congress after the war, recommended several steps toward strengthening the government: better fortifications, a standing army and a strong navy, a new national bank, effective protection of the new infant industries, a system of canals and roads for commercial and military use, and to top it off, a great national university. "The Republicans have out-Federalized Federalism," Josiah Quincy of Massachusetts remarked. Congress responded by authorizing a standing army of 10,000 and strengthening the navy as well.

THE BANK OF THE UNITED STATES   The trinity of economic nationalism—proposals for a second national bank, protective tariff, and internal improvements—inspired the greatest controversies of the time. After the national bank expired in 1811 the country had fallen into a financial muddle. State-chartered banks mushroomed with little or no control and their banknotes flooded the channels of commerce with money of uncertain value, which often was not accepted at par. And this was the money on which Americans depended. When the national bank liquidated its resources, it had to return about $7 million in gold to English investors, while most of the hard money remaining in the country found its way into New England banks because of the flourishing manufacturing and commercial economy there. Because hard money had been so short during the war, many state banks had suspended specie payments in redemption of their notes, thereby depressing the value of these notes further. The absence of the central bank had been a source of financial embarrassment to the government, which had neither a ready means of floating loans nor of transferring funds across the country.

Madison and most younger Republicans salved their constitutional scruples with a dash of pragmatism. The issue, Madison said, had been decided "by repeated recognitions . . . of the validity of such an institution in acts of the legislative, executive, and judicial branches of the Government, accompanied by . . . a concurrence of the general will of the nation." In 1816 Congress adopted over the protest of Old Republicans provision for a new Bank of the United States. Modeled after Hamilton's bank, it differed chiefly in that it was capitalized at $35 million instead of $10 million. Once again the charter ran for twenty years, once again the government owned a fifth of the stock and named five of the twenty-five directors, and again the bank served as the government depository. Its banknotes were accepted in payments to the government. In return for its privileges the bank had to take care of the government's funds without charge, lend the government $5 million on demand, and pay the government a cash bonus of $1.5 million.

The debate on the bank was noteworthy because of the leading roles played by the great triumvirate of John C. Calhoun of South Carolina, Henry Clay of Kentucky, and Daniel Webster of New Hampshire, later of Massachusetts. Calhoun, still in his youthful phase as a War Hawk nationalist, introduced the measure and pushed it through, justifying its constitutionality by the congressional power to regulate the currency, and pointing to the need for a uniform circulating medium. Clay, who had been in on the kill when Hamilton's bank expired in 1811, now confessed that he had failed to foresee the evils that resulted, and asserted that circumstances had made the bank indispensable. Webster, on the other hand, led the opposition of the New England Federalists, who did not want the banking center moved from Boston to Philadelphia. Later, after he moved from New Hampshire to Massachusetts, he would return to Congress as the champion of a much stronger national power, while events would carry Calhoun in the other direction.

A PROTECTIVE TARIFF   The shift of capital from commerce to manufactures, begun during the embargo, had speeded up during
the war. Peace in 1815 brought a sudden renewal of cheap British imports, and gave impetus to a movement for the protection
of infant industries. The self-interest of the manufacturers, who
as yet had little political impact, was reinforced by a patriotic desire for economic independence from Britain. Spokesmen for
New England shippers and southern farmers opposed the movement, but both sections had sizable minorities who believed that
the promotion of industry was vital to both sectional and national
welfare.

The Tariff of 1816, the first intended more for the protection
of industry against foreign competition than for revenue, passed
by a comfortable majority. The South and New England registered a majority of their votes against the bill, but the middle
states and Old Northwest cast only five negative votes altogether. Nathaniel Macon of North Carolina opposed the tariff
and defended the Old Republican doctrine of strict construction.
The power to protect industry, Macon said, like the power to establish a bank, rested on the doctrine of implied powers; Macon
worried that implied powers might one day be used to abolish
slavery. The minority of southerners who voted for the tariff, led
by William Lowndes and John C. Calhoun of South Carolina, had
good reason to expect that the South might itself become a manufacturing center. South Carolina was then developing a relatively diversified economy which included a few textile mills.
According to the census of 1810, the southern states had approximately as many manufactures as New England. Within a few
years New England moved ahead of the South, and Calhoun
went over to Macon's views against protection. The tariff then
became a sectional issue, with manufacturers, food growers,
wool, sugar, and hemp growers favoring higher tariffs, while
planters and shipping interests favored lower duties.

INTERNAL IMPROVEMENTS   The third major issue of the time was
internal improvements: the building of roads and the development of water transportation. The war had highlighted the shortcomings of existing facilities. Troop movements through the
western wilderness proved very difficult. Settlers found that unless they located near navigable waters, they were cut off from
trade and limited to a frontier subsistence.

The federal government had entered the field of internal
improvements under Jefferson, who went along with some
hesitation. He and both of his successors recommended a constitutional amendment to give the federal government undisputed

THE NATIONAL ROAD, 1811-1838
═══ Built 1811-1818
━━━ Built 1825-1838

power in the field, but lacking that, the constitutional grounds
for federal action rested mainly on provision for national defense
and expansion of the postal system. In 1803, when Ohio became
a state, Congress decreed that 5 percent of the proceeds from
land sales in the state would go to building a National Road from
the Atlantic coast into Ohio and beyond as the territory developed. In 1806 Jefferson signed a measure for a survey, and construction of the National Road got under way in 1811. By 1818 it
was open from Cumberland, Maryland, to Wheeling on the Ohio
River. Construction stopped temporarily during the business
panic of 1819, but by 1838 the road extended all the way to
Vandalia, Illinois.

In 1817 John C. Calhoun put through the House a bill to place
in a fund for internal improvements the $1.5 million bonus the
Bank of the United States had paid for its charter, as well as all
future dividends on the government's bank stock. Once again
opposition centered in New England and the South, which expected to gain least, and support came largely from the West,
which badly needed good roads. On his last day in office Madison
vetoed the bill. Sympathetic to its purpose, he could not overcome his "insuperable difficulty . . . in reconciling the bill with
the Constitution" and suggested instead a constitutional amendment. Internal improvements remained for another hundred
years, with few exceptions, the responsibility of states and private enterprise. Then and later Congress supported river and
harbor improvements, and scattered post roads, but nothing of a
systematic nature. The federal government did not enter the
field on a large scale until passage of the Federal Highways Act of
1916.

"Good Feelings"

JAMES MONROE   As Madison approached the end of a turbulent tenure he, like Jefferson, turned to a fellow Virginian, another secretary of state, as his successor: James Monroe. The Old Republicans, who had started a presidential campaign for Monroe in 1808, now turned to William H. Crawford of Georgia, who had replaced Gallatin at the Treasury. In the Republican caucus Monroe won the nomination, then overwhelmed his Federalist opponent, Rufus King of New York, 183 to 34 in the electoral college. The "Virginia Dynasty" continued. Like three of the four presidents before him, Monroe was a Virginia planter, but with a difference: Monroe came from the small-planter group. At the outbreak of the Revolution he was just beginning college at William and Mary. He joined the army at the age of sixteen, fought with Washington at Trenton, and was a lieutenant-colonel when the war ended. Later he studied law with Jefferson and absorbed Jeffersonian principles at the master's feet.

Monroe never showed the profundity of his Republican predecessors in scholarship or political theory, but what he lacked in intellect he made up in dedication to public service. His soul, Jefferson said, if turned inside out, would be found spotless. Monroe served in the Virginia assembly, as governor of the state, in the Confederation Congress and United States Senate, and as minister to Paris, London, and Madrid. Under Madison he had served as secretary of state, and twice doubled as secretary of

James Monroe, portrayed as he entered the presidency in 1816. [National Portrait Gallery, Smithsonian Institution]

war. Monroe, with his powdered wig, cocked hat, and knee-breeches, was the last of the revolutionary generation to serve in the White House and the last president to dress in the old style.

To the postwar generation there was an air of nostalgic solidity about him, even though little more than twenty years before, as minister to Paris, he had defended the French radicals during their bloodiest exploits. Firmly grounded in Republican principles, he was never quite able to keep up with the onrush of the new nationalism. He accepted as accomplished fact the bank and the protective tariff, but during his tenure there was no further extension of economic nationalism. Indeed there was a minor setback. He permitted the National (or Cumberland) Road to be carried forward, but in his veto of Cumberland Road Bill (1822) denied the authority of Congress to collect tolls for its repair and maintenance. Like Jefferson and Madison, he also suggested a constitutional amendment to remove all doubt about federal authority in the field of internal improvements, and in his last year in office did sign the General Survey Bill of 1824, which authorized estimates of roads and canals needed for military, commercial, and postal purposes.

Whatever his limitations, Monroe surrounded himself with some of the strongest and ablest young Republican leaders. John Quincy Adams became secretary of state. William Crawford of Georgia, his rival for the presidency, continued in office as secretary of the treasury. John C. Calhoun headed the War Department after Henry Clay refused the position in order to remain Speaker of the House. The new administration found the country in a state of well-being: America was at peace and the economy was flourishing. Soon after the inauguration Monroe embarked on a goodwill tour of New England. In Boston, lately a hotbed of wartime dissent, a Federalist paper, the *Columbian Centinel,* ran a general comment on the president's visit under the heading "Era of Good Feelings." The label became a popular catchphrase for Monroe's administration, and one that historians seized upon later. Like many a maxim, it conveys just enough truth to be sadly misleading. A resurgence of factionalism and sectionalism erupted just as the postwar prosperity collapsed in the Panic of 1819.

For two years, however, general harmony reigned, and even when the country's troubles revived, little of the blame sullied the name of Monroe. In 1820 he was reelected without opposition, even without needing nomination. The Federalists were too weak to put up a candidate, and the Republicans did not bother to call a caucus. Monroe got all the electoral votes except for three abstentions and one vote from New Hampshire for John Quincy Adams. The Republican party was dominant, or perhaps more accurately, was following the Federalists into oblivion. In the general political contentment the first party system was fading away, but rivalries for the succession soon commenced the process of forming new parties.

IMPROVING RELATIONS WITH BRITAIN Adding to the prevailing contentment after the war was a growing rapprochement with the recent enemy. Trade relations with Britain (and India) were restored by a Commercial Convention of 1815, which eliminated discriminatory duties on either side. The Peace of Ghent had left unsettled a number of minor disputes, but in the sequel two important compacts—the Rush-Bagot Agreement of 1817 and the Convention of 1818—removed several potential causes of irritation. In the first, effected by an exchange of notes between Acting Secretary of State Richard Rush and British Minister Charles Bagot, the threat of naval competition on the Great Lakes vanished with an arrangement to limit naval forces there to several revenue cutters. Although the exchange made no reference to the land boundary between the countries, its spirit gave rise to the tradition of an unfortified border, the longest in the world.

The Convention of 1818 covered three major points. The northern limit of the Louisiana Purchase was settled by extending the national boundary along the Forty-ninth Parellel west from Lake of the Woods to the crest of the Rocky Mountains. West of that point the Oregon country would be open to joint occupation, but the boundary remained unsettled. The right of Americans to fish off Newfoundland and Labrador, granted in 1783, was acknowledged once again.

The chief remaining problem was Britain's exclusion of American ships from the West Indies in order to reserve that lucrative trade for British ships. The Commercial Convention of 1815 did not apply there, and after the War of 1812 the British had once again closed the door. This remained a chronic irritant, and the United States retaliated with several measures. Under a Navigation Act of 1817, importation of West Indian produce was restricted to American vessels or vessels belonging to West Indian merchants. In 1818 American ports were closed to all British vessels arriving from a colony that was legally closed to vessels of the United States. In 1820 Monroe approved an act of Congress which specified total nonintercourse, in British vessels, with all British-American colonies, even in goods taken to England and reexported. The rapprochement with Britain therefore fell short of perfection.

JACKSON TAKES FLORIDA   The year 1819 was one of the more fateful years in American history, a time when a whole sequence of developments came into focus. The bumptious new nationalism reached a climax with the acquisition of Florida and the extension of the southwestern boundary to the Pacific, and with three major decisions of the Supreme Court. But nationalism quickly began to run afoul of domestic cross-currents that would set up an ever-widening swirl in the next decades. In the calculus of global power, it was perhaps long since reckoned that Florida would some day pass to the United States. Spanish sovereignty was more a technicality than an actuality, and extended little beyond St. Augustine on the east coast and Pensacola and St. Marks on the Gulf. The thinly held province had been a thorn in the side of the United States during the recent war, a center of British intrigue, a haven for Creek refugees, who there were beginning to take the name Seminole (runaway or separatist), and a harbor for runaway slaves and criminals. Florida also stood athwart the outlets of several important rivers flowing to the Gulf.

Spain was almost powerless at that point because of both internal and colonial revolt, and unable to enforce its obligations under the Pinckney Treaty of 1795 to pacify the frontiers. In 1816 American forces came into conflict with a group of escaped slaves who had taken over a British fort on the Appalachicola River. Seminoles who challenged the legality of Creek land cessions were soon fighting white settlers in the area. In November 1817 Americans burned the Seminole border settlement of Fowltown, killed four of its inhabitants, and dispersed the rest across the border into Florida.

At this point Secretary of War Calhoun authorized a campaign against the Seminoles, and summoned General Jackson from Nashville to take command. Jackson's orders allowed him to pursue the offenders into Spanish territory, but not to attack any Spanish post. A man of Jackson's direct purpose naturally felt hobbled by such a restriction, so he wrote to President Monroe that if the United States wanted Florida he could wind up the whole thing in sixty days. All he needed was private, unofficial word, which might be sent through Tennessee Rep. John Rhea. Soon afterward Jackson indeed got a letter from Rhea, and claimed that it transmitted cryptically the required authority, although Monroe always denied any such intention. The truth about the Rhea letter, which Jackson destroyed (at Monroe's request, he said), remains a mystery.

In any case, when it came to Spaniards or Indians, no white Tennessean—certainly not Andrew Jackson—was likely to bother with technicalities. Jackson pushed eastward through Florida, reinforced by Tennessee volunteers and a party of friendly Creeks, taking the Spanish post at St. Marks, and skirmishing with the Seminoles, destroying their settlements, and pursuing them to the Suwannee River. Two of their leaders, the prophet Francis and Chief Homollimico, Jackson hanged without any semblance of a trial. For two British intriguers in the area, a trader named Alexander Arbuthnot and a former British officer, Robert Ambrister, he convened a court-martial, but to the same end. Both had befriended the Seminoles, and Ambrister at least had offered them military training. In any case Jackson was convinced that the two were at the root of all the trouble, and the evidence did not much matter. Arbuthnot was hanged; Ambrister shot. Having mopped up the region from the Appalachicola to the Suwannee, Jackson then turned west and seized Pensacola, appointed one of his colonels civil and military governor of Florida, and returned home to Nashville. The whole thing had taken about four months; the Florida panhandle was in American hands by the end of May 1818.

The news created consternation in both Madrid and Washington. Spain demanded the return of its territory, reparations, and the punishment of Jackson, but Spain's impotence was plain for all to see. Monroe's cabinet was at first prepared to disavow Jackson's action, especially his direct attack on Spanish posts. Calhoun, as secretary of war, was inclined, at least officially, to discipline Jackson for disregard of orders—a stand which caused bad blood between the two men later—but privately confessed a certain pleasure at the outcome. In any case a man as popular as Jackson was almost invulnerable. And he had one important friend at court, Secretary of State John Quincy Adams, who realized that Jackson had strengthened his hand in negotiations already under way with the Spanish minister, Luís de Onís y Gonzalez. American forces withdrew from Florida, but negotiations resumed with the knowledge that the United States could take Florida at any time.

The fate of Florida was a foregone conclusion. Adams now had his eye on a larger purpose, a definition of the western boundary of the Louisiana Purchase and—his boldest stroke—extension of a boundary to the Pacific coast. In lengthy negotiations Adams gradually gave ground on claims to Texas, but stuck to his de-

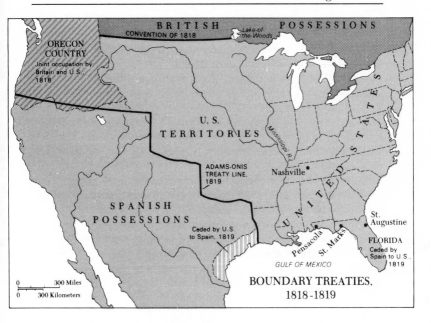

BRITISH POSSESSIONS
CONVENTION OF 1818
Lake-of-the-Woods

OREGON
COUNTRY
Joint occupation by
Britain and U.S.
1818

U. S.
TERRITORIES

Mississippi R.

ADAMS-ONIS
TREATY LINE,
1819

Nashville

UNITED STATES

SPANISH
POSSESSIONS

Ceded by U.S.
to Spain, 1819

St.
Augustine

Pensacola
St. Marks

FLORIDA
Ceded by
Spain to U.S.,
1819

GULF OF MEXICO

0   300 Miles
0   300 Kilometers

BOUNDARY TREATIES,
1818-1819

mand for a transcontinental line. Agreement finally came early in 1819. Spain ceded all of Florida in return for American assumption of private American claims against Spain up to $5 million. The western boundary of the Louisiana Purchase would run along the Sabine River and then in stair-step fashion up to the Red River, along the Red, and up to the Arkansas River. From the source of the Arkansas it would go north to the Forty-second Parallel and thence west to the Pacific coast. A dispute over land claims held up ratification for another two years, but those claims were revoked and final ratifications were exchanged in 1821. Florida became a territory, and its first governor briefly was Andrew Jackson. In 1845 Florida eventually achieved statehood.

"A Firebell in the Night"

THE PANIC OF 1819   Adams's Transcontinental Treaty was a triumph of foreign policy and the climactic event of the postwar nationalism. Even before it was signed in February 1819, however, two thunderclaps signaled the end of the brief "Era of Good Feelings" and gave warning of stormy weather ahead. The two portents were the financial Panic of 1819 and the controversy over statehood for Missouri. The occasion for the panic was the sudden collapse of cotton prices in the Liverpool market. At one point in 1818 cotton had soared to 32 1/2 cents a pound. The pressure of high prices forced British manufacturers to turn to cheaper East Indian cotton. It proved unsatisfactory, but only after severe damage had been done in American markets. In 1819 cotton averaged only 14.3 cents per pound at New Orleans. The price collapse in cotton was the catalytic event that set off a decline in the demand for other American goods, and suddenly revealed the fragility of the prosperity that followed the War of 1812.

Since 1815 a speculative bubble had grown with expectations that expansion would go on forever. But American industry began to run into trouble finding markets for its goods. Even the Tariff of 1816 had not been enough to eliminate British competition. What was more, businessmen, farmers, and land jobbers had inflated the bubble with a volatile expansion of credit. The sources of this credit were both government and banks. Under the Land Law of 1800 the government extended four years' credit to those who bought western lands. After 1804 one could buy as little as 160 acres at a minimum price of $1.64 per acre (although in auctions the best lands went for more). In many cases speculators took up large tracts, paying one-fourth down, and then sold them to settlers with the understanding that the settlers would pay the remaining installments. With the collapse of prices, and then of land values, both speculators and settlers found themselves caught short.

The inflation of credit was compounded by the reckless practices of state banks. To enlarge their loans they issued banknotes far beyond their means of redemption, and at first were under little pressure to promise redemption in specie. Even the second Bank of the United States, which was supposed to introduce some order, was at first caught up in the mania. Its first president, William Jones, had been a disaster at the Treasury, and seen his own business just go bankrupt. Jones yielded to the contagion of get-rich-quick fever that was sweeping the country.

Under the bank's charter its own stockholders were expected to pay a fourth of their subscription in specie. But with specie going at a premium, the hard-pressed stockholders were permitted to pay their last two installments in promissory notes secured by the value of their own stock. The proliferation of branches combined with little supervision from Philadelphia to carry the bank into the same reckless extension of loans that state banks had pursued. In 1819, just as alert businessmen began to take

The second Bank of the United States. [Historical Society of Pennsylvania]

alarm, a case of extensive fraud and embezzlement in the Baltimore branch came to light. The upshot of the disclosure was Jones's resignation, his replacement by Langdon Cheves, former congressman from South Carolina, and the establishment of a sounder policy.

Cheves reduced salaries and other costs, postponed dividends, restrained the extension of credit, and presented for redemption the state banknotes that came in, thereby forcing the wildcat banks to keep specie reserves. Cheves rescued the bank from near-ruin, but only by putting heavy pressure on state banks. State banks in turn put pressure on their debtors, who found it harder to renew old loans or get new ones. In 1823, his job completed, Cheves relinquished his position to Nicholas Biddle of Philadelphia. The Cheves policies were the result rather than the cause of the Panic, but they were anathema to debtors who found it all the more difficult to meet their obligations. Hard times lasted about three years, and the bank took much of the blame in the popular mind. The Panic passed, but resentment of the bank lingered. It never fully regained the confidence of the South and the West.

THE MISSOURI COMPROMISE   Just as the Panic was breaking over the country, another cloud appeared on the horizon, the onset of a sectional controversy over slavery. By 1819 it happened that the country had an equal number of slave and free states, eleven of each. The line between them was defined by the southern and western boundaries of Pennsylvania and the Ohio River. Although slavery still existed in some places north of the line, it was on the way to extinction there. Beyond the Mississippi, however, no move had been made to extend the dividing line across the Louisiana Purchase territory, where slavery had existed from the days when France and Spain had colonized the area. At the time the Missouri Territory embraced all of the Louisiana Purchase except the state of Louisiana (1812) and the Arkansas Territory (1819). In the westward rush of population, the old French town of St. Louis became the funnel through which settlers pushed on beyond the Mississippi. These were largely settlers from the south who brought their slaves with them.

In February 1819 the House of Representatives confronted legislation enabling Missouri to draft a state constitution, its population having passed the minimum of 60,000. At that point Rep. James Tallmadge, Jr., a congressman from New York, introduced a resolution prohibiting the further introduction of slaves into Missouri, which had some 10,000 in 1820, and providing freedom at age twenty-five for those born after the territory's admission as a state. Tallmadge's motives remain obscure, but may have been very simply a moral aversion to slavery or perhaps a political aversion to having slavery and three-fifths compromise extended any farther beyond the Mississippi River. After brief but fiery exchanges, the House passed the amendment on an almost strictly sectional vote and the Senate rejected it by a similar tally, but with several northerners joining in the opposition. With population at the time growing faster in the north, a balance between the two sections could be held only in the Senate. In the House, slave states had 81 votes while free states had 105; a balance was unlikely ever again to be restored in the House.

Congress adjourned in March, postponing further debate until the regular session in December. When the debate came, it was remarkable for the absence of moral argument, although repugnance to slavery and moral guilt about it were never far from the surface. The debate turned on the constitutional issue. Congress, Rufus King of New York asserted, was empowered to forbid slavery in Missouri as the Confederation Congress had done in the Northwest Territory. William Pinckney of Maryland asserted that the states were equal and that Congress could not bind a state. Southern leaders argued further that under the Fifth Amendment, slaveholders could not be denied the right to carry their property into the territory, which would be deprivation of property without due process of law. Henry Clay and others expressed a view, which Jefferson and Madison now shared, that the expansion and dispersal of slavery would ameliorate the condition of the slaves. Most of the constitutional arguments that would reverberate in later quarrels over slavery were already present in the argument over Missouri, but the moral issue of bondage had not yet reached the fevered condition it would later achieve, since few were yet prepared to defend slavery as a posi-

THE MISSOURI COMPROMISE (1820)

OREGON COUNTRY
Joint occupation by Britain and U.S.

UNORGANIZED TERRITORY *
(Free)

MICHIGAN TERRITORY

MAINE *
1820 (Free)

VT.
N.H.
MASS.
R.I.
CONN.

N.Y.

PENN.

N.J.
DEL.
MD.

OHIO
ILL. IND.
MO. *
1821
(Slave)

36°30'

SPANISH

POSSESSIONS

KY.

VA.

N.C.

S.C.

ARKANSAS *
TERRITORY
(Slave)

MISS. ALA. GA.

LA.

FLORIDA *
TERRITORY
(Slave)

Free states
Slave states
* States and territories covered by the compromise

tive good. In fact the general abhorrence of slavery was still strong enough that during 1820 Congress defined the illegal foreign slave trade as piracy, subjecting those engaged in it to the death penalty. This penalty was not actually imposed, however, until the outbreak of the Civil War.

Maine's application for statehood made it easier to arrive at an agreement. Since colonial times Maine had been the northern province of Massachusetts. The Senate linked its request for separate statehood with Missouri's and voted to admit Maine as a free state and Missouri as a slave state, thus maintaining the balance in the Senate. Sen. Jesse B. Thomas of Illinois further extended the compromise by an amendment to exclude slavery from the rest of the Louisiana Purchase north of 36° 30', Missouri's southern border. Slavery thus would continue in the Arkansas Territory and be excluded from the remainder of the area. But that was country which Zebulon Pike's and Stephen Long's reports had persuaded the public was the Great American Desert, unlikely ever to be settled. For this reason the arrangement seemed to be a victory for the slave states. The House at first refused to accept the arrangement, but the question went to a conference committee of the two houses for which Speaker Henry Clay had carefully chosen malleable members who accepted the Senate compromise. By a very close vote it passed the House on March 2, 1820.

Once that issue was settled, however, another problem arose.

Henry Clay's compromise deflected a confrontation on the expansion of slavery. Clay is portrayed here in 1822. [Library of Congress]

The proslavery elements which dominated Missouri's constitutional convention inserted in the new state constitution a proviso excluding free Negroes and mulattoes from the state. This clearly violated the requirement of Article IV, Section 2, of the Constitution: "The Citizens of each State shall be entitled to all Privileges and Immunities of Citizens in the Several States." Free Negroes were citizens of many states, including the slave states of North Carolina and Tennessee where, until the mid-1830s, they also voted.

The renewed controversy threatened final approval of Missouri's admission until Henry Clay, now beginning to earn his later title of the "Great Compromiser," formulated a "Second Missouri Compromise." Admission of Missouri as a state depended on assurance from the Missouri legislature that it would never construe the offending clause in such a way as to sanction denial of privileges that citizens held under the Constitution. It was one of the more artless dodges in American history, for it required the legislature to affirm that the state constitution did not mean what it clearly said, but the compromise worked. The Missouri legislature duly adopted the pledge, but qualified it by denying that the legislature had any power to bind the people of the state. On August 10, 1821, President Monroe proclaimed the admission of Missouri as the twenty-fourth state. For the time the controversy was settled. "But this momentous question," the aging Thomas Jefferson wrote to a friend after the first compromise, "like a firebell in the night awakened and filled me with terror. I considered it at once as the knell of the Union."

JUDICIAL NATIONALISM

JOHN MARSHALL, CHIEF JUSTICE   Meanwhile nationalism was still flourishing in the Supreme Court, where another Virginian, Chief Justice John Marshall, preserved Hamiltonian Federalism for another generation. Marshall, survivor of the Revolution, was among those who had been forever nationalized by the experience. In later years he said: "I was confirmed in the habit of considering America as my country and Congress as my government." The habit persisted through a successful legal career punctuated by service in Virginia's legislature and ratifying convention, as part of the "XYZ" mission to France, and as a member of Congress. Never a judge before he became chief justice in 1801, he established the power of the Supreme Court by the force of his mind and his determination. His influence was scarcely lessened when Jefferson and Madison filled vacancies on the Court with William Johnson (1804) of South Carolina and Joseph Story (1811) of Massachusetts. Once confirmed and beyond the reach of presidents, these Republican justices fell under the spell of Marshall. Story became a close collaborator.

During Marshall's early years on the Court (altogether he served thirty-four years) he affirmed the principle of judicial review. In *Marbury v. Madison* (1803) and *Fletcher v. Peck* (1810) the Court first struck down a federal law and then a state law as unconstitutional. In the cases of *Martin v. Hunter's Lessee* (1816) and *Cohens v. Virginia* (1821) the Court assumed the right to

Chief Justice John Marshall, pillar of judicial nationalism. [Library of Congress]

take appeals from state courts on the grounds that the Constitution, laws, and treaties of the United States could be kept uniformly the supreme law of the land only if the Court could review decisions of state courts. In the first case the Court overruled Virginia's confiscation of Loyalist property because this violated treaties with Great Britain; in the second it upheld Virginia's right to forbid the sale of lottery tickets.

PROTECTING CONTRACT RIGHTS   In the fateful year 1819 came two more decisions of major importance in checking the states and building the power of the central government: *Dartmouth College v. Woodward*, and *McCulloch v. Maryland*. The Dartmouth College case involved an attempt by the New Hampshire legislature to alter a charter granted Dartmouth by George III in 1769 under which the trustees became a self-perpetuating board. In 1816 the state's Republican legislature, offended by this relic of monarchy and even more by the Federalist majority on the board, placed Dartmouth under a new board named by the governor. The original trustees sued, lost in the state courts, but with Daniel Webster as counsel won on appeal to the Supreme Court. The charter, Marshall said for the Court, was a valid contract which the legislature had impaired, an act forbidden by the Constitution. This implied a new and enlarged definition of contract which seemed to put private corporations beyond the reach of the states that chartered them. But thereafter states commonly wrote into charters and general laws of incorporation provisions making them subject to modification. Such provisions were then part of the "contract."

STRENGTHENING THE FEDERAL GOVERNMENT   Marshall's single most important interpretation of the constitutional system came in the case of *McCulloch v. Maryland*. McCulloch, a clerk in the Baltimore branch of the Bank of the United States, failed to affix state revenue stamps to banknotes as required by a Maryland law taxing the notes. Indicted by the state, McCulloch, acting for the bank appealed to the Supreme Court, which handed down a unanimous judgment upholding the power of Congress to charter the bank and denying any right of the state to tax the bank. In a lengthy opinion Marshall examined and rejected Maryland's argument that the federal government was the creature of sovereign states. Instead, he argued, it arose directly from the people acting through the conventions which ratified the Constitution. While sovereignty was divided between the states and the national government, the latter, "though limited in its powers, is supreme within its sphere of action."

Marshall then went on to endorse the doctrine of broad construction and implied powers set forth by Hamilton in his bank message of 1791. The "necessary and proper" clause, he argued, did not mean "absolutely indispensable." The test of constitutionality he summed up in almost the same words as Hamilton: "Let the end be legitimate, let it be within the scope of the constitution, and all means which are appropriate, which are plainly adapted to that end, which are not prohibited, but consistent with the letter and spirit of the constitution, are constitutional."

The state's effort to tax the bank conflicted with the supreme law of the land. One great principle which "entirely pervades the constitution," Marshall wrote, was "that the constitution and the laws made in pursuance thereof are supreme: that they control the constitution and laws of the respective states, and cannot be controlled by them." The tax therefore was unconstitutional for "the power to tax involves the power to destroy"—which was precisely what the legislatures of Maryland and several other states had in mind with respect to the bank.

REGULATING INTERSTATE COMMERCE   Marshall's last great decision, *Gibbons v. Ogden* (1824), established national supremacy in regulating interstate commerce. In 1808 Robert Fulton and Robert Livingston, who pioneered commercial use of the steamboat, got

This 1810 lithograph shows Fulton's steamboat The Clermont, *going up the Hudson from New York to Albany. [New York Public Library]*

from the New York legislature the exclusive right to operate steamboats on the state's waters. From them in turn Aaron Ogden got the exclusive right to navigation across the Hudson between New York and New Jersey. Thomas Gibbons, however, operated a coastal trade under a federal license and came into competition with Ogden. On behalf of a unanimous Court, Marshall ruled that the monopoly granted by the state conflicted with the federal Coasting Act under which Gibbons operated. Congressional power to regulate commerce, the Court said, "like all others vested in Congress, is complete in itself, may be exercised to its utmost extent, and acknowledges no limitations other than are prescribed in the constitution." The opinion stopped just short of stating an exclusive federal power over commerce, and later cases would clarify the point that states had a concurrent jurisdiction so long as it did not come into conflict with federal action. For many years there was in fact little federal regulation, so that in striking down the monopoly created by the state Marshall had opened the way to extensive development of steamboat navigation and, soon afterward, steam railroads. Economic expansion was often consonant with judicial nationalism.

Nationalist Diplomacy

THE NORTHWEST   In foreign affairs, too, nationalism continued to be an effective force. Within two years after final approval of Adams's Transcontinental Treaty, the secretary of state was able to draw another important transcontinental line. In 1819 Spain had abandoned her claim to the Oregon country above the Forty-second Parallel. Russia, however, had claims along the Pacific coast as well. In 1741 Vitus Bering, in the employ of Russia, had explored the strait which now bears his name, and in 1799 the Russian-American Company had been formed to exploit the resources of Alaska. Some Russian outposts reached as far south as the California coast. In September 1821 the Russian czar issued an *ukase* (proclamation) claiming the Pacific coast as far south as 51°, which in the American view lay within the "Oregon country." In 1823 Secretary of State Adams contested "the right of Russia to any territorial establishment on this continent." The American government, he informed the Russian minister, assumed the principle "that the American continents are no longer subjects for any new European colonial establishments." The upshot of his protest was a treaty signed in 1824 whereby Russia accepted the line of 54° 40′ as the southern boundary of its claim. In 1825 a similar agreement between Russia and Britain gave the Oregon country clearly defined boundaries, although it was still subject to joint occupation by the United States and Great Britain under their agreement of 1818.

LATIN AMERICA Adams's disapproval of further colonization also had clear implications for Latin America. One consequence of the Napoleonic wars and French occupation of Spain and Portugal had been a series of wars of liberation in Latin America. Within little more than a decade after the flag of rebellion was first raised in 1811, Spain had lost its entire continental empire. All that was left were the islands of Cuba, Puerto Rico, and Santo Domingo. The only continental possessions left to European powers, 330 years after Columbus, were Russian Alaska, Canada, British Honduras, and Dutch, French, and British Guiana.

That Spain could not regain her empire seems clear enough in retrospect. The British navy would not permit it because Britain's trade with the area was too important. For a time, however, the temper of Europe after Napoleon was to restore "legitimacy" everywhere. The great European peace conference, the Congress of Vienna (1814–1815), returned that continent, as nearly as possible, to its status before the French Revolution and set out to make the world safe for monarchy. To that end the major powers (Great Britain, Prussia, Russia, and Austria) set up the Quadruple Alliance (it became the Quintuple Alliance after France entered in 1818) to police the continent. In 1821 the Alliance, with Britain dissenting, authorized Austria to put down liberal movements in Italy. The British government was no champion of liberal revolution, but neither did it feel impelled to police the entire continent. In 1822, when the allies met in the Congress of Verona, they authorized France to suppress the constitutionalist movement in Spain and restore the authority of Ferdinand VII. At that point the British withdrew from the Concert of Europe, which in a few more years fell apart in a dispute over support of Greek rebellion against the Turks.

THE MONROE DOCTRINE But in 1823 French troops crossed the Spanish border, put down the rebels, and restored King Ferdinand VII to absolute authority. Rumors began to circulate that France would also try to restore Ferdinand's "legitimate" power over Spain's American empire. Monroe and Secretary of War Calhoun were alarmed at the possibility, although John Quincy Adams took the more realistic view that such action was unlikely.

After the break with the Quadruple Alliance, British Foreign Minister George Canning sought to reach an understanding with the American minister to London that the two countries jointly undertake to forestall action by the Quadruple Alliance against Latin America. Monroe at first agreed, with the support of his sage advisors Jefferson and Madison.

Adams, however, urged upon Monroe and the cabinet the independent course of proclaiming a unilateral policy against the restoration of Spain's colonies. "It would be more candid," Adams said, "as well as more dignified, to avow our principles explicitly to Russia and France, than to come in as a cock-boat in the wake of the British man-of-war." Adams knew that the British navy would stop any action by the Quadruple Alliance in Latin America and he suspected that the alliance had no real intention to intervene anyway. The British wanted, moreover, the United States to agree not to acquire any more Spanish territory, including Cuba, Texas, or California, and Adams preferred to avoid such a commitment.

Indeed unbeknownst to Adams at the time Canning had already procured from French Foreign Minister Jules de Polignac a statement which renounced any purpose to reconquer or annex the former Spanish colonies. The Polignac Agreement was still unknown in the United States when Monroe incorporated the substance of Adams's views in his annual message to Congress on December 2, 1823. The Monroe Doctrine, as it was later called, comprised four major points: (1) that "the American continents . . . are henceforth not to be considered as subjects for future colonization by any European powers"; (2) the political system of European powers was different from that of the United States, which would "consider any attempt on their part to extend their system to any portion of this hemisphere as dangerous to our peace and safety"; (3) the United States would not interfere with existing European colonies; and (4) the United States would keep out of the internal affairs of European nations and their wars.

At the time the statement drew little attention either in the United States or abroad. Canning was more chagrined than anything else, since he had already achieved Monroe's objective two months before in the Polignac Agreement. In time the Monroe Doctrine, not even so called until 1852, became one of the cherished principles of American foreign policy, but for the time being it slipped into obscurity for want of any occasion to invoke it. In spite of Adams's affirmation, the United States came in as a cock boat in the wake of the British man-of-war after all, for the effectiveness of the doctrine depended on British naval supremacy. The doctrine had no standing in international law. It was merely a statement of intent by an American president to the Congress, and did not even draw enough interest at the time for European powers to renounce it.

ONE-PARTY POLITICS

Almost from the start of Monroe's second term the jockeying for the presidential succession had begun. Three members of Monroe's cabinet were active candidates: Calhoun, Crawford, and Adams. Henry Clay, longtime Speaker of the House, hungered and thirsted after the office. And on the fringes of the Washington scene a new force appeared in the person of Sen. Andrew Jackson, the scourge of the British, Spaniards, Creeks, and Seminoles, the epitome of what every frontiersman admired. All were Republicans, for again no Federalist stood a chance, but they were competing in a new political world, complicated by the cross-currents of nationalism and sectionalism. With only one party there was in effect no party, for there existed no generally accepted method for choosing a "regular" candidate.

PRESIDENTIAL NOMINATIONS   Selection by congressional caucus, already under attack in 1816, had disappeared in the wave of unanimity which reelected Monroe in 1820 without the formality of a nomination. The friends of Crawford sought in vain to breathe life back into "King Caucus," but only sixty-six congressmen appeared in answer to the call. They duly named Crawford for president and Albert Gallatin for vice-president, but the endorsement was so weak as to be more a handicap than an advantage. Crawford was in fact the logical successor to the Virginia dynasty, a native of the state though a resident of Georgia. He had flirted with nationalism, but swung back to states' rights and strict construction, and assumed leadership of a faction, called the Radicals, which included Old Republicans and those who distrusted the nationalism of Adams and Calhoun. Crawford's candidacy was a forlorn cause from the beginning, for the candidate had been stricken in 1823 by some unknown disease which left him half-paralyzed and half-blind. His friends protested that he would soon be well but he never did fully recover.

Long before the rump caucus met on February 14, 1824, indeed for two years before, the country had broken out in a rash of presidential endorsements by legislatures and public meetings.

On July 20, 1822, the Tennessee legislature named Andrew Jackson. In March 1824 a mass meeting of Pennsylvanians in Harrisburg added their endorsement and Jackson, who had previously kept silent, responded that while the presidency should not be sought, it could not with propriety be declined. The same meeting named Calhoun for vice-president, and Calhoun accepted. The youngest of the candidates, he was content to retire from the presidential contest and take second place for the time being. Meanwhile the Kentucky legislature named its favorite son, Clay, on November 18, 1822. The Massachusetts legislature named Adams in 1824.

Of the four candidates only two had clearly defined programs, and the outcome was an early lesson in the danger of being committed on the issues too soon. Crawford's friends emphasized his devotion to the "principles of 1798," states' rights and strict construction. Clay, on the contrary, took his stand for the "American System," which he outlined in a lengthy speech to the House on March 30–31, 1824: he favored the national bank, the protective tariff, and a national program of internal improvements to bind the country together and build its economy. Adams was close to Clay, openly dedicated to internal improvements but less strongly committed to the tariff. Jackson, where issues were concerned, remained an enigma and carefully avoided commitment. His managers hoped that, by being all things to all men, Jackson could capitalize on his popularity as the hero of New Orleans.

THE "CORRUPT BARGAIN" The outcome turned on personalities and sectional allegiance more than on issues. Adams, the only northern candidate, carried New England, the former bastion of Federalism, and most of New York's electoral votes. Clay took Kentucky, Ohio, and Missouri. Crawford carried Virginia, Georgia, and Delaware. Jackson swept the Southeast, plus Illinois and Indiana, and with Calhoun's support, the Carolinas, Pennsylvania, Maryland, and New Jersey. All candidates got scattered votes elsewhere. In New York, where Clay was strong, his supporters were outmaneuvered in the legislature, which still chose the presidential electors. Martin Van Buren, trying to hold the old Virginia–New York axis for Crawford, also lost out to the Adams forces under Thurlow Weed.

The result was inconclusive in both the electoral vote and the popular vote, wherever the state legislature permitted the choice of electors by the people. In the electoral college Jackson had 99, Adams 84, Crawford 41, Clay 37. In the popular vote it ran about the same: Jackson 154,000, Adams 109,000, Crawford 47,000, and Clay 47,000. Whatever might have been said about the outcome, one thing seemed apparent. It was a defeat for Clay's American System: New England and New York opposed him on internal improvements; the South and Southwest on the protective tariff. Sectionalism had defeated the national program, yet the advocate of the American System now assumed the role of president-maker, since the election was thrown into the House of Representatives, where Speaker Clay's influence was decisive. Clay had little trouble in choosing, since he regarded Jackson as unfit for the office. He kept his own counsel until near the end, then threw his support to Adams. The final vote in the House, which was by state, carried Adams to victory with thirteen votes to Jackson's seven and Crawford's four.

It was a pyrrhic victory, for the result was to unite Adams's foes and to cripple his administration before it got under way. There is no evidence that Adams entered into any bargain with Clay to win his support, but the charge was made and widely believed after Adams made Clay his secretary of state, and thus put him in the office from which three successive presidents had risen. Adams's Puritan conscience could never quite overcome its sense of guilt at the maneuverings that were necessary to gain his election, but a "corrupt bargain" was too much out of character for credence. Yet credence it had with a large number of people, and on that cry a campaign to elect Jackson next time was launched almost immediately after the 1824 decision. The Crawford people, including Martin Van Buren, the "Little Magician" of New York politics, soon moved into the Jackson camp.

JOHN QUINCY ADAMS'S PRESIDENCY   John Quincy Adams was one of the ablest men and finest intellects ever to enter the White House, but he sadly lacked the common touch and the politician's gift for maneuver. He firmly refused to play the game of patronage, on the simple grounds that it would be dishonorable to dismiss "able and faithful political opponents to provide for my own partisans." In four years he removed only twelve officeholders. His first annual message to Congress was a grandiose blueprint for national development, set forth in such a blunt way that it became a disaster of political ineptitude. In the boldness and magnitude of its conception, the Adams plan outdid both Hamilton and Clay. The central government, the president said, should promote internal improvements, set up a national university, finance scientific explorations, build astronomical observatories ("lighthouses of the skies"), reform the patent laws, and

John Quincy Adams, a president of great intellect but without the common touch, in a portrait by Thomas Sully. [New York State Bureau of Historic Sites]

create a new Department of the Interior. Ample powers to do all these things existed in "the power to exercise exclusive legislation in all cases whatsoever over the District of Columbia; . . . to lay and collect taxes, duties, imposts, and excises, to pay the debts and provide for the common defense and general welfare of the United States. . . . " In general terms he proposed "laws promoting the improvement of the agriculture, commerce, and manufactures, the cultivation and encouragement of the mechanic and of the elegant arts, the advancement of literature, and the progress of the sciences, ornamental and profound. . . . "

To refrain from using these powers "would be treachery to the most sacred of trusts." Officers of the government, he said, should not "fold up our arms and proclaim to the world that we are palsied by the will of our constituents. . . . " Whatever grandeur of conception the message had, it was obscured by an unhappy choice of language. For a minority president to demean the sovereignty of the voter was tactless enough. For the son of John Adams to cite the example "of the nations of Europe and of their rulers" was downright suicidal. At one fell swoop he had revived all the Republican suspicions of the Adamses. To the aging Jefferson his message seemed like Federalism run riot, looking to "a single and splendid government of an aristocracy, founded on banking institutions, and moneyed incorporation under the guise and cloak of . . . manufactures, commerce, and navigation, riding and ruling over the plundered ploughman and beggared yeomanry." Jefferson did not see, though, that

Adams's presidential message was the beginning of the definition of a new party system. The minority who cast their lot with Adams and Clay were turning into National-Republicans; the opposition, the growing party of Jacksonians, were the Democratic-Republicans, who would eventually drop the name Republican and become Democrats.

Adams's headstrong plunge into nationalism and his refusal to play the game of politics condemned his administration to utter frustration. Congress ignored his domestic proposals, and in foreign affairs the triumphs that he had scored as secretary of state had no sequels. In relations with Britain Adams had overreached himself by a "Perilous experiment" begun when he was secretary of state. By trying to force upon the British acceptance of American shipping on the same basis as British shipping in the West Indies, he passed up a chance for compromise on favorable terms, with the result that American shipping was banned altogether in 1826.

Before the year 1826 was out, Adams faced a showdown with the state of Georgia and meekly backed off. The affair began in 1825 when a federal Indian commissioner signed the fraudulent Treaty of Indian Springs with a group of Creek chieftains by which the Creeks lost 4.7 million acres in Georgia. Adams at first signed the treaty, but on further inquiry withdrew it and worked out the somewhat less stringent Treaty of Washington in 1826. The Georgia legislature denounced this annulment of the previous treaty as invalid and, by some obscure reasoning, called it a violation of states' rights. Gov. George M. Troup mobilized the Georgia militia and notified Adams that the state would repel with force any attempt to void the earlier treaty. At this the administration simply abandoned the Creeks to their fate. The Cherokees were next on the agenda, but by the time Georgia got around to them, there was a president who supported the land grabbers.

The climactic effort to discredit Adams came on the tariff issue. The Panic of 1819 had given rise to action for a higher tariff in 1820, but the effort failed by one vote in the Senate. In 1824 the advocates of protection renewed the effort, with greater success. The Tariff of 1824 favored the Middle Atlantic and New England manufacturers with higher duties on woolen, cotton, iron, and other finished goods. Clay's Kentucky won a tariff on hemp, and a tariff on raw wool brought the wool-growing interests to the support of the measure. Additional revenues were provided by duties on sugar, molasses, coffee, and salt. The tariff on raw wool was in obvious conflict with that on manufactured woolens, but the two groups got together and reached an agreement. A bill to raise further the wool and woolens duties failed in 1827 only by the tie-breaking vote of Vice-President Calhoun, who was in retreat from his prior support of the tariff.

At this point the supporters of Jackson saw a chance to advance their candidate by an awkward piece of political skulduggery. The plan, as later divulged by one of its authors, John Calhoun, was to present a bill with such outrageously high tariffs on raw materials that the manufacturers of the East would join the commercial interests there and with the votes of the agricultural South and Southwest defeat the measure. In the process Jackson men in the Northeast could take credit for supporting the tariff, and Jackson men, wherever it best fitted their interests, could take credit for opposing it—while Jackson himself remained in the background. John Randolph saw through the ruse. The bill, he asserted, "referred to manufactures of no sort or kind, but the manufacture of a President of the United States." The measure served that purpose, but in the process Calhoun was hoist on his own petard. The idea was a shade too clever, and Calhoun calculated neither upon the defection of Van Buren, who supported a crucial amendment to satisfy the woolens manufacturers, nor upon the growing strength of manufacturing interests in New England. Daniel Webster, now a senator from Massachusetts, explained that he was ready to deny all he had said against the tariff because New England had built up her manufactures on the understanding that the protective tariff was a settled policy.

When the bill passed on May 11, 1828, it was Calhoun's turn to explain his newfound opposition to the gospel of protection, and nothing so well illustrates the flexibility of constitutional principles as the switch in positions by Webster and Calhoun. Back in his study at Fort Hill, Calhoun prepared the *South Carolina Exposition and Protest* (1828), which was issued anonymously along with a series of resolutions by the South Carolina legislature. In that document Calhoun set forth the right of a state to nullify an act of Congress which it found unconstitutional.

JACKSON SWEEPS IN   Thus far the stage was set for the election of 1828, which might more truly be called a revolution than that of 1800. But if the issues of the day had anything to do with the election, they were hardly visible in the campaign, in which politicians on both sides reached depths of scurrilousness that had not been plumbed since 1800. Jackson was denounced as a hot-tempered and ignorant barbarian, a co-conspirator with Aaron

This anti-Jackson cartoon, published during the 1828 campaign, shows him as a frontier ruffian. [New-York Historical Society]

"Jackson is to be President, and you will be HANGED."

Burr, a participant in repeated duels and frontier brawls, a man whose fame rested on his reputation as a killer, a man whom Thomas Jefferson himself had pronounced unfit because of the rashness of his feelings—a remark inspired by Jackson's brief tenure in the Senate in 1797. In addition to that, his enemies dredged up the old story that Jackson had lived in adultery with his wife Rachel before they had been legally married; in fact they had lived together for two years in the mistaken belief that her divorce from a former husband was final. The worry over this humiliation and her probable reception in Washington may have contributed to an illness from which she died before Jackson took office, and it was one thing for which he could never forgive his enemies.

The Jacksonians, however, got in their licks against Adams, condemning him as a man who had lived his adult life on the public treasury, who had been corrupted by foreigners in the courts of Europe, and who had allegedly delivered up an American girl to serve the lust of Czar Alexander I. They called him a gambler and a spendthrift for having bought a billiard table and a set of chessmen for the White House, and a puritanical hypocrite for despising the common people and warning Congress to ignore the will of its constituents. He had finally reached the presidency, the Jacksonians claimed, by a corrupt bargain with Henry Clay.

In the campaign of 1828 when, the historian George Danger-

Jackson Forever!

The Hero of Two Wars and of Or'eans!

The Man of the People!

HE WHO COULD NOT BARTER NOR BARGAIN FOR THE

PRESIDENCY!

Who, although "*A Military Chieftain*," valued the purity of Elections and of the Electors, MORE than the Office of PRESIDENT itself! Although the greatest in the gift of his countrymen, and the highest in point of dignity of any in the world,

BECAUSE
It should be derived from the

PEOPLE!

No Gag Laws! No Black Cockades! No Reign of Terror! No Standing Army or Navy Officers, when under the pay of Government, to browbeat, or

KNOCK DOWN

Old Revolutionary Characters, or our Representatives while in the discharge of their duty. To the Polls then, and vote for those who will support

OLD HICKORY
AND THE ELECTORAL LAW.

This 1828 handbill identifies Jackson, "The Man of the People," with the democratic impulse of the time. [New-York Historical Society]

field said, "to betray an idea was almost to commit a felony," Jackson held most of the advantages. As a military hero he had some claim on patriotism. As a son of the West he was almost unbeatable there. As a planter and slaveholder he had the trust of southern planters. Debtors and local bankers who hated the national bank turned to Jackson. Not least of all, Jackson benefited from a spirit of democracy in which the commonality were no longer satisfied to look to their betters for leadership, as they had done in the lost world of Thomas Jefferson. It had become politically fatal to be labeled an aristocrat. Jackson's coalition now included even a seasoning of young Federalists—James Buchanan of Pennsylvania, Rober B. Taney of Maryland, William Drayton of South Carolina—eager to shed the stigma of aristocracy and get on in the world.

Since the Revolution and especially since 1800 manhood suffrage had been gaining ground. The traditional story has been that a surge of Jacksonian Democracy came out of the West like a great wave, supported mainly by small farmers, leading the way for the East. But there were other forces working in the older states toward a wider franchise: the revolutionary doctrine of equality, and the feeling on the parts of the workers, artisans, and small merchants of the towns, as well as small farmers and landed grandees, that a democratic ballot provided a means to combat the rising commercial and manufacturing interests. From the beginning Pennsylvania had opened the way to the ballot box with a taxpayers' franchise; by 1790 Georgia and New Hampshire had similar arrangements. Vermont, in 1791, became the first state with manhood suffrage, having first adopted it in 1777. Kentucky, admitted in 1792, became the second. Tennessee (1796) had only a light taxpaying qualification. New Jersey in 1807, and Maryland and South Carolina in 1810, abolished property and taxpaying requirements, and the new states of the West after 1815 came in with either white manhood suffrage or a low tax-paying requirement. Connecticut (1818), Massachusetts (1821), and New York (1821) all abolished their property requirements.

Along with the broadening of the suffrage went a liberalization of other features of government. Representation was reapportioned more nearly in line with population. An increasing number of officials, even judges, were named by popular vote. Final disestablishment of the Congregational church in New England came in Vermont (1807), New Hampshire (1817), Connecticut (1818), Maine (1820), and Massachusetts (1834). In 1824 six state legislatures still chose the presidential electors. By 1828 the popular vote prevailed in all but South Carolina and Delaware, and by 1832 in all but South Carolina.

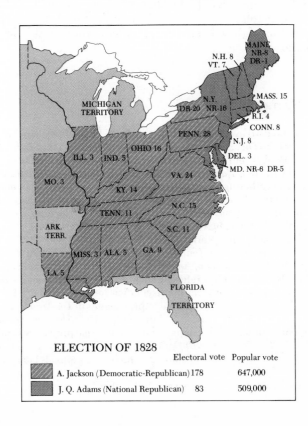

ELECTION OF 1828

	Electoral vote	Popular vote
A. Jackson (Democratic-Republican)	178	647,000
J. Q. Adams (National Republican)	83	509,000

The spread of the suffrage brought a new type of politician to the fore, the man who had special appeal to the masses or knew how to organize the people for political purposes, and who became a vocal advocate of the people's right to rule and the mystical concept that the voice of the people was the voice of God. Jackson fitted the ideal of this new political world, a leader sprung from the people rather than an aristocratic leader of the people, a frontiersman of humble origin who had scrambled up by will and tenacity, a fighter, a defender of the liberties of the people, a man who made no pretence of profound learning. "Adams can write," went one of the campaign slogans, "Jackson can fight." He could write too, but he once said that he had no respect for a man who could think of only one way to spell a word.

When the returns came in, it was clear that Jackson had won by a comfortable margin. The electoral vote was 178 to 83, and the popular vote (the figures vary) was about 647,000 to 509,000. Adams won all of New England, except for one of Maine's nine electoral votes, sixteen of the thirty-six from New York and six of the eleven from Maryland. All the rest belonged to Jackson.

FURTHER READING

A standard overview of the Era of Good Feelings remains George Dangerfield's *The Awakening of American Nationalism, 1815–1828* (1965).° Dangerfield also wrote *The Era of Good Feelings* (1952).° John Mayfield's *The New Nation, 1800–1845* (1981),° also treats events of this period. The gathering sense of a national spirit, hindered by an equally growing sectionalism, can be traced in Daniel J. Boorstin's *The Americans: The National Experience* (1965)° and in Paul C. Nagel's *One Nation Indivisible: The Union in American Thought, 1776–1861* (1964).

Background on the American System is handled in Frank W. Taussig's *The Tariff History of the United States* (1931) and in J. Van Fenstermaker's *The Development of American Commercial Banking, 1782–1837* (1965). Also good are the relevant chapters in Bray Hammond's *Banks and Politics in America from the Revolution to the Civil War* (1957).° George R. Taylor discusses internal improvements in *The Transportation Revolution, 1815–1860* (1951).° Phillip D. Jordan's *The National Road* (1948) concentrates on development of that internal project. Murray N. Rothbard's *The Panic of 1819* (1951) examines economics on the frontier. An overview of all the economic trends of the period is Douglass C.

°These books are available in paperback editions.

North's *The Economic Growth of the United States, 1790–1860* (1961).°

The political temper of the times is treated in biographical studies of principal figures: Harry Ammon's *James Monroe: The Quest for National Identity* (1971), Glyndon Van Deusen's *The Life of Henry Clay* (1937),° Clement Eaton's *Henry Clay and the Art of American Politics* (1957), Samuel F. Bemis's *John Quincy Adams and the Union* (1956), Richard W. Current's *John C. Calhoun* (1963), and C. C. Mooney's *William H. Crawford, 1772–1834* (1974). James S. Young's *The Washington Community, 1800–1828* (1961),° analyzes group leadership on the national level.

Diplomatic relations after 1812 are surveyed in several works, including C. C. Griffith's *The United States and the Disruption of the Spanish Empire* (1937) and Frank Thistlethwaite's *The Anglo-American Connection in the Early Nineteenth Century* (1959).° Ernest R. May's *The Making of the Monroe Doctrine* (1975) and Dexter Perkins's *A History of the Monroe Doctrine* (1963) provide clues to the formation of that policy.

In addition to works on the judiciary cited in Chapter 9, the following may also be consulted: Charles G. Haines's *The Role of the Supreme Court in American Government and Politics, 1789–1835* (1944), Robert K. Faulkner's *The Jurisprudence of John Marshall* (1968), Donald O. Dewey's *Marshall vs. Jefferson: The Background of Marbury v. Madison* (1970),° and Leonard Baker's *John Marshall: A Life at Law* (1974).°

Background on Andrew Jackson can be obtained from works cited in Chapter 11. The campaign which brought Jackson to the White House is analyzed in Robert V. Remini's *The Election of Andrew Jackson* (1963). Grant Foreman's *Indian Removal: The Emigration of the Five Civilized Tribes of Indians* (1932) and William W. Freehling's *Prelude to Civil War: The Nullification Controversy in South Carolina, 1816–1836* (1966)° treat specific issues of Jackson's first term.

11 ✒

THE JACKSONIAN IMPULSE

INAUGURATION Inauguration Day, March 4, 1829, came in a welcome spell of balmy weather after a bitterly cold winter. For days before, visitors had been crowding the streets and rooming houses of Washington in hope of seeing the people's hero take office. When Jackson emerged from his lodgings, dressed in black out of respect to his late wife Rachel, a great crowd filled both the east and west slopes of Capitol Hill. After Chief Justice Marshall administered the oath, the new president delivered his inaugural address in a voice so low that few of the crowd could hear a word of it. It mattered little, for Jackson's advisers had eliminated anything that might give offense. On the major issues of the tariff, internal improvements, and the Bank of the United States, Jackson remained enigmatic. Only a few points foreshadowed policies that the new chief executive would pursue: he favored retirement of the national debt, a proper regard for states' rights, a "just" policy toward Indians, and rotation in office, which he pronounced "a leading principle in the republican creed"—a principle his enemies would dub the "spoils system."

To that point all proceeded with dignity. Francis Scott Key, who witnessed the spectacle, declared: "It is beautiful, it is sublime!" After his speech Jackson mounted his horse and rode off to the White House, where a reception was scheduled for all who chose to come. The boisterous party that followed evoked the climate of turmoil that seemed always to surround Jackson. The crowd pushed into the White House, surged through the rooms, jostled the waiters, broke dishes, leaped on the furniture—all in an effort to shake the president's hand or at least get a glimpse of him. Surrounded by a group of his friends, the president soon

All creation Going to the White House. *The scene following Jackson's inauguration, according to satirist Robert Cruikshank.* *[Library of Congress]*

made his escape by a side door and went back to his lodgings for the night. Somebody then had the presence of mind to haul tubs of punch out on the White House lawn, where the unruly crowd followed. To Justice Story, "the reign of 'King Mob' seemed triumphant."

APPOINTMENTS AND POLITICAL RIVALRIES   To the office seekers who made up much of the restless crowd at the inaugural, some of Jackson's words held out high expectations that he planned to turn the rascals out and let the people rule. So it seemed when Jackson set forth a reasoned defense of rotation in office. The duties of government were reasonably simple, he said. Democratic principles supported the idea that a man should serve a term in government, then return to the status of private citizen, for officeholders who stayed too long became corrupted by a sense of power. And democracy, he argued, "is promoted by party appointments by newly elected officials." Jackson hardly foresaw how these principles would work out in practice, and it would be misleading to link him too closely with the "spoils system," which took its name from an 1832 partisan assertion by Democratic Sen. William L. Marcy of New York: "To the victor belong the spoils." Jackson in fact behaved with great moderation compared to the politicians of New York and Pennsylvania, where the spoils of office nourished extensive political machines. And a number of his successors made many more partisan appointments. During his first year in office Jackson replaced only

about 9 percent of the appointed officials in the federal government, and during his entire term fewer than 20 percent were replaced.

Jackson relied very little on his appointments to the cabinet,
which had little influence as an advisory group. More powerful
was a coterie of men who had the president's ear and were soon
dubbed his "Kitchen Cabinet." Among these, only Secretary of
State Martin Van Buren headed a department, but most of the
others were on the public payroll in some capacity. These included Amos Kendall of Kentucky, a former partisan of Clay,
Isaac Hill of New Hampshire, and Duff Green, editor of the
United States Telegraph, which had supported both Calhoun and
Jackson. Others in the group from time to time included William
B. Lewis of Tennessee, who had worked to make Jackson presi-
dent, and Jackson's nephew and secretary, Andrew Jackson
Donelson. The most influential members seem to have been
Kentuckians Amos Kendall and Frank Blair, Sr., editor of the ad-
ministration newspaper, the *Globe.*

Jackson's administration was from the outset a house divided
between the partisans of Van Buren of New York and Vice-President Calhoun of South Carolina. Much of the political history of
the next few years would turn upon the rivalry of the two, as each
man jockeyed for position as the heir apparent to Jackson. It soon
became clear in the political infighting for the succession that
Van Buren held most of the advantages, foremost among them
his skill at timing and tactics. As John Randolph put it, Van Buren
always "rowed to his objective with muffled oars." Jackson, new
to political administration, leaned heavily on him for advice and
for help in soothing the ruffled feathers of rejected office
seekers. Van Buren had perhaps more skill at maneuver than
Calhoun, and certainly more freedom of maneuver since his
home base of New York was more secure politically than Calhoun's base in South Carolina.

THE EATON AFFAIR   Van Buren also had luck on his side. Fate had
quickly handed him a trump card: the succulent scandal of the
Peggy Eaton affair. Peggy Eaton was the lively daughter of an
Irish innkeeper, William O'Neale, whose place had been a Washington hangout for politicians, including at times Senators Jackson and Eaton of Tennessee. She was the widow of a navy purser
named Timberlake, whose death (capital gossip had it) was a suicide brought on by her affair with Senator Eaton. Her marriage
to Eaton, three months before he entered the cabinet, had
scarcely made an honest woman of her in the eyes of the proper

ladies of Washington. Floride Calhoun, the vice-president's wife, pointedly snubbed her, and cabinet wives followed suit. Even Mrs. A. J. Donelson withdrew as White House hostess rather than accept a fallen woman.

Peggy's plight reminded Jackson of the gossip which had pursued his own Rachel, and he pronounced Peggy "chaste as a virgin." To a friend he wrote: "I did not come here to make a Cabinet for the Ladies of this place, but for the Nation." Despite the cabinet members' discomfort at Jackson's open displeasure, the cabinet members were unable to cure their wives of what Van Buren dubbed "the Eaton Marlaria." Van Buren, however, was a widower, and therefore free to lavish on poor Peggy all the attention that Jackson thought was her due. The bemused John Quincy Adams looked on from afar and noted in his diary that Van Buren had become the leader of the party of the frail sisterhood. Mrs. Eaton herself finally wilted under the chill, began to refuse invitations, and withdrew from society. The outraged Jackson came to link Calhoun with what he called a conspiracy, and drew even closer to Van Buren.

INTERNAL IMPROVEMENTS While capital society weathered the chilly winter of 1829–1830, Van Buren prepared some additional blows to Calhoun. It was easy to bring Jackson into opposition to internal improvements and thus to federal programs with which Calhoun had long been identified: the Bonus Bill of 1817, the General Survey Bill of 1824, and Calhoun's own report on internal improvements made when he was secretary of war. Jackson did not oppose roadbuilding per se, but he had the same constitutional scruples as Madison and Monroe about federal aid to local projects. In 1830 the Maysville Road Bill, passed by Congress, offered Jackson a happy chance for a dual thrust at both Calhoun and Clay. The bill authorized the government to buy stock in a road from Maysville to Clay's hometown of Lexington. The road lay entirely within the state of Kentucky, and though part of a larger scheme to link up with the National Road via Cincinnati, it could be viewed as a purely local undertaking. On that ground Jackson vetoed the bill as unconstitutional, to widespread popular acclaim.

But a foolish consistency about internal improvements was never Jackson's hobgoblin any more than it was his predecessors'. While Jackson continued to oppose federal aid to local projects, he supported interstate projects, such as the national road, as well as roadbuilding in the territories, and rivers and harbors bills, the "pork barrels" from which every congressman tried to pluck a morsel for his district. Even so, Jackson's attitude set an important precedent, on the eve of the railroad age, for limiting federal initiative in internal improvements. Railroads would be built altogether by state and private capital at least until 1850. And except for scattered post roads, the federal government did not aid roadbuilding again until 1916, with the coming of the automobile.

NULLIFICATION

CALHOUN'S THEORY   There is a fine irony to Calhoun's plight in the Jackson administration, for Calhoun was now in midpassage from his early phase as a War Hawk nationalist to his later phase as a states'-rights sectionalist—and open to thrusts on both flanks. Circumstances in his home state had brought on this change. Suffering from agricultural depression, South Carolina lost almost 70,000 people to emigration during the 1820s, and was fated to lose nearly twice that number in the 1830s. Most South Carolinians blamed the protective tariff, which tended to raise the price of manufactured goods and, insofar as it discouraged the sale of foreign goods in the United States, reduced the ability of British and French traders to acquire the American money and bills of exchange with which to buy American cotton. This worsened problems of low cotton prices and exhausted lands. The South Carolinians' malaise was further compounded by a growing reaction against the criticism of slavery. Hardly had

John C. Calhoun. A War Hawk nationalist during the 1810s and 1820s, Calhoun was now becoming a states'-rights sectionalist. [National Archives]

the country emerged from the Missouri controversy when Charleston was thrown into panic by the Denmark Vesey slave insurrection of 1822, though the Vesey plot was nipped before it erupted. The unexpected passage of the Tariff of Abominations (1828) left Calhoun no choice but to join those in opposition or abandon his home base.

Calhoun's *South Carolina Exposition and Protest* (1828), written in opposition to that tariff, actually had been an effort to check the most extreme states'-rights advocates with a fine-spun theory in which nullification stopped short of secession from the Union. The statement, unsigned by its author, accompanied resolutions of the South Carolina legislature against the tariff. Calhoun, it was clear, had not entirely abandoned his earlier nationalism. His object was to preserve the Union by protecting the minority rights which the agricultural and slaveholding South claimed. The fine balance he struck between states' rights and central authority, ironically, was not as far removed from Jackson's own philosophy as it might seem, but growing tension between the two men would complicate the issue. Jackson, in addition, was determined to draw the line at any defiance of federal law.

Nor would Calhoun's theory permit any state to take up such defiance lightly. The procedure of nullification, whereby a state could in effect repeal a federal law, would follow that by which the original thirteen states had ratified the Constitution. A special state convention, like the ratifying conventions embodying the sovereign power of the people, could declare a federal law null and void because it violated the Constitution, the original compact among the states. One of two outcomes would then be possible. Either the federal government would have to abandon the law or it would have to get a constitutional amendment removing all doubt as to its validity. The immediate issue was the constitutionality of a tariff designed mainly to protect American industries against foreign competition. The South Carolinians argued that the Constitution authorized tariffs for revenue only.

THE WEBSTER-HAYNE DEBATE South Carolina had proclaimed its dislike for the impost, but had postponed any action against its enforcement, awaiting with hope the election of 1828 in which Calhoun was the Jacksonian candidate for vice-president. The state anticipated a new tariff policy from the Jackson administration. There the issue stood until 1830, when the great Hayne-Webster debate sharpened the lines between states' rights and the Union. The immediate occasion for the debate, however, was the question of public lands. Late in 1829 Sen. Samuel A. Foot of Connecticut, an otherwise obscure figure, proposed an inquiry looking toward restriction of land sales in the West. When the Foot Resolution came before the Senate in January, Thomas Hart Benton of Missouri denounced it as a sectional attack designed to hamstring the settlement and development of the West so that the East might keep a supply of cheap factory labor. Robert Y. Hayne of South Carolina took Benton's side. Hayne saw in the issue a chance to strengthen the alliance of South and West that the vote for Jackson reflected. Perhaps by supporting a policy of cheap lands in the West the southerners could get in return western support for lower tariffs. The government, said Hayne, endangered the Union by any policy that would impose a hardship upon one section to the benefit of another. The use of public lands as a source of revenue to the central government would create "a fund for corruption—fatal to the sovereignty and independence of the states."

Daniel Webster of Massachusetts rose to defend the East. Denying that the East had ever shown an illiberal policy toward the West, he rebuked those southerners who, he said, "habitually speak of the Union in terms of indifference, or even of disparagement." Hayne had raised the false spectre of "Consolidation!—That perpetual cry, both of terror and delusion—consolidation!" Federal moneys, Webster argued, were not a source of corruption but a source of improvement. At this point the Foot Resolution and the issue of western lands vanished from sight. Webster had adroitly shifted the grounds of debate, and lured Hayne into defending states' rights and upholding the doctrine of nullification instead of pursuing coalition with the West.

Hayne took the bait. After some personal thrusts, in which he harked back to Webster's early career as a Federalist, he launched into a defense of the *South Carolina Exposition,* appealed to the example of the Virginia and Kentucky Resolutions of 1798, and called attention to the Hartford Convention in which New Englanders had taken much the same position against majority measures as South Carolina did. The Union was created by a compact of the states, he argued, and the federal government could not be the judge of its own powers, else its powers would be unlimited. Rather, the states remained free to judge when their agent had overstepped the bounds of its constitutional authority. The right of state interposition was "as full and complete as it was before the Constitution was formed."

In rebuttal to the state-compact theory, Webster defined a nationalistic view of the Constitution. From the beginning, he asserted, the American Revolution had been a crusade of the united colonies rather than of each separately. True sovereignty resided in the people as a whole, for whom both federal and state governments acted as agents in their respective spheres. If a single state could nullify a law of the general government, then the Union would be a "rope of sand," a practical absurdity. Instead the Constitution had created a Supreme Court with the final jurisdiction on all questions of constitutionality. A state could neither nullify a federal law nor secede from the Union. The practical outcome of nullification would be a confrontation leading to civil war.

Hayne may have had the better of the argument historically in advancing the state-compact theory, but the Senate galleries and much of the country at large thrilled to the eloquence of "the Godlike Daniel." His peroration became an American classic, reprinted in school texts and committed to memory by generations of schoolboy orators: "When my eyes shall be turned to behold, for the last time, the sun in heaven, may I not see him shining on the broken and dishonored fragments of a once glorious Union. . . . Let their last feeble and lingering glance, rather, behold the gorgeous ensign of the republic . . . blazing on all its ample folds, as they float over the sea and over the land . . . Liberty and Union, now and forever, one and inseparable." In the practical world of coalition politics Webster had the better of the

Massachusetts Sen. Daniel Webster in G. P. A. Healy's painting of the Webster-Hayne debate. [Boston Art Commission]

argument, for the Union and majority rule meant more to westerners, including Jackson, than the abstractions of state sovereignty and nullification. As for the public lands, the Foot
Resolution was soon defeated anyway. And whatever one might
argue about the origins of the Union, its evolution would more
and more validate Webster's position.

THE RIFT WITH CALHOUN   As yet, however, the enigmatic Jackson
had not spoken out on the issue. The nullificationists had given
South Carolina's electoral vote to him as well as to Calhoun in
1828. Jackson, like Calhoun, was a slaveholder, albeit a west-
erner, and might be expected to sympathize with South Carolina, his native state. Soon all doubt was removed, at least on the
point of nullification. On April 13, 1830, the Jefferson Day Dinner was held in Washington to honor the birthday of the former
president. It was a party affair, but the Calhounites controlled
the arrangements with an eye to advancing their own doctrine.
Jackson and Van Buren were invited as a matter of course, and
the two agreed that Jackson should present a toast which would
indicate his opposition to nullification. When his turn came, after
twenty-four toasts, many of them extolling states' rights, Jackson
raised his glass and, pointedly looking at Calhoun, announced:
"Our Union—It must be preserved!" (At the behest of Senator
Hayne the first words were later published as "Our Federal
Union.") Calhoun, who followed, trembled so that he spilled
some of the amber fluid from his glass (according to Van Buren),
but tried quickly to retrieve the situation with a toast to "The
Union, next to our liberty most dear! May we all remember that it
can only be preserved by respecting the rights of the States and
distributing equally the benefit and the burthen of the Union!"
But Jackson had set off a bombshell which exploded the plans of
the states'-righters.

Nearly a month afterward a final nail was driven into the coffin
of Calhoun's presidential ambitions. On May 12, 1830, Jackson
saw a letter from William H. Crawford giving final confirmation
to reports that had been reaching him of Calhoun's stand in
1818, when as secretary of war the South Carolinian had proposed to discipline Jackson for his Florida invasion. A tense correspondence between Jackson and Calhoun followed, and ended
with a curt note from Jackson cutting it off. "Understanding you
now," Jackson wrote on May 30, 1830, "no further communication with you on this subject is necessary."

One result of the growing rift between the men was the appearance of a new administration paper. Duff Green's *United
States Telegraph*, for two years the administration organ, was too

closely allied with Calhoun. Jackson and his "Kitchen Cabinet" arranged to have Francis Preston Blair, Sr., of Kentucky, move to Washington and set up the Washington *Globe,* the first issue of which appeared before the end of 1830. Another result was a cabinet shakeup by Jackson, who was resolved to remove all Calhoun partisans. According to a plan contrived by Van Buren, he and Secretary of War Eaton resigned, offering as their reason a desire to relieve Jackson of the embarrassment of awkward controversy. Jackson in turn requested and got resignations of the others, except Postmaster-General William T. Barry. Before the end of the summer of 1831 the president had a new cabinet entirely loyal to him.

Jackson then named Van Buren minister to London, pending Senate approval. The friends of Van Buren now importuned Jackson to repudiate his previous intention of only serving one term. It might have been hard, they felt, to get the nomination in 1832 for the New Yorker, who had been charged with intrigues against Calhoun, and the still-popular Carolinian might yet have carried off the prize. Jackson relented and in the fall of 1831 announced his readiness for one more term, with the idea of returning Van Buren from London in time to win the presidency in 1836. But in January 1832, when the Senate reconvened, Van Buren's enemies opposed his appointment as minister, and gave Calhoun, as vice-president, a chance to reject the nomination by a tie-breaking vote. "It will kill him, sir, kill him dead," Calhoun told Sen. Thomas Hart Benton. Benton disagreed: "You have broken a minister, and elected a Vice-President." So, it turned out, he had. Calhoun's vote against Van Buren provoked popular sympathy for the New Yorker, who would soon be nominated to succeed Calhoun.

Now that his presidential hopes were blasted, Calhoun came forth as the public leader of the nullificationists. These South Carolinians thought that, despite Jackson's gestures, tariff rates remained too high. Jackson, who accepted the principle of protection, nevertheless had called upon Congress in 1829 to modify duties by reducing tariffs on goods "which cannot come in competition with our own products." Late in the spring of 1830 Congress lowered duties on such consumer products as tea, coffee, salt, and molasses. In all it cut about $4.5 million from something over $20 million in tariff revenue. That and the Maysville veto, coming at about the same time, mollified a few South Carolinians, but nullifiers regarded the two actions as "nothing but sugar plums to pacify children." By the end of 1831 Jackson was calling for further reductions to take the wind out of the nullificationists' sails, and the tariff of 1832, pushed through by now

Rep. John Quincy Adams, cut revenues another $5 million, again mainly on unprotected items. Average tariff rates were about 25 percent, but rates on cottons, woolens, and iron remained up around 50 percent.

THE SOUTH CAROLINA ORDINANCE   In the South Carolina state elections of October 1832, all attention centered on the nullification issue. The nullificationists took the initiative in organization and agitation, and the Unionist party was left with a distinguished leadership but only small support, drawn chiefly from the merchants of Charleston and the yeoman farmers of the upcountry. A special session of the legislature in October called for the election of a state convention. The convention assembled at Columbia on November 19 and on November 24 overwhelmingly adopted an ordinance of nullification which repudiated the tariff acts of 1828 and 1832 as unconstitutional and forbade collection of the duties in the state after February 1, 1833. The reassembled legislature then provided that any citizen whose property was seized by federal authorities for failure to pay the duty could get a state court order to recover twice its value. The legislature also chose Hayne as governor and elected Calhoun to succeed him as senator. Calhoun promptly resigned as vice-president in order to defend nullification on the Senate floor.

JACKSON'S FIRM RESPONSE   In the crisis South Carolina found itself standing alone, despite the sympathy expressed elsewhere. The Georgia legislature called for a southern convention, but dismissed nullification as "rash and revolutionary." Alabama pronounced it "unsound in theory and dangerous in practice"; Mississippi stood "firmly resolved" to put down nullification. Jackson's response was measured and firm, but not rash—at least not in public. In private he threatened to hang Calhoun and all other traitors—and later expressed regret that he had failed to hang at least Calhoun. In his annual message on December 4, 1832, Jackson announced his firm intention to enforce the tariff, but once again urged Congress to lower the rates. On December 10 he followed up with his Nullification Proclamation, drafted by Secretary of State Edward Livingston, a document which characterized the doctrine as an "impractical absurdity." Jackson said in part: "I consider, then, the power to annul a law in the United States, assumed by one state, incompatible with the existence of the Union, contradicted expressly by the letter of the Constitution, unauthorized by its spirit, inconsistent with every principle on which it was founded, and destructive of the great object for which it was formed." He appealed to the people of his native state not to follow false leaders: "The laws of the United States must be executed. I have no discretionary power on the subject; my duty is emphatically pronounced in the constitution. Those who told you that you might peaceably prevent their execution, deceived you; they could not have been deceived themselves. . . . Their object is disunion. But be not deceived by names. Disunion by armed force is treason."

CLAY'S COMPROMISE   Jackson sent Gen. Winfield Scott to Charleston Harbor with reinforcements of federal soldiers, who were kept carefully isolated in the island posts at Fort Moultrie and Castle Pinckney to avoid incidents. A ship of war and seven revenue cutters appeared in the harbor, ready to enforce the tariff before ships had a chance to land their cargoes. The nullifiers mobilized the state militia while unionists in the state organized a volunteer force. In January 1833 the president requested from Congress a "Force Bill," specifically authorizing him to use the army to compel compliance with federal law in South Carolina. Under existing legislation he already had such authority, but this affirmation would strengthen his hand. At the same time he gave his support to a bill in Congress which would have lowered duties to a maximum of 20 percent within two years. The nullifiers postponed enforcement of their ordinances in anticipation of a compromise. Passage of the bill depended on the support of Henry Clay, who finally yielded to those urging him to save the day. On February 12, 1833, he brought forth a plan to reduce the tariff gradually until 1842, by which time no rate would be more than 20 percent. It was less than South Carolina would have preferred, but it got the nullifiers out of the corner into which they had painted themselves.

On March 1, 1833, the compromise tariff and the Force Bill passed Congress and the next day Jackson signed both. The South Carolina Convention then met and rescinded its nullification, and in a face-saving gesture, nullified the Force Bill, for which Jackson no longer had any need. Both sides were able to claim victory. Jackson had upheld the supremacy of the Union and South Carolina had secured a reduction of the tariff.

JACKSON'S INDIAN POLICY

On Indian affairs Jackson's attitude was the typically western one, that Indians were better off out of the way. Jackson had already done his part in the Creek and Seminole Wars to chastise them and separate them from their lands. By the time of his election in 1828 he was fully in accord with the view that a "just, humane, liberal policy toward Indians" dictated moving them onto the plains west of the Mississippi. The policy was by no means new or original with Jackson; the ideal had emerged gradually after the Louisiana Purchase in 1803. It had been formally set forth in 1823 by Calhoun, as secretary of war, and by now was generally accepted, that a permanent solution to the Indian "problem" would be their removal and resettlement in the "Great American Desert," which white men would never covet since it was thought fit mainly for horned toads and rattlesnakes.

INDIAN REMOVAL   In response to Jackson's message, Congress in 1830 approved the Indian Removal Act and appropriated $500,000 for the purpose. Jackson's presidency saw some ninety-four removal treaties negotiated, and by 1835 Jackson was able to announce that the policy had been carried out or was in process of completion for all but a handful of Indians. The policy was effected with remarkable speed, but even that was too slow for state authorities in the South and Southwest. Unlike the Ohio Valley–Great Lakes region, where flow of white settlement had constantly pushed the Indians westward before it, in the Old Southwest settlement moved across Kentucky and Tennessee and down the Mississippi, surrounding the Creeks, Choctaws,

The first issue of the Cherokee Phoenix *published the Constitution of the Cherokee nation, which embraced "the lands solemnly guaranteed and reserved forever to the Cherokee Nation by the Treaties concluded with the United States." [American Antiquarian Society]*

Chickasaws, Seminoles, and Cherokees. These tribes of the area had over the years taken on many of the features of white society. The Cherokees even had such appurtenances of "white civilization" as a constitution, a written language, and black slaves.

Most of the northern tribes were too weak to resist the importunings of Indian commissioners who, if necessary, used bribery and alcohol to woo the chiefs, and if sometimes the tribesmen rebelled, there was, on the whole, remarkably little resistance. In Illinois and Wisconsin Territory an armed clash sprang up from April to August 1832, which came to be known as the Black Hawk War, when the Sauk and Fox under Chief Black Hawk sought to reoccupy some lands they had abandoned in the previous year. Facing famine and hostile Sioux west of the Mississippi, they were simply seeking a place to get in a corn crop. The Illinois militia mobilized to expel them, chased them into Wisconsin Territory, and inflicted a gruesome massacre of women and children as they tried to escape across the Mississippi. The Black Hawk War came to be remembered later, however, less because of the atrocities inflicted on the Indians than because the participants included two native Kentuckians later pitted against each other; Lt. Jefferson Davis of the regular army and Capt. Abraham Lincoln of the Illinois volunteers.

In the South two nations, the Seminoles and Cherokees, put up a stubborn resistance. The Seminoles of Florida fought a protracted guerrilla war in the Everglades from 1835 to 1842. But most of the vigor went out of their resistance after 1837, when their leader Osceola was seized by treachery under a flag of truce to die a prisoner at Fort Moultrie in Charleston Harbor. After 1842 only a few hundred Seminoles remained, hiding out in the swamps. Most of the rest had been removed to the West.

THE CHEROKEES' TRAIL OF TEARS   The Cherokees had by the end of the eighteenth century fallen back into the mountains of northern Georgia and western North Carolina, onto land guaranteed to them in 1791 by treaty with the United States. But when Georgia ceded its western lands in 1802 it did so on the ambiguous condition that the United States extinguish all Indian titles within the state "as early as the same can be obtained on reasonable terms." In 1827 the Cherokees, relying on their treaty rights, adopted a constitution in which they said pointedly that they were not subject to any other state or nation. In 1828 Georgia responded with a law that after June 1, 1830, the authority of state law would extend over the Cherokees living within the boundaries of the state.

The discovery of gold in 1829 whetted the whites' appetite for Cherokee lands and brought bands of rough prospectors into the country. The Cherokees sought relief in the Supreme Court, but in *Cherokee Nation v. Georgia* (1831) John Marshall ruled that the Court lacked jurisdiction because the Cherokees were a "domestic dependent nation" rather than a foreign state in the meaning of the Constitution. In 1830 a Georgia law required whites in the territory to get licenses authorizing their residence there, and to take an oath of allegiance to the state. Two New England missionaries among the Indians refused and were sentenced to four years at hard labor. On appeal their case reached the Supreme Court as *Worcester v. Georgia* (1832) and the court held that the national government had exclusive jurisdiction in the Cherokee country and the Georgia law was therefore unconstitutional.

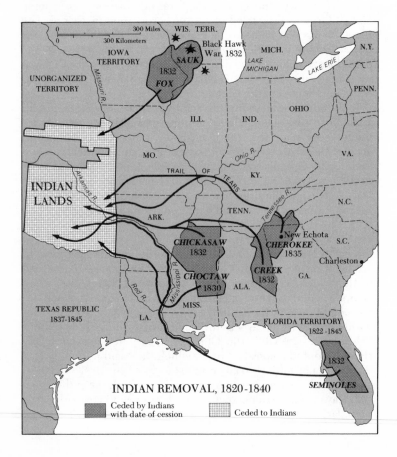

INDIAN REMOVAL, 1820–1840

Six years earlier Georgia had faced down President Adams when he tried to protect the rights of the Creeks. Now Georgia faced down the Supreme Court with the tacit consent of another president. Jackson is supposed to have said privately: "Marshall has made his decision, now let him enforce it!" Whether or not he actually put it so bluntly, Jackson did nothing to enforce the decision. In the circumstances there was nothing for the Cherokees to do but give in and sign a treaty, which they did in 1835. They gave up their lands in the Southeast in exchange for lands in the Indian Territory west of Arkansas, $5 million from the federal government, and expenses for transportation. By 1838 the Cherokees had departed on the "trail of tears" westward, following the Choctaws, Chickasaws, and Creeks on a journey marked by the cruelty and neglect of soldiers and private contractors, and scorn and pilferage by whites along the way. A few held out in the mountains and got a reservation from the state of North Carolina; thenceforth they were the "eastern band" of the Cherokees. A scattered few of the others remained in the Southeast, especially mixed-blood Creeks who could pass for white.

THE BANK CONTROVERSY

THE BANK'S OPPONENTS   The overriding national issue in the campaign of 1832 was neither Jackson's Indian policy nor South Carolina's obsession with nullification. It was the question of rechartering the Bank of the United States. On the bank issue, as on others, Jackson had made no public commitment, but his personal opposition to the bank was already formed. Jackson had absorbed the western attitude of hostility toward the bank after the Panic of 1819, and held to a conviction that it was unconstitutional no matter what Marshall had said in *McCulloch v. Maryland*. Banks in general had contributed to a speculative mania, and Jackson, suspicious of all banks, preferred a hard-money policy. The general felt in his bones that the bank was wrong and did not need to form his opinions out of an intimate knowledge of banking. He was in fact blissfully ignorant of the subject.

Under the management of Nicholas Biddle the Bank of the United States had prospered and grown. Coming from a well-to-do Philadelphia family, Biddle had previously followed a career as editor, diplomat, and politician. He had little acquaintance with business when Monroe appointed him a government director of the bank, but he proved a quick study and by the time he replaced Langdon Cheves as president of the bank in 1823 Bid-

dle was well versed in banking. The bank had worked to the benefit of business and performed the important function of
supplying a stable currency by its policy of forcing state banks to
keep a specie reserve (gold or silver) behind their notes. But ar-
rayed against the bank were powerful enemies: some of the state
and local banks which had been forced to reduce their note
issues, debtor groups which suffered from the reduction and
businessmen and speculators "on the make" who wanted easier
credit. States'-rights groups questioned the bank's constitutionality, though Calhoun, who had sponsored the original charter
and valued the bank's function of regulating the currency, was
not among them. Financiers of New York's Wall Street resented
the supremacy of the bank on Philadelphia's Chestnut Street.
Many westerners and workingmen, like Jackson, felt in their
bones that the bank was, in Thomas Hart Benton's words, a
"Monster," a monopoly controlled by a few of the wealthy with
power which was irreconcilable with a democracy. "I think it
right to be perfectly frank with you," Jackson told Biddle in
1829. "I do not dislike your Bank any more than all banks. But
ever since I read the history of the South Sea Bubble I have been
afraid of banks." This struck Biddle as odd, since he regarded his
conservative policies as a safeguard against speculative manias
like the eighteenth-century "South Sea Bubble," in which thousands of British investors had been fleeced. Jackson was perhaps
right in his instinct that the bank lodged too much power in private hands, but mistaken in his understanding of the bank's policies.

Biddle at first tried to conciliate Jackson and appointed a
number of Jackson men to branch offices of the bank. In his first
annual message (1829), though, Jackson questioned the bank's
constitutionality and asserted (whatever the evidence to the
contrary) that it had failed to maintain a sound and uniform currency. Jackson talked of a compromise, perhaps a bank completely owned by the government with its operations confined
chiefly to government deposits, its profits payable to the government, and its authority to set up branches in any state dependent
on the state's wishes. But Jackson would never commit himself
on the precise terms of compromise. Some of Jackson's cabinet
members cautiously favored the bank, but the opposition of
Amos Kendall and Francis P. Blair in the Kitchen Cabinet influenced him more. The bank's survival was left up to Biddle.

BIDDLE'S RECHARTER EFFORT Its twenty-year charter would run
through 1836, but Biddle could not afford the uncertainty of

waiting until then for a renewal. Biddle pondered whether to force the issue of recharter before the election of 1832 or after. On this point leaders of the National Republicans, especially Clay and Webster (who was counsel to the bank as well as a senator), argued that the time to move was before the election. Clay, already the candidate of the National Republicans, proposed to make the bank the central issue of the presidential canvass. Friends of the bank held a majority in Congress, and Jackson would risk loss of support in the election if he vetoed a renewal. But they failed to grasp the depth of prejudice against the bank, and succeeded mainly in handing to Jackson a popular issue on the eve of the election.

Both houses passed the recharter by comfortable margins, but without the two-thirds majority needed to override a veto. On July 10, 1832, Jackson vetoed the bill, sending it back to Congress with a ringing denunciation of monopoly and special privilege. In a message written largely by his confidant Amos Kendall, Jackson argued that the bank was unconstitutional, whatever the Court and Congress said. "Each public officer who takes an oath to support the Constitution swears that he will support it as he understands it, and not as it is understood by others. . . . The opinion of the judges has no more authority over Congress than the opinion of Congress had over the judges, and on that point the President is independent of both." Besides, there were sub-

This caricature shows King Andrew Jackson trampling the Constitution, internal improvements, and the U.S. Bank. Opponents considered Jackson's Maysville veto and bank veto abuses of power. [Library of Congress]

stantive objections aside from the question of constitutionality. Foreign stockholders in the bank had an undue influence. The bank had shown favors to members of Congress and exercised an improper power over state banks. The bill, he argued, demonstrated that "Many of our rich men have not been content with equal protection and equal benefits, but have besought us to make them richer by act of Congress." An effort to overrule the veto failed in the Senate; a vote of 22 to 19 for the bank fell far short of the needed two-thirds majority. Thus the stage was set for a nationwide financial crisis.

CAMPAIGN INNOVATIONS   The presidential campaign, as usual, was under way early, the nominations having been made before the bank veto, two in fact before the end of 1831. For the first time a third party entered the field. The Anti-Masonic party was, like the bank, the object of strong emotions then sweeping the new democracy. The group had grown out of popular hostility toward the Masonic order, members of which were suspected of having kidnapped and murdered a bricklayer of Batavia, New York, for revealing the "secrets" of his lodge. Opposition to a fraternal order was hardly the foundation on which to build a lasting party, but the Anti-Masonic party had three important "firsts" to its credit: in addition to being the first third party, it was the first party to hold a national nominating convention and the first to announce a platform, all of which it accomplished in September 1831 when it nominated William Wirt of Maryland for president.

The major parties followed its example by holding national conventions of their own. In December 1831 the delegates of the National Republican party assembled in Baltimore to nominate Henry Clay for president and John Sergeant of Pennsylvania, counsel to the bank and chief advocate of the recharter strategy, for vice-president. Jackson endorsed the idea of a nominating convention for the Democratic party (the name Republican was now formally dropped) to demonstrate popular support for its candidates. To that purpose the convention, also meeting at Baltimore, adopted the two-thirds rule for nomination (which prevailed until 1936), and then named Martin Van Buren as Jackson's running mate. The Democrats, unlike the other two parties, adopted no formal platform at their first convention, and relied to a substantial degree on hoopla and the personal popularity of the president to carry their cause.

The outcome was an overwhelming endorsement of Jackson in the electoral college by 219 votes to 49 for Clay, and a less overwhelming but solid victory in the popular vote, by 688,000 to

530,000. William Wirt carried only Vermont, with seven electoral votes. South Carolina, preparing for nullification and unable to stomach either Jackson or Clay, delivered its eleven votes to Gov. John Floyd of Virginia.

REMOVAL OF GOVERNMENT DEPOSITS   Jackson took the election as a mandate to proceed further against the bank. He asked Congress to investigate the safety of government deposits in the bank, since one of the current rumors told of empty vaults, carefully concealed. After a committee had checked, the Calhoun and Clay forces in the House of Representatives united in the passage of a resolution affirming that government deposits were safe and could be continued. The resolution passed, by chance, on March 2, 1833, the same day that Jackson signed the compromise tariff and Force Bill. With the nullification issue out of the way, however, Jackson was free to wage his unrelenting war on the bank, that "hydra of corruption," which still had nearly four years to run on its charter. Despite the House study and resolution, Jackson now resolved to remove all government deposits from the bank.

When Secretary of the Treasury McLane opposed removal of the government deposits and suggested a new and modified version of the bank, Jackson shook up his cabinet. He kicked McLane upstairs to head the State Department, which Edward Livingston left to become minister to France. To take McLane's place at the Treasury he chose William J. Duane of Philadelphia, but by some oversight Jackson failed to explore Duane's views fully or advise him of the presidential expectations. Duane was antibank, but he was consistent in his convictions. Dubious about banks in general, he saw no merit in removing deposits from the Monster for redeposit in countless state banks. Jackson might well have listened to Duane's warnings that such action would lead to speculative inflation, but the old general's combative instincts were too much aroused. He summarily dismissed Duane and moved Attorney-General Taney to the Treasury, where the new secretary gladly complied with the presidential wishes, which corresponded to his own views.

The procedure was to continue drawing on governmental accounts with Biddle's Bank, and to deposit all new governmental receipts in state banks. By the end of 1833 there were twenty-three state banks which had the benefit of governmental deposits, "pet banks" as they came to be called. The sequel to Jackson's headlong plunge into finance, it soon turned out, was the precise opposite of what he had sought. As so often happens

The Downfall of Mother Bank. *In this pro-Jackson cartoon of 1833, the bank crumbles and Jackson's opponents flee in the face of the heroic president's removal of government deposits. [New-York Historical Society]*

with complex public issues, dissatisfaction had become focused on a symbol. In this case the symbol was the "Monster of Chestnut Street," which had been all along the one institution able to maintain some degree of order in the financial world. The immediate result of Jackson's action was a contraction of credit by Biddle's bank in order to shore up its defenses against the loss of deposits. By 1834 the tightness of credit was creating complaints of business distress, which was probably exaggerated by both sides in the bank controversy for political effect: Biddle to show the evil consequences of the withdrawal of deposits, Jacksonians to show how Biddle abused his power.

The contraction brought about by the bank quickly gave way, however, to a speculative binge encouraged by the deposit of government funds in the pet banks. With the restraint of Biddle's bank removed, the state banks gave full rein to their wildcat tendencies. (The term "wildcat," used in this sense, originated in Michigan, where one of the fly-by-night banks featured a panther, or wildcat, on its worthless notes.) New banks mushroomed, printing banknotes with abandon for the purpose of lending to speculators. Sales of public lands rose from 4 million acres in 1834 to 15 million in 1835 and to 20 million in 1836. At the same time the states plunged heavily into debt to finance the building of roads and canals, inspired by the success of New York's Erie Canal. By 1837 total state indebtedness had soared to $170 million, a very large sum for this time. The supreme irony of Jackson's war on the bank then was that it preceded a speculative mania that dwarfed even the South Sea Bubble.

FISCAL MEASURES The new bubble reached its greatest extent in 1836, when a combination of events conspired suddenly to deflate it. Most important among these were the Distribution Act, passed in June 1836, and the Specie Circular of July 1836. Distribution of the government's surplus funds had long been a pet project of Henry Clay. One of its purposes was to eliminate the surplus thus removing one argument for cutting the tariff. Much of the surplus, however, was brought in by the "land office business" in western real estate, and was therefore in the form of banknotes that had been issued to speculators. Many westerners thought that the solution to the surplus was simply to lower the price of land; southerners preferred to lower the tariff—but such action would now upset the compromise achieved in the tariff of 1833. For a time the annual surpluses could be applied to paying off the government debt, but the debt, reduced to $7 million by 1832, was entirely paid off by January 1835.

Still the federal surplus continued to mount. Clay again proposed distribution, but Jackson had constitutional scruples about the process. Finally, a compromise was worked out whereby the government would distribute most of the surplus as loans to the states. To satisfy Jackson's scruples the funds were technically "deposits," but in reality they were never demanded back. Distribution was to be in proportion to each state's representation in the two houses of Congress, and was to be paid out in quarterly installments, beginning January 1, 1837.

About a month after passage of the Distribution Act came the Specie Circular of July 11, 1836, issued by the secretary of the treasury at Jackson's order. With that document the president belatedly applied his hard-money conviction to the sale of public lands. According to his order, the government after August 15 would accept only gold and silver in payment for lands—with the exception that for a brief time banknotes would be accepted for parcels up to 320 acres when bought by actual settlers or residents of the state in which the sale was made. The purposes declared in the circular were to "repress frauds," to withhold support "from the monopoly of the public lands in the hands of speculators and capitalists," and to discourage the "ruinous extension" of banknotes and credit.

Irony dogged Jackson to the end on this matter. Since few actual settlers could get their hands on specie, they were now left all the more at the mercy of speculators for land purchases. Both the distribution and the Specie Circular put many state banks in a precarious plight. The distribution reduced their deposits, or at least threw things into disarray by shifting them from bank to bank, and the increased demand for specie put an added strain on the supply of gold and silver.

BOOM AND BUST   But the boom and bust of the 1830s had causes larger even than Andrew Jackson, causes that were beyond his control. The inflation of mid-decade was rooted not in a prodigal expansion of banknotes, as it seemed at the time, but by an increase of specie flowing in from England and France, and especially from Mexico, for investment and for the purchase of American cotton and other commodities. At the same time British credits enabled Americans to buy British goods without having to export specie. Meanwhile the flow of hard cash to China, where silver had been much prized, declined. The Chinese now took in payment for their goods British credits which they could in turn use to cover rapidly increasing imports of opium from British India.

Contrary to appearances, therefore, the reserves of specie in American banks kept pace with the increase of banknotes, despite reckless behavior on the part of some banks. But by 1836 a tighter British economy caused a decline in British investments and in British demand for American cotton just when the new western lands were creating a rapid increase in cotton supply. Fortunately for Jackson, the Panic of 1837 did not break until he was out of the White House and safely back at the Hermitage. His successor would serve as the scapegoat.

In May 1837 New York banks suspended specie payments on their banknotes and fears of bankruptcy set off runs on banks around the country, many of which were soon overextended. A brief recovery followed in 1838, stimulated in part by a bad wheat harvest at home which forced the British to buy American wheat. But by 1839 that stimulus had passed. The same year a bumper cotton crop overloaded the market and a collapse of cotton prices set off a depression from which the economy did not fully recover until the mid-1840s.

Van Buren and the New Party System

THE WHIG COALITION   Before the crash, however, the Jacksonian Democrats reaped a political bonanza. Jackson had downed the dual monsters of nullification and the bank, and the people loved him for it. But out of the political wreckage that Jackson had inflicted on his opponents they began in 1834 to pull together a new coalition of diverse elements united chiefly by their hostility to Jackson. The imperial demeanor of that champion of democracy had given rise to the name of "King Andrew I"! His followers therefore were "Tories," supporters of the king, and his opponents took unto themselves the hallowed title of "Whigs," a name sanctioned by its honorable connotations in the American Revolution. This diverse coalition clustered around its center, the National Republican party of J. Q. Adams, Clay, and Webster. Into the combination came remnants of the Anti-Masons and Democrats who for one reason or another were alienated by Jackson's stands on the bank or state's rights. Of the forty-one Democrats in Congress who had voted to recharter the bank, twenty-eight had joined the Whigs by 1836.

Whiggery always had about it an atmosphere of social conservatism and superiority. The core Whigs were the supporters of Henry Clay, men whose vision was quickened by the vistas of his "American System." In the South the Whigs enjoyed the support of the urban banking and commercial interests, as well as their planter associates, owners of most of the slaves in the region. In the West, farmers who valued internal improvements joined the Whig ranks. Most states'-rights supporters eventually dropped away, and by the early 1840s the Whigs were becoming more clearly the party of Henry Clay's nationalism, even in the South. Throughout their two decades of strength the Whigs were a national party, strong both North and South, and a cohesive force for Union.

THE ELECTION OF 1836 By the presidential election of 1836 a new two-party system was emerging out of the Jackson and anti-Jackson forces, a system that would remain in fairly even balance for twenty years. In May 1835, eighteen months before the election, the Democrats held their second national convention and nominated Jackson's handpicked successor, Vice-President Martin Van Buren, the Red Fox of Kinderhook. The Whig coalition, united chiefly in its opposition to Jackson, held no convention but adopted a strategy of multiple candidacies, hoping to throw the election into the House of Representatives. The result was a free-for-all reminiscent of 1824, except that this time one candidate stood apart from the rest. It was Van Buren against the field. The Whigs put up three favorite sons: Daniel Webster, named by the Massachusetts legislature; Hugh Lawson White, chosen by anti-Jackson Democrats in the Tennessee legislature; and Wil-

Martin Van Buren, the "Little Magician." [Library of Congress]

liam Henry Harrison of Indiana, nominated by a predominantly Anti-Masonic convention in Harrisburg, Pennsylvania. In the South the Whigs made heavy inroads on the Democratic vote by arguing that Van Buren would be soft on antislavery advocates and that the South could trust only a southerner—i.e., White—as president.

In the popular vote Van Buren outdistanced the entire Whig field, with 765,000 votes to 740,000 votes for the Whigs, most of which were cast for Harrison. Van Buren had 170 electoral votes, Harrison 73, White 26, and Webster 14. In South Carolina, where the legislature still chose the electors, anti-Jackson Democrats threw 11 votes to Willie P. Mangum of North Carolina (soon to be a Whig himself).

Martin Van Buren, the eighth president, was the first of Dutch ancestry and at the age of fifty-five the first born under the Stars and Stripes. Son of a tavernkeeper in Kinderhook, New York, he had been schooled in a local academy, read law, and entered politics. Although he kept up a limited practice of law, he had been for most of his adult life a professional politician, so skilled in the arts of organization and manipulation that he came to be known as the "Little Magician." In New York politics he became leader of an organization known as the "Albany Regency," which backed his election as senator and later as governor. In 1824 he supported Crawford, then switched to Jackson in 1828, but continued to look to the Old Republicans of Virginia as the southern anchor of his support. After a brief tenure as governor of New York he resigned to join the cabinet, and because of Jackson's favor became minister to London and then vice-president.

THE PANIC OF 1837   Van Buren owed much of his success to good luck, to having backed the right horse, having been in the right place at the right time. But once he had climbed to the top of the greasy pole, luck suddenly deserted him. Van Buren had inherited Jackson's favor and a good part of his following, but he also inherited a financial panic. An already precarious economy was tipped over into crisis by depression in England, which resulted in a drop in the price of cotton from 17½¢ to 13½¢ a pound, and caused English banks and investors to cut back their commitments in the New World and refuse extensions of loans. This was a particularly hard blow since much of America's economic expansion depended on European—and mainly English—capital. On top of everything else, in 1836 there had been a failure of the wheat crop, the export of which in good years helped offset the drain of payments abroad. As creditors hastened to foreclose, the inflationary spiral went into reverse. States curtailed ambitious plans for roads and canals, and in many cases felt impelled to repudiate their debts. In the crunch a good many of the wildcat banks succumbed, and the government itself lost some $9 million it had deposited in pet banks.

Van Buren's advisors and supporters were inclined to blame speculators and bankers but at the same time to expect that the evildoers would get what they deserved in a healthy shakeout that would bring the economy back to stability. Van Buren did not believe that he or the government had any responsibility to rescue hard-pressed farmers or businessmen, or to provide public relief. He did feel obliged to keep the government itself in a healthy financial situation, however. To that end he called a special session of Congress in September 1837 which quickly voted to postpone indefinitely the distribution of the surplus because of a probable upcoming deficit, and also approved an issue of Treasury notes to cover immediate expenses.

AN INDEPENDENT TREASURY   But Van Buren devoted most of his message to his idea that the government cease risking its deposits in shaky banks and set up an Independent Treasury. Under this the government would keep its funds in its own vaults and do business entirely in hard money. Van Buren was opposed to the "bleeding of private interests with the operations of public business." The founders of the republic had "wisely judged that the less government interferes with private pursuits the better for the general prosperity." Webster's response typified the Whig reaction: "I feel . . . as if this could not be America when I see schemes of public policy proposed, having for their object the

THE TIMES. *The panic at the bank, the closed factory, and the beggars in the street all depict the effects of the depression of 1837, according to this anti-Jacksonian lithograph. [Library of Congress]*

convenience of Government only, and leaving the people to shift for themselves." The Whiggish approach, presumably, would have been some kind of Hamiltonian program of government promotion of economic development, perhaps in the form of tariff or currency legislation. Good Jacksonians disapproved of such programs, at least when they were run from Washington.

Passage of the Independent Treasury was held up by opposition from a combination of Whigs and conservative Democrats who feared deflation. It took Van Buren several years of maneuvering to get what he wanted. Calhoun signaled a return to the Democratic fold, after several years of flirting with the Whigs, when he came out for the Independent Treasury. Van Buren gained western support by backing a more liberal land policy. He finally got his Independent Treasury on July 4, 1840. Although it lasted little more than a year before the Whigs repealed it in 1841, it would be restored in 1846.

The drawn-out hassle over the Treasury was only one of several that kept Washington preoccupied through the Van Buren years. A flood of petitions for Congress to abolish slavery and the slave trade in the District of Columbia brought on tumultuous debate, especially in the House of Representatives. Border incidents growing out of a Canadian insurrection in 1837 and a dispute over the Maine boundary kept British-American animosity at a simmer, but Gen. Winfield Scott, the president's ace trouble-shooter, managed to keep the hotheads in check along the border. These matters will be discussed elsewhere, but basic to the spreading malaise of the time was the depressed condition of the economy that lasted through Van Buren's entire term. Fairly or not, the administration became the target of growing discontent. The president won renomination easily enough, but could not get the Democratic convention to agree on his vice-presidential choice, which the convention left up to the Democratic electors.

THE "LOG CABIN AND HARD CIDER" CAMPAIGN   The Whigs got an early start on their campaign when they met at Harrisburg, Pennsylvania, on December 4, 1839, to choose a candidate. Clay expected 1840 to be his year and had soft-pedaled talk of his American System in the interest of building broader support. Although he led on the first ballot, the convention was of a mind to look for a Whiggish Jackson, as it were, a military hero who could enter the race with few known political convictions or enemies. One possibility was Winfield Scott, but the delegates finally turned to William Henry Harrison, victor at the battle of Tippecanoe, former governor of the Indiana territory, briefly congressman and senator from Ohio, more briefly minister to Colombia. Another advantage of Harrison's was that the Anti-Masons liked him. To rally their states'-rights wing the Whigs chose for vice-president John Tyler of Virginia, a close friend of Clay.

The Whigs had no platform. That would have risked dividing a coalition united chiefly by opposition to the Democrats. But they had a slogan, "Tippecanoe and Tyler too," that went trippingly

In front of his log cabin, Old Tippecanoe pours the cider for cheering supporters. Jackson and Van Buren try to stop the flow. [New-York Historical Society]

on the tongue. And they soon had a rousing campaign theme which a Democratic paper unwittingly supplied them when the Baltimore *Republican* declared sardonically "that upon condition of his receiving a pension of $2,000 and a barrel of cider, General Harrison would no doubt consent to withdraw his pretensions, and spend his days in a log cabin on the banks of the Ohio." The Whigs seized upon the cider and log cabin symbols to depict Harrison as a simple man sprung from the people. Actually he sprang from one of the first families of Virginia and lived in a commodious farmhouse.

Substituting spectacle for argument, the Whig "Log Cabin and Hard Cider" campaign featured such sublime irrelevancy as the country had never seen before. Portable log cabins rolled through the streets along with barrels of potable cider to the tune of catchy campaign songs in support of

> The iron-armed soldier, the true-hearted soldier,
> The gallant old soldier of Tippecanoe.

His sweating supporters rolled huge victory balls along the highways to symbolize the snowballing majorities. All the devices of hoopla were mobilized: placards, emblems, campaign buttons, floats, effigies, transparencies, great rallies, and a campaign newspaper, *The Log Cabin.* Building on the example of the Jacksonians' campaign to discredit John Quincy Adams, the Whigs pictured Van Buren, who unlike Harrison came of humble origins as an aristocrat living in luxury at "the Palace":

> Let Van from his coolers of silver drink wine,
> And lounge on his cushioned settee;
> Our man on his buckeye bench can recline
> Content with hard cider is he!

The campaign left one lasting heritage in the American language, a usage now virtually worldwide. The expression "O.K." began as an abbreviation for "Old Kinderhook," an affectionate name for Van Buren, whose supporters organized "O.K. Clubs" during the campaign. The Whigs gave the initials a jocular turn and a new meaning when they attributed them to Andrew Jackson's creative spelling. Jackson had marked certain papers with the initials, he was said to have told Amos Kendall, to signify that they were "oll korrect." Thereafter Whig cider barrels carried the same seal of approval.

"We have taught them to conquer us!" the *Democratic Review*

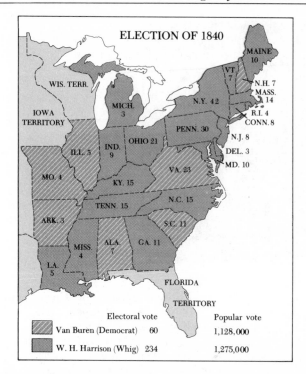

ELECTION OF 1840

	Electoral vote	Popular vote
Van Buren (Democrat)	60	1,128,000
W. H. Harrison (Whig)	234	1,275,000

lamented. The Whig party had not only learned its lessons well, it had learned to improve on its teachers in the art of campaigning. "Van! Van! Is a Used-up Man!" went one of the campaign refrains, and down he went by the thumping margin of 234 votes to 60 in the electoral college. In the popular vote it was closer: 1,275,000 for Old Tip, 1,128,000 for Van Buren.

Assessing the Jackson Years

The Jacksonian impulse had altered American politics permanently. Longstanding ambivalence about political parties had been purged in the fires of political conflict, and mass political parties had arrived to stay. They were now widely justified as a positive good. By 1840 both parties were organized down to the precinct level, and the proportion of adult white males who voted in the presidential election nearly tripled, from 26.5 percent in 1824 to 78.0 percent in 1840. That much is beyond dispute, but the phenomenon of Jackson, the great symbol for an

*Andrew Jackson in 1845.
Jackson died shortly after this
daguerrotype was taken.
[Library of Congress]*

age, has inspired among historians conflicts of interpretation as
spirited as those among his supporters and opponents at the time.
Jackson's personality itself seemed a compound of contradic-
tions. His first major biographer concluded from conflicting evidence that Jackson "was a patriot and a traitor. He was one of the
greatest of generals, and wholly ignorant of the art of war. A
writer brilliant, elegant, eloquent, without being able to com-
pose a correct sentence or spell words of four syllables. The first
of statesmen, he never devised, he never framed a measure. He
was the most candid of men, and was capable of the profoundest
dissimulation. A most law-defying, law-obeying citizen. A
stickler for discipline, he never hesitated to disobey his superior.
A democratic aristocrat. An urbane savage. An atrocious saint."

Interpretations of his policies, their sources, and their consequences have likewise differed. The earliest historians of the
Jackson era belonged largely to an eastern elite nurtured in a
"Whiggish" culture, men who could never quite forgive Jackson
for the spoils system which in their view excluded from office the
fittest and ablest. A later school of "progressive" historians depicted Jackson as the leader of a vast democratic movement
which welled up in the West and mobilized a farmer-labor alliance to sweep the "Monster" bank into the dustbin of history.
Some historians recently have focused attention on local power
struggles in which the great national debates of the time often
seem empty rhetoric or at most snares to catch the voters. One

view of Jackson makes him out to be essentially a frontier nabob, an opportunist for whom democracy "was good talk with which to win the favor of the people. . . ."

Another school has emphasized the importance of cultural-ethnic identity in deciding party loyalties. Jackson, according to this view, revitalized the Jeffersonian alliance of Virginia and New York, of individualistic southern planters and those elements of the North who stood outside the strait-laced Yankee culture created mainly by people of English origin. Though the political effects of ethnic identities were complex, in large measure such out-groups as the Scotch-Irish and the Catholic Irish felt more comfortable with the more tolerant Democratic party. If valid for the northern states, however, the cultural-ethnic interpretation needs qualification in the light of southern experience. Ethnic identities in the South had faded with the decline of immigration after the Revolution, but the South developed in the 1840s as vigorous a party division as the North.

There seems little question that, whatever else Jackson and his supporters had in mind, they followed an ideal of republican virtue, of returning to the Jeffersonian Arcadia of the Old Republic in which government would leave people largely to their own devices. In the Jacksonian view the alliance of government and business was always an invitation to special favors and an eternal source of corruption. The bank was the epitome of such evil. The right policy for government, at the national level in particular, was to refrain from granting special privileges and to let free competition in the marketplace regulate the economy.

In the bustling world of the nineteenth century, however, the idea of a return to agrarian simplicity was a futile exercise in nostalgia. Instead, laissez-faire policies opened the way for a host of aspiring entrepreneurs eager to replace the established economic elite with a new order of laissez-faire capitalism. And in fact there was no great conflict in the Jacksonian mentality between the farmer or planter who delved in the soil and the independent speculator and entrepreneur who won his way by other means. Jackson himself was all these things. What the Jacksonian mentality could not foresee was the degree to which, in a growing country, unrestrained enterprise could lead on to new economic combinations, centers of gigantic power largely independent of governmental regulation. But history is forever pursued by irony. Here the ultimate irony would be that the laissez-faire rationale for republican simplicity eventually became the justification for the growth of unregulated centers of economic power far greater than any ever wielded by Biddle's bank.

FURTHER READING

A survey of events covered in the chapter can be found in Glyndon Van Deusen's *The Jacksonian Era, 1828–1848* (1959).° The first of the modern interpretations of the Jacksonian period is Arthur M. Schlesinger, Jr.'s *The Age of Jackson* (1945),° which emphasizes the role played by antibusiness interests in the agrarian South and the urban North. Richard Hofstadter's *The American Political Tradition and the Men Who Made It* (1948)° challenges this thesis. Lee Benson's *The Concept of Jacksonian Democracy* (1964)° examines the ethnocultural basis for New York's politics of the common man. John W. Ward's *Andrew Jackson: Symbol for an Age* (1955)° assesses Jackson's impact on the psychology of mass politics. Also helpful is Marvin Meyer's *The Jacksonian Persuasion: Politics and Belief* (1960).° Robert Kelley treats these themes in two works: *The Transatlantic Persuasion: The Liberal-Democratic Mind in the Age of Gladstone* (1969) and *The Cultural Pattern in American Politics: The First Century* (1979). Edward E. Pessen's *Jacksonian America: Society, Personality, and Politics* (1978)° provides a recent overview of these arguments.

An introduction to development of political parties of the 1830s is in Richard P. McCormick's *The Second American Party System: Party Formation in the Jacksonian Era* (1966).° Richard Hofstadter's *The Idea of a Party System* (1969)° traces the roots of the theories of political opposition which carried over from the first party system. In addition to the work by Benson, illuminating case studies include Ronald P. Formisano's *The Birth of Mass Political Parties: Michigan, 1827–1861* (1971), Douglass T. Miller's *Jacksonian Aristocracy: Class and Democracy in New York, 1830–1860* (1967), and Harry L. Watson's *Jacksonian Politics and Community Conflict: The Emergence of the Second American Party System in Cumberland County, North Carolina* (1981).

Biographies of Jackson include Robert V. Remini's *Andrew Jackson* (1966),° which can serve as a good introduction. Also consult the two-volume work by Remini, *Andrew Jackson and the Course of American Empire, 1767–1821* (1977), and *Andrew Jackson and the Course of American Freedom, 1822–1832* (1981). A critical work is James C. Curtis's *Andrew Jackson and the Search for Vindication* (1976).° Marquis James's *Andrew Jackson: Portrait of a President* (1937) is more sympathetic. For Jackson's successor, consult Robert V. Remini's *Martin Van Buren and the Making of the Democratic Party* (1959) and James C. Curtis's *The Fox at Bay* (1970).

The political philosophies of those who came to oppose Jackson are treated in Daniel Walker Howe's *The Political Culture of the American Whigs* (1979). Biographies of leading Whigs include Charles M. Wiltse's *John C. Calhoun* (3 vols.; 1944–1951), Clement Eaton's *Henry Clay and*

°These books are available in paperback editions.

the Art of American Politics (1957), and Sydney Nathans's *Daniel Web-ster and Jacksonian Democracy* (1973).

A number of scholars have concentrated on the economics and fi-nance of the period. An overview is found in Peter Temin's *The Jackson-ian Economy* (1969).° Bray Hamond's *Banks and Politics in America from the Revolution to the Civil War* (1957) provides extensive background for the 1830s controversy. Robert V. Remini's *Andrew Jackson and the Bank War* (1967)° stresses the political differences. Thomas P. Govan's *Nicholas Biddle: Nationalist and Public Banker* (1959) provides a per-spective from the anti-Jackson side. John McFaul's *The Politics of Jack-sonian Finance* (1972) is a more recent treatment of all sides of the issue. Two studies of the impact of the bank controversy are William G. Shade's *Banks or No Banks: The Money Question in the Western States, 1832–1865* (1973), and James Roger Sharp's *The Jacksonians versus the Banks: Politics in the States after the Panic of 1837* (1970).

Among the best of all scholarship on the Jacksonian years is William W. Freehling's *Prelude to Civil War: The Nullification Controversy in South Carolina, 1816–1836* (1966).° Leonard D. White's *The Jackson-ians: A Study in Administrative History, 1829–1861* (1954),° examines the spoils system. Ronald N. Satz's *American Indian Policy in the Jack-sonian Era* (1975) surveys that tragedy. Other studies of Indian affairs include Arthur H. DeRosier, Jr.'s *The Removal of the Choctaw Indians* (1970)° and Michael P. Rogin's *Fathers and Children: Andrew Jackson and the Subjugation of the American Indian* (1975). The question of ris-ing inequality in American cities is treated in Edward E. Pesson's *Riches, Class, and Power before the Civil War* (1973) and Douglas T. Miller's *The Birth of Modern America, 1820–1850* (1970). Michael Feldberg's *The Turbulent Era: Riot and Disorder in Jacksonian America* (1980) discusses the ramifications of inequality.

12

THE DYNAMICS OF GROWTH

AGRICULTURE AND THE NATIONAL ECONOMY

COTTON "We are greatly, I was about to say fearfully, growing,"
John C. Calhoun told his congressional colleagues in 1816 when
he introduced his Bonus Bill for internal improvements. His pro-
phetic sentence expressed both the promise of national greatness and the threat of divisions that would blight Calhoun's own
ambition. But in the brief period of good feelings after the War of
1812, it was opportunity that seemed most conspicuously visible
to Americans everywhere, and nowhere more than in Calhoun's
native South Carolina. The reason was cotton, the new staple
crop of the South, which was spreading from South Carolina and
Georgia into the new lands of Mississippi and Alabama, where
Andrew Jackson had recently chastised the Creeks, and on into
Louisiana and Arkansas. Jackson himself had been set up as a
cotton planter at The Hermitage, near Nashville, Tennessee,
since the mid-1790s.

Cotton had been used from ancient times, but the Industrial
Revolution and its spread of textile mills created a rapidly growing market for the fluffy staple. Cotton had remained for many
years rare and expensive because of the need for hand labor to
separate the lint from the tenacious seeds of most varieties. But
by the mid-1780s in coastal Georgia and South Carolina a long-
staple "sea island" cotton was being grown commercially which
could easily be separated from its shiny black seeds by squeezing
it through rollers. Sea-island cotton, like the rice and indigo of
the colonial Tidewater, had little chance, though, in the soil and
climate of the upcountry. And the green seed of the upland cotton clung to the lint so stubbornly that the rollers crushed the
seed and spoiled the fiber. One person working all day could

manage to separate little if any more than a pound by hand. Cotton could not yet be king.

The rising cotton kingdom of the lower South came to birth at a plantation called Mulberry Hill in coastal Georgia, the home of Mrs. Nathanael Greene, widow of the Revolutionary War hero. At Mulberry Hill discussion often turned to the promising new crop and to speculation about better ways to remove the seeds. In 1792, on the way to a job as a tutor in South Carolina, young Eli Whitney, recently graduated from Yale, visited fellow graduate Phineas Miller, who was overseer at Mulberry Hill. Catherine Greene noticed her visitor's mechanical aptitude, which had been nurtured in boyhood by the needs of a Massachusetts farm. When she suggested that young Whitney devise a mechanism for removing the seed from upland cotton, he mulled it over and solved the problem in ten days. In the spring of 1793, his job as a tutor quickly forgotten, Whitney had a working model of a cotton gin.

By chance one of Mrs. Greene's daughters had bought some iron wire for a bird cage. Whitney used the wire to make iron pins which he inserted into a cylinder. When rotated, the cylinder passed cotton fiber through slots in an iron guard and the seeds dropped into a box below. Rotating brushes on the other side served as a doffer, removing the fiber as it passed through. With it one man could separate fifty times as much cotton as he could by hand. The device was an "absurdly simple contrivance," too much so as it turned out. A simple description was all any skilled worker needed to make a copy, and by the time

Whitney's cotton gin revolutionized the South's economy and breathed new life into slavery. [Merrimack Valley Textile Museum]

Whitney and Miller had secured a patent in 1794 a number of copies were already in use. Consequently the two men were never able to make good on the promise of riches that the gin offered, and spent most of their modest gains in expensive lawsuits. Improved models soon appeared. The use of a saw-toothed cylinder proved more effective than the original pins, and that device —which had occurred to Whitney at the start—appeared on the market as one of many designs contesting for patent rights.

Although Whitney realized little from his idea, he had unwittingly begun a revolution. Green-seed cotton first engulfed the upcountry hills of South Carolina and Georgia, and after the War of 1812 migrated into the former Creek, Choctaw, and Chickasaw lands to the west. Cotton production soared. Slavery had found a new and profitable use. Indeed thereafter slavery became almost synonymous with the Cotton Kingdom in the popular view. Planters migrated westward with their gangs of workers in tow, and a profitable trade began to develop in the sale of slaves from the coastal South to the West. The cotton culture became a way of life that tied the Old Southwest to the coastal Southeast in a common interest.

Not the least of the cotton gin's revolutionary consequences, although less apparent at first, was that cotton became almost immediately a major export commodity. Cotton exports averaged about $9 million in value from 1803 to 1807, about 22 percent of the value of all exports; from 1815 to 1819 they averaged over $23 million or 39 percent of the total, and from the mid-1830s to 1860 accounted for more than half the value of all exports. For the national economy as a whole, one historian asserted: "Cotton was the most important proximate cause of expansion." The South supplied the North both raw materials and markets for manufactures. Income from the North's role in handling the cotton trade then provided surpluses for capital investment. It was once assumed that the South supplied the Northwest with markets for foodstuffs, but recent research shows the Cotton Belt to have been self-sufficient in foodstuffs. The more likely explanation of growth in the Northwest now seems to be its own growing urban markets for foodstuffs, which supplemented the export market for grain.

FARMING THE WEST The westward flow of planters and their slave gangs to Alabama and Mississippi during these flush times was paralleled by another migration through the Ohio Valley and the Great Lakes region, where the Indians had been steadily pushed westward until the risk was minimal. "Old America seems to be

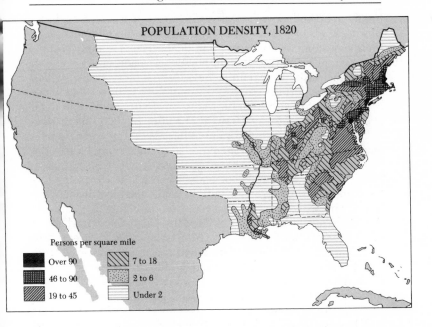

POPULATION DENSITY, 1820

Persons per square mile

Over 90
46 to 90
19 to 45
7 to 18
2 to 6
Under 2

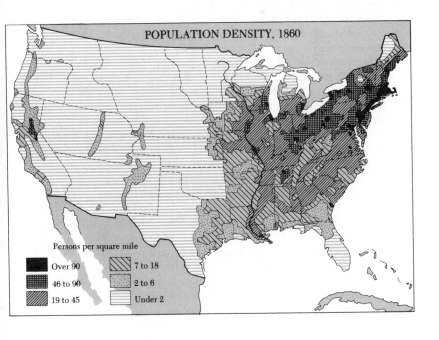

POPULATION DENSITY, 1860

Persons per square mile

Over 90
46 to 90
19 to 45
7 to 18
2 to 6
Under 2

breaking up and moving westward," an English traveler, Morris Birkbeck, observed in 1817 as he watched the migrants make their way along westward roads in Pennsylvania. Family groups, stages, light wagons, riders on horseback made up "a scene of bustle and business, extending over three hundred miles, which is truly wonderful." In 1800 some 387,000 settlers were counted west of the Atlantic states; by 1810, 1,338,000 lived over the mountains; by 1820, 2,419,000. By 1860 more than half the nation's expanded population resided in trans-Appalachia, and the restless movement had long since spilled across the Mississippi and touched the shores of the Pacific.

North of the expanding cotton belt in the Gulf states, the fertile woodland soils, riverside bottom lands, and black loam of the prairies drew farmers from the rocky lands of New England and the leached, exhausted soils of the Southeast. A new land law of 1820, passed after the Panic of 1819, eliminated the credit provisions of the 1800 act but reduced the minimum price from $1.64 to $1.25 per acre and the minimum plot from 160 to 80 acres. The settler could get a place for as little as $100, and over the years the proliferation of state banks made it possible to continue buying on credit. Even that was not enough for westerners who began a long—and eventually victorious—agitation for further relaxation of the land laws. They favored preemption, the right of squatters to purchase land at the minimum price, and graduation, the progressive reduction of the price on lands that did not sell.

Success came ultimately with two acts of Congress. Under the Preemption Act of 1830, a renewable law made permanent in the Preemption Act of 1841, squatters could stake out claims ahead of the land surveys and later get 160 acres at the minimum price of $1.25. In effect the law recognized a practice enforced more often than not by frontier vigilantes. Under the Graduation Act of 1854, which Sen. Thomas Hart Benton had plugged since the 1820s, prices of unsold lands were to go down in stages until the lands could sell for 12½¢ per acre after thirty years.

The progress of settlement followed the old pattern of girdling trees, clearing land, and settling down at first to a crude subsistence. The development of effective iron plows greatly eased the backbreaking job of breaking the soil. As early as 1797 Charles Newbold had secured a patent on an iron plow, but a superstition that iron poisoned the soil prevented much use until after 1819, when Jethro Wood of Scipio, New York, developed an improved version with separate parts that could be replaced without buying a whole new plow complete. The prejudice against iron suddenly vanished, and the demand for plows grew so fast that

Wood, like Whitney, could not supply the need and spent much of his remaining fifteen years fighting against patent infringements. The iron plow was a special godsend to those farmers who first ventured into the sticky black loams of the treeless prairies. Further improvements would follow in later years, including John Deere's steel plow (1837) and the chilled-iron and steel plow of John Oliver (1855).

TRANSPORTATION AND THE NATIONAL ECONOMY

NEW ROADS The pioneer's life of crude subsistence eventually gave way to staple farming for cash income, as markets for foodstuffs grew both in the South and Northwest. Improvements in transportation were beginning to make possible the development of a national market. As settlers moved west the demand went back east for better roads. In 1795 the Wilderness Road, along the trail blazed by Daniel Boone twenty years before, was opened to wagon traffic, thereby easing the route through the Cumberland Gap into Kentucky and along the Knoxville and Old Walton Roads, completed the same year, into Tennessee. "Stand at Cumberland Gap," Frederick Jackson Turner wrote years later, "and watch the procession of civilization marching single file—the buffalo following the trail to the salt springs, the Indian,

The primitive condition of American roads is evident in this early–nineteenth-century watercolor. [Museum of Fine Arts]

the fur-trader and hunter, the cattle-raiser, the pioneer farmer
—and the frontier has passed by." South of these roads there
were no such major highways. South Carolinians and Georgians
pushed westward on whatever trails or rutted roads had appeared.

To the northeast a movement for graded and paved roads
(macadamized with crushed stones packed down) gathered momentum after completion of the Philadelphia-Lancaster Turnpike in 1794 (the term derives from a pole or pike at the tollgate,
turned to admit the traffic). By 1821 some 4,000 miles of turnpikes had been completed, mainly connecting eastern cities, but
western traffic could move along the Frederick Pike to Cumberland and thence along the National Road, completed to Wheeling on the Ohio in 1818, and to Vandalia, Illinois, by about
mid-century; along the old Forbes Road from Philadelphia to

Pittsburgh; and along the Mohawk and Genesee Turnpike from the Massachusetts line through Albany to Buffalo, whence one could take ship for points on the Great Lakes.

RIVER TRANSPORT Once turnpike travelers had reached the Ohio they could float westward in comparative comfort. At Pittsburgh, Wheeling, and other points the emigrants could buy flatboats, commonly of two kinds: an ark with room for living quarters, possessions, and perhaps some livestock; or a keelboat —similar but with a keel. For large flatboats—a capacity of forty tons was common—crews were available for hire. At the destination the boat could be used again or sold for lumber. In the early 1820s an estimated 3,000 flatboats went down the Ohio every year, and for many years after that the flatboat remained the chief conveyance for heavy traffic downstream.

By the early 1820s the turnpike boom was giving way to new developments in water transportation: the river steamboat and the barge canal, which carried bulk commodities far more cheaply than did Conestoga wagons on the National Road. As early as 1787 John Fitch had launched a steamboat on the Delaware River, and in 1790 had one that carried passengers from Philadelphia to Trenton on a regular schedule, but technical problems continued to frustrate Fitch and other inventors. No commercially successful steamboat appeared until Robert Fulton and Robert R. Livingston sent the *Clermont* up the Hudson to Albany in 1807. After that the use of the steamboat spread rapidly to other eastern rivers, and in 1811 Nicholas Roosevelt, a business associate of Fulton, launched a sidewheeler, the *New Orleans*, at Pittsburgh and sent it down the Ohio and Mississippi; thus began an era of steamboat transportation that opened nearly half a continent to water traffic. The *New Orleans* itself thereafter plied between New Orleans and Natchez, but in 1815 the *Enterprise*, built by Henry Shreve, went all the way from New Orleans up the Ohio and another fifty miles up the Monongahela. In 1818 the *Walk-in-the-Water*, the first steamboat on Lake Erie, began a regular nine-day schedule between Buffalo and Detroit.

By 1836, 361 steamboats were registered to navigate the western waters. As the boats reached ever farther up the tributaries that connected to the main artery of the Mississippi, their design evolved toward the familiar "steamboat Gothic," the glorified keelboat which one wit called "an engine on a raft with $11,000 worth of jig-saw work." By the 1840s shallow-draft ships that traveled *on* rather than *in* the water carried 50–100 tons of freight on twenty-four-inch drafts. These steam-powered rafts, the scorn of ocean-going salts, became the basis of the rivermen's boast that they could navigate a heavy dew, that they were "so built that when the river is low and the sandbars come out for air, the first mate can tap a keg of beer and run the boat four miles on the suds." These boats ventured into far reaches of the Mississippi Valley, up such rivers as the Wabash, the Monongahela, the Cumberland, the Tennessee, the Missouri, and the Arkansas.

The miracle of these floating palaces became one of the romantic epics of America. The tradition was fixed early. In 1827 a lyrical writer for Cincinnati's *Western Monthly Review* let himself go with a description of the "fairy structures of oriental gorgeousness and splendor . . . rushing down the Mississippi . . . or plowing up between the forests . . . bearing speculators, merchants, dandies, fine ladies, everything real and everything af-

The sumptuous interior of the steamboat Princess. *[Anglo-American Art Museum, Louisiana State University]*

fected in the form of humanity, with pianos, and stocks of novels, and cards, and dice, and flirting, and love-making, and drinking, and champagne, and on the deck, perhaps, three hundred fellows, who have seen alligators and neither fear whiskey, nor gunpowder. A steamboat, coming from New Orleans, brings to the remotest villages of our streams, and the very doors of the cabins, a little Paris, a section of Broadway, or a slice of Philadelphia, to a ferment in the minds of our young people, the innate propensity for fashions and finery."

The prosaic flatboat, however, still carried to market most of the western wheat, corn, flour, meal, bacon, ham, pork, whiskey, soap and candles (the by-products of slaughterhouses), lead from Missouri, copper from Michigan, wood from the Rockies, and ironwork from Pittsburgh. But the steamboat, by bringing two-way traffic to the Mississippi Valley, created a continental market and an agricultural empire which became the new bread-basket of America. Farming evolved from a subsistence level to the ever-greater production of valuable staples. Along with the new farmers came promoters, speculators, and land-boomers. Villages at strategic trading points along the streams evolved into centers of commerce and urban life. The port of New Orleans grew in the 1830s and 1840s to lead all others in exports.

But by then the Erie Canal was drawing eastward much of the trade that once went down to the Gulf. In 1817 the New York

Flatboats in tow along the Erie Canal. The scene depicted is around 1830–1832. [New York Public Library]

legislature endorsed Gov. De Witt Clinton's dream of connecting the Hudson River with Lake Erie and authorized construction. Eight years later, in 1825, the canal was open for its entire 350 miles from Albany to Buffalo; branches soon put most of the state within reach of the canal. After 1828 the Delaware and Hudson Canal linked New York with the anthracite fields of northeastern Pennsylvania. The speedy success of the New York system inspired a mania for canals that lasted more than a decade and resulted in the completion of about 3,000 miles of waterways by 1837. But no canal ever matched the spectacular success of the Erie, which rendered the entire Great Lakes region an economic tributary to the port of New York. With the further development of canals spanning Ohio and Indiana from north to south, much of the upper Ohio Valley also came within the economic sphere of New York.

RAILROADS   The Panic of 1837 and the subsequent depression cooled the fever quickly. States which had borrowed heavily to finance canals in some cases had to repudiate their debts. The holders of repudiated bonds were left without recourse. Meanwhile a new and more versatile form of transportation was gaining on the canal: the railroad. Vehicles that ran on iron rails had long been in use, especially in mining, but now came a tremen-

dous innovation—the use of steam power—as the steam loco-
motive followed soon after the steamboat. As early as 1814
George Stephenson had built the first practical one in England.
In 1825, the year the Erie Canal was completed, the world's first
commercial steam railway began operations in England. By the
1820s the port cities of Baltimore, Charleston, and Boston were
alive with schemes to tap the hinterlands by rail.

On July 4, 1828, Baltimore got the jump on other cities when
Charles Carroll, the last surviving signer of the Declaration of
Independence, laid the first stone in the roadbed of the Baltimore and Ohio (B&O) Railroad. By 1832 the road reached
seventy-three miles west of Baltimore. The Charleston and
Hamburg Railroad, started in 1831 and finished in 1833, was at
that time the longest railroad under single management in the
world. It reached westward 136 miles to the hamlet of Hamburg,
opposite Augusta, where Charleston merchants hoped to divert
traffic from the Savannah River. Boston by 1836 had fanned out
three major lines to Lowell, Worcester, and Providence.

By 1840 the railroads, with a total of 3,328 miles, had outdistanced the canals by just two miles. Over the next twenty years,
though, railroads grew nearly tenfold to cover 30,626 miles;
more than a third of this total was built in the 1850s. Several
major east-west lines appeared, connecting Boston to Albany
and Albany with Buffalo; combined in 1853, these lines became
the New York Central. In 1851 the Erie Railroad spanned southern New York; by 1852 the Pennsylvania Railway connected
Philadelphia and Pittsburgh; in 1853 the B&O finally reached
Wheeling on the Ohio. By then New York had connections all
the way to Chicago, and in two years to St. Louis. Before 1860
the Hannibal and St. Joseph had crossed the state of Missouri.
Farther south, despite Charleston's early start on both canals and
railroads and despite the brave dream of a line to tap western
commerce at Cincinnati, the network of railroads still had many
gaps in 1860. By 1857 Charleston, Savannah, and Norfolk connected by way of lines into Chattanooga and thence along a single line to Memphis, the only southern route that connected the
east coast and the Mississippi. In 1860 the North and South had
only three major links: at Washington, Louisville, and Cairo, Illinois.

The proliferation of trunk lines had by then supplemented the
earlier canals to create multiple ties between the Northwest and
Northeast. But it was still not until the eve of the Civil War that
railroads surpassed canals in total haulage: in 1859 they carried a
little over 2 billion ton-miles compared to 1.6 billion on canals.

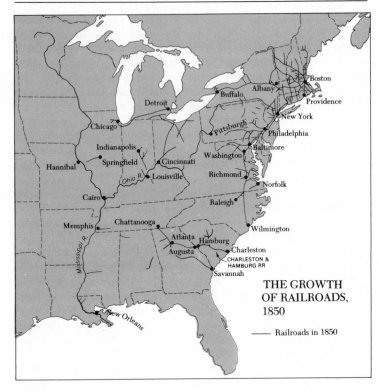

THE GROWTH
OF RAILROADS,
1850

—— Railroads in 1850

Travel on the early railroads was a chancy venture. Iron straps on top of wooden rails, for instance, tended to work loose and curl up into "snakesheads" which sometimes pierced railway coaches. The solution was the iron T-rail, introduced in 1831 and soon standard equipment on the best roads, but the strap-iron rail remained common because wood was so cheap. Wood was used for fuel too, and the sparks often caused fires along the way or damaged passengers' clothing. An English traveler, Harriet Martineau, reported seeing a lady's shawl ignited on one trip. She found in her own gown thirteen holes "and in my veil, with which I saved my eyes, more than could be counted." Creation of the "spark arrester" and the use of coal relieved but never overcame the hazard. Until after 1860 brakes had to be operated manually, crude pin-and-link couplings were used, and adequate springs were unknown. Different track widths often forced passengers to change trains until a standard gauge became national in 1882. Land travel, whether by stagecoach or train, was a

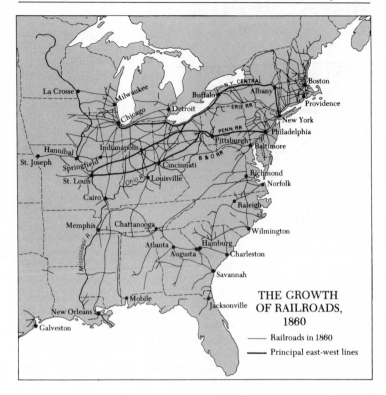

THE GROWTH
OF RAILROADS,
1860

—— Railroads in 1860

—— Principal east-west lines

jerky, bumpy, wearying ordeal. An early stage rider on the
Forbes Road said he alternately walked and rode and "though
the pain of riding exceeded the fatigue of walking, yet . . . it refreshed us by varying the weariness of our bodies."

Water travel, where available, offered far more comfort, but
railroads gained supremacy over other forms of transport because of their economy, speed, and reliability. By 1859 railroads
had reduced the cost of transportation services by $150–$175
million, accounting for a social saving that amounted to some 4
percent of the gross national product. By 1890 the saving would
run up to almost 15 percent. Railroads provided indirect benefits
by encouraging settlement and the expansion of farming. During
the antebellum period the reduced costs brought on by the
railroads aided the expansion of farming more than manufacturing, since manufacturers in the Northeast, especially New England, had better access to water transportation. The railroads'
demand for rail iron and equipment of various kinds, however,

The New-York Central Rail Road connected Albany with New England and "All Points West, Northwest, and Southwest." "Well ventilated Sleeping Cars" afforded "travelers the luxury of a Night's Sleep." [American Antiquarian Society]

did provide an enormous market for the industries that made these capital goods. And the ability of railroads to operate year round in all kinds of weather gave them an advantage in carrying finished goods too.

OCEAN TRANSPORT   For ocean-going traffic the start of service on regular schedules was the most important change of the early 1800s. In the first week of 1818 ships of the Black Ball Line inaugurated a weekly transatlantic packet service to and from New York and Liverpool. Beginning with four ships in all, the Black Ball Line thereafter had one ship leaving each port monthly at an announced time. With the business recovery in 1822 the packet business grew in a rush. Runs to London and Le Havre were added, and by 1845 some fifty-two transatlantic lines ran square-riggers on schedule from New York, with three regular sailings per week. Many others ran in the coastwide trade, to Charleston, Savannah, New Orleans, and elsewhere.

In the same year, 1845, came a great innovation with the building of the first clipper ship, the *Rainbow*, designed by Donald McKay. The clippers, built for speed, long and narrow with enormous sail areas, cut a dashing figure during their brief day of glory, which lasted less than two decades. In 1854 the *Flying Cloud* took eighty-nine days and eight hours to make the distance from New York to San Francisco, a speed that steamships took several decades to equal. But clippers, while fast, lacked ample cargo space, and after the Civil War would give way to the steamship.

The use of steam on ocean-going vessels lagged behind the development of steam riverboats because of the greater technological problems involved. The first steamship to cross the Atlantic, the *Savannah,* used steam power for only eighty hours during a twenty-seven day voyage from Savannah to Liverpool, relying on sails for most of the trip. It ended its days as a sailing vessel, stripped of its engines. On April 23, 1838, the British and American Steamship Navigation Company's ship *Sirius* arrived in New York, and another steamship, the *Great Western,* came in later the same day, but it would be another ten years before steamships began to threaten the sailing packets.

THE ROLE OF GOVERNMENT   The massive internal improvements of the era were the product of both governmental and private initiatives, sometimes undertaken jointly and sometimes separately. Private investment accounted for nearly all the turnpikes in New England and the middle states. Elsewhere states invested heavily in turnpike companies and in some cases, notably South Carolina and Indiana, themselves built and owned the turnpikes. Canals were to a much greater extent the product of state investment, and more commonly state-owned and operated. The Panic of 1837, however, caused states to pull back and leave railroad development mainly to private corporations. Most of the railroad capital came from private sources. Still, government had an enormous role in railroad development. Several states of the South and West built state-owned lines, such as Georgia's Western and Atlantic, completed from Atlanta to Chattanooga in 1851, although they generally looked to private companies to handle actual operations and in some cases sold the lines. States and localities along the routes invested in railroad corporations and granted loans; states were generous in granting charters and tax concessions.

The federal government helped too, despite the constitutional scruples of some against direct involvement. The government bought stock in turnpike and canal companies, and after the success of the Erie, extended land grants to several western states for the support of canal projects. Congress provided for railroad surveys by government engineers, and during 1830–1848 reduced the tariff duties on iron used in railroad construction. In 1850 Sen. Stephen A. Douglas of Illinois and others prevailed on Congress to extend a major land grant to support a north-south line connecting Chicago with Mobile. Grants of three square miles on alternate sides for each mile of railroad subsidized the building of the Illinois Central and the Mobile and Ohio Railroads. Regarded at the time a special case, the 1850 grant set a precedent for other bounties that totaled about 20 million acres by 1860—a small amount compared to the grants for transcontinental lines in the Civil War decade.

The Growth of Industry

While the South and West developed the agricultural basis for a national economy, the Northeast was laying foundations for an industrial revolution. Technology in the form of the cotton gin, the harvester, and improvements in transportation had quickened agricultural development and to some extent decided its direction. But technology altered the economic landscape even more profoundly by giving rise to the factory system.

EARLY TEXTILE MANUFACTURES   At the end of the colonial period manufacturing remained in the household or handicraft stage of development, or at best the "putting-out" stage, in which the merchant capitalist would distribute raw materials (say, leather patterns for shoes) to be worked up at home, then collected and sold. In 1815 *Niles' Weekly Register* described the town of Mount Pleasant, Ohio, with a population of barely over 500, as having some thirty-eight handicraft shops, including blacksmiths and bakers, and eight more shops engaged in tanning, textiles, and railmaking. Farmers themselves had to produce much of what they needed in the way of crude implements, shoes, and clothing, and in their crude workshops inventive genius was sometimes nurtured. As a boy Eli Whitney had set up a crude forge and manufactured nails in his father's rural workshop. The tran-

New England Factory Village, *around 1830. [New York State Historical Association]*

sition from such production to the factory was a slow process, but one for which a base had been laid before 1815.

In the eighteenth century Great Britain had jumped out to a long head start in industrial production, one that other countries were slow to overcome. The foundations of Britain's advantage were: the development of iron smelting by coke when sufficient wood was lacking; the invention of the steam engine by Thomas Newcomen in 1705 and its improvement by James Watt in 1765; and a series of inventions that mechanized the production of textiles, including John Kay's flying shuttle (1733), James Hargreaves's spinning jenny (1764), Richard Arkwright's "water frame" (1769), and Samuel Crompton's spinning mule (1779). The last could do the work of 200 spinners. Britain also carefully guarded its hard-won secrets, forbidding the export of machines or descriptions of them, even restricting the departure of informed mechanics. But the secrets could not be kept. In 1789 Samuel Slater arrived from England with the plan of Arkwright's water frame in his head. He contracted with Moses Brown, an enterprising merchant-manufacturer in Rhode Island, to build a mill in Pawtucket, and in this little mill, completed in 1790, nine children turned out a satisfactory cotton yarn, which was then worked up by the putting-out system. In 1793 the Schofield brothers, Englishmen from Yorkshire built the first woolens mill at Byfield, Massachusetts.

The beginnings in textiles were slow and faltering until Jefferson's embargo in 1807 and the War of 1812 restricted imports and encouraged the merchant capitalists of New England to switch their resources into manufacturing. New England, it happened, had one distinct advantage in that the fall line and the water power it provided stood near the coast where water transportation was also readily available. In 1813 Francis Cabot Lowell and a group of wealthy merchants known as the Boston Associates formed the Boston Manufacturing Company. At Waltham, Massachusetts, they built the first factory in which the processes of spinning and weaving by power machinery were brought under one roof, mechanizing every process from raw material to finished cloth. By 1815 textile mills numbered in the hundreds. A flood of British imports after the War of 1812 dealt a temporary setback to the infant industry, but the foundations of textile manufacture were laid, and they spurred the growth of garment trades and a machine-tool industry to build and service the mills.

TECHNOLOGY IN AMERICA Meanwhile American ingenuity was adding other bases for industrial growth. Oliver Evans of Philadelphia was a frustrated pioneer who had the misfortune to be ahead of his time. As a teenager he had been fascinated by steam engines but could not find the backing to pursue his ideas for steamboats and locomotives. As early as 1785 he built an automatic mill in which grain introduced at one end came out flour at the other, but could not get millers interested in trying it. Success eluded him until 1804, when he developed a high-pressure steam engine adapted to a variety of uses in ships and factories.

The practical bent of Americans was one of the outstanding traits noted by foreign visitors. In Europe, where class consciousness prevailed, Tocqueville wrote, men confined themselves to "the arrogant and sterile researches of abstract truths, whilst the social condition and institutions of democracy prepare them to seek immediate and useful practical results of the sciences." In 1814 Dr. Jacob Bigelow, a Harvard botanist, began to lecture on "The Elements of Technology," a word he did much to popularize. In his book of the same title he argued that technology constituted the chief superiority of moderns over the ancients, effecting profound changes in ways of living. Benjamin Silliman, Yale's first professor of chemistry, emphasized the application of science in his classes, publications (he founded the *American Journal of Science* in 1818), and public lectures.

One of the most striking examples of the connection between pure research and innovation, however, was in the researches of Joseph Henry, a Princeton physicist. His work in electromagnetism provided the basis for Samuel F. B. Morse's invention of the telegraph and for electrical motors later on. In 1846 Henry became head of the new Smithsonian Institution, founded with a bequest from the Englishman James Smithson "for the increase and diffusion of knowledge among men." The year 1846 also saw the founding of the American Association for the Advancement of Science.

It would be difficult to exaggerate the importance of science and technology in changing the ways people live. All aspects of life—the social, cultural, economic, and political—were and are shaped by it. Thomas Ewbank, a commissioner of patents in the mid–nineteenth century, pondered technology in reports widely publicized through Horace Greeley's New York *Tribune.* Ewbank, an English immigrant and hydraulic engineer, noted in his first report "a singular vagary" in the human mind, the delusion that the more abstract the study the nearer to the Great Spirit, "whereas God is the greatest of workers—the chief of artificers." Ewbank also emphasized the democratic implications of the machine which, he said, would bring equal opportunity within reach by reducing the costs of both necessities and luxuries.

Invention often brought about completely new enterprises, the steamboat and the railroad being the most spectacular, without which the pace of development would have been slowed immeasurably. Most basic inventions were imports from Europe. Preservation of food by canning, for instance, was unknown before the early nineteenth century when Americans learned of a new French discovery that food stayed fresh when cooked in airtight containers. By 1820 major canneries were in existence in Boston and New York. At the end of the 1830s glass containers were giving way to the "tin can" (tin-plated steel) brought in from England, and eventually used to market Gail Borden's new invention—a process for condensed milk. Among the other outstanding American originals were Cyrus Hall McCormick of Virginia and Obed Hussey of Massachusetts, who separately invented practical reapers for grain at about the same time, a development as significant to the Northwest as the cotton gin was to the South. Hussey got a patent in 1833, McCormick in 1834. Competition between the two brought a rapid growth in the industry, but McCormick finally emerged on top because he had the foresight in 1847 to put his main plant at Chicago near the emerging wheat belt and the wit to accept improvements more quickly than Hussey.

A spate of inventions in the 1840s foretokened future changes

"In this Field, July 25, 1831, will be Tried a new Patent Grain Cutter, worked by horsepower, invented by C. H. McCormick." [The Science Museum, London]

in American life. In 1844 Charles Goodyear patented a process for vulcanizing rubber. In the same year the first intercity telegraph message was transmitted from Baltimore to Washington on the device Morse had invented back in 1832. The telegraph was slow to catch on at first, but seventeen years after that demonstration, with the completion of connections to San Francisco, an entire continent had been wired for instant communications. In 1846 Elias Howe invented the sewing machine, soon improved by Allen B. Wilson and Isaac Merritt Singer. The sewing machine, incidentally, was one invention that slowed the progress of the factory. Since it was adapted to use in the home, it gave the "putting-out" system a new lease on life in the clothing industry.

Examples can do no more than hint at the magnitude of change in technology and manufacturing. A suggestive if flawed measure of this change was the growing number of patents issued. During the first twenty-one years of the Patent Office, 1790–1811, the number issued averaged only 77 per year; from 1820 to 1830 the average was up to 535; during the 1840s it was 646; and during the 1850s the number suddenly quadrupled to an average of 2,525 per year.

THE LOWELL SYSTEM   Before the 1850s the factory still had not become typical of American industry. Handicraft and domestic production (putting-out) remained common. In many industries they stayed for decades the chief agencies of growth. Hatmaking in Danbury, Connecticut, and shoemaking in eastern Massachusetts, for instance, grew mainly by the multiplication of small shops and their gradual enlargement. Not until the 1850s did either begin to adopt power-driven machinery, usually a distinctive feature of the factory system.

The factory system sprang full-blown upon the American scene at Waltham, Massachusetts, in 1813, in the plant of the Boston Manufacturing Company. In 1822 its promoters, the Boston Associates, developed a new center at a village, renamed Lowell, where the Merrimack River fell thirty-five feet. At this "Manchester of America" the Merrimack Manufacturing Company developed a new plant similar to the Waltham mill. Another sprang up in 1823 at Chicopee and before 1850 textile mills appeared at many other places in Massachusetts, New Hampshire, and Maine. By 1850, as good waterpower locations were occupied, steam power was becoming common in textile manufacture.

Companies organized on the Waltham plan produced by 1850 a fifth of the nation's total output of cotton cloth. The chief features of this plan were large capital investment, the concentration of all processes in one plant under unified management, and specialization in a relatively coarse cloth requiring minimum skill by the workers. In the public mind, however, the system then and afterward was associated above all with the recruitment of young women from New England farms who lived in dormitories while they worked in the mills. The system offered reassurance to parents by providing strait-laced discipline supervised by respectable housemothers, regular curfews, and compulsory church attendance. Many women were drawn by the chance to escape the routine of farm life and to earn money which might be used to help the family or improve their own circumstances. Despite their twelve-hour day and seventy-hour week some of them found the time and energy to form study groups, publish a literary magazine, and attend lectures by Ralph Waldo Emerson and other luminaries of the era. Foreign travelers were almost universally charmed by the arrangement. It was hardly an idyllic existence, but few if any of the young women saw their work as a lifetime career. It was, rather, at worst a temporary burden, at best a preparation for life or an exciting interlude before settling into the routine of domesticity.

It was but an interlude in the history of American labor too. The "Lowell girls" drew attention less because they were typical than because they were special. An increasingly common pattern for industry was the family system, sometimes called the Rhode

*A label for cloth "made and printed by the Merrimack Manufacturing Co., Lowell, Mass."
Women such as those at left typically worked twelve-hour days, seventy-hour weeks. [Merrimack Valley Textile Museum]*

Island or Fall River system, which prevailed in textile manufactures outside of northern New England. Factories that relied on waterpower often rose in unpopulated areas, and part of their construction included tenements or mill villages. Whole families might be hired, the men for heavy labor, the women and children for the lighter work. The system promoted paternalism. Employers dominated the life of the mill villages, often setting rules of good behavior. Wages under the system are hard to establish, for employers often paid in goods from the company store. The hours of labor often ran from sunup to sunset, and longer in winter—a sixty-eight- to seventy-two-hour week. Such hours were common on the farms of the time, but in factories the work was more intense and offered no seasonal let-up. The labor of children, common on the farm, excited little censure from communities still close to the soil. A common opinion at the time regarded the provision of gainful employment for the women and children of the lower orders as a community benefit.

CORPORATIONS AND INDUSTRY In manufacturing the corporate form of organization caught on slowly. Manufacturing firms usually took the form of individual proprietorships, family enterprises, or partnerships. The success of the Boston Associates at Waltham and Lowell, and the growth of larger units, particularly in textiles, brought the corporate device into greater use. But until 1860 most manufacturing was carried on by unincorporated enterprises.

The corporate organization was more common for banking, turnpike, canal, and railroad companies, since many then believed that the form should be reserved for such quasi-public and quasi-monopolistic functions. The irregular practices of "wildcat" banks gave corporations a bad name throughout the period. Corporations were regarded with suspicion as the beneficiaries of special privileges, as threats to individual enterprises. "The very object of the act of incorporation is to produce inequality, either in rights, or in the division of property," the lawyer-economist Daniel Raymond wrote in 1820. "*Prima facie,* therefore, all money corporations, are detrimental to national health. They are always for the benefit of the rich, and never for the poor." It would be many years before corporations came to be widely regarded as agencies of free enterprise.

Banks of the time supplied mainly short-term commercial loans and long-term secured loans, but even before 1815 some of them had become active as investment banks—that is, they would take government or private securities in wholesale lots and put them on the market. The New York Stock Exchange, started in 1817, soon became the chief exchange for these securities, and the Boston Stock Exchange was the one on which manufacturing securities were traded before the Civil War. Most of the capital that financed new factories through the purchase of securities came from profits made earlier in commerce. New England's head start in commerce fueled its head start in factories. Foreign investments were important in building the canals and railroads, but contributed little to manufacturing. The same was true of investments by the states.

As late as 1860 the United States was still preponderantly rural and agricultural. Industry was heavily concentrated in the Northeast. In southern New England, especially its coastal regions, and along the Hudson and Delaware Rivers, the concentration of industry rivaled that in any of the industrialized parts of Britain and exceeded that in most parts of the European continent.

In the 1860 Census of Manufactures cotton textiles stood ahead of all other categories in rank order of value added (value of product minus value of raw material). Recognizing the primacy of the fiber in exports as well, the census report began with these words: "The growth of the culture and manufacture of cotton in the United States constitutes the most striking feature of the industrial history of the last fifty years." In all, American industry in 1860 employed 1,311,000 workers in 140,000 establishments; with a capital investment of just over $1 billion, output amounted to $1.886 billion (up significantly from 1810's

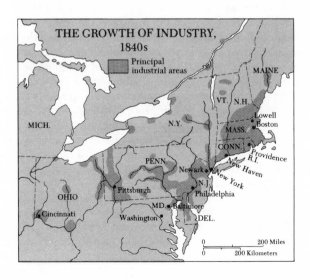

THE GROWTH OF INDUSTRY, 1840s

Principal industrial areas

MAINE

VT. N.H.

MICH.

N.Y.

Lowell
Boston

MASS.

CONN.

Providence
R.I.

PENN.

New Haven

Newark
New York

N.J.

Pittsburgh

Philadelphia

OHIO

MD. Baltimore

Cincinnati

Washington

DEL.

0   200 Miles

0   200 Kilometers

total output of $149 million), of which the value added by manufacturing was $854 million.

INDUSTRY AND CITIES The rapid growth of commerce and industry impelled a rapid growth of cities. Using the census definition of "urban" as places with 8,000 inhabitants or more, the proportion of urban population grew from 3.3 percent in 1790 to 16.1 percent in 1860. Modern cities have served three major economic functions: they have been centers of trade and distribution, centers of manufacturing, and centers of administration. Until near the mid–nineteenth century American cities grew mainly in response to the circumstances of transportation and trade. Because of their strategic locations the four great Atlantic seaports of New York, Philadelphia, Baltimore, and Boston held throughout the antebellum period the relative positions of leadership they had gained by the end of the Revolution. New Orleans became the nation's fifth-largest city from the time of the Louisiana Purchase. Its focus on cotton exports, to the neglect of imports, however, caused it eventually to lag behind its eastern competitors. New York outpaced both its competitors and the nation as a whole in its population growth. By 1860 it was the first American city to reach the size of more than a million, largely because of its superior harbor and its unique access to commerce.

Pittsburgh, at the head of the Ohio, was already a center of iron production by 1800, and Cincinnati, at the mouth of the Little Miami, soon surpassed all other centers of meatpacking, with pork a specialty. Louisville, because it stood at the falls of the Ohio, became an important stop for trade and remained so after the short Louisville and Portland Canal bypassed the falls in 1830. On the Great Lakes the leading cities also stood at important breaking points in water transportation: Buffalo, Cleveland, Detroit, Chicago, and Milwaukee. Chicago was especially well located to become a hub of both water and rail transportation on into the trans-Mississippi West. During the 1830s St. Louis tripled in size mainly because most of the trans-Mississippi fur trade was funneled down the Missouri River. By 1860 St. Louis and Chicago were positioned to challenge Boston and Baltimore for third and fourth places.

Before 1840 commerce dominated the activities of major cities, but early industry often created new concentrations of population at places convenient to waterpower or raw materials. During the 1840s and 1850s, however, the stationary steam engine and declining transportation costs more and more offset the

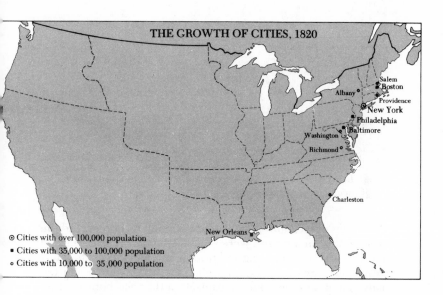

THE GROWTH OF CITIES, 1820

Salem
Boston
Albany
Providence
New York
Philadelphia
Washington
Baltimore
Richmond

Charleston

New Orleans

⊙ Cities with over 100,000 population
▪ Cities with 35,000 to 100,000 population
○ Cities with 10,000 to 35,000 population

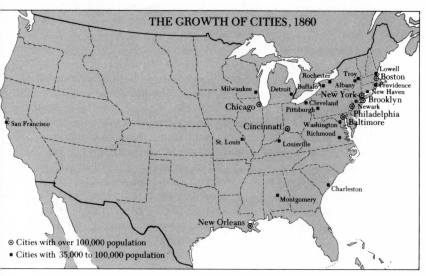

THE GROWTH OF CITIES, 1860

Lowell
Boston
Rochester
Troy
Providence
Buffalo
Albany
New Haven
Milwaukee
Detroit
New York
Brooklyn
Cleveland
Newark
Chicago
Pittsburgh
Philadelphia
Cincinnati
Washington
Baltimore
Richmond
St. Louis
Louisville
San Francisco

Charleston

Montgomery

New Orleans

⊙ Cities with over 100,000 population
▪ Cities with 35,000 to 100,000 population

St. Louis in the 1850s, looking east toward the Mississippi River.
[Chicago Historical Society]

advantages of locations near waterpower and resources, and the attractions of older cities were enhanced: pools of experienced labor, capital, warehousing and trading services, access to information, the savings of bulk purchasing and handling, and the many amenities of city life. Urbanization thus was both a consequence of economic growth and a positive force in its promotion.

IMMIGRATION

For all the new economic growth, one basic condition of American life carried over beyond the mid–nineteenth century: land remained plentiful and relatively cheap, while labor was scarce and relatively dear. A decline in the birth rate coinciding with the onset of industry and urbanization influenced this condition. The United States became a strong magnet to immigrants, offering them chances to take up farms in the country or jobs in the cities. Glowing reports from early arrivals who made good reinforced romantic views of America opportunity and freedom. "Tell Miriam," one immigrant wrote back, "there is no sending children to bed without supper, or husbands to work without dinner in their bags." A German immigrant in Missouri wrote home applauding the "absence of overbearing soldier, haughty clergymen, and inquisitive tax collectors."

During the forty years from the outbreak of the Revolution until the end of the War of 1812 immigration had slowed to a trickle. The wars of the French Revolution and Napoleon restricted travel until 1815. Within a few years, however, packet

lines had begun to cross the north Atlantic, and competing shippers who needed westbound payloads kept the transatlantic
fares as low as $30 per person. One informed estimate had it that
from 1783 to 1819 total arrivals numbered about 250,000, or
something under 7,000 per year. In 1820, when the govenment
began to keep records, the number was 8,385. Thereafter the
pace followed just behind the growth of business. For two decades the numbers rose steadily: 10,199 in 1825, 23,322 in 1830,
84,066 in 1840. After 1845 the tempo picked up rapidly. During
the 1830s total arrivals had numbered fewer than 600,000. In
the 1840s almost three times as many, or 1.7 million, immi-
grated, and during the 1850s 2.6 million more. In 1850 the annual count went above 300,000 for the first time, then rose
annually to a peak of 427,833 in 1854, a figure not equaled before 1880. The years from 1845 to 1854 saw the greatest proportionate influx of immigrants in American history, 2.4 million,
or about 14.5 percent of the total population in 1845.

THE IRISH   In 1860 more than one of every eight persons in
America was foreign born. The largest groups among them, by
far, were 1.6 million Irish, 1.3 million Germans, and 588,000
British (mostly English). The Catholic Irish were the most conspicuous new element in the population. Ireland had long
seethed with discontent at British rule, British landlords, and
British taxes to support the Church of England. What sent the
Irish fleeing their homeland was a chronic depression that set in
with the nineteenth century. By the 1830s their numbers in
America were growing annually, and after an epidemic of potato
rot in 1845 brought famine, the flow of Irish immigrants rose to a
flood. The Irish disaster coincided with the end of depression
and a rising tempo of business in the United States. In 1847 Irish
arrivals numbered above 100,000 and stayed above that level for
eight years, reaching a peak of 221,000 in 1851.

The Irish were mostly tenant farmers, but their experience
had left them little taste for farm work and little money to travel
or buy land. Great numbers of them hired on with construction
gangs building the canal and railways—about 3,000 set to work
on the Erie Canal as early as 1818. Few immigrants of any origin
found their way into the South, but the Irish who did sometimes
found work with planters who preferred not to risk valuable
slaves at hazardous tasks. For the most part, however, the Irish
congregated in the eastern cities, in or near their port of entry.
Generally they worked as domestic servants or unskilled laborers, and clustered together in shanty-towns and around

Catholic churches, both of which became familiar features of the urban scene.

Experienced at organized resistance to rent and tax collectors, the Irish formed blocs of voters and found their way into American politics more quickly than any other immigrant group. Drawn mainly to the party of Jefferson and Jackson, "the party of the common man," they set a pattern of identification with the Democrats that other ethnic groups by and large followed. They also stimulated the growth of the Catholic church with their numbers and their more aggressive spirit. Years of persecution had instilled in them a fierce loyalty to the doctrines of the church.

THE GERMANS   When the new wave of German migration got under way in the 1830s there were still large enclaves of Germans in Pennsylvania and Ohio who preserved their language and cultures, and in the Old World style, clustered in agricultural villages. The new German migration peaked just a few years after the Irish, in 1854 when 215,000 arrived. Unlike the Irish, the Germans included fair numbers of independent farmers, skilled workers, and shopkeepers who arrived with some means to get themselves established in skilled labor or on the land. Three major centers of new settlement developed in Missouri and southwestern Illinois (around St. Louis), in Texas (near San Antonio), and in Wisconsin (especially around Milwaukee). The German migrants also included a large number of professional people, some of them refugees from the failure of liberal revolution in Germany, among whom was Carl Schurz, later senator from Missouri. The larger German communities developed traditions of good food, beer, and music along with German *Turnvereine* (gymnastic societies), sharpshooter clubs, fire engine companies, and kindergartens (introduced by Mrs. Carl Schurz).

A Turnverein *in Cincinnati (1850). [Cincinnati Historical Society]*

THE BRITISH, SCANDINAVIANS, AND CHINESE   Among the British immigrants too were large numbers of professionals, independent
farmers, and skilled workers. Some British workers, such as Samuel Slater, helped transmit the technology of British factories
into the United States. Two other groups that began to arrive in
some number during the 1840s and 1850s were but the vanguard of greater numbers to come later. Annual arrivals from
Scandinavia did not exceed 1,000 until 1843, but by 1860 a total
of 72,600 Scandinavians lived in America. The Norwegians and
Swedes gravitated to Wisconsin and Minnesota where the climate and woodlands reminded them of home. By the 1850s the
sudden development of California was bringing in Chinese who,
like the Irish in the East, did the heavy work of construction. Infinitesimal in numbers until 1854, the Chinese in America numbered 35,500 by 1860.

NATIVISM   America had always been a land of immigrants, but the
welcome accorded them had often been less than cordial. For
many natives these waves of strangers in the land posed a threat
of unknown tongues and mysterious ways. The greatest single
group of newcomers were the Irish, who were mostly Catholic.
The Germans too included many Catholics. This massive increase naturally aroused antagonisms which were rooted in the
Protestant tradition of hostility to "popery" and aggravated by
job competition in the cities where immigrants gathered. A mili-
tant Protestantism growing out of revivals in the early nineteenth
century heated up the climate of opinion. There were fears of
radicalism among the Germans and of voting blocs among the
Irish, but above all hovered the menace of unfamiliar religious
practices. Catholic authoritarianism was widely perceived as a
threat to hard-won liberties, religious and political. The convenience of this, for political adventurers and fanatics, was that the
Catholic church in most places remained small enough to be attacked with impunity.

In the 1830s nativism was conspicuously on the rise. Pointing
to the Catholic missions sponsored by European groups, and to
the pope's trappings of monarchy in Italy, overheated patriots
envisaged conspiracy and subversion in America. Samuel F. B.
Morse, already at work on his telegraph, took time out from his
painting and inventing to write two books demonstrating his
theory that Catholicism in America was a plot of foreign monarchs to undermine American liberty before its revolutionary
message affected their own people. In 1836 he ran for mayor of
New York on a Native American ticket, and his books went
through numerous editions. But the literature of conspiracy

could scarcely compete with a profitable trade in books which, in the guise of attacking evil, exploited salacious fantasies of sex in Catholic nunneries.

At times this hostility rekindled the spirit of the wars of religion. In 1834 a series of anti-Catholic sermons by Lyman Beecher and others aroused feelings to the extent that a mob attacked and burned the Ursuline Convent in Charlestown, Massachusetts. In 1844 armed clashes between Protestants and Catholics in Philadelphia ended with about 20 killed and 100 injured. Sporadically, the nativist spirit took organized form in groups that proved their patriotism by hating foreigners and Catholics.

As early as 1837 a Native American Association was formed at Washington, but the most significant such group was the Order of the Star Spangled Banner, founded in New York in 1849. Within a few years this group had grown into a formidable third party. In July 1854 delegates from thirteen states gathered to form the American party, which had the trappings of a secret fraternal order. Members pledged never to vote for any foreign-born or Catholic candidate. When asked about the organization, they were to say "I know nothing." In popular parlance the American party became the Know-Nothing party. For a season it

Americans Shall Rule America. *This 1856 sketch satirizes Baltimore nativists out to bully German and Irish immigrants.*
[Maryland Historical Society]

seemed that the American party might achieve major-party status. In state and local campaigns during 1854 the Know-Nothings carried one election after another. In November they swept the Massachusetts legislature, winning all but two seats in the lower house. That fall they elected more than forty congressmen. For a while they threatened to control New England, New York, and Maryland, and showed strength elsewhere, but the movement collapsed when slavery became the focal issue of the 1850s.

The Know-Nothings demanded the exclusion of immigrants and Catholics from public office and extension of the period for naturalization from five to twenty-one years, but the party never gathered the political strength to effect such legislation. Nor did Congress act during the period to restrict immigration in any way. The first federal law on immigration, passed in 1819, enacted only safety and health regulations regarding supplies and the number of passengers on immigrant ships. This and subsequent acts designed to protect immigrants from overcrowding and unsanitary conditions were, however, poorly enforced.

IMMIGRANT LABOR   After 1840 immigration became critical to the dynamics of growth. The increase in population it brought contributed to economic growth and demand, whether the newcomer took up land or went into the city. The readiness of immigrant and native alike to go where jobs beckoned was important to rapid growth. By meeting the demand for cheap, unskilled labor immigrants made a twofold contribution. They moved into jobs vacated or bypassed by those who went into the factories; they themselves made up a pool of labor from which in time factory workers were drawn.

In New England the large numbers of Irish workers, accustomed to hard treatment, spelled the end of the "Lowell girls." By 1860 immigrants made up more than half the labor force in New England mills. Even so, their price was generally higher than that of the women and children who worked to supplement family incomes, and the flood of immigration never rose fast enough to stop the long-term rise in wages. So factory labor continued to draw people from the countryside. Work in the cities offered higher real wages than work on the farm, which kept manufacturers alert for ways to cut their labor costs by improving machines. The cost of labor also put a premium on mass production of low-priced goods for a mass market. Artisans who emphasized quality and craftsmanship for a custom trade found it hard to meet such competitive conditions. Many artisans in fact found that their skills were going out of style. Some took work as craftsmen in factories, while others went into small-scale manufacturing or shopkeeping, and some bought homesteads to practice their skills in the West.

ORGANIZED LABOR

EARLY UNIONS Few workers of the period belonged to unions, but in the 1820s and 1830s a growing fear that they were losing status led artisans of the major cities into intense activity in labor politics and unions. As early as the colonial period craftsmen had formed fraternal and mutual benefit societies, much like the medieval guilds, through which they regulated a system for training apprentices. These organizations continued to flourish well into the national period. After the Revolution, however, organizations of journeymen carpenters, masons, shipfitters, tailors, printers, and cordwainers (as shoemakers were called) became concerned with wages, hours, and working conditions and began to back up their demands with such devices as the strike and the closed shop. These organizations were local, often largely social in purpose, and frequently lasted only for the duration of the dispute. The longest-lived was Philadelphia's Federated Society of Journeymen Cordwainers, which flourished from 1794 to 1806.

Early labor unions faced serious legal obstacles. Unions were prosecuted as unlawful conspiracies. In 1806, for instance, Philadelphia shoemakers were found "guilty of a combination to raise their wages." The decision broke the union. Such precedents were used for many years to hamstring labor organizations until the Massachusetts Supreme Court made a landmark ruling in the case of *Commonwealth v. Hunt* (1842). In this case Chief Justice Shaw ruled that forming a trade union was not in itself illegal nor was a demand that employers hire only members of the union.

Until the 1820s labor organizations took the form of local trade unions, confined to one city and one craft. During the ten years from 1827 to 1837 organization on a larger scale began to take hold. Philadelphia, in 1827, had the first city central, formed after the carpenters had lost a strike for the ten-hour day. The Mechanics' Union of Trade Associations included carpenters, shoemakers, bricklayers, glaziers, and other groups associated for the purpose of pooling resources. In the mid-1830s still wider organizations were attempted. In 1834 the National Trades' Union was set up in the effort to federate the city societies. At the same time national craft unions were established by the shoemakers, printers, combmakers, carpenters, and hand-

*Early labor unions were hampered
by legal obstacles. These boot and
shoemakers were found guilty of a
"conspiracy to raise their wages."
[New York Public Library]*

loom weavers, but all the national groups and most of the local
ones vanished in the economic collapse of 1837.

LABOR POLITICS   With the removal of property qualifications for
voting nearly everywhere, labor politics flourished briefly. In
this, as in other respects, Philadelphia was in the forefront. A
Working Men's party, formed there in 1828, gained the balance
of power in the city council that fall. This success inspired other
Working Men's parties in New York, Boston, and about fifteen
states. In 1829 the New York party elected the head of the carpenters' union to the state legislature. The Working Men's parties were broad reformist groups devoted to the interests of
labor. But they admitted to their ranks many who were not
workers by any strict definition, and their leaders were mainly
reformers and small businessmen. The labor parties faded
quickly for a variety of reasons: the inexperience of labor politicians, which left the parties prey to manipulation by political
professionals; the fact that some of their causes were espoused
also by the major parties; and their vulnerability to attack on
grounds of extreme radicalism or dilettantism. Additionally, they
often splintered into warring factions, limiting their effectiveness.

Once the parties had faded, however, many of their supporters found their way into a radical wing of the Jacksonian

Democrats. This wing became the Equal Rights party and in 1835 acquired the name "Locofocos" when their opponents from New York City's regular Democratic organization, Tammany Hall, turned off the gas lights at their meeting and the Equal Rights supporters produced candles, lighting them with the new friction matches known as Locofocos. The Locofocos soon faded as a separate group, but endured as a radical faction within the Democrat party.

While the labor parties elected few candidates they did succeed in drawing notice to their demands, many of which attracted the support of middle-class reformers. Above all they carried on an agitation for free public education and the abolition of imprisonment for debt, causes that won widespread popular support. The labor parties and unions actively promoted the ten-hour day. In 1836 President Jackson established the ten-hour day at the Philadelphia Navy Yard in response to a strike, and in 1840 President Van Buren extended the limit to all government offices and projects. In private jobs the ten-hour day became increasingly common, although by no means universal, before 1860. Other reforms put forward by the workingman's parties included mechanics' lien laws, to protect workers against nonpayment of wages; reform of a militia system which allowed the rich to escape service with fines but forced the poor to face jail terms; the abolition of "licensed monopolies," especially banks; measures to ensure hard money and to protect workers against inflated banknote currency; measures to restrict competition from prison labor; and the abolition of child labor.

LABOR AND REFORM   After the Panic of 1837 the nascent labor movement went into decline, and during the 1840s the focus of its radical spirit turned toward the promotion of cooperative societies. During the 1830s there had been sporadic efforts to provide self-employment through producers' cooperatives, but the movement began to catch on after the iron molders of Cincinnati set up a successful shop in 1848. Soon the tailors of Boston had a cooperative workshop which employed thirty to forty men. New York was an especially strong center, with cooperatives among tailors, shirtmakers, bakers, shoemakers, and carpenters. Consumer cooperatives became much more vigorous and involved more people. The New England Protective Union, formed in 1845, organized a central purchasing agency for co-op stores and by 1852 was buying more than $1 million worth of goods while affiliated stores were doing in excess of $4 million in trade. Both the producers' and consumers' movement benefited from the support of Associationists, who saw it as a possible first step on the road to utopia, but more people probably were drawn to the movement for practical reasons: to reduce their dependence on employers or to reduce the cost of purchases. After peaking in the early 1850s, however, cooperatives went into decline. The high mobility of Americans and the heterogenous character of the population as immigration increased created unfavorable conditions. Insufficient capital and weak, inexperienced management also plagued the cooperative movement.

THE REVIVAL OF UNIONS   The high visibility of reform efforts, however, should not obscure the continuing activity of unions, which began to revive with improved business conditions in the early 1840s. Still, the unions remained local, weak, and given to sporadic activity. Often they came and went with a single strike. The greatest single labor dispute before the Civil War came on February 22, 1860, when shoemakers at Lynn and Natick, Massachusetts, walked out for higher wages. Before the strike ended it had spread through New England, involving perhaps twenty-five towns and 20,000 workers. It stood out also as a strike the workers won. Most of the employers agreed to wage increases and some also agreed to recognize the union as a bargaining agent.

This reflected the growing tendency of workers to view their unions as permanent. Workers emphasized union recognition and regular collective bargaining agreements. They shared a growing sense of solidarity. In 1852 the National Typographical Union revived the effort to organize skilled crafts on a national scale. Others followed: the Hat Finishers National Association in 1854, the Journeymen Stone Cutters Association in 1855, the National Union of Iron Molders in 1859. By 1860 about twenty such organizations had appeared, although none was strong enough as yet to do much more than hold national conventions and pass resolutions.

JACKSONIAN INEQUALITY

During the years before the Civil War the United States had begun to develop a distinctive working class, most conspicuously in the factories and the ranks of common labor, often including many Irish or German immigrants. More and more craftsmen, aware that they were likely to remain wage earners, became receptive to permanent unions. But the American legend of "rags to riches," the image of the self-made man, was a durable myth. "In America," Tocqueville wrote, "most of the rich men were formerly poor." Speaking to the Senate on the tariff in 1832, Henry Clay said that almost all the successful factory owners he knew were "enterprising self-made men, who have whatever wealth they possess by patient and diligent labor." The legend had just enough basis in fact to lend credence. John Jacob Astor, the wealthiest man in America, worth more than $20 million at his death in 1848, came of humble if not exactly destitute origins. Son of a minor official in the Duchy of Baden, he arrived in 1784 with little or nothing, made a fortune first on the western fur trade, then parlayed that into a large fortune in New York real estate. But his and similar cases were more exceptional than common.

Researches by Edward Pessen on the rich in major eastern cities show that while men of moderate means could sometimes run their inheritances into fortunes by good management and prudent speculation, those who started with the handicap of poverty and ignorance seldom made it to the top. In 1828 the top 1 percent of New York's families (owning $34,000 or more) held 40 percent of the wealth, and the top 4 percent held 76 percent. Similar circumstances prevailed in Philadelphia, Boston, and other cities.

A supreme irony of the times was that the "age of the common man," "the age of Jacksonian Democracy," seems actually to have been an age of increasing social rigidity. Years before, the colonists had brought to America conceptions of a social hierarchy which during the eighteenth century corresponded imperfectly with the developing reality. In the late eighteenth century, slavery aside, American society probably approached equality more closely than any population its size anywhere else in the world. During the last half of the 1700s, the historian Jackson T. Main has argued, social mobility was higher than either before or since. By the time popular egalitarianism caught up with reality, reality was moving back toward greater inequality.

Why this happened is difficult to say, except that the boundless wealth of the untapped frontier narrowed as the land was occupied and claims on various opportunities were staked out. Such developments took place in New England towns even before the end of the seventeenth century. But despite growing social distinctions, it seems likely that the white population of America, at least, was better off than the general run of European peoples. New frontiers, geographical and technological, raised the level of material well-being much as a rising tide raises boats of all sizes.

FURTHER READING

On economic developments in the nation's early decades, see W. Elliott Brownlee's *Dynamics of Ascent: A History of the American Economy* (1979), which provides the most current overview. Older, yet still valuable, are Stuart Bruchey's *The Roots of American Economic Growth, 1607–1861* (1965),° Douglass C. North's *The Economic Growth of the United States, 1790–1860* (1961),° and Thomas C. Cochran and William Miller's *The Age of Enterprise: A Social History of Industrial America* (1961).°

The resilient classic on transportation as a basis for growth is George R. Taylor's *The Transportation Revolution, 1815–1861* (1951).° Specialized accounts of water travel and trade are Erik F. Haites, James Mak, and Gary M. Walter's *Western Rivers Transportation: The Era of Early Internal Improvements* (1975), Walter Havighurst's *Voices on the River: The Story of the Mississippi Water Ways* (1964), Ronald Shaw's *Erie Water West: A History of the Erie Canal* (1966), and Carter Goodrich's *Government Promotion of Canals and Railroads, 1800–1890* (1960). Scholarly works concentrating on railroads include John F. Stover's *Iron Road to the West: American Railroads in the 1850s* (1978), Albert Fishlow's *American Railroads and the Transformation of the American Economy* (1965), and Robert W. Fogel's *Railroads and American Economic Growth* (1964). Phillip D. Jordan's *The National Road* (1948) treats one of the first government transportation projects. For background on the merchant marine, consult Samuel E. Morison's *Maritime History of Massachusetts, 1789–1860* (1921), and A. H. Clark's *The Clipper Ship Era* (1910).

Concurrent with transportation innovations was industrial growth. Thomas C. Cochran's *Frontiers of Change: Early Industrialism in America* (1981)° is a recent survey. The business side of industrial growth can be studied in the surveys cited above, as well as in Elisha P. Douglass's *The Coming of Age of American Business* (1971) and Edwin M. Dodd's *American Business Corporations until 1860* (1954). The impact of technology is traced in David J. Jeremy's *Transatlantic Industrial Revolution: The Diffusion of Textile Technologies between Britain and America* (1981), Nathan Rosenberg's *Technology and American Economic Growth* (1972),° H. J. Habakkuk's *American and British Technology in the Nineteenth Century* (1962),° and Merritt R. Smith's *Harper's Ferry Armory and the New Technology: The Challenge of Change* (1977).

What Americans thought about the changes wrought by technology and industry is surveyed in Joseph Dorfman's *The Economic Mind in American Civilization* (vols. 1–4, 1946–1959). Richard D. Brown's *Modernization: The Transformation of American Life, 1600–1865* (1976),° assesses the impact of technology on living patterns. How American values were affected by the new industrial system is assessed in John F. Kasson's

°These books are available in paperback editions.

Civilizing the Machine: Technology and Republican Values in America, 1776–1900 (1977),° and Leo Marx's *The Machine in the Garden: Technology and the Pastoral Ideal in America* (1964).° Roger Burlingame's *The March of the Iron Men* (1960) gauges the role of technology in American social history, and Paul Johnson's *A Shopkeepers Millennium: Society and Revivals in Rochester, New York, 1815–1837* (1978),° studies the role religion played in the emerging industrial order.

The attitude of the worker during this time of transition is surveyed in Joseph G. Rayback's *A History of American Labor* (1966).° More narrative in treatment are John R. Commons's *A History of Labour in the United States* (vol. 1, 1918) and Norman Ware's *The Industrial Worker, 1840–1860* (1924). Edward E. Pessen's *Most Uncommon Jacksonians: The Radical Leaders of the Early Labor Movement* (1967)° concentrates on political reactions. Detailed case studies of working communities include Anthony F. C. Wallace's *Rockdale: The Growth of an American Village in the Early Industrial Revolution* (1978),° Thomas Dublin's *Women at Work: The Transformation of Work and Community in Lowell, Massachusetts, 1826–1860* (1979),° Alan Dawley's *Class and Community: The Industrial Revolution in Lynn* (1976),° and Bruce Laurie's *The Working People of Philadelphia, 1800–1850* (1980).

For introductions to the development of urbanization, see Sam Bass Warner, Jr.'s *The Urban Wilderness* (1972),° Richard C. Wade's *The Urban Frontier* (1964), and Howard P. Chudacoff's *The Evolution of American Urban Society* (1981). A recent valuable case study is Edward K. Spann's *The New Metropolis: New York, 1840–1857* (1981). Studies of the origins of immigration include Oscar Handlin's *The Uprooted* (1951),° Phillip Taylor's *The Distant Magnet: European Emigration to the USA* (1971),° Carl Wittke's *The Irish in America* (1956), Robert Ernest's *Immigrant Life in New York City, 1825–1863* (1949), and Jay P. Dolan's *The Immigrant Church: New York's Irish and German Catholics, 1815–1865* (1975). Ray Billington's *The Protestant Crusade, 1800–1860* (1938), examines nativist sentiments toward the immigrants. Walter E. Hugins's *Jacksonian Democracy and the Working Class* (1960) surveys the Working-Men's party and Locofocos of New York City.

13 ✍

AN AMERICAN RENAISSANCE:
ROMANTICISM AND REFORM

RATIONAL RELIGION

The American novelist Nathaniel Hawthorne once lamented "the difficulty of writing a romance about a country where there is no shadow, no antiquity, no mystery, no picturesque and gloomy wrong. . . . Romance and poetry, ivy, lichens, and wall-flowers, need ruin to make them grow." Unlike nations of the Old World, rooted in shadow and mystery, in historic cultures and traditions, the United States had been rooted in the ideas of the Enlightenment. Those ideas, most vividly set forth in Jefferson's Declaration, had in turn a universal application. In the eyes of many if not most citizens, the "first new nation" had a mission to stand as an example to the world, much as John Winthrop's "city upon a hill" had once stood as an example to erring humanity. The concept of mission in fact still carried spiritual overtones, for the religious fervor quickened in the Great Awakening had reinforced the idea of national purpose. In turn the sense of high calling infused the national character with an element of perfectionism—and an element of impatience when reality fell short of expectations. The combination brought major reforms and advances in human rights. It also brought disappointments that could fester into cynicism and alienation.

DEISM The currents of the Enlightenment and the Great Awakening, now mingling, now parting, flowed on into the nineteenth century. By the turn of the century both had worked changes in

the Calvinist orthodoxy of American religion. Many leaders of
the Revolutionary War era, like Jefferson and Franklin, became
deists, even while nominally attached to existent churches.
Deism, which arose in eighteenth-century Europe, simply carried the logic of Sir Isaac Newton's world machine to its logical
conclusion. The God of the deist, the Master Clockmaker in Voltaire's words, had planned the universe, built it, and then set it in
motion. But men, on their own, by the use of reason might grasp
the natural laws which govern the universe. Deism tended to be
a benevolent force. Thomas Paine in *The Age of Reason* (1794)
defined religious duties as "doing justice, loving mercy and en-
deavoring to make our fellow creatures happy," a message of
Quaker-like simplicity. But ever the controversialist, Tom Paine
felt obliged to assail the "superstition" of the Scriptures and the
existing churches—"human inventions set up to terrify and enslave mankind and monopolize power and profit." Orthodox
churchmen could hardly distinguish such doctrine from atheism.

The old Puritan churches around Boston ironically proved
most vulnerable to the logic of the Enlightenment. A strain of rationalism had run through Puritan belief all along in its stress on
the need for right reason to interpret the Scriptures. Boston's
progress from Puritanism to prosperity had persuaded many rising families that they were anything but sinners in the hands of
an angry God. Drawn toward less strenuous doctrines, some
went back to the traditional rites of the Episcopal church. More
of them simply dropped or qualified their adherence to Calvinism while remaining in the Congregational churches.

UNITARIANISM   By the end of the eighteenth century they were
drifting into Unitarianism, a belief which emphasized the oneness of God and put reason and conscience ahead of creeds and
confessions. One stale jest had it that Unitarians believed in the
fatherhood of God, the brotherhood of man, and the neighborhood of Boston. Boston was very much the center of the movement and it flourished chiefly within Congregational churches
which kept their standing in the established order until controversy began to smoke them out.

It began in 1805 with the election of a liberal clergyman,
Henry Ware, as Hollis Professor of Divinity at Harvard, followed
by the choice of four more liberal professors in as many years. In
protest against Unitarian Harvard, the Rev. Jedediah Morse, the
noted geographer, led a movement to establish Andover Theological Seminary as a center of orthodoxy. Thereafter more and
more liberal churches accepted the name of Unitarian.

William Ellery Channing of Boston's Federal Street Church emerged as the chief spokesman for the liberal position. "I am surer that my rational nature is from God," he said, "than that any book is an expression of his will." A "Conference of Liberal Ministers," formed in 1820, became in 1826 the American Unitarian Association with 125 churches (all but 5 of them in Massachusetts) including 20 of the 25 oldest Calvinist churches in the United States. That same year, when the Presbyterian minister Lyman Beecher moved to Boston, he lamented: "All the literary men of Massachusetts were Unitarian; all the trustees and professors of Harvard College were Unitarian, all the elite of wealth and fashion crowded Unitarian churches."

UNIVERSALISM A parallel movement, Universalism, attracted a different social stratum: workers and the more humble. In 1779 John Murray, who had come from England as a missionary for the new doctrine, founded the first Universalist church at Gloucester, Massachusetts. In 1794 a Universalist convention in Philadelphia organized the sect. Universalism held to a belief in the salvation of all men and women, while holding intact most Calvinist doctrines. God, they taught, was too merciful to condemn anyone to eternal punishment. True believers could escape altogether through Christ's atonement; the unregenerate would suffer in proportion to their sins, but eventually all souls would come into harmony with God. "Thus, the Unitarians and Universalists were in fundamental agreement," wrote one historian of religion, "the Universalists holding that God was too good to damn man; the Unitarians insisting that man was too good to be damned."

THE SECOND AWAKENING

For all the impact of rationalism, however, Americans remained a profoundly religious people. There was, Alexis de Tocqueville asserted, "no country in the world where the Christian religion retains a greater influence over the souls of men than in America." Around 1800 a revival of faith began to manifest itself. Soon it grew into a Second Awakening. An early exemplar of the movement, Timothy Dwight, became president of Yale College in 1795 and set about to purify a place which, in Lyman Beecher's words, had turned into "a hotbed of infidelity," where students openly discussed French radicalism, deism, and perhaps things even worse. Like his grandfather, Jonathan Edwards,

"Pope Timothy" had the gift of moving both mind and spirit, of reaching both the lettered and the unlettered. The result was a series of revivals that swept the student body and spread to all New England as well. "Wheresoever students were found," wrote a participant in the 1802 revival, "the reigning impression was, 'surely God is in this place.'"

After the founding in 1808, Jedediah Morse's Andover Seminary reinforced orthodoxy and the revival spirit so forcefully that its location came to be known as "Brimstone Hill." "Let us guard against the insidious encroachments of *innovation*—that evil and beguiling spirit which is now stalking to and fro in the earth, seeking whom it may devour." To avoid the fate of Harvard, Morse and his associates made professors give their assent to an Andover Creed of double-distilled Calvinism. The religious intensity and periodic revivals at Andover and Yale had their counterparts in many colleges for the next fifty years, since most were under the control of evangelical denominations. Hampden-Sydney College in Virginia had in fact got the jump on New England with a revival in 1787 which influenced many leaders of the awakening in the South.

REVIVALS ON THE FRONTIER   In its frontier phase the Second Awakening, like the first, generated great excitement and strange manifestations. It gave birth, moreover, to a new institution, the camp meeting, in which the fires of faith were repeatedly rekindled. Missionaries found ready audiences among lonely frontiersmen hungry for a sense of community. Among the

While Methodist preachers address the crowd at this camp meeting, a man in the foreground is overcome with religious ecstacy. [Library of Congress]

established sects, the Presbyterians were entrenched among the Scotch-Irish from Pennsylvania to Georgia. They gained further from the Plan of Union worked out in 1801 with the Congregationalists of Connecticut and later other states. Since the two groups agreed on doctrine and differed mainly on the form of church government, they were able to form unified congregations and call a minister from either church. The result through much of the Old Northwest was that New Englanders became Presbyterians by way of the "Presbygational" churches.

The Baptists had a simplicity of doctrine and organization which appealed to the common people of the frontier. Since each congregation was its own highest authority, a frontier congregation need appeal to no hierarchy before setting up shop and calling a minister or naming one of their own. Sometimes whole congregations moved across the mountains as a body. As Theodore Roosevelt described it in *The Winning of the West:* "Baptist preachers lived and worked exactly as their flocks. . . . they cleared the ground, split rails, planted corn, and raised hogs on equal terms with their parishioners."

But the Methodists may have had the most effective method of all, the circuit rider who sought out people in the most remote areas with the message of salvation as a gift free for the taking. The system began with Francis Asbury, the founder. "When he came to America," a biographer wrote, "he rented no house, he hired no lodgings, he made no arrangements to board anywhere, but simply set out on the Long Road, and was traveling forty-five years later when death caught up with him." By the 1840s the Methodists had grown into the largest Protestant church in the country, with over a million members.

The frontier phase of the Second Awakening got its start in Logan County, Kentucky, an area notorious as a Rogue's Harbor, a refuge of thieves and cutthroats. James McGready, a Presbyterian minister of Pennsylvania Scotch-Irish background, arrived there in 1796 after threats drove him out of the North Carolina Piedmont, where he was accused of running people distracted with his revivals. He had been influenced in his course by the Hampden-Sydney revival. Over the next few years he prepared a way for the Lord in the West. In 1800 a Methodist preacher named John McGee conducted a meeting in the neighborhood. So much excitement attended his preaching that other meetings were held near each of McGready's three churches and through the summer people came from far and wide, prepared to stay on the grounds for several days. Among those drawn to the Logan County, or Cumberland, Revival was Barton W. Stone, minister of two Presbyterian churches in Bourbon County. He soon began to preach the revival in his own churches and the result was the greatest of all camp meetings at Cane Ridge. During August 1801 the preachings drew great crowds variously estimated at from 10,000 to 25,000.

The Great Revival spread quickly through the West and into more settled regions back east. Camp meetings came to be held typically in late summer or fall, when crops could be laid-by temporarily. People came from far and wide, camping in wagons, tents, brush arbors or crude shacks. Mass excitement swept up even the most stable onlookers and the spirit moved participants to strange manifestations. Some went into cataleptic trances, others contracted the "jerks," laughed the "holy laugh," babbled in unknown tongues, danced like David before the Ark of God, or got down on all fours and barked like dogs to "tree the Devil." More sedate and prudent believers thought such rousements might be the work of the devil, out to discredit the true faith. But to dwell on the bizarre aspects of the camp meetings would be to distort an institution that offered social outlet to an isolated people, that brought a more settled community life through the churches that grew out of it, that spread a more democratic faith among the common people. Indeed with time camp meetings became much more sedate and dignified affairs.

THE "BURNED-OVER DISTRICT" But little wonder that regions swept by such fevers might be compared to forests devastated by fire. Western New York state all the way from Lake Ontario to the Adirondacks achieved the name of the "Burned-Over District" long before 1821, when a "mighty baptism of the Holy Ghost" overwhelmed a young lawyer in the town of Adams. The spirit went through him "in waves and waves of liquid love," Charles Grandison Finney wrote years later. The next day he announced a new profession: "I have a retainer from the Lord Jesus Christ to plead his case," he told a caller. In 1823 the St. Lawrence Presbytery ordained Finney and for the next decade he subjected the Burned-Over District to yet another scorching.

Finney went on to become the greatest single exemplar of revivalism and, some would argue, the very inventor of professional revivalism. The saving of souls did not have to wait for a miracle, he argued; it could come from careful planning. Nor did Finney shrink from comparing his methods to those of politicians who used advertising and showmanship to get attention. The revivalist planned carefully to arouse excitement, not for its own sake but to rivet attention on the Word. "New measures are necessary from time to time to awaken attention and bring the gospel to bear on the public mind." To those who challenged such use of emotion Finney had a frank answer: "The results justify my methods." Finney carried the methods of the frontier revival into the cities of the East and as far as Great Britain.

Untrained in theology, Finney read the Bible, he said, as he would a law book, and worked out his own theology of free will. His gospel combined faith and good works: one led to the other. "All sin consists in selfishness," he said, "and all holiness or virtue, in disinterested benevolence." Regeneration therefore was "a change from selfishness to benevolence, from having a supreme regard to one's own interest to an absorbing and controlling choice of the happiness and glory of God's Kingdom."

In 1835 Finney took the chair of theology in the new Oberlin College, founded by pious New Englanders in Ohio's Western Reserve. Later he served as its president. From the start Oberlin radiated a spirit of reform predicated on faith; it was the first college in America to admit either women or Negroes, and it was a hotbed of antislavery doctrine. Finney himself, however, held that men must be reformed from within, and cautioned against political action. In this, he held to a view which deeply influenced American social thought and action, a view which the historian John L. Thomas called romantic perfectionism: "Since social evils were simply individual acts of selfishness compounded, . . . it followed that . . . deep and lasting reform . . . meant an educational crusade based on the assumption that

Ohio's Oberlin College was the first in America to admit women or blacks. This graduating class is from the later nineteenth century. [Oberlin College Archives]

when a sufficient number of individual Americans had seen the light, they would automatically solve the country's social problems."

On the other hand the ardor aroused by revivals led to narrow sectarian bickerings, repeated schisms, and the phenomenon known as "come-outism" which further multiplied the sects—a phenomenon almost always noted by foreign travelers. James McGready's first revivals in Kentucky, for instance, created a tremendous demand for preachers which the Cumberland Presbytery met by ordaining men who lacked proper educational credentials. After a prolonged quarrel with the Kentucky Synod, the revivalists formed the Cumberland Presbyterian church to which McGready himself adhered before he returned to a more orthodox faith. Likewise, when the synod began to investigate two ministers connected with Barton W. Stone's Cane Ridge Revival, Stone and others pulled out in 1803 and adopted the name "Christian Church"—a name they claimed had no sectarian bias. Each congregation was independent and recognized no other authority than the Bible. A similar movement arose independently in western Pennsylvania in 1809 led by Thomas and Alexander Campbell. The Campbellites, like the Stonites, adopted the name "Christian" and the practice of baptism by immersion. In 1832 a movement started in Lexington, Kentucky, to unite these churches as the Disciples of Christ—a name that came to be used interchangeably with Christian church.

THE MORMONS   The Kentucky sects remained pretty much within the bounds of previous experience. The Burned-Over District, by contrast, gave rise to several new departures, of which the most important was the Church of Jesus Christ of Latter Day Saints, or the Mormons. The founder, Joseph Smith, Jr., born in Vermont, was the fourth child of wandering parents who finally settled in the village of Palmyra, New York. In 1820 young Smith (then fourteen) had a vision of "two Personages, whose brightness and glory defy all description." They identified themselves as the Savior and God the Father and cautioned him that all existing beliefs were false. About three years later the angel Moroni led Smith to the hill of Gumorah (its ancient name), where he found the Book of Mormon engraved on golden tablets in "reformed Egyptian." Later, with the aid of the magic stones Urim and Thummim, he rendered into English what he found to be a lost section of the Bible. This was the story of ancient Hebrews who had inhabited the New World and to whom Jesus had made an appearance.

After a slow start the church, founded April 6, 1830, gathered converts by the thousands. From the outset the Mormon saints upset the "gentiles" with their close pattern of community and their assurance of righteousness. In their search for a refuge from persecution the Mormons moved from New York to Kirtland, Ohio, then to several places in Missouri, and finally in 1839 to Nauvoo, Illinois, where they settled and grew in number for some five years. Through bloc voting they soon gathered political power in the Illinois state house, but eventually offended both major parties with their demands. In 1844 a crisis arose when dissidents accused Smith of justifying polygamy and published in the *Nauvoo Expositor* an exposé of polygamy in theory and practice. When Smith tried to suppress the paper, the upshot was a schism in the church, a gathering movement in the neighboring counties to attack Nauvoo, and the arrest of Smith and his brother Hyrum. On June 27, 1844, an anti-Mormon lynch mob stormed the feebly defended jail and took out and shot both Joseph and Hyrum Smith.

In Brigham Young, successor to Joseph Smith and president of the Quorum of the Twelve, the Mormons found a leader of uncommon qualities: strong-minded, intelligent, and decisive. After the murder of the founder, Young patched up an unsure peace with the neighbors by promising to plan an early exodus from Nauvoo, Illinois. Before that year was out Young had chosen the place, sight unseen, from promotional literature on the West. It lay near the Great Salt Lake, guarded by mountains to the east and north, deserts to the west and south, yet itself fed by mountain streams of melted snow—"Truly a bucolic region," in John Charles Frémont's words. Despite its isolation, moreover, it was close enough to the Oregon Trail for the saints to prosper by trade with passing gentiles.

Brigham Young trusted God, but believed in making preparations—no wandering in the wilderness for the Mormon Moses. As a result, the Mormon trek was better organized and less burdensome than most of the overland migrations of the time. Early in 1846 a small band crossed the frozen Mississippi into Iowa to set up the Camp of Israel, the first in a string of way stations along the route. By the fall of 1846 all 15,000 of the migrants had reached the prepared winter quarters on the Missouri River, where they paused until the first bands set out the next spring for the Promised Land. The first arrivals at Salt Lake in July 1847 found only "a broad and barren plain hemmed in by mountains . . . the paradise of the lizard, the cricket and the rattlesnake." But by the end of 1848 the Mormons had developed an efficient

THE MORMON TREK, 1830-1851

OREGON TERRITORY

MINNESOTA TERRITORY

WIS.

N.Y. Palmyra 1830

Kirtland 1831-1837

PENN.

Winter quarters 1846-1848

Nauvoo 1840-1845

OHIO

IND.

Great Salt Lake
Ogden

Virginia City

UTAH
Salt Lake City 1847

Carson City

TERRITORY

Platte R.

Independence 1831-1839

ILL.

MO.

Ohio R.

CAL.

Cedar City

Las Vegas

San Bernardino 1851

Colorado R.

NEW MEXICO TERR.

Los Angeles

San Diego

Phoenix

TEXAS

MEXICO

ROCKY MTS.

INDIAN COUNTRY

Missouri R.

Mississippi R.

APPALACHIAN MTS.

0   300 Miles

0   300 Kilometers

☆ Mormon settlements

← The Mormon Trail, 1830-1851

Proposed state of Deseret

irrigation system and over the next decade, by cooperative labor, they brought about the greening of the desert. The Mormons had scarcely arrived when their land became part of the United States. They organized at first their own state of Deseret (meaning "land of the honey bee," according to Young) with ambitious boundaries that reached the Pacific in southern California. But the Utah Territory, which Congress created, afforded them almost the same control with Gov. Brigham Young the chief political and theocratic authority.

MILLENNIALISM   In the 1840s the Burned-Over District was once more swept by religious fervor, this time centered on millennialism and spiritualism. One William Miller, a Baptist farmer-preacher in upstate New York near the Vermont line, had become persuaded that the signs of the times pointed to an early Second Advent of Christ. The year 1843, which Miller called the last sure "year of time," brought widespread excitement and religious delusions. Miller had set no exact date, but when 1843 passed, some of his followers set October 22, 1844, as the date of the second coming. Even after that final disappointment Miller and others held to the belief that the millennium was near, however wrong their mathematics. In 1845 a loose organization was formed, which grew into the Advent Christian Association, from which in 1846 the Seventh Day Adventists broke away on the question of observing the Jewish Sabbath instead of the new Lord's Day.

Hard on the heels of the Millerite frenzy came the craze of "spirit-rapping" which began with Kate and Margaret Fox, daughters of a farmer near Rochester. In 1848 strange knocking sounds in the house began to keep their family awake. The girls soon identified the sounds as messages from the spirit world. As the word spread, the curious gathered for their revelations, and the Fox sisters were launched on a professional career of demonstrations as far away as England. Before long spirit mediums by the hundreds were staging seances, communicating with the dead, and spreading the vogue through spiritualist magazines.

This revival of faith was very much attuned to the rising democratic belief in the power and wisdom of the common man, with its preference for heart over head. No one expressed the hopefulness of this belief better that President Andrew Jackson:

> I believe that man can be elevated; man can become more and more endowed with divinity; and as he does he becomes more God-like in his character and capable of governing himself. Let us go on elevating our people, perfecting our institutions, until democracy shall reach such a point of perfection that we can acclaim with truth that the voice of the people is the voice of God.

ROMANTICISM IN AMERICA

Another great victory of heart over head was the romantic movement in thought, literature, and the arts. By the 1780s a revolt was brewing in Europe against the well-ordered world of the Enlightened thinkers. Were there not, after all, more things in this world than reason and logic can box up and explain: moods, impressions, feelings; mysterious, unknown, and half-seen things? A clear and lucid idea, organized and understandable, might well be superficial. Americans took readily to the romantics' emphasis on individualism, idealizing now the virtues of the common man, now the idea of original or creative genius in the artist, the author, or the great personality.

Where the Enlightened had scorned the Middle Ages, the romantic now looked back to the period with fascination. America, lacking a feudal history, nonetheless had an audience for the novels of Sir Walter Scott and copied the Gothic and even more exotic styles in architecture. More congenial to the American scene were the new themes in art. In contrast to well-ordered classical scenes, romantic artists such as Thomas Cole (1801–1848) and Thomas Doughty (1793–1856) preferred wild and misty landscapes which often evoked more than they showed.

The German philosopher Immanuel Kant gave the movement a summary definition in the title of his *Critique of Pure Reason* (1781), an influential book which emphasized the limits of human science and reason in explaining the universe. People have conceptions of conscience and beauty, the romantics believed, and religious impulses too strong to be dismissed as illusions. Where science can neither prove nor disprove, people are justified in having faith. The impact of such ideas was stated succinctly by a historian of American cultural life: "By degrees intuitive knowledge, during the period 1770–1830, took on validity equal to, or superior to, rational knowledge."

TRANSCENDENTALISM The most intense expression of such thought came in the Transcendentalist Movement of New England, which drew its name from its emphasis on those things which transcended (or rose above) the limits of reason. Transcendentalism, said its chronicler O. B. Frothingham, assumed "certain fundamental truths not derived from experience, not susceptible of proof, which transcend human life, and are perceived directly and intuitively by the human mind." If transcendentalism drew much from Kant, it was also rooted in New England Puritanism, to which it owed a pervasive moralism, and had a close affinity with the Quaker doctrine of the inner light. The inner light, a gift from God's grace, was transformed into intuition, a faculty of man's mind.

An element of mysticism had always lurked in Puritanism, even if viewed as a heresy—Anne Hutchinson, for instance, had been banished for claiming direct revelation. The reassertion of mysticism had something in common, too, with the meditative religions of the Orient—with which New England now had a flourishing trade. Transcendentalists steeped themselves in the teachings of Buddha, the Mohammedan Sufis, the Upanishads, and the Bhagavadgita.

In 1836 an informal discussion group soon named the Transcendental Club began to meet from time to time at the homes of members in Boston and Concord. A floating group, it drew at different times clergymen such as Theodore Parker, George Ripley, and James Freeman Clarke; writers such as Henry Thoreau,

Bronson Alcott, Jones Very, Nathaniel Hawthorne, and Orestes Brownson; and learned women like Elizabeth and Sophia Peabody and Margaret Fuller, who edited the group's quarterly review, *The Dial* (1840–1844), for two years before the duty fell to Ralph Waldo Emerson, soon to become the acknowledged high priest of transcendentalism.

EMERSON More than any other person, Emerson spread the Transcendentalist gospel across the country. Sprung from a line of New England ministers, he set out to be a Unitarian parson, then quit before he was thirty. After travel to Europe, where he met such literary lights as Wordsworth, Coleridge, and Carlyle (a lifelong correspondent), Emerson settled in Concord to take the life of an essayist, poet, and popular speaker on the lecture circuit. On the road he took up a new ministry preaching the good news of optimism, self-reliance, and man's unlimited potential.

Emerson's lectures and writings hold the core of the Transcendentalist worldview. His notable lecture delivered at Harvard in 1837 "The American Scholar," essentially summarized his first book *Nature*, published the previous year. In that lecture he urged his hearers to put aside their awe of European culture and explore their own new world. It was "our intellectual Declaration of Independence," said Oliver Wendell Holmes, Sr. Emerson's lecture on "The Over-soul" set forth a kind of pantheism, in which the souls of all men commune with the great universal soul, of which they are part and parcel. His essay on "Self-Reliance" (1841) has a timeless appeal to youth with its message of individualism and the cultivation of one's personality. Like most of Emerson's writings, it is crammed with quotable quotes:

Ralph Waldo Emerson, author of Nature, *America's "intellectual Declaration of Independence." [The Warder Collection]*

Whoso would be a man, must be a nonconformist. . . . Nothing is at last sacred but the integrity of your own mind. . . . It is easy in the world to live after the world's opinion; it is easy in solitude to live after our own; but the great man is he who in the midst of a crowd keeps with perfect sweetness the independence of solitude. . . . A foolish consistency is the hobgoblin of little minds, adored by little statesmen and philosophers and divines. . . . Speak what you think in hard words and tomorrow speak what tomorrow thinks in hard words again, though it contradict everything you said today. . . . To be great is to be misunderstood.

THOREAU   Emerson's friend and Concord neighbor, Henry David Thoreau, practiced the self-reliance that Emerson preached. "If a man does not keep pace with his companion," Thoreau wrote, "perhaps it is because he hears a different drummer." And Thoreau marched to a different drummer all his life. After Harvard, where he exhausted the resources of the library in gargantuan bouts of reading, and after a brief stint as a teacher in which he got in trouble by his preference for persuasion over discipline, Thoreau settled down to eke out a living through his family's cottage industry of pencil making. But he made frequent escapes to drink in the beauties of nature. Not for him the contemporary scramble for wealth. "The mass of men," he wrote, "lead lives of quiet desperation."

His first book, *A Week on the Concord and Merrimack Rivers* (1849), used the story of a boat trip with his brother as the thread on which to string his comments on life and literature. The second, *Walden, or Life in the Woods* (1854), used an account of his experiment in self-sufficiency to much the same purpose. On July 4, 1845, Thoreau took to the woods to live in a cabin he had built beside Walden Pond. He was out to demonstrate that a person could free himself from the products of commercialism and industrialism. His purpose was not to lead a hermit's life, but to test the possibilities. He would return to town to dine with his friends, and although he used manufactured lime to caulk his walls, he gathered clamshells and made enough himself to show it could be done. "I went to the woods because I wished to live deliberately," he wrote, ". . . and not, when I came to die, discover that I had not lived."

While Thoreau was at Walden the Mexican War broke out. Believing it an unjust war to advance the cause of slavery, he refused payment of his state poll tax as a gesture of opposition, for which he was put in jail (only for one night; an aunt paid the tax). The incident was so trivial as to be almost comic, but out of it grew the classic essay "Civil Disobedience" (1849) which was

Henry David Thoreau, author of the American classics Walden *and "Civil Disobedience." [The Warder Collction]*

later to influence the passive-resistance movements of Mahatma Gandhi in India and Martin Luther King in the American South. "If the law is of such a nature that it requires you to be an agent of unjustice to another," Thoreau wrote, "then, I say, break the law. . . ."

The broadening ripples of influence more than a century after Thoreau's death show the impact a contemplative man can have on the world of action. Although both men lent their voices to worthy causes, Thoreau, like Emerson, shied away from involvement in public life. The Transcendentalists primarily supplied the force of an idea: men must follow their consciences. If these thinkers attracted only a small following among the public at large in their own time, they had much to do with pushing along reform movements and were the quickening force for a generation of writers that produced the first great classic age of American literature.

THE FLOWERING OF AMERICAN LITERATURE

HAWTHORNE Nathaniel Hawthorne, the supreme artist of the New England group, never shared the sunny optimism of his neighbors nor their belief in reform. A sometime resident of Concord, but a native and longtime resident of Salem, he was haunted by the knowledge of evil bequeathed to him by his Puritan forebears—one of whom had been a judge at the Salem witchcraft trial. After college at Bowdoin, he worked for some time in obscurity in Salem, gradually began to place a few stories,

Nathaniel Hawthorne, in the center, with his publishers Ticknor and Fields. [The Warder Collection]

and finally emerged to a degree of fame with his collection of *Twice-Told Tales* (1837). In these, as in most of his later work, his themes were the examination of sin and its consequences: pride and selfishness, secret guilt, selfish egotism, the impossibility of rooting sin out of the human soul. His greatest novels explored such burdens. In *The Scarlet Letter* (1850) Hester Prynne, an adultress tagged with a badge of shame by the Puritan authorities, won redemption by her suffering, while the Rev. Arthur Dimmesdale was destroyed by his gnawing guilt and Roger Chillingworth by his obsession with vengeance.

The flowering of New England featured, too, a foursome of poets who shaped the American imagination in a day when poetry was still accessible to a wide public: Henry Wadsworth Longfellow, John Greenleaf Whittier, Oliver Wendell Holmes, Sr., and James Russell Lowell. But a fifth, Emily Dickinson, the most original of the lot, remained a recluse in the family home in Amherst. Only two of her poems had been published (anonymously) before her death in 1886 and the full corpus of her work remained unknown for years after that.

The half-decade of 1850–1855 saw the publication of *Representative Men* by Emerson, *Walden* by Thoreau, *The Scarlet Letter* and *The House of the Seven Gables* by Nathaniel Hawthorne, *Moby-Dick* by Herman Melville, and *Leaves of Grass* by Walt Whitman. As the critic F. O. Mathiessen wrote in his book *American Renaissance:* "You might search all the rest of American literature without being able to collect a group of books equal to these in imaginative quality."

It had been little more than thirty years since the noted British critic Sydney Smith asked in 1820: "In the four quarters of the

Globe, who reads an American book?'' Quoted out of context, the question rubbed Americans the wrong way, but Smith, an admirer of American institutions, foresaw a future flowering in the new country. He did not have long to wait, for within a year Washington Irving's *The Sketch Book* (1820), James Fenimore Cooper's *The Spy* (1821), and William Cullen Bryant's *Poems* (1821) were drawing wide notice in Britain as well as in America. Bryant's energies were drawn into journalism by his need to earn a living. As editor of the New York *Evening Post* he wielded an important influence in American life. He is remembered as a poet mainly for two poems of his youth: "Thanatopsis" and "To a Waterfowl." But Irving and Cooper went on to greater literary triumphs, and made New York for a time the national literary capital.

IRVING AND COOPER Irving in fact stood as a central figure in the American literary world from the time of his satirical *Diedrich Knickerbocker's A History of New York* (1809) until his death fifty years later. He showed that an American could, after all, make a career of literature, and was a confidant and advocate of numerous other writers. During those years a flood of histories, biographies, essays, and stories poured from his pen. A talented writer, Irving was the first to show that authentic American themes could draw a wide audience. Yet, as Melville later noted, he was less a creative genius than an adept imitator. Even the most "American" of his stories, "Rip Van Winkle" and "The Legend of Sleepy Hollow," drew heavily on German folk tales.

Cooper, a country gentleman, got his start as a writer on a bet with his wife that he could write a better novel than one they had just read. *Precaution* (1820) was an imitative story of manners in English high society, but the following year he brought out *The Spy* (1821), a historical romance based on a real incident of the American Revolution. In 1823 Cooper in *The Pioneers* introduced Natty Bumppo, an eighteenth-century frontiersman destined to be the hero of five novels known collectively as *The Leather-Stocking Tales.* Natty Bumppo, a deadshot also known as Hawkeye, and his Indian friend Chingachgook, the epitome of the noble savage, took a place among the most unforgettable heroes of world literature. The tales of man pitted against nature in the backwoods, of hairbreadth escapes and gallant rescues, were the first successful romances of frontier life and models for the later cowboy novels and movies set in the Far West. In addition to the backwoods tales, Cooper also was the virtual creator of the sea novel in *The Pilot* (1823), another romance of the Revolution.

Edgar Allan Poe, perhaps the most inventive American writer of the period. [American Antiquarian Society]

POE AND THE SOUTH   By the 1830s and 1840s new major talents had come on the scene. Edgar Allan Poe, a native of Boston but reared in Virginia, was arguably America's most inventive genius in the first half of the century, and probably the most important American writer of the times in the critical esteem of Europeans. Poe's success had many dimensions. As a critic, he argued that the object of poetry was beauty (not truth) and that the writer should calculate his effect on the reader with precision. To that end he favored relatively short poems and stories, and wrote only one novel in his brief career. His poems, such as "The Raven," exemplified his theory, and although relatively few in number, won great fame. He was moreover a master of gothic horror in the short story and the inventor of the detective story and its major conventions. But the tormented, hard-drinking wanderer that Poe became hardly fit his countrymen's image of the proper man of letters.

Neither did a group of southern writers who came to be called the southwestern humorists. With stories of the backwoods from Georgia westward they exploited frontier tall tales and the raw, violent life of the region. Their number included Davy Crockett, a sort of real-life Natty Bumppo, George Washington Harris, whose hero Sut Lovingood lived up to his name, and Johnson Jones Hooper, author of *Some Adventures of Captain Simon Suggs* (1845), about a peerless con man whose motto became a national joke: "It is good to be shifty in a new country." Augustus Baldwin Longstreet, author of *Georgia Scenes* (1835), would hardly be remembered but for his stories about Ransy Sniffle and

other examples of backwoods low life. Dismissed at the time as
subliterary amusement, southwestern humor was later raised to
the level of high art by Mark Twain.

Among southern authors, William Gilmore Simms best exemplified the genteel man of letters. Editor and writer in many
genres, he had a prodigious output of poems, novels, histories,
biographies, essays, short stories, and drama. He gained a wide
audience with *Guy Rivers* (1834), first of a series of "Border Romances" set in frontier Georgia, but the peak of his achievement
was in two novels published in 1835: *The Yemassee*, a story of Indian war in 1715, and *The Partisan*, first of seven novels about the
Revolution in South Carolina. In his own time he was the preemi-
nent southern author and something of a national figure, but he
finally dissipated his energies in politics and the defense of slavery. He went down steadily in critical esteem, and most critics
would agree with his own epitaph, that he had "left all his better
works undone."

The duc de La Rochefoucauld-Liancourt, who visited the
south in the 1790s, noted some cultural characteristics that continued to prevail in the nineteenth century: "In spite of the Virginian love for dissipation, the taste for reading is commoner
there among men of the first class than in any other part of
America; but the populace is perhaps more ignorant there than
elsewhere." The readers of "the first class," however, tended to
take their cues in literary and aesthetic matters from London or
New York. They usually read English and northern authors to the
neglect of their own, and took northern rather than southern
magazines. And "men of the first class" who read widely tended
to look upon literature as ornamental and a less praiseworthy activity than the high arts of oratory and statesmanship.

MELVILLE Those southerners who followed the literary prefer-
ences of the North are likely to have passed over the work of
Herman Melville, whose literary reputation went into a decline
after his initial successes. In the twentieth century Melville's
good reputation was dramatically revived, elevating him into the
literary pantheon occupied by only the finest American authors.
Born of distinguished ancestry on both sides, Melville suffered a
sharp reversal of fortunes when his father died a bankrupt, and
after various odd jobs, he shipped out as a seaman at age twenty.
Some time later, after eighteen months aboard a whaler, he
fetched up in the South Seas and jumped ship with a companion
in the Marquesas Islands. After several weeks spent with a
friendly tribe in the valley of the Typees, he signed onto an Aus-

Whaling off the Acushnet. *Melville's experiences on the ship informed his great novel,* Moby-Dick *(1851). [Peabody Museum of Salem]*

tralian whaler, jumped ship again in Tahiti, and finally returned home as a seaman aboard a frigate of the United States Navy. An embroidered account of his exotic adventures in *Typee* (1846) became an instant popular success, which he repeated in *Omoo* (1847), based on his stay in Tahiti.

So many readers took his accounts as fictional (as in part they were) that Melville was inspired to write novels of nautical adventures, and scored two successes after an initial failure. Then just five years after his first success, he produced one of the world's great novels in *Moby-Dick* (1851). In the story of Captain Ahab and his obsessive quest for the white whale which had caused the loss of his leg, Melville explored the darker recesses of the soul just as his good friend Hawthorne had done. The book was aimed at two audiences. On one level it was a ripping good yarn of adventure on the high seas. But Ahab's single-minded mission to slay the evildoer turned the captain himself into a monster of destruction who sacrificed his ship, his crew, and himself to his folly, leaving as the one survivor the narrator of the story. Unhappily, neither the public nor the critics at the time accepted the novel on either level. After that Melville's career wound down into futility. He supported himself for years with a job in the New York Custom House and turned to poetry, much of which, especially the Civil War *Battle-Pieces* (1866), gained acclaim in later years.

WHITMAN   Walt Whitman of Brooklyn had from the age of twelve worked mainly as a handyman and newspaperman, and remained relatively obscure until the first edition of *Leaves of Grass* (1855) caught the eye of contemporaries. Emerson found it "the most extraordinary piece of wit and wisdom that America has yet contributed," and greeted Whitman "at the beginning of a great career, which yet must have had a long foreground somewhere, for such a start"—an endorsement Whitman brazenly seized upon to promote the book. Yet it was appropriate that Emerson should endorse it for Whitman had taken to heart his argument that an American poet must exploit great American themes. The two greatest influences on him, Whitman said, were hearing Italian opera and reading Emerson: "I was simmering, simmering, simmering; Emerson brought me to a boil."

Whitman's life thereafter was in large measure given to "hackling" at his gargantuan *Leaves of Grass*, enlarging and reshaping it in successive editions. The growth of the book he identified with the growth of the country, which he proclaimed in all its variety. "I hear America singing," he wrote, "the varied carols I hear." He sounded his "barbaric yawp over the roofs of the world," and wrote unabashedly:

> Do I contradict myself?
> Very well then I contradict myself,
> (I am large, I contain multitudes.)

While he celebrated America, he also set out to "celebrate myself and sing myself."

To his Victorian generation Whitman was a startling figure with his frank reminders of sexuality and "the body electric," which were not without homoerotic overtones. And he stood out from the pack of fellow writers in rejecting the idea that woman's proper sphere was a supportive and dependent role, just as he rejected the "empty dish, gallantry."

Later, during the Civil War, Whitman went to Washington to see about his injured brother. The injury was slight, but "the good gray poet" stayed on to visit the sick and wounded, to serve as attendant and nurse when needed. Out of his wartime service came *Drum Taps* (1865), containing his masterpiece of the 1860s, an elegy on the death of Lincoln: "When lilacs last in the dooryard bloomed." In much of his prose Whitman vigorously defended democracy. In the postbellum *Democratic Vistas* (1871) he summoned Americans to higher goals than materialism.

THE POPULAR PRESS   The renaissance in literature came at a time of massive expansion in the popular press. The steam-driven Napier press, introduced from England in 1825, could print 4,000 sheets of newsprint in an hour. Richard Hoe of New York improved on it, inventing in 1847 the Hoe Rotary Press, which printed 20,000 sheets an hour. Like many advances in technology, this was a mixed blessing. The high cost of such a press made it harder for a man of small means to break into publishing. On the other hand it expedited production of cheap newspapers, magazines, and books—which were often cheap in more ways than one.

The New York *Sun*, in 1833 the first successful penny daily, and others like it, often ignored the merely important in favor of scandals and sensations, true or false. James Gordon Bennett, a native of Scotland, perfected this style on the New York *Herald*, which he founded in 1835. His innovations drew readers by the thousands: the first Wall Street column, the first society page (which satirized the well-to-do until it proved more gainful to show readers their names in print), pictorial news, telegraphic news, and great initiative in getting scoops. Eventually, however, the *Herald* suffered from dwelling so much on crime, sex, and depravity in general.

The chief beneficiary of a rising revulsion was the New York *Tribune*, founded as a Whig organ in 1841. Horace Greeley, who became the most important journalist of the era, announced that it would be a cheap but decent paper avoiding the "matters which have been allowed to disgrace the columns of our leading Penny Papers." And despite occasional lapses, Greeley's "Great Moral Organ" typically amused its readers with wholesome human-interest stories. Greeley also won a varied following by plugging the reforms of the day—those few he did not espouse he reported nonetheless. Socialism, land reform, feminism, abolitionism, temperance, the protective tariff, internal improvements, improved methods of agriculture, vegetarianism, spiritualism, trade unions—all got a share of attention. The *Tribune*, moreover, set a new standard in reporting literary news. Margaret Fuller briefly served as critic; in 1856 the *Tribune* became the first daily to have a regular book-review column. For a generation it was probably the most influential paper in the country. By 1860 its weekly edition had a national circulation of 200,000. The number of newspapers around the country grew from about 1,200 in 1833 to about 3,000 in 1860.

Magazines found a growing market too. Periodicals of the eighteenth century typically had brief lives, but *The Port Folio* (1801–1827) of Philadelphia lasted an unusually long time. A monthly literary review edited at one time by Nicholas Biddle, it gave much attention to politics as well, from a Federalist viewpoint. *Niles' Weekly Register* (1811–1849) of Baltimore and Washington, founded by the printer Hezekiah Niles, was an early version of the twentieth-century news magazine. Niles got credit for accurate reports on the War of 1812 and made a reputation for good and unbiased coverage of public events—all of which make it a basic source for historians. The *North American Review* of Boston (1815–1940), started by a young graduate of Harvard, achieved high standing among scholarly readers. Its editor adorned the journal with materials on American history and biography. It also featured coverage of European literature.

More popular and more widely circulated than the others was *Graham's Magazine* of Philadelphia (1826–1858). Started as *The Casket: Flowers of Literature, Wit and Sentiment*, the magazine became a highly profitable enterprise after George R. Graham bought it in 1839, spicing it up with a "magazinish" style in contrast to the heavy review style of the day and decorating it with original artwork. As a result of the liberal payment he offered, Graham published the best authors of the day: Bryant, Longfellow, Cooper, Lowell, and Poe all appeared in its pages.

Harpers' Magazine (1850–present), originally the organ of the publishers Harper and Brothers, went Graham one better. Instead of showing that liberal rewards to authors paid off, the publisher built on a practice already profitable in book publishing—pirating the output of popular English writers in the absence of an international copyright agreement. Gradually, however, faced with an outcry against the practice, *Harpers'* instituted payment and published original material by American authors. *Frank Leslie's Illustrated Newspaper* (1855–1922) in New York used large and striking pictures to illustrate its material, and generally followed its founder's motto: "Never shoot over the heads of the people." *Leslie's* and a vigorous competitor of somewhat higher quality, *Harper's Illustrated Weekly* (1857–1916), appeared in time to provide a thoroughgoing pictorial record of the Civil War.

The boom in periodicals gave rise to more journals directed to specialized audiences. Worthy of mention, among others, are such magazines as *Godey's Lady's Book* (1830–1898), *The Southern Literary Messenger* (1834–1864), *Hunt's Merchants' Magazine* (1839–1870), *DeBow's Commercial Review of the South and West* (1846–1880), and *The American Farmer* (1819–1897), the first important agricultural journal. The new methods of production and distribution gave a boost to the book market as well. The publisher Samuel Goodrich estimated gross sales of

Without the protection of international copyright laws (not enacted until the late nineteenth century), many British authors found their works pirated by unscrupulous American publishers. With book sales growing, this cartoon of an "American Bookman Scalping an English Author" became more apt. [Punch, *London*]

books in America at $2 million in 1820, $12 million in 1850, and nearly $20 million in 1860. From 1820 to 1850, he estimated, moreover, books by American authors increased their share of the market from about a third to about two-thirds.

EDUCATION

EARLY PUBLIC SCHOOLS Literacy was surprisingly widespread, given the condition of public education. By 1840, according to census data, some 78 percent of the total population and 91 percent of the white population could read and write. Ever since the colonial period, in fact, Americans had the highest literacy rate in the Western World. Most children learned their letters from church or private "dame" schools, formal tutors, or from their families. When Abraham Lincoln came of age, he said, he did not know much. "Still, somehow, I could read, write and cipher to the rule of three, but that was all." At that time, about 1830, no state had a school system in the modern sense, although Massachusetts had for nearly two centuries required towns to maintain schools. Some major cities had the resources to develop real systems on their own. The Public School Society of New York, for instance, built a model system of free schools in the city, with state aid after 1815. In 1806 the society introduced the Lancasterian schools (after Joseph Lancaster, an English Quaker) in which teachers used monitors to instruct hundreds of pupils at once. By 1853 when the state took over its properties the society had provided schooling for more than 600,000 pupils.

A scattered rural popularion, however, did not lend itself so readily to the development of schools. In 1860, for instance, Louisiana had a population density of 11 per square mile, Virginia 14, while Massachusetts had 127. In many parts of the country, as in South Carolina after 1811, the state provided some aid to schools for children of indigent parents, but such institutions were normally stigmatized as "pauper schools," to be shunned by the better sort.

Beginning with Connecticut as early as 1750, and New York in 1782, most states built up "literary" or school funds—an idea which gained momentum when Ohio, upon achieving statehood in 1803, also got the sixteenth section of each township as endowment for education. The funds were applied to various purposes—usually at first to aid local schools either public or private.

By the 1830s the demand for public schools was rising fast. Reformers argued that popular government presupposed a literate and informed electorate. With the lowering of barriers to the ballot box the argument carried all the more force. Workers wanted free schools to give their children an equal chance. In 1830 the Working Men's party of Philadelphia resolved in favor of "a system of education that shall embrace equally all the children of the state, of every rank and condition." Education, it was argued, would be a means of reform. It would improve manners and at the same time lessen crime and poverty. Opposition was minor, but when it came it was from taxpayers who held education to be a family matter and from those church groups which maintained schools at their own expense.

Horace Mann of Massachusetts stood out in the early drive for statewide school systems. Trained as a lawyer, Mann sponsored through the legislature the creation of a state board of education, which he then served as secretary. Mann went on to sponsor many reforms in Massachusetts, including the first state-supported normal school for teachers, teacher-training institutes for refresher courses, a state association of teachers, and a minimum school year of six months. He made his twelve annual reports into instruments of propaganda for public education. In these papers he explored problems of methods, curriculum, school management, and much more. His final report in 1848 defended the school system as the way to social stability and equal opportunity. It had never happened, he argued, and never could happen, that an educated people could be permanently poor. "Education then, beyond all other devices of human origin, is a great equalizer of the conditions of men—the balance wheel of the social machinery."

In the South the state of North Carolina led the way. There Calvin H. Wiley played a role like that of Mann, building from a law of 1839 which provided support to localities willing to tax themselves for the support of schools. As the first state superintendent of public instruction he traveled to every county drumming up support for the schools. By 1860, as a result of his activities, North Carolina enrolled more than two-thirds of its white school population for an average term of four months. But the educational pattern in the South continued to reflect the aristocratic pretensions of the region: the South had a higher percentage of college students than any other region, but a lower percentage of public school students. And the South had some 500,000 white illiterates, more than half the total number in the country.

For all the effort, conditions for public education were seldom ideal. Funds were insufficient for buildings, books, and equipment; teachers were poorly paid, and often so poorly prepared as to be little ahead of their charges in the ability to read, write, and cipher. In many a rural schoolhouse the teacher's first task was to thrash the huskiest youth in the class in order to encourage the others. The teachers, consequently, were at first mostly men, often young men who did not regard teaching as a career but as a means of support while preparing for a career as a lawyer or preacher, or as part-time work during slack seasons on the farm. With the encouragement of educational reformers, however, teaching was beginning to be regarded as a profession. As the schools multiplied and the school term lengthened, women increasingly entered the field.

Still, given the condition of their preparation, teachers were heavily dependent on textbooks and publishers were happy to oblige them. The most common texts were Noah Webster's *Blue-Backed Spellers* and a series of six graded *Eclectic Readers* which William Holmes McGuffey, a professor and university president in Ohio, began to bring out in 1836 and completed in 1857. His books taught children to recite "Twinkle, Twinkle,

Little Star," "The Boy Stood on the Burning Deck," "The Boy Who Cried Wolf," and the patriotic words of Washington, Patrick Henry, Webster, and Clay. The readers were replete with parables designed to instill thrift, morality, and patriotism. At the same time they carried selections from the masters of English prose and verse.

Most students going beyond the elementary grades went to private academies, often subsidized by church and public funds. Such schools, begun in colonial days, multiplied until there were in 1850 more than 6,000 of them. In 1821 the Boston English High School opened as the first free public secondary school, set up mainly for students not going on to college. By a law of 1827 Massachusetts required a high school in every town of 500; in towns of 4,000 or more the school had to offer Latin, Greek, rhetoric, and other college preparatory courses. Public high schools became well established in school systems only after the Civil War. In 1860 there were barely 300 in the whole country.

POPULAR EDUCATION   Beyond the schools there grew up many societies and institutes to inform the general public: mechanics' and workingmen's "institutes," "young men's associations," "debating societies," "literary societies," and such. Outstanding in the field was the Franklin Institute, founded at Philadelphia in 1824 to inform the public mainly in the fields of science and industry. Similar institutes were sponsored by major philanthropists like Lowell in Boston, Peabody in Baltimore, and Cooper in New York. Some cities offered evening classes to those who could not attend day schools. The most widespread and effective means of popular education, however, was the lyceum movement, which aimed to diffuse knowledge through public lectures. Professional agencies provided speakers and performers of all kinds, in literature, science, music, humor, travel, and other fields. Most of the major savants of the age at one time or another rode the lecture circuit: Emerson, Melville, Lyman Beecher, Daniel Webster, Harriet Beecher Stowe, Louis Agassiz, Benjamin Silliman.

Akin to the lyceum movement and ultimately reaching more people was the movement for public libraries. Benjamin Franklin's Philadelphia Library Company (1731) had given impulse to the growth of subscription or association libraries. In 1803 Salisbury, Connecticut, opened a free library for children and in 1833 Peterborough, New Hampshire, established a tax-supported library open to all. The opening of the Boston Public Library in 1851 was a turning point. By 1860 there were approximately 10,000 public libraries (not all completely free) housing some 8 million volumes.

HIGHER EDUCATION   The postrevolutionary proliferation of colleges continued after 1800 with the spread of small church schools and state universities. Nine colleges had been founded in the colonial period, all of which survived; but not many of the fifty that sprang up between 1776 and 1800 lasted. Among those that did were Hampden-Sydney, Charleston, Bowdoin, and Middlebury, all of which went on to long and fruitful careers. Of the seventy-eight colleges and universities in 1840, fully thirty-five had been founded after 1830, almost all as church schools. A postrevolutionary movement for state universities flourished in those southern states which had had no colonial university. Federal policy abetted the spread of universities into the West. When Congress granted statehood to Ohio in 1803, it set aside two townships for the support of a state university and kept up that policy in other new states.

The coexistence of state and religious schools, however, set up conflicts over funding and curriculum. Beset by the need for funds, as colleges usually were, denominational schools often competed with tax-supported schools. Regarding curricula, the new Awakening led many of the church schools to emphasize theology at the expense of science and the humanities. On the other hand America's development required broader access to education and programs geared to vocations. The University of Virginia, "Mr. Jefferson's University," founded in 1819 within sight of Monticello, introduced in 1826 a curriculum which reflected Jefferson's own view that education ought to combine pure knowledge with "all the branches of science useful *to us*, and *at this day.*" The model influenced the other new state universities of the South and West.

Technical education grew slowly. The United States Military Academy at West Point, founded in 1802, trained a limited number of engineers. More were trained by practical experience with railroad and canal companies, and apprenticeship to experienced technologists. Similarly, most aspiring lawyers went to "read law" with an established attorney, and doctors served their apprenticeships with practicing physicians. Francis Wayland, president of Brown University, remarked that there were forty-two theological schools and forty-seven law schools, but none to provide "the agriculturalist, the manufacturer, the mechanic, and the merchant with any kind of professional preparation." There were few schools of this sort before 1860, but a

Jefferson's design for the rotunda at the University of Virginia, founded in 1819. [University of Virginia Manuscript Department]

promise for the future came in 1855 when Michigan and Pennsylvania each established an agricultural and mechanical college, now Michigan State and Pennsylvania State.

Elementary education for girls, where available for boys, met with general acceptance, but training beyond that level did not. Many men and women thought higher education unsuited to woman's destiny in life. Some did argue that education would make better wives and mothers, but few were ready yet to demand equality on principle. Progress began with the academies, some of which taught boys and girls alike. Good "female seminaries" like those founded by Emma Willard at Troy, New York (1824), and Mary Lyon at Mount Holyoke, Massachusetts (1836), prepared the way for women's colleges. Many of them, in fact, grew into such colleges, but Georgia Female College (later Wesleyan) at Macon, chartered in 1836, first offered women the A.B. in 1840. The work in female seminaries usually differed from the courses in men's schools, giving more attention to the social amenities and such "embellishments" as music and art. Vassar, opened at Poughkeepsie, New York, in 1865, is usually credited with being the first women's college which gave priority to academic standards. Oberlin College in Ohio, founded in 1833, opened as both a biracial and a coeducational institution. Its first women students were admitted in 1837. In general the West gave the greatest impetus to coeducation, with state universities in the lead.

SOME MOVEMENTS FOR REFORM

Alexis de Tocqueville, a French traveler who wrote a classic report on American society, *Democracy in America* (1835), commented on many things, including the role of education in the United States. Another matter caught his special attention: nothing, he wrote, "in my view, more deserves attention than the intellectual and moral associations in America." During his extended visit in 1831 he heard that 100,000 men had pledged to abstain from alcohol. At first he thought it was a joke. Why should these abstemious citizens not quietly drink water by their own firesides? Then he understood that "Americans of all ages, all stations to life and all types of dispositions are forever forming associations. There are not only commercial and industrial associations in which all take part, but others of a thousand different types—religious, moral, serious, futile, very general and very limited, very large and very minute."

Emerson spoke for his generation, as he so often did, when he asked: "What is man born for, but to be a Reformer, a Remaker of what man has made?" The urge to eradicate evil from nineteenth-century America had its roots in the ubiquitous sense of mission, which in turn drew upon rising faith in the perfectibility of man. Belief in perfectibility had both evangelical and liberal bases. Transcendentalism, the spirit of which infected even those unfamiliar with the philosophy, offered a romantic faith in the individual and the belief that human intuition led to right thinking.

Few things escaped the ministrations of the reformers, however trivial or weighty: observance of the Sabbath, dueling, crime and punishment, the hours and conditions of work, poverty, vice, care of the handicapped, pacifism, foreign missions, temperance, women's rights, the abolition of slavery. Some crusaders challenged a host of evils; others focused on pet causes. Dr. William Alcott of Massachusetts, for example, insisted that "a vegetable diet lies at the basis of all reforms." The greatest dietary reformer of the age, however, was Sylvester Graham, who started as a temperance speaker in 1830 and moved on to champion a natural diet of grains, vegetables, and fruits, and abstinence from alcohol, coffee, tea, tobacco, and many foods. The Graham cracker is one of the movement's legacies to later times. Graham's ideas evolved into a way of life requiring proper habits of dress, hygiene, sex, and mind. The movement became a major industry, sponsoring health clubs, camps, sanitariums, magazines, and regular lecture tours by Graham, "the Peristaltic Persuader."

TEMPERANCE The temperance crusade, at which Tocqueville marvelled, was perhaps the most widespread of all, with the possible exception of the public school movement. The cause drew its share of spoilsports, but it also drew upon concern with a real problem. The census of 1810 reported some 14,000 distilleries producing 25 million gallons of spirits each year. With a hard-drinking population of just over 7 million, the "alcoholic republic" was producing well over three gallons per year for every man, woman, and child, not counting beer, wine, and cider. And the census takers no doubt missed a few stills. William Cobbett, an English reformer who traveled in the United States, noted in 1819 that one could "go into hardly any man's house without being asked to drink wine or spirits, even *in the morning.*"

The movement for temperance rested on a number of arguments. First and foremost was the demand of religion that "sol-

Intemperance was an important step on the way of evil, leading to "everlasting Punishment." [Library of Congress]

diers of the cross" lead blameless lives. The bad effects of distilled beverages on body and mind were noted by the respected physician Benjamin Rush as early as 1784. The dynamic new economy, with factories and railroads moving on strict schedules, made tippling by the labor force a far greater problem than it had been in a simple economy. Humanitarians emphasized the relations between drinking and poverty. Much of the movement's propaganda focused on the sufferings of innocent mothers and children. "Drink," said a pamphlet from the Sons of Temperance, "is the prolific source (directly or indirectly) of nearly all the ills that afflict the human family."

In 1826 a group of ministers in Boston organized the American Society for the Promotion of Temperance. The society worked through lecturers, press campaigns, prize essay contests, and the formation of local and state societies. A favorite device was to ask each person who took the pledge to put by his signature a T for Total Abstinence. With that a new word entered the language: "teetotaler."

In 1833 the society called a national convention in Philadelphia where the American Temperance Union was formed. The convention revealed internal tensions, however: Was the goal moderation or total abstinence, and if the latter, abstinence merely from ardent spirits or also from wine, cider, and beer? Should the movement work by persuasion or by legislation? Like nearly every movement of the day, temperance had a wing of perfectionists who rejected counsels of prudence. They would brook no compromise with Demon Rum, and carried the day with a resolution that the liquor traffic was morally wrong and ought to be prohibited by law. The union, at its spring convention in 1836, called for abstinence from all alcoholic beverages —a pyrrhic victory that caused moderates to abstain from the movement instead.

The demand for the prohibition of alcoholic beverages led in the 1830s and thereafter to experiments with more stringent regulations and local option laws. In 1838 Massachusetts forbade the sale of spirits in lots of less than fifteen gallons, thereby cutting off sales in taverns and to the poor—who could not handle it as well as their betters, or so their betters thought. After repeal of the law in 1840, prohibitionists in Massachusetts turned to the towns, about a hundred of which were dry by 1845. In 1839 Mississippi restricted sales to no less than a gallon, but the movement went little further in the South. In 1846 Maine enacted a law against sales of less than twenty-eight gallons; five years later Maine forbade the manufacture or sale of *any* intoxicants. By 1855 thirteen states had such laws. Rum-soaked New England had gone legally dry, along with New York and parts of the Midwest. But most of the laws were poorly drafted and vulnerable to court challenge. Within a few years they survived only in northern New England. Still, between 1830 and 1860 the temperance agitation drastically reduced the per-capita consumption of alcohol.

PRISONS AND ASYLUMS   The sublime optimism of the age, the liberal belief that people are innately good and capable of improvement, brought major changes in the treatment of prisoners, the handicapped, and dependent children. Public institutions arose dedicated to the treatment and cure of social ills. Earlier these had been "places of last resort," David Rothman wrote in *The Discovery of the Asylum*. Now they "became places of first resort, the preferred solution to the problems of poverty, crime, delinquency, and insanity." Removed from society, the needy and deviant could be made whole again. Unhappily, this ideal kept running up against the dictates of convenience and economy. The institutions had a way of turning into breeding grounds of brutality and neglect.

In the colonial period prisons were usually places for brief confinement before punishment, which was either death or some kind of pain or humiliation: whipping, mutilation, confinement in stocks, ducking, branding, and the like. A new attitude began to emerge after the Revolution. American reformers argued against the harshness of the penal code and asserted that the certainty of punishment was more important than its severity. Society, moreover, would benefit more from the prevention than the punishment of crime. The Philadelphia Society for Alleviating the Miseries of Public Prisons, founded in 1787, took the lead in spreading the new doctrines. Gradually the idea of the penitentiary developed. It would be a place where the guilty experienced penitence and underwent rehabilitation, not just punishment.

An early model of the new system, widely copied, was the Auburn Penitentiary, commissioned by New York in 1816. The prisoners at Auburn had separate cells and gathered for meals and group labor. Discipline was severe. The men were marched out in lock step and never put face to face or allowed to talk. But prisoners were at least reasonably secure from abuse by other prisoners. The system, its advocates argued, had a beneficial effect on the prisoners and saved money since the workshops supplied prison needs and produced goods for sale at a profit. By 1840 there were twelve prisons of the Auburn type.

It was still more common, and the persistent curse of prisons, for inmates to be thrown together willy-nilly. In an earlier day of corporal punishments jails housed mainly debtors. But as practices changed, debtors found themselves housed with convicts. In New York City, investigation showed about 2,000 debtors confined during 1816, as many as 600 at one time. Of the annual total, over 1,000 were held for debts less than $50, 700 for debts under $25. Without provision for food, furniture, or fuel, the debtors would have expired but for charity. The absurdity of the system was so obvious that the tardiness of reform seems strange. New York in 1817 made $25 the minimum for which one could be imprisoned, but no state eliminated the practice altogether until Kentucky acted in 1821. Ohio acted in 1828 and other states gradually fell in line, but it was still more than three decades before debtors' prisons became a thing of the past.

The reform impulse naturally found outlet in the care of the insane. The Philadelphia Hospital (1752), one of the first in the country, had a provision in its charter that it should care for "lunaticks," but before 1800 few hospitals provided care for the mentally ill. There were in fact few hospitals of any kind. The insane were merely confined at home with hired keepers or in jails and almshouses. In the years after 1815, however, asylums which housed the disturbed separately from criminals began to appear. Early efforts led to such optimism that a committee reported to the Massachusetts legislature in 1832 that with the right treatment "insanity yields with more readiness than ordinary diseases." These high expectations gradually faded with experience.

The most important figure in arousing the public conscience to

Dorothea Dix, one of the most influential of American reformers. [Schlesinger Library, Radcliffe College]

the plight of these unfortunates was Dorothea Lynde Dix. A Boston schoolteacher called upon to instruct a Sunday school class at the East Cambridge House of Correction in 1841, she found there a roomful of insane persons completely neglected and left without heat on a cold March day. She then commenced a two-year investigation of jails and almshouses in Massachusetts. In a memorial to the state legislature in 1843 she began "I tell what I have seen," and went on to report "the *present* state of insane persons confined within the Commonwealth, in *cages, closets, cellars, stalls, pens! Chained, naked, beaten with rods, and lashed into obedience!"* Keepers of the institutions charged "slanderous lies," but she got the support of leading reformers and won a large appropriation. From Massachusetts she carried her campaign throughout the country and abroad. By 1860 she had gotten twenty states to heed her advice. Of Dorothea Dix it was truly said that "Few persons have ever had such far-reaching effect on public policy toward reform."

WOMEN'S RIGHTS While Dorothea Dix stood out as an example of the opportunity reform gave middle-class women to enter public life, Catherine Beecher, a leader in the education movement and founder of women's schools in Connecticut and Ohio, published a guide prescribing the domestic sphere for women. *A Treatise on Domestic Economy* (1841) became the leading handbook of what historians have labeled the "cult of domesticity." While Beecher upheld high standards in women's education, she also accepted the prevailing view that "woman's sphere" was the home and argued that young women should be trained in the domestic arts. Her guide, designed for use also as a textbook, led prospective wives and mothers through the endless rounds from Monday washing to Saturday baking, with instructions on health, food, clothing, cleanliness, care of domestics and children, gardening, and hundreds of other household details. Such duties, Beecher emphasized, should never be taken as "petty, trivial or unworthy" since "no statesman . . . had more frequent calls for wisdom, firmness, tact, discrimination, prudence, and versatility of talent."

The social custom of assigning the sexes different roles of course did not spring full-blown into life during the nineteenth century. In earlier agrarian societies sex-based functions were closely tied to the household and often overlapped. As the more complex economy of the nineteenth century matured, economic production came to be increasingly separated from the home, and the home in turn became a refuge from the cruel world outside, with separate and distinctive functions. Some have argued that the home became a trap for women, a prison that hindered fulfillment. But others have noted that it often gave women a sphere of independence in which they might exercise a degree of initiative and leadership. The so-called cult of true womanhood idealized woman's moral role in civilizing husband and family.

The status of women remained much as it had been in the colonial era. Legally, a woman was disfranchised, denied control of her property and even of her children. A wife could not make a will, sign a contract, or bring suit in court without her husband's permission. Her legal status was like that of a minor, a slave, or a free Negro. The organized movement for women's rights in fact had its origins in 1840, when the American antislavery movement split over the question of women's right to participate. American women decided then that they needed to organize on behalf of their own emancipation too.

In 1848 Lucretia Mott and Elizabeth Cady Stanton decided to call a convention to discuss "the social, civil, and religious condition and rights of women." The hastily called Seneca Falls Convention, the first of its kind, issued on July 19, 1848, a clever paraphrase of Jefferson's Declaration, the Declaration of Sentiments, mainly the work of Mrs. Stanton. The document proclaimed the self-evident truth that "all men and women are created equal," and the attendant resolutions said that all laws which placed woman "in a position inferior to that of men, are contrary to the great precept of nature, and therefore of no force or authority."

From 1850 until the Civil War the women's rights leaders held annual conventions, and carried on a program of organizing, lecturing, and petitioning. The movement had to struggle in the face of meager funds and antifeminist women and men. What success the movement had was due to the work of a few undaunted women who refused to be overawed by the odds against them. Susan B. Anthony, already active in temperance and antislavery groups, joined the crusade in the 1850s. As one observer put it, Mrs. Stanton "forged the thunderbolts and Miss Anthony hurled them." Both were young when the movement started and both lived into the twentieth century, focusing after the Civil War on demands for woman suffrage. Many of the feminists like Stanton, Lucretia Mott, and Lucy Stone had supportive husbands, and the movement won prominent male champions like Emerson, William Ellery Channing, and William Lloyd Garrison. Editor Horace Greeley gave the feminists sympathetic attention in the New York *Tribune*. The fruits of the movement were slow to ripen. The women did not gain the ballot, but there were some legal gains. The state of Mississippi, seldom regarded as a hotbed

Elizabeth Cady Stanton (left) and Susan B. Anthony. Mrs. Stanton "forged the thunderbolts and Miss Anthony hurled them." [The Warder Collection]

of reform, was in 1839 the first to grant married women control over their property; by the 1860s eleven more states had such laws, and other rights followed.

Still, the only jobs open to educated women in any numbers were nursing and teaching, both of which extended the domestic roles of health care and nurture into the world outside. Both brought relatively lower status and pay than "man's work" despite the skills, training, and responsibility involved. Against the odds, a hardy band of women carved out professional careers. With the rapid expansion of schools, women moved into the teaching profession first. If women could be teachers, Susan Anthony asked, why not lawyers or doctors? Harriet Hunt of Boston was a teacher who, after nursing her sister through a serious illness, set up shop in 1835 as a self-taught physician and persisted in medical practice although twice rejected by Harvard Medical School. Voted into Geneva Medical College in western New York as a joke, Elizabeth Blackwell of Ohio had the last laugh when she finished at the head of her class in 1849. She founded the New York Infirmary for Women and Children and later had a long career as a professor of gynecology in the London School of Medicine for Women.

An intellectual prodigy among women of the time—the derisory term was "bluestocking"—was Margaret Fuller. A precocious child, she was forced-fed education by a father who set her at Latin when she was six. As a young adult she moved in the literary circles of Boston and Concord, edited the *The Dial* for two years, and became literary editor and critic for Horace Greeley's New York *Tribune*. From 1839 to 1844 she conducted "conversations" with the cultivated ladies of Boston. From this

Margaret Fuller, an influential American intellectual. [Metropolitan Museum of Art]

classroom-salon emerged many of the ideas that went into her book *Woman in the Nineteenth Century* (1845), a plea for removal of all intellectual and economic disabilities. Minds and souls were neither masculine nor feminine, she argued. Genius had no sex. "What woman needs," she wrote, "is not as a woman to act or rule, but as a nature to grow, as an intellect to discern, as a soul to live freely and unimpeded, to unfold such powers as were given her when we left our common home."

UTOPIAN COMMUNITIES   The quest for utopia flourished in the climate of reform. "We are all a little mad here with numberless projects of social reform," Emerson wrote to Thomas Carlyle in 1840. "Not a reading man but has a draft of a new community in his pocket." Drafts of new communities had long been an American passion, at least since the Puritans set out to build a Wilderness Zion. The visionary communes of the nineteenth century often had purely economic and social objectives, but those that were rooted in religion proved most durable. An early instance, an offshoot of the Mennonites in 1732, the Ephrata Community in Pennsylvania practiced an almost monastic life into the early nineteenth century. Founder Johann Conrad Beissel's emphasis on music left a lasting imprint on American hymnology. In 1803 George Rapp led about 600 Lutheran come-outers from Württemberg to Pennsylvania. They took the Bible literally, and like Beissel's group, renounced sex. Since the millennium was near they had to keep ready. No quarrel went unsettled overnight, and all who had sinned confessed to Rapp before sleeping. Industrious and disciplined, the Rappites prospered, and persevered to the end of the century.

Sixteen utopian communities sprang up between 1820 and

1830, forty-two in the palmy days from 1830 to 1850, ten more between 1850 and 1870—in all more than a hundred between 1800 and 1900. Among the most durable were the Shakers, officially the United Society of Believers, founded by Ann Lee Stanley (Mother Ann), who reached New York state with eight followers in 1774. Believing religious fervor a sign of inspiration from the Holy Ghost, they had strange fits in which they saw visions and prophesied. These manifestations later evolved into a ritual dance—hence the name Shakers. Shaker doctrine held God to be a dual personality: in Christ the masculine side was manifested, in Mother Ann the feminine element. Mother Ann preached celibacy to prepare Shakers for the perfection that was promised them. The church would first gather in the elect, and eventually in the spirit world convert and save all mankind.

Mother Ann died in 1784, but the group found new leaders. From the first community at Mount Lebanon, New York, the movement spread to new colonies in New England, and soon afterward into Ohio and Kentucky. By 1830 about twenty groups were flourishing. In Shaker communities all property was held in common. Governance of the colonies was concentrated in the hands of select groups chosen by the ministry, or "Head of Influence" at Mount Lebanon. To outsiders this might seem almost despotic, but the Shakers emphasized equality of labor and reward, and members were free to leave at will. The Shakers' farms yielded a surplus for the market. They were among the leading sources of garden seed and medicinal herbs, and many of their manufactures, including clothing, household items, and especially furniture, were prized for their simple beauty. By the mid–twentieth century, however, few members remained alive; they had reached the peak of activity in the years 1830–1860.

John Humphrey Noyes, founder of the Oneida Community, got religion at one of Charles G. Finney's revivals and entered the ministry. He was forced out, however, when he concluded that with true conversion came perfection and a complete release from sin. In 1836 he gathered a group of "Perfectionists" around his home in Putney, Vermont. Ten years later Noyes announced a new doctrine of complex marriage, which meant that every man in the community was married to every woman and vice versa. To outsiders it looked like simple promiscuity and Noyes was arrested. He fled to New York and in 1848 established the Oneida Community, which numbered more than 200 by 1851.

The group eked out a living with farming and logging until the mid-1850s, when the inventor of a new steel trap joined the community. Oneida traps were soon known as the best. The community then branched out into sewing silk, canning fruits, and making silver spoons. The spoons were so popular that, with the addition of knives and forks, tableware became the Oneida speciality. Community Plate is still made. In 1879, however, the community faced a crisis when Noyes fled to Canada to avoid prosecution for adultery. The members then abandoned complex marriage, and in 1881 decided to convert into a joint-stock company, the Oneida Community, Ltd. A similar fate overtook the Amana Society, or Community of True Faith, a German group that migrated to New York state in 1843 and on to Iowa in 1850. Eventually, in 1932, beset by the problems of the Great Depression, they incorporated as a joint-stock company making refrigerators and eventually a great variety of home appliances.

In contrast to these communities, Robert Owen's New Harmony was based on a secular principle. A British capitalist who worried about the social effects of the factory system, Owen built a model factory town, supported labor legislation, and set forth a scheme for a model community in his pamphlet *A New View of Society* (1813). Later he snapped at a chance to buy the Rappites' town of Harmony, Indiana, and promptly christened it New Harmony. In Washington an audience including President Monroe crowded the hall of the House of Representatives to hear Owen tell about his high hopes.

In 1825 a varied group of about 900 colonists gathered in New Harmony for a period of transition from Owen's ownership to the new system of cooperation. The group began to run the former Rappite industries, and after only nine months' trial Owen turned over management of the colony to a town meeting of all residents and a council of town officers. The high proportion of learned participants generated a certain intellectual electricity about the place. Schools sprang up quickly. Owen's two sons started a sprightly paper, the *New Harmony Gazette.* There were frequent lectures and social gatherings with music and dancing.

For a time it looked like a brilliant success, but New Harmony soon fell into discord. The *Gazette* complained of "grumbling, carping, and murmuring" members and others who had the "disease of laziness." The problem, it seems, was a problem common to reform groups. Every idealist wanted his own patented plan put into practice. In 1827 Owen returned from a visit to England to find New Harmony insolvent. The following year he dissolved the project and sold or leased the lands on good terms, in many cases to the settlers. All that remained he turned over to his sons, who remained and became American citizens.

The 1840s brought a flurry of interest in the ideas of Fourieristic socialism. Charles Fourier, a Frenchman, proposed to reorder society into small units, or "phalanxes," ideally of 1,620 members. All property would be held in common and each phalanx would produce that for which it felt itself best suited; the joy of work and communal living would supply the incentive. By example the phalanxes would eventually cover the earth and displace capitalism. Fourier remained a prophet without honor in his own country, but Arthur Brisbane's book *The Social Destiny of Man* (1840) brought Fourierism before the American public and Horace Greeley's New York *Tribune* kept it there.

Greeley was in such a hurry to try out the idea, however, that Brisbane thought him rash. Brisbane was right. The first community, the Sylvania Phalanx in northern Pennsylvania, founded with Greeley's help in 1842, lasted but a year. Sylvania picked up 2,300 acres of land at little cost because it was remote and infertile. During their only season about 100 members produced just eleven bushels of grain on the four acres of arable land. Greeley lost $5,000. In all some forty or fifty phalansteries sprang up, but lasted on the average about two years.

Brook Farm was surely the most celebrated of all the utopian communities because it had the support of Emerson, Lowell, Whittier, and countless other well-known literary figures of New England. Nathaniel Hawthorne, a member, later memorialized its failure in his novel *The Blithedale Romance* (1852). George Ripley, a Unitarian minister and Transcendentalist, conceived of Brook Farm as a kind of early-day "think tank," combining high thinking and plain living. The place survived, however, mainly because of an excellent community school that drew tuition-paying students from outside. In 1844 Brook Farm converted itself into a phalanstery, but when a new central building burned down on the day of its dedication in 1846, the community spirit expired in the embers.

Utopian communities, with few exceptions, quickly ran into futility. Soon after Hawthorne left Brook Farm he wrote: "It already looks like a dream behind me." His life there was "an unnatural and unsuitable, and therefore an unreal one." Such experiments, performed in relative isolation, had little effect on the real world outside, where reformers wrestled with the sins of the multitudes. Among all the targets of reformers' wrath, one great evil would finally take precedence over the others— human bondage. The paradox of American slavery coupled with American freedom, of "the world's fairest hope linked with man's foulest crime," in Herman Melville's words, would inspire the climactic crusade of the age, abolitionism, one that would ultimately move to the center of the political stage and sweep the nation into an epic struggle.

FURTHER READING

Few single-volume works cover the diversity of early American reform. A good start is Perry Miller's *The Life of the Mind in America: From the Revolution to the Civil War* (1966),° on the intellectual evolution which ran concurrent with reformist behavior. Russel B. Nye's *Society and Culture in America, 1830–1860* (1974), provides a wide-ranging survey. Everyday behavior is stressed more in Carl Bode's *The Anatomy of American Popular Culture, 1840–1861* (1959). On reform itself, consult Alice F. Tyler's *Freedom's Ferment: Phases of American Social History to 1860* (1944).°

Sydney E. Ahlstrom's *A Religious History of the America People* (1972) gives a solid survey of antebellum religious movements and developments. More interpretative is Martin E. Marty's *Righteous Empire: The Protestant Experience in America* (1970). Henry F. May traces the legacy of rationalist thinking in *The Enlightenment in America* (1976).° Theodore D. Bozeman's *Protestants in an Age of Science: The Baconian Ideal and Antebellum American Religious Thought* (1977) examines similar themes for a later period. The development of the rationalist-oriented sects is the subject of Daniel W. Howe's *The Unitarian Conscience: Harvard Moral Philosophy, 1805–1861* (1970), David P. Edgell's *William Ellery Channing: An Intellectual Portrait* (1955), and H. M. Morais's *Deism in Eighteenth Century America* (1934). Revivals are covered in Whitney R. Cross's *The Burned Over District* (1950),° John B. Boles's *The Great Revival* (1972), and William G. McLoughlin's *Modern Revivalism: Charles Grandison Finney to Billy Graham* (1959). Donald G. Mathews, in *Religion in the Old South* (1977),° dissects the concept of the evangelical mind.

For splinter sects, the scholarship is most voluminous on the Mormons. Consult Klaus J. Hansen's *Mormonism and the American Experience* (1981), Leonard Arrington's *Great Basin Kingdom* (1958), and Fawn M. Brodie's *No Man Knows My History: The Life of Joseph Smith* (1945).

Francis O. Matthiessen's *American Renaissance* (1941),° examines the literary history of the antebellum period. Good for the interpretive contents are Richard W. B. Lewis's *The American Adam: Innocence, Tragedy, and Tradition in the Nineteenth Century* (1955) and Charles Feidelson, Jr.'s *Symbolism and American Art* (1953). The best introduction to transcendentalist thought are the writings of the transcendentalists themselves, collected in Perry Miller (ed.), *The Transcendentalists* (1950).° Also see Gay Wilson Allen's *Waldo Emerson: A Biography* (1981)° and Joel Porte's *Representative Man: Ralph Waldo Emerson in His Time* (1979). For Emerson's protégé, see Walter Harding's *Thoreau: Man of Concord* (1960), Sherman Paul's *The Shores of America: Thoreau's Inward Exploration* (1961), and Richard LeBeaux's *Young Man*

°These books are available in paperback editions.

Thoreau (1977).° A recent treatment of the poet Whitman is Justin Kaplan's *Walt Whitman: A Life* (1980).° Henry Nash Smith's *Virgin Land: The American West as Symbol and Myth* (1950),° examines some important themes of the romantics. A solid introduction to antebellum newspapers is Frank L. Mott's *American Journalism* (1962), while Glyndon Van Deusen's *Horace Greeley, Nineteenth-Century Crusader* (1953) documents the life of that famous editor. Barbara Novak's *Nature and Culture: American Landscape and Painting, 1825–1875* (1980),° provides an overview of the Hudson River School.

Lawrence Cremin's *American Education: The National Experience, 1783–1876* (1980),° traces early school reform. Other views on the topic appear in Stanley K. Schultze's *The Culture Factory: Boston Public Schools, 1789–1860* (1973), Michael Katz's *The Irony of Early School Reform* (1968),° and Jonathan Messerli's *Horace Mann* (1972).

Ronald G. Walters's *American Reformers* (1978),° surveys the general bounds of the reform impulse. For temperance, see W. G. Rorabaugh's *The Alcoholic Republic: An American Tradition* (1979),° Frank L. Byrne's *Prophet of Prohibition: Neal Dow and His Crusade* (1961), and Clifford S. Griffin's *Their Brother's Keeper: Moral Stewardship in the United States, 1800–1865* (1960). For the religious context of reform, consult Carroll Smith-Rosenberg's *Religion and the Rise of the American City: The New York Mission Movement* (1971). On prison reform and other humanitarian projects, see David J. Rothman's *The Discovery of the Asylum* (1971),° Helen D. Marshall's *Dorothea Dix: Forgotten Samaritan* (1937), and Gerald N. Grob's *Mental Institutions in America* (1973).

The literature on feminism is both voluminous and diverse. Surveys of feminist history which extend into the antebellum period include Carl N. Degler's *At Odds: Women and Family in America from the Revolution to the Present* (1980),° William L. O'Neill's *Everyone Was Brave: The Rise and Fall of Feminism in America* (1970),° Gerda Lerner's *The Woman in American History* (1970), and Mary P. Ryan's *Womanhood in America* (1975).° More specific are Eleanor Flexner's *Century of Struggle: The Women's Rights Movement in the United States* (1975)° and Linda Gordon's *Woman's Body, Woman's Right: A Social History of Birth Control in America* (1976).° More particular to the antebellum period are Keith Melder's *The Beginnings of Sisterhood* (1977), Nancy Cott's *The Bonds of Womanhood: "Women's Sphere" in New England, 1780–1835* (1977),° Barbara J. Berg's *The Remembered Gate: Origins of American Feminism—The Woman and the City, 1800–1860* (1977), and Ellen C. DuBois's *Feminism and Suffrage: The Emergence of an Independent Women's Movement in America, 1848–1869* (1978).° Biographical studies include Alma Lutz's *Susan B. Anthony* (1959), Lois Banner's *Elizabeth Cady Stanton* (1980),° and Paula Blanchard's *Margaret Fuller: From Transcendentalism to Revolution* (1978).°

Michael Fellman's *The Unbounded Frame: Freedom and Community in Nineteenth Century Utopianism* (1973) and Mark Holloway's *Heavens on Earth* (1951) survey the utopian movements. J. F. C. Harrison's *Quest for the New Moral World: Robert Owen and the Owenites in Britain and*

America (1969); Robert O. Thomas's *The Man Who Would Be Perfect* (1977), on John Humphrey Noyes; Marin L. Carden's *Oneida* (1969); and Henri Desroche's *The American Shakers from Neo-Christianity to Pre-Socialism* (1971) all treat specific experiments. Also helpful is Lawrence Foster's *Religion and Sexuality: Three American Communal Experiments of the Nineteenth Century* (1981).

Perspectives on family life during the times of reforms can be gained from Milton Rugoff's *The Beechers: An American Family in the Nineteenth Century* (1981) and Mary P. Ryan's *Cradle of the Middle Class: The Family in Oneida Country, New York, 1790–1865* (1981).

14

MANIFEST DESTINY

The Tyler Years

When William Henry Harrison took office in 1841, elected like Jackson mainly on the strength of his military record and without commitment on issues, the Whig leaders expected him to be a figurehead. At first it did seem that he would be a tool in the hands of Webster and Clay. Webster became secretary of state and, while Clay preferred to stay in the Senate, the cabinet was filled with his friends. Within a few days of the inauguration there were signs of strain between Harrison and Clay, whose disappointment at missing the nomination had made him peevish and arrogant. But the enmity never had a chance to develop, for Harrison served the shortest term of any president—after the longest inaugural address. At the inauguration on a cold and rainy day he caught cold. The importunings of office seekers in the following month filled his days and sapped his strength. On April 4, 1841, exactly one month after the inauguration, he died of pneumonia.

Thus John Tyler of Virginia, the first vice-president to succeed on the death of a president, was to serve practically all of Harrison's term. And if there was ambiguity about where Harrison stood, there was none about Tyler. At age fifty-one he already had a long career behind him as legislator, governor, congressman, and senator, and was on record on all the important issues. At an earlier time he might have been called an Old Republican, stubbornly opposed to everything that was signified by Clay's American System—protective tariffs, a national bank, or internal improvements at national expense—and in favor of strict construction and states' rights. Once a Democrat, he had broken with Jackson's stand on nullification and his imperious use of executive authority. Tyler had been chosen to "balance" the

509

ticket, with no belief that he would wield power. And to compound the irony, because he was known as a friend of Clay, his choice had been designed in part to pacify Clay's disappointed followers.

DOMESTIC AFFAIRS   Given more finesse on Clay's part, personal friendship might have enabled him to bridge the policy divisions among the Whigs. But for once, driven by disappointment and ambition, the "Great Pacificator" had lost his instinct for compromise. When Congress met in special session at the end of May 1841 Clay introduced, and the Whig majority passed, a series of resolutions designed to supply the platform which the party had evaded in the previous election. The chief points were repeal of the Independent Treasury, establishment of a third Bank of the United States, distribution to the states of proceeds from public land sales, and a higher tariff. Clay then set out to push his program through Congress. Despite the known views of Tyler, he remained hopeful. "Tyler dares not resist me. I will drive him before me," he said. Tyler, it turned out, was not easily driven.

By 1842 Clay's program was in ruins. He had failed to get a new bank, and distribution was abandoned with adoption of the high 1842 tariff. Even his successes were temporary—a Democratic Congress and president in 1846 restored the Independent Treasury and cut the tariff, leaving preemption (which legalized the frontier tradition of "squatter's rights") as the only major permanent achievement of the Whigs, something that had been no part of Clay's original scheme. If the program was in ruins, however, Clay's leadership of his party was fixed beyond question, and Tyler was left in the position of a president without a party.

FOREIGN AFFAIRS   In foreign relations, on the other hand, developments of immense significance were taking place. Several unsettled issues had arisen to trouble relations between Britain and the United States. In 1837 a forlorn insurrection in Upper Canada led to the seizure of the American steamboat *Caroline* by Canadians who set it afire and let it drift over Niagara Falls. In the course of the incident one American was killed. The British ignored all protests, but President Van Buren called out militia under Gen. Winfield Scott to prevent frontier violations in either direction. The issue faded until 1840 when Alexander McLeod, a Canadian, was arrested and brought to trial in New York state after he boasted of his participation in the incident and his responsibility for the killing. The British government now did admit that it had ordered destruction of the vessel and argued that McLeod could not be held personally responsible. The incident fortunately was closed when McLeod proved to have an air-tight alibi—he was miles away and his story had been nothing but barroom braggadocio.

Another issue involved the suppression of the African slave trade, which both the United States and Britain had outlawed in 1808. In August 1841 Prime Minister Palmerston asserted the right of British patrols off the coast of Africa to board and search vessels flying the American flag to see if they carried slaves, but the American government remembered the impressments and seizures during the Napoleonic Wars and refused to accept it. Relations were further strained late in 1841 when American slaves on a brig, the *Creole,* bound from Hampton Roads to New Orleans, mutinied and sailed into Nassau, where the British set them free. Webster demanded that the slaves be returned as American property, but the British refused.

Fortunately at this point a new British ministry under Sir Robert Peel decided to accept Webster's overtures for negotiations and sent Lord Ashburton to Washington. Ashburton was widely known to be friendly to Americans, and the talks proceeded smoothly. The Maine boundary was settled in what Webster later called "the battle of the maps." Webster settled for about seven-twelfths of the contested lands along the Maine boundary, and except for Oregon, which remained under joint occupation, he settled the other border disputes by accepting the existing line between the Connecticut and St. Lawrence rivers, and by compromising on the line between Lake Superior and the Lake of the Woods. This last was important because it gave the United States most of the Mesabi iron range, which was apparently known to

THE WEBSTER-ASHBURTON TREATY, 1842

Tyler and Webster but not to Ashburton. The Webster-Ashburton treaty (1842) also provided for joint patrols off Africa to repress the slave trade.

Moving West

In the early 1840s the American people were no more stirred by the quarrels of Tyler and Clay over such issues as banking, tariffs, and distribution, important as they were, than students of history would be at a later date. Nor was the pulse much quickened by the adjustment of boundaries supposedly settled in 1783. What stirred the blood was the mounting evidence that the "empire of freedom" was hurdling the barriers of the "Great American Desert" and the Rocky Mountains, reaching out toward the Pacific coast. In 1845 John Louis O'Sullivan, editor of the *United States Magazine and Democratic Review*, gave a name to this bumptious spirit of expansion. "Our manifest destiny," he wrote, "is to overspread the continent allotted by Providence for the free development of our yearly multiplying millions." Traders and trappers, as always, were the harbingers of empire, and an unguarded boundary was no barrier to their entering Mexican borderlands sparsely peopled and scarcely governed from the remote capital.

REACHING THE ROCKIES   One of the first magnets to draw Americans was Santa Fe, a remote outpost of Spanish empire founded in the seventeenth century, the capital and trading center for a population of perhaps 60,000 in New Mexico. In September 1821 William Becknell, an enterprising merchant, gathered a party to head up the Arkansas River on a horse-trading expedition. Becknell and his men stumbled onto a group of Mexican soldiers who received them hospitably with the news that Mexico was newly independent and that American traders were welcome in Santa Fe, where Becknell sold his goods for Spanish silver dollars. His second expedition in 1822 followed a new desert route along the Cimarron River. Word spread quickly and every spring thereafter merchants gathered at Independence, Missouri, for the long journey of wagon trains along the Santa Fe Trail. The trade never involved more than one or two hundred merchants, but it was a profitable enterprise in which American goods were traded for the gold, silver, and furs of the Mexicans. In 1843 trouble over the Texas question caused the Mexican government to close the trade once again.

The Santa Fe traders had pioneered more than a new trail.

They showed that heavy wagons could cross the plains and penetrate the mountains, and they developed the technique of organized caravans for mutual protection. They also began to
discover the weakness of Mexico's control over its northern borderlands, and to implant in American minds their contempt for
the "mongrel" population of the region. From the 1820s on,
however, that population had begun to include a few Americans
who lingered in Santa Fe or Taos, using them as jumping-off
points for hunting and trapping expeditions northward and westward.

The more important avenue for the fur trade, however, was
the Missouri River with its many tributaries. The heyday of the
mountain fur trade began in 1822 when a Missouri businessman,
William H. Ashley, sent his first trading party to the upper Missouri. In 1825 Ashley devised the "rendezvous system," in
which trappers, traders, and Indians from all over the Rocky
Mountain country gathered annually at some designated place,
usually in or near the Grand Tetons, in order to trade. But by
1840 the great days of the western fur trade were over. The
streams no longer teemed with beavers. The country was
trapped out, and the animals were saved from extinction only by
the caprice of fashion, which now decreed that men's dress hats
should be made of silk rather than beaver skins. But during the
1820s and 1830s the trade had sired a uniquely reckless breed of
"mountain men," who deserted civilization for the pursuit of the
beaver, reverted to a primitive existence in the wilderness,
sometimes in splendid isolation, sometimes in the shelter of
primitive forts, and sometimes among the Indians. They were the
first to find their way around in the Rocky Mountains and they pioneered the trails over which settlers by the 1840s were beginning to flood the Oregon country and trickle across the border
into California.

THE OREGON COUNTRY Beyond the mountains the Oregon country stretched from the Forty-second Parallel north to 54° 40′,
between which Spain and Russia had given up their claims, leaving Great Britain and the United States as the only claimants.
Under the Convention of 1818 the two countries had agreed to
"joint occupation." Until the 1830s, however, joint occupation
had been a legal technicality, because the only American presence was the occasional mountain man who wandered into the
Pacific slope or the infrequent trading vessel from Boston, Salem,
or New York.

The effective impulse for American settlement came finally
from an unlikely source. In 1833 the *Christian Advocate and*

Herald, a Methodist journal, published a fanciful letter from
William Walker, an educated Wyandot Indian. It told of western
tribesmen who wanted the white man's "Book of Heaven" and
missionaries to instruct them in the Christian faith. Soon every
pulpit and church paper was echoing this fictitious request, and
before the year was ended the Methodist Missionary Society had
sent out the Rev. Jason Lee, who established a mission in the fertile Willamette Valley, south of the Columbia.

Lee sent back glowing reports and returned east to speak on
the attractions of Oregon; his mission in the fertile Willamette
Valley became the chief magnet for settlement. By the late
1830s a trickle of emigrants was flowing along the Oregon Trail.
In 1841 and 1842 the first sizable wagon trains made the trip,
and in 1843 the movement began to assume the proportions of
mass migrations. That year about a thousand overlanders followed the trail westward from Independence, Missouri, along

WAGON TRAILS WEST

the Platte River into Wyoming, through South Pass down to Fort Bridger (abode of a celebrated Mountain Man, Jim Bridger), then down the Snake River to the Columbia and along the Columbia to their goal in the Willamette Valley. By 1845 there were about 5,000 settlers in the region.

EYEING CALIFORNIA   California, thinly peopled by mission friars and Mexican rancheros, had drawn New England ships into an illegal traffic in sea-otter skins before the end of the eighteenth century. By the late 1820s American trappers wandered in from time to time and American ships began to enter the "hide and tallow" trade. The ranchos of California produced cowhide and beef tallow in large quantity and both products enjoyed a brisk demand, cowhides mainly for shoes and the tallow chiefly for candles. Ships from Boston, Salem, or New York, well stocked with trade goods, struggled southward around Cape Horn and northward to the customs office at the California capital of Monterey. From there the ships worked their way down the coast, stopping to sell their goods and take on return cargoes. Richard Henry Dana's *Two Years before the Mast* (1840), a classic account of his adventures as a seaman in the trade, brought the scene vividly to life for his many readers and focused their attention on the romance and the potential of California.

By the mid-1830s shippers began setting up agents on the scene to buy the hides and store them until a company ship arrived. One of these agents, Thomas O. Larkin at Monterey, was destined to play a leading role in the American acquisition of California. Larkin stuck pretty much to his trade, operating a retail business on the side, while others branched out and struck it rich in ranching. The most noteworthy of the alien nabobs, however, was not American, but Swiss. John A. Sutter had tried the Santa Fe trade first, then found his way to California via Oregon, Hawaii, and Alaska. In Monterey he persuaded the Mexican governor to give him land on which to plant a colony of Swiss emigrés.

At the juncture of the Sacramento and American Rivers (later the site of Sacramento) he built an enormous enclosure that guarded an entire village of settlers and shops. At New Helvetia (Americans called it Sutter's Fort), completed in 1843, no Swiss colony materialized, but the enclosure became the chief mecca for Americans bent on settling the Sacramento country. It stood at the end of what became the most traveled route through the Sierras, the California Trail which forked off from the Oregon Trail and led through the mountains south of Lake Tahoe. By the start of 1846 there were perhaps 800 Americans in California, along with some 8,000–12,000 Californios of Spanish descent.

*John Charles Frémont, the
Pathfinder. [Library of
Congress]*

The premier press agent for California, and the Far West generally, was John Charles Frémont, the Pathfinder—who found mainly paths that the Mountain Men showed him. In the early 1840s his new father-in-law, Missouri Sen. Thomas Hart Benton, arranged the explorations toward Oregon that made him famous. In 1842 he mapped the Oregon Trail beyond South Pass—and met Christopher Carson, one of the most knowledgeable of the mountain men, who became his frequent associate, and as Kit Carson, the most famous frontiersman after Daniel Boone. In 1843–1844 Frémont went on to Oregon, then made a heroic sweep down the eastern slopes of the Sierras, headed southward through the central valley of California, bypassed the mountains in the south, and returned via Great Salt Lake. His reports on both expeditions, published together in 1845, enjoyed a career rare for a government document. In numerous popular reprints they gained a wide circulation.

American presidents, beginning with Jackson, tried to acquire at least northern California, down to San Francisco Bay, by purchase from Mexico. Jackson reasoned that as a free state California could balance the future admission of Texas as a slave state. But Jackson's agent Anthony Butler had to be recalled after a clumsy effort to bribe Mexican officials. Tyler's minister to Mexico resumed talks, but they ended abruptly after a bloodless comic-opera conquest of Monterey by the commander of the American Pacific Fleet.

Rumors flourished that the British and French were scheming to grab California, though neither government had such intentions. Political conditions in Mexico left the remote territory in near anarchy much of the time, as governors came and went in rapid succession. Amid the chaos substantial Californios reasoned that they would be better off if they cut the ties to Mexico altogether. Some favored an independent state, perhaps under French or British protection. A larger group, led by a Sonoma cattleman, Mariano G. Vallejo, admired the balance of central and local authority in the United States and felt their interests might best be served by American annexation. By the time the Americans were ready to fire the spark of rebellion, there was little will to resist.

ANNEXING TEXAS

AMERICAN SETTLEMENTS   Manifest Destiny was most clearly at work in the most accessible of all the Mexican borderlands, Texas. There more Americans were resident than in all the other coveted regions combined. Many claimed in fact, if with little evidence, that Texas had been part of the Louisiana Purchase, abandoned only when John Quincy Adams had accepted a boundary at the Sabine River in 1819. Adams himself, as president, tried to make up for the loss by offering to buy Texas for $1 million, but Mexico refused both that and a later offer of $5 million, from Jackson. Meanwhile, however, it was rapidly turning into an American province, for Mexico welcomed American settlers there.

First and foremost among the promoters of Anglo-American settlement was Stephen F. Austin, a resident of Missouri, who gained from Mexico confirmation of a huge land grant originally given to his father by Spanish authorities. Indeed before Mexican independence was fully won he had begun a colony on the lower Brazos River late in 1821 and by 1824 had more than 2,000 settlers on his lands. In 1825, under a National Colonization Law, the state of Coahuila-Texas offered large tracts to *empresarios* who promised to sponsor immigrants. Most of the newcomers were southern farmers drawn to rich new cotton lands going for only a few cents an acre. By 1830 the coastal region of eastern Texas had approximately 20,000 white settlers and 1,000 Negro slaves brought in to work the cotton.

At that point the Mexican government took alarm at the flood of strangers who threatened to engulf the province. A new edict forbade further immigration, and troops moved to the frontier to enforce the law. But illegal immigrants moved across the long border as easily as illegal immigrants would later cross over in the other direction. By 1835 the American population had grown to around 30,000, about ten times the number of Mexicans in Texas. Friction mounted in 1832 and 1833 as Americans organized conventions to demand a state of their own, separate from Coahuila. Instead of granting Texans their own state, General Santa Anna, who had seized power in Mexico, dissolved the national congress late in 1834, abolished the federal system, and became dictator of a centralized state. Texans rose in rebellion, summoned a convention which, like the earlier Continental Congress, adopted a "Declaration of Causes" for taking up arms, and pledged to fight for the old Mexican constitution. On March 2, 1836, however, the Texans declared their independence as Santa Anna approached with an army of conquest.

INDEPENDENCE FROM MEXICO   The Mexican army delivered its first blow at San Antonio, where it had already brought under siege a small Texas garrison holed up behind the adobe walls of an abandoned mission, the Alamo. On March 6, four days after the declaration of independence, the Mexican force of 4,000 launched a frontal assault and, taking fearful losses, finally swarmed over the walls and annihiliated the 187 Texans in the Alamo, including their commander William B. Travis and the frontier heroes Davy Crockett and Jim Bowie, slave smuggler and inventor of the Bowie knife. It was a complete victory, but a costly one. The defenders of the Alamo sold their lives at the cost of 1,544 Mexicans, and inspired the rest of Texas to fanatical resistance.

Commander-in-chief of the Texas forces was Sam Houston, a Tennessee frontiersman who had learned war under the tutelage of Old Hickory at Horseshoe Bend, had later represented the Nashville district in Congress, and had moved to Texas only

Sam Houston, president of the Republic of Texas before it was annexed by the United States. [Library of Congress]

three years before. Houston beat a strategic retreat eastward, gathering reinforcements as he went, including volunteer recruits from the United States. Just west of the San Jacinto River he finally paused near the site of the city that later bore his name, and on April 21 surprised a Mexican encampment there. The Texans charged, yelling "Remember the Alamo," overwhelmed the Mexican force within fifteen minutes, and took Santa Anna prisoner. The Mexican dictator bought his freedom at the price of a treaty recognizing Texan independence, with the Rio Grande as the boundary. The Mexican Congress repudiated the treaty, but the war was at an end.

THE MOVE FOR ANNEXATION   The Lone Star Republic then drafted a constitution, made Houston its first president, and voted almost unanimously for annexation to the United States as soon as the opportunity arose. Houston's old friend Jackson was still president, but even Old Hickory could be discreet when delicacy demanded it. The addition of a new slave state at a time when Congress was beset with abolitionist petitions threatened a serious sectional quarrel which might endanger the election of Van Buren. Worse than that, it raised the spectre of war with Mexico. Jackson kept his counsel and even delayed recognition of the Texas Republic until his last day in office. Van Buren shied away from the issue during his entire term as president.

Rebuffed in Washington, Texans turned their thoughts to a separate destiny. Under President Mirabeau Bonaparte Lamar, elected in 1838, they began to talk of expanding to the Pacific as a new nation that would rival the United States. France and Britain extended recognition and began to develop trade relations. Texas supplied them an independent source of cotton, new markets, and promised also to become an obstacle to American expansion. The British, who had emancipated slaves in their colonies in 1833, hoped Texans might embrace abolition as the price of guarantees against Mexico.

The Texans, however, had never abandoned their hopes of annexation. Reports of growing British influence created anxieties in the United States government and among southern slaveholders, who became the chief advocates of annexation. In 1843 Abel P. Upshur, Tyler's secretary of state, opened secret negotiations with Texas. Before the negotiations were far advanced, Upshur met an untimely death aboard a navy frigate when a cannon exploded, killing both him and the secretary of the navy. In April John C. Calhoun, the new secretary of state, completed a treaty which went to the Senate for ratification.

Calhoun chose this moment also to send the British minister,

Richard Pakenham, a letter instructing him on the blessings of slavery and stating that annexation of Texas was needed to foil the British abolitionists. Publication of the note fostered the claim that annexation was planned less in the national interest than to promote the expansion of slavery. It was so worded, Francis P. Blair wrote Jackson, as to "drive off every northern man from the support of the measure." Sectional division, plus fear of a war with Mexico, contributed to the Senate's overwhelming rejection of the treaty. Solid Whig opposition contributed more than anything to its defeat.

POLK'S PRESIDENCY

THE ELECTION OF 1844   Prudent leaders in both political parties had hoped to keep this divisive issue out of the 1844 campaign. Clay and Van Buren, the leading candidates, had reached the same conclusion about Texas: when the treaty was submitted to the Senate, they both wrote letters opposing annexation because it would create the danger of war. Both letters, dated three days apart, appeared in separate Washington newspapers on April 27, 1844. Clay's "Raleigh letter" (written while he was on a southern tour) added that annexation was "dangerous to the integrity of the Union . . . and not called for by any general expression of public opinion." The outcome of the Whig convention in Baltimore seemed to bear out his view. Party leaders showed no qualms about Clay's stance. The convention nominated him unanimously, and the Whig platform omitted any reference to Texas.

The Democratic convention was a different story. Van Buren's southern supporters, including Jackson, left him. Expansionist forces got the convention to adopt the two-thirds rule once again. It had served Van Buren's cause before, but this time it doomed his chances. With the convention deadlocked, on the eighth ballot the expansionists brought forward James K. Polk of Tennessee, and on the ninth ballot he became the first "dark horse" candidate to win a major-party nomination. The party platform took an unequivocal stand favoring expansion, and to win support in the North and West as well as the South it linked the questions of Oregon and Texas: "our title to the whole of the territory of Oregon is clear and unquestionable," the party proclaimed, and called for "the reoccupation of Oregon and the reannexation of Texas."

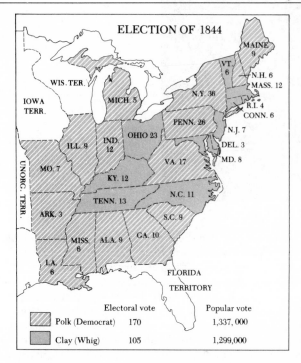

ELECTION OF 1844

	Electoral vote	Popular vote
Polk (Democrat)	170	1,337,000
Clay (Whig)	105	1,299,000

The combination of southern and western expansionism was a winning strategy, so popular that Clay began to hedge his statement on Texas. While he still believed the integrity of the Union the chief consideration, he had "no personal objection to the annexation of Texas" if it could be achieved "without dishonor, without war, with the common consent of the Union, and upon just and fair terms." His explanation seemed clear enough, but prudence was no match for spread-eagle oratory and the emotional pull of Manifest Destiny. The net result of Clay's stand was to turn more antislavery votes to the Liberty party, which increased its count from about 7,000 in 1840 to more than 62,000 in 1844. In the western counties of New York the Liberty party drew enough votes away from the Whigs to give the state to Polk. With New York, Clay would have carried the election by seven electoral votes. Polk won a narrow plurality of 38,000 popular votes nationwide (the first president to win without a majority) but a clear majority of the electoral college, 170 to 105.

"Who is James K. Polk?" the Whigs scornfully asked in the campaign. But the man was not as obscure as they implied. He

James Knox Polk, in a daguerrotype by Mathew Brady. [Library of Congress]

was a dark horse only in the sense that he was not a candidate before the convention. Born near Charlotte, North Carolina, trained in mathematics and the classics at the University of North Carolina, Polk had moved to Tennessee as a young man. A successful lawyer and planter, he had entered politics early, served fourteen years in Congress (four as Speaker of the House) and two as governor of Tennessee. Young Hickory, as his partisans liked to call him, had none of Jackson's charisma, but shared his prejudices and made up for his lack of color by stubborn determination and hard work, which destroyed his health during four years in the White House. March 4, 1845, was dark and rainy; Polk delivered his inaugural address to "a large assemblage of umbrellas," as John Quincy Adams described it. The speech was as colorless as the day, a recitation of Jeffersonian and Jacksonian principles in which Polk denounced protective tariffs, national banks, and implied powers, and again claimed title to Oregon.

POLK'S PROGRAM   In domestic affairs Young Hickory hewed to the principle of the old hero, but the new Jacksonians subtly reflected the growing influence of the slaveholding South within the party. Abolitionism, Polk warned, could bring the dissolution of the Union. Antislavery northerners had already begun to drift away from the Democratic party, which New York Rep. Lemuel Stetson complained was coming to represent the slaveholding interest.

Soon after Polk took office he explained his objectives to the historian George Bancroft, his navy secretary. His major objectives were reduction of the tariff, reestablishment of the Independent Treasury, settlement of the Oregon question, and the acquisition of California. He got them all. The Tariff of 1846 replaced specific or flat duties with *ad valorem* (or percentage) duties and reduced the tariff to an average level of about 26.5 percent. In the same year Polk persuaded Congress to restore the Independent Treasury, which the Whigs had eliminated. Twice Polk vetoed internal improvement bills. In each case his blows to the American System of Henry Clay's Whigs satisfied the urges of the slaveholding South, but at the cost of annoying northern protectionists and westerners who wanted internal improvements.

THE STATE OF TEXAS   But the chief focus of Polk's concern remained geographical expansion. He privately vowed to Bancroft his purpose of acquiring California, and New Mexico as well, preferably by purchase. The acquisition of Texas was already under way before Polk took office. President Tyler, taking Polk's election as a mandate to act, asked Congress to accomplish annexation by joint resolution, which required only a simple majority in each house and avoided the two-thirds Senate vote needed to ratify a treaty. Congress had read the election returns too, and after a bitter debate over slavery, the resolution passed by votes of 27 to 25 in the Senate and 120 to 98 in the House. Tyler signed the resolution on March 1, 1845, offering to admit Texas to statehood. The new state would keep its public lands but pay its own war debt, and with its own consent might be divided into as many as five states in the near future. A Texas convention accepted the offer in July, the voters of Texas ratified the action in October, and the new state formally entered the Union on December 29, 1845.

OREGON   Meanwhile the Oregon issue heated up as expansionists aggressively insisted that Polk abandon previous offers to settle on the Forty-ninth Parallel and stand by the platform pledge to take all of Oregon. The bumptious expansionists were prepared to risk war with Britain while relations with Mexico were simultaneously moving toward the breaking point. "Fifty-four forty or fight," they intoned. "All of Oregon or none." In his inaugural address Polk declared the American title to Oregon "clear and unquestionable," but privately he favored a prudent compromise. War with Mexico was brewing; the territory up to 54° 40′ seemed of less importance than Puget Sound or the ports of California, on which the British also were thought to have an eye. Since Monroe each administration had offered to extend the boundary along the Forty-ninth Parallel. In July 1845 Polk and Buchanan renewed the offer, only to have it refused by the British minister, Richard Pakenham.

Polk withdrew the offer and went back to his claim to all of Oregon. In the annual message to Congress at year's end, he asked for permission to give a year's notice that joint occupation would be abrogated, and revived the Monroe Doctrine with a new twist: "The people of *this continent* alone have the right to decide their own destiny." To a hesitant congressman he avowed that "the only way to treat John Bull was to look him straight in the eye." After a long and bitter debate Congress adopted the resolution, but Polk was playing a bluff game. War with Mexico seemed increasingly certain and Secretary of State Buchanan privately informed the British government that any new offer would be submitted to the Senate.

Fortunately for Polk the British government had no enthusiasm for war over that remote wilderness at the cost of profitable trade relations with the United States. From the British viewpoint, the only land in dispute all along had been between the Forty-ninth Parallel and the Columbia River. Now the fur trade

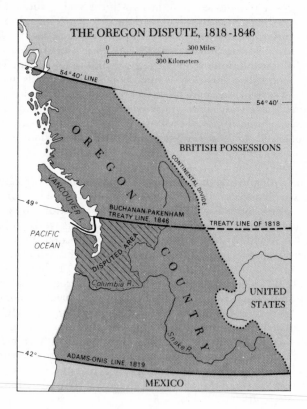

THE OREGON DISPUTE, 1818-1846

of the region was a dying industry. In early June 1846 the British government submitted a draft treaty to extend the border along the Forty-ninth Parallel and through the main channel south of Vancouver Island. On June 15 Buchanan and British Minister Pakenham signed it, and three days later it was ratified in the Senate, where the only opposition came from a group of bitter-end expansionists representing the Old Northwest who wanted more. Most of the country was satisfied. Southerners cared less about Oregon than Texas, and northern business interests valued British trade more than they valued Oregon. Besides, the country was already at war with Mexico.

THE MEXICAN WAR

THE OUTBREAK OF WAR Relations with Mexico had gone from bad to worse. On March 6, 1845, two days after Polk took office, the Mexican ambassador broke off relations and left for home to protest the annexation of Texas. When an effort at negotiation failed, Polk focused his efforts on unilateral initiatives. Already he was egging on American intrigues in California. On October 17, 1845, he had written Consul Thomas O. Larkin in Monterey that the president would make no effort to induce California into the Union, but "if the people should desire to unite their destiny with ours, they would be received as brethren." Larkin, who could take a hint, began to line up Americans and sympathetic Californios. Meanwhile Polk ordered American troops under Gen. Zachary Taylor to take up positions on the Rio Grande in the new state of Texas. These positions lay in territory that was doubly disputed: Mexico recognized neither the American annexation of Texas nor the Rio Grande boundary.

The last hope for peace died when John Slidell, sent to Mexico City to negotiate a settlement, finally gave up on his mission in March. After receiving him back in early May 1846, Polk resolved that he could achieve his purposes only by force. He sought and got the cabinet's approval of a war message to Congress. That very evening, May 9, the news arrived that Mexicans had attacked American soldiers north of the Rio Grande. Eleven Americans were killed, five wounded, and the remainder taken prisoner.

In his war message Polk could now take the high ground that the war was a response to aggression, a recognition that war had been forced upon the United States. "The cup of forbearance had been exhausted" before the incident; now, he said, Mexico "has passed the boundary of the United States, has invaded our territory, and shed American blood upon the American soil." The House quickly passed the war resolution, 174 to 14, the Senate on the next day by 40 to 2 with 3 abstentions, including Calhoun who feared that acquiring new territory would inflame the slavery issue. Polk signed the declaration of war on May 13. Both votes exaggerated the extent of support for the war. In the House twenty-seven members favored an amendment stating that the resolution should not be construed as approval of Polk's moving troops into the disputed area between the Nueces and the Rio Grande. The House authorized a call for 50,000 volunteers and a war appropriation of $10 million, but sixty-seven Whigs voted against that measure, another token of rising opposition to the war.

OPPOSITION TO THE WAR   In the Mississippi Valley, where expansion fever ran high, the war was immensely popular. The farther away from the scene of action, as a general rule, the less the enthusiasm for "Mr. Polk's War." Whigs ranged from lukewarm to hostile. John Quincy Adams, who voted against participation, called it "a most unrighteous war," and an obscure one-term congressman from Illinois named Abraham Lincoln, upon taking his seat in December 1847, began introducing "spot resolutions," calling on Polk to name the spot where American blood had been shed on American soil. If he were Mexican, Sen. Thomas Corwin of Ohio said, he would ask: "Have you not room in your own country to bury your dead men? If they come into mine, we will greet you, with bloody hands, and welcome you to hospitable graves."

Once again, as in 1812, New England was a hotbed of opposition, largely in the belief that this war was the work of "Land-Jobbers and Slave-Jobbers." As the Massachusetts poet James Russell Lowell put it in his *Biglow Papers*:

> They just want this Californy
> So's to lug new slave-states in
> To abuse ye, an' to scorn ye,
> An' to plunder ye like sin.

Some New England men, including Lowell, were ready to separate from the slave states, and the Massachusetts legislature formally pronounced the conflict a war of conquest. But before the war ended some antislavery men had a change of heart. Mexican territory seemed so unsuited to plantation staples that they endorsed expansion in hope of enlarging the area of free soil. Manifest Destiny exerted a potent influence even on those who opposed the war. *The Harbinger*, house organ of Brook Farm, managed to have it both ways. "This plundering aggression," the paper editorialized, "is monstrously iniquitous, but after all it seems to be completing a more universal design of Providence of extending the power and intelligence of advanced civilized nations."

PREPARING FOR BATTLE Both the United States and Mexico approached the war ill-prepared. American policy had been incredibly reckless, risking war with both Britain and Mexico while doing nothing to strenghten the armed forces until war came. At the outset of war the United States' regular army numbered barely over 7,000 in contrast to the Mexican force of 32,000. Before the war ended the American force grew to 104,000, of whom about 31,000 were regular army troops and marines. Most of these were six- and twelve-month volunteers from the West. Volunteer militia companies, often filled with frontier toughs, made up as raunchy a crew as ever graced the American military—innocent of uniforms, standard equipment, and discipline alike. One observer watched a band of such recruits with "torn and dirty shirts—uncombed heads—unwashed faces" trying to drill, "all hollowing, cursing, yelling like so many incarnate fiends." Repeatedly, despite the best efforts of the commanding generals, these undisciplined forces ran out of control in plunder, rape, and murder.

Nevertheless, being used to a rough-and-tumble life, they overmatched larger Mexican forces which had their own problems with training, discipline and munitions. Mexican artillery pieces were generally obsolete and the powder was so faulty that American soldiers could often dodge cannon balls that fell short and bounced ineffectively along the ground.

The United States entered the war without even a tentative plan of action. One had to be worked out hastily, and politics complicated things. What Polk wanted, Thomas Hart Benton wrote later, was "a small war, just large enough to require a treaty of peace, and not large enough to make military reputations, dangerous for the presidency." Winfield Scott, general-in-chief of the army, was both a Whig and politically ambitious. Nevertheless Polk named him at first to take charge of the Rio Grande front. When Scott fell into disputes with Secretary of War William L. Marcy, the exasperated Polk had Marcy withdraw the appointment. Scott, already known as "Old Fuss and Feathers" for his insistence on proper uniform, had also a genius for absurd turns of phrase. He began an indignant reply to Marcy with the remark that he got the secretary's letter as he "sat down to take a hasty plate of soup." One Washington wit promptly dubbed him Marshal Tureen.

There seemed now a better choice. Zachary Taylor's men had scored two victories over Mexican forces north of the Rio Grande, at Palo Alto (May 8) and Resaca de la Palma (May 9). On May 18 Taylor crossed over and occupied Matamoros, which a demoralized and bloodied Mexican army had abandoned. These quick victories brought Taylor instant popularity and the president responded willingly to the demand that he be made commander for the conquest of Mexico. "Old Rough and Ready" Taylor, a thickset and none-too-handsome man of sixty-one, seemed unlikely stuff from which to fashion a hero and impressed Polk as less of a political threat than Scott. Taylor acted at least as cautiously as Scott, awaiting substantial reinforcements and supplies before moving any deeper into Mexico. But without a major battle he had achieved Polk's main objective, the conquest of Mexico's northern provinces.

ANNEXATION OF CALIFORNIA   Along the Pacific coast, conquest was under way before definite news of the Mexican war arrived. Near the end of 1845 John C. Frémont brought out a band of sixty frontiersmen ostensibly on another exploration of California and Oregon. "Frémont's conduct was extremely mysterious," John A. Sutter wrote. "Flitting about the country with an armed body of men, he was regarded with suspicion by everybody." When José Castro, commandant at Monterey, ordered him out of the

Zachary Taylor, "Old Rough and Ready." This daguerrotype was made around the time of the Mexican War. [Chicago Historical Society]

Salinas Valley, he occupied the peak of Gavilan Mountain and defied the Mexicans to oust him, but soon changed his mind and headed for Oregon. In June 1846 Frémont and his men moved south into the Sacramento Valley. Americans in the area fell upon Sonoma on June 14, proclaimed William B. Ide president of the "Republic of California," and hoisted the hastily designed Bear Flag, a California Grizzly and star painted on white cloth—an idealized version of which became the state flag.

By the end of June Frémont had endorsed the Bear Flag Republic and set out for Monterey. Before he arrived, Commodore John D. Sloat of the Pacific Fleet, having heard of the outbreak of hostilities, sent a party ashore to raise the American flag and proclaim California a part of the United States. The Republic of California had lasted less than a month and most Californians of whatever origin welcomed a change that promised order in preference to the confusion of the unruly Bear Flaggers.

Before the end of July Commodore Robert F. Stockton replaced the ailing Sloat and began preparations to move against southern California. As senior officer on the scene, Sloat enlisted Frémont's band as the California Battalion and gave Frémont the rank of major. This group he sent down to San Diego too late to overtake the fleeing Mexican loyalists. In a more leisurely fashion, then, Stockton occupied Santa Barbara and Los Angeles. By mid-August resistance had dissipated. On August 17 Stockton declared himself governor, with Frémont as military commander in the north and Lieutenant Gillespie in the south.

By August another expedition was closing on Santa Fe. On August 18 Stephen Kearny and his men entered the Mexican town, whence an irresolute governor had fled with its defenders. After setting up a civilian governor, Kearny divided his remaining force, leading 300 dragoons west toward California in late September. On October 6 they encountered a band of frontiersmen under Frémont's old helper, Kit Carson, who was riding eastward with news that California had already fallen. Kearny sent 200 of his men back and with the remaining 100 pushed west with Carson serving as a reluctant guide.

But after Carson's departure from the coast, the picture had changed. In southern California, where most of the poorer Mexicans and Mexicanized Indians resented American rule, a rebellion broke out. By the end of October the rebels had ousted the token American force that remained in southern California. Kearny walked right into this rebel zone when he arrived. At San Diego he met up with Stockton and joined him in the reconquest of southern California, which they achieved after two brief

The Battle of the Plains of Mesa took place just before American forces entered Los Angeles. This sketch was made at the scene. [The Warder Collection]

clashes when they entered Los Angeles on January 10, 1847. Rebel forces capitulated on January 13.

TAYLOR'S BATTLES   Both California and New Mexico had been taken before Gen. Zachary Taylor fought his first major battle in northern Mexico. Having waited for more men and munitions, Taylor finally moved out of his Matamoros base in September 1846 and headed southward toward the heart of Mexico. His first goal was the fortified city of Monterrey, in Nuevo Leon, which he took after a five-day seige. Polk, however, was none too happy with the easy terms to which Taylor agreed, nor with Taylor's growing popularity. The whole episode merely confirmed the president's impression that Taylor was too passive to be trusted further with the major campaign. Besides, his victories, if flawed, were leading to talk of Taylor as the next Whig candidate for president.

But Polk's grand strategy was itself flawed. Having never seen the Mexican desert, Polk wrongly assumed that Taylor could live off the country and need not depend on resupply. Polk therefore misunderstood the general's reluctance to strike out across several hundred miles of barren land in front of Mexico City. The president was simply duped on another point. The old dictator Santa Anna, forced out in 1844, got word to Polk from his exile in Havana that in return for the right considerations he could bring about a settlement. Polk in turn assured the Mexican leader that Washington would pay well for any territory taken through a settlement. In August, after another overturn in the Mexican government, Santa Anna was permitted to pass through the American blockade into Vera Cruz. Soon he was again in command of the Mexican army and then was named president once more. The consequence of Polk's intrigue was to put perhaps the ablest Mexican general back in command of the enemy army, where he busily organized his forces to strike at Taylor.

By then another front had been opened and Taylor was consigned to inactivity. In October 1846 Polk and his cabinet decided to move against Mexico City by way of Vera Cruz. Polk would have preferred a Democratic general, but for want of a better choice named Winfield Scott to the field command. In January 1847 Taylor was required to give up most of his regulars to Scott's force gathering at Tampico. Taylor, miffed at his reduction to a minor role, disobeyed orders and advanced beyond Saltillo.

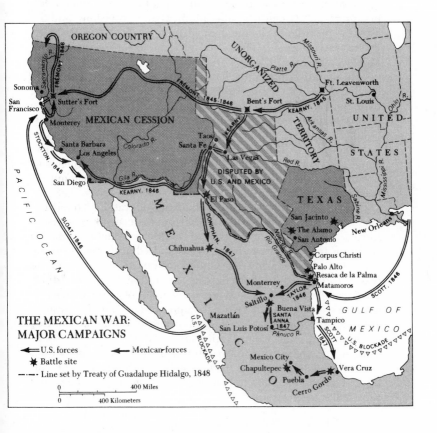

THE MEXICAN WAR: MAJOR CAMPAIGNS

⇐ U.S. forces　　← Mexican forces
✱ Battle site
–·–· Line set by Treaty of Guadalupe Hidalgo, 1848

0 — 400 Miles
0 — 400 Kilometers

There, near the hacienda of Buena Vista, Santa Anna met Taylor's untested volunteers with a large but ill-trained and tired army. In the hard-fought Battle of Buena Vista (February 22–23, 1847) neither side could claim victory on the strength of the outcome, but Taylor was convinced that only his lack of regulars prevented him from striking a decisive blow. In any case it was the last major action on the northern front, and Taylor was granted leave to return home.

SCOTT'S TRIUMPH   The long-planned assault on the enemy capital had begun on March 9, 1847, when Scott's army landed on the beaches south of Vera Cruz. It was the first major amphibious operation by American military forces, carried out without loss. Vera Cruz surrendered on March 27 after a weeklong siege. Scott then set out on the route taken by Cortes more than 300 years before. Santa Anna tried to set a trap for him at the mountain pass of Cerro Gordo, but Scott's men took more than 3,000 prisoners, large quantities of equipment and provisions, and the Mexican president's personal effects.

On May 15 Scott's men entered Puebla, the second city of Mexico. There Scott lost about a third of his army. Men whose twelve-month enlistments had expired felt free to go home, leaving Scott with about 7,000 troops in all. There was nothing to do but hang on until reinforcements and new supplies came up from the coast. After three months, with his numbers almost doubled, Scott set out on August 7 through the mountain passes into the valley of Mexico, cutting his supply line to the coast. The aging duke of Wellington, following the campaign from afar, predicted: "is lost—he cannot capture the city and he cannot fall back upon his base."

But Scott directed a brilliant flanking operation around the lakes and marshes which guarded the eastern approaches to Mexico City, then another around the Mexican defenses at San Antonio. In the battles of Contreras and Churubusco (both on August 20) Scott's army overwhelmed Mexican defenses on the way to the capital. In those defeats Santa Anna lost a third of his forces and had to fall back within three miles of the city. In fighting renewed after a lull, two strong points guarding the western approaches to Mexico City fell in the Battles of Molino del Rey (September 8) and Chapultepec (September 12–13). On September 13 American forces entered Mexico City and within three days mopped up the remnants of resistance. At the National Palace a batallion of marines ran up the flag and occupied the "halls of Montezuma."

Winfield Scott takes Mexico City after his defeat of Santa Anna. [The Warder Collection]

THE TREATY OF GUADALUPE HIDALGO   After the fall of the capital, Santa Anna resigned and a month later left the country. Meanwhile Polk had appointed as chief peace negotiator Nicholas P. Trist, chief clerk of the State Department and a Virginia Democrat of impeccable partisan credentials. Trist was frustrated for want of anybody to negotiate with. In October Polk decided that the Mexican delays required a stronger stand and ordered Trist recalled, but before the message reached Mexico City things had changed. On November 11 the Mexican Congress elected an interim president, and on November 22 the new administration told Trist it had named commissioners to deal with him. Trist, having just received the recall notice, decided to go ahead with negotiations anyway. A sixty-five-page letter of justification did nothing to persuade Polk that he was anything but an "impudent and unqualified scoundrel," but Trist reasoned that it was better to continue than to risk a return of the war party or the disintegration of all government in Mexico.

Formal talks got under way on January 2, 1848, at the village of Guadalupe Hidalgo just outside the capital, and dragged out through the month. Finally Trist, fearing stronger orders from Washington at any time, threatened to end the negotiations and the Mexicans yielded. By the treaty of Guadalupe Hidalgo, signed on February 2, 1848, Mexico gave up all claims to Texas above the Rio Grande and ceded California and New Mexico to the United States. In return the United States agreed to pay

Mexico $15 million and assume the claims of American citizens against Mexico up to a total of $3¼ million.

Miffed that Trist had ignored his orders, Polk nevertheless had little choice but to submit the treaty to the Senate. A growing movement to annex all of Mexico had impelled him to hold out for more. But as Polk confided to his diary, rejecting the treaty would be too risky. If he should reject a treaty made in accord with his own original terms in order to gain more territory, "the probability is that Congress would not grant either men or money to prosecute the war." In that case he might eventually have to withdraw the army and lose everything. The treaty went to the Senate, which ratified it on March 10, 1848, by a vote of 38 to 14. By the end of July the last remaining American soldiers had boarded ship in Vera Cruz.

THE WAR'S LEGACIES   The Mexican War had cost the United States 1,721 killed, 4,102 wounded, and far more, 11,155 dead of disease. The military and naval expenditures had been $97.7 million. For this price, and payments made under the treaty, the United States acquired more than 500,000 square miles of territory (more than a million counting Texas), including the great Pacific harbors of San Diego, Monterey, and San Francisco, with uncounted millions in mineral wealth. Except for a small addition by the Gadsden Purchase of 1853, these annexations rounded out the continental United States. Several important "firsts" are associated with the Mexican War: the first successful offensive war, the first major amphibious operation, the first occupation of an enemy capital, the first in which martial law was declared on foreign soil, the first in which West Point graduates played a major role, and the first reported by modern war correspondents like George W. Kendall of the New Orleans *Picayune*.

Manifest Destiny and images of the Golden West fired the imaginations of Americans, then and since. But the Mexican War somehow never became entrenched in the national legends. Within a few years it fell in the shadow of another and greater conflict, and was often recalled as a kind of preliminary bout in which Grant, Lee, and other great generals learned their trade as junior officers. The Mexican War never took on the dimensions of a moral crusade based on the defense of great principles. It was, transparently, a war of conquest provoked by a president bent on the acquisition of territory. One might argue that Polk merely hastened, and possibly achieved at less cost in treasure and human misery, what the march of the restless frontier would soon have achieved anyway. During one term in office he annexed to Jefferson's "empire of liberty" more land than Jefferson himself, but the imperishable glamor that shone about the names of Caesar, Cortés, or Napoleon never brightened the name of Polk. For a brief season, however, the glory of conquest did shed luster on the names of Zachary Taylor and Winfield Scott. Despite Polk's best efforts, he had manufactured the next, and last two Whig candidates for president. One of them, Taylor, would replace him in the White House, with the storm of sectional conflict already on the horizon.

FURTHER READING

While no recent survey of Whig party history has been completed, Glyndon G. Van Deusen's *The Jacksonian Era* (1959),° Richard P. McCormick's *The Second American Party System* (1966),° and William R. Brock's *Parties and Political Conscience* (1979), as well as other works cited in Chapter 11, provide background on Whig programs and activities. More focused on the values which inspired Whig programs is Daniel Walker Howe's *The Political Culture of the American Whigs* (1979). Robert G. Gundersen's *The Log Cabin Campaign* (1957) examines the election of 1840. To understand more fully the Tyler administration, consult Oscar D. Lambert's *Presidential Politics in the United States, 1841–1844* (1936), and Robert J. Morgan's *A Whig Embattled* (1954). The border disputes of the period are covered in Albert B. Corey's *The Crisis of 1830–1842 in Canadian-American Relations* (1941).

Several works help interpret the concept of Manifest Destiny. Frederick Merk's *Manifest Destiny and Mission in American History* (1963)° and Edward M. Burns's *The American Idea of Mission: Concepts of National Purpose and Destiny* (1957) study the ideological background. Merk takes a more diplomatic slant in *The Monroe Doctrine and American Expansion, 1843–1849* (1966). Other works which explore the same themes are Norman A. Graebner's *Empire on the Pacific: A Study in American Continental Expansion* (1955), Albert K. Weinberg's *Manifest Destiny* (1936), and Henry Nash Smith's *Virgin Land* (1950).°

Ray A. Billington's *Westward Expansion* (1974) and *The Far Western Frontier, 1830–1860* (1956),° narrate well the story of pioneer movement. Bernard DeVoto's *Across the Wide Missouri* (1947) concentrates on the fur trappers and the Mountain Men. Robert L. Duffus's *The Santa Fe Trail* (1930) covers some of the same material. William H. Goetzmann's *Army Exploration in the American West, 1803–1863* (1959), looks at the military involvement. A recent interpretation is John D. Unruh's *The Plains Across: The Overland Emigrants and the TransMissis-*

°These books are available in paperback editions.

sippi West, 1840–1860 (1978). Francis Parkman's *The Oregon Trail* (1849)° is an enduring classic on the subject.

Since California was the promised land for many, several scholars have concentrated on that area. Kevin Starr's *America and the California Dream, 1850–1915* (1973), is a good introduction. Also valuable are Leonard Pitt's *The Decline of the Californias* (1970), Walter Bean's *California: An Interpretative History* (1968), and Earl Pomeroy's *The Pacific Slope: A History* (1965). Pomeroy is also helpful for the early history of Oregon. How the Mormons came to Utah is covered in Wallace Stegner's *The Gathering of Zion: The Story of the Mormon Trail* (1964),° as well as works cited in Chapter 13.

The settlement of Texas is presented by William C. Binkley in *The Texas Revolution* (1952)° and *The Expansionist Movement in Texas, 1836–1850* (1925). Eugene C. Barker adds a nationalistic perspective in *Mexico and Texas, 1821–1835* (1928). Marquis James's *The Raven* (1929)° remains a fine biography of Sam Houston. The controversy over annexation is analyzed in David M. Pletcher's *The Diplomacy of Annexation: Texas, Oregon, and the Mexican War* (1973) and Frederick Merk's *Slavery and the Annexation of Texas* (1972).

Gene M. Brack's *Mexico Views Manifest Destiny, 1821–1846* (1975), takes Mexico's viewpoint on American designs on the West. The views of the expansionist president are gauged in Charles G. Sellers's *James K. Polk: Continentalist, 1843–1849* (1966), while John H. Schroeder's *Mr. Polk's War* (1973) is more critical. Surveys of the military conflict are provided in Otis Singletary's *The Mexican War* (1960)° and K. Jack Bauer's *The Mexican War, 1846–1848* (1974). Biographies of two leading generals are Charles W. Elliott's *Winfield Scott* (1937) and Holman Hamilton's *Zachary Taylor: Soldier of the Republic* (1941).

15 ✑

THE OLD SOUTH:
AN AMERICAN TRAGEDY

MYTH, REALITY, AND THE OLD SOUTH

SOUTHERN MYTHOLOGY Southerners, North Carolina editor Jonathan Daniels once wrote, are "a mythological people, created half out of dream and half out of slander, who live in a still legendary land." Most Americans, including southerners, carry an assorted mental baggage of myths about the South in which a variety of elements have been assembled. But the main burden of southern mythology is still carried in those images of the Old South set during the nineteenth-century sectional conflict, or in modernized versions of them: the Sunny South of the plantation tradition or the Benighted South of the Savage Ideal, the "dream" and the "slander."

The pattern of the first appeared full-blown at least as early as 1832 in John Pendleton Kennedy's romance, *Swallow Barn*. Every American is familiar with the euphoric pattern of kindly old massa with his mint julep on the white-columned piazza, happy "darkies" singing in fields perpetually white to the harvest, coquettish belles wooed by slender gallants underneath the moonlight and magnolias. The legend of the Southern Cavalier seemed to fulfill some psychic need for an American counterweight to the mental image of the grasping, money-grubbing Yankee.

But there are other elements in the traditional pattern. Off in the piney woods and erosion-gutted clay hills, away from gentility, dwelt a depraved group known as the poor white trash: the crackers; hillbillies; sand-hillers; squatters; rag, tag, and bobtail; po' buckra to the blacks. Somewhere in the pattern the respectable small farmer was lost from sight, perhaps neither romantic enough nor outrageous enough to fit in. He was absent too from the image of the Benighted South, in which the plantation myth simply appeared in reverse, as a pattern of corrupt opulence resting on human exploitation. Gentle old massa became the arrogant, haughty, imperious potentate, the very embodiment of sin, the central target of antislavery attack. He kept a seraglio in the slave quarters; he bred Negroes like cattle and sold them "down the river" to certain death in the sugar mills, separating families if that suited his purpose, while southern women suffered in silence the guilty knowledge of their men's infidelity. The "happy darkies" in this picture became white men in black skins, an oppressed people longing for freedom, the victims of countless atrocities, forever seeking a chance to follow the North Star to freedom. The masses of the white folks were, once again, poor whites, relegated to ignorance and degeneracy by the slavocracy.

THE SOUTHERN CONDITION   Everyone of course recognizes these pictures as overdrawn stereotypes, but as one historian has said, myths are made of tough stuff. Once implanted in the mind, they are hard to shake, partly because they have roots in reality. But to comprehend the distinctiveness of the Old South we must first identify the forces and factors that gave it a sense of unity. Efforts to do so usually turn on two lines of thought: the causal effects of environment (geography and climate), and the causal effects of human decisions and actions. The name of the historian Ulrich B. Phillips is associated with both. At the outset of his *Life and Labor in the Old South* (1929) Phillips wrote: "Let us begin by discussing the weather, for that has been the chief agency in making the South distinctive." It fostered the growing of staple crops, and thus the plantation system and black slavery. These things in turn brought sectional conflict and Civil War.

But while geography may render certain things possible and others impossible, explanations that involve human agency are more persuasive. In the 1830s Alexis de Tocqueville found the origins of southern distinctiveness in the institution of slavery. U. B. Phillips argued nearly a century later that with large numbers of blacks in the population, "the central theme" of southern history became "a common resolve indomitably maintained" by whites that they should retain their control. And this resolve in turn led to a sense of racial unity that muted class conflict among whites. But in the long run, the biracial character of the population influenced far more aspects of life than Phillips acknowledged. In making the culture of the South, W. J. Cash asserted in *The Mind of the South* (1941), "Negro entered into white man as profoundly as white man entered into Negro—subtly influencing every gesture, every word, every emotion and idea, every attitude." In shaping patterns of speech and folklore, of music and literature, black southerners immeasurably influenced and enriched the culture of the region.

The South differed from other sections too in its high proportion of native population, both white and black. Despite a great diversity of origins in the colonial population, the South drew few immigrants after the Revolution. One reason was that the main shipping lines went to northern ports; another, that the prospect of competing with slave labor was unattractive to immigrants. The South, one writer has said, "was created by the need to protect a peculiar institution from threats originating outside the region." After the Missouri Controversy of 1819–1821 the South became more and more a conscious minority, its population growth lagging behind that of other sections, its peculiar institution of slavery more and more an isolated and odious thing in Western civilization. Attitudes of defensiveness strongly affected its churches. The religious culture of the white South retreated from the liberalism of the Revolutionary War era into orthodoxy, which provided one line of defense against new doctrines of any kind, while black southerners found in a similar religious culture a refuge from the hardships of their lot, a promise of release on some future day of Jubilee.

Other ways in which the South was said to be different included its architecture, its peculiar work ethic, its penchant for the military, and its country-gentlemen ideal. One author, tongue in cheek, even suggested that the South was where the mule population was highest. The preponderance of farming remained a distinctive characteristic, whether pictured as the Jeffersonian yeoman living by the sweat of his brow or the lordly planter dispatching his slave gangs. In an agricultural society like the South there tended to be a greater "personalness" of human relations in contrast to the organized and contractual nature of relations in a more complex urban environment. But in the end what made the South distinctive was its people's belief, and other people's belief, that they *were* distinctive. Southernism, one historian asserted, was too elusive for a clear definition. "Poets," he wrote, "have done better in expressing the oneness of the South than historians in explaining it."

Cotton, the South's most important staple crop, being prepared for the gin on J. J. Smith's plantation, Beaufort, South Carolina, 1862. [Library of Congress]

STAPLE CROPS The idea of the Cotton Kingdom is itself something of a mythic stereotype. Although cotton was the most important of the staple, or market, crops, it was a latecomer. Tobacco, the first staple crop, had earlier been the mainstay of Virginia and Maryland, and important in North Carolina. After the Revolution pioneers carried it over the mountains into Kentucky and as far as Missouri. Indigo, an important crop in colonial South Carolina, vanished with the loss of British bounties, but rice growing continued in a coastal strip that lapped over into North Carolina and Georgia. Rice growing was limited to the Tidewater because it required frequent flooding and draining of the fields, and along that sector of the coast the tides rose and fell six or seven feet. Since rice growing required substantial capital for floodgates, ditches, and machinery, its plantations were large and relatively few in number.

Sugar, like rice, called for a heavy capital investment in machinery to grind the cane, and was limited in extent because the cane was extremely susceptible to frost. An influx of refugees from the revolution in Haiti helped the development of a sugar belt centered along the Mississippi River above New Orleans. Some sugar grew in a smaller belt of eastern Texas. But it was always something of an exotic growth, better suited to a tropical climate. Since it needed the prop of a protective tariff, it produced the anomaly in southern politics of pro-tariff congressmen from Louisiana. Hemp had something of the same effect in the

Kentucky Blue Grass region and northwestern Missouri. Both flax and hemp were important to backcountry farmers at the end of the colonial era. Homespun clothing was most apt to be linsey-woolsey, a combination of linen and wool. But flax never developed more than a limited commercial market, and that mostly for linseed oil. Hemp, on the other hand, developed commercial possibilities in rope and cotton baling cloth, although it suffered heavy competition from a higher quality Russian product.

Cotton, the last of the major staples, eventually outpaced all the others put together. At the end of the War of 1812 production was estimated at less than 150,000 bales; in 1860 it was reported at 3.8 million. Two things accounted for the growth: the voracious market in British and French textiles, and the cultivation of new lands in the Southwest. Much of the story of the southern people—white and black—from 1820 to 1860 was their movement to fertile cotton lands farther west. The crop flourished best in the hot growing season of the Deep South. By 1860 the center of the cotton belt stretched from eastern North Carolina through the fertile Alabama-Mississippi black belts (so called for the color of both people and soil), on to Texas, and up the Mississippi Valley as far as southern Illinois. Cotton prices fell sharply after the Panic of 1837, and remained below 10¢ a pound through most of the 1840s, but they advanced above 10¢ late in 1855 and stayed there until 1860, reaching 15¢ in 1857—despite a business setback and a constantly increasing supply.

AGRICULTURAL DIVERSITY   The focus on cotton and the other cash crops has obscured the degree to which the South fed itself from its own fields. With 29.5 percent of the country's area in 1860, and 38.9 percent of its population, the slave states produced 52 percent of the nation's corn, 28.9 percent of the wheat, 19.2 percent of the oats, 19.4 percent of the rye, 10 percent of the white potatoes, and 94 percent of the sweet potatoes. The upper South in many areas practiced general farming in much the same way as the Northwest. Cyrus McCormick first tested his harvester in the wheatfields of Virginia. Corn grew everywhere, but went less into the market than into local consumption by man and beast, as feed and fodder, as hoecake and grits. On many farms and plantations the rhythms of the growing season permitted the labor force to alternate attention between the staples and the food crops.

Livestock added to the diversity of the farm economy. The South had in 1860 half of the nation's cattle, over 60 percent of

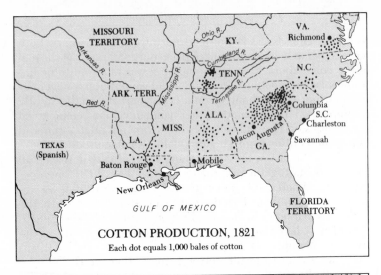

COTTON PRODUCTION, 1821

Each dot equals 1,000 bales of cotton

**POPULATION GROWTH and
COTTON PRODUCTION, 1821-1859**

Percentage increase in population, 1821-1859

Under 200%

200% to 499%

500% to 1,000%

Over 1,000%

Each dot equals
1,000 bales of cotton

the swine, nearly 45 percent of the horses, 52 percent of the oxen, nearly 90 percent of the mules, and nearly a third of the sheep, the last mostly in the upper South. Cattle herding prevailed on the southern frontier at one time, and persisted in areas less suited to farming, such as the piney woods of the coastal plains, the Appalachians, and the Ozarks and their foothills. Plantations and farms commonly raised livestock for home consumption.

Yet the picture was hardly one of unbroken prosperity. The

South's staple crops quickly exhausted the soil, and open row crops like tobacco, cotton, and corn left the bare ground in between subject to leaching and erosion. Much of eastern Virginia by 1800 had abandoned tobacco, and in some places had turned to scrabbling wheat from the soil for the northern market. One ex-slave later recalled what he saw as a slave trader carried him across Virginia about 1805: "For several days we traversed a region, which had been deserted by the occupants—being no longer worth culture—and immense thickets of young red cedars now occupied the fields." In low-country South Carolina Sen. Robert Y. Hayne spoke of "Fields abandoned; and hospitable mansions of our fathers deserted. . . . " The older farming lands had trouble competing with the newer soils farther west. But when the Panic of 1837 ended the flush times of Alabama and Mississippi, farm prices everywhere remained low until the mid-1850s. Soon western lands too began to show wear and tear. By 1855 Sen. C. C. Clay was writing of his home country in northern Alabama: "Our small planters, after taking the cream off their lands . . . are going further west and south in search of other virgin lands which they may and will despoil and impoverish in like manner." This of course happened all along the frontier. "If the Old South had greater ruins than did the other sections,"historian Avery Craven insisted, "it was largely because it had been more successful in quickly and cheaply garnering the riches which Nature offered and spending them in the far-away markets where the comforts and luxuries of a more advanced life might be secured."

So the Southeast and then the Southwest faced a growing sense of economic crisis as the century advanced. Proposals to deal with it followed two lines. Some argued for agricultural reform, and others for diversification through industry and trade. Edmund Ruffin of Virginia stands out as perhaps the greatest of the reformers. After studying the chemistry of soils, he reasoned that most exhausted soils of the upper South had acid conditions which needed to be neutralized before they could become productive again. He turned his plantations into laboratories in which he discovered that marl from a shell deposit in eastern Virginia did the trick. His *Essay on Calcareous Manures* (1832) a Department of Agriculture expert pronounced at the end of the century the "most thoughtful piece of work on a special agricultural subject ever published in the English language." Such publications and farm magazines in general, however, reached but a minority of farmers, mostly the larger and more successful planters. The same was true of the agricultural associations which sprang up in the Old South, though some of these sponsored experimental farms and agricultural fairs which became fairly common by the 1840s and 1850s, reaching farmers with examples put before their very eyes.

MANUFACTURING AND TRADE   By 1840 many thoughtful southerners reasoned that by staking everything on agriculture the region had wasted chances in manufacturing and trade. The census of 1810 had shown the South with more various and numerous manufactures than New England. The War of 1812 provided the South some stimulus for manufacturing, but the momentum was lost in the postwar flood of British imports. Then cotton growing swept everything before it. As the spread of landholding rendered concern with industry sporadic, the South became increasingly dependent on northern manufacturing and trade. Cotton and tobacco were exported mainly in northern vessels. In 1830 southern ship tonnage of 109,000 was less than a third of the North's 360,000; by 1860 the South's 855,000 was little more than a fifth of the North's 4 million. Southerners also relied on connections in the North for imported goods. The South became, economically if not formally, a kind of colonial dependency on the North.

The South's dependence on the North inspired a series of commercial conventions which commenced with a meeting at Augusta, Georgia, in 1837, and continued almost every year through the next two decades. The call for the first convention set forth a theme that would run through them all. The merchants of northern cities, it said, "export our immense valuable productions, and import our articles of consumption and from this agency they derive a profit which has enriched them . . . at our expense."

Along with the call for direct trade in southern ships went a movement for a more diversified economy, for native industries to balance agriculture and trade. Southern publicists called attention to the section's great resources: its raw materials, labor supply, waterpower, wood and coal, and markets. The chief vehicle for the advocates of economic development, and the leading economic journal of the South, came to be *The Commercial Review of the South and the Southwest*, edited by James D. B. De Bow.

De Bow's contemporary, William Gregg, began promoting textiles in South Carolina during the 1840s, when he bought into an early cotton mill near Edgefield and successfully reorganized it. After travels in New England, he wrote a series of articles for a Charleston paper advocating southern industrial development.

These pieces appeared in 1845 as a pamphlet: *Essays on Domestic Industry.* About a year later he began construction of the Graniteville Manufacturing Company. Built of native granite by local labor, the mill still survives. Adjoining the mill he built a model village with good homes, a school, library, churches, infirmary, and recreational facilities. The project was a success from the start, paying dividends in a few years of up to 8 percent.

In Richmond, Virginia, the Tredegar Iron Works grew into the most important single manufacturing enterprise in the Old South. Launched in 1837, the company in 1848 fell under the control of Joseph Reid Anderson, for several years its sales agent, before that a graduate of West Point and an army engineer. His military connections brought Tredegar contracts for cannon, shot, and shell, but the firm also made axes, saws, bridge materials, boilers, and steam engines, including locomotives. Unlike Gregg, Anderson used mainly slave workers, either hired from their owners or, more and more, owned by him outright.

Daniel Pratt of Alabama built Prattville, which grew into a model of diversified industry. Prattville ultimately had a gristmill, a shingle mill, a carriage factory, foundries, a tin mill, and a blacksmith shop. Pratt then launched into the iron business and coal mining, while on the side experimenting with vineyards and truck farming. Like Anderson he used both black and white labor; like Gregg he practiced paternalism. Profits from his company store went into churches, schools, a library, an art gallery, and a printing establishment—and into handsome dividends.

These men and others like them directed a program of industry that gathered momentum in the 1850s, and in its extent and diversity belied the common image of a strictly agricultural South. Manufactures were supplemented by important extractive industries such as coal, iron, lead, copper, salt, and gold, the

The Tredegar Iron Works in Richmond, Virginia. [Library of Congress]

last chiefly in North Carolina and Georgia. In manufacturing, altogether in 1860 the slave states had 22 percent of the country's plants, 17 percent of its labor, 20 percent of the capital invested, 17 percent of the wages generated, and 16 percent of the output, an impressive showing but still not up to the South's 29½ percent of the population. Also, southern industry was concentrated in the border states, which had many economic conditions in common with neighboring states of the North.

ECONOMIC DEVELOPMENT There were two major explanations generally put forward for the lag in southern industrial development. First, blacks were presumed unsuited to factory work, perhaps because they could not adjust to the discipline of work by the clock. Second, the ruling orders of the Old South were said to have developed a lordly disdain for the practice of trade, because a certain aristocratic prestige derived from owning land and slaves, and from conspicuous consumption. But any argument that black labor was incompatible with industry simply flew in the face of the evidence, since factory owners bought or hired slave operatives for just about every kind of manufacture. Given the opportunity, a number of blacks displayed managerial skills as overseers. Nor should one take at face value the legendary indifference of aristocratic planters to the balance sheet. On the southwestern frontiers of the Cotton Kingdom, those who did fit that description became pathetic objects of humor, pushed aside by the hustlers.

More often than not the successful planter was a driving newcomer bent on maximizing profits. While the profitability of slavery has been a long-standing subject of controversy, in recent years economic historians, applying new tools of statistics and theory, have reached the conclusion that slaves on the average supplied about a 10 percent return on their cost. Slave ownership was, moreover, a reasonable speculation, for slave prices tended to move upward. By a strictly hardnosed and hardheaded calculation, investment in slaves and cotton lands was the most profitable investment available at the time in the South.

Despite the South's lag in trade and industry, incomes in the region fared well indeed, especially in the newer cotton lands of the Southwest. The census region comprising Arkansas, Louisiana, Texas, and the Indian Territory (later Oklahoma) had a higher per-capita income than any other census region in 1860, $184 to a national average of $128. Since these calculations included the total population, slave and free, some of the southwestern slaveholders clearly were rich beyond the dreams of avarice. The wealthiest regions at the time were the Southwest and the Northeast, which had a per-capita income of $181 in 1860. The new cotton lands and the expanding factories enjoyed the most dynamic growth of the time.

The notion that the South was economically backward emerged from the sectional quarrels of the times, in which southerners took a poorer-than-thou attitude, so to speak, in order to bolster their claims of northern exploitation. Antislavery elements also contributed to this notion by way of arguing the failure of a slave economy. It was true that in any comparison of the South with the North, the South usually came off second best. But in comparison with the rest of the world, the South as a whole was well off: its average per-capita income in 1860 ($103) was about the same as that of Switzerland, and was exceeded only by Australia, the North, and Great Britain, in that order.

WHITE SOCIETY IN THE SOUTH

If an understanding of the Old South must begin with a knowledge of social myths, it must end with a sense of tragedy. White southerners had won short-term gains at the cost of both long-term development and moral isolation in the eyes of the world. The concentration on land and slaves, and the paucity of cities and immigrants, deprived the South of the dynamic bases of innovation. The slaveholding South hitched its wagon not to a star, but to the world (largely British) demand for cotton, which had not slackened from the start of the Industrial Revolution. In the piping times of the late 1850s, it seemed that prosperity would never end. The South, "safely entrenched behind her cotton bags . . . can defy the world—for the civilized world depends on the cotton of the South," said a Vicksburg newspaper in 1860. "No power on earth dares to make war upon it," said James H. Hammond of South Carolina. "Cotton is king." The only perceived threat to King Cotton was the growing antislavery sentiment. The unperceived threat was an imminent slackening of the cotton market. The hey-day of expansion in British textiles was over by 1860, but by then the Deep South was locked into cotton production for generations to come.

THE PLANTERS Although great plantations were relatively few in number, they set the tone of economic and social life in the South. What distinguished the plantation from the farm, in addition to its size, was the use of a large labor force, under separate control and supervision, to grow primarily staple crops for profit. A clear-cut distinction between management and labor set the planter apart from the small slaveholder, who often worked side by side with his bondsmen at the same tasks.

If, to be called a planter, one had to own 20 slaves, the South in 1860 numbered only 46,274 planters. Fewer than 8,000 owned 50 or more slaves, and the owners of over 100 numbered 2,292. The census enumerated only 11 with 500 and just 1 with as many as 1,000 slaves. Yet this small, privileged group tended to think of their class interest as the interest of the South, and to perceive themselves as community leaders in much the fashion of the English gentry. The planter group owned more than half the slaves, produced most of the cotton, tobacco, and hemp, and all of the sugar and rice. In a white population numbering just over 8 million in 1860, the total number of slaveholders came to only 383,637. But assuming that each family numbered five people, the whites with some proprietary interest in slavery came to 1.9 million, or roughly one-fourth of the white population. While the preponderance of southern whites belonged to the small-farmer class, the presumptions of the planters were seldom challenged. Too many small farmers aspired to rise in the world.

Often the planter did live in the splendor which legend attributed to him, with the wealth and leisure to cultivate the arts of hospitality, good manners, learning, and politics. More often the scene was less charming. Some of the mansions on closer inspection turned out to be modest houses with false fronts. A style of housing derived from the frontier log cabin grew to be surprisingly common. The one-room cabin would expand by the building of a second room with a sheltered open "dog trot" in the middle. As wealth increased, larger houses evolved from the plain log cabin and the dog trot grew into a central hall from the front

The Fairntosh plantation house, North Carolina. [North Carolina State Archives]

to the rear of the house. In larger houses halls to one or both sides might be added.

The planter commonly had less leisure than legend would suggest, for he in fact managed a large enterprise. At the same time he often served as the patron to whom workers appealed the actions of their foremen. The quality of life for the slaves was governed far more by the attitude of the master than by the formal slave codes, which were seldom enforced strictly except in times of troubles. The mistress of the plantation, like the master, seldom led a life of idle leisure. She was called upon to supervise the domestic household in the same way the planter took care of the business, to see after food, linens, housecleaning, the care of the sick, and a hundred other details. Mary Boykin Chesnut of South Carolina complained that "there is no slave like a wife."

THE MIDDLE CLASS   Overseers on the largest plantations generally came from the middle class of small farmers or skilled workers, or were younger sons of planters. Most aspired to become slaveholders themselves, and sometimes rose to that status, but others were constantly on the move in search of better positions. And their interests did not always coincide with the long-term interests of the planter. "Overseers are not interested in raising negro children, or meat, in improving land, or improving productive qualities of seed or animals," a Mississippi planter complained to Frederick Law Olmstead, a northern visitor. "Many of them do not care whether property has depreciated or improved, so they make a crop to boast of." Occasionally there were black overseers, but the highest management position to which a slave could aspire was usually that of driver or leader, placed in charge of a small group of slaves with the duty of getting them to work without creating dissension.

The most numerous white southerners were the middle-class yeoman farmers. W. J. Cash, in his classic *The Mind of the South*, called the small farmer "the man at the center." The most prosperous of these generally lived in the mountain-sheltered valleys from the Shenandoah of Virginia down to northern Alabama, areas with rich soil but without ready access to markets, and so less suitable for staple crops or slave labor. But the more numerous yeomen lived in the interstices of the plantation economy. Probably about 80 percent of them owned land. "Nearly all of them," Cash wrote, "enjoyed some measure of a kind of curious half-thrifty, half-shiftless prosperity—a thing of sagging rail fences, unpainted houses, and crazy barns which yet bulged with corn." The yeomen adapted from the planters certain traits of character. "The result was a kindly courtesy, a level eyed pride, an easy quietness, a barely perceptible flourish of bearing, which for all its obvious angularity and fundamental plainness, was one of the finest things the Old South produced."

THE "POOR WHITES" But outside observers often had trouble telling yeomen apart from the true "poor whites," a degraded class crowded off into the pine barrens. Stereotyped views of southern society had prepared many travelers to see only planters and "poor whites," and many a small farmer living in rude comfort, his wealth concealed in cattle and swine off foraging in the woods, was mistaken for "white trash." The type was a familiar one from the frontier days, living on the fringes of polite society. William Byrd of Virginia found them in "Lubberland" (his name for North Carolina) as early as 1730, and in the literature of the South, both fiction and nonfiction, their descendants appeared right on down to the twentieth-century Jeeter Lester of *Tobacco Road* and the Snopeses of William Faulkner's novels. D. R. Hundley wrote in 1860: "There is no . . . method by which they can be weaned from leading the lives of vagrom-men, idlers, and squatters, useless to themselves and to the rest of mankind." They were characterized by a pronounced lankness and sallowness, given over to hunting and fishing, to hound dogs and moonshine whiskey.

Speculation had it that they were descended from indentured servants or convicts transported to the colonies, or that they were the weakest of the frontier population, forced to take refuge in the sand land, the pine barrens, and the swamps after having been pushed aside by the more enterprising and successful. But the problem was less heredity than environment, the consequence of infections and dietary deficiencies which gave rise to a trilogy of "lazy diseases": hookworm, malaria, and pellagra, all of which produced an overpowering lethargy. Many poor whites displayed a morbid craving to chew clay, from which they got the name "dirt eaters"; the cause was a dietary deficiency, although a folklore grew up about the nutritional and medicinal qualities of certain clays. Around 1900 modern medicine discovered the causes and cures for these diseases and by 1930 they had practically disappeared, taking with them many stereotypes of poor whites.

PROFESSIONALS AND OTHERS "The social system of the South may be likened to a three-story white structure on a mudsill of black," as one historian put it. But that hardly exhausted the complexity of things. Manufacturers held their own with the planters, as did merchants, often called brokers or factors, who handled the planters' crops and acted as purchasing agents for their needs, supplying credit along the way. Professional people, including lawyers, doctors, and editors, stood in close relationship to the planter and merchant classes which they served and to which they sometimes belonged.

There was a degree of fluidity and social mobility in the class structure of the white South. Few indeed were the "cotton snobs" who lorded it over the lower orders. Planters were acknowledged as the social models and natural leaders of society by consensus. Planters risen from the ranks as often as not had close relatives still among the less well-to-do. Those who aspired to public office, especially, could not afford to take a lordly attitude, for every southern state by 1860 allowed universal white male suffrage. The voters, while perhaps showing deference to their "betters," could nevertheless pick and choose among them at election time.

Other groups stood farther from the mainstream. The mountain people of Appalachia engaged in subsistence farming, employed few or no slaves, and in attitude stood apart from the planter society, sometimes in open hostility toward it. Scattered in many of the flatland counties were small groups who sometimes fell even below the poor whites in the social scale. In some places the advance of the frontier had left behind pockets of Indians with whom passing whites and escaped slaves eventually mingled. The triple admixture of races produced islands of peoples known variously as brass ankles, Turks, redbones, yellow hammers, and Melungeons (derived apparently from "mélange," mixture).

Black Society in the South

"FREE PERSONS OF COLOR" Free Negroes, or "free persons of color," occupied an uncertain status, balanced somewhere between slavery and freedom, subject to legal restrictions not imposed on whites. In the seventeenth century a few blacks had been freed on the same basis as indentured servants. Over the years some slaves were able to purchase their freedom, while some gained freedom as a reward for service in American wars. Others were simply freed by conscientious masters, either in their wills, as in the case of George Washington, or during their lifetimes, as in the case of John Randolph. In one incredible case, a prince of the kingdom of Fita Jallon (in present-day Guinea), captured in warfare, turned up as a slave in Natchez, and after

*A badge, issued in Charleston, South
Carolina, to be worn by free blacks.
[Charleston Museum]*

some years managed to get a letter in Arabic to the sultan of
Morocco, who intervened in his favor. In 1827, after thirty-nine
years of slavery, he gained his freedom and returned to Africa.

The free persons of color included a large number of mulattoes. In urban centers like Charleston and especially New Orleans, "colored" society become virtually a third caste, a new
people who occupied a status somewhere between black and
white. Some of them built substantial fortunes and even became
slaveholders. They often operated inns serving a white clientele.
Jehu Jones, for instance, was the "colored" proprietor of one of
Charleston's best hotels, which he bought in 1815 for $13,000.
In Louisiana a mulatto, Cyprien Ricard, bought an estate with
ninety-one slaves for $250,000. In Natchez William Johnson,
son of a white father and mulatto mother, operated three bar-
bershops and owned 1,500 acres of land and several slaves.

But such cases were rare. Free blacks more often were skilled
artisans (blacksmiths, carpenters, cobblers), farmers, or common
laborers. The increase in their numbers slowed as legislatures
put more and more restrictions on the right to free slaves, but by
1860 there were 262,000 free blacks in the slave states, a little
over half the national total of 488,000. They were most numerous in the upper South. In Maryland the number of free Negroes
very nearly equaled the number still held in slavery; in Delaware
free Negroes made up 91.7 percent of the black population.

THE TRADE IN SLAVES   The slaves stood at the bottom of the social
hierarchy. From the first census in 1790 to the eighth in 1860
their numbers had grown from 698,000 to almost 4 million. The
rise in the slave population came mainly through a natural increase, the rate of which was very close to that of whites at the
time. When the African slave trade was outlawed in 1808, it

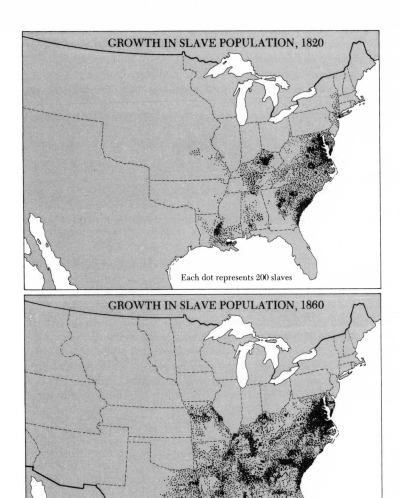

GROWTH IN SLAVE POPULATION, 1820

Each dot represents 200 slaves

GROWTH IN SLAVE POPULATION, 1860

Each dot represents 200 slaves

seemed to many a step toward the extinction of slavery, but the expansion of the cotton belt, with its voracious appetite for workers, soon created such a vested interest in slaves as to dash such hopes. Shutting off the import of slaves only added to the value of those already present. Prices for prime fieldhands ranged between $300 and $400 in the 1790s, up to $1,000–$1,300 in the 1830s, peaked just before the onset of depression in 1837, and rose again in the great prosperity of the 1850s to $1,500-$2,000. Slaves with special skills cost even more.

The rise in slave value tempered some of the harsher features of the peculiar institution. Valuable slaves, like valuable livestock, justified some minimal standards of care. "Massa was purty good," one ex-slave recalled later. "He treated us jus' 'bout like you would a good mule." Another said his master "fed us reg'lar on good, 'stantial food, jus' like you'd tend to you hoss, if you had a real good one." Some owners hired wage laborers, often Irish immigrants, for ditching and other dangerous work rather than risk the lives of valuable slaves.

The end of the foreign slave trade gave rise to a flourishing domestic trade, with slaves moving mainly from the used-up lands of the Southeast into the booming new country of the Southwest. The trade peaked just before 1837, then slacked off, first because of depression, then because agricultural reform and recovery renewed the demand for slaves in the upper South. Many slaves moved south and west with their owners, but there also developed an organized business with brokers, slave pens, and auctioneers. Franklin and Armfield, the leading traders, had their offices and collecting pens in Alexandria, Virginia, where they fattened and spruced up slaves for the auction block. From Alexandria slave coffles moved overland through the Ohio Valley or down the Piedmont, making sales along the way. Other groups went out by sea to Wilmington, Charleston, Savannah, or directly to Mobile, New Orleans, and on to Natchez, a leading market for the new districts.

While the mainstream of the trade moved southwestward, every town of any size had public auctioneers and dealers willing to buy and sell slaves—along with other merchandise—or handle sales on a commission. The worst aspect of the slave trade was

Slave pens inside Pine, Birch & Co., dealers in slaves, Alexandria, Virginia. [Library of Congress]

Gathering Cotton on a South Carolina Plantation. *Sketch by William Waud. [The Historic New Orleans Collection]*

its breakup of families. Only Louisiana and Alabama (from 1852) forbade selling a child under ten from its mother, and no state forbade separation of husband from wife. Many such sales are matters of record, and although the total number is controversial, it took only a few to have a damaging effect on the morale of all.

PLANTATION SLAVERY   The typical lot of the slave was plantation labor. More than half of all slaves in 1860 worked on plantations, and most of those were fieldhands. The best jobs were those of household servants and skilled workers, including blacksmiths, carpenters, and coopers. Others might get special assignments as, say, boatmen or cooks. Housing for the fieldhands was usually in simple one- or two-room wooden shacks with dirt floors, some without windows. Of food there was usually a rough sufficiency, but one slave recalled that "de flour dat we make the biscuits out of wus de third-grade shorts." A distribution of clothing commonly came twice a year, but shoes were generally provided only in winter. On larger plantations there was sometimes an infirmary and regular sick call, but most planters resorted to doctors mainly in cases of sickness. In a material way slaves probably fared about as well as the poor in the rest of the world, perhaps better than the peasants of eastern Europe.

To some extent, chiefly in the rice and tobacco belts, work was parceled out by the task. But more commonly fieldhands worked long hours from dawn to dusk, or "from kin [see] to kaint." The slave codes gave little protection from long hours. South Carolina's limit of fifteen hours in winter and sixteen in summer exceeded the hours of daylight most of the year. The slave codes adopted in each state concerned themselves mainly with the owner's interests, and subjected the slaves not only to his governance but to surveillance by patrols of county militiamen, who struck fear into the slave quarters by abusing slaves found at large without a good explanation. Evidence suggests that a majority of both planters and small farmers used the whip, which the slave codes authorized. The difference between a good owner and a bad one, according to one ex-slave, was the difference between one who did not "whip too much" and one who "whipped till he's bloodied you and blistered you."

The ultimate recourse of slaves was rebellion or flight, but most recognized the futility of such measures with whites wielding most of the power and weapons. In the nineteenth century only three slave insurrections drew much notice, and two of those were betrayed before they got under way. In 1800 a slave named Gabriel on a plantation near Richmond hatched a plot involving perhaps a thousand others in a scheme to seize key points in Richmond and start a general slaughter of whites. Twenty-five slaves involved in the plot were executed and ten others deported. The Denmark Vesey plot in Charleston, discovered in 1822, was the plan of a free black to fall upon the white population of the town, seize ships in the harbor, and make for Santo Domingo. In this case thirty-five were executed and thirty-four deported. Only the Nat Turner insurrection of 1831 in rural Southhampton County, Virginia, got beyond the planning stage. Turner, a black overseer, was also a religious exhorter who professed a divine mission in leading the movement. The revolt began when a small group killed Turner's master's household and set off down the road repeating the process at other farmhouses, where other slaves joined the marauders. Before it ended at least fifty-five whites were killed. Eventually trials resulted in seventeen hangings and seven deportations, but the militia killed large numbers of slaves indiscriminately in the process of putting down the rebels.

Slaves more often retaliated against oppression by malingering, by pretending literal-mindedness in following orders, or by outright sabotage. There were constraints on such behavior, however, for laborers would likely eat better on a prosperous plantation than on one they had reduced to poverty. And the shrewdest slaveholders knew that they would more likely benefit from holding out rewards than from inflicting pain. Plantations based on the profit motive fostered between slaves and owners mutual dependency as well as natural antagonism. And in an agrarian society where personal relations counted for much, blacks could win concessions which moderated the harshness of slavery, permitting them a certain degree of individual and community development.

FORGING THE SLAVE COMMUNITY   To generalize about slavery is to miss elements of diversity from place to place and from time to time. The experience could be as varied as people are. Historians of slavery in recent years have transferred their perspectives from the institutional aspects of slavery to the human aspects: what it was like to be held in bondage. At its worst, the historian Stanley M. Elkins has argued, slavery, like the concentration camps of Nazi Germany, dehumanized its victims, and turned them into creatures who internalized their masters' image of them. The slave thus actually became what he seemed to whites to be, a "Sambo" who in Elkins's words "was docile but irresponsible, loyal but lazy, humble but chronically given to lying and stealing," an adult "full of infantile silliness" and "utter dependence and childlike attachment." Some slaves were no doubt so beaten down as to fit the description, but slave lore was too full of stories about "puttin' on ole massa" to permit the belief that Sambo was often anything more than a protective mask put on to meet the white folks' expectations—and not all slaves would demean themselves in that way.

Slaves were victims, there was no question about that. But to stop with so obvious a perception would be to miss an important story of endurance and achievement. If ever there was a melting pot in American history, the most effective may have been that in which Africans from a variety of ethnic, linguistic, and tribal origins fused into a new community and a new culture as Afro-Americans.

Recent scholarship on slavery has looked inside the slave community, once thought inaccessible, mainly by taking seriously firsthand accounts previously discounted as unreliable. Most useful among these have been the slave narratives, life stories of slaves and former slaves published in the 1800s. Among the more interesting are *The Narrative of the Life of Frederick Douglass* (1845) and *Twenty Years a Slave* (1853) by Solomon Northrup, a free man in the North who was kidnapped and sold south into slavery.

Members of the slave community were bound together in helping and protecting one another, which in turn created a sense of cohesion and pride. Slave culture incorporated many African survivals, especially in areas where whites were few.

Among the Gullah Negroes of the South Carolina and Georgia coast, a researcher found as late as the 1940s more than 4,000 words still in use from the languages of twenty-one African tribes. But the important point, as another researcher put it, was not survivals which served "as quaint reminders of an exotic culture sufficiently alive to render the slaves picturesquely different but little more." The point was one of transformations in a living culture. Elements of African cultures thus "have continued to exist . . . as dynamic, living, creative parts of life in the United States," and have interacted with other cultures in which they came in contact.

SLAVE RELIGION AND FOLKLORE   Among the most important manifestations of slave culture was the slaves' religion, a mixture of African and Christian elements. Most Africans brought with them a concept of a Creator, or Supreme God, whom they could recognize in Jehovah, and lesser gods whom they might identify with Christ, the Holy Ghost, and the saints, thereby reconciling their earlier beliefs with the new Christian religion. Alongside the church they maintained beliefs in spirits, many of them benign magic, and conjuring. Belief in magic is in fact a common human response to conditions of danger or helplessness. Conjurors plied a brisk trade in the slave community, and often exercised considerable influence by promising protection against floggings, separations, and other dangers.

But slaves found greater comfort in the church. Masters sought to instill lessons of humility and obedience, but blacks could identify their plight with that of the Israelites in Egypt or of the God who suffered as they did. And the ultimate hope of a better world gave solace in this one. Some owners openly encouraged religious meetings among their slaves, but those who were denied the open use of "praise houses" held "bush meetings" in secret. The preachers and exhorters who sprang up in the slave world commonly won the acceptance of the owners if only because efforts to get rid of them proved futile. The peculiar cadences of their exhortations, chants, and spirituals were to the whites at best exotic but fundamentally mystifying. The ecstatic "ring shout," in which the celebrants moved rhythmically in a circle, was not a dance—as whites tended to believe—because, the worshippers said, they never crossed their feet. Because slave religion was so widely misperceived by whites, one historian has called it the "invisible institution" of the antebellum South.

"African culture was much more resistant to the bludgeon of slavery than historians have hitherto suspected," John Blassingame wrote in *The Slave Community* (1972). African cultural forms influenced a music of great rhythmic complexity, forms of dance and body language, spirituals and secular songs, and folk tales. Among oppressed peoples humor often becomes a means of psychological release, and there was a lively humor in the West African "trickster tales" of rabbits, tortoises, or Anansi the spider—relatively weak creatures who outwitted stronger animals. Afro-American folklore tended to be realistic in its images of wish-fulfillment. Until after emancipation there were few stories of superhuman heroes like Davy Crockett or Mike Fink, except for tales about captive Africans who escaped slavery by flying back home across the ocean. For the most part whites remained strangely blind and deaf to the black culture around them.

THE SLAVE FAMILY Whites showed much the same ambivalence toward the slaves' instinct for family life. Slave marriages had no legal status, but slaveowners generally seem to have accepted marriage as a stabilizing influence on the plantation. Sometimes they performed marriages themselves or had a minister celebrate a formal wedding with all the trimmings. A common practice was the "broomstick wedding," in which the couple was married by simply jumping over a broomstick, a custom of un-

Several generations of a family raised in slavery. Plantation of J. J. Smith, Beaufort, South Carolina, 1862. [Library of Congress]

certain origin. But whatever the formalities, the norm for the slave community as for the white was the nuclear family of parents and children, with the father regarded as head of the family. Slaves also displayed a lively awareness of the extended family of cousins. Most slave children were socialized into their culture through the nuclear family, which afforded some degree of independence from white influence.

Slaves were not always allowed to realize this norm. In some cases the matter of family arrangements was ignored or left entirely up to the slaves on the assumption that black females were simply promiscuous—a convenient rationalization for sexual exploitation, to which the presence of many mulattoes attested. The census of 1860 reported 412,000 persons of mixed ancestry in the United States, or about 10 percent of the Negro population, probably a drastic undercount. That planters and their sons took advantage of female slaves was widely admitted, and sometimes defended on the grounds that the practice protected the chastity of white women. "Like the patriarchs of old," wrote Mary Boykin Chesnut, a plantation mistress of South Carolina, "our men live all in one house with their wives and concubines." And, she observed, "any lady is ready to tell you who is the father of all the mulatto children in everybody's household but her own."

Antislavery Movements

early opposition to slavery   From the Revolution to the early 1830s, few southern whites showed much disposition to defend the peculiar institution. But in the oft-used figure of speech, they had the wolf by the ears and could not let go. Such scattered antislavery groups and publications as existed in those years in fact were found mainly in the upper South. In 1815, for instance, Charles Osborn, a Quaker preacher, founded the Tennessee Manumission Society, and in 1819 Elihu Embree began the *Manumission Intelligencer*, soon renamed *The Emancipator*, in Jonesboro, Tennessee. In 1821 Benjamin Lundy established in Ohio the *Genius of Universal Emancipation*, later published at Greenville, Tennessee, and Baltimore. In 1827 Lundy counted 106 emancipation societies, with 5,150 members, in the slave states and only 24, with 1,475 members, in the free states. The North Carolina Manumission Society held meetings as late as 1834. These groups and publications urged masters to free their slaves voluntarily.

The emancipation movement got a new thrust with the formation of the American Colonization Society in 1817. The society proposed to colonize freed slaves in Africa, or as one historian put it, "more truly, away from America." Its supporters included such prominent figures as James Madison, James Monroe, Henry Clay, John Marshall, and Daniel Webster, and it appealed to diverse opinions. Some backed it as an antislavery group, while others saw it as a way to bolster slavery by getting rid of potentially troublesome free Negroes. Articulate elements of the free black community denounced it from the start. About a month after the group's founding, when James Forten, a successful sailmaker and Revolutionary War veteran, called upon the assembled free blacks of Philadelphia to vote on the proposition, he got a long, tremendous "No" which, he wrote, "seemed as if it would bring down the walls of the building." America, the blacks insisted, was their native land.

In 1821, nevertheless, agents of the Society acquired from local chieftains in West Africa a parcel of land which became the nucleus of a new country. In 1822 the first freed slaves arrived there, and twenty-five years later the society relinquished control to the independent republic of Liberia. But given its uncertain purpose, the colonization movement fell between two stools. It got meager support from either antislavery or proslavery elements. In all, up to 1860 only about 15,000 blacks migrated to Africa, approximately 12,000 with the help of the Colonization Society. The number was infinitesimal compared to the number of slave births.

A certificate of membership in the New York City Colonization Society. Natives of Liberia welcome society members and a ship carrying freed slaves from America. [Oberlin College Archives]

FROM GRADUALISM TO ABOLITIONISM   Meanwhile in the early 1830s the antislavery movement took a new departure. Three dramatic events marked its transition from favoring gradualism to demanding the immediate end of slavery. In 1829 a pamphlet appeared in Boston: *Walker's Appeal . . . to the Colored Citizens of the World.* Its author, David Walker, born a free Negro in North Carolina, preached insurrection and violence as a proper response to the wrongs that blacks suffered. Over the next few years Walker circulated the pamphlet widely among blacks and white sympathizers. While free Negroes in parts of the South were known to have read it, the message appears to have reached few slaves.

Two other major events followed in close sequence during 1831. On January 1, William Lloyd Garrison began publication in Boston of a new antislavery newspaper, *The Liberator.* Garrison, who rose from poverty in Newburyport, Massachusetts, had been apprenticed to a newspaperman and had edited a number of papers. For two years he worked on Benjamin Lundy's *Genius of Universal Emancipation* in Baltimore, but became restless with Lundy's moderation. In the first issue of his new paper he renounced "the popular but pernicious doctrine of gradual emancipation" and vowed: "I will be as harsh as truth, and as uncompromising as justice. On this subject, I do not wish to think, or speak, or write, with moderation. . . . I am in earnest—I will not equivocate—I will not excuse—I will not retreat a single inch AND I WILL BE HEARD."

And he was heard, mainly at first because his language provoked outraged retorts from slaveholders who publicized the paper more than his own supporters did. Circulation in fact was never very large, but copies went to papers with much wider cir-

William Lloyd Garrison. [Metropolitan Museum of Art]

culations. In the South, literate blacks would more likely encounter Garrison's ideas in the local papers than in what few
copies of *The Liberator* found their way to them. Slaveholders'
outrage mounted higher after the Nat Turner insurrection in August 1831. Garrison, they assumed, bore a large part of the responsibility for the affair, but there is no evidence that Nat
Turner had ever heard of him, and Garrison said that he had not a
single subscriber in the South at the time. What is more, however
violent his language, Garrison was a pacifist, opposed to the use
of physical violence.

THE AMERICAN ANTI-SLAVERY SOCIETY A period of organization followed these events. In 1832 Garrison and his followers set up the
New England Anti-Slavery Society. In 1833 two wealthy New
York merchants, Arthur and Lewis Tappan, founded a similar
group in their state and the same year took the lead in starting a
national society with the help of Garrison and a variety of other
antislavery people. They hoped to exploit the publicity gained
by the British antislavery movement, which that same had
induced Parliament to end slavery, with compensation to slaveholders, throughout the British Empire.

The American Anti-Slavery Society conceded in its constitution the right of each state to legislate on its domestic institutions, but set a goal of convincing fellow citizens "that
Slaveholding is a heinous crime in the sight of God, and that the
duty, safety, and best interests of all concerned, require its *immediate abandonment*, without expatriation." The society went
beyond the issue of emancipation to argue that blacks should
"share an equality with the whites, of civil and religious privileges."

The group set about organizing a barrage of propaganda for its
cause, including periodicals, tracts, agents, lecturers, organizers,
and fund-raisers. Probably its most effective single agent was
Theodore Dwight Weld of Ohio, a convert and disciple of the
great evangelist Charles Grandison Finney. In 1834 Weld led a
group of students at Lane Theological Seminary in Cincinnati in
a protracted discussion of abolition. Efforts of its president,
Lyman Beecher, and the trustees to repress this interruption of
normal routine led to a mass secession from Lane and the start of
a new theological school at the recently opened Oberlin College.
The move won the financial and moral support of the Tappans.
Weld and a number of the "Lane rebels" set out to evangelize
the country for abolition. Weld earned the reputation of trouble-
maker and "the most mobbed man in the United States," but at
the same time he displayed a genius for turning enemies into dis-

ciples. In 1836 Weld conducted a New York training school for lecturers from which seventy apostles went out two by two to weave a network of abolitionist organizations across the North. Publications by Weld included *The Bible Against Slavery* (1837) and *American Slavery as It Is: Testimony of a Thousand Witnesses* (1839), the latter including examples of atrocities against slaves gathered from news accounts. The book sold 100,000 copies in its first year.

THE MOVEMENT SPLITS   As the movement spread, debates over tactics inevitably grew. The Garrisonians, mainly New Englanders, were radicals who felt that American society had been corrupted from top to bottom and needed universal reform. Garrison embraced just about every important reform movement that came down the pike in those years: antislavery, temperance, pacifism, and women's rights. Deeply affected by the perfectionism of the times, he refused to compromise principle for expediency, to sacrifice one reform for another. Abolition was not enough. He opposed colonization of freed slaves and stood for equal rights. He broke with the organized church, which to his mind was in league with slavery. The federal government, with its Fugitive Slave Law, was all the more so. The Constitution, he said, was "a covenant with death and an agreement with hell." Garrison therefore refused to vote. He was, however, prepared to collaborate with those who did or with those who disagreed with him on other matters.

Other reformers saw American society as fundamentally sound and concentrated their attention on purging it of slavery. Garrison struck them as an impractical fanatic. A showdown came in 1840 on the issue of women's rights. Women had joined the movement from the start, but quietly and largely in groups without men. The activities of the Grimké sisters brought the issue of women's rights forward. Sarah and Angelina Grimké, daughters of a prominent South Carolina family, had moved north to embrace antislavery and other reforms. Their publications included Angelina's *Appeal to the Christian Women of the South* (1836), calling on southern women to speak and act against slavery, and Sarah's *Letter on the Equality of the Sexes and the Condition of Women* (1838). Having attended Weld's school for antislavery apostles in New York (Angelina later married Weld), they set out speaking to women in New England and slowly widened their audiences to "promiscuous assemblies" of both men and women. Such unseemly behavior inspired the Congregational clergy of Massachusetts to pontificate in a pastoral letter: "If the vine . . . thinks to assume the independence and overshadowing nature of the elm, it will not only cease to bear fruit, but fall in shame and dishonor in the dust." But the Grimké sisters declined the role of clinging vines.

At the Anti-Slavery Society's meeting in 1840 the Garrisonians insisted on the right of women to participate equally in the organization, and carried their point. They did not commit the group to women's rights in any other way, however. Contrary opinion, mainly from the Tappans' New York group, ranged from outright antifeminism to simple fear of scattering shots on too many reforms. The New Yorkers broke away to form the American and Foreign Anti-Slavery Society. Weld, who had probably done more than anybody else to build the movement, declined to go with either group. Like the New Yorkers, he preferred to focus on slavery as the central evil of the times, but he could not accept their "anti-woman" attitude, as he saw it. Discouraged by the bickering, he drifted away from the movement he had done so much to build and into a long-term teaching career.

BLACK ANTISLAVERY   Antislavery men also balked at granting full recognition to black abolitionists of either sex. Often blindly patronizing, white leaders expected blacks to take a back seat in the movement. Not all blacks were easily put down, and most became exasperated at whites' tendency to value purity over results, to strike a moral posture at the expense of action. But despite the invitation to form separate black groups, black leaders were active in the white societies from the beginning. Three attended the organizational meeting of the American Anti-Slavery Society in 1833, and some became outstanding agents for the movement, notably the former slaves who could speak from firsthand experience. Garrison pronounced such men as Henry Bibb and William Wells Brown, both escapees from Kentucky, and Frederick Douglass, who fled Maryland, "the best qualified to address the public on the subject of slavery." Douglass, blessed with an imposing frame and a gift of eloquence, became the best known black man in America. "I appear before the immense assembly this evening as a thief and a robber," he told a Massachusetts group in 1842. "I stole this head, these limbs, this body from my master, and ran off with them." Fearful of capture after publishing his *Narrative of the Life of Frederick Douglass* (1845), he left for an extended lecture tour of the British Isles and returned two years later with enough money to purchase his freedom. He then started an abolitionist newspaper for blacks, the *North Star*, in Rochester, New York.

Douglass's *Narrative* was but the best known among a hundred or more such accounts. Escapees often made it out on their own

Frederick Douglass (left) and Sojourner Truth (right) were both leading abolitionists. [Library of Congress; New-York Historical Society]

—Douglass borrowed a pass from a free black seaman—but many were aided by the Underground Railroad, which grew in legend into a vast system to conceal runaways and spirit them to freedom, often over the Canadian border. Levi Coffin, a North Carolina Quaker who moved to Cincinnati and did help many fugitives, was the reputed president. Actually, there seems to have been more spontaneity than system about the matter, and blacks contributed more than was credited in the legend. Experience had conditioned escapees to distrust whites. One escapee recalled later: "We did not dare ask [for food], except when we found a slave's or a free colored person's house remote from any other, and then we were never refused, if they had food to give." A few intrepid refugees actually ventured back into slave states to organize escapes. Harriet Tubman, the most celebrated, went back nineteen times. Most refugees came from the upper South. Among the few who made it out of the Deep South, William and Ellen Craft of Macon, Georgia, devised one of the cleverest ruses. Being light-skinned she disguised herself as a decrepit planter accompanied north for medical aid by a faithful servant.

REACTIONS TO ANTISLAVERY   Even the road north, many blacks found to their dismay, did not lead to the Promised Land. North of slavery, they encountered much of the discrimination and segregation that freed slaves would later encounter in the southern states. When Prudence Crandall of Connecticut admitted a black girl to her private school in 1833, she lost most of her white pupils. She held out in the face of insults, vandalism, and a law which made her action illegal, but closed the school after eighteen months and left the state. Garrison, Douglass, Weld, and other abolitionists had to face down hostile crowds who disliked blacks or found antislavery agitation bad for business. In 1837 a hostile mob killed the antislavery editor Elijah P. Lovejoy, in Alton, Illinois, giving the movement a martyr to both abolition and freedom of the press.

By then proslavery southerners, by seeking to suppress discussion of emancipation, had already given abolitionists ways to link antislavery with the cause of civil liberties for whites. In the summer of 1835 a mob destroyed several sacks of abolitionist literature in the Charleston post office. The postmaster had announced that he would not try to deliver such matter. Bitter debates in Congress ensued. President Jackson wanted a law against handling "incendiary literature," but Congress failed to oblige him. The postmaster-general, nevertheless, did nothing about forcing delivery.

One shrewd political strategy, promoted by Weld, was to deluge Congress with petitions for abolition in the District of Columbia. Most such petitions were presented by former President John Quincy Adams, elected to the House from Massachusetts in 1830. In 1836, however, the House adopted a rule to lay abolition petitions automatically on the table, in effect ignoring them. Adams, "Old Man Eloquent," stubbornly fought this "Gag Rule" as a violation of the First Amendment, and hounded its supporters until the Gag Rule was finally repealed in 1844.

Meanwhile, in 1840, the year of the schism in the antislavery movement, a small group of abolitionists called a convention in Albany, New York, and launched the Liberty party, with James G. Birney, one-time slaveholder of Alabama and Kentucky, as its candidate for president. Birney, converted to the cause by Weld, had tried without success to publish an antislavery paper in Danville, Kentucky. He then moved it to Ohio and in 1837 became executive secretary of the American Anti-Slavery Society. In the 1840 election he polled only 7,000 votes, but in 1844 his vote rose to 60,000, and from that time forth an antislavery party contested every national election until Abraham Lincoln won the presidency.

THE DEFENSE OF SLAVERY Birney was but one among a number of southerners propelled north during the 1830s by the South's growing hostility to emancipationist ideas. Antislavery in the upper South had its last stand in 1831–1832 when the Virginia legislature debated a plan of gradual emancipation and colonization, then rejected it by a vote of 73 to 58. Thereafter, leaders of southern thought worked out an elaborate intellectual defense of slavery, presenting it as a positive good rather than, in the words of Tennessee's constitutional convention of 1834, "a great evil" that "the wisest heads and most benevolent hearts" had not been able to dispose of.

In 1832 Prof. Thomas R. Dew of the College of William and Mary published the most comprehensive defense of slavery produced to that time, his *Review of the Debate of the Virginia Legislature of 1831 and 1832*. In it he made the practical argument that the natural increase of the slave population would outrun any colonization effort. But he went on to justify slavery as required by the circumstances of southern life and the condition of human inequality, citing as authorities the Bible, Aristotle, and Edmund Burke.

The biblical argument became one of the most powerful. The evangelical churches, which had widely condemned slavery at one time, gradually turned proslavery. Ministers of all denominations joined in the argument. Had not the patriarchs of the Old Testament held bondsmen? Had not Noah, upon awakening from a drunken stupor, cursed Canaan, son of Ham, from whom the Negroes were descended? Had not Saint Paul advised servants to obey their masters and told a fugitive servant to return to his master? And had not Jesus remained silent on the subject, at least so far as the Gospels reported his words? In 1844–1845 disputes over slavery split two great denominations and led to the formation of the Methodist Episcopal Church, South, and the Southern Baptist Convention.

Another, and fundamental, feature of the proslavery argument developed a theory of the intrinsic inferiority of Negroes. Most whites, blind and deaf to the complexity of black culture, assumed that the evidence of their eyes and ears confirmed their own superiority. The weight of scientific opinion, which was not above prejudice on such matters, was on their side, but it is doubtful that many felt the need of science to prove what seemed so obvious to them. Stereotyping the poor and powerless as inferior is an old and seemingly ineradicable human habit. There was in fact a theory championed by Dr. Josiah C. Nott, a physician of Mobile, Alabama, that blacks were the product of a separate creation, but this challenged orthodox faith in the biblical account of creation and was generally rejected.

Other arguments took a more "practical" view of slavery. Not only was slavery profitable, it was a matter of social necessity. Jefferson, for instance, in his *Notes On Virginia* (1785), had argued that emancipated slaves and whites could not live together without risk of race war growing out of the recollection of past injustices. What is more, it seemed clear that blacks could not be expected to work under conditions of freedom. They were too shiftless and improvident, the argument went, and in freedom would be a danger to themselves as well as to others. White workmen, on the other hand, feared their competition. Whites were struck with fear too by the terrible example of the bloody rebellion in Santo Domingo.

In 1856 William J. Grayson of Charleston published a lengthy poem, *The Hireling and the Slave*, which defended slavery as better for the worker than the "wage slavery" of northern industry. George Fitzhugh of Virginia developed the same argument, among others, in two books: *Sociology for the South; or, The Failure of a Free Society* (1854) and *Cannibals All! or, Slaves Without Masters* (1857). Few if any socialists ever waxed more eloquent over the evils of industrial capitalism than these proslavery theorists. The factory system had brought abuses and neglect far worse than those of slavery. Slavery, Fitzhugh argued, was the truest form of socialism, for it provided security for the workers in sickness and old age, whereas workers in the North were exploited for profit and then cast aside without compunction. Men were not born equal, he insisted: "It would be far nearer the truth to say that some were born with saddles on their backs, and others booted and spurred to ride them—and the riding does them good." Fitzhugh argued for an organic, hierarchical society, much like the family, in which each had a place with both rights and obligations. Calhoun endorsed slavery with the more popular argument that it freed masters from drudgery to pursue higher things, and thus made possible a Greek democracy—or what one historian has more aptly tagged a "Herrenvolk [master race] democracy."

Within one generation such ideas had triumphed in the white South over the postrevolutionary apology for slavery as an evil bequeathed by the forefathers. Opponents of the orthodox faith in slavery as a positive good were either silenced or exiled. Freedom of thought in the Old South had become a victim of the nation's growing obsession with slavery.

FURTHER READING

Those interested in the problem of separating myth from reality in the southern experience should consult Patrick Gerster and Nicholas

° These books are available in paperback editions.

Cord (eds.), *Myth and Southern History* (vol. 1, 1974)°, for various essays on the topic. William R. Taylor's *Cavalier and Yankee: The Old South and American National Character* (1961)° is also helpful. W. J. Cash's *The Mind of the South* (1940)° remains a classic on the subject.

I. A. Newby's *The American South* (1979), Monroe Billington's *The American South* (1971), and Clement Eaton's *A History of the Old South* (1975) offer good surveys of the antebellum period. More specific are Charles S. Syndnor's *The Development of Southern Sectionalism, 1819–1848* (1948),° and Avery O. Craven's *The Growth of Southern Nationalism, 1848–1860* (1953).°

The dominance of the plantation system is analyzed in Ulrich B. Phillips's *Life and Labor in the Old South* (1929)° and Lewis C. Gray's *History of Agriculture in the Southern United States to 1860* (vol. 2, 1933). Frank L. Owsley's *Plain Folk of the South* (1949)° argues that yeomen farmers were dominant in many aspects of antebellum agriculture. A Marxist analysis of the plantations system is Eugene Genovese's *The World the Slaveholders Made* (1969),° while Gavin Wright's *The Political Economy of the Cotton South* (1978)° is more economic in approach.

A firsthand description of cotton growing in the South comes from Frederick Law Olmstead's *The Cotton Kingdom* (1861, 1953), based on his travels in the region just before the Civil War. The concept of agricultural reform is handled in Avery O. Craven's *Edmund Ruffin, Southerner* (1932),° and Betty L. Mitchell's *Edmund Ruffin, A Biography* (1981). The support system of merchants, factors, and bankers is described in both Harold Woodman's *King Cotton and His Retainers* (1968) and Lewis Atherton's *The Southern Country Store, 1800–1860* (1948). How southerners distributed their agricultural produce is the subject of Samuel Hilliard's *Hog Meat and Hoe Cake: Food Supply in the Antebellum South, 1840–1860* (1972).

Why southern industry lagged behind agriculture is treated in relevant chapters of Eugene Genovese's *The Political Economy of Slavery* (1962).° The life of a pioneer southern industrialist is documented in Broadus Mitchell's *William Gregg* (1928). Ernest Lander's *Antebellum Textiles in South Carolina* (1969) handles the origins of Piedmont cotton mills. Thomas Weiss and Fred Bateman's *A Deplorable Scarcity* (1981) explores the unfulfilled potential for southern industrial growth. Robert Starobin's *Industrial Slavery in the Old South* (1970)° and Claudia Goldin's *Urban Slavery in the South, 1820–1860* (1976), take opposing viewpoints on the use of bondsmen in nonagricultural labor.

The historiography of slavery and racism contains some of the most exciting and controversial scholarship in American letters. The first major work, U. B. Phillips's *American Negro Slavery* (1919), stressed a benign paternalism among planters. That view went generally unchallenged until Kenneth Stampp's *The Peculiar Institution* (1956)° showed how slaves resisted the oppression they faced. The idea of a creative black personality was challenged in Stanley Elkins's *Slavery: A Problem in American Intellectual Life* (1963).° More recent scholarship emphasizes the self-generative, dynamic character of black society under slavery. Harold Rawick's *From Sunup to Sundown* (1967), John W.

Blassingame's *The Slave Community: Plantation Life in the Antebellum South* (1972),° Eugene Genevese's *Roll, Jordan, Roll: The World the Slaves Made* (1974),° and Herbert Gutman's *The Black Family in Slavery and Freedom* (1976)° all stress the theme of a persisting and identifiable slave culture.

Most controversial has been the profitability of slavery. Harold A. Woodman handles the topic in *Slavery and the Southern Economy* (1966). Robert W. Fogel and Stanley L. Engerman sparked controversy with *Time on the Cross: The Economics of Negro Slavery* (1974),° which argues that not only did planters benefit from bondage, but that slaves themselves incorporated a Victorian work ethic based on incentives. Herbert Gutman reviews this controversy in *Slavery and the Numbers Game* (1975).°

Other recent works on slavery include R. C. Wade's *Slavery in the Cities* (1964), Leslie H. Owens's *This Species of Property* (1976),° Nathan I. Huggins's *Black Odyssey* (1977),° Lawrence W. Levine's *Black Culture and Black Consciousness: Afro-American Folk Thought from Slavery to Freedom* (1977),° Albert J. Raboteau's *Slave Religion: The "Invisible Institution" in the Antebellum South* (1978),° and Joel Williamson's *New People: Miscegenation and Mulattoes in the United States* (1982). Much of the oral history used to construct some of the new concepts on slavery is in John W. Blassingame (ed.), *Slave Testimony* (1977).°

Quite a number of overviews of abolitionism are worth inspection. For background on the origins of antislavery thought in Western civilization, consult David Brion Davis's *The Problem of Slavery in Western Culture* (1966).° Other surveys include Louis Filler's *The Crusade against Slavery* (1960)° Merton L. Dillon's *The Abolitionists: The Growth of a Dissenting Minority* (1974),° Ronald G. Walters's *The Anti-Slavery Appeal* (1976), and James B. Stewart's *Holy Warriors: The Abolitionists and American Slavery* (1976).° Also valuable is a collection of documents edited by Donald G. Mathews, *Agitators for Freedom: The Abolitionist Movement* (1972).

For particular emphasis on the religious background of abolitionism, see Gilbert H. Barnes's *The Anti-Slavery Impulse* (1933), which imparts a central role to Theodore Dwight Weld. For a contrasting viewpoint, see Aileen S. Kraditor's *Means and Ends in Anti-Slavery Thought* (1967), with its stress on the role of the Garrisonians. More philosophical is Lewis Perry's *Radical Abolitionists: Anarchy and the Government of God in Anti-Slave Thought* (1973). A comparative approach is Lewis Perry and Michael Fellman (eds.), *Anti-Slavery Reconsidered: New Perspectives on the Abolitionists* (1979).

Numerous biographies of the leading abolitionists contribute to an understanding of the movement: Betty Fladefeld's *James Gillespie Birney: Slaveholder to Abolitionist* (1955), Walter M. Merrill's *Against Wind and Tide: A Biography of William Lloyd Garrison* (1963), John L. Thomas's *The Liberator: William Lloyd Garrison* (1963), Gerda Lerner's *The Grimké Sisters from South Carolina: Rebels against Slavery* (1967),° Bertram Wyatt-Brown's *Lewis Tappan and the Evangelical War against Slavery* (1969), James B. Stewart's *Joshua Giddings and the Tactics of*

Radical Politics (1970), and Robert Abzug's *Passionate Liberator: Theodore Dwight Weld and the Dilemma of Reform* (1980).°

The role free blacks played in the antislavery movement appears in Benjamin Quarles's *Black Abolitionists* (1969)°. Jane H. and William H. Pease also examine the role of black abolitionists in *They Who Would Be Free* (1974)°. The legend and the reality of the underground railroad is explored in Larry Gara's *The Liberty Line* (1961)°. A recent work on the leading black abolitionist is Arna Bontemps's *Free at Last: The Life of Frederick Douglass* (1971). Surveys of black history for the period include John Hope Franklin's *From Slavery to Freedom* (1974),° Leon F. Litwack's *North of Slavery: The Negro in the Free States, 1790–1860* (1961),° and Ira Berlin's *Slaves without Masters* (1975),° on southern free blacks.

The literature on white reaction to the antislavery movement includes Russel B. Nye's *Fettered Freedom: Civil Liberties and the Slavery Controversy* (1963), Leonard L. Richards's *"Gentlemen of Property and Standing": Anti-Abolition Mobs in Jacksonian America* (1970), and Thomas O. Morris's *Free Men All: The Personal Liberty Laws of the North, 1780–1861* (1974).

For the proslavery argument as it developed in the South, see William J. Cooper's *The South and the Politics of Slavery, 1828–1856* (1978),° and James Oakes's *The Ruling Race: A History of American Slaveholders* (1982).° Harvey Wish's *George Fitzhugh* (1943) examines the role of the leading southern apologist for slavery. The role which churches played in the argument appears in H. Shelton Smith's *In His Image, But. . . : Racism in Southern Religion, 1780–1910* (1972). Also helpful for the conflict within one denomination is Donald G. Mathews's *Methodism and Slavery* (1965). The problems leading southerners had in justifying slavery is explored in Drew G. Faust's *A Sacred Circle: The Dilemma of the Intellectual in the Old South, 1840–1860* (1977), and Carl N. Degler's *The Other South: Southern Dissenters in the Nineteenth Century* (1974).° How one family coped with ambiguous feelings about slavery is shown in Drew G. Faust's *James Henry Hammond and the Old South* (1982). Dickson D. Bruce, Jr., explores the white tendency toward a physical defense of slavery in *Violence and Culture in the Antebellum South* (1979). George M. Frederickson's *The Black Image in the White Mind* (1971)° examines a variety of racial stereotypes held by white southerners.

16

THE CRISIS OF UNION

SLAVERY IN THE TERRITORIES

John C. Calhoun and Ralph Waldo Emerson had little else in common, but both men sensed in the Mexican War the omens of a greater disaster. Mexico was "the forbidden fruit; the penalty of eating it would be to subject our institutions to political death," Calhoun warned. "The United States will conquer Mexico," Emerson conceded, "but it will be as the man swallows the arsenic. . . . Mexico will poison us." Wars, as both men knew, have a way of breeding new wars, often in unforseen ways. Like Britain's conquest of New France, the winning of the Southwest gave rise in turn to quarrels over newly acquired lands. In each case the quarrels set in train a series of disputes: Britain's crisis of empire had its counterpart in America's crisis of union.

THE WILMOT PROVISO The Mexican War was less than three months old when the seeds of a new conflict began to sprout. On Saturday evening, August 8, 1846, a sweltering House of Representatives reassembled to clear its calendar for adjournment. Polk had sent Congress that noon a hurried request for $2 million to expedite negotiations with Mexico. He expected little hindrance, since party discipline had already whipped through most of his program. But the House, resentful of Polk's triumphs, was ripe for revolt when a freshman Democrat from Pennsylvania, David Wilmot, stood up. He favored expansion, Wilmot explained, even the annexation of Texas as a slave state. But slavery had come to an end in Mexico, and if free soil should be acquired, "God forbid that we should be the means of planting this institution upon it." Drawing upon the words of the Northwest Ordinance, he offered a fateful amendment: in lands acquired from

573

Mexico, "neither slavery nor involuntary servitude shall ever exist in any part of said territory, except for crime, whereof the party shall first be duly convicted."

Within ten minutes an otherwise obscure congressman had immortalized his name. The Wilmot Proviso, although never a law, politicized slavery once and for all. For a generation, since the Missouri Controversy of 1819–1821, the issue had been lurking in the wings, kept there most of the time by politicians who feared its disruptive force. From that day forth, for two decades the question would never be far from center stage.

The first flurry of excitement passed quickly, however. The House adopted the Wilmot Proviso that Saturday night. The following Monday the Senate refused to concur and Congress adjourned without giving Polk his $2 million. When Congress reconvened in December Polk prevailed on Wilmot to withhold his amendment when he asked for the money again, but by then others were ready to take up the cause. When Preston King of New York revived the proviso he signaled a revolt by the Van Burenites in concert with the antislavery forces of the North. Once again the House approved the amendment. Once again the Senate refused. In March the House finally gave in, but in one form or another Wilmot's idea kept cropping up. Abraham Lincoln later recalled that during one term as congressman, 1847–1849, he voted for it "as good as forty times."

John C. Calhoun meanwhile devised a thesis to counter the proviso and set it before the Senate in four resolutions on February 19, 1847. The Calhoun Resolutions, which never came to a vote, argued that since the territories were the common possession of the states, Congress had no right to prevent any citizen from taking his slaves into them. To do so would violate the Fifth Amendment, which forbade Congress to deprive any person of life, liberty, or property without due process of law, and slaves were property. Thus by a clever stroke of logic Calhoun took that basic guarantee of liberty, the Bill of Rights, and turned it into a basic guarantee of slavery. The irony was not lost on his critics, but the point became established southern dogma— echoed by his colleagues and formally endorsed by the Virginia legislature.

Thomas Hart Benton of Missouri, himself a slaveholder but also a Jacksonian nationalist, found in Calhoun's resolutions a set of abstractions "leading to no result." Wilmot and Calhoun between them, he said, had fashioned a pair of shears. Neither blade alone would cut very well, but joined together they could sever the ties of union. Within another year Benton was complaining that the slavery issue had become like the plague of frogs in Pharaoh's Egypt, with "this black question, forever on the table, on the nuptial couch, everywhere."

POPULAR SOVEREIGNTY Many others, like Benton, refused to be polarized, seeking to bypass the conflict that was brewing. President Polk was among the first to suggest extending the Missouri Compromise dividing free and slave territory at latitude 36° 30' all the way to the Pacific. Sen. Lewis Cass of Michigan suggested that the citizens of a territory "regulate their own internal concerns in their own way," like the citizens of a state. Such an approach would combine the merits of expediency and democracy. It would take the issue out of the national arena and put it in the hands of those directly affected.

Popular sovereignty, or squatter sovereignty, as the idea was alternatively called, had much to commend it, including an ambiguity which improved the presidential prospects of Cass. Without directly challenging the slaveholders' access to the new lands, it promised to open them quickly to free farmers who would almost surely dominate the territories. With this tacit understanding the idea prospered in Cass's Old Northwest, where Stephen A. Douglas of Illinois and other prominent Democrats soon endorsed it. Popular sovereignty, they hoped, might check the magnetic pull toward the opposite poles of Wilmot and Calhoun.

When the Mexican War ended in 1848, the question of bondage in the new territories was no longer hypothetical—unless one reasoned, as many did, that their arid climate excluded plantation crops and therefore excluded slavery. For Calhoun, who leaned to that opinion, that was beside the point since the right to carry slaves into the territories was the outer defense line of the peculiar institution, not be yielded without opening the way to further assaults. In fact there is little reason in retrospect to credit the argument that slavery had reached its natural limits of expansion. Slavery had been adapted to occupations other than plantation agriculture. Besides, on irrigated lands, cotton later became a staple crop of the Southwest.

Nobody doubted that Oregon would become free soil, but it too was drawn into the maelstrom of controversy. Territorial status, pending since 1846, was delayed because its provisional government had excluded slavery. To concede that provision would imply an authority drawn from the powers of Congress, since a territory was created by Congress. Finally, a Senate committee proposed to let Oregon exclude slavery but to deny the territories of California and New Mexico any power to legislate at all on the subject, thus passing the issue to the courts. The question of slavery, previously outlawed under Mexican rule, could rise on appeal to the Supreme Court and thus be kept out of the political arena. The Senate accepted this but the House rejected it, and finally an exhausted Congress let Oregon organize without slavery, but postponed decision on the Southwest. Polk signed the bill on the principle that Oregon was north of 36°30′.

Polk had promised to serve only one term; exhausted by his labors and having reached his major goals, he refused to run again. In the Democratic convention Lewis Cass took an early lead and won nomination on the fourth ballot. The Democratic party had endorsed the author of squatter sovereignty, but its platform simply denied the power of Congress to interfere with slavery in the states and criticized all efforts to bring the question before Congress. The Whigs devised an even more artful shift. Once again, as in 1840, they passed over their party leader for a general, Zachary Taylor, whose fame and popularity had grown since the Battle of Buena Vista. He was a legal resident of Louisiana who owned more than a hundred slaves, an apolitical figure who had never voted in a national election. Once again, as in 1840, the party adopted no platform at all. While most of Taylor's support came from the South, Thurlow Weed and William H. Seward of New York had favored him and helped engineer a vice-presidential nomination for New Yorker Millard Fillmore.

THE FREE-SOIL COALITION But the antislavery impulse was not easily squelched. Wilmot had raised a standard to which a broad coalition could rally. Men who shied away from abolitionism could readily endorse the exclusion of slavery from the territories. The Northwest Ordinance and the Missouri Compromise supplied honored precedents. By doing so, moreover, one could strike a blow for liberty without caring about slavery itself, or about the slaves. One might simply want free soil for white farmers, while keeping the unwelcome blacks far away in the South, where they belonged. Free soil, therefore, rather than abolition, became the rallying point—and also the name of a new party.

Three major groups entered the free-soil coalition: rebellious Democrats, antislavery Whigs, and members of the Liberty party, which dated from 1840. Disaffection among the Democrats centered in New York, where the Van Burenite "Barnburners" squared off against the pro-administration "Hunkers" in a factional dispute which had as much to do with personal ambitions as with local politics. Each group gave the other its name, the one for its alleged purpose to rule or ruin like the farmer who burned his barn to get rid of the rats, the other for hankering or "hunkering" after office.

As their conflict grew, however, the Barnburners seized on the free-soil issue as a means of winning support. When the Democratic convention voted to divide the state's votes between contesting delegations, they bolted the party and named Van Buren as their candidate for president on a free-soil platform. Other Wilmot Democrats, including Wilmot himself, joined the revolt. Revolt among the Whigs centered in Massachusetts where a group of "conscience" Whigs battled the "cotton" Whigs. The latter, according to Charles Sumner, belonged to a coalition of northern businessmen and southern planters, "the lords of the lash and the lords of the loom." Conscience Whigs rejected the slaveholder, Taylor. The third group in the coalition, the abolitionist Liberty party, had already nominated Sen. John P. Hale of New Hampshire for president.

In August these groups—Barnburners, Conscience Whigs, and Liberty party men—organized the Free Soil party in a convention at Buffalo. Its presidential nomination went to Martin Van Buren by a close margin over Hale, while the vice-presidential nomination went to Charles Francis Adams, a Conscience Whig. The old Jacksonian and the son of John Quincy Adams made strange bedfellows indeed! The old Liberty party was rewarded with a platform plank which pledged the government to

An 1848 Free Soil party banner. The party's slogan was "Free Soil, Free Labor, Free Speech." [Library of Congress]

abolish slavery whenever such action became constitutional, but the party's main principle was the Wilmot Proviso and it entered the campaign with the catchy slogan of "free soil, free speech, free labor, and free men."

Its impact on the election was mixed. The Free Soilers split the Democractic vote enough to throw New York to Taylor, and the Whig vote enough to give Ohio to Cass, but Van Buren's total of 291,000 votes was far below the popular totals of 1,361,000 for Taylor and 1,222,000 for Cass. Taylor won with 163 to 127 electoral votes, and both major parties retained a national following. Taylor took eight slave states and seven free; Cass just the opposite, seven slave and eight free.

TOWARD STATEHOOD FOR CALIFORNIA   Meanwhile a new dimension had been introduced into the question of the territories. On January 24, 1848, nine days before Trist signed the Mexican peace treaty, gold was discovered in California. The word spread quickly, and Polk's confirmation of the discovery in his last annual message, on December 5, 1848, turned the gold-fever into a worldwide contagion.

During 1849, by the best estimates, more than 80,000 persons reached California. Probably 55,000 went overland; the rest went by way of Panama or Cape Horn. Along the western slopes of the Sierra Nevada they thronged the valleys and canyons in a wide belt from LaPorte southward to Mariposa. The village of San Francisco, located near the harbor entrance Frémont had aptly named Golden Gate, grew rapidly into a city. The influx quickly reduced the Mexicans to a minority, and sporadic conflicts with the Indians of the Sierra Nevada foothills decimated the native peoples. In 1850 Americans already accounted for 68 percent of the population and there was a cosmopolitan array of "Sydney Ducks" from Australia, "Kanakas" from Hawaii, "Limies" from London, "Paddies" from Ireland, "Coolies" from China, and "Keskydees" from Paris (who were always asking "Qu'est-ce qu'il dit?").

Zachary Taylor did not remain an enigma for long. Born in Virginia, raised in Kentucky, he had been a soldier most of his adult life, with service in the War of 1812, the Black Hawk and Seminole Wars, as well as in Mexico. Constantly on the move, he had acquired a home in Louisiana and a plantation in Mississippi. Southern Whigs had rallied to his support, expecting him to uphold the cause of slavery. Instead they had turned up a southern man with Union principles, who had no more use for Calhoun's proslavery abstractions than Jackson had for his nullification doctrine. Innocent of politics Taylor might be, and to southern Whigs it was ominous that the antislavery Seward had his ear, but "Old Rough and Ready" had the direct mind of the soldier he was. Slavery should be upheld where it existed, he felt, but he had little patience with abstract theories about slavery in territories where it probably could not exist. Why not make California and New Mexico into states immediately, he reasoned, and bypass the whole issue?

But the Californians, in need of organized government, were already ahead of him. By December 1849, without leave of Congress, California had a free-state government in operation. New Mexico responded more slowly, but by June 1850 Americans there had adopted another free-state constitution. The Mormons around Salt Lake, meanwhile, drafted a basic law for the imperial state of Deseret, which embraced most of the Mexican Cession, including a slice of the coast from Los Angeles to San Diego.

In Taylor's annual message on December 4, 1849, he endorsed immediate statehood for California and enjoined Congress to "abstain from . . . those exciting topics of sectional character which have hitherto produced painful apprehensions in the public mind." The new Congress, however, was in no mood for simple solutions. For three weeks the House, where fifteen Free Soilers held the balance of power, remained snarled in an angry contest over the choice of a Speaker.

THE COMPROMISE OF 1850

THE GREAT DEBATE   The spotlight, however, fell on the Senate, where a stellar cast enacted one of the great dramas of American politics, the Compromise of 1850: the great triumvirate of Clay, Calhoun, and Webster, with a supporting cast that included William H. Seward, Stephen A. Douglas, Jefferson Davis, and Thomas Hart Benton. Henry Clay once again took the role of "Great Pacificator," which he had played in the Missouri and nullification controversies. In January he presented a package of eight resolutions which wrapped up solutions to all the disputed issues. He proposed to (1) admit California as a free state, (2) organize the remainder of the Southwest without restriction as to slavery, (3) deny Texas its extreme claim to a Rio Grande boundary up to its source, (4) compensate Texas for this by assuming the Texas debt, (5) uphold slavery in the District of Columbia, but (6) abolish the slave trade across its boundaries, (7) adopt a more effective fugitive slave act, and (8) deny congressional authority to interfere with the interstate slave trade. His proposals, in substance, became the Compromise of 1850, but only after a prolonged debate, the most celebrated, if not the greatest, in the annals of Congress—and the final great debate for Calhoun, Clay and Webster. Calhoun, already dying, would be gone on March 31, and Clay and Webster two years later, in 1852.

On February 5–6 the aging Clay summoned all his resources of eloquence in a defense of the settlement. In the interest of "peace, concord and harmony" he called for an end to "passion, passion—party, party—and intemperance." California should be admitted on the terms that its own people had approved. As to the remainder of the new lands, he told northerners: "You have got what is worth more than a thousand Wilmot provisos. You have nature on your side. . . ." Secession, he warned southerners, would inevitably bring on war. Even a peaceful secession, however unlikely, would gain none of the South's demands. Slavery in the territories and the District, the return of fugitives—all would be endangered.

The debate continued sporadically through February, with Sam Houston rising to the support of Clay's compromise, Jefferson Davis defending the slavery cause on every point, and none rising to any effective defense of President Taylor's straightforward plan. Then on March 4 Calhoun left his sickbed to sit, a gaunt figure with his cloak draped about his shoulders, as Senator Mason of Virginia read the "sentiments" he had "reduced to writing."

"I have, Senators, believed from the first that the agitation of the subject of slavery would, if not prevented by some timely and effective measure, end in disunion," said Calhoun. Neither Clay's compromise nor Taylor's efforts would serve the Union. The South needed but an acceptance of its rights: equality in the territories, the return of fugitive slaves, and some guarantee of "an equilibrium between the sections." The last, while not spelled out in the speech, referred to Calhoun's notion of a "concurrent majority" by which each section could gain security through a veto power, perhaps through a dual executive, an idea which would be elaborated in his posthumous *Discourse on the Constitution*.

Three days later Calhoun returned to hear Daniel Webster. The assumption was widely held that the "godlike Daniel," long since acknowledged the supreme orator of an age of oratory, would stick to his mildly free-soil views. In a sense he did, but his central theme, as in the classic debate with Hayne, was the preservation of the Union: "I wish to speak today, not as a Massachusetts man, not as a Northern man, but as an American. . . . I speak today for the preservation of the Union. 'Hear me for my cause.'" The extent of slavery was already determined, he insisted, by the Northwest Ordinance, by the Missouri Compromise, and in the new lands by the law of nature. The Wilmot Proviso was superfluous: "I would not take pains to reaffirm an ordinance of nature nor to re-enact the will of God." Both sections, to be sure, had legitimate grievances: on the one hand the excesses of "infernal fanatics and abolitionists" in the North; and on the other hand southern efforts to expand slavery and southern slurs on northern workingmen. But "Secession! Peaceable secession! Sir, your eyes and mine are never destined to see that miracle." Instead of looking into such "caverns of darkness," let men "enjoy the fresh air of liberty and union." Let them look to a more hopeful future.

The March 7 speech was a supreme gesture of conciliation, and Webster had knowingly brought down a storm upon his head. New England antislavery leaders virtually exhausted the vocabulary of abuse against this new "Benedict Arnold" who had betrayed his section. John Greenleaf Whittier lamented in "Ichabod":

> So fallen! so lost! the light withdrawn
> Which once he wore!
> The glory from his gray hairs gone
> Forevermore!

But Webster had also revived hopes of compromise in both North and South. Agreement, wrote the New England historian George Ticknor, "will be mainly owing to the conciliatory tone taken by Mr. Webster." Georgia's Senator Toombs found "a tolerable prospect for a proper settlement of the slavery question, probably along the lines backed by Webster."

On March 11 William H. Seward, freshman Whig senator from New York, gave the antislavery reply to Webster. As the confidant of Taylor he might have been expected to defend the president's program. Instead he stated his own view that compromise with slavery was "radically wrong and essentially vicious." There was, he said, "a higher law than the Constitution," thus leaving some doubt, according to the historian David Potter, whether he was floor leader for Zachary Taylor or for God.

In mid-April a select Committee of Thirteen bundled Clay's suggestions (insofar as they concerned the Mexican cession) into one comprehensive bill, which the committee reported to the

Senate early in May. The measure was quickly dubbed the "Omnibus" bill because it resembled the contemporary vehicle that carried many riders. Taylor continued to oppose Clay's compromise and the two men came to an open break which threatened to split the Whig party wide open. Another crisis loomed when word came near the end of June that a convention in New Mexico was applying for statehood, with Taylor's support, and with boundaries that conflicted with the Texas claim to the east bank of the Rio Grande.

TOWARD A COMPROMISE   On July 4 friends of the Union staged a grand rally at the base of the unfinished Washington Monument. Taylor went to hear Henry S. Foote, but lingered for other ceremonies in the hot sun. Back at the White House he quenched his thirst with iced water and milk, ate some cherries, cucumbers, or cabbage, and was stricken with cholera morbus (gastroenteritis). Five days later he was dead. The outcome of the sectional quarrel, had he lived, probably would have been different, whether for better or worse one cannot know. In a showdown Taylor had put everyone on notice that he would be as resolute as Jackson. "I can save the Union without shedding a drop of blood," he said. On the other hand a showdown might have provoked civil war ten years before it came, years during which the northern states gained in population and economic strength.

Taylor's sudden death, however, strengthened the chances of compromise. The soldier in the White House was followed by a politician, Millard Fillmore. The son of a poor farmer in upper New York, Fillmore had come up through the school of hard

Millard Fillmore. His support of the Compromise of 1850 helped the Union muddle through the crisis. [Library of Congress]

knocks. Largely self-educated, he had made his own way in the profession of law and the rough-and-tumble world of New York politics. Experience had taught him caution, which some thought was indecision, but he had made up his mind to support Clay's compromise and had so informed Taylor. It was a strange switch. Taylor, the Louisiana slaveholder, had been ready to make war on his native region; Fillmore, whom southerners thought was antislavery, was ready to make peace.

At this point young Sen. Stephen A. Douglas of Illinois, a rising star of the Democratic party, came to the rescue of Clay's faltering compromise. Never sanguine about the Omnibus, he had refused service on the Committee of Thirteen, and with Clay's consent, kept himself ready to lead an alternative strategy. His strategy was in fact the same one that Clay had used to pass the Missouri Compromise thirty years before. Reasoning that nearly everybody objected to one or another provision of the Omnibus, Douglas worked on the principle of breaking it up into six (later five) separate measures. Few members were prepared to vote for all of them, but from different elements Douglas hoped to mobilize a majority for each.

It worked. Thomas Hart Benton described the sequel. The separate items were like "cats and dogs that had been tied together by their tails four months, scratching and biting, but being loose again, every one of them ran off to his own hole and was quiet." By September 17 it was over, and three days later Fillmore had signed the last of the five measures into law. The Union had muddled through, and the settlement went down in history as the Compromise of 1850. For the time it defused an explosive situation and settled each of the major points at issue.

First, California entered the Union as a free state, ending forever the old balance of free and slave states. Second, the Texas and New Mexico Act made New Mexico a territory and set the Texas boundary at its present location. In return for giving up its claims east of the Rio Grande Texas was paid $10 million, which secured payment of the Texas debt and brought a powerful lobby of bondholders to the support of compromise. Third, the Utah Act set up another territory. The territorial act in each case omitted reference to slavery except to give the territorial legislature authority over "all rightful subjects of legislation" with provision for appeal to federal courts. For the sake of agreement the deliberate ambiguity of the statement was its merit. Northern congressmen could assume that territorial legislatures might act to exclude slavery on the unstated principle of popular sovereignty. Southern congressmen assumed that they could not.

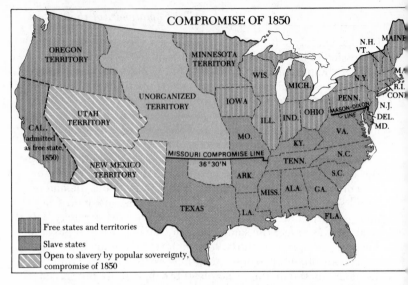

COMPROMISE OF 1850

OREGON TERRITORY

MINNESOTA TERRITORY

WIS.

MICH.

UNORGANIZED TERRITORY

IOWA

UTAH TERRITORY

OHIO

PENN.

MASON-DIXON LINE

N.Y.

N.H. VT. MAINE

MA

R.I.

CONN

N.J.

DEL.

MD.

CAL. (admitted as free state, 1850)

ILL. IND.

MO.

KY.

VA.

MISSOURI COMPROMISE LINE 36°30'N

NEW MEXICO TERRITORY

TENN.

N.C.

ARK.

S.C.

MISS. ALA. GA.

TEXAS

LA.

FLA.

Free states and territories

Slave states

Open to slavery by popular sovereignty, compromise of 1850

Fourth, a new Fugitive Slave Act put the matter wholly under federal jurisdiction and stacked the cards in favor of slave-catchers. Fifth, as a gesture to antislavery forces the slave trade, but not slavery itself, was abolished in the District of Columbia: more specifically, no slave could be brought into the District for the purpose of sale or be held in a depot for transfer and sale elsewhere. The spectacle of slave coffles passing through the streets of the capital was brought to an end. Calling these five measures the Compromise of 1850 was an afterthought. Actually they were the result less of a sectional bargain than of a parliamentary maneuver. They were nevertheless an accomplished fact, and a large body of citizens welcomed the outcome, if not with joy, at least with relief. Millard Fillmore's message to Congress in December 1850 pronounced the measures "a final settlement."

Still, doubts lingered that either North or South could be reconciled to the measures permanently. In the South the disputes of 1846–1850 had transformed the abstract doctrine of secession into a movement animated by such fire-eaters as Robert Barnwell Rhett of South Carolina, William Lowndes Yancey of Alabama, and Edmund Ruffin of Virginia.

But once the furies aroused by the Wilmot Provisio were spent, the compromise left little on which to focus a proslavery agitation. The state of California was an accomplished fact, and, ironically, tended to elect proslavery men to Congress. New Mexico and Utah were far away, and in any case at least hypothetically open to slavery. Both in fact adopted slave codes, but the census of 1860 reported no slaves in New Mexico and only twenty-nine in Utah. The Fugitive Slave Law was something else again. It was the one clear-cut victory for the cause of slavery, but a pyrrhic victory if ever there was one.

THE FUGITIVE SLAVE LAW Southern intransigence had presented abolition its greatest gift since the Gag Rule, a new focus for agitation and one that was far more charged with emotion. The fugitive slave law did more than stack the deck in favor of slave-catchers; it offered a strong temptation to kidnap free Negroes by denying alleged fugitives a jury trial and by providing a fee of $10 for each fugitive delivered. In addition federal marshals could require citizens to help in enforcement; violators could be imprisoned up to six months and fined $1,000. Anson Burlingame of Massachusetts said it fixed the value of a Carolina slave at $1,000, of a Yankee soul at $5.

"This filthy enactment was made in the nineteenth century, by people who could read and write," Emerson marveled in his journal. He advised neighbors to break it "on the earliest occasion." The occasion soon arose in many places, if not in Emerson's Concord. Within a month of the law's enactment claims were filed in New York, Philadelphia, Harrisburg, Detroit, and

Practical Illustration of the Fugitive Slave Law. *Depicts the divisive effects of the law. [The Smithsonian Institution]*

other cities. Trouble soon followed. In Detroit only military force stopped the rescue of an alleged fugitive by an outraged mob in October 1850.

There were relatively few such incidents, however. In the first six years of the fugitive act only three fugitives were forcibly rescued from the slave-catchers. On the other hand probably fewer than 200 were remanded to bondage during the same years. More than that were rescued by stealth, often through the Underground Railroad. Still, the Fugitive Slave Act had tremendous effect in widening and deepening the antislavery impulse in the North.

UNCLE TOM'S CABIN Antislavery forces found their most persuasive appeal not in the fugitive slave law but in the fictional drama of Harriet Beecher Stowe's *Uncle Tom's Cabin,* a combination of unlikely saints and sinners, stereotypes and melodramatic escapades—and a smashing commercial success. The long-suffering Uncle Tom, the villainous Simon Legree, the angelic Eva, the desperate Eliza taking her child to freedom across the icy Ohio —all became stock characters of the American imagination. Slavery, seen through Mrs. Stowe's eyes, subjected its victims either to callous brutality or, at the hands of indulgent masters, to the indignity of extravagant ineptitude and bankruptcy. It took time for the novel to work its effect on public opinion, however. Neither abolitionists nor fire-eaters represented their sections at the time. The country was enjoying a surge of prosperity, and the course of the presidential campaign in 1852 reflected a common desire to lay sectional quarrels to rest.

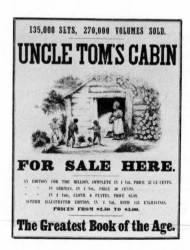

"*The Greatest Book of the Age.*" Uncle Tom's Cabin, *as this advertisement indicates, was a tremendous commercial success.* [New-York Historical Society]

FOREIGN ADVENTURES

The Democrats, despite a fight over the nomination, had some success in papering over the divisions within their party. As their nominee for president they turned finally to Franklin Pierce of New Hampshire; William R. King of Alabama was nominated for vice-president. The platform pledged the Democrats to "abide by and adhere to a faithful execution of the acts known as the Compromise measures. . . . " The candidates and the platform generated a surprising reconciliation of the party's factions. Pierce rallied both the Southern Rights men and the Barnburners, who at least had not burned their bridges with the Democrats. The Free Soilers, as a consequence, mustered only 156,000 votes for John P. Hale in contrast to the 291,000 they got for Van Buren in 1848.

The Whigs were less fortunate. They repudiated the lackluster Fillmore, who had faithfully supported the Compromise, and once again tried to exploit martial glory. It took fifty-three ballots, but the convention finally chose Winfield Scott, the hero of Lundy's Lane and Mexico City, a native of Virginia backed mainly by northern Whigs, including Seward. The convention dutifully endorsed the Compromise, but with some opposition from the North. Scott, an able commander but politically inept, had gained a reputation for antislavery and nativism, alienating German and Irish ethnic voters. In the end Scott carried only Tennessee, Kentucky, Massachusetts, and Vermont. Pierce overwhelmed him in the electoral college 254 to 42, although the popular vote was closer: 1.6 million to 1.4 million.

Pierce, an undistinguished but handsome and engaging figure, a former congressman, senator, and brigadier in Mexico, was, like Polk, touted as another "Young Hickory." But he turned out to be made of more pliable stuff, unable to dominate the warring factions of his party, trying to be all things to all men, but looking more and more like a "Northern man with Southern principles."

"YOUNG AMERICA" Foreign diversions now distracted attention from domestic quarrels. After the Mexican War the spirit of Manifest Destiny took on new life in an amorphous movement called "Young America." The Spirit of Young America was full of spread-eagle bombast, buoyant optimism, and enthusiasm for economic growth and territorial expansion. The dynamic force of American institutions would somehow transform the world. On February 21, 1848, just two days after word of the Mexican treaty reached Washington, an uprising in Paris signaled the liberal Revolutions of 1848, which set Europe ablaze. The Young Americans greeted that new dawn with all the ardor Jeffersonians had lavished on the first French Revolution. And when it all collapsed, the result seemed all the more to confirm the belief that Europe was, in the words of Stephen A. Douglas, "antiquated, decrepit, tottering on the verge of dissolution . . . a vast graveyard."

CUBA Closer to home, Cuba, one of Spain's earliest and one of its last possessions in the New World, continued to be an object of American concern. In the early 1850s a crisis arose over expeditions launched against Cuba from American soil. Spanish authorities retaliated against these provocations by harassment of American ships. In 1854 the Cuban crisis expired in one final outburst of braggadocio, the Ostend Manifesto. That year the Pierce administration instructed Pierre Soule, the minister in Madrid, to offer $130 million for Cuba, which Spain peremptorily spurned. Soule then joined the American ministers to France and Britain in drafting the Ostend Manifesto. It declared that if Spain, "actuated by stubborn pride and a false sense of honor refused to sell," then the United States must ask itself, "does Cuba, in the possession of Spain, seriously endanger our internal peace and existence of our cherished Union?" If so, "then, by every law, human and divine, we shall be justified in wresting it from Spain. . . ." Publication of the supposedly confidential dispatch left the administration no choice but to disavow what northern opinion widely regarded as a "slaveholders' plot." The last word on this and other such episodes perhaps should go to the staid London *Times*, which commented near the end of 1854: "The diplomacy of the United States is certainly a very singular profession."

So was the practice of filibustering which, again, was more bluster than action. Little wonder the word has come to suggest gas-bag as well as freebooter, and the double-meaning is appropriate for the 1850s. William Walker, a Tennessean by birth who went to California and began to fancy himself a new Cortés, reached his supreme moment in 1855 when the "grey-eyed man of destiny" sailed with sixty followers, "the immortals," to mix in a Nicaraguan civil war. Before the year was out he had made himself president of a republic which Franklin Pierce promptly recognized. Walker was deposed in 1857, and in 1860 was executed by a firing squad in Honduras.

DIPLOMATIC GAINS IN THE PACIFIC In the Pacific, however, American diplomacy scored some positive achievements. American

trade with China dated from 1785, but was allowed only through
the port of Canton. In 1844 the United States and China signed
the Treaty of Wanghsia, which opened four ports, including
Shanghai, to American trade and for the first time granted America "extraterritoriality," or special privileges, including the right
of Americans to remain subject to their own law in certain areas.
The Treaty of Tientsin (1858) opened eleven more ports and
granted Americans the right to travel and trade throughout
China. China quickly became a special concern of American Protestant missionaries as well. About fifty were already there by
1855, and for nearly a century China remained far and away the
greatest mission field for Americans.

Japan meanwhile had remained for two centuries closed to
American trade. Moreover, American whalers wrecked on the
shores of Japan had been forbidden to leave the country. Mainly
in their interest President Fillmore entrusted a special Japanese
expedition to Commodore Matthew C. Perry, who arrived in
Tokyo on July 8, 1853. Japan's actual ruler, the Tokugawa sho-
gun, was already under pressure from merchants and the educated classes to seek wider contacts in the world. He agreed to
deliver Perry's letter to the emperor. Negotiations followed, and
in the Treaty of Kanagawa (March 31, 1854) Japan agreed to an
American consulate, promised good treatment to castaways, and
permitted visits in certain ports for supplies and repairs. Broad
commercial relations came after the first envoy, Townsend
Harris, negotiated the Harris Convention of 1858, which opened
five ports to American trade and made certain tariff concessions.
In 1860 a Japanese diplomatic mission, the first to enter a Western country, visited the United States for three months.

A Japanese view of Commodore Perry's landing in Yokohama Harbor.
[Library of Congress]

THE KANSAS-NEBRASKA CRISIS

During the 1850s the only land added to the United States was a barren stretch of some 30,000 square miles south of the Gila River in present New Mexico and Arizona. This Gadsden Purchase of 1853, which cost the United States $10 million, was made to acquire land offering a likely route for a Pacific railroad. The idea of building a railroad linking together the new continental domain of the United States, though a great national goal, spawned sectional rivalries in still another quarter and reopened the slavery issue. Among the many transcontinental routes projected, the four most important were the northern route from Milwaukee to the Columbia River, a central route from St. Louis to San Francisco, another from Memphis to Los Angeles, and a more southerly route from New Orleans to San Diego via the Gadsden Purchase.

DOUGLAS'S PROPOSAL   Stephen A. Douglas of Illinois had an even better idea: Chicago ought to be the eastern terminus. In 1852 and 1853 Congress debated and dropped several likely proposals. For various reasons, including terrain, climate, and sectional interest, Secretary of War Jefferson Davis favored the southern route and encouraged the Gadsden Purchase. Any other route, moreover, would go through the Indian country which stretched from Texas to the Canadian border.

Since 1845, therefore, Douglas and others had offered bills for

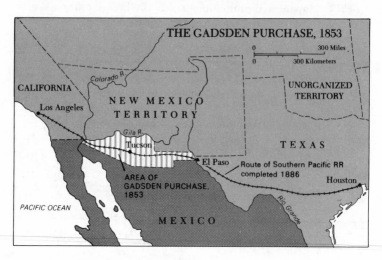

a new territory in the lands west of Missouri and Iowa, bearing the Indian name Nebraska. In January 1854, as chairman of the committee on territories, Senator Douglas reported yet another Nebraska bill. Unlike the others this one included the entire un-organized portion of the Louisiana Purchase to the Canadian border. At this point fateful connections began to transform his proposal from a railroad bill to a proslavery bill. To carry his point Douglas needed the support of southerners, and to win that support he needed to make some concession on slavery. This he did by writing popular sovereignty into the bill in language which specified that "all questions pertaining to slavery in the Territories, and in the new states to be formed therefrom are to be left to the people residing therein, through their appropriate representatives."

It was a clever dodge since the Missouri Compromise would still exclude slaves until the territorial government had made a decision, preventing slaveholders from getting established be-fore a decision was reached. Southerners quickly spotted the barrier and Douglas as quickly made two more concessions. He supported an amendment for repeal of the Missouri Compromise insofar as it excluded slavery north of 36°30', and then agreed to organize two territories, Kansas, west of Missouri; and Nebraska, west of Iowa and Minnesota.

Douglas's motives are unclear. Railroads were surely foremost in his mind, but he was influenced also by his proslavery friend, Sen. David Atchison of Missouri, by the desire to win support for his bill in the South, by the hope that popular sovereignty would quiet the slavery issue and open the Northwest, or by a chance to split the Whigs. But he had blundered, had damaged his presidential chances, and had set his country on the road to civil war. The tragic flaw in his plan was his failure to gauge the depth of antislavery feelings. Douglas himself preferred that the territories become free. Their climate and geography excluded plantation agriculture, he reasoned, and he could not comprehend how people could get so wrought up over abstract rights. Yet he had in fact opened the possibility that slavery might gain a foothold in Kansas.

The agreement to repeal the Missouri Compromise was less than a week old before six antislavery congressmen published a protest, the "Appeal of the Independent Democrats." The tone of moral indignation which informed their protest quickly spread among those who opposed Douglas. The document arraigned his bill "as a gross violation of a sacred pledge," and as "part and parcel of an atrocious plot" to create "a dreary region of despotism, inhabited by masters and slaves." They called upon their fellow citizens to protest against this "atrocious crime."

Across the North editorials, sermons, speeches, and petitions echoed this indignation. What had been radical opinion was fast becoming the common view of people in the North. But Douglas had the votes and, once committed, forced the issue with tireless energy. President Pierce impulsively added his support. Southerners lined up behind Douglas, with notable exceptions like Texas Sen. Sam Houston, who denounced the violation of two solemn compacts: the Missouri Compromise and the confirmation of the territory to the Indians "as long as grass shall grow and water run." He was not the only one to think of the Indians, however. Federal agents were already busy extinguishing Indian titles. But Douglas and Pierce whipped reluctant Democrats into line (though about half the northern Democrats refused to yield), pushing the bill to final passage in May by 37 to 14 in the Senate and 113 to 100 in the House.

Very well, many in the North reasoned, if the Missouri Compromise was not a sacred pledge, then neither was the Fugitive Slave Act. On June 2 Boston witnessed the most dramatic demonstration against the act. After several attempts had failed to rescue a fugitive named Anthony Burns, a force of soldiers and marines marched him to a waiting ship through streets lined with people shouting "Kidnappers!" past buildings draped in black, while church bells tolled across the city. The event cost the federal government $14,000. Burns was the last to be returned from Boston, and was himself soon freed through purchase by the black community of Boston.

THE EMERGENCE OF THE REPUBLICAN PARTY   What John C. Calhoun had called the cords holding the Union together had already begun to part. The national church organizations of Baptists and Methodists, for instance, had split over slavery by 1845. The national parties, which had created mutual interests transcending sectional issues, were beginning to unravel under the strain. The Democrats managed to postpone disruption for yet a while, but their congressional delegation lost heavily in the North, enhancing the influence of the southern wing.

The strain of the Kansas-Nebraska Act, however, soon destroyed the Whig party. Southern Whigs now tended to abstain from voting while Northern Whigs moved toward two new parties. One was the new American (Know Nothing) party, which had raised the banner of native Americanism and the hope of serving the patriotic cause of Union. More Northern Whigs joined with independent Democrats and Free Soilers in spontaneous antislavery coalitions with a confusing array of names, including "anti-Nebraska," "Fusion," and "People's party." These coalitions finally converged in 1854 on the name "Republican," evoking the memory of Jefferson. The Know-Nothings and the Republicans, paradoxically, appealed to overlapping constituencies. As the historian David Potter aptly pointed out, "much of the rural, Protestant, puritan-oriented population of the North was sympathetic to antislavery and temperance and nativism and unsympathetic to the hard-drinking Irish Catholics."

"BLEEDING" KANSAS   After passage of the Kansas-Nebraska Act, attention swung to the plains of Kansas where opposing elements gathered to stage a rehearsal for civil war. All agreed that Nebraska would be free, but Kansas soon exposed the potential for mischief in popular sovereignty. The ambiguity of the law, useful to Douglas in getting it passed, only added to the chaos. The people of Kansas were "perfectly free to form and regulate their domestic institutions in their own way, subject only to the Constitution." That in itself was subject to conflicting interpretations, but the law was completely silent as to the time of decision, adding to each side's sense of urgency about getting control of the territory.

The settlement of Kansas therefore differed from the usual pioneering efforts. Groups sprang up North and South to hurry right-minded settlers westward. The first and best known was Eli Thayer's New England Emigrant Aid Society. During 1855 and 1856 it sent fewer than 1,250 colonists, but its example encouraged other groups and individuals to follow suit. Southern efforts of the same kind centered in Missouri, which was separated from Kansas only by a surveyor's line. When Kansas's first governor, Andrew H. Reeder of Pennsylvania, arrived in October 1854, he found several thousand settlers already on the ground. He ordered a census and scheduled an election for a territorial legislature in March 1855. When the election took place, several thousand "Border Ruffians" crossed over from Missouri and swept the polls for proslavery forces. Reeder denounced the vote as a fraud, but did nothing to alter the results. The legislature so elected expelled the few antislavery members, adopted a drastic slave code, and made it a capital offense to aid a fugitive slave and a felony even to question the legality of slavery in the territory.

Free-state men rejected this "bogus" government and moved directly toward application for statehood. In October 1855 a constitutional convention, the product of an extralegal election, met in Topeka, drafted a state constitution excluding both slavery and free Negroes from Kansas, and applied for admission to the Union. By March 1856 a free-state "governor" and "legislature" were functioning in Topeka. But the prospect of getting any government to command general authority in Kansas seemed dim, and both sides began to arm. The Emigrant Aid Society was soon in the business of gun-running as well as helping settlers. The Rev. Henry Ward Beecher's name became especially identified with gun-running because of "Beecher's Bibles," rifles supplied by his congregation.

Finally, confrontation began to slip into conflict. In May 1856 a proslavery mob entered the free-state town of Lawrence and began a wanton destruction of property. They smashed newspaper presses and tossed them into the river, set fire to the free-state governor's home, stole property that was not nailed down, and trained five cannon on the Free State Hotel, destroying it.

The "sack of Lawrence" resulted in just one casualty, but the excitement aroused a fanatical free-soiler named John Brown,

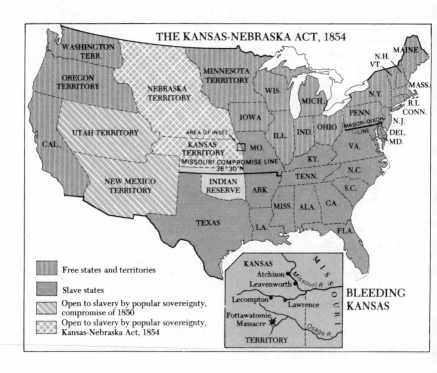

who had a history of instability. A minister with whom he stayed in Kansas described him later as one "impressed with the idea that God had raised him up on purpose to break the jaws of the wicked." Two days after the sack of Lawrence, Brown set out with four sons and three other men toward Pottawatomie Creek, site of a proslavery settlement, where they killed five men in cold blood, ostensibly as revenge for the deaths of free-state men. The Pottawatomie Massacre (May 24–25, 1856) set off a running guerrilla war in the territory which lasted through the fall when a new governor, John W. Geary of Pennsylvania, restored a semblance of order with the help of federal soldiers. Altogether, by the end of 1856 Kansas lost about 200 killed and $2 million in property destroyed.

VIOLENCE IN THE SENATE   Violence in Kansas spilled over into the rhetoric of Congress, where angry legislators began to trade recriminations, coming to the verge of blows. On May 22, the day after the sack of Lawrence, two days before the Pottawatomie Massacre, a sudden flash of violence on the Senate floor electrified the whole country. Just two days earlier Sen. Charles Sumner of Massachusetts had finished a speech on "The Crime against Kansas." Sumner, elected five years earlier by a coalition of Free Soilers and Democrats, was a complex mixture of traits: capable at once of eloquence and excess, a man of principle with limited tolerance for opinions different from his own. He had intended his speech to be "the most thorough philippic" ever heard.

What he produced was an exercise in pedantry and studied insult. The treatment of Kansas was "the rape of a virgin territory," he said, " . . . and it may be clearly traced to a depraved longing for a new slave State, the hideous offspring of such a crime. . . ." Sen. A. P. Butler of South Carolina became a special target of his censure. Like Don Quixote in choosing Dulcinea, Butler had "chosen a mistress . . . who . . . though polluted in the sight of the world, is chaste in his sight—I mean the harlot, Slavery." Sumner said that Butler betrayed "an incapacity of accuracy," a constant "deviation of truth."

Sumner's rudeness might well have discredited the man, if not his cause, had it not been for Preston S. Brooks, a congressman from Edgefield, South Carolina. For two days Brooks brooded over the insult to his uncle, Senator Butler. Knowing that Sumner would refuse a challenge to a duel, he considered but rejected the idea of taking a horsewhip to him. Finally, on May 22 he found Sumner writing at his Senate desk after an adjournment,

"Bully" Brooks's attack on Charles Sumner. The incident increased the strains on the Union. [New York Public Library]

accused him of libel against South Carolina and Butler, and commenced beating him about the head with a cane. Sumner, struggling to rise, wrenched the desk from the floor and collapsed.

Brooks had created a martyr for the antislavery cause. Like so many other men in those years, he betrayed the hotspur's gift for snatching defeat from the jaws of victory. For two and a half years Sumner's empty seat was a solemn reminder of the violence done to him. Some thought the senator was feigning injury, others that he really was physically disabled. In fact, although his injuries were bad enough, including two gashes to the skull, he seems to have suffered a psychosomatic shock which left him incapable of functioning adequately. When the House censured Brooks, he resigned, went home to Edgefield, and returned after being triumphantly reelected. His admirers showered him with new canes. Southerners who never would have done what Brooks did now hastened to make excuses for him. Northerners who never would have said what Sumner said now hastened to his defense. Men on each side, appalled at the behavior of the other, reasoned that North and South had developed into different civilizations, with incompatible standards of honor. "I do not see," Emerson confessed, "how a barbarous community and a civilized community can constitute one state. We must either get rid of slavery, or get rid of freedom."

SECTIONAL POLITICS   Within the span of five days in May "Bleeding Kansas," "Bleeding Sumner," and "Bully Brooks" had set the tone for another presidential year. The major parties could no longer evade the slavery issue. Already in February it had split the hopeful American party wide open. Southern delegates, with help from New York, killed a resolution to restore the Missouri Compromise, and nominated Millard Fillmore for president and Andrew Jackson Donelson for vice-president. Later, what was left of the Whig party endorsed the same candidates.

At its first national convention the new Republican party passed over its leading figure, William H. Seward, who was awaiting a better chance in 1860. Following the Whig tradition they sought out a military hero, John C. Frémont, the "Pathfinder" and leader in the conquest of California. The Republican platform owed much to the Whigs too. It favored a transcontinental railroad and, in general, more internal improvements. It condemned the repeal of the Missouri Compromise, the Democratic policy of expansion, and "those twin relics of barbarism—Polygamy and Slavery." The campaign slogan echoed that of the Free Soilers: "Free soil, free speech, and Frémont." It was the first time a major party platform had taken a stand against slavery.

The Republican position on slavery, the historian Eric Foner has argued, developed from an ideology of free labor. "Political anti-slavery was not merely a negative doctrine, an attack on southern slavery and the society built on it," Foner wrote; "it was an affirmation of the superiority of the social system of the North—a dynamic expanding capitalist society, whose achievements and destiny were almost wholly the result of the dignity and opportunities which it offered the average laboring man." Such a creed, he argued, could accommodate a variety of opinions on race, economics, or other issues, but it was "an ideology which blended personal and sectional interest with morality so perfectly that it became the most potent political force in the nation."

The Democrats, meeting two weeks earlier in June, had rejected Pierce, the hapless victim of so much turmoil. Douglas too was left out because of the damage done by his Kansas-Nebraska Act. The party therefore turned to its old wheelhorse, James Buchanan of Pennsylvania, who had long sought the nomination. The party and its candidate nevertheless hewed to the policies of Pierce. The platform endorsed the Kansas-Nebraska Act and nonintervention. Congress, it said, should not interfere with slavery in either states or territories. The party reached out to its newly acquired ethnic voters by condemning nativism and endorsing religious liberty.

The campaign of 1856 resolved itself into two sectional cam-

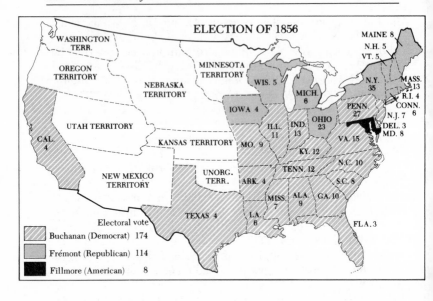

ELECTION OF 1856

Electoral vote

Buchanan (Democrat) 174

Frémont (Republican) 114

Fillmore (American) 8

paigns. The "Black Republicans" had few southern supporters, and only a handful in the border states, where fears of disunion held many Whigs in line. Buchanan thus went to the country as the candidate of the only remaining national party. Although Fillmore won a larger vote in the South than Scott had, the slave states were safe for Buchanan. Frémont swept the northernmost states, with 114 electoral votes, but Buchanan added five free states to his southern majority for a total of 174: Pennsylvania, New Jersey, Illinois, Indiana, and California, all but the last of which bordered on slave states.

Few presidents before Buchanan had a broader experience in politics and diplomacy. His career went back to 1815 when he started as a Federalist legislator in Pennsylvania before switching to Jackson in the 1820s. He had been over twenty years in Congress, minister to Russia and Britain, and Polk's secretary of state in between. His long quest for the presidency had been built on a southern alliance, and his political debts reinforced his belief that saving the Union depended on concessions to the South. Republicans belittled him as another "doughface" like Pierce, lacking the backbone to stand up to the southerners who dominated the Democratic majorities in Congress. His choice of four slave-state and only three free-state men for his cabinet seemed another bad omen.

THE DEEPENING SECTIONAL CRISIS

THE DRED SCOTT CASE   An old saying has it that troubles come in threes. In 1856 Lawrence, the Brooks-Sumner affair, and Pottawotamie came in quick succession. During Buchanan's first six months in 1857 he encountered the Dred Scott decision, new troubles in Kansas, and a business panic. On March 6, 1857, two days after the inauguration, the Supreme Court rendered a decision in the long-pending case of *Dred Scott v. Sandford.* Dred Scott, born a slave in Virginia about 1800, had been taken to St. Louis and sold to an army surgeon, Dr. John Emerson. In 1834 Emerson took him as body servant to Fort Armstrong, Illinois, then to Fort Snelling in Wisconsin Territory (later Minnesota), and finally returned him to St. Louis in 1838. After Emerson's death in 1843 Scott apparently had tried to buy his freedom. In 1846, with help from white friends, he brought suit in Missouri courts claiming that residence in Illinois and Wisconsin Territory had made him free. A jury decided in his favor, but the state supreme court ruled against him. When the case rose on appeal to the Supreme Court, the country anxiously awaited its opinion on the issue of slavery in the territories.

Each of the eight justices filed a separate opinion, except one who concurred with Chief Justice Taney. By different lines of reasoning seven justices ruled that Scott remained a slave. The aging Taney, whose opinion stood as the opinion of the Court, ruled that Scott lacked standing in court because he lacked citizenship. Taney argued that one became a federal citizen either by birth or by naturalization, which ruled out any former slave.

Dred Scott. The Supreme Court's decision on his suit for freedom fanned the flames of discord. [Missouri Historical Society]

He further argued that no state had ever accorded citizenship to Negroes—a statement demonstrably in error. At the time the Constitution was adopted, Taney further said, Negroes "had for more than a century been regarded as . . . so far inferior, that they had no rights which the white man was bound to respect."

To nail down further the definition of Scott's status, Taney moved to a second major question. Residency in a free state had not freed him since, in line with precedent, the decision of the state court governed. This left the question of residency in a free territory. On this point Taney argued that the Missouri Compromise had deprived citizens of property in slaves, an action "not warranted by the constitution." He strongly implied, but never said explicitly, that the compromise had violated the due process clause of the Fifth Amendment, as Calhoun had earlier argued. The upshot was that the Supreme Court had declared an act of Congress unconstitutional for the first time since *Marbury v. Madison* (1803), and a major act for the first time ever. Congress had repealed the Missouri Compromise in the Kansas-Nebraska Act three years earlier, but the decision now pointed a thrust at popular sovereignty. If Congress could not exclude slavery from the territories, then presumably slavery could not be lawfully excluded by any other means short of changing the constitution.

By this decision six justices of the Supreme Court had thought to settle a question which Congress had dodged ever since the Wilmot Proviso surfaced. But far from settling it, they had only fanned the flames of dissension. Little wonder that Republicans protested: the Court had declared their program unconstitutional. It had also reinforced the suspicion that the slavocracy was hatching a conspiracy. Were not all but one of the justices who joined Taney southerners? And had not Buchanan chatted with the chief justice at the inauguration and then urged the people to accept the early decision as a final settlement, "Whatever this may be"? (Actually, Buchanan already knew the outcome because two other justices had spilled the beans in private letters.) Besides, if Dred Scott were not a citizen and had no standing in court, there was no case before it. The majority ruling was an *obiter dictum*—a statement not essential to deciding the case and therefore not binding, "entitled to just so much moral weight as would be the judgment of a majority of those congregated in any Washington bar-room."

Proslavery elements, of course, greeted the court's opinion as binding. Now the fire-eaters among them were emboldened to yet another demand. It was not enough to deny Congress the right to interfere with slavery in the territories; Congress had an obligation to protect the property of slaveholders, making a federal slave code the next step. The idea, first broached by Alabama Democrats in the "Alabama Platform" of 1848, soon became orthodox southern doctrine.

THE LECOMPTON CONSTITUTION Out in Kansas, meanwhile, the struggle continued. Just before Buchanan's inauguration the proslavery legislature called an election of delegates to a constitutional convention. Since no provision was made for a referendum on the constitution, Governor Geary vetoed the measure and the legislature overrode his veto. Geary resigned on the day Buchanan took office and the new president replaced him with Robert J. Walker. A native Pennsylvanian who made a political career in Mississippi and a former member of Polk's cabinet, Walker had greater prestige than his predecessors, and like contemporaries such as Houston of Texas, Foote of Mississippi, and Benton of Missouri, put the Union above slavery in his scale of values. In Kansas he scented a chance to advance the cause of both the Union and his party. Under popular sovereignty, fair elections would produce a state that was both free and Democratic. Walker arrived in May, and, with Buchanan's approval, pledged to the free-state elements that the new constitution would be submitted to a fair vote. But in spite of his pleas, he arrived too late to persuade free-state men to vote for convention delegates in elections they were sure had been rigged against them. Later, however, Walker did persuade the free-state leaders to vote in the October election of a new territorial legislature.

As a result a polarity arose between an antislavery legislature and a proslavery constitutional convention. The convention, meeting at Lecompton, drew up a constitution under which Kansas would become a slave state. A referendum on the document was cunningly contrived so that voters could not vote against the proposed constitution. They could only accept it "with slavery" or "with no slavery," and even the latter meant that property in slaves already in Kansas would "in no measure be interfered with." The vote was set for December 21, 1857, with rules and officials chosen by the convention.

Although Kansas had only about 200 slaves at the time, free-state men boycotted the election on the claim that it was rigged. At this point President Buchanan took a fateful step. Influenced by southern advisers and politically dependent upon southern congressmen, he decided to renege on his pledge to Walker and support the action of the Lecompton Convention. Walker resigned and the election went according to form: 6,226 for the constitution with slavery, 569 for the constitution without slavery. Meanwhile, Frederick P. Stanton of Tennessee, the acting governor, had convened the antislavery legislature, which called for another election to vote the Lecompton Constitution up or down. The result on January 4, 1858, was overwhelming: 10,226 against the constitution, 138 for the constitution with slavery, 24 for the constitution without slavery.

The combined results suggested a clear majority against slavery, but Buchanan stuck to his support of the Lecompton Constitution, driving another wedge into the Democratic party. Senator Douglas, up for reelection, could not afford to run as a champion of Lecompton. He broke dramatically with the president in a tense confrontation, but Buchanan persisted in trying to drive Lecompton "naked" through the Congress. In the Senate, administration forces held firm, and in March 1858 Lecompton was passed. In the House, enough anti-Lecompton Democrats combined to put through an amendment for a new and carefully supervised popular vote in Kansas. Enough senators went along to permit passage of the House bill. Southerners were confident the vote would favor slavery, because to reject slavery the voters would have to reject the constitution, which would postpone statehood until the population reached 90,000. On August 2, 1858, Kansas voters nevertheless rejected Lecompton by 11,300 to 1,788. With that vote Kansas, now firmly in the hands of its antislavery legislature, ended its main role in the sectional controversy.

THE PANIC OF 1857 The third crisis of Buchanan's first half year in office, a financial crisis, broke in August 1857. It was brought on by a reduction in demand for American grain caused by the end of the Crimean War (1854–1856), a surge in manufacturing which outran the growth of markets, and the continued weakness and confusion of the state banknote system. Failure of the Ohio Life Insurance and Trust Company on August 24, 1857, precipitated the panic, which was followed by a depression from which the country did not emerge until 1859.

Everything in those years seemed to get drawn into the vortex of sectional conflict, and business troubles were no exception. Northern businessmen tended to blame the depression on the Democratic Tariff of 1857, which had put rates at their lowest level since 1816. The agricultural South weathered the crisis better than the North. Cotton prices fell, but slowly, and world markets for cotton quickly recovered. The result was an exalted notion of King Cotton's importance to the world, and apparent confirmation of the growing argument that the southern system was superior to the free-labor system of the North.

DOUGLAS VS. LINCOLN Amid the recriminations over Dred Scott, Kansas, and the depression, the center could not hold. The Lecompton battle put severe strains on the one substantial cord of Union left, the Democratic party. To many, Douglas seemed the best hope, one of the few remaining Democratic leaders with support in both sections. But now Douglas was being whipsawed between the extremes. Kansas-Nebraska had cast him in the role of "doughface." His opposition to Lecompton, the fraudulent fruit of popular sovereignty, however, had alienated him from Buchanan's southern junta. But for all his flexibility and opportunism, Douglas had convinced himself that popular sovereignty was a point of principle, a bulwark of democracy and local self-government. In 1858 he faced reelection to the Senate against the opposition of Buchanan Democrats and Republicans. The year 1860 would give him a chance for the presidency, but first he had to secure his home base in Illinois.

To oppose him Illinois Republicans named Abraham Lincoln of Springfield, former Whig state legislator and one-term congressman, a moderately prosperous small-town lawyer. Lincoln's early life had been the hardscrabble existence of the frontier farm. Born in a Kentucky log cabin in 1809, raised on frontier farms in Indiana and Illinois, the young Lincoln had the wit and will to rise above his beginnings. With less than twelve months of sporadic schooling he learned to read, studied such books as came to hand, and eventually developed a prose style as muscular as the man himself. He worked at various farm tasks, operated a ferry, and made two trips down to New Orleans as a flatboatman. Striking out on his own, he managed a general store in New Salem, Illinois, learned surveying, served in the Black Hawk War (1832), won election to the legislature in 1834 at the age of twenty-five, read law, and was admitted to the bar in 1836. As a Whig regular, he adhered to the philosophy of Henry Clay. He stayed in the legislature until 1842, and in 1846 won a term in Congress. After a single term he retired from active politics to cultivate his law practice.

In 1854 the Kansas-Nebraska debate drew him back into active politics. When Douglas appeared in Springfield to defend his stand, Lincoln spoke in refutation from the same platform. In Peoria he repeated the performance of what was known thereafter as the "Peoria Speech." This speech began the journey toward his appointment with destiny, preaching an old but oft-neglected doctrine: hate the sin but not the sinner.

> When Southern people tell us they are no more responsible for the origin of slavery, than we; I acknowledge the fact. When it is said that the institution exists; and that it is very difficult to get rid of it, in any satisfactory way, I can understand and appreciate the saying. . . .
>   But all this, to my judgment, furnishes no more excuse for permitting slavery to go into our own free territory, than it would for reviving the African slave trade by law.

At first Lincoln held back from the rapidly growing new party, but in 1856 he threw in his lot with the Republicans, getting over 100 votes for their vice-presidential nomination, and gave some fifty speeches for the Frémont ticket in Illinois and nearby states. By 1858 he was the obvious choice to oppose Douglas himself, and Douglas knew he was up against a formidable foe. Lincoln resorted to the classic ploy of the underdog: he challenged the favorite to debate with him. Douglas had little relish for drawing attention to his opponent, but agreed to meet him in seven places around the state. Thus the legendary Lincoln-Douglas debates took place, August 21 to October 15.

At the time and since, much attention focused on the second debate, at Freeport, where Lincoln asked Douglas how he could reconcile popular sovereignty with the Dred Scott ruling that

A scene from Lincoln's 1858 senatorial campaign. The tall figure at the right of the doorway is Abraham Lincoln. [Library of Congress]

citizens had the right to carry slaves into any territory. Douglas's answer, thenceforth known as the Freeport Doctrine, was to state the obvious. Whatever the Supreme Court might say about slavery, it could not exist anywhere unless supported by local police regulations.

Douglas tried to set some traps of his own. It is standard practice, of course, to put extreme constructions upon an adversary's stand. Douglas intimated that Lincoln belonged to the fanatical sect of abolitionists who planned to carry the battle to the slave states, just as Lincoln intimated the opposite about Douglas. Douglas accepted, without any apparent qualms, the conviction of black inferiority which most whites, North and South, shared at the time, and sought to pin on Lincoln the stigma of advocating racial equality. The question was a hot potato, which Lincoln handled with caution. There was "A physical difference between the white and black races" and it would "forever forbid the two races living together on terms of social and political equality," he said. He simply favored the containment of slavery where it existed so that "the public mind shall rest in the belief that it is in the course of ultimate extinction." But the basic difference between the two men, Lincoln insisted, lay in Douglas's professed indifference to the moral question of slavery: "He says he 'don't care whether it is voted up or voted down' in the territories. . . . Any man can say that who does not see anything wrong in slavery, but no man can logically say it who does see a wrong in it; because no man can logically say he don't care whether a wrong is voted up or down. . . . "

If Lincoln had the better of the argument, at least in the long view, Douglas had the better of the election. The voters actually had to choose a legislature, which would then elect the senator. Lincoln men won the larger total vote, but its distribution gave Douglas the legislature, 54 to 41. As the returns trickled in from the fall elections in 1858—there was still no common election date—they recorded one loss after another for Buchanan men. When they were over, the administration had lost control of the House. But the new Congress would not meet in regular session until December 1859.

STORM WARNINGS   After the Lecompton fiasco the slavery issue was no longer before Congress in any direct way. The gradual return of prosperity in 1859 offered hope that the storms of the 1850s might yet pass. But the issue still haunted the public mind, and like sheet lightning on the horizon, warned that a storm was still pending. In the spring there were two warning flashes. The

Supreme Court finally ruled in the case of *Ableman v. Booth,* which had arisen in 1854 when an abolitionist editor in Milwaukee, Sherman M. Booth, roused a mob to rescue a fugitive slave. Convicted in federal court of violating the Fugitive Slave Act, he got the Wisconsin Supreme Court to order him freed on the ground that the act was unconstitutional. A unanimous Supreme Court made short work of Wisconsin's interposition. Chief Justice Taney's opinion denied the right of state courts to interfere and reaffirmed the constitutionality of the Fugitive Slave Act. The Wisconsin legislature in turn responded with states'-rights resolutions that faintly echoed the Virginia and Kentucky Resolutions of 1798–1799.

The episode, like others at the time, illustrated the significant fact that both North and South seized on nationalism or states' rights for their own purposes—neither was a point on which many men could claim consistency. Since the early 1840s the Garrisonian abolitionists had openly championed disunion, but they were a small, if vocal, minority in the North. In the South few denied a state's right to dissolve the bond of Union in the same way that the original states had ratified it. And as the South became increasingly a conscious minority, beset by antislavery forces and aware of its growing isolation in the Western world, more and more were willing to consider secession a possibility. By 1855, when Peru acted to abolish slavery, the peculiar institution was left only in Brazil, in the Spanish colonies of Cuba and Puerto Rico, in the Dutch colonies of Guiana and the West Indies, and in the American South.

JOHN BROWN'S RAID   For a season, however, sectional agitations were held in check. But in October 1859 John Brown once again surfaced. Since the Pottawatomie Massacre in 1856 Brown had led a furtive existence, engaging in fundraising and occasional bushwhacking. Finally, on October 16, 1859, he was ready for his supreme gesture. From a Maryland farm he crossed the Potomac with nineteen men, including five Negroes, and under cover of darkness occupied the federal arsenal in Harper's Ferry, Virginia (now West Virginia). His scheme was foredoomed from the start, and any attempt at a rational explanation probably misses the point. His notion seems to have been that he would arm the many slaves who would flock to his cause, set up a black stronghold in the mountains of western Virginia, and provide a nucleus of support for slave insurrections across the South. What he actually did was to take the arsenal by surprise, seize a few hostages, and sit there until he was surrounded and captured. He had even

John Brown. [The Warder Collection]

forgotten to bring food. Militiamen from the surrounding country rallied by the next afternoon, and the next evening Lt. Col. Robert E. Lee, U.S. Cavalry, arrived with his aide, Lt. J. E. B. Stuart, and a force of marines. On the morning of October 18 Brown refused a call to surrender and the marines stormed the arsenal and took Brown prisoner, with a painful wound. Altogether Brown's men killed four people (including one marine) and wounded nine. Of their own force, ten died (including two of Brown's sons), five escaped, and seven were captured.

Brown was turned over to Virginia authorities, quickly tried for treason against the state and conspiracy to incite insurrection, convicted on October 31, and hanged on December 2 at Charles Town. Six others died on the gallows later. If Brown had failed in his purpose—whatever it was—he had achieved two things. He had become a martyr for the antislavery cause, and he had set off panic throughout the slaveholding South. At his sentencing he delivered one of the classic American speeches: "Now, if it is deemed necessary that I should forfeit my life for the furtherance of the ends of justice, and mingle my blood further with the blood of my children and with the blood of millions in this slave country whose rights are disregarded by wicked, cruel, and unjust enactments, I say, let it be done."

When Brown, still unflinching, met his end, it was a day of solemn observances in the North. Prominent Republicans, including Lincoln and Seward, repudiated Brown's coup, but the discovery of Brown's correspondence revealed that he had enjoyed support among prominent antislavery leaders who, whether or not they knew at the time what they were getting into, later defended his deeds. "That new saint," Emerson said,

" . . . will make the gallows as glorious as the cross." Garrison, the lifelong pacifist, now wished "success to every slave insurrection at the South and in every slave country."

By far the gravest after-effect of Brown's raid was to leave southerners in no mood to distinguish between John Brown and the Republican party. The southern mind now merged those who would contain slavery with those who would drown it in blood. All through the fall and winter of 1859–1860 rumors of conspiracy and insurrection swept the region. Every northern visitor, commercial traveler, or schoolteacher came under suspicion, and many were driven out. "We regard every man in our midst an enemy to the institutions of the South," said the Atlanta *Confederacy*, "who does not boldly declare that he believes African slavery to be a social, moral, and political blessing." Francis Lieber, a German exile, political scientist, and dedicated nationalist, survived in discomfort for yet a while at the College of South Carolina. But relations between the sections reminded him of what Thucydides had said about the Peloponnesian War: "The Greeks did not understand each other any longer, though they spoke the same language."

THE CENTER COMES APART

The first session of the new Congress, which convened three days after the death of John Brown, confirmed Lieber's melancholy thought. The Democrats still controlled the Senate, but the House once again was thrown into deadlock over the choice of a Speaker. John Sherman of Ohio, the Republican candidate for Speaker, had committed the unforgivable sin in southern eyes of supporting the distribution of Hinton R. Helper's *The Impending Crisis of the South* (1857). Helper was a former North Carolinian who sought to demonstrate that slavery had impoverished nonslaveholding white southerners. The issue of "Helperism" kept enough votes from Sherman to prevent his selection. The House finally turned to William Pennington of New Jersey, an old Whig who supported the Fugitive Slave Act but also favored exclusion of slavery from the territories. He soon lined up with the Republicans. On the day after Pennington's election as Speaker, Jefferson Davis stood up in the Senate to introduce a set of resolutions for the defense of slavery, the main burden of which was a demand that the federal government extend "all needful protection" to slavery in the territories. Davis in effect asked for a federal slave code.

THE DEMOCRATS DIVIDE   Thus amid emotional hysteria and impossible demands the nation ushered in the year of another presidential election, destined to be the most fateful in its history. Four years earlier, in a moment of euphoria, the Democrats had settled on Charleston, South Carolina, as the site for their 1860 convention. Charleston in April, with the azaleas ablaze, was perhaps the most enticing city in the United States, but the worst conceivable place for such a meeting. It was a hotbed of extremist sentiment, and lacked adequate accommodations for the crowds thronging in. South Carolina itself had chosen a remarkably moderate delegation, but the extreme southern-rights men held the upper hand in the delegations from the Gulf states.

Douglas men preferred to stand by the platform of 1856, which simply promised congressional noninterference with slavery. Southern firebrands, however, were now demanding federal protection for slavery in the territories. Buchanan supporters, hoping to stop Douglas, encouraged the strategy. The platform debate reached a heady climax when the Alabama fire-eater Yancey informed the northern Democracy that its error had been the failure to defend slavery as a positive good. Sen. George E. Pugh of Ohio offered a blunt reply: "Gentlemen of the South," he said, "you mistake us—you mistake us. We will not do it."

When the southern planks lost, Alabama walked out of the convention, followed by the other Gulf states, Georgia, South Carolina (except for two stubborn upcountry Unionists), and parts of the delegations from Arkansas and Delaware. This pattern foreshadowed with some fidelity the pattern of secession, in which the Deep South left the Union first. The convention then decided to leave the overwrought atmosphere of Charleston and reassemble in Baltimore on June 18. The Baltimore convention finally nominated Douglas on the 1856 platform. The Charleston seceders met first in Richmond, then in Baltimore, where they adopted the slave-code platform defeated in Charleston, and named Vice-President John C. Breckinridge of Kentucky for president. Thus another cord of union had snapped: the last remaining national party.

LINCOLN'S ELECTION   The Republicans meanwhile gathered in Chicago, in a gigantic hall jocosely called the "Wigwam." There everything suddenly came together for "Honest Abe" Lincoln, "the Railsplitter," the uncommon common man. Lincoln had suddenly emerged in the national view during his senatorial campaign two years before, and had since taken a stance de-

Abraham Lincoln at the time of his nomination for the presidency. [Library of Congress]

signed to make him available for the nomination. He was strong enough on the containment of slavery to satisfy the abolitionists, yet moderate enough to seem less threatening than they were. In February 1860 he had gone east to address an audience of influential Republicans at the Cooper Union in New York, where he emphasized his view of slavery "as an evil, not to be extended, but to be tolerated and protected only because of and so far as its actual presence among us makes that toleration and protection a necessity."

Chicago provided surroundings which gave Lincoln's people many advantages. His managers, for instance, could pack the galleries with noisy supporters. They started out with little more support than the Illinois delegation, but worked to make Lincoln everybody else's second choice. William H. Seward was the early leader, but he had been tagged, perhaps wrongly, as an extremist for his earlier statements about an "irrepressible conflict" and a "higher law." On the first ballot Lincoln finished in second place. On the next ballot he drew almost even with Seward, and when he came within one and a half votes of a majority on the third count, Ohio quickly switched four votes to put him over the top. Later the same day Sen. Hannibal Hamlin of Maine, a former Democrat, became the vice-presidential nominee.

The platform foreshadowed future policy better than most. It denounced John Brown's raid as "among the gravest of crimes," and promised the "maintenance inviolate of the right of each state to order and control its own domestic institutions." The party reaffirmed its resistance to the extension of slavery, and in an effort to gain broader support, endorsed a protective tariff for manufacturers, a more liberal naturalization law, and internal improvements, including a Pacific railroad. With this platform Republicans made a strong appeal to eastern businessmen, western farmers, and the large immigrant population.

Both major conventions revealed that opinion tended to become more radical in the upper North and Deep South. Attitude followed latitude. In the border states a sense of moderation, perhaps due to a sense that the border areas would bear the brunt of any calamity, aroused the diehard Whigs there to make one more try at reconciliation. Meeting in Baltimore a week before the Republicans met in Chicago, they reorganized into the Constitutional Union party and named John Bell of Tennessee for president. Their only platform was "the Constitution of the Country, the Union of the States, and the Enforcement of the Laws."

Of the four candidates not one was able to command a national following, and the campaign resolved into a choice between Lincoln and Douglas in the North, Breckinridge and Bell in the South. One consequence of these separate campaigns was that each section gained a false impression of the other. The South never learned to distinguish Lincoln from the radicals; the North failed to gauge the force of southern intransigence—and in this Lincoln was among the worst. He stubbornly refused to offer the South assurances or to amplify his position, which he said was a matter of public record. The one man who tried to break through the veil that was falling between the sections was Douglas, who tried to mount a national campaign. Only forty-seven, but al-

The Carolina Clothing Depot's advertisement drums up business while beating the drums of disunion in South Carolina. [The Bettmann Archive]

ready weakened by drink, ill-health, and disappointments, he wore himself out in one final glorious campaign. Early in October, at Cedar Rapids, Iowa, he got the news of Republican state victories from Pennsylvania and Indiana. "Mr. Lincoln is the next President," he said. "We must try to save the Union. I will go South." Down through the hostile areas of Tennessee, Georgia, and Alabama he carried appeals on behalf of the Union. "I do not believe that every Breckinridge man is a disunionist," he said, "but I do believe that every disunionist is a Breckinridge man." He was in Mobile when the election came.

By midnight of November 6 Lincoln's victory was clear. In the final count he had about 39 percent of the total popular vote, but a clear majority with 180 votes in the electoral college. He carried every one of the eighteen free states, and by a margin enough to elect him even if the votes for the other candidates had been combined. Among all the candidates, only Douglas had electoral votes from both slave and free states, but his total of 12 was but a pitiful remnant of Democratic Unionism. He ran last. Bell took Virginia, Kentucky, and Tennessee for 39 votes, and Breckinridge swept the other slave states to come in second with 72.

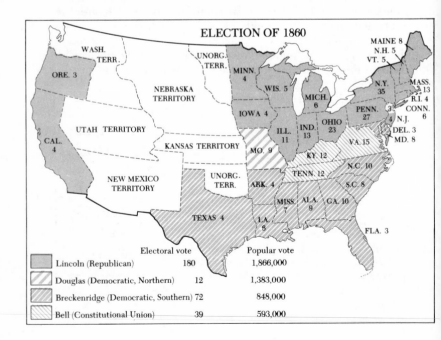

ELECTION OF 1860

	Electoral vote	Popular vote
Lincoln (Republican)	180	1,866,000
Douglas (Democratic, Northern)	12	1,383,000
Breckenridge (Democratic, Southern)	72	848,000
Bell (Constitutional Union)	39	593,000

CHARLESTON

MERCURY

EXTRA:

Passed unanimously at 1.15 o'clock, P.M. December 20th, 1860.

AN ORDINANCE

To dissolve the Union between the State of South Carolina and other States united with her under the compact entitled "The Constitution of the United States of America."

UNION
IS
DISSOLVED!

A handbill announcing South Carolina's secession from the Union. [New York Public Library]

SECESSION OF THE DEEP SOUTH   Soon after the election the South Carolina legislature, which had assembled to choose the state's electors, set a special election for December 6 to choose delegates to a convention. In Charleston on December 20 the convention unanimously voted an Ordinance of Secession, declaring the state's ratification of the Constitution repealed and the union with other states dissolved. A Declaration of the Causes of Secession reviewed the threats to slavery, and asserted that a sectional party had elected to the presidency a man "whose opinions and purposes are hostile to slavery," who had declared "Government cannot endure permanently half slave, half free," and "that the public mind must rest in the belief that Slavery is in the course of ultimate extinction."

By February 1, 1861, six more states had declared themselves out of the Union. Texas was the last to act because its governor, staunch old Jacksonian Sam Houston, had refused to assemble the legislature for a convention call, but secessionist leaders called an irregular convention which authorized secession. Only there was the decision submitted to a referendum, which the secessionists carried handily. In some places the vote for delegates revealed a close division, especially in Georgia and Louisiana, but secession carried. On February 4, a convention of the seven states met in Montgomery; on February 7 they adopted a provisional constitution for the Confederate States of America, and two days later they elected Jefferson Davis its president. He was inaugurated February 18, with Alexander Stephens of Georgia as vice-president.

In all seven states of the southernmost tier a solid majority had voted for secessionist delegates, but their combined vote would not have been a majority of the presidential vote in November. What happened, it seemed, was what often happens in revolutionary situations: a determined and decisive group acted quickly in an emotionally charged climate and carried its program against a confused and indecisive opposition. Trying to decide whether or not a majority of the whites actually favored secession probably is beside the point—a majority were vulnerable to the decisive action of the secessionists.

BUCHANAN'S WAITING GAME   History is full of might-have-beens. A bold stroke, even a bold statement, by the president at this point might have changed things, but there was no Jacksonian flourish in Buchanan. Besides, a bold stroke might simply have hastened the conflict. No bold stroke came from Lincoln either, nor would he consult with the administration during the long months before his inauguration on March 4. He inclined all too strongly to the belief that secession was just another bluff and kept his public silence. Buchanan followed his natural bent, the policy on which he had built a career: make concessions, seek a compromise to mollify the South. In his annual message on December 3 Buchanan made a forthright argument that secession was illegal, but that he lacked authority to coerce a state. "Seldom have we known so strong an argument come to so lame and impotent a conclusion," the Cincinnati *Enquirer* editorialized. There was, however, a hidden weapon in the president's reaffirmation of a duty to "take care that the laws be faithfully executed" insofar as he was able. If the president could enforce the law upon all citizens, he would have no need to "coerce" a state. Indeed his position became the policy of the Lincoln administration, which fought a war on the theory that individuals but not states as such were in rebellion.

Buchanan held firmly to his resolve, with some slight stiffening by the end of December when secession became a fact and the departure of two southerners removed the region's influence in his cabinet. He would retain positions already held, but would make no effort to assert federal authority provocatively. As the secessionists seized federal property, arsenals, and forts, this policy soon meant holding to isolated positions at Fort Pickens in Pensacola Harbor, some remote islands off southern Florida, and Fort Sumter in Charleston Harbor. On the day after Christmas the small garrison at Fort Moultrie had been moved into the nearly completed Fort Sumter by Maj. Robert Anderson, a Kentucky Unionist. Anderson's move, designed to achieve both disengagement and greater security, struck South Carolina authorities as provocative, a violation of an earlier "gentleman's agreement" that the administration would make no changes in its arrangements, and commissioners of the newly "independent" state peremptorily demanded withdrawal of all federal forces. They had overplayed their hand. Buchanan's cabinet, with only one southerner left, insisted it would be a gross violation of duty, perhaps grounds for impeachment, for the president to yield. His backbone thus stiffened, he sharply rejected the South Carolina ultimatum to withdraw: "This I cannot do: this I will not do." His nearest approach to coercion was to dispatch a steamer, *Star of the West*, to Fort Sumter with reinforcements and provisions. As the ship approached Charleston Harbor, Carolina batteries at Fort Moultrie and Morris Island opened fire and drove it away on January 9. It was in fact an act of war, but Buchanan chose to ignore the challenge. He decided instead to hunker down and ride out the remaining weeks of his term, hoping against hope that one of several compromise efforts would yet prove fruitful.

LAST EFFORTS AT COMPROMISE   Forlorn efforts at compromise continued in Congress until dawn of inauguration day. On December 18 Sen. John J. Crittenden of Kentucky had proposed a series of amendments and resolutions the central features of which were the recognition of slavery in the territories south of 36° 30′; and guarantees to maintain slavery where it already existed. A Senate Committee of Thirteen named to consider the proposal proved unable to agree. A House Committee of Thirty-three under Thomas Corwin of Ohio adopted two concessions to the South: an amendment guaranteeing slavery where it existed and granting statehood to New Mexico, presumably as a slave state. But the committee finished by submitting a set of proposals without endorsing any of them. The fight for a compromise was carried to the floor of each house by Crittenden and Corwin, and subjected to intensive debate during January and February.

Meanwhile a Peace Conference met in Willard's Hotel in February at the call of the Virginia legislature. Twenty-one states sent delegates and former president John Tyler presided, but the convention's proposal, substantially the same as the Crittenden Compromise, failed to win the support of either house of Congress. The only compromise proposal that met with any success was Corwin's amendment to guarantee slavery where it existed. Many Republicans, including Lincoln, were prepared to go that far to save the Union, but they were unwilling to repudiate their stand against slavery in the territories. As it happened, after passing the House the amendment passed the Senate without a vote to spare, by 24 to 12, on the dawn of inauguration day. It would have become the Thirteenth Amendment, with the first use of the word "slavery" in the Constitution, but the states never ratified it. When a Thirteenth Amendment was ratified in 1865, it did not guarantee slavery—it abolished slavery.

FURTHER READING

Two works which survey the coming of the Civil War are Allan Nevins's *Ordeal of the Union* (4 vols.; 1947) and David M. Potter's *The Impending Crisis, 1848–1861* (1976).° Interpretive essays can be studied in Edwin C. Rozwenc (ed.), *The Causes of the American Civil War* (1972), and Eric Foner's *Politics and Ideology in the Age of the Civil War* (1980).°

Numerous works cover various aspects of the political crises of the 1850s. C. W. Morrison's *Democratic Politics and Sectionalism: The Wilmot Proviso Controversy* (1967) focuses on the initial dispute. Joseph G. Rayback's *Free Soil: The Election of 1848* (1970), Frederick J. Blue's *Free Soilers: Third Party Politics, 1848–1854* (1973), and William R. Brock's *Parties and Political Conscience: American Dilemmas, 1840–1850* (1979), all examine the disruption of the two-party balance. Holman Hamilton's *Prologue to Conflict: The Crisis and Compromise of 1850* (1964)° probes that crucial dispute. Michael F. Holt's *The Political Crisis of the 1850s* (1978)° traces the demise of the Whigs. Eric Foner provides a good introduction to how events and ideas combined to form a new political party in *Free Soil, Free Labor, Free Men: The Ideology of the Republican Party before the Civil War* (1970).° Michael F. Holt's *Forging a Majority: The Republican Party in Pittsburgh, 1848–1860* (1969), explores how ethnic tensions led to local political realignments. Also good on the Republicans is Hans L. Trefousse's *The Radical Republicans: Lincoln's Vanguard for Racial Justice* (1969) and David H. Donald's *Charles Sumner and the Coming of the Civil War* (1970).°

Robert W. Johansen's *Stephen A. Douglass* (1973) analyzes the issue of popular sovereignty, and Paul W. Gates details the violence in Kansas in *Fifty Million Acres: Conflicts over Kansas Land Policy, 1854–1890* (1954).° A more national perspective is provided in James A. Rawley's *Race and Politics: "Bleeding Kansas" and the Coming of the Civil War* (1969). Two works which treat the role played by one abolitionist in Kansas are James C. Malin's *John Brown and the Legend of Fifty-Six* (1970) and Stephen B. Oates's *To Purge This Land with Blood: A Biography of John Brown* (1970).° Also useful is Malin's *The Nebraska Question: 1852–1854* (1953).

° These books are available in paperback editions.

The links between foreign policy aims and the desire for slavery expansion can be studied in Robert E. May's *The Southern Dream of a Caribbean Empire* (1973), Basil Rauch's *American Interest in Cuba, 1848–1855* (1948), and E. S Wallace's *Destiny and Glory* (1957). America's Asian interests are explored in Tyler Dennett's *America in East Asia* (1941), Arthur Walworth's *Black Ships off Japan* (1946), and Alfred W. Griswold's *The Far Eastern Policy of the United States* (1938).

Stanley W. Campbell's *The Slave Catchers: Enforcement of the Fugitive Slave Law, 1840–1860* (1968), traces the problems caused by the Compromise of 1850. Richard H. Sewell's *Ballots for Freedom: Anti-Slavery Politics in the United States, 1847–1860* (1976),° and Louis Filler's *The Crusade against Slavery, 1830–1860* (1960),° stress the role of abolitionists. William J. Cooper's *The South and the Politics of Slavery, 1828–1865* (1978),° presents the opposing viewpoint. A wonderful primary document of antebellum attitudes is Harriet Beecher Stowe's *Uncle Tom's Cabin*, edited and annotated by Phillip Van Doren Stern (1964).° For details of the Dred Scott case, consult Don E. Fehrenbacher's *The Dred Scott Case: Its Significance in American Law and Politics* (1978).°

The growing alienation of southerners from national trends is explored in David M. Potter's *The South and the Sectional Conflict* (1968), Avery O. Craven's *The Growth of Southern Nationalism, 1848–1861* (1953), and Jesse T. Carpenter's *The South as a Conscious Minority* (1930). Studies of southern states include J. Mills Thornton III's *Politics and Power in a Slave Society: Alabama, 1800–1860* (1978),° Michael Johnson's *Toward a Patriarchial Society: The Secession of Georgia* (1977), Steven A. Channing's *Crisis of Fear: Secession in South Carolina* (1970),° and William L. Barney's *The Road to Secession: A New Perspective on the Old South* (1972)° and *The Secessionist Impulse: Alabama and Mississippi* (1974). Also consult R. A. Wooster's *The Secession Conventions of the South* (1962). How the North reacted is studied in Kenneth M. Stampp's *And the War Came: The North and the Secession Crisis, 1860–61* (1950).°

To gauge the role played by Lincoln in the coming crisis of war, see the biographies listed in Chapter 17. Particularly good for Lincoln during the 1850s is Don E. Fehrenbacher's *Prelude to Greatness* (1962).° Harry V. Jaffa's *Crisis of the House Divided* (1959) details the Lincoln-Douglas debates, and Richard N. Current's *Lincoln and the First Shot* (1963)° treats the Fort Sumter controversy.

17

THE WAR OF THE UNION

END OF THE WAITING GAME

During the four long months between his election and in-auguration Lincoln would say little about future policies and less about past positions. "If I thought a *repetition* would do any good I would make it," he wrote to an editor in St. Louis. "But my judgment is it would do positive harm. The secessionists *per se,* believing they had alarmed me, would clamor all the louder." So he stayed in Springfield until February 11, 1861, biding his time. He then boarded a train for a long, roundabout trip, and began to drop some hints to audiences along the way. To the New Jersey legislature, which responded with prolonged cheering, he said: "The man does not live who is more devoted to peace than I am. . . . But it may be necessary to put the foot down." At the end of the journey he reluctantly yielded to rumors of plots against his life, passed unnoticed on a night train through Baltimore, and slipped into Washington before daybreak on February 23.

The ignominious end to his journey reinforced the fears of eastern sophisticates that the man lacked style. Lincoln, to be sure, lacked a formal education and training in the rules of eti-quette. His clothing was hardly modish, even for the times. His tall frame shambled awkwardly, and he had an unseemly pen-chant for funny stories. But the qualities that first called him to public attention would soon manifest themselves. His prose, at least, had style—and substance. So did his politics. What Hawthorne called his "Yankee shrewdness and not-to-be caughtness" guided him through the traps laid for the unwary in Washington. Whatever else people might think of him, they soon learned that he was not easily dominated.

LINCOLN'S INAUGURATION   Buchanan called for Lincoln at Willard's Hotel on a bright and blustery March 4. Together they rode in an open carriage to the Capitol, where Chief Justice Taney administered the oath on a platform outside the East Portico. At the start, Stephen A. Douglas reached out to hold Lincoln's hat as a gesture of unity. In his inaugural address Lincoln repeated views already on record by quoting from an earlier speech: "I have no purpose, directly or indirectly, to interfere with the institution of slavery in the States where it exists. I believe I have no lawful right to do so, and I have no inclination to do so."

But the immediate question had shifted from slavery to secession, and most of the speech emphasized Lincoln's view that "the Union of these States is perpetual." The Union, he asserted, was older than the Constitution itself, dating from the Articles of Association in 1774, "matured and continued" by the Declaration of Independence and the Articles of Confederation. But even if the United States were only a contractual association, "no State upon its own mere motion can lawfully get out of the Union." Lincoln promised to hold areas belonging to the government, collect duties and imposts, and deliver the mails unless repelled, but beyond that "there will be no invasion, no using of force against or among the people anywhere." The final paragraph, based on a draft by Seward, was an eloquent appeal for harmony:

> I am loath to close. We are not enemies, but friends. We must not be enemies. Though passion may have strained, it must not break, our bonds of affection. The mystic chords of memory, stretching from every battlefield and patriot grave to every living heart and hearthstone all over this broad land, will yet swell the chorus of the Union, when again touched, as surely they will be, by the better angels of our nature.

Lincoln not only entered office amid the gravest crisis yet faced by a president, but he also faced unusual problems of transition. Republicans, in power for the first time, crowded Washington, hungry for office. Four of the seven new cabinet members had been rivals for the presidency: William H. Seward at State, Salmon P. Chase at the Treasury, Simon Cameron at the War Department, and Edward Bates as attorney-general. Four were former Democrats and three were former Whigs. They formed a group of better than average ability, though most were so strong-minded they thought themselves better qualified to lead than Lincoln. It was only later than they were ready to acknowledge with Seward that "he is the best man among us."

THE FALL OF FORT SUMTER   For the time being Lincoln's combination of firmness and moderation differed little in effect from his predecessor's stance. Harsh judgments of Buchanan's waiting game overlook the fact that Lincoln kept it going. Indeed his only other choices were to accept secession as an accomplished fact or to use force right away. On the day after he took office, however, word arrived from Charleston that time was running out. Major Anderson had supplies for a month to six weeks, and Fort Sumter was being surrounded by a Confederate "ring of fire." Most cabinet members favored evacuation of Fort Sumter and defense of Fort Pickens at Pensacola, where relief ships were already offshore.

Events moved quickly to a climax in the next two weeks. On April 4 Lincoln decided to reinforce Fort Pickens and resupply Fort Sumter. On April 6 he notified the governor of South Carolina that "an attempt will be made to supply Fort Sumter with provisions only. . . . " On April 9 President Jefferson Davis and his cabinet in Montgomery decided against permitting Lincoln to maintain the status quo. On April 11 Confederate Gen. Pierre G. T. Beauregard demanded a speedy surrender of Sumter. Major Anderson refused, but said his supplies would be used up in

The Fourth Regiment, Georgia Volunteer Army, Confederate States of America. These troops were guarding Fort Sumter in April 1861.
[*Library of Congress*]

three more days. With the relief ships approaching, Anderson received an ultimatum to yield. He again refused, and at 4:30 A.M. on April 12 the first gun sounded at Fort Johnson on James Island, and Fort Sumter quickly came under a crossfire from Sullivan's and Morris Islands as well. After more than thirty hours, his ammunition exhausted, Anderson agreed to give up, and on April 14 he lowered his flag. The only fatalities, ironically, were two men killed in an explosion during a final salute to the colors, the first in a melancholy train of war dead.

The guns of Charleston signaled the end of the waiting game. On the day after Anderson's surrender, Lincoln called upon the loyal states to supply 75,000 militiamen to subdue a combination "too powerful to be suppressed by the ordinary course of judicial proceedings." Volunteers rallied around the flag at the recruiting stations. On April 19 Lincoln proclaimed a blockade of southern ports which, as the Supreme Court later ruled, confirmed the existence of war.

TAKING SIDES   In the free states and the Confederate states the proclamation reinforced the patriotic fervor of the day. In the upper South it brought dismay, and another wave of secession which swept four more states into the Confederacy. Many in those states, like Jonathan Worth of North Carolina, abhorred both abolitionists and secessionists, but faced with a call for troops to suppress their sister states, decided to abandon the Union. Virginia acted first. Its convention had met intermittently since February 13; now it convened again and passed an ordinance of secession on April 17. On May 21 the Confederate Congress chose Richmond as its new capital, and the government moved there in June.

Three other states followed Virginia in little over a month: Arkansas on May 6, Tennessee on May 7, and North Carolina on May 20. The Tar Heel state, next to last to ratify the Constitution, was last in secession. All four of the holdout states, especially Tennessee and Virginia, had mountain areas where both slaves and secessionists were scarce and where Union sentiment ran strong. In Tennessee the mountain counties would supply more volunteers to the Union than to the Confederate cause. Unionists in western Virginia, bolstered by a Union army from Ohio under Gen. George B. McClellan, contrived a loyal government of Virginia which gave its consent to the formation of a new state. In 1863 Congress admitted West Virginia to the Union with a constitution that provided for gradual emancipation of the few slaves there.

Of the other slave states, Delaware, with but a token number of slaves, remained firmly in the Union, but Maryland, Kentucky, and Missouri went through bitter struggles for control. The secession of Maryland would have made Washington but a Union enclave within the Confederacy, and in fact Baltimore's mayor for a time did cut all connections to the capital. On April 19 a mob attacked the Sixth Massachusetts Regiment on its way through Baltimore and inflicted a toll of four dead and thirty-six wounded. To hold the state Lincoln took drastic measures of dubious legality: he suspended the writ of habeas corpus (under which judges could require arresting officers to produce their prisoners and justify their arrest) and rounded up pro-Confederate leaders and threw them in jail. The fall elections ended the threat of Maryland's secession by returning a solidly Unionist majority in the state.

Kentucky, native state of both Lincoln and Davis, home of Crittenden and Breckinridge, was torn by divided loyalties. But May and June elections for a state convention returned a thumping Unionist majority, and the state legislature proclaimed Kentucky's "neutrality" in the conflict. Lincoln recognized the strategic value of his native state, situated on the south bank of

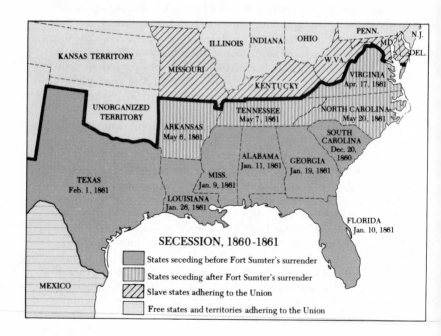

SECESSION, 1860-1861

■ States seceding before Fort Sumter's surrender

▥ States seceding after Fort Sumter's surrender

▨ Slave states adhering to the Union

□ Free states and territories adhering to the Union

the Ohio. "I think to lose Kentucky is nearly the same as to lose the whole game," he said. He promised to leave the state alone so long as the Confederates did likewise, and reassured its citizens that a war against secession was not a war against slavery. Kentucky's fragile neutrality lasted until September 3, when a Confederate force occupied Hickman and Columbus. Gen. Ulysses S. Grant then moved Union soldiers into Paducah, at the mouth of the Tennessee River. Kentucky, though divided in allegiance, for the most part remained with the Union. It joined the Confederacy, some have said, only after the war.

Lincoln's effort to hold a middle course in Missouri was upset by the maneuvers of less patient men in the state. Unionists there had a numerical advantage, but Confederate sympathies were strong and St. Louis had large numbers of both. For a time the state, like Kentucky, kept an uneasy peace. But elections for a convention brought an overwhelming Union victory, while a pro-Confederate militia under Gov. Claiborne F. Jackson began to gather near St. Louis. In the city Unionist forces rallied under Nathaniel Lyon and Francis P. Blair, Jr., brother of the postmaster-general, and on May 10 they surprised and disarmed the militia at its camp. Lyon pursued the pro-Confederate forces into the southwestern part of the state, and after a temporary setback at Wilson's Creek on August 10, in which Lyon lost his own life, the Unionists pushed the Confederates back again, finally breaking their resistance at the battle of Pea Ridge (March 6–8, 1862), just over the state line in Arkansas. Thereafter border warfare continued in Missouri, pitting rival bands of gunslingers who kept up their feuding and banditry for years after the war was over.

A "BROTHERS' WAR" Robert E. Lee epitomized the agonizing choice facing many men of the border states. Son of "Lighthorse Harry" Lee, a Revolutionary War hero, and married to a descendant of Martha Washington, Lee had served in the United States Army for thirty years. Master of Arlington, an estate which faced Washington across the Potomac, he was summoned by Gen. Winfield Scott, another Virginian, and offered command of the Federal forces in the field. After a sleepless night pacing the floor, Lee told Scott that he could not go against his "country," meaning Virginia. He resigned his commission, retired to his estate, and soon answered a call to the Virginia—later the Confederate—service. The course of the war might have been different had Lee made another choice.

The conflict sometimes became literally a "brothers' war." At

Hilton Head, South Carolina, Percival Drayton commanded a Federal gunboat while his brother, Brig. Gen. Thomas F. Drayton, led Confederate land forces. Franklin Buchanan, who commanded the *Virginia* (formerly the *Merrimac*), sank the Union ship *Congress* with his brother on board. John J. Crittenden of Kentucky had a son in each army. J. E. B. Stuart of the Confederate cavalry was chased around the peninsula below Richmond by his Federal father-in-law, Philip St. George Cooke. Lincoln's attorney-general Edward Bates had a son in the Confederate army, and Mrs. Lincoln herself had a brother, three half-brothers, and three brothers-in-law in the Confederate forces.

Neither side was ready for war, not even for the kind that had been fought before. And certainly neither could foresee the consuming force of this one, with its total mobilization of men and materials. This first of "modern" wars brought into use devices and techniques never before employed on such a scale: railroad transport, artillery, repeating rifles, ironclad ships, the telegraph, balloons, the Gatling gun (a rudimentary machine-gun), trenches, and wire entanglements.

ECONOMIC ADVANTAGES If the South seceded in part out of a growing awareness of its minority status in the nation, a balance sheet of the sections in 1860 shows the accuracy of that perception. To begin, the Union held twenty-three states, including four border slave states, while the Confederacy had eleven, claiming also Missouri and Kentucky. Ignoring conflicts of allegiance within various states, which might roughly cancel each other out, the population count was about 22 million in the Union to 9 million in the Confederacy, and about 3½ million of the latter were slaves. The Union therefore had an edge of about four to one in potential manpower.

An even greater advantage for the North was its industry. In gross value of manufactures, the Union states had a margin of better than ten to one in 1860. The states which joined the Confederacy produced just under 7.4 percent of the nation's manufactures on the eve of conflict. What made the disparity even greater was that little of this was in heavy industry. The only iron industry of any size in the Confederacy was the Tredegar Iron Works in Richmond, which had long supplied the United States Army. Tredegar's existence strengthened the Confederacy's will to defend its capital. The Union states, in addition to making most of the country's shoes, textiles, and iron products, turned out 97 percent of the firearms and 96 percent of the railroad equipment produced in the nation. They had most of the trained mechanics, most of the shipping and mercantile firms, and the bulk of the banking and financial resources.

Even in farm production the northern states overshadowed the bucolic South, for most of the North's population was still rooted in the soil. As the progress of the war upset southern output, northern farms managed to increase theirs, despite the loss of workers to the army. The Confederacy produced enough to meet minimal needs, but the disruption of transport caused shortages in many places. One consequence was that the North produced a surplus of wheat for export at a time when drought and crop failures in Europe created a critical demand. King Wheat supplanted King Cotton as the nation's main export, the chief means of acquiring foreign money and bills of exchange to pay for imports from abroad.

The North's advantage in transport weighed heavily as the war went on. The Union had more wagons, horses, and ships than the Confederacy, and an impressive edge in railroads: about 20,000 miles to the South's 10,000. The actual discrepancy was even greater, for southern railroads were mainly short lines built to different gauges, and had few replacements for rolling stock which broke down or wore out. The Confederacy had only one east-west connection, between Memphis and Chattanooga. The latter was an important rail hub with connections via Knoxville into Virginia and down through Atlanta to Charleston and Savannah. The North, on the other hand, already had an intricate network. Three major lines gave western farmers an outlet to the eastern seaboard and greatly lessened their former dependence on the Mississippi River.

MILITARY ADVANTAGES Against the weight of such odds the wonder was that the Confederacy managed to survive more than four years. Yet at the start certain things evened the odds. At first the South had more experienced military leaders. A number of circumstances had given rise to a military tradition in the South: the long-standing Indian danger, the fear of slave insurrection, an archaic punctilio about points of honor, and a history of expansionism. Military careers had prestige, and military schools multiplied in the antebellum years, the most notable West Points of the South being the Citadel and Virginia Military Institute. West Point itself drew many southerners, producing an army corps dominated by men from the region, chief among them Winfield Scott. Many northern West Pointers, like George B. McClellan and Ulysses S. Grant, dropped out of the service for civilian careers. A large proportion of the army's southern officers resigned their commissions to follow their states into the Confederacy. The head of the Louisiana Seminary of Learning and Military Academy (precursor of Louisiana State University), William Tecumseh Sherman, went the other way, rejoining the United States Army.

The general loyalty of the navy, which retained most of its southern officers, provided an important balance to the North's losses of army men. At the start Union seapower relied on about 90 ships, though only 42 were on active service and most were at distant stations. But under the able guidance of Secretary Gideon Welles and his assistant Gustavus V. Fox, the Union navy eventually grew to 650 vessels of all types. It never completely sealed off the South, but it raised to desperate levels the hazards of blockade running. On the inland waters navy gunboats and transports played an even more direct role in ultimately securing the Union's control of the Mississippi and its larger tributaries, which provided easy routes into the center of the Confederacy.

THE WAR'S EARLY COURSE   Amid the furies of passion after the fall of Fort Sumter, hearts lifted on both sides with the hope that the war might end with one sudden bold stroke, the capture of Washington or the fall of Richmond. Strategic thought at the time remained under the spell of Napoleon, holding that everything would turn on one climactic battle in which a huge force, massed against an enemy's point of weakness, would demoralize its armies and break its will to resist. Such ideas had been instilled in a generation of West Point cadets through their study of the baron de Jomini, a French interpreter of Napoleonic strategy, and the works of American strategists such as Henry W. Halleck's *Elements of Military Art and Science* (1846) and Dennis Mahan's *Elementary Treatise on Advance Guard, Out-Post, and Detachment Service of Troops . . .* (1847), commonly known by the short title *Out-Post*. But these ideas neglected the massive losses Napoleon had suffered, losses that finally turned his victories into defeat.

General Scott, the seventy-five-year-old commander of the Union army, saw a long road ahead. Being older—his career dated from the War of 1812—he fell under the Napoleonic spell less than others. He proposed to use the navy to blockade the long Atlantic and Gulf coastlines, and then to divide and subdivide the Confederacy by pushing southward along the main water routes: the Mississippi, Tennessee, and Cumberland Rivers. As word leaked out, the newspapers impatiently derided his "Anaconda" strategy, which they judged far too slow, indica-

tive of the commander's old age and caution. To the end, however, the Anaconda strategy of attrition remained Union policy:
there was no Napoleonic climax.

Like Lincoln, President Davis was under pressure to strike for
a quick decision. Davis let the battle-hungry Gen. P. G. T.
Beauregard hurry his main forces in Virginia to Manassas Junction, about twenty-five miles from Washington. Lincoln seems
meanwhile to have been persuaded that Gen. Irwin McDowell's
newly recruited army of some 30,000 might overrun the outnumbered Confederates and quickly march on to Richmond. But
Gen. Joseph E. Johnston had another Confederate force of some
12,000 in the Shenandoah Valley around Winchester. These men
slipped over the Blue Ridge and down the Manassas Gap
Railroad. Most arrived on the scene the day before the battle.

On July 21, 1861, McDowell's forces encountered Beauregard's army dug in behind a little stream called Bull Run. The
generals adopted markedly similar plans—each would turn the
other's left. Beauregard's orders went astray, while the Federals
nearly achieved their purpose early in the afternoon. Beauregard then rushed his reserves to meet the offensive, which
reached its climax around the Henry House Hill. Amid the fury,
Gen. Barnard Bee rallied his South Carolina volunteers by pointing to Thomas J. Jackson's brigade: "There stands Jackson like a
stone wall." After McDowell's last assault had faltered, he de-

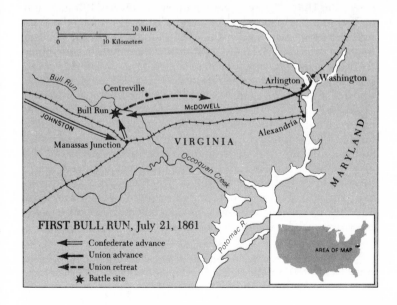

FIRST BULL RUN, July 21, 1861

- Confederate advance
- Union advance
- Union retreat
- ★ Battle site

cided that discretion was the better part of valor. An orderly retreat in battle is one of the most difficult of maneuvers, and as it
happened, was too much for the raw Federal recruits. On the
road back to Washington a bridge at Cub Run collapsed, and in
the traffic jam that ensued, retreat turned into panic.

Fortunately for the Federals, the Confederates were about as
demoralized by victory as the Federals by defeat. In any case a
summer downpour the next day turned roads into sloughs. The
quick decision for which both sides had reached proved beyond
their grasp. Beauregard, however, was promoted to full general,
one of five in the Confederate service, while the Union set about
building Washington's defenses. To replace the hapless McDowell, Lincoln named Gen. George B. McClellan, fresh from his
victories in western Virginia where he had secured the route of
the Baltimore and Ohio Railroad.

Military Deadlock

MOBILIZING VOLUNTEERS After the Battle of Bull Run (or Manassas)° both sides realized that the war would be more than a triumphant march. But even then mobilization was so haphazard
that a Prussian general later remarked that the war was fought by
little more than armed mobs on both sides. When secession
came, the United States Army numbered only 16,400 men and
officers, most of whom were out west. The army remained a separate and very small part of the Union forces. Both sides, in the
time-honored American way of war, looked to militia and volunteers to beef up their armies, and in the beginning were
swamped with lighthearted recruits.

Lincoln's first emergency call for 75,000 militiamen produced
about 80,000, but most of these three-month men were nearly
due to go home by the time of Bull Run. On May 3 Lincoln called
for 45,000 volunteers in 40 regiments to serve for three years.
So overwhelming was the response that 208 regiments quickly
materialized. This was the beginning of a great volunteer army.
Meeting in special session on July 4, 1861, Congress authorized
a call for 500,000 more men, and after Bull Run added another
500,000. By the end of the year the first half million had enlisted,
as a result mainly of state initiative and in many cases the efforts

---

°The Federals most often named battles for natural features, the Confederates for nearby towns, thus Bull Run (Manassas), Antietam (Sharpsburg),
Stone's River (Murfreesboro), and the like.

of groups, towns, and even individuals who raised and equipped regiments. This pell-mell mobilization left the army with a large number of "political" officers, commissioned by state governors or elected by the recruits.

The Confederate record was much the same. The first mass enlistment put an even greater strain on limited means. By act of February 28, 1861, the Provisional Congress authorized President Davis to accept for terms of one year state troops or volunteer units offered by governors. On March 6 Davis was empowered to call 100,000 twelve-month volunteers and to employ state militia up to six months. In May, once the fighting had started, he was authorized to raise up to 400,000 three-year volunteers "without the delay of a formal call upon the respective states." Thus by early 1862, despite the leavening of three-year men, most of the veteran Confederate soldiers were nearing the end of their terms without having encountered much significant action. They were also resisting the incentives of bonuses and furloughs for reenlistment.

THE DRAFT   The Confederates were driven to adopt conscription first. By act of April 16, 1862, all male white citizens, eighteen to thirty-five, were declared members of the army for three years and those already in service were required to serve out three years. In September 1862 the upper age was raised to forty-five, and in February 1864 the age limits were further extended to cover all from seventeen to fifty, with those under eighteen and over forty-five reserved for state defense.

Comprehensive as the law appeared on its face, it was weakened in practice by two loopholes. First, a draftee might escape service either by providing an able-bodied substitute not of draft age or by paying $500 in commutation. Second, exemptions, designed to protect key civilian work, were all too subject to abuse by men seeking "bombproof" jobs. Exemption of state officials, for example, was flagrantly abused by governors like Joseph E. Brown of Georgia and Zebulon B. Vance of North Carolina, who were in charge of defining the vital jobs. The exclusion of teachers with twenty pupils inspired a sudden educational renaissance, and the exemption of one white man for each plantation with twenty or more slaves led to bitter complaints about "a rich man's war and a poor man's fight."

The Union took nearly another year to decide that volunteers would be too few once the first excitement had passed. Congress flirted with conscription in the Militia Act of July 1862, which invited states to draft 300,000 militiamen, but this move pro-

duced only about 65,000 soldiers. Then Congress offered bounties of $100 ($300 by 1864) for enlistments, but the system was
grossly abused by "bounty-jumpers" who would collect in one
place and then move on to enlist somewhere else.

Congress finally acted in March 1863 to draft men aged
twenty to forty-five. Exemptions were granted to specified federal and state officeholders and to others on medical or compas-
sionate grounds, but one could still buy a substitute or, for $300,
have his service commuted. An elaborate machinery of enforcement passed down quotas to states and districts; conscription was
used only where the number of volunteers fell short of the quota,
an incentive for communities to supplement the federal bounties. In both the North and the South conscription spurred men
to volunteer, either to collect bounties or to avoid the disgrace of
being drafted. Eventually the draft in the North produced only
46,000 conscripts and 118,000 substitutes, or about 6 percent of
the Union armies.

The draft flouted an American tradition of voluntary service
and was widely held to be arbitrary and unconstitutional. In the
South the draft also sullied the cause of states' rights by requiring
the exercise of a central power. It might have worked better had
it operated through the states, some of which had set up their
own drafts to meet the calls of President Davis. Governor Brown
of Georgia, who had one of the best records for raising troops at
first, turned into a bitter critic of the draft, pronouncing it unconstitutional and trying to obstruct its enforcement. Few of the
other governors gave it unqualified support, and Vice-President
Stephens remained unreconciled to it throughout the war.

Widespread opposition limited enforcement of the draft acts
both North and South. In New York City, which had long enjoyed commercial ties with the South, the announcement of a
draft lottery on July 11, 1863, led to a week of rioting in which
mobs turned on black scapegoats, lynched Negroes caught on
the streets, and burned down a Negro orphanage. The violence
and pillaging ran completely out of control; seventy-four persons
died, and an estimated $2 million in property was destroyed be-
fore soldiers brought from Gettysburg restored order.

As important as the problem of manpower were those of supply and logistics. If wars bring forth loyalty, they also bring forth
greed, and this war's pell-mell mobilization offered much room
for profiteering. Simon E. Cameron, the machine politician
whom Lincoln appointed secretary of war to round out his political coalition, tolerated wholesale fraud. Lincoln eased him out in
January 1862, and his successor, Edwin M. Stanton, brought
order and efficiency into the department. But he was never able

entirely to eliminate the plague of overcharging for shoddy goods.

NAVAL ACTIONS   After Bull Run, both sides mobilized for a longer war, and for the rest of 1861 into early 1862 the most important actions involved naval war and blockade. The one great threat to the Union navy proved to be short-lived. The Confederates in Norfolk fashioned an ironclad ship from an abandoned Union steam frigate, the *Merrimack*. Rechristened the *Virginia,* it ventured out on March 8, 1862, and wrought havoc among Union ships at the Chesapeake entrance. But as luck would have it, a new Union ironclad, the *Monitor,* arrived from New York in time to engage the *Virginia* on the next day. They fought to a draw and the *Virginia* returned to port, where the Confederates destroyed it when they had to give up Norfolk soon afterward.

Gradually the "anaconda" tightened its grip on the South. At Fortress Monroe, Virginia, Union forces under Benjamin F. Butler held the tip of the peninsula between the James and the York, the scene of much colonial and revolutionary history. The navy extended its bases farther down the coast in the late summer and fall of 1862. Ben Butler's troops then captured Hatteras Inlet on the Outer Banks of North Carolina in August, a foothold soon extended to Roanoke Island and New Bern on the mainland. In November 1861 a Federal flotilla appeared at Port Royal, South Carolina, pounded the fortifications into submission, and seized the port and nearby sea islands.

From there the navy's progress extended southward along the Georgia-Florida coast. To the north the Federals laid siege to Charleston; by 1863 Fort Sumter and the city itself had come under bombardment from Morris Island. In the spring of 1862 Flag Officer David Glasgow Farragut forced open the lower Mississippi and surprised New Orleans, which had expected any attack to come downstream. He won a surrender on May 1, then moved quickly to take Baton Rouge in the same way. An occupation force moved in under General Butler.

ACTIONS IN THE WEST   Except for the amphibious thrusts along the southern coast, little happened in the Eastern Theater (east of the Appalachians) before May 1862. The Western Theater (from the mountains to the Mississippi), on the other hand, flared up with several encounters and an important penetration of the Confederate states. In January, Gen. George H. Thomas cleared eastern Kentucky by a decisive defeat of the Confederates at Mill Springs. The main routes southward, however, lay farther west. There Confederate Gen. Albert Sidney Johnston had perhaps

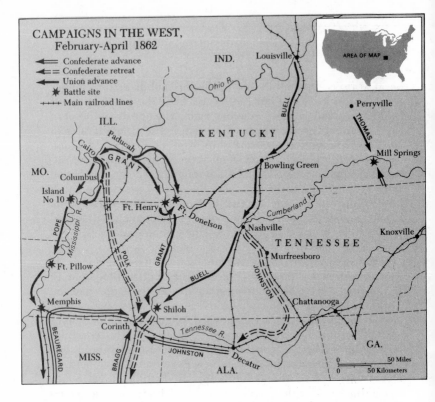

40,000 men stretched over some 150 miles, with concentrations
at Columbus and Bowling Green, Kentucky, each astride a major
north-south railroad. At the center, however, only about 5,500
men held Fort Henry on the Tennessee and Fort Donelson on the
Cumberland.

Early in 1862 Ulysses S. Grant made the first thrust against
Johnston's center. Moving out of Cairo and Paducah with a gunboat flotilla under Commodore Andrew H. Foote, he swung
southward up the Tennessee River toward Fort Henry. After a
pounding from the Union gunboats, Fort Henry fell on February
6. Grant then moved quickly overland to attack Fort Donelson,
while Foote ran his gunboats back to the Ohio and up the Cumberland. Donelson proved a harder nut to crack, but on February
16 it gave up with some 12,000 men. Grant's terms, "unconditional surrender," and his quick success sent a thrill through the
Union. U. S. "Unconditional Surrender" Grant had not only
opened a water route to Nashville, but had thrust his forces between the two strongholds of the western Confederates. A. S.
Johnston therefore had to give up his foothold in Kentucky and
abandon Nashville to Don Carlos Buell's Army of the Ohio (Feb-

ruary 25) in order to reunite his forces at Corinth, Mississippi, along the Memphis and Chattanooga Railroad.

SHILOH Thus, quickly, the Union regained most of Kentucky and western Tennessee, and stood poised to strike at the Deep South. On the Mississippi itself, Confederate strong points at Island No. 10 and at Fort Pillow fell on April 7 and 13 respectively, and Memphis on June 6, to a combined force under Commodore Foote and Gen. John Pope. Meanwhile Grant moved farther southward along the Tennessee River, hoping to link up with Buell's army near the southern border of Tennessee. At Pittsburg Landing, their rendezvous, Grant made a deadly mistake. While planning his attack on Corinth, he failed to set up defensive lines. The morning of April 6 the Confederates struck suddenly at Shiloh, a country church, and after a day of bloody confusion, pinned Grant's men against the river. But under the cover of gunboats and artillery at Pittsburg Landing, reinforcements from Buell's army arrived overnight. The next day the tide turned and the Rebels withdrew to Corinth, with Grant's army too battered to pursue.

Shiloh was the costliest battle in which Americans had ever engaged, although worse was yet to come. Combined casualties of nearly 25,000 exceeded the total dead and wounded of the Revolution, the War of 1812, and the Mexican War combined. Among the dead was Albert Sidney Johnston, an artery in his leg severed by a gunshot. The Union, too, lost for a while the full services of its finest general. Grant had been caught napping and was too shattered by his heavy losses to press the advantage. The Confederates had missed their chance to prevent Grant's linkage with Buell, but as at Bull Run, the victors were as demoralized by victory as the losers by defeat.

Gen. Henry W. Halleck, who first replaced Frémont in Missouri and then took overall command in the West, now arrived to take personal command of the Union forces in the field. He shelved Grant in an insignificant position as second in command, giving the troops Grant had been leading to George H. Thomas. Halleck, "Old Brains," the textbook strategist of offensive war, proved in the field to be unaccountably timid. Determined not to repeat Grant's mistake, he moved with profound caution on Corinth, taking at face value every inflated report of Rebel strength. But outnumbered better than two to one, P. G. T. Beauregard (Johnston's successor) abandoned Corinth to the Federals on May 30, falling back on Tupelo.

Halleck let slip the chance to overwhelm Beauregard. Instead, before being summoned back to Washington in June, he split up

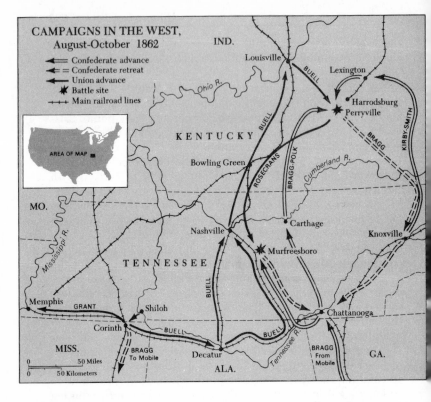

CAMPAIGNS IN THE WEST,
August–October 1862

◄══ Confederate advance
◄ ═ Confederate retreat
◄── Union advance
✸ Battle site
┼┼┼ Main railroad lines

AREA OF MAP ■

IND.

Louisville

Lexington

Harrodsburg
Perryville

KIRBY-SMITH

BRAGG

Ohio R.

BUELL

KENTUCKY

BUELL

Bowling Green

Cumberland R.

ROSECRANS

BRAGG-POLK

MO.

Mississippi R.

Carthage

Knoxville

Nashville

Murfreesboro

TENNESSEE

BUELL

Chattanooga

Memphis   GRANT   Shiloh

Corinth

BUELL

BUELL

Tennessee R.

BRAGG
From
Mobile

GA.

MISS.

0   50 Miles
0   50 Kilometers

BRAGG
To Mobile

Decatur

ALA.

his army in several directions. Grant remained on the scene,
guarding Corinth and other points. Buell withdrew to Nashville
to prepare an offensive against Chattanooga. The Confederate
force, commanded by Braxton Bragg after the loss of Corinth,
moved via Mobile to Chattanooga. For the remainder of 1862
the chief action in the Western Theater was a series of inconclusive maneuvers and two sharp engagements. Bragg took his army
to Kentucky, threatened Louisville, and was stopped by Buell's
Army of the Ohio at Perryville on October 8. Kentuckians failed
to rally to the Confederate flag and Bragg pulled back into Tennessee. Buell, meanwhile, under pressure to sever the rail line at
Chattanooga, proved to be one of the many Union generals who
Lincoln said had "the slows." The administration replaced him
with William S. Rosecrans, who moved out of Nashville and met
Bragg in the costly engagement at Murfreesboro (or Stone's
River), December 31 to January 3, after which Bragg cleared out
of central Tennessee and fell back on Chattanooga. But Lincoln
still coveted eastern Tennessee both for its many Unionists and
for its railroads, which he wanted to cut to get between the
Rebels and their "hog and hominy."

MCCLELLAN'S PENINSULAR CAMPAIGN The Eastern Theater, aside from the coastal operations, remained fairly quiet for nine months after Bull Run. When George B. McClellan took command in Washington after Bull Run, he vigorously set about getting men back to their units, getting them organized, and keeping them busy—in short, he built an army out of the fragments left from the first battle. In November, upon General Scott's retirement, which McClellan impatiently awaited, he became general-in-chief. The newspapers dubbed him Little Napoleon, and a photographer posed him with his right hand inside his jacket. But these impressions were misleading. On the surface McClellan exuded confidence and poise, and a certain flair for parade-ground showmanship. Yet his knack for organization never went much beyond that.

Time passed, the army grew, and McClellan kept building his forces to meet the superior numbers that always seemed to be facing him. His intelligence service, headed by the private detective Allen Pinkerton, tended to estimate enemy forces at double their actual size. Before moving, there was always the need to do this or that, to get 10,000 or 20,000 more men, always something. McClellan's Army of the Potomac was nine months in gestation after Bull Run, and then moved mainly because Lincoln insisted. In General Order No. 1, the president directed McClellan to begin forward movement by Washington's Birthday, February 22. The president's idea was that the army should move directly toward Richmond, keeping itself between the Confederate army and Washington. But McClellan had another idea, and despite his reluctance to move, very nearly pulled it off. The idea was to enter Richmond by the side door, so to speak, up the neck of land between the York and James Rivers, site of Jamestown, Williamsburg, and Yorktown, at the tip of which Federal forces already held Fortress Monroe, about seventy-five miles from Richmond.

Lincoln consented but specified, to McClellan's chargin, that a force be left under McDowell to guard Washington. In mid-March 1862 McClellan's army finally embarked. Advancing slowly up the thinly defended peninsula, taking no chances, McClellan brought Yorktown under siege from April 5 until May 4, when the Confederates slipped away, having accomplished their purpose of allowing Gen. Joseph E. Johnston to get his army in front of Richmond. Before the end of May McClellan's advance units sighted the church spires of Richmond. But his army was divided by the Chickahominy River, which splits the peninsula north and east of Richmond, and though Richmond lay south of the Chickahominy, part of the Confederate army was on the north bank to counter any southward move from Washington by McDowell.

McDowell, however, was delayed by more urgent matters, or what seemed so. President Davis, at the urging of military adviser Robert E. Lee, sent Stonewall Jackson into the Shenandoah Valley on what proved to be a brilliant diversionary action. From March 23 to June 9, Jackson and some 18,000 men pinned down two separate armies with more than twice his numbers by striking first at Frémont in the western Virginia mountains, then at Nathanial P. Banks at the northern end of the valley. While McDowell braced to defend Washington, Jackson hastened back to defend Richmond.

On May 31 Johnston struck at Union forces isolated on the south bank by the flooded river. In the battle of Seven Pines (Fair Oaks), only the arrival of reinforcements, who somehow crossed the swollen river, prevented a disastrous Union defeat. Both

THE PENINSULAR CAMPAIGN, 1862

sides took heavy casualties, and General Johnston was severely wounded. At this point Robert E. Lee assumed command of the Army of Northern Virginia. Lee quickly sized up the situation. Reunited with the elusive Jackson, Lee would hit the Union forces north of the Chickahominy with everything he had, leaving a token force in front of Richmond.

On June 26, Lee and Jackson struck the Union's extreme right at Mechanicsville, and kept up the assault on successive days at Gaines' Mill, Savage's Station, and White Oak Swamp. As the Federals withdrew they inflicted heavy losses on the Rebels, frustrating Lee's purpose of crushing the right flank. McClellan managed to get his main forces on the south side of the river, and established a new base at Harrison's Landing on the James. Lee's final desperate attack came at Malvern Hill (July 1), where the Confederates suffered heavy losses from Union artillery and gunboats in the James. The Seven Days' Battles (June 25 to July 1) had failed to dislodge the Union forces. McClellan was still near Richmond, with good supply lines on the James River.

On July 9, when Lincoln visited McClellan's headquarters on the James, the general complained that the administration had failed to support him adequately and handed the president a strange document, the "Harrison's Landing Letter," in which, despite his critical plight, he instructed the president at length on war policies. It was ample reason to remove the general. Instead Lincoln returned to Washington and on July 11 called Henry Halleck from the west to take charge as general-in-chief, a post that McClellan had temporarily vacated.

SECOND BATTLE OF MANASSAS   The new high command decided to evacuate the peninsula, which had become the graveyard of the last hope for a short war. McClellan was ordered to leave the peninsula and join the Washington defense force, now under John Pope, for a new overland move on Richmond. As McClellan's Army of the Potomac began to pull out, Lee moved northward to strike at Pope before McClellan arrived. Once again he adopted an audacious stratagem. Dividing his forces, he sent Jackson on a sweep around Pope's right flank to attack his supply lines. At Cedar Mountain on August 9 Jackson pushed back an advance party under General Banks, and on August 26 issued suddenly down Thoroughfare Gap to seize and destroy the Federal supply base at Manassas Junction. At Second Bull Run (or Second Manassas), fought on almost the same site as the earlier battle, Pope assumed that he faced only Jackson, but Lee's main army by that time had joined in. On August 30 a crushing attack on Pope's flank by James Longstreet's corps of 30,000 drove the Federals from the field. In the next few days the Union forces pulled back into the fortifications around Washington, where McClellan once again took command and reorganized.

ANTIETAM   But Lee gave him little time. Still on the offensive, early in September he invaded western Maryland. His purpose was in part to get the fighting out of Virginia during harvest season, in part to score a victory on Union soil for the sake of prestige and possible foreign recognition. By a stroke of fortune a

CAMPAIGNS IN VIRGINIA
& MARYLAND, 1862

◄══ Confederate advance   ◄── Union advance
◄═ = Confederate retreat   ◄-─- Union retreat
✹ Battle site

Lincoln and his staff at Antietam, 1862. [National Archives]

Union soldier picked up a bundle of cigars with an order from Lee wrapped around them. The paper revealed that Lee had again divided his army, sending Jackson off to take Harpers Ferry. But McClellan delayed, still worried about enemy strength, and Lee got most of his army back together behind Antietam Creek. On September 17, at the Battle of Antietam (Sharpsburg), just as the Confederate lines seemed ready to break, the last of Jackson's men arrived to bolster them. At this point McClellan backed away, letting Lee get away across the Potomac. Lincoln, discouraged by McClellan's failure to follow up, removed him once and for all and assigned him to recruiting duty in Trenton, New Jersey. McClellan would never again have a command.

FREDERICKSBURG In his search for a fighting general Lincoln now made the worst choice of all. He turned to Ambrose E. Burnside, whose main achievements to that time had been to capture Roanoke Island and grow his famous side-whiskers. Burnside had twice before turned down the job on the grounds that he felt unfit for so large a command. But if the White House wanted him to fight, he would fight even in the face of oncoming winter. On December 13 he sent his men across the Rappahannock River to face Lee's forces, entrenched behind Fredericksburg on Marye's Heights. Confederate artillery and small-arms fire chewed up the blue columns as they crossed a mile of bottomland outside the town. Six times the Union's suicidal assaults melted under the murderous fire issuing from protected positions above and below them. After taking more than 12,000 casualties compared to fewer than 6,000 for the Confederates, Burnside retired across the river.

The year 1862 ended with forces in the East deadlocked and the Union advance in the West stalled since mid-year. Union morale reached a low ebb. Northern Democrats were calling for negotiated peace. At the same time Lincoln was under pressure from the Radicals of his own party who were pushing for more stringent war measures, questioning the competence of the president, and demanding the removal of Secretary of State Seward. Burnside was under fire from his own officers, some of whom were ready to testify publicly to his shortcomings.

But the deeper currents of the war were turning in favor of the Union: in a lengthening war its resources began to tell. In both the Eastern and Western Theaters the Confederate counterattack had been turned back. The year ended with forces under Rosecrans and Bragg locked in combat at Stone's River (Murfreesboro) in Tennessee. There again, after three more days of bloody stalemate, the Confederates fell back. And even while the armies clashed on that darkling plain in Tennessee, Lincoln by the stroke of a pen had changed the conflict from a war for the Union into a revolutionary struggle for abolition. On January 1, 1863, he signed the Emancipation Proclamation.

EMANCIPATION

It was the product of long and painful deliberation. In Lincoln's annual message of December 3, 1861, he had warned Congress to be "anxious and careful" that the war did not "degenerate into a violent and remorseless revolutionary struggle." At the outset he had upheld the promise of his party's platform to restore the Union but accept slavery where it existed. Congress too endorsed that position in the Crittenden-Johnson Resolutions which passed both houses soon after the Battle of Bull Run, with few dissenting votes. Once fighting began, the need to hold the border states dictated caution on the issue of emancipation. Beyond that, some other things deterred action. For one, Lincoln had to cope with a deep-seated racial prejudice in the North. Even the antislavery impulse derived often from the will to keep both slavery and blacks in the South. Lincoln himself harbored doubts about his authority to act so long as he clung to the view that the states remained legally in the Union. The only way around the problem would be to justify emancipation on the bases of military necessity and the president's war powers, as in fact John Quincy Adams had foreseen many years before.

Former slaves, or "contrabands," on Mr. Foller's farm, Cumberland Landing, Virginia, 1862. [Library of Congress]

A MEASURE OF WAR The war forced the issue. Fugitive slaves began to turn up in Union camps. In May 1861 at Fortress Monroe, Virginia, Benjamin F. Butler declared them "contraband of war" and put them to work on his fortifications. "Contrabands" soon became a common name for runaways in Union lines. But John C. Frémont pressed the issue one step too far. As commander of the Department of the West, on August 30, 1861, he simply liberated the slaves of all who actively helped the Rebel cause, an action which risked unsettling the yet-doubtful border states. Lincoln demanded that Frémont conform to the Confiscation Act of 1861, which freed only those slaves used by Rebel military services, as Butler's first "contrabands" had been. On May 9, 1862, Gen. David Hunter declared free all slaves in South Carolina, Georgia, and Florida. He had no runaway slaves in his lines, he said, although some runaway masters had fled the scene. Lincoln quickly revoked the order, and took the brunt of the rising outrage among congressional Radicals.

Lincoln himself meanwhile edged toward emancipation. In March 1862 he proposed that federal compensation be offered any state which began gradual emancipation. The cost in the border states, he estimated, would about equal the cost of eighty-seven days of the war. The plan failed in Congress because of border-state opposition, but on April 16, 1862, Lincoln signed an act which abolished slavery in the District of Columbia, with compensation to owners; on June 19 another act excluded slavery from the territories, without offering owners compensation. A Second Confiscation Act, passed on July 17, liberated the slaves of all persons aiding the rebellion. Still another act forbade the army to help return runaways.

To save the Union, Lincoln finally decided, complete emancipation would be required for several reasons: slave labor bolstered the Rebel cause, sagging morale in the North needed the lift of a moral cause, and public opinion was swinging that way as the war dragged on. Proclaiming a war on slavery, moreover, would end forever any chance that France or Britain would suport the Confederacy. In July 1862 Lincoln first confided to his cabinet that he had in mind a proclamation that under his war powers would free the slaves of the enemy. At the time Seward advised him to wait for a Union victory in order to avoid any semblance of desperation.

The delay lasted through the long weeks during which Lee invaded Maryland and Bragg moved into Kentucky. As late as August 22, 1862, Lincoln responded to Horace Greeley's plea for emancipation: "My paramount object in this struggle is to save the Union and is not either to save or destroy slavery." The time to act finally came a month later, after Antietam. It was a dubious victory, but it did result in Lee's withdrawal. On September 22 Lincoln issued a preliminary Emancipation Proclamation, in which he repeated all his earlier stands: that his object was mainly to restore the Union and that he favored proposals for compensated emancipation and colonization. But the main burden of the document was his warning that on January 1, 1863, "all persons held as slaves within any state, or designated part of a state, the people whereof shall be in rebellion against the United States, shall be then, thenceforward and forever free."

In his annual message of December 1862 Lincoln once again raised the question of border-state compensation and ended with one of his most eloquent passages:

> We, even we here, hold the power and bear the responsibility. In giving freedom to the slave we assure freedom to the free—honorable alike in what we give and what we preserve. We shall nobly save or meanly lose the last, best hope of earth. Other means may succeed; this could not fail. The way is plain, peaceful, generous, just—a way which if followed the world will forever applaud and God must forever bless.

But this peroration was delivered with one eye to justifying the emancipation he had already promised. On January 1, 1863, Lincoln signed the second Emancipation Proclamation, giving effect to his promise of September, again emphasizing that this was a war measure based on his war powers. He also urged blacks to abstain from violence except in self-defense, and added that free blacks would now be received into the armed service of the

*Two views of the Emancipation Proclamation. The Union view (top)
shows a thoughtful Lincoln composing the Proclamation with the
Constitution and the Holy Bible in his lap. The Confederate view (bottom)
shows a demented Lincoln with his foot on the Constitution using an
inkwell held by the devil. [Library of Congress]*

United States. For all its eloquence, the document set forth its points in commonplace terms. *Die Presse*, a newspaper in far-away Austria, got the point better than many closer home: "Lincoln is a figure *sui generis* in history. No pathos, no idealistic flights of eloquence, no posing, no wrapping himself in the toga of history. The most formidable decrees which he hurls against the enemy and which will never lose their historic significance, resemble—as the author intends them to—ordinary summonses sent by one lawyer to another on the opposing side. . . . " But as Henry Adams wrote from the London embassy, the Proclamation had created "an almost convulsive reaction in our favour."

REACTIONS TO EMANCIPATION Among the Confederate states, Tennessee and the occupied parts of Virginia and Louisiana were exempted from its effect. The document, with few exceptions, freed no slaves who were within Union lines at the time, as cynics noted. Moreover, it went little further than the Second Confiscation Act. But these objections missed a point which black slaves readily grasped. "In a document proclaiming liberty," wrote the historian Benjamin Quarles, "the unfree never bother to read the fine print." Word spread quickly in the quarters, and in some cases masters learned of it first from their slaves. Though most slaves deemed it safer just to wait for the "day of jubilee" when Union forces arrived, some actively claimed their freedom. One spectacular instance was that of the black pilot Robert Smalls, who one night in May 1862 took over a small Confederate gunboat, the *Planter*, and sailed his family through Charleston Harbor out to the blockading Union fleet. Later he served the Union navy as a pilot and still later became a congressman.

BLACKS IN THE MILITARY From very early in the war Union commanders found "contrabands" like Smalls useful as guides to unfamiliar terrain and waterways, informants on the enemy, and at the very least common laborers. While menial labor by blacks was familiar enough, military service was something else again. Though not unprecedented, it aroused in whites instinctive fears. For more than a year the administration warily evaded the issue, although the navy began to enlist blacks before the end of 1861.

Even after Congress authorized the enlistment of Negroes in the Second Confiscation Act of July 1862, the administration ordered no general mobilization of black troops. It did, however, permit Gen. Rufus Saxton to raise five regiments in the Sea Island, forming the First South Carolina Volunteer Regiment under Col. Thomas Wentworth Higginson, which sallied forth in late 1862 on raids along the Georgia-Florida coast. On January 1, 1863, Lincoln's Emancipation Proclamation reaffirmed the policy that blacks could enroll in the armed services and sparked new efforts to organize all-black units. Gov. John A. Andrew swiftly mustered the Massachusetts Fifty-fourth Regiment as the first northern all-Negro unit, under Col. Robert Gould Shaw. Rhode Island and other states soon followed suit. In May the War Department authorized general recruitment of blacks all over the country.

By mid-1863 black units were involved in significant action in both the Eastern and Western Theaters. On July 18 the Massachusetts Fifty-fourth led a gallant if hopeless assault on Battery Wagner, at the entrance to Charleston Harbor. This action, and the use of Negro units in the Vicksburg campaign, did much to win acceptance for both black soldiers and for emancipation, at least as a proper strategem of war. Commenting on Union victories at Port Hudson and Milliken's Bend, Mississippi, Lincoln reported that "some of our commanders . . . believe that . . . the use of colored troops constitutes the heaviest blow yet dealt to the rebels, and that at least one of these important successes could not have been achieved . . . but for the aid of black soldiers."

Altogether, between 180,000 and 200,000 black Americans served in the Union army, providing around 10 percent of its total. Some 38,000 gave their lives. In the Union navy the 29,500 blacks accounted for about a fourth of all enlistments; of

Company E of the Fourth U.S. Colored Infantry. These determined soldiers helped defend Washington, D.C. [Library of Congress]

these more than 2,800 died. Not only black men but black women as well served in the war; Harriet Tubman and Susie King Taylor, for instance, were nurses with Clara Barton in the Sea Islands.

As the war entered its final months freedom emerged more fully as a legal reality. Three major steps occurred in January 1865 when both Missouri and Tennessee abolished slavery by state action and the House of Representatives passed an abolition amendment introduced by Sen. Lyman Trumbull of Illinois the year before. Upon ratification by three-fourths of the states, the Thirteenth Amendment became part of the Constitution on December 18, 1865, and removed any lingering doubts about the legality of emancipation. By then, in fact, slavery remained only in the border states of Kentucky and Delaware.

GOVERNMENT DURING THE WAR

Striking the shackles from 3.5 million slaves was a momentous social and economic revolution. But an even broader revolution got under way as power shifted from South to North with secession. Before the war southern congressmen had been able at least to frustrate the designs of both Free Soil and Whiggery. But once the secessionists abandoned Congress to the Republicans, a dramatic change occurred. The protective tariff, a transcontinental railroad, a homestead act—all of which had been stalled by sectional controversy—were adopted before the end of 1862. The National Banking Act followed in 1863. These were supplemented by the Morrill Land Grant Act (1862), which provided federal aid to state colleges of "agriculture and mechanic arts," and the Contract Labor Act (1864), which aided the importation of immigrant labor. All of these had great long-term significance.

UNION FINANCES   The more immediate problem for Congress was how to finance the war, because expenditures generally ran ahead of expectations while revenues lagged behind. Three expedients were open: higher taxes, issues of paper money, and borrowing. The higher taxes came chiefly in the form of the Morrill Tariff and excise duties which one historian said "might be described with a near approach to accuracy as a tax on everything." Excises taxed manufactures and the practice of nearly every profession. A butcher, for example, had to pay thirty cents for every head of beef he slaughtered, ten cents for every hog, five for every sheep. On top of the excises came an income tax which started in 1861 at 3 percent of incomes over $800 and increased in 1864 to a graduated rate rising from 5 percent of incomes over $600 to 10 percent of incomes over $10,000. To collect these the Revenue Act of 1862 created a Bureau of Internal Revenue.

But tax revenues trickled in so slowly—in the end they would meet 21 percent of wartime expenditures—that Congress in 1862 forced upon a reluctant Treasury Secretary Chase the expedient of printing paper money, backed up only by the proviso that it was legal tender for all debts. Beginning with the Legal Tender Act of February 1862, Congress ultimately authorized $450 million of the notes, which soon became known as "greenbacks" because of their color. The amount of greenbacks issued was limited enough to tide the Union over its financial crisis without causing the ruinous inflation which the unlimited issue of paper money caused in the Confederacy.

The net wartime issue of $431 million in greenbacks was only about a sixth of the total wartime indebtedness. From the beginning Chase had intended to rely for funds chiefly on the sale of bonds. Sales went slowly at first, although the issue of greenbacks, which depreciated in value against gold, encouraged the purchase of 6 percent bonds with the cheaper currency. But after October 1862 a Philadelphia banker named Jay Cooke (sometimes tagged "The Financier of the Civil War") mobilized a nationwide machinery of agents and patriotic propaganda for the sale of bonds. Eventually bonds amounting to more than $2 billion were sold, but not all by the ballyhoo of Jay Cooke and Company. New banks formed under the National Banking Act were required to invest part of their capital in the bonds, and encouraged to invest even more as security for the national banknotes they could issue.

For many businessmen wartime ventures brought quick riches which were made visible all too often in vulgar display and extravagance. "The world has seen its iron age, its silver age, its golden age and its brazen age," the New York *Herald* commented. "This is the age of shoddy . . . shoddy brokers in Wall Street, or shoddy manufacturers of shoddy goods, or shoddy contractors for shoddy articles for shoddy government. Six days a week they are shoddy businessmen. On the seventh day they are shoddy Christians." Not all the wartime fortunes, however, were made dishonestly. And their long-run importance was in promoting the capital accumulation with which American businessmen fueled later expansion. Wartime business laid the groundwork for the fortunes of such nabobs as Morgan, Rockefeller, Mellon, Carnegie, Stanford, Huntington, Armour, and Swift.

CONFEDERATE FINANCES   Confederate finances were a disaster from the start. Treasury Secretary Christopher Memminger was appointed more to give South Carolina a place in the cabinet than for his financial skill or tact. But even the most tactful genius might never have overcome popular reluctance, congressional stalling, and limited governmental structure, all of which hindered efforts to finance the Confederacy. In the first year of its existence the Confederacy levied export and import duties, but exports and imports were low. It enacted a tax of one-half of 1 percent on most forms of property, which should have yielded a hefty income, but the Confederacy farmed out its collection to the states, promising a 10 percent rebate on the take. The result was chaos. All but three states raised their quota by floating loans, which only worsened inflation.

In April 1863 Memminger extracted from the Confederate Congress a measure which, like Union excises, taxed nearly everything. A 10 percent tax in kind on all agricultural products did more to outrage farmers and planters than to supply the army, however. Enforcement was so poor and evasion so easy that the taxes produced only negligible amounts of depreciated currency.

Altogether, taxes covered no more than 5 percent of Confederate costs, perhaps less; bond issues accounted for less than 33 percent; and treasury notes more than 66 percent. The last resort, the printing press, was in fact one of the early resorts. The first issue of $1 million in treasury notes in February 1861 was only the beginning: $20 million was authorized in May and $100 million in August, launching the Confederacy on an extended binge for which the only cure was more of the same. Altogether the Confederacy turned out more than $1 billion in paper money. J.B. Jones, a clerk at the War Department in Richmond, reported in March 1864 a wild turkey offered in the market for $100, flour at $425 a barrel, home calls by doctors at $30, meal at $72 a bushel, and bacon at $10 a pound. Country folk were likely to have enough for subsistence, perhaps a little surplus to barter, but townspeople on fixed incomes were caught in a merciless squeeze.

CONFEDERATE DIPLOMACY   Civil wars often become international conflicts. The foundation of Confederate diplomacy in fact was the hope of help from the outside in the form of supplies, diplomatic recognition, or perhaps even intervention. The South indulged the pathetic expectation that diplomatic recognition would prove decisive, when in fact it more likely would have followed decisive victory in the field, which never came. An equally fragile illusion was the conviction that King Cotton, as an Atlanta newspaper affirmed, would "bring more wooing princes to the feet of the Confederate states than Penelope had."

Indeed, to help foreign leaders make up their minds, the Confederates imposed a voluntary embargo on shipments of cotton until the Union blockade began to strangle their foreign trade. European textile manufacturers meanwhile subsisted on the carryover from their purchase of the record crops of 1859 and 1860. By the time they needed cotton, it was available from new sources in Egypt, India, and elsewhere. Cotton textiles aside, the British economy was undergoing a boom from wartime trade with the Union and blockade-running into the Confederacy.

The first Confederate emissaries to England and France took hope when Foreign Minister Lord John Russell received them informally after their arrival in London in May 1861; they even got a promise from Napoleon III to recognize the Confederacy if Britain would lead the way. The key was therefore in London, but Russell refused to receive the Confederates again, partly because of Union pressures and partly out of British self-interest.

One incident early in the war threatened to upset British equanimity. In November 1861 Cap. Charles Wilkes's Union warship *San Jacinto* stopped a British mail packet, the *Trent*, and took into custody two Confederate commissioners, James M. Mason and John Slidell, en route from Havana to Europe. Celebrated as a heroic deed by a northern public still starved for victories, the *Trent* affair roused a storm of protest in Britain. An ultimatum for the captives' release was delivered to Washington, confronting Lincoln and Seward with an explosive crisis. But the interference with a neutral ship on the high seas violated long-settled American principle, and Seward finally decided to face down popular clamor and release Mason and Slidell, much to their own chagrin. As martyrs in Boston's Fort Warren they were more useful to their own cause than they could ever be in London and Paris.

In contrast to the futility of King Cotton diplomacy, Confederate commissioners scored some successes in getting supplies. The most spectacular feat was James D. Bulloch's procurement of Confederate raiding ships. Although British law forbade the sale of warships to belligerents, Bulloch contrived to have the ships built and then, on trial runs, to escape to the Azores or elsewhere for outfitting with guns. In all, eighteen such ships were activated and saw action in the Atlantic, Pacific, and Indian Oceans, where they sank hundreds of Yankee ships and threw terror into the rest. The most spectacular of the Confederate raiders were the first two, the *Florida* and the *Alabama*, which took thirty-eight and sixty-four prizes respectively.

A much greater threat to Union seapower came when Bulloch contracted with England's Laird Shipyard for fast ironclad ships with pointed prows. Named the "Laird rams," they were meant to smash the Union's wooden vessels, break its blockade, and maybe even attack northern ports. Perhaps in response to news of Union victories at Gettysburg and Vicksburg, however, the British government decided to hold the Laird rams in port. Thereafter the British showed little disposition to ignore Confederate transgressions, although one Rebel raider, the *Shenandoah*, did escape British port in October 1864, and was still burning Yankee whalers in the Bering Sea as late as July 1865, when a passing British ship brought word that the war was over.

UNION POLITICS AND CIVIL LIBERTIES   On the home fronts there was no moratorium on politics, North or South. Within his own party Lincoln faced a Radical wing composed mainly of prewar abolitionists. By the end of 1861 they were getting restless with the policy of fighting solely to protect the Union. The congressional Joint Committee on the Conduct of the War, created December 20,1861, became an instrument of their cause. Led by men like Thaddeus Stevens and George W. Julian in the House, and Charles Sumner, Benjamin F. Wade (the chairman), and Zachariah Chandler in the Senate, they pushed for confiscation and emancipation, and a more vigorous prosecution of the war. Still, the greater body of Republicans backed Lincoln's more cautious approach. And the party was generally united on economic policy.

The Democratic party was set back by the loss of its southern wing and the death of its leader, Stephen A. Douglas, in June 1861. By and large, northern Democrats supported a war for the "Union as it was" before 1860 giving reluctant support to war policies but opposing wartime restraints on civil liberties and the new economic legislation. "War Democrats" like Sen. Andrew Johnson and Secretary of War Edwin M. Stanton fully supported Lincoln's policies, however, while a Peace Wing of the party preferred an end to the fighting, even at risk to the Union. An extreme fringe of the Peace Wing even flirted with outright disloyalty. The "Copperheads," as they were called, organized secret orders with such names as Sons of Liberty for purposes that were none too clear and often suspect. They were strongest in states such as Ohio, Indiana, and Illinois, all leavened with native southerners, some of whom were pro-Confederate.

Coercive measures against disloyalty were perhaps as much a boost as a hindrance to Democrats, who took up the cause of civil liberty. Early in the war Lincoln assumed the power to suspend the writ of habeas corpus and subjected "disloyal" persons to martial law—often just on vague suspicion. The Constitution said only that it should be suspended in cases of rebellion or invasion, but congressional leaders argued that Congress alone had authority to act, since the provision fell in Article 1, which deals with the powers of Congress. When Congress, by the Habeas Corpus Act of March 1863, finally authorized the president to suspend the writ, it required officers to report the names of all arrested persons to the nearest district court, and provided that if the grand jury found no indictment, those arrested could be released upon taking an oath of allegiance.

There were probably more than 14,000 arrests made without a writ of habeas corpus. One celebrated case arose in 1863 when Federal soldiers hustled Clement L. Vallandigham out of his home in Dayton, Ohio. Brought before a military commission, Ohio's most prominent Copperhead was condemned to confinement for the duration of the war because he had questioned arbitrary arrests. The muzzling of a political opponent proved such an embarrassment to Lincoln that he commuted the sentence, but only by another irregular device, banishment behind the Confederate lines. Vallandigham eventually found his way to Canada. In 1863 he ran as Democratic candidate for governor *in absentia*, and in 1864 slipped back into the country. He was left alone at Lincoln's order, took part in the Democratic national convention, and ultimately proved more of an embarrassment to the Democrats than to the president.

In the midterm elections of 1862, the Democrats exploited war weariness and resentment of Lincoln's war measures to gain a startling recovery, though not control of Congress. At their 1864 national convention in Chicago the Democrats called for an armistice to be followed by a national convention which would restore the Union. They named Gen. George B. McClellan as their candidate, but McClellan distanced himself from the peace platform by declaring that agreement on Union would have to precede peace.

Radical Republicans, who still regarded Lincoln as soft on treason, trotted out two candidates, first Salmon P. Chase, who failed to get the support of his own state, then John C. Frémont, but too late. Lincoln outmaneuvered them at every turn, and without public announcement of a choice, brought about the vice-presidential nomination of Andrew Johnson, a War Democrat from Tennessee, on the "National Union" ticket, so named to minimize partisanship. As the war dragged on through 1864, with Grant taking heavy losses in Virginia, Lincoln fully expected to lose. Then Admiral Farragut's capture of Mobile in August and Sherman's capture of Atlanta on September 2 turned the tide. McClellan carried only New Jersey, Delaware, and Kentucky, with 21 electoral votes to Lincoln's 212, and 1.8 million popular votes (45 percent) to Lincoln's 2.2 million (55 percent).

CONFEDERATE POLITICS   Unlike Lincoln, Jefferson Davis never had to contest a presidential election. Both Davis and Vice-President Stephens, named first by the Provisional Congress, were elected without opposition in 1861 and began single terms of six years on Washington's Birthday, February 22, 1862. But discontent flourished as things went from bad to worse, and came very close to home in the Richmond bread riot of April 2, 1863, which ended only when Davis himself persuaded the mob to disperse. After the congressional elections of 1863, the second and last in the confederacy, about a third of the legislators were antiadministration. Although parties as such did not figure in the elections, it was noteworthy that many ex-Whigs and other opponents of secession were chosen.

Davis, like Lincoln, had to contend with dissenters. Large pockets of Union loyalists appeared in the German counties of Texas, the hill country of Arkansas, and most of all along the Appalachian spine that reached as far as Alabama and Georgia. Many Unionists followed their states into the Confederacy reluctantly, and were receptive to talk of peace. They were less troublesome to Davis, however, than the states'-rights men who had embraced secession and then guarded states' rights against the Confederacy as zealously as they had against the Union. Georgia under Gov. Joseph E. Brown, and to a lesser degree North Carolina under Gov. Zebulon B. Vance, were strongholds of such sentiment, which prevailed widely elsewhere as well. They challenged, among other things, the legality of conscription, taxes on farm produce, and above all the suspension of habeas corpus. Never mind that Davis, the legal-minded leader of a revolution, never suspended habeas corpus until granted congressional authority on February 27, 1862, and then did so sparingly. Vice-President Alexander Stephens carried on a running battle against

Davis's effort to establish "military despotism," left Richmond to sulk at his Georgia home for eighteen months, and warned the Georgia legislature in 1864, on the eve of Sherman's march, against the "siren song, 'Independence first and liberty afterwards.' " The ultimate failure of the Confederacy has been attributed to many things. One of many ironies was that the fight for slavery suffered from a doctrinaire defense of liberty. Among other things, the Confederacy died of dogma.

THE FALTERING CONFEDERACY

In 1863 the hinge of fate began to close the door on the brief career of the Confederacy. After the Union disaster at Fredericksburg, Lincoln's search for a general turned to one of Burnsides's disgruntled lieutenants, Joseph E. Hooker, whose pugnacity had given him the name of "Fighting Joe." Hooker took over the Army of the Potomac near the end of January. After the appointment, Lincoln wrote his new commander, "there are some things in regard to which, I am not quite satisfied with you." Hooker had been saying the country needed a dictator, and word reached Lincoln. "Only those generals who gain successes can set up dictators," the president wrote. "What I now ask of you is military success, and I will risk the dictatorship." But the risk was not great. Hooker was no more able than Burnside to deliver the goods. He failed the test at Chancellorsville, May 1–5.

CHANCELLORSVILLE With a force of perhaps 130,000, the largest Union army yet gathered, and a brilliant plan, he suffered a loss of control, perhaps a failure of nerve, at the critical juncture. Lee, with perhaps half that number, staged what became a textbook classic of daring and maneuver. Hooker's plan was to leave his base, opposite Fredericksburg, on a sweeping movement upstream across the Rappahannock and Rapidan to flank Lee's position. John N. Sedgwick was to cross below the town for a major diversion with 40,000 men. Lee, however, leaving about 10,000 men at Marye's Heights, pulled his main forces back to meet Hooker. At Chancellorsville, after a preliminary skirmish, Lee divided his army again, sending Jackson with more than half the men on a long march to hit the enemy's exposed right flank.

On May 2, toward evening, Jackson surprised the right flank at the edge of a wooded area called the Wilderness, throwing things into chaos, but the fighting died out in confusion as dark-

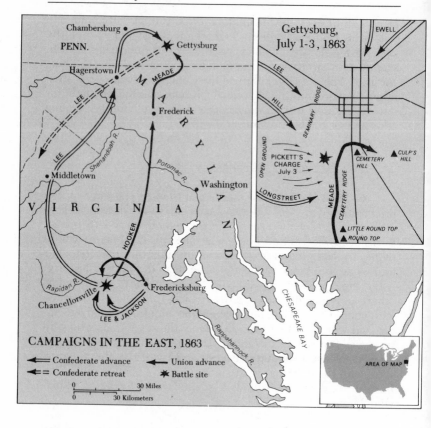

Gettysburg, July 1-3, 1863

CAMPAIGNS IN THE EAST, 1863

Confederate advance — Union advance
Confederate retreat — Battle site

0   30 Miles
0   30 Kilometers

AREA OF MAP

ness fell. The next day, while Jeb Stuart held Hooker at bay, Lee had to turn around and fend off Sedgwick, who had stormed Marye's Heights and advanced on Lee's rear. Lee struck him and counterattacked on May 3–4, after which Sedgwick recrossed the Rappahannock. The following day Hooker did the same, although he was still left in a strong position. It was the peak of Lee's career, but Chancellorsville was his last significant victory. And his costliest: the South suffered some 12,000 casualties and more than 1,600 killed, among them Stonewall Jackson, mistakenly felled by his own men upon his return from a reconnaisance.

VICKSBURG   While Lee held the Federals at bay in the East, they had resumed a torturous advance in the West. Since the previous fall Ulysses Grant had been groping his way toward Vicksburg,

which along with Port Hudson, Louisiana, was one of the last two
Rebel strongholds on the Mississippi. Located on a bluff 200 feet
above the river, Vicksburg had withstood naval attacks and a
downriver expedition led by William T. Sherman, which had
stormed Chickasaw Bluffs north of the city in December. Because the rail lines were vulnerable to hit-and-run attacks, Grant
resolved to use naval supply lines downriver. He positioned his
army about fifteen miles north of the city, but the Delta region
there was laced with bayous which baffled efforts to reach the
goal. At first Grant thought to use these waterways to advantage,
and during the winter he made bold efforts along two routes.
Well to the north, opposite Helena, Arkansas, he blasted a hole
in the levee and floated gunboats and transports through to the
Tallahatchie River. There ensued a strange progress along winding waterways choked with vegetation and covered by over-
hanging branches, where the Union navy stood in danger of
capture by the Confederate army. That effort, and a similar try
up Steele's Bayou farther south, was soon abandoned.

Grant finally gave up the idea of a northern approach. He
crossed over to Louisiana at Milliken's Bend, and while the navy
ran gunboats and transports past the Confederate batteries at

VICKSBURG, 1863

← Union forces   ✸ Battle site

Vicksburg, he moved south to meet them, crossed back, and fetched up on dry ground south of Vicksburg at the end of April. From there Grant adopted a new expedient. He would forget supply lines and live off the country. John C. Pemberton, Confederate commander at Vicksburg, thoroughly baffled, was further confused by two diversions: a feint by General Sherman at Chickasaw Bluffs and a cavalry raid by Col. Benjamin Grierson, who cut a swath through central Mississippi with fewer than 1,000 men and reentered Union lines at Baton Rouge. Grant himself swept eastward on a campaign which Lincoln later called "one of the most brilliant in the world," took Jackson, where he seized or destroyed supplies, then turned westward and on May 18 emerged from the "tunnel" he had entered two weeks before to pin Pemberton's army of 30,000 inside Vicksburg.

GETTYSBURG   The plight of Vicksburg put the Confederate high command in a quandary. Joseph E. Johnston, now in charge of the western forces but with few men under his personal command, would have preferred to focus on the Tennessee front and thereby perhaps force Grant to relax his grip. Robert E. Lee had another idea for a diversion. If he could win a victory on northern soil he might do more than just relieve the pressure at Vicksburg. In June he moved into the Shenandoah Valley and northward across Maryland.

Hooker followed, keeping himself between Lee and Washington, but demoralized by defeat at Chancellorsville and quarrels with Halleck, he turned in his resignation. On June 28 Maj.-Gen. George C. Meade took command. Neither side chose Gettysburg, Pennsylvania, as the site for the climactic battle, but a Confederate party entered the town in search of shoes and encountered units of Union cavalry on June 30. The main forces quickly converged on that point. On July 1 the Confederates pushed the Federals out of the town, but into stronger positions on high ground to the south. Meade hastened reinforcements to his new lines along the heights; on the map these resembled an inverted fishook with Culp's Hill and Cemetery Hill curved around the top, and Cemetery Ridge extended three miles down the shank to Round Top and Little Round Top. On July 2 Lee mounted assaults at both the extreme left and right flanks of Meade's army, but in vain.

On July 3 Lee staked everything on one final assault on the Union center on Cemetery Ridge. Confederate artillery raked the ridge, but with less effect than intended. About 2 P.M. 15,000 men of Gen. George E. Pickett's command emerged from

Harvest of Death. *T. H. O'Sullivan's grim photograph of the dead at Gettysburg. [Library of Congress]*

the woods west of Cemetery Ridge and began their advance across open ground commanded by Union artillery. It was as hopeless as Burnside's assault at Fredericksburg. Only 5,000 of Pickett's men finally reached the ridge, and the few who got within range of hand-to-hand combat were quickly overwhelmed.

With nothing left to do but retreat, on July 4 Lee's dejected army, with about a third of its number gone, began to slog back through a driving rain. They had failed in all their purposes, not the least being to relieve the pressure on Vicksburg. On that same July 4 Pemberton reached the end of his tether and surrendered his entire garrison of 30,000 men, whom Grant paroled and permitted to go home. Four days later the last remaining Confederate stronghold on the Mississippi, Port Hudson, under siege since May by Union forces, gave up. "The father of waters," Lincoln said, "flows unvexed to the sea." The Confederacy was irrevocably split, and had Meade pursued Lee he might have delivered the *coup de grace* before the Rebels could get back across the flooded Potomac.

CHATTANOOGA   The third great Union victory of 1863 occurred in fighting around Chattanooga, the railhead of eastern Tennessee and gateway to northern Georgia. In the late summer Rosecrans's Union army moved southeastward from Murfreesboro, and Bragg pulled out of Chattanooga to gain room for maneuver. Rosecrans took the city on September 9 and then rashly pursued Bragg into Georgia, where his forces met the Confederates at Chickamauga. The battle (September 19–20) had the makings of a Union disaster, since it was one of the few times when the Confederates had a numerical advantage (about 70,000 to 56,000). On the second day Bragg smashed the Federal right, and only the stubborn stand of the left under George H. Thomas (thenceforth "the Rock of Chickamauga") prevented a general rout. The battered Union forces fell back into Chattanooga, while Bragg cut the railroad from the west and held the city virtually under siege from the heights to the south and east.

Rosecrans seemed stunned and apathetic, but Lincoln urged him to hang on: "If we can hold Chattanooga, and East Tennessee, I think rebellion must dwindle and die." Following the Con-

BATTLES NEAR CHATTANOOGA, 1863

Gen. Ulysses S. Grant. [Library of Congress]

federate example the Union command sent Joe Hooker with reinforcements from Virginia, Grant and Sherman with more from the west. Grant, given overall command of the West on October 16, pushed his way into Chattanooga a few days later, forcing open a supply route as he came. He replaced Rosecrans, putting Thomas in command. On November 24 the Federals began to move, with Hooker and Sherman hitting the Confederate flanks at Lookout Mountain and Signal Hill while Thomas created a diversion at the center. Hooker took Lookout Mountain in what was mainly a feat of mountaineering, but Sherman was stalled. On the second day of the battle Grant ordered Thomas forward to positions at the foot of Misssionary Ridge. Successful there, but still exposed, the men spontaneously began to move on up toward the crest 400 to 500 feet above. They might well have been cut up badly, but the Rebels were unable to lower their big guns enough and in the face of thousands swarming up the hill they panicked and fled.

Bragg was unable to get his forces together until they were many miles to the south, and the Battle of Chattanooga was the end of his active career. Jefferson Davis, who had backed him against all censure, reluctantly replaced him with Johnston and called Bragg back to Richmond as an advisor. Soon after the battle the Federals linked up with Burnside, who had taken Knoxville, and proceeded to secure their control of Eastern Tennessee, where the hills were full of Unionists.

Chattanooga had another consequence. If the battle was won by the rush on Missionary Ridge, against orders, the victory nonetheless confirmed the impression of Grant's genius. Lincoln had at last found his general. In March 1864 Grant arrived in Washington to assume the rank of lieutenant-general and a new position as general-in-chief. Halleck became chief-of-staff and continued in his role as channel of communication between the president and commanders in the field. Within the Union armies at least, a modern command system was emerging; the Confederacy never had a unified command.

THE CONFEDERACY'S DEFEAT

The main targets now were Lee's army in Virginia and Johnston's in Georgia. Grant personally would accompany Meade, who retained direct command over the Army of the Potomac; operations in the West were entrusted to Grant's long-time lieutenant, William T. Sherman. As Sherman put it later, "he was to go for Lee, and I was to go for Joe Johnston. That was his plan."

GRANT'S PURSUIT OF LEE   They began to go for both of them in May, while lesser offensives kept the Confederates occupied all across the map. The Army of the Potomac, numbering about 115,000 to Lee's 65,000, moved south across the Rappahannock and the Rapidan into the Wilderness, where Hooker had come to grief in the Battle of Chancellorsville. In the Battle of the Wilderness (May 5–6) the armies fought blindly through the woods, the horror and suffering of the scene heightened by crackling brush fires. Grant's men took heavier casualties than the Confederates, but the Rebels were running out of replacements. Always before, Lee's adversaries had pulled back to nurse their wounds, but Grant slid off to his left and continued his relentless advance, now toward Spotsylvania Court House.

There Lee's advance guard barely arrived in time to stall the movement and the armies settled down for five days of bloody warfare, May 8–12, in which the Federals failed to break the Confederate center, the "Bloody Angle." Before it was over Grant sent word back to Halleck: "I propose to fight it out along this line if it takes all summer." But again Grant slid off to his left, tested Lee's defenses along the North Anna River (May 16–23), and veered off again over the Pamunkey and back to the scenes of McClellan's Peninsula Campaign. There, along the Chickaho-

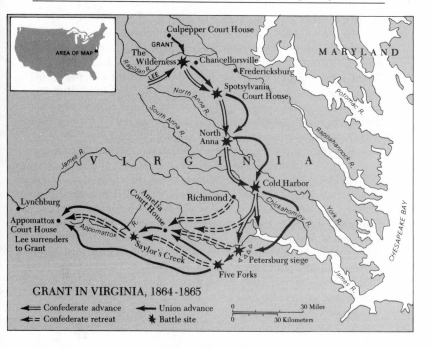

AREA OF MAP

GRANT IN VIRGINIA, 1864-1865

◄══ Confederate advance   ◄─ Union advance
◄═ Confederate retreat   ✹ Battle site

0   30 Miles
0   30 Kilometers

miny, occurred the pitched battle of Cold Harbor (June 1–3).
Battered and again repulsed, Grant cut away yet again. For several days Lee lost sight of the Federals while they crossed the
James on a pontoon bridge and headed for Petersburg, the junction of railroads into Richmond from the south.

Petersburg was thinly held by Confederates under Beauregard, but before Grant could bring up his main force Lee's men
moved into the defenses. Grant dug in for a siege along lines that
extended for twenty-five miles above and below Petersburg. On
July 30 a huge mine exploded in a tunnel under the Confederate
line. In the ensuing Battle of the Crater, the soldiers who were
supposed to exploit the opening milled around aimlessly in the
pit while Rebels shot them like fish in a pond. For nine months
the two armies faced each other down while Grant kept pushing
toward his left flank to break the railroad arteries that were Lee's
lifeline. He would fight it out along *this* line all summer, all autumn, and all winter, generously supplied by Union vessels moving up the James while Lee's forces, beset by hunger, cold, and
desertion, wasted away. Petersburg had become Lee's prison
while disasters piled up for the Confederacy elsewhere.

SHERMAN'S MARCH   When Grant headed south, so did Sherman—toward the railroad hub of Atlanta, with 90,000 men against Joe Johnston's 60,000. Sherman's campaign, like Grant's, developed into a war of maneuver, but without the pitched battles. As Grant kept slipping off to his left, Sherman kept moving to his right, but Johnston was always one step ahead of him—turning up in secure positions along the North Georgia ridges, drawing him farther from his Chattanooga base, harassing his supply lines with Joe Wheeler's cavalry, and keeping his own main force intact. But Johnston's skillful use of Fabian tactics caused an impatient President Davis finally to replace him with the combative but reckless John B. Hood. Three times in eight days Hood lashed out, first at Peachtree Creek (July 20) on the Union center, then at the Battle of Atlanta (July 22) to the east, and Ezra Church (July 28) to the west, each time meeting a bloody rebuff. Sherman at first resorted to a siege of Atlanta, then slid off to the right again, cutting the rail lines below Atlanta. Hood evacuated on September 1, but kept his army intact.

Sherman now laid plans for a march through central Georgia where no organized armies remained. Hood meanwhile had hatched an equally audacious plan. He would cut away to northern Alabama and push on into Tennessee, forcing Sherman into

SHERMAN'S CAMPAIGNS, 1864-1865

William Tecumseh Sherman.
[National Archives]

pursuit. Sherman refused to take the bait, although he did send
Thomas back to Tennessee to keep watch with 30,000 men. So
the curious spectacle unfolded of the main armies moving off in
opposite directions. But it was a measure of the Confederates'
plight that Sherman could cut a swath across Georgia with impunity while Hood was soon outnumbered again. In the Battle of
Franklin (November 30), Hood sent his army across two miles of
open ground. Six waves broke against the Union lines, leaving
the ground strewn with Confederates. Total Rebel casualties
numbered 6,000. With what he had left, Hood dared not attack
Nashville, nor did he dare withdraw for fear of final disintegration. Finally, in the Battle of Nashville (December 15–16),
Thomas broke and scattered what was left of the Confederate
Army of Tennessee. The Confederate front west of the Appalachians had collapsed, leaving only Nathan Bedford Forrest's cavalry and a few other scattered units in the field, mainly around
Mobile.

During all this Sherman was marching through Georgia, pioneering the modern practice of total war against a people's resources and against their will to resist. On November 15, 1864,
he destroyed Atlanta's warehouses and railroad facilities while
spreading fires consumed about a third of the city. The Union
army moved out in four columns over a front twenty to sixty
miles wide, living off the land and destroying any stores or provisions that might serve Confederate forces. Bands of stragglers
and deserters from both armies joined in looting along the flanks,
while Joe Wheeler's cavalry destroyed Rebel stores to keep
them out of enemy hands. When, after a month, Sherman
fetched up near Savannah he had cut a swath of desolation 250

Robert E. Lee. Mathew Brady took this photograph in Richmond eleven days after Lee's surrender at Appomattox. [Library of Congress]

miles long. On December 21 Sherman marched into Savannah, and three days later Lincoln got a dispatch tendering the city as a Christmas gift.

Pushing across the river into that "hell-hole of secession," South Carolina, his men wrought even greater destruction. More than a dozen towns were consigned to the flames in whole or part, including the state capital of Columbia, captured February 17. On the day Sherman entered Columbia, Charleston's defenders abandoned the city and pulled north to join an army which Joseph E. Johnston was desperately pulling together. Johnston was able to mount one final attack on Sherman's left wing at Bentonville (March 19–20), but that was his last major battle.

APPOMATTOX During this final season of the Confederacy, Grant kept pushing, probing, and battering the Petersburg defenses. Raids by Philip H. Sheridan had desolated Lee's breadbasket in the Shenandoah Valley, and winter left his men on short rations. News of Sherman's progress added to the gloom and the impulse to desert. By March the Confederate lines had thinned out to about 1,000 men per mile. Lee began to lay plans to escape and join Johnston in North Carolina. At Five Forks (April 1, 1865) Grant finally cut the last rail line to Petersburg, and the next day Lee abandoned Richmond and Petersburg in a desperate flight toward Lynchburg and rails south. President Davis gathered what archives and treasure he could and made it out by train ahead of the advancing Federals, only to be captured on May 10 at Irwinton, Georgia, by James H. Wilson's Union cavalry, which had been ranging across Mississippi and Alabama.

By then the Confederacy was already dead. Lee moved out with Grant in hot pursuit, and soon found his escape route cut by forces under Sheridan. On April 9 (Palm Sunday) he met Grant in the parlor of the McLean home at Appomattox to tender his surrender, four years to the day after Davis and his cabinet decided to attack Fort Sumter. Grant, at Lee's request, let the Rebel officers keep their side arms and permitted soldiers to keep private horses and mules. On April 18, Johnston surrendered to Sherman at the Bennett house near what would soon be the thriving tobacco town of Durham. On May 4 at Citronelle, Alabama, General Taylor surrendered the remaining forces east of the Mississippi to General Canby, leaving only the forces under Edmund Kirby Smith west of the river. On May 26 Kirby Smith capitulated to Canby at New Orleans.

In Charleston, the Confederate "holy of holies," the first occupation troops to arrive in February were black units, including the Third and Fourth South Carolina Regiments, some of whom had been among the city's slaves in 1860. It was little more than four years since the secession convention had met at Institution Hall, not quite five years since the disruption of the Democratic party in the same building. Soon after the occupation the War Department began plans for a massive celebration at Fort Sumter on the fourth anniversary of its fall. On April 14, 1865, the fort filled with dignitaries, including William Lloyd Garrison and Henry Ward Beecher, the orator of the day, and a few hundred black soldiers brought out by the *Planter,* the boat on which Capt. Robert Smalls had fled slavery two years before. At noon Major Anderson ran up the flag he had lowered just four years previously, while gaily decorated ships and all the forts in the harbor sounded a salute.

The same day President Lincoln spent the afternoon discussing postwar policy with his cabinet. That night Mr. and Mrs. Lincoln went to the theater.

FURTHER READING

The most comprehensive treatment of the Civil War period is Allan Nevins's *The War for the Union* (4 vols.; 1959–1971). Also good for an overview are James G. Randall and David Donald's *The Civil War and Reconstruction* (1969) and James M. McPherson's *Ordeal by Fire: The Civil War and Reconstruction* (1982). The many military histories by

Bruce Catton are extremely readable; begin with *This Hallowed Ground* (1956).°

More interpretative treatments are William L. Barney's *Flawed Victory* (1975)° and Peter Prish's *The American Civil War* (1975). Principal themes of the period are discussed in David Donald (ed.), *Why the North Won the War* (1960),° Irwin Unger's *Essays on the Civil War and Reconstruction* (1970), and Eric Foner's *Politics and Ideology in the Age of the Civil War* (1980).°

The Civil War period is also blessed with a number of firsthand accounts of personal experiences. Among the better are C. Vann Woodward (ed.), *Mary Chestnutt's Civil War* (1981),° and Robert M. Myers (ed.), *The Children of Pride* (1972).° Stephen Crane's *The Red Badge of Courage* (1895)° remains a literary classic of the conflict. Also revealing are MacKinley Kantor's *Andersonville* (1955)° and Michael Shaara's *The Killer Angels* (1969),° about Gettysburg. The life of the common soldier is well treated by Bell I. Wiley in *The Life of Johnny Reb* (1943)° and *The Life of Billy Yank* (1952).° The values held by the soldiers on both sides are explored in Michael Barton's *Good Men: The Character of Civil War Soldiers* (1981).

For emphasis on the South, turn first to Emory M. Thomas's *The Confederate Nation* (1979).° Older, but still reliable, is Clement Eaton's *A History of the Southern Confederacy* (1954). More interpretive is Emory M. Thomas's *The Confederacy as a Revolutionary Experience* (1971),° which looks at the problems of states'-rights doctrine. Also helpful is Henry S. Commager's *The Defeat of the Confederacy* (1964). Stress on the role of Confederate leadership is provided in E. M. Coulter's *The Confederate States of America, 1861–65* (1950), and Frank VanDiver's *Their Tattered Flags* (1965). The most recent work on the president of the Confederacy is Clement Eaton's *Jefferson Davis* (1977). Thomas L. Connelly and Archer Jones also deal with Davis in *The Politics of Command* (1973). Rudolph Von Abele's *Alexander Stephens* (1946) is good for the interpretation of Confederate politics. Also see Thomas B. Alexander and Richard E. Beringer's *The Anatomy of the Confederate Congress* (1972). Background on problems of supply can be gleaned from Charles B. Dew's *Ironmaker to the Confederacy* (1966) and Frank VanDiver's *Ploughshares into Swords* (1952).

Shelby Foote's *The Civil War* (3 vols.; 1958–1973) gives the most thorough treatment of the military conflict from the southern perspective. The war in the Eastern Theater is handled in the several biographies of Robert E. Lee, among them Douglass S. Freeman's *Lee: A Biography* (4 vols.; 1934–1935) and Thomas L. Connelly's *Marble Man* (1971).° The war in the West is the subject of Thomas L. Connelly's *Army of the Heartland: The Army of Tennessee, 1861–62* (1967) and *Autumn of Glory: The Army of Tennessee, 1862–65* (1971). Studies of other generals include Hal Bridges's *Lee's Maverick General: Daniel Harvey Hill* (1962), Frank VanDiver's *Mighty Stonewall* (1957), Grady McWhiney's *Braxton Bragg and the Confederate Defeat* (1969), Robert L. Kerby's *Kirby-*

° These books are available in paperback editions.

Smith's Confederacy (1972), and Richard M. Murray's *John Bell Hood and the War for Southern Independence* (1982). A cultural interpretation of Confederate military behavior is Grady McWhiney's *Attack and Die* (1982).

Treatments of northern politics during the war include David Donald's *Charles Sumner and the Rights of Man* (1971),° Harold M. Hyman's *A More Perfect Union* (1973),° and Allan G. Bogue's *The Earnest Men: Republicans of the Civil War Senate* (1981). Diplomatic relations with Europe are covered in Glyndon G. Van Deusen's *William Henry Seward* (1967) and Martin B. Duberman's *Charles Francis Adams* (1961).°

The central political figure, Abraham Lincoln, is the subject of many books. Good single-volume biographies are Stephen B. Oates's *With Malice toward None* (1979)° and Benjamin P. Thomas's *Abraham Lincoln* (1952). Carl Sandburg's *Lincoln: The War Years* (4 vols.; 1939)° gives the fullest treatment of his presidential career. Varying interpretations of Lincoln can be found in David Donald's *Lincoln Reconsidered* (1956)° and Richard N. Current's *The Lincoln Nobody Knows* (1958). Also valuable is the chapter on Lincoln in Daniel Walker Howe's *The Political Culture of the American Whigs* (1979).

The emphasis is also on Lincoln in a number of works dealing with northern military strategy. Most voluminous is Kenneth P. Williams's *Lincoln Finds a General* (5 vols.; 1949–1959). A fine interpretive work is T. Harry Williams's *Lincoln and His Generals* (1952). Biographical studies of the northern military leaders include T. Harry Williams's *McClellan, Sherman and Grant* (1962), Lloyd Lewis's *Sherman* (1932), and William S. McFeely's *Grant: A Biography* (1981).° A review of the careers of all the Eastern Theater commanders appears in Bruce Catton's *The Army of the Potomac* (3 vols.; 1951–1954). Naval operations are detailed in Virgil C. Jones's *The Civil War at Sea* (3 vols.; 1960–1962), and John Niven's *Gideon Welles: Lincoln's Secretary of the Navy* (1973).

Life behind the battle lines is the topic of several works. Emerson D. Fite's *Social and Industrial Conditions in the North during the Civil War* (1910) remains the standard introduction. Political dissent is handled in Frank L. Klement's *The Copperheads in the Middle West* (1960). Paul C. Gates treats the disruption of farming in *Agriculture and the Civil War* (1965). Mary E. Massey's *Bonnet Brigades* (1966) examines the contributions of women. Adrian Cook's *The Armies of the Streets* (1974) analyzes the antidraft riots of New York City, and Eugene C. Murdock's *One Million Men* (1971) examines reaction to the draft in general. The views of northern intellectuals is the subject of George Frederickson's *The Inner Civil War* (1965).°

How the emancipated slave fared during the war has drawn recent scholarly attention. The standard overview is Benjamin Quarles's *The Negro in the Civil War* (1953).° The career of the black soldier is found in Dudley T. Cornish's *The Sable Arm* (1966). Willie Lee Rose's *Rehearsal for Reconstruction: The Port Royal Experiment* (1964)° and Louis Gerteis's *From Contraband to Freedman: Federal Policy toward Southern Blacks, 1861–1865* (1973), both trace the federal government's policies. For Lincoln's viewpoint, see Lawanda Cox's *Lincoln and Black Freedom:*

A Study in Presidential Leadership (1981). The Confederate viewpoint is handled in Robert F. Durden's *The Gray and the Black* (1972). Peter Kolchin's *First Freedom* (1972) examines what blacks themselves thought, as does Leon F. Litwack in the early chapters of *Been in the Storm So Long* (1979).°

18 ✑

RECONSTRUCTION:
NORTH AND SOUTH

THE WAR'S AFTERMATH

In the spring of 1865 the weary war was over, a war whose cost in casualties was greater than all foreign wars down to World War II, and in proportion to population, greater than all other American wars down to the present day. At this frightful cost some old and tenacious issues were finally resolved. As the historian David Potter so graphically put it, "slavery was dead, secession was dead, and six hundred thousand men were dead." American nationalism emerged triumphant, its victory ratified in 1869 when the Supreme Court stamped its approval on the decision of arms. In the case of *Texas v. White*, the Court firmly denied any legality to Rebel state governments while it affirmed the existence of "an indestructible Union, composed of indestructible states." Pursued at first to preserve that Union, the war had turned into a crusade for the total abolition of chattel slavery. Before the end of 1865 all but two border states had voted emancipation. Ratification of the Thirteenth Amendment in December 1865 ended the remnants of slavery in Delaware and Kentucky and overrode any lingering doubts about the legitimacy of Lincoln's Emancipation Proclamation.

DEVELOPMENT IN THE NORTH   The war had been, in the words of Charles and Mary Beard, a Second American Revolution. It was more truly a social revolution than the War of Independence, for it reduced the once-dominant power of planter agrarians in the national councils and elevated that of the "captains of industry."

It is easy to exaggerate the profundity of this change, but government did become subtly more friendly to businessmen and unfriendly to those who would probe into their activities. The Republican Congress had delivered on the major platform promises of 1860, which had cemented the allegiance of northeastern businessmen and western farmers to the party of free labor.

In the absence of southern members, Congress had passed the Morrill Tariff of 1861 which, with later revisions, brought the average level of duties up to about double what it had been on the eve of conflict. The National Banking Act of 1863, reframed in 1864, created a uniform system of banking and banknote currency, and helped to finance the war. Under laws of 1862 and 1864 Congress guaranteed that the first transcontinental railroad would run along a north-central route from Omaha to Sacramento, and donated public lands and public bonds to ensure its financing. In the Homestead Act of 1862, moreover, Congress voted free homesteads of 160 acres to actual settlers who occupied the land for five years, and in the Morrill Land Grant Act of the same year conveyed to each state 30,000 acres of public land per member of Congress from the state, the proceeds from the sale of which went to colleges of "agriculture and mechanic arts."

DEVASTATION IN THE SOUTH   The South, where most of the fighting had occurred, offered a sharp contrast to the victorious North. Along the path of the army led by General Sherman, Carl Schurz reported in 1866, the countryside still "looked for many miles like a broad black streak of ruin and desolation." Columbia, South Carolina, said another observer, was "a wilderness of ruins," Charleston a place of "vacant houses, of widowed women, of rotting wharves, of deserted warehouses, of weed-wild gardens, of miles of grass-grown streets, of acres of pitiful and voiceless barrenness." In the valley of the Tennessee, the British visitor Robert Somers reported: "The trail of war is visible . . . in burnt-up gin houses, ruined bridges, mills, and factories." The border states of Missouri and Kentucky had gone through a guerrilla war which lapsed into postwar anarchy perpetrated by marauding bands of bushwhackers turned bank robbers, such as the notorious Younger brothers, Coleman and Jim, and the even more notorious James boys, Frank and Jesse.

Property values had collapsed. Confederate bonds and money became worthless, railroads and rolling stock were damaged or destroyed. Stores of cotton which had escaped destruction were seized as Confederate property or in forfeit of federal taxes. Emancipation at one stroke wiped out perhaps $4 billion in-

Virginia's Capitol, designed by Thomas Jefferson, looms over the ruins of Richmond, Virginia, April 1865. [Library of Congress]

vested in human flesh and left the labor system in disarray. The great age of expansion in the cotton market was over. Not until 1879 would the cotton crop again equal the record crop of 1860; tobacco production did not regain its prewar level until 1880; the sugar crop of Louisiana not until 1893; and the old rice industry of the Tidewater and the hemp industry of the Kentucky Blue Grass never regained their prewar status.

LEGALLY FREE, SOCIALLY BOUND   The newly freed slaves suffered most of all. According to Frederick Douglass, the black abolitionist, the former bondsman "was free from the individual master but a slave of society. He had neither money, property, nor friends. He was free from the old plantation, but he had nothing but the dusty road under his feet. He was free from the old quarter that once gave him shelter, but a slave to the rains of summer and the frosts of winter. He was turned loose, naked, hungry, and destitute to the open sky."

According to a former Confederate general, recently freed blacks had "nothing but freedom." [Library of Congress]

Even dedicated abolitionists in large part shrank from the measures of land reform that might have given the freedmen more self-support and independence. Citizenship and legal rights were one thing, wholesale confiscation and land distribution quite another. Instead of land or material help the freedmen more often got what the historian Leon Litwack called "the moral and economic injunctions and shibboleths that were standard fare in nineteenth-century American society: success came ultimately to the hard-working, the sober, the honest, and the educated, to those individuals who engaged in 'faithful industry,' practiced 'judicious economy,' cultivated habits of thrift and temperance, made their homes 'models of neatness,' and led moral, virtuous, Christian lives."

In 1865 Rep. George Julian of Indiana and Sen. Charles Sumner of Massachusetts proposed to give freedmen forty-acre homesteads carved out of Rebel lands taken under the Confiscation Act of 1862. But their plan for outright grants was replaced by a program of rentals since, under the law, confiscation was effective only for the lifetime of the offender. Discussions of land distribution, however, fueled rumors that freedmen would get "forty acres and a mule," a slogan that swept the South at the end of the war. Its source remains unknown, but the aspirations which gave rise to it are clear enough. As one black man in Mississippi put it: "Gib us our own land and we take care ourselves; but widout land, de ole massas can hire us or starve us, as dey please." More lands were seized as "abandoned lands" under an act of 1864, and for default on the direct taxes which Congress levied in 1861 and 1862, than under the Confiscation Act. The most conspicuous example of confiscation was the estate of Robert E. Lee and the Custis family, which became Arlington National Cemetery, but larger amounts were taken in the South Carolina Sea Islands and elsewhere. Some of these lands were sold to freedmen, some to Yankee speculators.

THE FREEDMEN'S BUREAU On March 3, 1865, Congress set up within the War Department the Bureau of Refugees, Freedmen, and Abandoned Lands, to provide "such issues of provisions, clothing, and fuel" as might be needed to relieve "destitute and suffering refugees and freedmen and their wives and children." The Freedmen's Bureau would also take over abandoned and confiscated land for rental in forty-acre tracts to "loyal refugees and freedmen," who might buy the land at a fair price within three years. But the amount of such lands was limited. Under Gen. Oliver O. Howard as commissioner, and assistant commis-

Sketch of a primary school set up by the Freedmen's Bureau, Vicksburg, Mississippi, 1866. [The Historic New Orleans Collection]

sioners in each state of the former Confederacy, agents were entrusted with negotiating labor contracts (something new for both freedmen and planters), providing medical care, and setting up schools, often in cooperation with northern agencies like the American Missionary Association and the Freedmen's Aid Society. The bureau had its own courts to deal with labor disputes and land titles, and its agents were further authorized to supervise trials involving Negroes in other courts.

This was as far as Congress would go. Beyond such temporary measures of relief, no program of reconstruction ever incorporated much more than constitutional and legal rights for freedmen. These were important in themselves, of course, but the extent to which even these should go was very uncertain, to be settled more by the course of events than by any clear-cut commitment to equality.

THE BATTLE OVER RECONSTRUCTION

The problem of reconstruction arose first at the very beginning of the Civil War, when the western counties of Virginia refused to go along with secession. In 1861 a loyal state government of Virginia was proclaimed at Wheeling and this government in turn consented to the formation of a new state called West Virginia, duly if irregularly admitted to the Union in 1863. The loyal government of Virginia under Gov. Francis H. Pierpont then carried on from Alexandria, its reach limited to that part of the state which the Union controlled. As Union forces advanced into the South, Lincoln in 1862 named military governors for Tennessee, Arkansas, and Louisiana. By the end of the following year he had formulated a plan for regular governments in those states and any others that might qualify.

LINCOLN'S PLAN AND CONGRESS'S RESPONSE   Acting under his pardon power, President Lincoln issued on December 8, 1863, a Proclamation of Amnesty and Reconstruction under which any Rebel state could form a Union government whenever a number equal to 10 percent of those who had voted in 1860 took an oath of allegiance to the Constitution and Union and received a presidential pardon. Participants also had to swear support for laws and proclamations dealing with emancipation. Excluded from the pardon, however, were certain groups: civil and diplomatic officers of the Confederacy; high officers of the Confederate army and navy; judges, congressmen, and military officers of the United States who had left their posts to aid the rebellion; and those accused of failure to treat captured Negro soldiers and their officers as prisoners of war.

Under this plan loyal governments appeared in Tennessee, Arkansas, and Louisiana, but Congress recognized them neither by representation nor in counting the electoral votes of 1864. In the absence of any specific provisions for reconstruction in the Constitution, there was disagreement as to where authority properly rested. Lincoln claimed the right to direct reconstruction under Article II, Section 2, which set forth the presidential pardon power, and also under Article IV, Section 4, which imposed an obligation on the United States to guarantee each state a republican form of government. Republican congressmen, however, argued that Article IV, Section 4, implied a power of Congress to act. The first congressional plan for reconstruction appeared in the Wade-Davis Bill, sponsored by Sen. Benjamin Wade of Ohio and Rep. Henry Winter Davis of Maryland, which proposed much more stringent requirements than Lincoln had. In contrast to Lincoln's 10 percent plan, the Wade-Davis Bill required that a majority of white male citizens declare their allegiance and that only those who could take an "ironclad" oath (required of federal officials since 1862) attesting to their *past* loyalty could vote or serve in the state constitutional conventions. The conventions, moreover, would have to abolish slavery, exclude from political rights high-ranking civil and military officers of the Confederacy, and repudiate debts incurred "under the sanction of the usurping power."

Passed during the closing day of the session, the bill was subjected to a pocket veto by Lincoln, who refused to sign it but issued an artful statement that he would accept any state which preferred to present itself under the congressional plan. The sponsors responded by issuing to the newspaper the Wade-Davis Manifesto, which accused the president, among other sins, of usurping power and attempting to use readmitted states to ensure his reelection.

Lincoln's last public words on reconstruction came in his last public address, on April 11, 1865. Speaking from the White House balcony, he pronounced the theoretical question of whether the Confederate states were in the Union "bad as the basis of a controversy, and good for nothing at all—a mere pernicious abstraction." These states were simply "out of their proper practical relation with the Union," and the object was to get them "into their proper practical relation." It would be easier to do this by merely ignoring the abstract issue: "Finding themselves safely at home, it would be utterly immaterial whether they had been abroad." At a cabinet meeting on April 14, Lincoln proposed to get state governments in operation before Congress met in December. Secretary Gideon Welles later reported him to have said: "There were men in Congress who, if their motives were good, were nevertheless impracticable, and who possessed feelings of hate and vindictiveness in which he did not sympathize and could not participate." He wanted "no persecution, no bloody work."

THE ASSASSINATION OF LINCOLN   That evening Lincoln went to Ford's Theater and his rendezvous with death. Shot by John Wilkes Booth, a crazed actor who thought he was doing something for the South, the president died the next morning in a room across the street. Accomplices had also targeted Vice-President Johnson and Secretary of State Seward. Seward and four others, including his son, were victims of severe but not fatal stab wounds. Johnson escaped injury, however, because his chosen assassin got cold feet and wound up in the barroom of Johnson's hotel. Had Johnson been murdered, the presidency would have gone to a man whose name is virtually unknown today: Lafayette Sabine Foster, president pro tem of the Senate, a moderate Republican from Connecticut.

Martyred in the hour of victory, Lincoln entered into the national mythology even while the funeral train took its mournful burden north to New York and westward home to Springfield. The nation extracted a full measure of vengeance from the conspirators. Pursued into Virginia, Booth was trapped and shot in a burning barn. Three collaborators were brought to trial by a military commission and hanged, along with Mrs. Mary Surratt, at whose boarding house they had plotted. Against her the court had no credible evidence of complicity. Three others got life sentences, including a Maryland doctor who set the leg Booth had broken when he jumped to the stage. A stagehand at Ford's Theater got six years. All were eventually pardoned by President Johnson, except one who died in prison. The doctor achieved lasting fame by making common a once obscure expression. His name was Mudd. Apart from those cases, however, there was only one other execution in the aftermath of war: Henry Wirz, who commanded the infamous prison at Andersonville, Georgia, where Union prisoners were probably more the victims of war conditions than of deliberate cruelty.

JOHNSON'S PLAN   Lincoln's death suddenly elevated to the White House Andrew Johnson of Tennessee, a man whose state was still in legal limbo and whose party affiliation was unclear. He was a War Democrat who had been put on the Union ticket in 1864 as a gesture of unity. Of humble origins like Lincoln, Johnson had moved as a youth from his birthplace in Raleigh, North Carolina, to Greeneville, Tennessee, where he became proprietor of a moderately prosperous tailor shop. Self-educated with the help of his wife, he had made himself into an effective orator of the rough-and-tumble school, and had become an advocate of the yeomanry against the privileges of the aristocrats. He was one of the few southern men who championed a homestead act. He had served as mayor, congressman, governor, and senator, then as military governor of Tennessee before he became vice-president.

Andrew Johnson. [Library of Congress]

Some of the most advanced Radicals at first thought Johnson, unlike Lincoln, to be one of them—an illusion created by Johnson's gift for strong language. "Treason is a crime and must be punished," he had said. "Treason must be made infamous and traitors must be impoverished." Ben Wade was carried away with admiration. "Johnson, we have faith in you," he said. "By the gods, there will be no trouble now in running this government." But Wade would soon find him as untrustworthy as Lincoln, if for different reasons. Johnson's very loyalty to the Union sprang from a strict adherence to the Constitution. Given to dogmatic abstractions which were alien to Lincoln's temperament, he nevertheless arrived by a different route at similar objectives. The states should be brought back into their proper relation to the Union not by ignoring as a pernicious abstraction the theoretical question of their status, but because the states and the Union were indestructible. And like many other whites, he found it hard to accept the growing Radical movement toward suffrage for blacks. By May he was saying "there is no such thing as reconstruction. Those States have not gone out of the Union. Therefore reconstruction is unnecessary."

Johnson's plan of Reconstruction thus closely resembled Lincoln's. A new Proclamation of Amnesty (May 29, 1865) added to those Lincoln excluded from pardon everybody with taxable property worth more than $20,000. These were the people Johnson believed had led the South into secession. But special applications for pardon might be made by those in the excluded groups, and before the year was out Johnson had issued some 13,000 such pardons. In every case Johnson ruled that pardon, whether by general amnesty or special clemency, restored one's property rights in land. He defined as "confiscated" only lands already sold under court decree. This included lands set aside by General Sherman's expansive Special Field Order No. 15, which had allocated for the exclusive use of freed Negroes a coastal strip thirty miles wide from Charleston south to the St. John's River in Florida.

Johnson's rulings nipped in the bud an experiment in land distribution that had barely begun. More than seventy years later one Thomas Hall, born a slave in Orange County, North Carolina, spoke bluntly of his dashed hopes: "Lincoln got the praise for freeing us, but did he do it? He give us freedom without giving us any chance to live to ourselves and we still had to depend on the southern white man for work, food and clothing, and he held us through our necessity and want in a state of servitude but little better than slavery." Later, a South Carolina Land Commission, established by the Radical state government in 1869, distributed lands to more than 5,000 black families. One black community in the upcountry, Promised Land, still retained its identity more than a century later, an obscure reminder of what might have been.

On the same day that Johnson announced his amnesty, he issued another proclamation which applied to his native state of North Carolina, and within six more weeks came further edicts for the other Rebel states not already organized by Lincoln. In each a native Unionist became provisional governor with authority to call a convention elected by loyal voters. Lincoln's 10 percent requirement was omitted. Johnson called upon the conventions to invalidate the secession ordinances, abolish slavery, and repudiate all debts incurred to aid the Confederacy. Each state, moreover, was to ratify the Thirteenth Amendment. Lincoln had privately advised the governor of Louisiana to consider a grant of suffrage to some blacks, "the very intelligent and those who have fought gallantly in our ranks." In his final public address he publicly endorsed a limited black suffrage. Johnson repeated Lincoln's advice. He reminded the provisional governor of Mississippi, for example, that the state conventions might "with perfect safety" extend suffrage to blacks with education or with military service so as to "disarm the adversary"—the adversary being "radicals who are wild upon Negro franchise."

The state conventions for the most part met Johnson's requirements, although South Carolina and Mississippi did not repudiate their debt and the new Mississippi legislature refused to ratify the Thirteenth Amendment. Presidential agents sent south to observe and report back for the most part echoed General Grant's finding after a two-month tour: "I am satisfied that the mass of thinking men of the south accept the present situation of affairs in good faith." But Carl Schurz of Missouri found "an *utter absence of national feeling* . . . and a desire to preserve slavery . . . as much and as long as possible." The discrepancy between the two reports is perhaps only apparent: southern whites accepted the situation because they thought so little had changed after all. Emboldened by Johnson's indulgence they ignored his counsels of expediency. Suggestions of Negro suffrage were scarcely raised in the conventions, and promptly squelched when they were.

SOUTHERN INTRANSIGENCE When Congress met in December, for the first time since the end of the war, it had only to accept the accomplished fact that state governments were functioning in the South. But there was the rub. Southern voters had acted with extreme disregard of northern feelings. Among the new members presenting themselves were Georgia's Alexander H. Stephens, late vice-president of the Confederacy, now claiming a seat in the Senate, four Confederate generals, eight colonels, six cabinet members, and a host of lesser Rebels. That many of them had counseled delay in secession, like Stephens, or actually opposed it until it happened, made little difference given the temper of the times. The Congress forthwith excluded from the roll call and denied seats to all members from the eleven former Confederate states. It was too much to expect, after four bloody years, that Unionists would welcome Rebels like prodigal sons.

Furthermore, the action of southern legislatures in passing repressive Black Codes seemed to confirm Schurz's view that they intended to preserve slavery as nearly as possible. The codes extended to blacks certain rights they had not hitherto enjoyed, but universally set them aside as a separate caste subject to special restraints. Details varied from state to state, but some provisions were common. Existing marriages, including common-law marriages, were recognized, and testimony of Negroes was accepted in cases involving Negroes—in six states in all cases. Blacks could hold property. They could sue and be sued in the courts. On the other hand Negroes could not own farm lands in Mississippi or city lots in South Carolina. In some states they could not carry firearms without a license to do so.

The codes' labor provisions seemed to confirm the worst suspi-

Slavery Is Dead (?) *Thomas Nast's cartoon suggested that, in 1866, slavery was only legally dead.* [Harper's Weekly]

cions. Blacks were required to enter into annual labor contracts, with provision for punishment in case of violation. Dependent children were subject to compulsory apprenticeship and corporal punishment by masters. Vagrants were punished with severe fines and could be sold into private service if unable to pay. To many people it indeed seemed that slavery was on the way back in another guise. The new Mississippi penal code virtually said so: "All penal and criminal laws now in force describing the mode of punishment of crimes and misdemeanors committed by slaves, free negroes, or mulattoes are hereby re-enacted, and decreed to be in full force against all freedmen, free negroes and mulattoes."

Faced with such evidence of southern intransigence, moderate Republicans drifted more and more toward Radical views. Having excluded southern members, the new Congress set up a Joint Committee on Reconstruction, with nine members from the House and six from the Senate, to gather evidence and submit proposals. Headed by the moderate Sen. William Pitt Fessenden, the committee fell under greater Radical influence as a parade of witnesses testified to the Rebels' impenitence. Initiative on the committee fell to determined Radicals who knew what they wanted: Ben Wade of Ohio, George W. Julian of Indiana, Henry Wilson of Massachusetts, Zachary Chandler of Michigan, James M. Ashley of Ohio—and most conspicuously of all, Thaddeus Stevens of Pennsylvania and Charles Sumner of Massachusetts.

THE RADICALS Their motivations were mixed, and perhaps little purpose is served in attempting to sort them out. Purity of motive is rare in an imperfect world. Most Radicals had been connected with the antislavery cause. While one could be hostile to both slavery and blacks, many whites approached the question of Negro rights with a humanitarian impulse. Few could escape the bitterness bred by the long and bloody war, however, or remain unaware of the partisan advantage that would come to the Republican party from Negro suffrage. But the party of Union and freedom, after all, could best guarantee the fruits of victory, they reasoned, and Negro suffrage could best guarantee Negro rights.

The growing conflict of opinion brought about an inversion in constitutional reasoning. Secessionists—and Johnson—were now arguing that their states had remained in the Union, and some Radicals were contriving arguments that they had left the Union after all. Rep. Thaddeus Stevens spun out a theory that the Confederate states were now conquered provinces, subject to the absolute will of the victors. Sen. Charles Sumner advanced a

Two leading Radicals: Sen. Charles Sumner (left) and Rep. Thaddeus Stevens. [Library of Congress; National Archives]

thesis that the southern states, by their pretended acts of secession, had in effect committed suicide and reverted to the status of unorganized territories subject to the will of Congress. But few ever took such ideas seriously. Republicans converged instead on the "forfeited rights theory" first advanced by Rep. Samuel Shellabarger of Ohio and later embodied in the report of the Joint Committee on Reconstruction. This theory held that the states as entities continued to exist, but by the acts of secession and war had forfeited "all civil and political rights under the constitution." And Congress was the proper authority to determine conditions under which such rights might be restored.

JOHNSON'S BATTLE WITH CONGRESS   A long year of political battling remained, however, before this idea triumphed. Radical views had gained a majority in Congress, if one not yet large enough to overide presidential vetoes. But the critical year 1866 saw the gradual waning of Johnson's power and influence; much of this was self-induced, for he betrayed as much addiction to "pernicious abstraction" as any Radical. Johnson first challenged Congress in February, when he vetoed a bill to extend the life of the Freedmen's Bureau. The measure, he said, assumed that wartime conditions still existed, whereas the country had returned "to a state of peace and industry." No longer valid as a war measure, the bill violated the Constitution in several ways. It made the federal government responsible for the care of indigents. It was passed by a Congress in which eleven states were denied seats. And it used vague language in defining the "civil rights and immunities" of Negroes. The Congress soon moved to correct that particular defect, but for the time being Johnson's prestige remained sufficiently intact that the Senate upheld his veto.

Three days after the veto, however, Johnson undermined his already weakening prestige with a gross assault on Radical leaders during an impromptu speech on Washington's Birthday. The Joint Committee on Reconstruction, he said, was "an irresponsible central directory" which had repudiated the principle of an indestructible Union and accepted the legality of secession by entertaining conquered-province and state-suicide theories. From that point forward moderate Republicans backed away from a president who had opened himself to counterattack. He was "an alien enemy of a foreign state," Stevens declared. He was "an insolent drunken brute," Sumner asserted—and Johnson was open to the charge because of an incident at his vice-presidential inauguration. Weakened by illness at the time, he had taken a belt of brandy to get him through the ceremony and, under the influence of fever and alcohol, had become incoherent.

In mid-March 1866 Congress passed the Civil Rights Act, which Sen. Lyman Trumbull of Illinois had introduced along with the Freedmen's Bureau Bill. A response to the Black Codes, this bill declared that "all persons born in the United States and not subject to any foreign power, excluding Indians not taxed," were citizens entitled to "full and equal benefit of all laws." The grant of citizenship to native-born blacks, Johnson fulminated, went beyond anything formerly held to be within the scope of federal power. It would, moreover, "foment discord among the races." This time, on April 9, 1866, Congress overrode the presidential veto. On July 16 it enacted a revised Bureau Bill, again overriding a veto. From that point on Johnson steadily lost ground.

THE FOURTEENTH AMENDMENT   To remove all doubt about the constitutionality of the new Civil Rights Act, which was justified as implementing freedom under the Thirteenth Amendment, the Joint Committee recommended a new amendment which passed Congress on June 16, 1866, and was ratified by July 28, 1868. The Fourteenth Amendment, however, went far beyond the Civil Rights Act. It merits close scrutiny because of its broad impact on subsequent laws and litigation. In the first section it did four things: it reaffirmed state and federal citizenship for persons born or naturalized in the United States, it forbade any *state* (the word "state" was important in later litigation) to abridge the "privileges and immunities" of citizens; to deprive any *person* (again an important term) of life, liberty, or property without "due process of law"; or to deny any person "the equal protection of the laws." The last three of these clauses have been the subject of long and involved lawsuits resulting in applications not widely, if at all, foreseen at the time. The "due process clause" has come in the twentieth century to mean that state as well as federal power is subject to the Bill of Rights, and the "due process clause" has been used to protect corporations, as legal "persons," from "unreasonable" regulation by the states. Other provisions of the amendment had less far-reaching effect. Section 4 specified that the debt of the United States "shall not be questioned," but declared "illegal and void" all debts contracted in aid of the rebellion. Section 5 specified the power of Congress to pass laws enforcing the amendment.

Johnson's home state was among the first to ratify. In Tennessee, which had harbored probably more Unionists than any other Confederate state, the government had fallen under Radical control. Gov. W. G. "Parson" Brownlow, in reporting the results to the secretary of the Senate, added: "Give my respects to the dead dog of the White House." His words afford a fair sample of the growing acrimony on both sides of the reconstruction debates. In May and July bloody race riots in Memphis and New Orleans added fuel to the flames. Both incidents amounted to indiscriminate massacres of blacks by local police and white mobs. The carnage, Radicals argued, was the natural fruit of Johnson's policy. "Witness Memphis, witness New Orleans," Sumner cried. "Who can doubt that the President is the author of these tragedies?"

RECONSTRUCTING THE SOUTH

THE TRIUMPH OF CONGRESSIONAL RECONSTRUCTION   As 1866 drew to an end, the congressional elections promised to resolve differences in the direction of policy. In August Johnson's friends staged a National Union Convention in Philadelphia. Men from Massachusetts and South Carolina marched down the aisle arm in arm to symbolize national reconciliation. The Radicals countered with a convention of their own and organized a congressional campaign committee to coordinate their propaganda. Johnson responded with a stumping tour of the Midwest, a "swing around the circle," which turned into an undignified contest of vituperation. Subjected to heckling and attacks on his integrity, Johnson responded in kind. "I have been called Judas Iscariot and all that," he said in St. Louis. "If I have played the Judas, who has been my Christ that I have played the Judas with? Was it Thad Stevens? Was it Wendell Phillips? Was it Charles Sumner?" Johnson may have been, as Secretary Seward claimed, the best stump speaker in the country. The trouble was, as Secretary Welles responded, the president ought not to be a stump speaker. It tended to confirm his image as a "ludicrous boor" and "drunken imbecile," which Radical papers projected. When the returns came in, the Republicans had well over a two-thirds majority in each house, by counts of 42 to 11 in the Senate and 143 to 49 in the House, a comfortable margin with which to override any presidential vetoes.

The Congress in fact enacted a new program even before new members took office. Two acts passed in January 1867 extended the suffrage to Negroes in the District of Columbia and the territories. Another law provided that the new Congress would meet on March 4 instead of the following December, depriving Johnson of a breathing spell. On March 2, 1867, two days before the old Congress expired, it passed three basic laws of congressional reconstruction over Johnson's vetoes: the Military Reconstruction Act, the Command of the Army Act (an amendment to an army appropriation), and the Tenure of Office Act.

The first of the three acts prescribed new conditions under which the formation of southern state governments should begin all over again. The other two sought to block obstruction by the president. The Army Act required that all orders from the commander-in-chief go through the headquarters of the general of the army, then Ulysses S. Grant, who could not be reassigned outside Washington without the consent of the Senate. The Radicals had faith in Grant, who was already leaning their way. The Tenure of Office Act required the consent of the Senate for the president to remove any officeholder whose appointment the Senate had to confirm in the first place. The purpose of at least some congressmen was to retain Secretary of War Edwin M. Stanton, the one Radical sympathizer in Johnson's cabinet, but an ambiguity crept into the wording of the act. Cabinet officers, it said, should serve during the term of the president who appointed them—and Lincoln had appointed Stanton, although, to be sure, Johnson was serving out Lincoln's term.

The Military Reconstruction Act, often hailed or denounced as the triumphant victory of "Radical" Reconstruction, actually fell short of a thoroughgoing radicalism. It emerged, the historian Michael Les Benedict wrote, "only after furious tugging and hauling among various Republican factions." As first reported from the Reconstruction committee by Stevens, it would have given military commanders in the South ultimate control over law enforcement and would have left open indefinitely the terms of future restoration. More moderate elements, however, pushed through the "Blaine amendment," which scrapped the prolonged national control under which Radicals hoped to put through the far more revolutionary program of reducing the Rebel states to territories, plus programs of land confiscation and education. With the Blaine amendment in place the Reconstruction program boiled down to little more than a requirement that southern states accept black suffrage and ratify the Fourteenth Amendment. Years later Albion W. Tourgée, after a career as a carpetbagger in North Carolina, wrote: "Republicans gave the ballot to men without homes, money, education, or security, and then told them to use it to protect themselves. . . . It was cheap patriotism, cheap philanthropy, cheap success!"

The act began with a pronouncement that "no legal state governments or adequate protection for life and property now exists in the rebel States. . . . " One state, Tennessee, which had ratified the Fourteenth Amendment, was exempted from the application of the act. The other ten were divided into five military districts, and the commanding officer of each was authorized to keep order and protect the "rights of persons and property." To that end he might use military tribunals in place of civil courts when he judged it necessary. The Johnson governments remained intact for the time being, but new constitutions were to be framed "in conformity with the Constitution of the United States," in conventions elected by male citizens twenty-one and older "of whatever race, color, or previous condition." Each state constitution had to provide the same universal male suffrage. Then, once the constitution was ratified by a majority of voters and accepted by Congress, and once the state legislature had ratified the Fourteenth Amendment, and once the amendment became part of the Constitution, any given state would be entitled to representation in Congress once again. Persons excluded from officeholding by the proposed amendment were also excluded from participation in the process.

Johnson reluctantly appointed military commanders under the act, but the situation remained uncertain for a time. Some people expected the Supreme Court to strike down the act, and for the time being no machinery existed for the new elections.

Congress quickly remedied that on March 23 with the Second Reconstruction Act, which directed the commanders to register for voting all adult males who swore they were qualified. A Third Reconstruction Act, passed on July 19, directed registrars to go beyond the loyalty oath and determine each person's eligibility to take it, and also authorized district commanders to remove and replace officeholders of any existing "so-called state" or division thereof. Before the end of 1867 new elections had been held in all the states but Texas.

Having clipped the president's wings, the Republican Congress moved a year later to safeguard its program from possible interference by the Supreme Court. In two important cases during 1866 the Court had shown a readiness to question certain actions. In *Ex parte Milligan* it struck down the wartime conviction of an Indiana Copperhead tried by court-martial for conspiracy to release and arm Rebel prisoners. The civil courts, the opinion noted, were duly operating in the area, which was far from the front. In *Cummings v. Missouri* the Court ruled void, as *ex post facto*, a Missouri statute which excluded ex-Confederates from certain professions. In *Ex parte Garland* (1867) it made a similar ruling against a test oath which barred ex-Confederates from practice before the Court. On the other hand it had evaded decision on two suits which directly challenged military Reconstruction, *Mississippi v. Johnson* and *Georgia v. Stanton*, on the ground that the suits involved political questions. Nevertheless, another case arising from Mississippi, *Ex parte McCardle*, raised the issue in a different form. McCardle, a Vicksburg editor arrested for criticizing General Ord's administration of the Fourth Military District, sought release under the Habeas Corpus Act of 1867. Congress responded on March 27, 1868, by simply removing the power of the Supreme Court to review cases arising under the law, which Congress clearly had the right to do under its power to define the Court's appellate jurisdiction (Article III, Section 2). The Court accepted this curtailment on the same day it affirmed the notion of an "indestructible Union" in *Texas v. White* (1869). In that case it also asserted the right of Congress under Article IV, Section 4, to reframe state governments.

THE IMPEACHMENT AND TRIAL OF JOHNSON Congress's move to restrain the Supreme Court preceded by just two days the trial of the president in the Senate on an impeachment brought in by the House. Johnson, though hostile to the congressional program, had gone through the motions required of him. He continued, however, to pardon former Confederates in wholesale lots and replaced several district commanders whose Radical sympathies offended him. He and his cabinet members, moreover, largely ignored the Test Oath Act of 1862 by naming former Confederates to post offices and other federal positions. Nevertheless a lengthy investigation by the House Judiciary Committee, extending through most of the year 1867, failed to convince the House that grounds for impeachment existed.

The occasion for impeachment came when Johnson deliberately violated the Tenure of Office Act in order, he said, to test its constitutionality in the courts. Secretary of War Stanton had become a thorn in the president's side, refusing to resign despite his disagreements with the president's policy. On August 12, 1867, during a recess of Congress, Johnson suspended Stanton and named General Grant in his place. Grant's political stance was ambiguous at the time, but his acceptance implied cooperation with Johnson. When the Senate refused to confirm Johnson's action, however, Grant returned the office to Stanton. The president thereupon named Gen. Lorenzo Thomas as secretary of war after a futile effort to interest Gen. William T. Sherman. Three days later, on February 24, 1868, the House voted impeachment, to be followed by specific charges. In due course a special committee of seven brought in its report.

Of the eleven articles of impeachment, eight focused on the charge that he had unlawfully removed Stanton and had failed to give the Senate the name of a successor. Article 9, the "Emory article," accused the president of issuing orders directly to Gen. William H. Emory in violation of the Army Act. The last two in effect charged him with criticizing Congress by "inflammatory and scandalous harangues" and by claiming that the Congress was not legally valid without southern representatives. But Article 11 accused Johnson of "unlawfully devising and contriving" to violate the Reconstruction Acts, contrary to his obligation to execute the laws. At the least, Johnson had tried to obstruct Congress's will while observing the letter of the law.

The Senate trial opened on March 5 and continued until May 26, with Chief Justice Salmon P. Chase presiding. Seven managers from the House, including Thaddeus Stevens and Benjamin F. Butler, directed the prosecution. The president was spared the humiliation of a personal appearance, and was ably represented by Attorney-General Henry Stanbery, William H. Evarts, Benjamin R. Curtis, and William S. Groesbeck. The defense counsel shrewdly insisted on narrowing the trial to questions that would be indictable offenses under the law, and steered the

Johnson, impeached by the House, barely survived his trial in the Senate. [Harper's Weekly, *April 11, 1868*]

questions away from Johnson's manifest wish to frustrate the will of Congress. Such questions, they contended, were purely political in nature. In the end enough Republican senators, the "recusants," joined their pro-Johnson colleagues to prevent conviction. On May 16 the crucial vote came on Article 9: 35 votes guilty and 19 not guilty, one vote short of the two-thirds needed to convict. On Articles 2 and 3 the vote was exactly the same, and the trial adjourned.

In a parliamentary system Johnson probably would have been removed as leader of the government long before then. But by deciding the case on the narrowest grounds, the Senate made it unlikely that any future president could ever be removed except for the gravest personal offenses, and almost surely not for flouting the will of Congress in his execution of the laws. Impeachment of Johnson was in the end a great political mistake, for the failure to remove the president was damaging to Radical morale and support. Nevertheless the Radical cause did gain something. To blunt the opposition, Johnson agreed not to obstruct the process of Reconstruction, named as secretary of war Gen. John M. Schofield, who was committed to enforcing the new laws, and sent to Congress the new Radical constitutions of Arkansas and South Carolina. Thereafter his obstruction ceased and Radical Reconstruction got under way.

REPUBLICAN RULE IN THE SOUTH   In June 1868 Congress agreed that seven states had met the conditions for readmission, all but

Virginia, Mississippi, and Texas. Congress rescinded Georgia's admission, however, when the state legislature expelled twenty-eight black members on the pretext that the state constitution had failed to specify their eligibility, and seated some former Confederate leaders. The military commander of Georgia then forced the legislature to reseat the Negro members and remove the Confederates, and the state was compelled to ratify the Fifteenth Amendment before being admitted in July 1870. Mississippi, Texas, and Virginia had returned earlier in 1870, under the added requirement that they too ratify the Fifteenth Amendment. This amendment, submitted to the states in 1869, ratified in 1870, forbade the states to deny any person the vote on grounds of race, color, or previous condition of servitude.

Long before the new governments were established, Republican groups began to spring up in the South, chiefly under the aegis of the Union League, founded at Philadelphia in 1862 to promote support for the Union. Emissaries of the league enrolled Negroes and loyal whites, initiated them into the secrets and rituals of the order, and instructed them "in their rights and duties." The league emphasized the display of such symbols as the Bible, the flag, the Constitution, and the Declaration of Independence. The sign of recognition was the recital of the "four Ls": Lincoln, Liberty, Loyal, League. Agents of the Freedmen's Bureau, northern missionaries, teachers, and soldiers aided the cause and spread its influence. When the time came for political action, they were ready. In October 1867, for instance, on the eve of South Carolina's choice of convention delegates, the league reported eighty-eight chapters, which claimed to have enrolled almost every adult black male in the state.

BLACKS IN SOUTHERN POLITICS   It was the new role of Negroes in politics on which attention focused then and afterward. If largely illiterate and inexperienced in the rudiments of politics, they were little different from millions of whites enfranchised in the age of Jackson or immigrants herded to the polls by political bosses in New York and other cities after the war. Some freedmen frankly confessed their disadvantages. Beverly Nash, a black delegate in the South Carolina convention of 1868, told his colleagues: "I believe, my friends and fellow-citizens, we are not prepared for this suffrage. But we can learn. Give a man tools and let him commence to use them, and in time he will learn a trade. So it is with voting."

Brought suddenly into politics in times that tried the most skilled of statesmen, a surprising number of blacks rose to the occasion. Yet it would be absurd to claim, in the phrase of the times, that the "bottom rail" ever got on top. To call what happened "black Reconstruction" is to exaggerate black influence, which was limited mainly to voting, and to overlook the large numbers of white Republicans, especially in the mountain areas of the upper South. Only one of the new conventions, South Carolina's, had a black majority, 76 to 41. Louisiana's was evenly divided between blacks and whites, and in only two other conventions were more than 20 percent of the members black: Florida's, with 40 percent, and Virginia's, with 24 percent. The Texas convention was only 10 percent and North Carolina's 11 percent—but that did not stop a white newspaper from calling it "Ethiopian minstrelsy, Ham radicalism in all its glory," a body consisting of "baboons, monkeys, mules, Tourgée, and other jackasses."

In the new state governments, any Negro participation was a novelty, but no black man ever served as governor and few as judges. There were two Negro senators in Congress, Hiram Revels and Blanche K. Bruce, both from Mississippi, and fourteen black members of the House during Reconstruction. Among these were some of the ablest congressmen of the time. Blacks served in every state legislature, but only in South Carolina did they ever make up a majority in both houses and that only for two years.

CARPETBAGGERS AND SCALAWAGS   The top positions in southern state governments went for the most part to white Republicans, whom the opposition whites soon labeled "carpetbaggers" and "scalawags," depending on their place of birth. The men who al-

Hiram R. Revels. Senator from Mississippi, Revels was also a Methodist minister and, later, president of Alcorn College. [Library of Congress]

legedly came south with all their belongings in carpetbags to pick up the political pelf were more often than not men who had arrived as early as 1865 or 1866, drawn south by the hope of economic opportunity and by other attractions that many of them had seen in Union service. Many were teachers or preachers who came on missionary endeavors. Albion W. Tourgée, for instance, a badly wounded Union veteran, moved to North Carolina in 1865, seeking a milder climate for reasons of health. He invested $5,000 in a nursery, and promptly lost it. He would have needed a fine crystal ball indeed to see two years in advance the chance for political office under the Radical program. As it turned out, he served in the state constitutional convention of 1868 and later as a state judge.

The "scalawags," or native white Republicans, were even more reviled and misrepresented. Most had opposed secession, forming a Unionist majority in many mountain counties as far south as Georgia and Alabama, and especially in the Tennessee hills. Not a few in both hills and flatlands attested to the power of what has been labeled "persistent Whiggery." Old Whigs often found Republican economic policies to be in keeping with Henry Clay's American System. Unionists, whether Whig or Democratic before the war, and even some secessionists, agreed with Georgia's Joseph E. Brown, confederate governor and later Democratic senator: "The statesman like the businessman should take a practical view of questions as they arise." For the time a practical view dictated joining the Republicans. Mississippi's James L. Alcorn, wealthy planter and former Whig, was among the prominent whites who joined the Republicans in the hope of moderating Radical policies. Such men were ready to concede Negro suffrage in the hope of influencing Negro voters. Alcorn became the first Republican governor of Mississippi.

THE REPUBLICAN RECORD   The new state constitutions were objectionable to adherents of the old order more because of their origins than because of their contents, excepting their provisions for Negro suffrage and civil rights. Otherwise the documents were in keeping with other state constitutions of the day, their provisions often drawn from the basic laws of northern states. Most remained in effect for some years after the end of Radical control, and later constitutions incorporated many of their features. Conspicuous among Radical innovations were such steps toward greater democracy as requiring universal manhood suffrage, reapportioning legislatures more nearly according to population, and making more state offices elective.

Given the circumstances in which the Radical governments arose and the intense hostility which met them, they made a surprisingly good record of positive achievement. For the first time in most of the South they established state school systems, however inadequate and ill-supported at first. The testimony is almost universal that Negroes eagerly sought education for themselves and their children. Some 600,000 black pupils were in schools by 1877. State governments under the Radicals gave more attention than ever before to poor relief and to public institutions for the disadvantaged and handicapped: orphanages, asylums, institutions for the deaf, dumb, and blind of both races. Public roads, bridges, and buildings were repaired or rebuilt. Blacks achieved new rights and opportunities that would never again be taken away, at least in principle: equality before the law, and the right to own property, carry on business, enter professions, attend schools, and learn to read and write.

In the annals of Reconstruction, partisan historians long denounced the Republican regimes for unparalleled corruption and abuse. That abuses proliferated in those years there is no question. Public money and public credit were often voted to privately owned corporations, especially railroads, under conditions which invited influence-peddling. But governmental subsidies were common before and after Reconstruction, especially for transportation, and the extension of public aid had general support among all elements, including the Radicals and their enemies. Contracts were let at absurd prices and public officials took their cut. Taxes and public debt rose in every state. Yet the figures of taxation and debt hardly constitute an unqualified indictment of Radical governments, since they then faced unusual and inflated costs for the physical reconstruction of public works in the South. Most states, moreover, had to float loans at outrageous discounts, sometimes at 50–75 percent of face value, because of uncertain conditions.

Nor, for that matter, were the breaches of public morality limited to the South or to Republicans. The Democratic Tweed Ring at the time was robbing New York City of more than $75 million, while the Republican "Gas Ring" in Philadelphia was lining its pockets. In national politics it was the time of the Crédit Mobilier, the Whiskey Ring, and other scandals that plagued the Grant administration. Corruption was neither invented by the Radical regimes, nor did it die with them. In Louisiana, the carpetbag governor Henry C. Warmoth found a certain Latin zest in the game: "Why," he said, "down here everybody is demoralized. Corruption is the fashion." In three years Louisiana's printing bill ran to $1.5 million, about half of which went to a newspaper belonging to young Warmoth, who left office with a tidy nest egg and settled down to a long life as a planter. But a later Democratic state treasurer, Maj. E. A. Burke, who decamped for Tegucigalpa in 1890 with the accounts over $1 million short, far outstripped Warmoth's record or anybody else's. About the same time Mississippi's Democratic state treasurer was found to have embezzled over $315,000. During Republican rule in Mississippi, on the other hand, there was no evidence of major corruption.

WHITE TERROR   The case of Mississippi strongly suggests that whites were hostile to Republican regimes less because of their corruption than their inclusion of blacks. Most white southerners remained unreconstructed, so conditioned by slavery that they were unable to conceive of blacks as citizens or even free agents. In some places hostility to the new regimes took on the form of white terror. The prototype of terrorist groups was the Ku Klux Klan, first organized in 1866 by some young men of Pulaski, Tennessee, as a social club with the costumes, secret ritual, and mumbo-jumbo common to fraternal groups. At first a group of Merry Andrews devoted to practical jokes, the founders eventually realized, as two of them wrote in a later account, that they "had evoked a spirit from 'the vasty deep' [which] would not down at their bidding." Pranks turned into intimidation of blacks and white Republicans, and the KKK and imitators like Louisiana's Knights of the White Camellia spread rapidly across the South in answer to the Union League. Klansmen rode about the

Two "carpetbaggers" hanged by the Klan, in the Tuscaloosa Independent Monitor, *1868. [Alabama State Department of Archives and History]*

countryside hiding under masks and robes, spreading horren-
dous rumors, issuing threats, harassing assertive Negroes, and
occasionally running amok in violence and destruction. "Typically the Klan was a reactionary and racist crusade against equal
rights which sought to overthrow the most democratic society or
government the South had yet known," wrote its historian, Allan
W. Trelease. During its brief career it "whipped, shot, hanged,
robbed, raped, and otherwise outraged Negroes and Republicans across the South in the name of preserving white civilization."

Militia groups formed by the Radical regimes were hardly able
to cope with the underground tactics of the Klan, although their
presence may have prevented worse violence. Congress struck
back with three Enforcement Acts (1870–1871) to protect
Negro voters. The first of these measures levied penalties on
persons who interfered with any citizen's right to vote. A second
placed the election of congressmen under surveillance by federal election supervisors and marshals. The third (the Ku Klux
Klan Act) outlawed the characteristic activities of the Klan—
forming conspiracies, wearing disguises, resisting officers, and
intimidating officials—and authorized the president to suspend
habeas corpus where necessary to suppress "armed combinations." President Grant, in October 1871, singled out nine counties in upcountry South Carolina as an example, suspended
habeas corpus, and pursued mass prosecutions which brought an
abrupt halt to the Klan outrages. Elsewhere the Justice Department carried out a campaign of prosecution on a smaller scale,
while a congressional committee gathered testimony on Klan activity which ran to twelve volumes. The program of federal enforcement broke the back of the Klan, whose outrages declined
steadily as conservative southerners resorted to more subtle
methods.

CONSERVATIVE RESURGENCE   The Klan in fact could not take credit
for the overthrow of Republican control in any state. Perhaps its
most important effect, Allen Trelease suggested, was to weaken
Negro and Republican morale in the South and strengthen in the
North a growing weariness with the whole "southern question."
Yankees had other fish to fry anyway. Onrushing expansion into
the West, Indian wars, economic growth, and political controversy over the tariff and the currency distracted attention from
southern outrages. Republican control in the South gradually
loosened as "Conservative" parties—Democrats used that name
to mollify former Whigs—mobilized the white vote. Scalawags,
and many carpetbaggers, drifted away from the Radical ranks

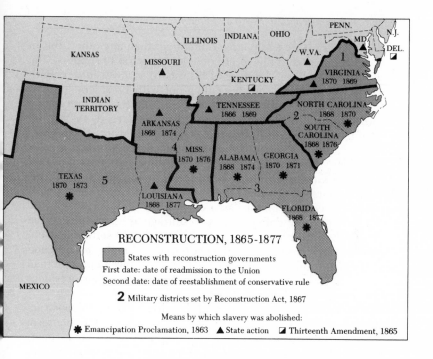

RECONSTRUCTION, 1865-1877

☐ States with reconstruction governments
First date: date of readmission to the Union
Second date: date of reestablishment of conservative rule

2 Military districts set by Reconstruction Act, 1867

Means by which slavery was abolished:
✳ Emancipation Proclamation, 1863 ▲ State action ◪ Thirteenth Amendment, 1865

under pressure from their white neighbors. Few of them had joined the Republicans out of concern for Negro rights in the first place.

Republican control collapsed in Virginia and Tennessee as early as 1869, in Georgia and North Carolina in 1870, although there was a Republican governor in North Carolina until 1876. Reconstruction lasted longest in the Deep South states with the heaviest Negro population, where whites abandoned Klan masks for barefaced intimidation in paramilitary groups like the Mississippi Rifle Club and the South Carolina Red Shirts. By 1876 Radical regimes survived only in Louisiana, South Carolina, and Florida, and these all collapsed after the elections of that year. Later Daniel H. Chamberlain, the last carpetbag governor of South Carolina, told William Lloyd Garrison that "the uneducated negro was too weak, no matter what his numbers, to cope with the whites."

THE GRANT YEARS

GRANT'S ELECTION Ulysses S. Grant, who presided over this fiasco, brought to the presidency less political experience than any man who ever occupied the office, except perhaps Zachary Taylor, and arguably less political judgment than any other. But in 1868 the rank-and-file voter could be expected to support "the Lion of Vicksburg" because of his record as a war leader. Both parties wooed him, but his falling-out with President Johnson pushed him toward the Republicans and built trust in him among the Radicals. They were, as Thad Stevens said, ready to "let him into the church." Impeachment proceedings were still in progress when the Republicans gathered in Chicago to name their candidate. Grant was the unanimous choice and House Speaker Schuyler Colfax of Indiana became his running mate. The platform endorsed the Reconstruction policy of Congress, congratulating the country on the "assured success" of the program. One plank cautiously defended Negro suffrage as a necessity in the South, but a matter each northern state should settle for itself. Another urged payment of the national debt "in the utmost good faith to all creditors," which meant in gold. More important than the platform were the great expectations of a soldier-president and his slogan: "Let us have peace."

The Democrats took an opposite position on both Reconstruction and the debt. The Republican Congress, the platform charged, instead of restoring the Union, had "so far as in its power, dissolved it, and subjected ten states, in the time of profound peace, to military despotism and Negro supremacy." As to the public debt, the party endorsed Rep. George H. Pendleton's "Ohio idea" that since most bonds had been bought with depreciated greenbacks, they should be paid off in greenbacks unless they specified payment in gold. With no conspicuously available candidate in sight, the convention turned to Horatio Seymour, war governor of New York and chairman of the convention. His friends had to hustle him out of the hall to prevent his withdrawal. With Francis P. Blair of Missouri in the second place on the ticket, the Democrats made a closer race of it than showed up in the electoral vote. Eight states, including New York and New Jersey, went for Seymour. While Grant swept the electoral college by 214 to 80, his popular majority was only 307,000 out of a total of over 5.7 million votes. More than 500,000 black voters accounted for Grant's margin of victory.

EARLY APPOINTMENTS   Grant had proven himself a great leader in the war, but in the White House he seemed blind to the political forces and influence peddlers around him. He was awe-struck by men of wealth and unaccountably loyal to some who betrayed his trust. The historian Henry Adams, who lived in Washington at the time, noted that to his friends "Grant appeared as intermittent energy, immensely powerful when awake, but passive and plastic in repose. . . . They could never measure his character or be sure when he would act. They could never follow a mental process in his thought. They were not sure that he did think." His conception of the presidency was "Whiggish." The chief executive carried out the laws; in the formulation of policy he passively followed the lead of Congress. This approach endeared him at first to party leaders, but it left him at last ineffective and others disillusioned with his leadership.

At the outset Grant consulted nobody on his cabinet appointments. Some of his choices indulged personal whims; others simply betrayed bad judgment. In some cases appointees learned of their nomination from the newspapers. The first secretary of state, former Rep. Elihu B. Washburne, an old friend from Illinois, served an honorific term of one week before going to his destined post as minister to France. Secretary of the Navy Adolph E. Borie was a casual dinner-table acquaintance and political contributor. A. T. Stewart, a wealthy merchant nominated as secretary of the treasury, was ineligible because of a law which barred anyone in "trade or commerce." As time went by Grant betrayed a fatal gift for losing men of talent and integrity from his cabinet. Secretary of State Hamilton Fish of New York turned out to be a happy exception; he guided foreign policy throughout the Grant presidency.

At first it looked as if Grant's free-wheeling style of choosing a cabinet signaled a sharp departure from the spoils system. But once Grant had taken care of his friends and relatives, he began to take care of party leaders. Cabinet members who balked at the procedure were soon eased out. This strengthened a nascent movement for a merit system in the civil service, modeled on systems recently adopted in Great Britain, Germany, and France. Grant finally approved a measure to set up a commission to look into the matter in 1872, a good gesture in a political year. The group duly brought in recommendations which in turn were duly shelved and forgotten once the election was over.

THE GOVERNMENT DEBT The "sound money" men had more success than the reformers. They claimed that Grant's election had been a mandate to save the country from the Democrats' "Ohio idea." The underlying purpose of the movement to pay off the government debt in greenbacks was to bring about an inflation of the currency. Many debtors and aggressive businessmen rallied to the cause of "easy money," joined by a large number of Radicals who thought a combination of high tariffs and easy money would bring about more rapid economic growth. But creditors stood to gain from payment in gold, and they had the greater influence in Republican circles. They also had the benefit of a strong Calvinistic tendency in the public mind to look upon the cause of hard money as a moral one; depreciated currency was somehow a fraud. In his inaugural address Grant endorsed payment of the debt in gold not as a point of policy but as a point of national honor. On March 18, 1869, the Public Credit Act endorsing that principle became the first act of Congress he signed. Under the Refunding Act of 1870 the Treasury was able to replace 6 percent Civil War bonds with a new issue promising 4–5 percent in gold.

But whatever Grant's convictions respecting a "sound currency," he was not ready to risk a sharp contraction of the greenbacks in circulation. After the war the Treasury had assumed that the $400 million in greenbacks would be retired from circulation. To that end in 1866 Congress gave the Treasury discretionary power to begin the process at a rate of $10 million in the first six months and $4 million a month thereafter. In 1868, however, "soft money" elements in Congress stopped the process, leaving $356 million outstanding. There matters stood when Grant took office.

REFORM AND SCANDAL   Long before Grant's first term was out, a reaction against the Reconstruction measures, and against incompetence and corruption in the administration, had incited mutiny within the Republican ranks. Open revolt broke out first in Missouri where Carl Schurz, a German immigrant and war hero, led a group which elected a governor with Democratic help in 1870 and sent Schurz to the Senate. In 1872 the Liberal Republicans (as they called themselves) held a national convention at Cincinnati which produced a compromise platform condemning the party's southern policy and favoring civil service reform, but remained silent on the protective tariff. The meeting, moreover, was stampeded toward an anomalous presidential candidate: Horace Greeley, editor of the New York *Tribune*, a strong protectionist, and longtime champion of just about every reform of his times. His image as a visionary eccentric was complemented by his record of hostility to Democrats, whose support the Liberals needed. The Democrats nevertheless swallowed the pill and gave their nomination to Greeley as the only hope of beating Grant.

The result was a foregone conclusion. Republican regulars duly endorsed Radical Reconstruction and the protective tariff.

Grant still had seven carpetbag states in his pocket, generous support from business and banking interests, and the stalwart support of the Radicals. Above all he still evoked the imperishable glory of Missionary Ridge and Appomattox. Greeley, despite an exhausting tour of the country—still unusual for a presidential candidate—carried only six southern and border states and none in the North. Greeley's wife had died during the campaign, and worn out with grief and fatigue, he too was gone three weeks after the election.

Within less than a year of his reelection Grant was adrift in a cesspool of scandal. The first hint of scandal had touched Grant in the summer of 1869, when the crafty Jay Gould and the flamboyant Jim Fisk connived with the president's brother-in-law, Abel R. Corbin, to corner the gold market. Gould concocted an argument that the government should refrain from selling gold on the market because a rise in gold prices would raise temporarily depressed farm prices. Grant apparently smelled a rat from the start, but was seen in public with the speculators. Corbin convinced his associates that the president had bought the argument. As the rumor spread on Wall Street, gold rose from $132 to $163 an ounce. When Grant finally persuaded Corbin to pull out of the deal, Gould began quietly selling out. Finally, on "Black Friday," September 24, 1869, Grant ordered the Treasury to sell a large quantity of gold and the bubble burst. Fisk got out by repudiating his agreements and hiring thugs to intimidate his creditors. "Nothing is lost save honor," he said.

During the campaign of 1872 the public first learned about the financial buccaneering of the Crédit Mobilier, a construction company which had milked the Union Pacific Railroad for exorbitant fees to line the pockets of insiders who controlled both firms. Rank-and-file Union Pacific shareholders were left holding the bag. Rep. Oakes Ames had distributed Crédit Mobilier shares at bargain rates where, he said, "it will produce much good to us." The beneficiaries had included Speaker Schuyler Colfax, later vice-president, and Rep. James A. Garfield, later president. This chicanery had transpired before Grant's election in 1868, but it touched a number of prominent Republicans. Of thirteen members of Congress involved, only two were censured by a Congress which, before it adjourned in March 1873, voted itself a pay raise from $5,000 to $7,500—retroactive, it decided, for two years. A public uproar forced repeal, leaving the raises voted the president ($25,000 to $50,000) and Supreme Court justices.

Even more odious disclosures soon followed, and some in-

The People's Handwriting on the Wall. *An 1872 engraving comments on the corruption engulfing Grant. [Library of Congress]*

volved the president's cabinet. Secretary of War W. W. Belknap, it turned out, had accepted bribes from Indian traders at army posts in the West. He was impeached, but resigned in time to elude trial by the Senate. Post-office contracts, it was revealed, went to carriers who offered the highest kickbacks. Secretary of the Treasury W. A. Richardson had awarded a commission of 50 percent for the collection of overdue taxes by John D. Sanborn, a political friend of Massachusetts Rep. Benjamin F. Butler. In St. Louis a "Whiskey Ring" bribed tax collectors to bilk the government of millions in revenue. Grant's private secretary, Orville Babcock, was enmeshed in that scheme, taking large sums of money and other valuables in return for inside information. Before Grant's second term ended, the corruption crossed the Atlantic when Gen. Robert Schenck, minister to London, unloaded worthless stock in "Emma Mines" on gullible Britons. Only a plea of diplomatic immunity and a sudden exit spared him from British justice. There is no evidence that Grant himself was ever involved in, or that he personally profited from, any of the fraud, but his poor choice of associates earned him the public censure that was heaped upon his head.

PANIC AND REDEMPTION Economic distress followed close upon public scandal. Contraction of the money supply and expansion of the railroads into sparsely settled areas had made investors cautious. During 1873 the market for railroad bonds turned sour as some twenty-five roads defaulted on their interest payments before the end of August. The investment banking firm of Jay Cooke and Company, unable to sell the bonds of the Northern Pacific Railroad, financed them with short-term deposits in hope that a European market would develop. But in 1873 the opposite happened when a financial panic in Vienna forced many financiers to unload American stocks and bonds. Caught short, Cooke and Company went bankrupt on September 18, 1873. The ensuing stampede forced the stock market to close for ten days. The Panic of 1873 set off a depression that lasted for six years, the longest and most severe that Americans had yet suffered, marked by widespread bankruptcies, unemployment, and a drastic slowdown in railroad building.

Hard times and scandals hurt Republicans in the midterm elections of 1874. The Democrats won control of the House of Representatives and gained in the Senate. The new Democratic House immediately launched inquiries into the scandals and unearthed further evidence of corruption in high places. The panic meanwhile focused attention once more on greenback currency.

Since greenbacks were valued less than gold, they had become the chief circulating medium. Most people spent greenbacks first and held their gold or used it to settle foreign accounts, which drained much gold out of the country. The postwar retirement of greenbacks had made for tight money. To relieve deflation and stimulate business, therefore, the Treasury reissued $26 million in greenbacks previously withdrawn, raising the total in circulation to about $382 million.

For a time the advocates of easy money were riding high. Early in 1874 they pushed through a bill to issue greenbacks up to the wartime level of $400 million. Here the administration drew the line, however. Grant vetoed the bill in April and in his annual message of December 1874 called for the gradual resumption of specie payments—that is, the redemption of greenbacks in gold. This would make greenbacks "good as gold" and raise their value to a par with the gold dollar. In January, before the Republicans gave up control of the House, Congress obliged by passing the Resumption Act of 1875. The redemption in specie began on January 1, 1879, after the Treasury had built a gold reserve for the purpose and reduced the value of greenbacks in circulation.

THE COMPROMISE OF 1877   Grant, despite everything, was eager to run again in 1876, but the recent scandals discouraged any challenge to the two-term tradition. James G. Blaine of Maine, late Speaker of the House, emerged as the Republican front-runner, but he too bore the taint of scandal. Letters in the possession of James Mulligan of Boston linked Blaine to some dubious railroad dealings. Blaine cajoled Mulligan into turning over a packet of letters, from which he read to Congress selected passages exonerating him. But the performance was a shade too clever. It left doubts which were strengthened by the disclosure of still other "Mulligan letters" that found their way into print.

The Republican convention in Cincinnati therefore eliminated Blaine and several other hopefuls in favor of Ohio's favorite son, Rutherford B. Hayes. Three times elected governor of Ohio, most recently as an advocate of sound money, Hayes had also made a name as a civil service reformer. But his chief virtue was that he offended neither Radicals nor reformers. As Henry Adams put it, he was "a third rate nonentity, whose only recommendation is that he is obnoxious to no one." The vice-presidential nod went to William A. Wheeler of New York.

The Democratic convention in St. Louis was abnormally harmonious from the start. The nomination went on the second ballot to Samuel J. Tilden, millionaire corporation lawyer and reform governor of New York who had directed a campaign to overthrow first the Tweed Ring in New York City and then another ring in Albany which had bilked the state of millions. The convention named Thomas A. Hendricks of Indiana for vice-president.

The campaign generated no burning issues. Both candidates favored the trend toward conservative rule in the South. During one of the most corrupt elections ever, both candidates favored civil service reform. In the absence of strong differences, Democrats waved the Republicans' dirty linen. In response, Republicans waved the bloody shirt, which is to say that they engaged in verbal assaults on former Confederates and the spirit of Rebellion. The phrase "waving the bloody shirt" originated at the impeachment trial of President Johnson when Benjamin F. Butler, speaking for the prosecution, displayed the bloody shirt a Mississippi carpetbagger had been wearing when hauled out of bed and beaten by Ku Kluxers. Reporting such atrocities came to be known to Democrats as "grinding the outrage mills." "Our strong ground," Hayes wrote to Blaine, "is the dread of a solid South, *rebel rule*, etc., etc. . . . It leads people away from 'hard times,' which is our deadliest foe."

On the night of the election early returns pointed to a victory for Tilden, but Republican National Chairman Zachariah Chandler refused to concede. As it fell out, Tilden had 184 electoral votes, just one short of a majority, but Republicans claimed nineteen doubtful votes from Florida, Louisiana, and South Carolina, while Democrats laid a counterclaim to one vote from Oregon. But the Republicans had clearly carried Oregon. In the South the outcome was less certain, and given the fraud and intimidation perpetrated on both sides, nobody will ever know what might have happened if, to use a slogan of the day, "a free ballot and a fair count" had prevailed. As good a guess as any may be, as one writer suggested, that the Democrats stole the election first and the Republicans stole it back.

In all three of the disputed southern states rival canvassing boards sent in different returns. In Florida, Republicans conceded the state election, but in Louisiana and South Carolina rival state governments also appeared. The Constitution offered no guidance in this unprecedented situation. Even if Congress was empowered to sort things out, the Democratic House and the Republican Senate proved unable to reach an agreement.

Finally, on January 29, 1877, the two houses decided to set up a special Electoral Commission which would investigate and report back its findings. It had fifteen members, five each from the House, the Senate, and the Supreme Court. Members were so chosen as to have seven from each major party with Justice David Davis of Illinois as the swing man. Davis, though appointed to the Court by Lincoln, was no party regular and was in fact thought to be leaning toward the Democrats. Republicans who voted for the commission, James A. Garfield said, were "fair-minded asses" who thought that "truth is always half way between God and the Devil." The panel appeared to be stacked in favor of Tilden.

But as it turned out, the panel got restacked the other way. Short-sighted Democrats in the Illinois legislature teamed up with minority Greenbackers to name Davis their senator. Davis accepted, no doubt with a sense of relief. From the remaining justices, all Republicans, the panel chose Joseph P. Bradley to fill the vacancy. The decision on each state went by a vote of 8 to 7, along party lines, in favor of Hayes. After much bluster and threat of filibuster by Democrats, the House voted on March 2 to accept the report and declare Hayes elected by an electoral vote of 185 to 184.

Critical to this outcome was the defection of southern Democrats who had made several informal agreements with the Republicans. On February 26, 1877, a bargain was struck at the Wormley House, a Washington hotel, between prominent Ohio Republicans, including Sen. John Sherman and Rep. James A.

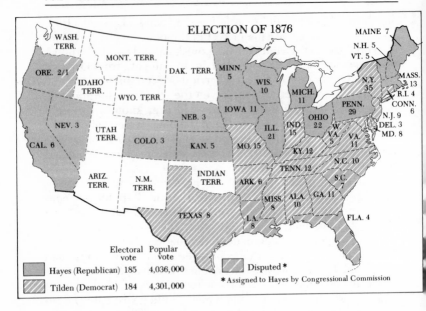

ELECTION OF 1876

	Electoral vote	Popular vote
Hayes (Republican)	185	4,036,000
Tilden (Democrat)	184	4,301,000
Disputed *		

* Assigned to Hayes by Congressional Commission

Garfield, and powerful southern Democrats, including Sen. John Brown Gordon of Georgia and Rep. L. Q. C. Lamar of Mississippi. The Republicans promised that, if elected, Hayes would withdraw federal troops from Louisiana and South Carolina, letting the Republican governments there collapse. In return the Democrats promised to withdraw their opposition to Hayes, to accept in good faith the Reconstruction amendments, and to refrain from partisan reprisals against Republicans in the South.

With this agreement in hand, southern Democrats could justify deserting Tilden because this so-called Compromise of 1877 brought a final "redemption" from the "Radicals" and a return to "home rule," which actually meant rule by white Democrats. Other, more informal promises, less noticed by the public, bolstered the Wormley House agreement. Hayes's friends pledged more support for Mississippi levees and other internal improvements, including federal subsidy for a transcontinental railroad along a southern route. Southerners extracted a further promise that Hayes would name a white southerner as postmaster-general, the cabinet position with the most patronage jobs at hand. In return, southerners would let Republicans make James A. Garfield Speaker of the new House.

THE END OF RECONSTRUCTION   After Hayes took office, most of these promises were either renounced or forgotten. They had served their purpose of breaking the crisis. In April, Hayes withdrew federal troops from the state houses in Louisiana and South Carolina, and the Republican governments there collapsed—along with much of Hayes's claim to legitimacy. Hayes chose a Tennessean, former Confederate David M. Key, as postmaster-general. But after southern Democrats failed to permit the choice of Garfield as Speaker, Hayes expressed doubt about any further subsidy for railroad building, and none was voted.

As to southern promises regarding the civil rights of blacks, only a few Democratic leaders such as Wade Hampton and Francis T. Nicholls, the new governors of South Carolina and Louisiana, remembered them for long. Over the next three decades those rights crumbled under the pressure of white rule in the South and the force of Supreme Court decisions narrowing the application of the Reconstruction amendments. The Compromise of 1877, viewed in the light of its consequences, might justly bear the label which one historian gave it: "The betrayal of the Negro." But "betrayal" implies that a promise was made in the first place, and Reconstruction never offered more than an uncertain commitment to equality before the law. Yet it left an enduring legacy, the Thirteenth, Fourteenth, and Fifteenth Amendments—not dead but dormant, waiting to be warmed back into life.

FURTHER READING

Over time the various interpretations of Reconstruction have made that period "a dark and bloody ground" for historians. Those interested in following the interplay of interpretation might first turn to works of fiction to understand how the adversaries line up. Albion W. Tourgée's *A Fool's Errand* (1880, 1966)° provides a northern carpetbagger's idealistic view, while Thomas Dixon's *The Clansman* (1905)° applauds the defeated South's heroic casting off of the tyranny of corrupt occupation. This pro-southern viewpoint came to dominate professional scholarship as well after 1900. William A. Dunning's *Reconstruction, Political and Economic, 1865–1877* (1907), sets the tone for numerous monographs sympathetic to white southern suffering under "black rule."

Among the early challengers to the Dunning school are Charles and Mary Beard, whose sweeping *Rise of American Civilization* (1927) assigns largely economic motives to the actors in Reconstruction politics. Howard Beale's *The Critical Year* (1930) sees the Radical Republicans as fanatics who served business interests, and Andrew Johnson as a commonsensical mediator in the controversies of 1866. Among the strongest

°These books are available in paperback editions.

challengers of the pro-southern view is W. E. B. Du Bois's *Black Reconstruction* (1935), which maintains that the Republicans held valid ideals in their defense of freedmen rights.

The civil rights movement of the 1950s and 1960s brought new freshness to the topic. Among the surveys which reflect a new sympathy for the aims of the Radicals and the plight of freedmen are John Hope Franklin's *Reconstruction after the Civil War* (1961) and Kenneth M. Stampp's *The Era of Reconstruction* (1964).° More detailed, but equally valuable, are Rembert W. Patrick's *The Reconstruction of the Nation* (1967), James G. Randall and David Donald's *Civil War and Reconstruction* (1969), and James M. McPherson's *Ordeal by Fire: The Civil War and Reconstruction* (1982).

More specialized works give closer scrutiny to the aims of the principal political figures. William B. Hesseltine's *Lincoln's Plan of Reconstruction* (1960) argues that the president planned postwar policy in the same pragmatic fashion as he directed the Civil War. Peyton McCrary's *Abraham Lincoln and Reconstruction* (1978) deals with the Lincoln policies as they were carried out in Louisiana. Claude G. Bower's *The Tragic Era* (1929) is sympathetic to Johnson, while Eric McKitrick's *Andrew Johnson and Reconstruction* (1960),° John H. and LaWanda C. Cox's *Politics, Principle, and Prejudice* (1963), and William R. Brock's *An American Crisis* (1963) sharply criticize the behavior of a president who obstructed Republican policies. Why Johnson was impeached is detailed in Michael L. Benedict's *The Impeachment of Andrew Johnson* (1973)° and H. L. Trefousse's *Impeachment of a President* (1975).

Recent scholars have been far more sympathetic to the aims and motives of the Radical Republicans. Surveys of congressional behavior are Hans F. Trefousse's *The Radical Republicans* (1969)° and Herman Belz's *Reconstructing the Union* (1969). Clearest in dealing with the ideology of these Radicals is Michael L. Benedict's *A Compromise of Principle: Congressional Republicans and Reconstruction* (1974). Biographies of Radical leaders include Fawn M. Brodie's *Thaddeus Stevens* (1959)° and David Donald's *Charles Summer and the Rights of Man* (1970).° For an emphasis on the relations of the courts and these congressmen, consult Stanley I. Kutler's *The Judicial Power and Reconstruction Policies* (1968) or Charles Fairman's *Reconstruction and Reunion* (1971).

The intransigence of southern white attitudes is examined in Michael Perman's *Reunion without Compromise* (1973) and Joe G. Taylor's *Louisiana Reconstructed* (1974). Allen W. Trelease's *White Terror* (1971) covers the various organizations which practiced vigilante tactics, chiefly the Ku Klux Klan. The difficulties former planters had in adjusting to the new labor system are documented in James L. Roark's *Masters without Slaves* (1977).°

Numerous works have appeared on the freedmen's experience in the South. Start with Leon Litwack's *Been in the Storm So Long* (1979),° which wonderfully covers the transition from slavey to freedom. Among the best state-level studies are those dealing with South Carolina blacks. Willie Lee Rose's *Rehearsal for Reconstruction* (1964)° examines Union efforts to define the social role of former slaves during wartime emancipation. Joel Williamson's *After Slavery* (1965)° argues that South Carolina freedmen took an active role in pursuing their political and economic rights. A study of Alabama freedmen—Peter Kolchin's *First Freedom* (1974)—should also be consulted. The role of the Freedman's Bureau is explored in George R. Bentley's *A History of the Freedman's Bureau* (1955), William S. McFeely's *Yankee Stepfather: O. O. Howard and the Freedman* (1980),° and Robert C. Morris's *Reading, 'Riting and Reconstruction: The Education of Freedmen in the South, 1861–1870* (1981).

The role of white Republicans in one southern state in the immediate postwar years is traced in William C. Harris's *The Day of the Carpetbagger: Republican Reconstruction in Mississippi* (1979). The land confiscation issue is discussed in Eric Foner's *Politics and Ideology in the Age of the Civil War* (1980),° Beth Bethel's *Promiseland* (1981) on a South Carolina black community, and Janet S. Hermann's *The Pursuit of a Dream* (1981)° on the Davis Bend experiment.

The politics of corruption outside the South is depicted in Allan Nevin's *Hamilton Fish: The Inner History of the Great Administration* (1936) and William S. McFeeley's *Grant: A Biography* (1981).° The influence of Horace Greeley in postwar politics is treated in Eric S. Lunde's *Horace Greeley* (1980). The political maneuvers of the election of 1876 and the resultant crisis and compromise are explained in C. Vann Woodward's *Reunion and Reaction* (1966)° and William Gillette's *Retreat from Reconstruction, 1869–1879* (1979).°

APPENDIX

THE DECLARATION OF INDEPENDENCE

WHEN IN THE COURSE OF HUMAN EVENTS, it becomes necessary for one people to dissolve the political bands which have connected them with another, and to assume the Powers of the earth, the separate and equal station to which the Laws of Nature and of Nature's God entitle them, a decent respect to the opinions of mankind requires that they should declare the causes which impel them to the separation.

We hold these truths to be self-evident, that all men are created equal, that they are endowed by their Creator with certain unalienable rights, that among these are Life, Liberty, and the pursuit of Happiness. That to secure these rights, Governments are instituted among Men, deriving their just powers from the consent of the governed. That whenever any Form of Government becomes destructive of these ends, it is the Right of the People to alter or to abolish it, and to institute new Government, laying its foundation on such principles and organizing its powers in such form, as to them shall seem most likely to effect their Safety and Happiness. Prudence, indeed, will dictate that Governments long established should not be changed for light and transient causes; and accordingly all experience hath shown, that mankind are more disposed to suffer, while evils are sufferable, than to right themselves by abolishing the forms to which they are accustomed. But when a long train of abuses and usurpations, pursuing invariably the same Object evinces a design to reduce them under absolute Despotism, it is their right, it is their duty, to throw off such Government, and to provide new Guards for their future security.—Such has been the patient sufferance of these Colonies; and such is now the necessity which constrains them to alter their former Systems of Government. The history of the present King of Great Britain is a history of repeated injuries and usurpations, all having in direct object the establishment of an absolute Tyranny over these States. To prove this, let Facts be submitted to a candid world.

He has refused his Assent to Laws, the most wholesome and necessary for the public good.

He has forbidden his Governors to pass Laws of immediate and pressing importance, unless suspended in their operation till his Assent should be obtained; and when so suspended, he has utterly neglected to attend to them.

He has refused to pass other Laws for the accommodation of large districts of people, unless those people would relinquish the right of Representation in the Legislature, a right inestimable to them and formidable to tyrants only.

He has called together legislative bodies at places unusual, uncomfortable, and distant from the depository of their public Records, for the sole purpose of fatiguing them into compliance with his measures.

He has dissolved Representative Houses repeatedly, for opposing with manly firmness his invasions on the rights of the people.

He has refused for a long time, after such dissolutions, to cause others to be elected; whereby the Legislative powers, incapable of Annihilation, have returned to the People at large for their exercise; the State remaining in the mean time exposed to all dangers of invasion from without, and convulsions within.

He has endeavoured to prevent the population of these States; for that purpose obstructing the Laws of Naturalization of Foreigners; refusing to pass others to encourage their migrations hither, and raising the conditions of new Appropriations of Lands.

He has obstructed the Administration of Justice, by refusing his Assent to Laws for establishing Judiciary powers.

He has made Judges dependent on his Will alone, for the tenure of their offices, and the amount and payment of their salaries.

He has erected a multitude of New Offices, and sent hither swarms of Officers to harass our People, and eat out their substance.

He has kept among us, in times of peace, Standing Armies without the Consent of our legislature.

He has affected to render the Military independent of and superior to the Civil Power.

He has combined with others to subject us to a jurisdiction foreign to our constitution, and unacknowledged by our laws; giving his Assent to their Acts of pretended Legislation:

For quartering large bodies of armed troops among us:

For protecting them, by a mock Trial, from Punishment for any Murders which they should commit on the Inhabitants of these States:

For cutting off our Trade with all parts of the world:

For imposing taxes on us without our Consent:

For depriving us of many cases, of the benefits of Trial by jury:

For transporting us beyond Seas to be tried for pretended offences:

For abolishing the free System of English Laws in a neighbouring Province, establishing therein an Arbitrary government, and enlarging its Boundaries so as to render it at once an example and fit instrument for introducing the same absolute rule into these Colonies:

For taking away our Charters, abolishing our most valuable Laws, and altering fundamentally the Forms of our Governments:

For suspending our own Legislatures, and declaring themselves invested with Power to legislate for us in all cases whatsoever.

He has abdicated Government here, by declaring us out of his Protection and waging War against us.

He has plundered our seas, ravaged our Coasts, burnt our towns, and destroyed the lives of our people.

He is at this time transporting large armies of foreign mercenaries to compleat the works of death, desolation, and tyranny, already begun with circumstances of Cruelty & perfidy scarcely paralleled in the most barbarous ages, and totally unworthy the Head of a civilized nation.

He has constrained our fellow Citizens taken Captive on the high Seas to bear Arms against their Country, to become the executioners of their friends and Brethren, or to fall themselves by their Hands.

He has excited domestic insurrections amongst us, and has endeavoured to bring on the inhabitants of our frontiers, the merciless Indian Savages, whose known rule of warfare, is an undistinguished destruction of all ages, sexes, and conditions.

In every stage of these Oppressions We have Petitioned for Redress in the most humble terms: Our repeated Petitions have been answered only by repeated injury. A Prince, whose character is thus marked by every act which may define a Tyrant, is unfit to be the ruler of a free people.

Nor have We been wanting in attention to our British brethren. We have warned them from time to time of attempts by their legislature to extend an unwarrantable jurisdiction over us. We have reminded them of the circumstances of our emigration and settlement here. We have appealed to their native justice and magnanimity, and we have conjured them by the ties of our common kindred to disavow these usurpations, which, would inevitably interrupt our connections and correspondence. They too must have been deaf to the voice of justice and of consanguinity. We must, therefore, acquiesce in the necessity, which denounces our Separation, and hold them, as we hold the rest of mankind, Enemies in War, in Peace Friends.

WE, THEREFORE, the Representatives of the UNITED STATES OF AMERICA, in General Congress, Assembled, appealing to the Supreme Judge of the world for the rectitude of our intentions, do, in the Name, and by Authority of the good People of these Colonies, solemnly publish and declare, That these United Colonies are, and of Right ought to be FREE AND INDEPENDENT STATES; that they are Absolved from all Allegiance to the British Crown, and that all political connection between them and the State of Great Britain, is and ought to be totally dissolved; and that as Free and Independent States, they have full Power to levy War, conclude Peace, contract Alliances, establish Commerce, and to do all other Acts and Things which Independent States may of right do. And for the support of this Declaration, with a firm reliance on the Protection of Divine Providence, we mutually pledge to each other our Lives, our Fortunes, and our sacred Honor.

The foregoing Declaration was, by order of Congress, engrossed, and signed by the following members:

John Hancock

NEW HAMPSHIRE
Josiah Bartlett
William Whipple
Matthew Thornton

MASSACHUSETTS BAY
Samuel Adams
John Adams
Robert Treat Paine
Elbridge Gerry

RHODE ISLAND
Stephen Hopkins
William Ellery

CONNECTICUT
Roger Sherman
Samuel Huntington
William Williams
Oliver Wolcott

NEW YORK
William Floyd
Philip Livingston
Francis Lewis
Lewis Morris

NEW JERSEY
Richard Stockton
John Witherspoon
Francis Hopkinson
John Hart
Abraham Clark

PENNSYLVANIA
Robert Morris
Benjamin Rush
Benjamin Franklin
John Morton
George Clymer
James Smith
George Taylor
James Wilson
George Ross

DELAWARE
Caesar Rodney
George Read
Thomas M'Kean

MARYLAND
Samuel Chase
William Paca
Thomas Stone
Charles Carroll,
  of Carrollton

VIRGINIA
George Wythe
Richard Henry Lee
Thomas Jefferson
Benjamin Harrison
Thomas Nelson, Jr.
Francis Lightfoot Lee
Carter Braxton

NORTH CAROLINA
William Hooper
Joseph Hewes
John Penn

SOUTH CAROLINA
Edward Rutledge
Thomas Heyward, Jr.
Thomas Lynch, Jr.
Arthur Middleton

GEORGIA
Button Gwinnett
Lyman Hall
George Walton

Resolved, That copies of the Declaration be sent to the several assemblies, conventions, and committees, or councils of safety, and to the several commanding officers of the continental troops; that it be proclaimed in each of the United States, at the head of the army.

ARTICLES OF CONFEDERATION

To all to whom these Presents shall come, we the undersigned Delegates of the States affixed to our Names send greeting.

Whereas the Delegates of the United States of America in Congress assembled did on the fifteenth day of November in the Year of our Lord One Thousand Seven Hundred and Seventy-seven, and in the Second Year of the Independence of America agree to certain articles of Confederation and perpetual Union between the States of Newhampshire, Massachusetts-bay, Rhodeisland and Providence Plantations, Connecticut, New York, New Jersey, Pennsylvania, Delaware, Maryland, Virginia, North-Carolina, South-Carolina and Georgia in the Words following, viz.

"Articles of Confederation and perpetual Union between the States of Newhampshire, Massachusetts-bay, Rhodeisland and Providence Plantations, Connecticut, New-York, New-Jersey, Pennsylvania, Delaware, Maryland, Virginia, North-Carolina, South-Carolina and Georgia.

Article I. The stile of this confederacy shall be "The United States of America."

Article II. Each State retains its sovereignty, freedom and independence, and every power, jurisdiction and right, which is not by this confederation expressly delegated to the United States, in Congress assembled.

Article III. The said States hereby severally enter into a firm league of friendship with each other, for their common defense, the security of their liberties, and their mutual and general welfare, binding themselves to assist each other, against all force offered to, or attacks made upon them, or any of them, on account of religion, sovereignty, trade or any other pretence whatever.

ARTICLE IV. The better to secure and perpetuate mutual friendship and intercourse among the people of the different States in this Union, the free inhabitants of each of these States, paupers, vagabonds and fugitives from justice excepted, shall be entitled to all privileges and immunities of free citizens in the several States; and the people of each State shall have free ingress and regress to and from any other State, and shall enjoy therein all the privileges of trade and commerce, subject to the same duties, impositions and restrictions as the inhabitants thereof respectively, provided that such restrictions shall not extend so far as to prevent the removal of property imported into any State, to any other State of which the owner is an inhabitant; provided also that no imposition, duties or restriction shall be laid by any State, on the property of the United States, or either of them.

If any person guilty of, or charged with treason, felony, or other high misdemeanor in any State, shall flee from justice, and be found in any of the United States, he shall upon demand of the Governor or Executive power, of the State from which he fled, be delivered up and removed to the State having jurisdiction of his offence.

Full faith and credit shall be given in each of these States to the records, acts and judicial proceedings of the courts and magistrates of every other State.

ARTICLE V. For the more convenient management of the general interests of the United States, delegates shall be annually appointed in such manner as the legislature of each State shall direct, to meet in Congress on the first Monday in November, in every year, with a power reserved to each State, to recall its delegates, or any of them, at any time within the year, and to send others in their stead, for the remainder of the year.

No State shall be represented in Congress by less than two, nor by more than seven members; and no person shall be capable of being a delegate for more than three years in any term of six years; nor shall any person, being a delegate, be capable of holding any office under the United States, for which he, or another for his benefit receives any salary, fees or emolument of any kind.

Each State shall maintain its own delegates in a meeting of the States, and while they act as members of the committee of the States.

In determining questions in the United States, in Congress assembled, each State shall have one vote.

Freedom of speech and debate in Congress shall not be impeached or questioned in any court, or place out of Congress, and the members of Congress shall be protected in their persons from arrests and imprisonments, during the time of their going to and from, and attendance on Congress, except for treason, felony, or breach of the peace.

ARTICLE VI. No State without the consent of the United States in Congress assembled, shall send any embassy to, or receive any embassy from, or enter into any conference, agreement, alliance or treaty with any king, prince or state; nor shall any person holding any office of profit or trust under the United States, or any of them, accept of any present, emolument, office or title of any kind whatever from any king, prince or foreign state; nor shall the United States in Congress assembled, or any of them, grant any title of nobility.

No two or more States shall enter into any treaty, confederation or alliance whatever between them, without the consent of the United States in Congress assembled, specifying accurately the purposes for which the same is to be entered into, and how long it shall continue.

No State shall lay any imposts or duties, which may interfere with any stipulations in treaties, entered into by the United States in Congress assembled, with any king, prince or state, in pursuance of any treaties already proposed by Congress, to the courts of France and Spain.

No vessels of war shall be kept up in time of peace by any State, except such number only, as shall be deemed necessary by the United States in Congress assembled, for the defence of such State, or its trade; nor shall any body of forces be kept up by any State, in time of peace, except such number only, as in the judgment of the United States, in Congress assembled, shall be deemed requisite to garrison the forts necessary for the defense of such State; but every State shall always keep up a well regulated and disciplined militia, sufficiently armed and accoutred, and shall provide and constantly have ready for use, in public stores, a due number of field pieces and tents, and a proper quantity of arms, ammunition and camp equipage.

No State shall engage in any war without the consent of the United States in Congress assembled, unless such State be actually invaded by enemies, or shall have received certain advice of a resolution being formed by some nation of Indians to invade such State, and the danger is so imminent as not to admit of a delay, till the United States in Congress assembled can be consulted: nor shall any State grant commissions to any ships or vessels of war, nor letters of marque or reprisal, except it be after a declaration of war by the United States in Congress assembled, and then only against the kingdom or state and the subjects thereof, against which war has been so declared, and under such regulations as shall be established by the United States in Congress assembled, unless such State be infested by pirates, in which case vessels of war may be fitted out for that occasion, and kept so long as the danger shall continue, or until the United States in Congress assembled shall determine otherwise.

ARTICLE VII. When land-forces are raised by any State of the common defence, all officers of or under the rank of colonel, shall be appointed by the Legislature of each State respectively by whom such forces shall be raised, or in such manner as such State shall direct, and all vacancies shall be filled up by the State which first made the appointment.

ARTICLE VIII. All charges of war, and all other expenses that shall be incurred for the common defense or general welfare, and allowed by the United States in Congress assembled, shall be defrayed out of a common treasury, which shall be supplied by the several States, in proportion to the value of all land within each State, granted to or surveyed for any person, as such land and the buildings and improvements thereon shall be estimated according to such mode as the United States in Congress assembled, shall from time to time direct and appoint.

The taxes for paying that proportion shall be laid and levied by the authority and direction of the Legislatures of the several States within the time agreed upon by the United States in Congress assembled.

ARTICLE IX. The United States in Congress assembled, shall have the sole and exclusive right and power of determining on peace and war, except in the cases mentioned in the sixth article—of sending and receiving ambassadors—entering into treaties and alliances, provided that no treaty of commerce shall be made whereby the legislative power of the respective States shall be restrained from imposing such imposts and duties on foreigners, as their own people are subjected to, or from prohibiting the exportation or importation of and species of goods or commodities whatsoever—of establishing rules for deciding in all cases, what captures on land or water shall be legal, and in what manner prizes taken by land or naval forces in the service of the United States shall be divided or appropriated—of granting letters of marque and reprisal in times of peace—appointing courts for the trial of piracies and felonies committed on the high seas and establishing courts for receiving and determining finally appeals in all cases of captures, provided that no member of Congress shall be appointed a judge of any of the said courts.

The United States in Congress assembled shall also be the last resort on appeal in all disputes and differences now subsisting or that hereafter may arise between two or more States concerning boundary, jurisdiction or any other cause whatever; which authority shall always be exercised in the manner following. Whenever the legislative or executive authority or lawful agent of any State in controversy with another shall present a petition to Congress, stating the matter in question and praying for a hearing, notice thereof shall be given by order of Congress to the legislative or executive authority of the other State in controversy, and a day assigned for the appearance of the parties by their lawful agents, who shall then be directed to appoint by joint consent, commissioners or judges to constitute a court for hearing and determining the matter in question: but if they cannot agree, Congress shall name three persons out of each of the United States, and from the list of such persons each party shall alternately strike out one, the petitioners beginning, until the number shall be reduced to thirteen; and from that number not less than seven, nor more than nine names as Congress shall direct, shall in the presence of Congress be drawn out by lot, and the persons whose names shall be so drawn or any five of them, shall be commissioners or judges, to hear and finally determine the controversy, so always as a major part of the judges who shall hear the cause shall agree in the determination: and if either party shall neglect to attend at the day appointed, without reasons, which Congress shall judge sufficient, or being present shall refuse to strike, the Congress shall proceed to nominate three persons out of each State, and the Secretary of Congress shall strike in behalf of such party absent or refusing; and the judgment and sentence of the court to be appointed, in the manner before prescribed, shall be final and conclusive; and if any of the parties shall refuse to submit to the authority of such court, or to appear or defend their claim or cause, the court shall nevertheless proceed to pronounce sentence, or judgment, which shall in like manner be final and decisive, the judgment or sentence and other procedings being in either case transmitted to Congress, and lodged among the acts of Congress for the security of the parties concerned: provided that every commissioner, before he sits in judgment, shall take an oath to be administered by one of the judges of the supreme or superior court of the State where the cause shall be tried, "well and truly to hear and determine the matter in question, according to the best of his judgment, without favour, affection or hope of reward:" provided also that no State shall be deprived of territory for the benefit of the United States.

All controversies concerning the private right of soil claimed under different grants of two or more States, whose jurisdiction as they may respect such lands, and the states which passed such grants are adjusted, the said grants or either of them being at the same time claimed to have originated antecedent to such settlement of jurisdiction, shall on the petition of either party to the Congress of the United States, be finally determined as near as may be in the same manner as is before prescribed for deciding disputes respecting territorial jurisdiction between different States.

The United States in Congress assembled shall also have the sole and exclusive right and power of regulating the alloy and value of coin struck by their own authority, or by that of the respective States—fixing the standard of weights and measures throughout the United States—regulating the trade and managing all affairs with the Indians, not members of any of the States, provided that the legislative right of any State within its own limits be not infringed or violated—establishing and regulating post-offices from one State to another, throughout all of the United States, and exacting such postage on the papers passing thro' the same as may be requisite to defray the expenses of the said office—appointing all officers of the land forces, in the service of the United States, excepting regimental officers—appointing all the officers of the naval forces, and commissioning all officers whatever in the service of the United States—making rules for the government and regulation of the said land and naval forces, and directing their operations.

The United States in Congress assembled shall have authority to appoint a committee, to sit in the recess of Congress, to be denominated "a Committee of the States," and to consist of one delegate from each State; and to appoint such other committees and civil officers as may be necessary for managing the general affairs of the United States under their direction—to appoint one of their number to preside, provided that no person be allowed to serve in the office of president more than one year in any term of three years; to ascertain the necessary sums of money to be raised for the service of the United States, and to appropriate and apply the same for defraying the public expenses—to borrow money, or emit bills on the credit of the United States, transmitting every half year to the respective States an account of the sums of money so borrowed or emitted,—to build and equip a navy—to agree upon the number of land forces, and to make requisitions from each State for its quota, in proportion to the number of white inhabitants in such State; which requisition shall be binding, and thereupon the Legislature of each State shall appoint the regimental officers, raise the men and cloath, arm and equip them in a soldier like manner, at the expense of the United States; and the officers and men so cloathed, armed and equipped shall march to the place appointed, and within the time agreed on by the United States in Congress assembled: but if the United States in Congress assembled shall, on consideration of circumstances judge proper that any State should not raise men, or should raise a smaller number of men than the quota thereof, such extra number shall be raised, officered, cloathed, armed and equipped in the same manner as the quota of such State, unless the legislature of such State shall judge that such extra number cannot be safely spared out of the same, in which case they shall raise officer, cloath, arm and equip as many of such extra number as they judge can be safely spared. And the officers and men so cloathed, armed and equipped, shall march to the place appointed, and within the time agreed on by the United States in Congress assembled.

The United States in Congress assembled shall never engage in a war, nor grant letters of marque and reprisal in time of peace, nor enter into any treaties or alliances, nor coin money, nor regulate the value thereof, nor ascertain the sums and expenses necessary for the defence and welfare of the United States, or any of them, nor emit bills, nor borrow money on the credit of the United States, nor appropriate money, nor agree upon the number of vessels to be built or purchased, or the number of land or sea forces to be raised, nor appoint a commander in chief of the army or navy, unless nine States assent to the same: nor shall a question on any other point, except for adjourning from day to day be determined, unless by the votes of a majority of the United States in Congress assembled.

The Congress of the United States shall have power to adjourn to any time within the year, and to any place within the United States, so that no period of adjournment be for a longer duration than the space of six months, and shall publish the journal of their proceedings monthly, except such parts thereof relating to treaties, alliances or military operations, as in their judgment require secresy; and the yeas and nays of the delegates of each State on any question shall be entered on the Journal, when it is desired by any delegate; and the delegates of a State, or any of them, at his or their request shall be furnished with a transcript of the said journal, except such parts as are above excepted, to lay before the Legislatures of the several States.

ARTICLE X. The committee of the States, or any nine of them, shall be authorized to execute, in the recess of Congress, such of the powers of Congress as the United States in Congress assembled, by the consent of nine States, shall from time to time think expedient to vest them with; provided that no power be delegated to the said committee, for the exercise of which, by the articles of confederation, the voice of nine States in the Congress of the United States assembled is requisite.

ARTICLE XI. Canada acceding to this confederation, and joining in the measures of the United States, shall be admitted into, and entitled to all the advantages of this Union: but no other colony shall be admitted into the same, unless such admission be agreed to by nine States.

ARTICLE XII. All bills of credit emitted, monies borrowed and debts contracted by, or under the authority of Congress, before the assembling of the United States, in pursuance of the present confederation, shall be deemed and considered as a charge against the United States, for payment and satisfaction whereof the said United States, and the public faith are hereby solemnly pledged.

ARTICLE XIII. Every State shall abide by the determinations of the United States in Congress assembled, on all questions which by this confederation are submitted to them. And the articles of this confederation shall be inviolably observed by every State, and the Union shall be perpetual; nor shall any alteration at any time hereafter be made in any of them; unless such alteration be agreed to in a Congress of the United States, and be afterwards confirmed by the Legislatures of every State.

And whereas it has pleased the Great Governor of the world to incline the hearts of the Legislatures we respectively represent in Congress, to approve of, and to authorize us to ratify the said articles of confederation and perpetual union. Know ye that we the undersigned delegates, by virtue of the power and authority to us given for that purpose, do by these presents, in the name and in behalf of our respective constituents, fully and entirely ratify and confirm each and every of the said articles of confederation and perpetual union, and all and singular the matters and things therein contained: and we do further solemnly plight and engage the faith of our respective constituents, that they shall abide by the determinations of the United States in Congress assembled, on all questions, which by the said confederation are submitted to them. And that the articles thereof shall be inviolably observed by the States we respectively represent, and that the Union shall be perpetual.

In witness thereof we have hereunto set our hands in Congress. Done at Philadelphia in the State of Pennsylvania the ninth day of July in the year of our Lord one thousand seven hundred and seventy-eight, and in the third year of the independence of America.

THE CONSTITUTION OF THE UNITED STATES

WE THE PEOPLE OF THE UNITED STATES, in order to form a more perfect Union, establish Justice, insure domestic Tranquility, provide for the common defence, promote the general Welfare, and secure the Blessings of Liberty to ourselves and our Posterity, do ordain and establish this Constitution for the United States of America.

ARTICLE. I.

Section. 1. All legislative Powers herein granted shall be vested in a Congress of the United States, which shall consist of a Senate and House of Representatives.

Section. 2. The House of Representatives shall be composed of Members chosen every second Year by the People of the several States, and the Electors in each State shall have the Qualifications requisite for Electors of the most numerous Branch of the State Legislature.

No Person shall be a Representative who shall not have attained to the Age of twenty five Years, and been seven Years a Citizen of the United States, and who shall not, when elected, be an Inhabitant of that State in which he shall be chosen.

Representatives and direct Taxes shall be apportioned among the several States which may be included within this Union, according to their respective Numbers, which shall be determined by adding to the whole Number of free Persons, including those bound to Service for a Term of Years, and excluding Indians not taxed, three fifths of all other Persons. The actual Enumeration shall be made within three Years after the first Meeting of the Congress of the United States, and within every subsequent Term of ten Years, in such Manner as they shall by Law direct. The Number of Representatives shall not exceed one for every thirty Thousand, but each State shall have at Least one Representative; and until such enumeration shall be made, the State of New Hampshire shall be entitled to chuse three, Massachusetts eight, Rhode-Island and Providence Plantations one, Connecticut five, New-York six, New Jersey four, Pennsylvania eight, Delaware one, Maryland six, Virginia ten, North Carolina five, South Carolina five, and Georgia three.

When vacancies happen in the Representation from any state, the Executive Authority thereof shall issue Writs of Election to fill such Vacancies.

The House of Representatives shall chuse their Speaker and other Officers; and shall have the sole Power of Impeachment.

Section. 3. The Senate of the United States shall be composed of two Senators from each State, chosen by the legislature thereof, for six Years; and each Senator shall have one Vote.

Immediately after they shall be assembled in Consequence of the first Election, they shall be divided as equally as may be into three Classes. The Seats of the Senators of the first Class shall be vacated at the Expiration of the second Year, of the second Class at the Expiration of the fourth Year, and of the third Class at the Expiration of the sixth Year, so that one third maybe chosen every second Year; and if Vacancies happen by Resignation, or otherwise, during the Recess of the Legislature of any State, the Executive thereof may make temporary Appointments until the next Meeting of the Legislature, which shall then fill such Vacancies.

No Person shall be a Senator who shall not have attained to the Age of thirty Years, and been nine Years a Citizen of the United States, and who shall not, when elected, be an Inhabitant of that State for which he shall be chosen.

The Vice President of the United States shall be President of the Senate, but shall have no Vote, unless they be equally divided.

The Senate shall chuse their other Officers, and also a President pro tempore, in the Absence of the Vice President, or when he shall exercise the Office of President of the United States.

The Senate shall have the sole Power to try all Impeachments. When sitting for that Purpose, they shall be on Oath or Affirmation. When the President of the United States is tried, the Chief Justice shall preside: And no Person shall be convicted without the Concurrence of two thirds of the Members present.

Judgment in Cases of Impeachment shall not extend further than to removal from Office, and disqualification to hold and enjoy any Office of honor, Trust or Profit under the United States: but the Party convicted shall nevertheless be liable and subject to Indictment, Trial, Judgment and Punishment, according to Law.

Section. 4. The Times, Places and Manner of holding Elections for Senators and Representatives, shall be prescribed in each State by the Legislature thereof, but the Congress may at any time by Law make or alter such Regulations, except as to the Places of chusing Senators.

The Congress shall assemble at least once in every Year, and such Meeting shall be on the first Monday in December, unless they shall by Law appoint a different Day.

Section. 5. Each House shall be the Judge of the Elections, Returns and Qualifications of its own Members, and a Majority of each shall constitute a Quorum to do Business; but a smaller Number may adjourn from day to day, and may be authorized to compel the Attendance of absent Members, in such Manner, and under such Penalties as each House may provide.

Each House may determine the Rules of its Proceedings, punish its Members for disorderly Behaviour, and, with the Concurrence of two thirds, expel a Member.

Each House shall keep a Journal of its Proceedings, and from time to time publish the same, excepting such Parts as may in their Judgment require Secrecy; and the Yeas and Nays of the Members of either House on any question shall, at the Desire of one fifth of those Present, be entered on the Journal.

Neither House, during the Session of Congress, shall, without the Consent of the other, adjourn for more than three days, nor to any other Place than that in which the two Houses shall be sitting.

Section. 6. The Senators and Representatives shall receive a Compensation for their Services, to be ascertained by Law, and paid out of the Treasury of the United States. They shall in all Cases, except Treason, Felony and Breach of the Peace, be privileged from Arrest during their Attendance at the Session of their respective Houses, and in going to and returning from the same; and for any Speech or Debate in either House, they shall not be questioned in any other Place.

No Senator or Representative shall, during the Time for which he was elected, be appointed to any civil Office under the Authority of the United States, which shall have been created, or the Emoluments whereof shall have been encreased during such time; and no Person holding any Office under the United States, shall be a Member of either House during his Continuance in Office.

Section. 7. All Bills for raising Revenue shall originate in the House of Representatives; but the Senate may propose or concur with Amendments as on other Bills.

Every Bill which shall have passed the House of Representatives and the Senate shall, before it become a Law, be presented to the President of the United States; If he approve he shall sign it, but if not he shall return it, with his Objections to that House in which it shall have originated, who shall enter the Objections at large on their Journal, and proceed to reconsider it. If after such Reconsideration two thirds of that House shall agree to pass the Bill, it shall be sent, together with the Objections, to the other House, by which it shall likewise be reconsidered, and if approved by two thirds of that House, it shall become a Law. But in all such Cases the Votes of both Houses shall be determined by yeas and Nays, and the Names of the Persons voting for and against the Bill shall be entered on the Journal of each House respectively. If any Bill shall not be returned by the President within ten Days (Sundays excepted) after it shall have been presented to him, the Same shall be a Law, in like Manner as if he had signed it, unless the Congress by their Adjournment prevent its Return, in which Case it shall not be a Law.

Every Order, Resolution, or Vote to which the Concurrence of the

Senate and House of Representatives may be necessary (except on a question of Adjournment) shall be presented to the President of the United States; and before the Same shall take Effect, shall be approved by him, or being disapproved by him, shall be repassed by two thirds of the Senate and House of Representatives, according to the Rules and Limitations prescribed in the Case of a Bill.

Section. 8. The congress shall have Power To lay and collect Taxes, Duties, Imposts and Excises, to pay the Debts and provide for the common Defence and general Welfare of the United States; but all Duties, Imposts and Excises shall be uniform throughout the United States.

To borrow Money on the credit of the United States;

To regulate Commerce with foreign Nations, and among the several States, and with the Indian Tribes;

To establish an uniform Rule of Naturalization, and uniform Laws on the subject of Bankruptcies throughout the United States;

To coin Money, regulate the Value thereof, and of foreign Coin, and fix the Standard of Weights and Measures;

To provide for the Punishment of counterfeiting the Securities and current Coin of the United States;

To establish Post Offices and Post Roads;

To promote the Progress of Science and useful Arts, by securing for limited Times to Authors and Inventors the exclusive Right to their respective Writings and Discoveries;

To constitute Tribunals inferior to the supreme Court;

To define and punish Piracies and Felonies committed on the high Seas, and Offences against the Law of Nations;

To declare War, grant Letters of Marque and Reprisal, and make Rules concerning Captures on land and Water;

To raise and support Armies, but no Appropriation of Money to that Use shall be for a longer Term than two Years;

To provide and maintain a Navy;

To make Rules for the Government and Regulation of the land and naval Forces;

To provide for calling forth the Militia to execute the Laws of the Union, suppress Insurrections and repel Invasions;

To provide for organizing, arming, and disciplining, the Militia, and for governing such Part of them as may be employed in the Service of the United States, reserving to the States respectively, the Appointment of the Officers, and the Authority of training the Militia according to the discipline prescribed by Congress;

To exercise exclusive Legislation in all Cases whatsoever, over such District (not exceeding ten Miles square) as may, by Cession of particular States, and the Acceptance of Congress, become the Seat of the Government of the United States, and to exercise like Authority over all Places purchased by the Consent of the Legislature of the State in which the Same shall be, for the Erection of Forts, Magazines, Arsenals, dock-Yards, and other needful Buildings;—And

To make all Laws which shall be necessary and proper for carrying into Execution the foregoing Powers, and all other Powers vested by this Constitution in the Government of the United States, or in any Department or Officer thereof.

Section. 9. The Migration or Importation of such Persons as any of the States now existing shall think proper to admit, shall not be prohibited by the Congress prior to the Year one thousand eight hundred and eight, but a Tax or duty may be imposed on such Importation, not exceeding ten dollars for each Person.

The Privilege of the Writ of Habeas Corpus shall not be suspended, unless when in Cases of Rebellion or Invasion the public Safety may require it.

No Bill of Attainder or ex post facto Law shall be passed.

No Capitation, or other direct, Tax shall be laid, unless in Proportion to the Census or Enumeration herein before directed to be taken.

No Tax or Duty shall be laid on Articles exported from any State.

No Preference shall be given by any Regulation of Commerce or Revenue to the Ports of one State over those of another: nor shall Vessels bound to, or from, one State, be obliged to enter, clear, or pay Duties in another.

No Money shall be drawn from the Treasury, but in Consequence of Appropriations made by Law, and a regular Statement and Account of the Receipts and Expenditures of all public Money shall be published from time to time.

No Title of Nobility shall be granted by the United States: And no Person holding any Office of Profit or trust under them, shall, without the Consent of the Congress, accept of any present, Emolument, Office, or Title, of any kind whatever, from any King, prince, or foreign State.

Section. 10. No State shall enter into any Treaty, Alliance, or Confederation; grant Letters of Marque and Reprisal; coin Money; emit Bills of Credit; make any Thing but gold and silver Coin a Tender in Payment of Debts; pass any Bill of Attainder, ex post facto Law, or Law impairing the Obligation of Contracts, or grant any Title of Nobility.

No State shall, without the Consent of the Congress, lay any Imposts or Duties on Imports or Exports, except what may be absolutely necessary for executing it's inspection Laws: and the net Produce of all Duties and Imposts, laid by any State on Imports or Exports, shall be for the Use of the Treasury of the United States; and all such Laws shall be subject to the Revision and Controul of the Congress.

No State shall, without the Consent of Congress, lay any Duty of Tonnage, keep Troops, or Ships of War in time of Peace, enter into any Agreement or Compact with another State, or with a foreign Power, or engage in War, unless actually invaded, or in such immiment Danger as will not admit of delay.

ARTICLE. II.

Section. 1. The executive Power shall be vested in a President of the United States of America. He shall hold his Office during the term of four

Years, and, together with the Vice President, chosen for the same Term, be elected, as follows.

Each State shall appoint, in such Manner as the Legislature thereof may direct, a Number of Electors, equal to the whole Number of Senators and Representatives to which the State may be entitled in the Congress: but no Senator or Representative, or Person holding an Office of Trust or Profit under the United States, shall be appointed an Elector.

The Electors shall meet in their respective States, and vote by Ballot for two Persons, of whom one at least shall not be an Inhabitant of the same State with themselves. And they shall make a List of all the Persons voted for, and of the Number of Votes for each; which List they shall sign and certify, and transmit sealed to the Seat of the Government of the United States, directed to the President of the Senate. The President of the Senate shall, in the Presence of the Senate and House of Representatives, open all the Certificates, and the Votes shall then be counted. The Person having the greatest Number of Votes shall be the President, if such Number be a Majority of the whole Number of Electors appointed; and if there be more than one who have such Majority, and have an equal Number of Votes, then the House of Representatives shall immediately chuse by Ballot one of them for President; and if no Person have a Majority, then from the five highest on the List the said House shall in like Manner chuse the President. But in chusing the President, the Votes shall be taken by States, the Representation from each State having one Vote; A quorum for this Purpose shall consist of a Member or Members from two thirds of the States, and a Majority of all the States shall be necessary to a Choice. In every Case, after the Choice of the President, the Person having the greatest Number of Votes of the Electors shall be the Vice President. But if there should remain two or more who have equal Votes, the Senate shall chuse from them by Ballot the Vice President.

The Congress may determine the Time of chusing the Electors, and the Day on which they shall give their Votes; which Day shall be the same throughout the United States.

No Person except a natural born Citizen, or a Citizen of the United States, at the time of the Adoption of this Constitution, shall be eligible to the Office of President; neither shall any Person be eligible to that Office who shall not have attained to the Age of thirty five Years, and been fourteen Years a Resident within the United States.

In Case of the Removal of the President from office, or of his Death, Resignation, or Inability to discharge the Powers and Duties of the said Office, the Same shall devolve on the Vice President, and the Congress may by Law provide for the Case of Removal, Death, Resignation or Inability, both of the President and Vice President, declaring what Officer shall then act as President, and such Officer shall act accordingly, until the Disability be removed, or a President shall be elected.

The President shall, at stated Times, receive for his Services, a Compensation, which shall neither be encreased or diminished during the Period for which he shall have been elected, and he shall not receive within that Period any other Emolument from the United States, or any of them.

Before he enters on the Execution of his Office, he shall take the following Oath or Affirmation:—"I do solemnly swear (or affirm) that I will faithfully execute the Office of President of the United States, and will to the best of my Ability, preserve, protect and defend the Constitution of the United States."

Section. 2. The President shall be Commander in Chief of the Army and Navy of the United States, and of the Militia of the several States, when called into the actual Service of the United States; he may require the Opinion, in writing, of the principal Officer in each of the executive Departments, upon any Subject relating to the Duties of their respective Offices, and he shall have Power to grant Reprieves and Pardons for Offences against the United States, except in Cases of Impeachment.

He shall have Power, by and with the Advice and Consent of the Senate, to make Treaties, provided two thirds of the Senators present concur; and he shall nominate, and by and with the Advice and Consent of the Senate, shall appoint Ambassadors, other public Ministers and Consuls, Judges of the supreme Court, and all other Officers of the United States, whose Appointments are not herein otherwise provided for, and which shall be established by Law; but the Congress may by Law vest the Appointment of such inferior Officers, as they think proper, in the President alone, in the Courts of Law, or in the Heads of Departments.

The President shall have Power to fill up all Vacancies that may happen during the Recess of the Senate, by granting Commissions which shall expire at the End of their next Session.

Section. 3. He shall from time to time give to the Congress Information of the State of the Union, and recommend to their Consideration such Measures as he shall judge necessary and expedient; he may, on extraordinary Occasions, convene both Houses, or either of them, and in Case of Disagreement between them, with Respect to the Time of Adjournment, he may adjourn them to such Time as he shall think proper; he shall receive Ambassadors and other public Ministers; he shall take Care that the Laws be faithfully executed, and shall Commission all the Officers of the United States.

Section. 4. The President, Vice President and all civil Officers of the United States, shall be removed from Office on Impeachment for, and Conviction of, Treason, Bribery, or other high Crimes and Misdemeanors.

ARTICLE. III.

Section. 1. The judicial Power of the United States, shall be vested in one supreme Court, and in such inferior Courts as the Congress may from time to time ordain and establish. The Judges, both of the supreme and inferior Courts, shall hold their Offices during good Behavior, and shall, at stated Times, receive for their Services, a Compensation, which shall not be diminished during their Continuance in Office.

Section. 2. The judicial Power shall extend to all Cases, in Law and Equity, arising under this Constitution, the Laws of the United States, and Treaties made, or which shall be made, under their Authority;—to all Cases affecting Ambassadors, other public Ministers and Consuls;—to all Cases of admiralty and maritime Jurisdiction;—to Controversies to which the United States shall be a Party;—to Controversies between two or more States;—between a State and Citizens of another State;—between Citizens of different States;—between Citizens of the same State claiming Lands under Grants of different States, and between a State, or the Citizens thereof, and foreign States, Citizens or Subjects.

In all cases affecting Ambassadors, other public Ministers and Consuls, and those in which a State shall be Party, the supreme Court shall have original Jurisdiction. In all the other Cases before mentioned, the supreme Court shall have appellate Jurisdiction, both as to Law and Fact, with such Exceptions, and under such Regulations as the Congress shall make.

The Trial of all Crimes, except in Cases of Impeachment, shall be by Jury; and such Trial shall be held in the State where the said Crimes shall have been committed; but when not committed within any State, the Trial shall be at such Place or Places as the Congress may by Law have directed.

Section. 3. Treason against the United States, shall consist only in levying War against them, or in adhering to their Enemies, giving them Aid and Comfort. No Person shall be convicted of Treason unless on the Testimony of two Witnesses to the same overt Act, or on Confession in open Court.

The Congress shall have Power to declare the Punishment of Treason, but no Attainder of Treason shall work Corruption of Blood, or Forfeiture except during the Life of the Person attainted.

ARTICLE. IV.

Section. 1. Full Faith and Credit shall be given in each State to the public Acts, Records, and judicial Proceedings of every other State. And the Congress may by general Laws prescribe the Manner in which such Acts, Records and Proceedings shall be proved, and the Effect thereof.

Section. 2. The Citizens of each State shall be entitled to all Privileges and Immunities of Citizens in the several States.

A Person charged in any State with Treason, Felony, or other Crime, who shall flee from Justice, and be found in another State, shall on Demand of the executive Authority of the State from which he fled, be delivered up, to be removed to the State having Jurisdiction of the Crime.

No Person held to Service or Labour in one State, under the Laws thereof, escaping into another, shall, in Consequence of any Law or Regulation therein, be discharged from such Service or Labour, but shall be delivered up on Claim of the Party to whom such Service or Labour may be due.

Section. 3. New States may be admitted by the Congress into this Union; but no new State shall be formed or erected within the Jurisdiction of any other State; nor any State be formed by the Junction of two or more States, or Parts of States, without the consent of the Legislatures of the States concerned as well as of the Congress.

The Congress shall have Power to dispose of and make all needful Rules and Regulations respecting the Territory or other Property belonging to the United States; and nothing in this Constitution shall be so construed as to Prejudice any Claims of the United States, or of any particular States.

Section. 4. The United States shall guarantee to every State in this Union a Republican Form of Government, and shall protect each of them against Invasion; and on Application of the Legislature, or of the Executive (when the Legislature cannot be convened) against domestic Violence.

ARTICLE. V.

The Congress, whenever two thirds of both Houses shall deem it necessary, shall propose Amendments to this Constitution, or, on the Application of the Legislatures of two thirds of the several States shall call a Convention for proposing Amendments, which, in either Case, shall be valid to all Intents and Purposes, as Part of this Constitution, when ratified by the Legislatures of three fourths of the several States, or by Conventions in three fourths thereof, as the one or the other Mode of Ratification may be proposed by the Congress; Provided that no Amendment which may be made prior to the Year One thousand eight hundred and eight shall in any Manner affect the first and fourth Clauses in the Ninth Section of the first Article; and that no State, without its Consent, shall be deprived of it's equal Suffrage in the Senate.

ARTICLE. VI.

All Debts contracted and Engagements entered into, before the Adoption of this Constitution, shall be as valid against the United States under this Constitution, as under the Confederation.

This Constitution, and the Laws of the United States which shall be made in Pursuance thereof; and all Treaties made, or which shall be made, under the Authority of the United States, shall be the supreme Law of the Land; and the Judges in every State shall be bound thereby, any Thing in the Constitution or Laws of any State to the Contrary notwithstanding.

The Senators and Representatives before mentioned, and the Members of the several State Legislatures, and all executive and judicial Officers, both of the United States and of the several States, shall be bound by Oath or Affirmation, to support this Constitution; but no religious Test shall ever be required as a Qualification to any Office or public Trust under the United States.

ARTICLE. VII.

The Ratification of the Conventions of nine States, shall be sufficient for the Establishment of this Constitution between the States so ratifying the Same.

Done in Convention by the Unanimous Consent of the States present the Seventeenth Day of September in the Year of our Lord one thousand seven hundred and Eighty seven and of the Independence of the United States of America the Twelfth. In witness thereof We have hereunto subscribed our Names,

G°: WASHINGTON—Presid⸀
and deputy from Virginia

New Hampshire	John Langdon Nicholas Gilman		Geo: Read Gunning Bedford jun
Massachusetts	Nathaniel Gorham Rufus King	**Delaware**	John Dickinson Richard Bassett Jaco: Broom
Connecticut	Wᵐ Samˡ Johnson Roger Sherman		James McHenry Dan of Sᵗ Thoˢ
New York	Alexander Hamilton	**Maryland**	Jenifer Danˡ Carroll
New Jersey	Wil: Livingston David A. Brearley. Wᵐ Paterson. Jona: Dayton	**Virginia**	John Blair— James Madison Jr.
Pennsylvania	B. Franklin Thomas Mifflin Robᵗ Morris Geo. Clymer Thoˢ. FitzSimons Jared Ingersoll James Wilson Gouv Morris	**North Carolina**	Wᵐ. Blount Richᵈ Dobbs Spaight. Hu Williamson
		South Carolina	J. Rutledge Charles Cotesworth Pinckney Charles Pinckney Pierce Butler.
		Georgia	William Few Abr Baldwin

AMENDMENTS TO THE CONSTITUTION

ARTICLES IN ADDITION TO, and Amendment of the Constitution of the United States of America, proposed by Congress, and ratified by the Legislatures of the several States, pursuant to the fifth Article of the original Constitution.

AMENDMENT I.

Congress shall make no law respecting an establishment of religion, or prohibiting the free exercise thereof; or abridging the freedom of speech, or of the press; or the right of the people peaceably to assemble, and to petitition the Government for a redress of grievances.

AMENDMENT II.

A well regulated Militia, being necessary to the security of a free State, the right of the people to keep and bear Arms, shall not be infringed.

AMENDMENT III.

No Soldier shall, in time of peace be quartered in any house, without the consent of the Owner, nor in time of war, but in a manner to be prescribed by law.

AMENDMENT IV.

The right of the people to be secure in their persons, houses, papers, and effects, against unreasonable searches and seizures, shall not be violated, and no Warrants shall issue, but upon probable cause, supported by Oath or affirmation, and particularly describing the place to be searched, and the persons or things to be seized.

AMENDMENT V.

No person shall be held to answer for a capital, or otherwise infamous crime, unless on a presentment or indictment of a Grand Jury, except in cases arising in the land or naval forces, or in the Militia, when in actual service in time of War or public danger; nor shall any person be subject for the same offence to be twice put in jeopardy of life or limb; nor shall be compelled in any criminal case to be a witness against himself, nor be deprived of life, liberty, or property, without due process of law; nor shall private property be taken for public use, without just compensation.

AMENDMENT VI.

In all criminal prosecutions, the accused shall enjoy the right to a speedy and public trial, by an impartial jury of the State and district wherein the crime shall have been committed, which district shall have been previously ascertained by law, and to be informed of the nature and cause of the accusation; to be confronted with the witnesses against him; to have compulsory process for obtaining witnesses in his favor, and to have the Assistance of Counsel for his defence.

AMENDMENT VII.

In Suits at common law, where the value in controversy shall exceed twenty dollars, the right of trial by jury shall be preserved, and no fact tried by a jury, shall be otherwise re-examined in any Court of the United States, than according to the rules of the common law.

AMENDMENT VIII.

Excessive bail shall not be required, nor excessive fines imposed, nor cruel and unusual punishments inflicted.

AMENDMENT IX.

The enumeration in the Constitution, of certain rights, shall not be construed to deny or disparage others retained by the people.

AMENDMENT X.

The powers not delegated to the United States by the Constitution, nor prohibited by it to the States, are reserved to the States respectively, or to the people. [The first ten amendments went into effect December 15, 1791.]

AMENDMENT XI.

The Judicial power of the United States shall not be construed to extend to any suit in law or equity, commenced or prosecuted against one of the United States by Citizens of another State, or by Citizens or Subjects of any Foreign State. [January 8, 1798.]

AMENDMENT XII.

The Electors shall meet in their respective states, and vote by ballot for President and Vice-President, one of whom, at least, shall not be an inhabitant of the same state with themselves; they shall name in their ballots the person voted for as President, and in distinct ballots the person voted for as Vice-President, and they shall make distinct lists of all persons voted for as President, and of all persons voted for as Vice-President, and of the number of votes for each, which lists they shall sign and certify, and transmit sealed to the seat of the government of the United States, directed to the President of the Senate;—The President of the Senate shall, in the presence of the Senate and House of Representatives, open all the certificates and the votes shall then be counted;—The person having the greatest number of votes for President, shall be the President, if such number be a majority of the whole number of Electors appointed; and if no person have such majority, then from the persons having the highest numbers not exceeding three on the list of those voted for as President, the House of Representatives shall choose immediately, by ballot, the President. But in choosing the President, the votes shall be taken by states, the representation from each state having one vote; a quorum for this purpose shall consist of a member or members from two-thirds of the states, and a majority of all the states shall be necessary to a choice. And if the House of Representatives shall not choose a President whenever the right of choice shall devolve upon them, before the fourth day of March next following, then the Vice-President shall act as President, as in the case of the death or other constitutional disability of the President.—The person having the greatest number of votes as Vice-President, shall be the Vice-President, if such number be a majority of the whole number of Electors appointed, and if no person have a majority, then from the two highest numbers on the list, the Senate shall choose the Vice-President; a quorum for the purpose shall consist of two-thirds of the whole number of Senators, and a majority of the whole number shall be necessary to a choice. But no person constitutionally ineligible to the office of President shall be eligible to that of Vice-President of the United States. [September 25, 1804.]

AMENDMENT XIII.

Section 1. Neither slavery nor involuntary servitude, except as a punishment for crime whereof the party shall have been duly convicted, shall exist within the United States, or any place subject to their jurisdiction.

Section 2. Congress shall have power to enforce this article by appropriate legislation. [December 18, 1865.]

AMENDMENT XIV.

Section 1. All persons born or naturalized in the United States, and subject to the jurisdiction thereof, are citizens of the United States and of the State wherein they reside. No State shall make or enforce any law which shall abridge the privileges or immunities of citizens of the United States; nor shall any State deprive any person of life, liberty, or property, without due process of law; nor deny to any person within its jurisdiction the equal protection of the laws.

Section 2. Representatives shall be apportioned among the several States according to their respective numbers, counting the whole number of persons in each State, excluding Indians not taxed. But when the right to vote at any election for the choice of electors for President and Vice President of the United States, Representatives in Congress, the Executive and Judicial officers of a State, or the members of the Legislature thereof, is denied to any of the male inhabitants of such State, being twenty-one years of age, and citizens of the United States, or in any way abridged, except for participation in rebellion, or other crime, the basis of representation therein shall be reduced in the proportion which the number of such male citizens shall bear to the whole number of male citizens twenty-one years of age in such State.

Section 3. No person shall be a Senator or Representative in Congress, or elector of President and Vice President, or hold any office, civil or military, under the United States, or under any State, who, having previously taken an oath, as a member of Congress, or as an officer of the United States, or as a member of any State legislature, or as an executive or judicial officer of any State, to support the Constitution of the United States, shall have engaged in insurrection or rebellion against the same, or given aid or comfort to the enemies thereof. But Congress may by a vote of two-thirds of each House, remove such disability.

Section 4. The validity of the public debt of the United States, authorized by law, including debts incurred for payment of pensions and bounties for services in suppressing insurrection or rebellion, shall not be questioned. But neither the United States nor any State shall assume or pay any debt or obligation incurred in aid of insurrection or rebellion against the United States, or any claim for the loss or emancipation of any slave; but all such debts, obligations and claims shall be held illegal and void.

Section 5. The Congress shall have power to enforce, by appropriate legislation, the provisions of this article. [July 28, 1868.]

AMENDMENT XV.

Section 1. The right of citizens of the United States to vote shall not be denied or abridged by the United States or by any State on account of race, color, or previous condition of servitude—

Section 2. The Congress shall have power to enforce this article by appropriate legislation.—[March 30, 1870.]

AMENDMENT XVI.

The Congress shall have power to lay and collect taxes on incomes, from whatever source derived, without apportionment among the several States, and without regard to any census or enumeration. [February 25, 1913.]

Amendment XVII.

The Senate of the United States shall be composed of two senators from each State, elected by the people thereof, for six years; and each Senator shall have one vote. The electors in each State shall have the qualifications requisite for electors of the most numerous branch of the State legislature.

When vacancies happen in the representation of any State in the Senate, the executive authority of such State shall issue writs of election to fill such vacancies: *Provided,* That the legislature of any State may empower the executive thereof to make temporary appointments until the people fill the vacancies by election as the legislature may direct.

This amendment shall not be so construed as to affect the election or term of any senator chosen before it becomes valid as part of the Constitution. [May 31, 1913.]

Amendment XVIII.

After one year from the ratification of this article, the manufacture, sale, or transportation of intoxicating liquors within, the importation thereof into, or the exportation thereof from the United States and all territory subject to the jurisdiction thereof for beverage purposes is hereby prohibited.

The Congress and the several States shall have concurrent power to enforce this article by appropriate legislation.

This article shall be inoperative unless it shall have been ratified as an amendment to the Constitution by the legislatures of the several States, as provided in the Constitution, within seven years from the date of the submission thereof to the States by Congress. [January 29, 1919.]

Amendment XIX.

The right of citizens of the United States to vote shall not be denied or abridged by the United States or by any State on account of sex.

The Congress shall have power by appropriate legislation to enforce the provisions of this article. [August 26, 1920.]

Amendment XX.

Section 1. The terms of the President and Vice-President shall end at noon on the twentieth day of January, and the terms of Senators and Representatives at noon on the third day of January, of the years in which such terms would have ended if this article had not been ratified; and the terms of their successors shall then begin.

Section 2. The Congress shall assemble at least once in every year, and such meeting shall begin at noon on the third day of January, unless they shall by law appoint a different day.

Section 3. If, at the time fixed for the beginning of the term of the President, the President-elect shall have died, the Vice-President-elect shall become President. If a President shall not have been chosen before the time fixed for the beginning of his term, or if the President-elect shall have failed to qualify, then the Vice-President-elect shall act as President until a President shall have qualified; and the Congress may by law provide for the case wherein neither a President-elect nor a Vice-President-elect shall have qualified, declaring who shall then act as President, or the manner in which one who is to act shall be selected, and such person shall act accordingly until a President or Vice-President shall have qualified.

Section 4. The Congress may by law provide for the case of the death of any of the persons from whom the House of Representatives may choose a President whenever the right of choice shall have devolved upon them, and for the case of the death of any of the persons from whom the Senate may choose a Vice-President whenever the right of choice shall have devolved upon them.

Section 5. Sections 1 and 2 shall take effect on the 15th day of October following the ratification of this article.

Section 6. This article shall be inoperative unless it shall have been ratified as an amendment to the Constitution by the legislatures of three-fourths of the several States within seven years from the date of its submission. [February 6, 1933.]

AMENDMENT XXI.

Section 1. The eighteenth article of amendment to the Constitution of the United States is hereby repealed.

Section 2. The transportation or importation into any State, Territory or possession of the United States for delivery or use therein of intoxicating liquors, in violation of the laws thereof, is hereby prohibited.

Section 3. This article shall be inoperative unless it shall have been ratified as an amendment to the Constitution by convention in the several States, as provided in the Constitution, within seven years from the date of the submission thereof to the States by the Congress. [December 5, 1933.]

AMENDMENT XXII.

Section 1. No person shall be elected to the office of the President more than twice, and no person who has held the office of President, or acted as President, for more than two years of a term to which some other person was elected President shall be elected to the office of the President more than once. But this Article shall not apply to any person holding the office of President when this Article was proposed by the Congress, and shall not prevent any person who may be holding the office of President, or acting as President, during the term within which this Article becomes operative from holding the office of President or acting as President during the remainder of such term.

Section 2. This article shall be inoperative unless it shall have been ratified as an amendment to the Constitution by the legislatures of three-fourths of the several states within seven years from the date of its submission to the States by the Congress. [February 27, 1951.]

AMENDMENT XXIII.

Section 1. The District constituting the seat of government of the United States shall appoint in such manner as the Congress may direct:

A number of electors of President and Vice-President equal to the whole number of Senators and Representatives in Congress to which the District would be entitled if it were a State, but in no event more than the least populous State; they shall be in addition to those appointed by the States, but they shall be considered, for the purposes of the election of President and Vice-President, to be electors appointed by a State; and they shall meet in the District and perform such duties as provided by the twelfth article of amendment.

Section 2. The Congress shall have the power to enforce this article by appropriate legislation. [March 29, 1961.]

AMENDMENT XXIV.

Section 1. The right of citizens of the United States to vote in any primary or other election for President or Vice President, for electors for President or Vice President, or for Senator or Representative in Congress, shall not be denied or abridged by the United States or any State by reason of failure to pay any poll tax or other tax.

Section 2. The Congress shall have power to enforce this article by appropriate legislation. [January 23, 1964.]

AMENDMENT XXV.

Section 1. In case of the removal of the President from office or of his death or resignation, the Vice President shall become President.

Section 2. Whenever there is a vacancy in the office of Vice President, the President shall nominate a Vice President who shall take office upon confirmation by a majority vote of both Houses of Congress.

Section 3. Whenever the President transmits to the President pro tempore of the Senate and the Speaker of the House of Representatives his written declaration that he is unable to discharge the powers and duties of his office, and until he transmits to them a written declaration to the contrary, such powers and duties shall be discharged by the Vice President as Acting President.

Section 4. Whenever the Vice President and a majority of either the principal officers of the executive departments or of such other body as Congress may by law provide, transmit to the President pro tempore of the Senate and the Speaker of the House of Representatives their written declaration that the President is unable to discharge the powers and duties of his office, the Vice President shall immediately assume the powers and duties of the office as Acting President.

Thereafter, when the President transmits to the President pro tempore of the Senate and the Speaker of the House of Representatives his written declaration that no inability exists, he shall resume the powers and duties of his office unless the Vice President and a majority of either the principal officers of the executive departments or of such other body as Congress may by law provide, transmit within four days to the President pro tempore of the Senate and the Speaker of the House of Representatives their written declaration that the President is unable to discharge the powers and duties of his office. Thereupon Congress shall decide the issue, assembling within forty-eight hours for that purpose if not in session. If the Congress, within twenty-one days after receipt of the latter written declaration, or, if Congress is not in session, within twenty-one days after Congress is required to assemble, determines by two-thirds vote of both Houses that the President is unable to discharge the powers and duties of his office, the Vice President shall continue to discharge the same as Acting President; otherwise, the President shall resume the powers and duties of his office. [February 10, 1967.]

Amendment XXVI.

Section 1. The right of citizens of the United States, who are eighteen years of age or older, to vote shall not be denied or abridged by the United States or by any State on account of age.

Section 2. The Congress shall have power to enforce this article by appropriate legislation [June 30, 1971.]

PRESIDENTIAL ELECTIONS

Year	Number of States	Candidates	Parties	Popular Vote	% of Popular Vote	Electoral Vote	% Voter Participation
1789	11	**GEORGE WASHINGTON**	No party designations			69	
		John Adams				34	
		Other candidates				35	
1792	15	**GEORGE WASHINGTON**	No party designations			132	
		John Adams				77	
		George Clinton				50	
		Other candidates				5	
1796	16	**JOHN ADAMS**	Federalist			71	
		Thomas Jefferson	Democratic-Republican			68	
		Thomas Pinckney	Federalist			59	
		Aaron Burr	Democratic-Republican			30	
		Other candidates				48	
1800	16	**THOMAS JEFFERSON**	Democratic-Republican			73	
		Aaron Burr	Democratic-Republican			73	
		John Adams	Federalist			65	
		Charles C. Pinckney	Federalist			64	
		John Jay	Federalist			1	

Year	Number of States	Candidates	Parties	Popular Vote	% of Popular Vote	Electoral Vote	% Voter Participation
1804	17	**THOMAS JEFFERSON**	Democratic-Republican			162	
		Charles C. Pinckney	Federalist			14	
1808	17	**JAMES MADISON**	Democratic-Republican			122	
		Charles C. Pinckney	Federalist			47	
		George Clinton	Democratic-Republican			6	
1812	18	**JAMES MADISON**	Democratic-Republican			128	
		DeWitt Clinton	Federalist			89	
1816	19	**JAMES MONROE**	Democratic-Republican			183	
		Rufus King	Federalist			34	
1820	24	**JAMES MONROE**	Democratic-Republican			231	
		John Quincy Adams	Independent			1	
1824	24	**JOHN QUINCY ADAMS**	Democratic-Republican	108,740	30.5	84	26.9
		Andrew Jackson	Democratic-Republican	153,544	43.1	99	
		Henry Clay	Democratic-Republican	47,136	13.2	37	
		William H. Crawford	Democratic-Republican	46,618	13.1	41	

Year	Number of States	Candidates	Parties	Popular Vote	% of Popular Vote	Electoral Vote	% Voter Participation
1828	24	**ANDREW JACKSON**	Democratic	647,286	56.0	178	57.6
		John Quincy Adams	National Republican	508,064	44.0	83	
1832	24	**ANDREW JACKSON**	Democratic	688,242	54.5	219	55.4
		Henry Clay	National Republican	473,462	37.5	49	
		William Wirt	Anti-Masonic	101,051	8.0	7	
		John Floyd	Democratic			11	
1836	26	**MARTIN VAN BUREN**	Democratic	765,483	50.9	170	57.8
		William H. Harrison	Whig	739,795	49.1	73	
		Hugh L. White	Whig			26	
		Daniel Webster	Whig			14	
		W. P. Mangum	Whig			11	
1840	26	**WILLIAM H. HARRISON**	Whig	1,274,624	53.1	234	80.2
		Martin Van Buren	Democratic	1,127,781	46.9	60	
1844	26	**JAMES K. POLK**	Democratic	1,338,464	49.6	170	78.9
		Henry Clay	Whig	1,300,097	48.1	105	
		James G. Birney	Liberty	62,300	2.3		
1848	30	**ZACHARY TAYLOR**	Whig	1,360,967	47.4	163	72.7
		Lewis Cass	Democratic	1,222,342	42.5	127	
		Martin Van Buren	Free Soil	291,263	10.1		

Year	Number of States	Candidates	Parties	Popular Vote	% of Popular Vote	Electoral Vote	% Voter Participation
1852	31	**FRANKLIN PIERCE**	Democratic	1,601,117	50.9	254	69.6
		Winfield Scott	Whig	1,385,453	44.1	42	
		John P. Hale	Free Soil	155,825	5.0		
1856	31	**JAMES BUCHANAN**	Democratic	1,832,955	45.3	174	78.9
		John C. Frémont	Republican	1,339,932	33.1	114	
		Millard Fillmore	American	871,731	21.6	8	
1860	33	**ABRAHAM LINCOLN**	Republican	1,865,593	39.8	180	81.2
		Stephen A. Douglas	Democratic	1,382,713	29.5	12	
		John C. Breckinridge	Democratic	848,356	18.1	72	
		John Bell	Constitutional Union	592,906	12.6	39	
1864	36	**ABRAHAM LINCOLN**	Republican	2,206,938	55.0	212	73.8
		George B. McClellan	Democratic	1,803,787	45.0	21	
1868	37	**ULYSSES S. GRANT**	Republican	3,013,421	52.7	214	78.1
		Horatio Seymour	Democratic	2,706,829	47.3	80	
1872	37	**ULYSSES S. GRANT**	Republican	3,596,745	55.6	286	71.3
		Horace Greeley	Democratic	2,843,446	43.9		
1876	38	**RUTHERFORD B. HAYES**	Republican	4,036,572	48.0	185	81.8
		Samuel J. Tilden	Democratic	4,284,020	51.0	184	
1880	38	**JAMES A. GARFIELD**	Republican	4,453,295	48.5	214	79.4
		Winfield S. Hancock	Democratic	4,414,082	48.1	155	
		James B. Weaver	Greenback-Labor	308,578	3.4		

Year	Number of States	Candidates	Parties	Popular Vote	% of Popular Vote	Electoral Vote	% Voter Participation
1884	38	GROVER CLEVELAND	Democratic	4,879,507	48.5	219	77.5
		James G. Blaine	Republican	4,850,293	48.2	182	
		Benjamin F. Butler	Greenback-Labor	175,370	1.8		
		John P. St. John	Prohibition	150,369	1.5		
1888	38	BENJAMIN HARRISON	Republican	5,477,129	47.9	233	79.3
		Grover Cleveland	Democratic	5,537,857	48.6	168	
		Clinton B. Fisk	Prohibition	249,506	2.2		
		Anson J. Streeter	Union Labor	146,935	1.3		
1892	44	GROVER CLEVELAND	Democratic	5,555,426	46.1	277	74.7
		Benjamin Harrison	Republican	5,182,690	43.0	145	
		James B. Weaver	People's	1,029,846	8.5	22	
		John Bidwell	Prohibition	264,133	2.2		
1896	45	WILLIAM McKINLEY	Republican	7,102,246	51.1	271	79.3
		William J. Bryan	Democratic	6,492,559	47.7	176	
1900	45	WILLIAM McKINLEY	Republican	7,218,491	51.7	292	73.2
		William J. Bryan	Democratic; Populist	6,356,734	45.5	155	
		John C. Wooley	Prohibition	208,914	1.5		

Year	Number of States	Candidates	Parties	Popular Vote	% of Popular Vote	Electoral Vote	% Voter Participation
1904	45	**THEODORE ROOSEVELT**	Republican	7,628,461	57.4	336	65.2
		Alton B. Parker	Democratic	5,084,223	37.6	140	
		Eugene V. Debs	Socialist	402,283	3.0		
		Silas C. Swallow	Prohibition	258,536	1.9		
1908	46	**WILLIAM H. TAFT**	Republican	7,675,320	51.6	321	65.4
		William J. Bryan	Democratic	6,412,294	43.1	162	
		Eugene V. Debs	Socialist	420,793	2.8		
		Eugene W. Chafin	Prohibition	253,840	1.7		
1912	48	**WOODROW WILSON**	Democratic	6,296,547	41.9	435	58.8
		Theodore Roosevelt	Progressive	4,118,571	27.4	88	
		William H. Taft	Republican	3,486,720	23.2	8	
		Eugene V. Debs	Socialist	900,672	6.0		
		Eugene W. Chafin	Prohibition	206,275	1.4		
1916	48	**WOODROW WILSON**	Democratic	9,127,695	49.4	277	61.6
		Charles E. Hughes	Republican	8,533,507	46.2	254	
		A. L. Benson	Socialist	585,113	3.2		
		J. Frank Hanly	Prohibition	220,506	1.2		
1920	48	**WARREN G. HARDING**	Republican	16,143,407	60.4	404	49.2
		James M. Cox	Democratic	9,130,328	34.2	127	
		Eugene V. Debs	Socialist	919,799	3.4		
		P. P. Christensen	Farmer-Labor	265,411	1.0		
1924	48	**CALVIN COOLIDGE**	Republican	15,718,211	54.0	382	48.9
		John W. Davis	Democratic	8,385,283	28.8	136	
		Robert M. La Follette	Progressive	4,831,289	16.6	13	

Year	Number of States	Candidates	Parties	Popular Vote	% of Popular Vote	Electoral Vote	% Voter Participation
1928	48	**HERBERT C. HOOVER**	Republican	21,391,993	58.2	444	56.9
		Alfred E. Smith	Democratic	15,016,169	40.9	87	
1932	48	**FRANKLIN D. ROOSEVELT**	Democratic	22,809,638	57.4	472	56.9
		Herbert C. Hoover	Republican	15,758,901	39.7	59	
		Norman Thomas	Socialist	881,951	2.2		
1936	48	**FRANKLIN D. ROOSEVELT**	Democratic	27,752,869	60.8	523	61.0
		Alfred M. Landon	Republican	16,674,665	36.5	8	
		William Lemke	Union	882,479	1.9		
1940	48	**FRANKLIN D. ROOSEVELT**	Democratic	27,307,819	54.8	449	62.5
		Wendell L. Willkie	Republican	22,321,018	44.8	82	
1944	48	**FRANKLIN D. ROOSEVELT**	Democratic	25,606,585	53.5	432	55.9
		Thomas E. Dewey	Republican	22,014,745	46.0	99	
1948	48	**HARRY S TRUMAN**	Democratic	24,179,345	49.6	303	53.0
		Thomas E. Dewey	Republican	21,991,291	45.1	189	
		J. Strom Thurmond	States' Rights	1,176,125	2.4	39	
		Henry A. Wallace	Progressive	1,157,326	2.4		
1952	48	**DWIGHT EISENHOWER**	Republican	33,936,234	55.1	442	63.3
		Adlai E. Stevenson	Democratic	27,314,992	44.4	89	

Year	States	Candidates	Parties	Popular Vote	% Popular Vote	Electoral Vote	% Voter Participation
1956	48	**DWIGHT D. EISENHOWER** Adlai E. Stevenson	Republican Democratic	35,590,472 26,022,752	57.6 42.1	457 73	60.6
1960	50	**JOHN F. KENNEDY** Richard M. Nixon	Democratic Republican	34,226,731 34,108,157	49.7 49.5	303 219	64.0
1964	50	**LYNDON B. JOHNSON** Barry M. Goldwater	Democratic Republican	43,129,566 27,178,188	61.1 38.5	486 52	61.7
1968	50	**RICHARD M. NIXON** Hubert H. Humphrey George C. Wallace	Republican Democratic American Independent	31,785,480 31,275,166 9,906,473	43.4 42.7 13.5	301 191 46	60.6
1972	50	**RICHARD M. NIXON** George S. McGovern John G. Schmitz	Republican Democratic American	47,169,911 29,170,383 1,099,482	60.7 37.5 1.4	520 21	55.5
1976	50	**JIMMY CARTER** Gerald R. Ford	Democratic Republican	40,830,763 39,147,793	50.1 48.0	297 240	54.3
1980	50	**RONALD REAGAN** Jimmy Carter John B. Anderson Ed Clark	Republican Democratic Independent Libertarian	43,901,812 35,483,820 5,719,722 921,188	50.7 41.0 6.6 1.1	489 49	53.0

Candidates receiving less than 1 percent of the popular vote have been omitted. Thus the percentage of popular vote given for any election year may not total 100 percent.
Before the passage of the Twelfth Amendment in 1804, the Electoral College voted for two presidential candidates; the runner-up became vice president.

ADMISSION OF STATES

Order of Admission	State	Date of Admission	Order of Admission	State	Date of Admission
1	Delaware	December 7, 1787	26	Michigan	January 26, 1837
2	Pennsylvania	December 12, 1787	27	Florida	March 3, 1845
3	New Jersey	December 18, 1787	28	Texas	December 29, 1845
4	Georgia	January 2, 1788	29	Iowa	December 28, 1846
5	Connecticut	January 9, 1788	30	Wisconsin	May 29, 1848
6	Massachusetts	February 7, 1788	31	California	September 9, 1850
7	Maryland	April 28, 1788	32	Minnesota	May 11, 1858
8	South Carolina	May 23, 1788	33	Oregon	February 14, 1859
9	New Hampshire	June 21, 1788	34	Kansas	January 29, 1861
10	Virginia	June 25, 1788	35	West Virginia	June 30, 1863
11	New York	July 26, 1788	36	Nevada	October 31, 1864
12	North Carolina	November 21, 1789	37	Nebraska	March 1, 1867
13	Rhode Island	May 29, 1790	38	Colorado	August 1, 1876
14	Vermont	March 4, 1791	39	North Dakota	November 2, 1889
15	Kentucky	June 1, 1792	40	South Dakota	November 2, 1889
16	Tennessee	June 1, 1796	41	Montana	November 8, 1889
17	Ohio	March 1, 1803	42	Washington	November 11, 1889
18	Louisiana	April 30, 1812	43	Idaho	July 3, 1890
19	Indiana	December 11, 1816	44	Wyoming	July 10, 1890
20	Mississippi	December 10, 1817	45	Utah	January 4, 1896
21	Illinois	December 3, 1818	46	Oklahoma	November 16, 1907
22	Alabama	December 14, 1819	47	New Mexico	January 6, 1912
23	Maine	March 15, 1820	48	Arizona	February 14, 1912
24	Missouri	August 10, 1821	49	Alaska	January 3, 1959
25	Arkansas	June 15, 1836	50	Hawaii	August 21, 1959

POPULATION OF THE UNITED STATES

Year	Number of States	Population	Percent Increase	Population per Square Mile
1790	13	3,929,214		4.5
1800	16	5,308,483	35.1	6.1
1810	17	7,239,881	36.4	4.3
1820	23	9,638,453	33.1	5.5
1830	24	12,866,020	33.5	7.4
1840	26	17,069,453	32.7	9.8
1850	31	23,191,876	35.9	7.9
1860	33	31,443,321	35.6	10.6
1870	37	39,818,449	26.6	13.4
1880	38	50,155,783	26.0	16.9
1890	44	62,947,714	25.5	21.2
1900	45	75,994,575	20.7	25.6
1910	46	91,972,266	21.0	31.0
1920	48	105,710,620	14.9	35.6
1930	48	122,775,046	16.1	41.2
1940	48	131,669,275	7.2	44.2
1950	48	150,697,361	14.5	50.7
1960	50	179,323,175	19.0	50.6
1970	50	203,235,298	13.3	57.5
1980	50	226,504,825	11.4	64.0

PRESIDENTS, VICE-PRESIDENTS, AND SECRETARIES OF STATE

President	Vice-President	Secretary of State
1. George Washington, Federalist 1789	John Adams, Federalist 1789	T. Jefferson 1789 E. Randolph 1794 T. Pickering 1795
2. John Adams, Federalist 1797	Thomas Jefferson, Dem.-Rep. 1797	T. Pickering 1797 John Marshall 1800
3. Thomas Jefferson, Dem.-Rep. 1801	Aaron Burr, Dem.-Rep. 1801 George Clinton, Dem.-Rep. 1805	James Madison 1801
4. James Madison, Dem.-Rep. 1809	George Clinton, Dem.-Rep. 1809 Elbridge Gerry, Dem.-Rep. 1813	Robert Smith 1809 James Monroe 1811
5. James Monroe, Dem.-Rep.-1817	D. D. Tompkins, Dem.-Rep. 1817	J. Q. Adams 1817
6. John Quincy Adams, Dem.-Rep. 1825	John C. Calhoun, Dem.-Rep. 1825	Henry Clay 1825
7. Andrew Jackson, Democratic 1829	John C. Calhoun, Democratic 1829 Martin Van Buren, Democratic 1833	M. Van Buren 1829 E. Livingston 1831 Louis McLane 1833 John Forsyth 1834
8. Martin Van Buren, Democratic 1837	Richard M. Johnson, Democratic 1837	John Forsyth 1837
9. William H. Harrison, Whig 1841	John Tyler, Whig 1841	Daniel Webster 1841

President	Vice-President	Secretary of State
10. John Tyler, Whig and Democratic 1841		Daniel Webster 1841 Hugh S. Legare 1843 Abel P. Upshur 1843 John C. Calhoun 1844
11. James K. Polk, Democratic 1845	George M. Dallas, Democratic 1845	James Buchanan 1845
12. Zachary Taylor, Whig 1849	Millard Fillmore, Whig 1848	John M. Clayton 1849
13. Millard Fillmore, Whig 1850		Daniel Webster 1850 Edward Everett 1852
14. Franklin Pierce, Democratic 1853	William R. D. King, Democratic 1853	W. L. Marcy 1853
15. James Buchanan, Democratic 1857	John C. Breckinridge, Democratic 1857	Lewis Cass 1857 J. S. Black 1860
16. Abraham Lincoln, Republican 1861	Hannibal Hamlin, Republican 1861 Andrew Johnson, Unionist 1865	W. H. Seward 1861
17. Andrew Johnson, Unionist 1865		W. H. Seward 1865
18. Ulysses S. Grant, Republican 1869	Schuyler Colfax, Republican 1869 Henry Wilson, Republican 1873	E. B. Washburne 1869 H. Fish 1869
19. Rutherford B. Hayes, Republican 1877	William A. Wheeler, Republican 1877	W. M. Evarts 1877

President	Vice-President	Secretary of State
20. James A Garfield, Republican 1881	Chester A. Arthur, Republican 1881	J. G. Blaine 1881
21. Chester A. Arthur, Republican 1881		F. T. Frelinghuysen 1881
22. Grover Cleveland, Democratic 1885	T. A. Hendricks, Democratic 1885	T. F. Bayard 1885
23. Benjamin Harrison, Republican 1889	Levi P. Morton, Republican 1889	J. G. Blaine 1889 J. W. Foster 1892
24. Grover Cleveland, Democratic 1893	Adlai E. Stevenson, Democratic 1893	W. Q. Gresham 1893 R. Olney 1895
25. William McKinley, Republican 1897	Garret A. Hobart, Republican 1897 Theodore Roosevelt, Republican 1901	J. Sherman 1897 W. R. Day 1897 J. Hay 1898
26. Theodore Roosevelt, Republican 1901	Chas. W. Fairbanks, Republican 1905	J. Hay 1901 E. Root 1905 R. Bacon 1909
27. William H. Taft, Republican 1909	James S. Sherman, Republican 1909	P. C. Knox 1909
28. Woodrow Wilson, Democratic 1913	Thomas R. Marshall, Democratic 1913	W. J. Bryan 1913 R. Lansing 1915 B. Colby 1920
29. Warren G. Harding, Republican 1921	Calvin Coolidge, Republican 1921	C. E. Hughes 1921
30. Calvin Coolidge, Republican 1923	Charles G. Dawes, Republican 1925	C. E. Hughes 1923 F. B. Kellogg 1925

President	Vice-President	Secretary of State
31. Herbert Hoover, Republican 1929	Charles Curtis, Republican 1929	H. L. Stimson 1929
32. Franklin D. Roosevelt, Democratic 1933	John Nance Garner, Democratic 1933 Henry A. Wallace, Democratic 1941 Harry S Truman, Democratic 1945	C. Hull 1933 E. R. Stettinius, Jr. 1944
33. Harry S Truman, Democratic 1945	Alben W. Barkley, Democratic 1949	J. F. Byrnes 1945 G. C. Marshall 1947 D. G. Acheson 1949
34. Dwight D. Eisenhower, Republican 1953	Richard M. Nixon, Republican 1953	J. F. Dulles 1953 C. A. Herter 1959
35. John F. Kennedy, Democratic 1961	Lyndon B. Johnson, Democratic 1961	D. Rusk 1961
36. Lyndon B. Johnson, Democratic 1963	Hubert H. Humphrey, Democratic 1965	D. Rusk 1963
37. Richard M. Nixon, Republican 1969	Spiro T. Agnew, Republican 1969 Gerald R. Ford, Republican 1973	W. P. Rogers 1969 H. A. Kissinger 1973
38. Gerald R. Ford, Republican 1974	Nelson Rockefeller, Republican 1974	H. A. Kissinger 1974
39. Jimmy Carter, Democratic 1977	Walter Mondale, Democratic 1977	C. Vance 1977 E. Muskie 1980
40. Ronald Reagan, Republican 1981	George Bush, Republican 1981	A. Haig 1981 G. Schultz 1982

INDEX